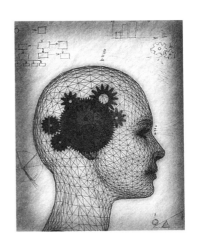

American Women in Technology

D1518646

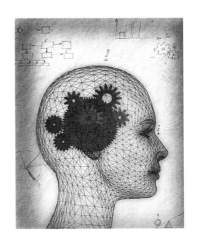

American Women in Technology
An Encyclopedia

Linda Zierdt-Warshaw, Alan Winkler,
and Leonard Bernstein

ABC-CLIO

Santa Barbara, California
Denver, Colorado
Oxford, England

Acknowledgments

Numerous people provided assistance to the authors in the preparation of this book in the form of research, reviewing, revising, and clerical aid. The authors wish to extend their gratitude to these individuals by acknowledging them here. Our sincere thanks go to Evelyn Rothschild and the staff of the Oceanside Public Library, Brian Leddy and the staff of the New Milford Public Library, and the student and professional staff of the Wolfgram Memorial Library of Widener University, Ann Bailey, Christine Beck, Jennifer Beck, and Barbara Littman Eisenberg.

The authors also extend their gratitude and deepest appreciation to family and friends for their support and understanding for time spent away from home during the research and writing of this book.

Library of Congress Cataloging-in-Publication Data

Zierdt-Warshaw, Linda.
    American women in technology : an encyclopedia / Linda Zierdt-Warshaw,
  Alan Winkler, and Leonard Bernstein.
      p.   cm.
    Includes bibliographical references and index.
    ISBN 1-57607-072-7 (alk. paper)
     1. Women in Technology—United States—Encyclopedias. I. Winkler, Alan.
  II. Bernstein, Leonard. III. Title.
  T36.Z54   2000
  604'.82'0973—dc21   00-021997

06 05 04 03 02 01   10 9 8 7 6 5 4 3 2

ABC-CLIO, Inc.
130 Cremona Drive, P.O. Box 1911
Santa Barbara, California 93116-1911

This book is printed on acid-free paper ∞ .
Manufactured in the United States of America

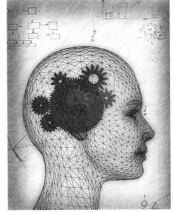

Contents

Contents

Contents

In 1987, the month of March was designated by an act of Congress as National Women's History Month. National Women's History Month was established to encourage people to reflect upon the contributions and achievements of women in business, scholarship, humanities, science, medicine, engineering, technology, and invention. Since the creation of National Women's History Month, more complete media coverage of current events involving women's achievements has helped to increase public awareness; however, the contributions of women in the past often remain largely unknown.

The study of women's contributions to technology is complicated by the lack of agreement about what constitutes technology. At the outset of this project, the authors focused their research on women who in some way had applied a particular science to industrial, commercial, or household uses. However, as work progressed, it became clear that this definition was too limited in its scope, since it did not account for the contributions of women to fields such as medicine, pharmacology, space exploration, and agriculture, among others—contributions that clearly required an application of scientific ideas and principles and that in many cases resulted in great individual and societal benefits. Thus, our definition of technology was broadened to include not only the application of science to the development of processes and products that have industrial, commercial, or household uses but also those that in some way improve the daily lives of humans (individually or collectively).

Because it draws on science, technology has traditionally been considered as falling within the realm of "men's work." The traditional view of the inherent masculinity of science and technology, combined with the entrenched idea that a woman's place is in the home, often prevented women from participating in technological endeavors and from receiving due recognition when they did venture to participate. The contributions of women to technology were often overlooked.

The idea that the role of women in society was to take care of the home and bear and rear children came to the Americas with the earliest colo-

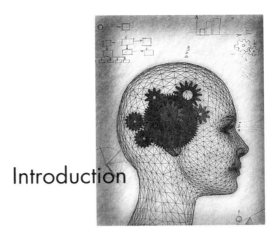

Introduction

nists. In addition, women often were expected to assist in raising crops, caring for animals, and making products for use by their families. Very often, this diversity of responsibility and the hardships it created led women to conceive of devices and means by which they might lessen their burden and that of other members of their family. At this time in history, most of the colonies had laws that prohibited women from owning property. For this reason, when a device or process that constituted an invention was developed by a woman, credit for that device was often attributed to a male family member, especially when a patent was involved. The story of Thomas and Sybilla Masters, who in the early 1700s lived in Philadelphia, a colony of England, illustrates this problem. In 1712, the Masterses traveled to England for the purpose of obtaining patents on inventions developed by Sybilla. Thomas Masters was issued British Patent No. 401 for "a new invention found out by Sybilla, his wife, for cleaning and curing the Indian corn growing in the several colonies in America." Although this patent clearly acknowledges that the process involved is the invention of Sybilla rather than Thomas Masters, the patent, nonetheless, was issued in Thomas's name.

In 1776, America gained its independence from England; however, many of the laws that had governed the colonies remained in place. The first patent act of the United States was created in 1790 by President George Washington. Although this law did not expressly prohibit women from obtaining patents, colonial laws that prevented women from owning property remained in place. Thus, inventions developed by women were often still credited to men. An interesting twist on this law happened when Hannah Wilkinson Slater developed an improved cotton thread. In 1793, Slater obtained a patent on this invention, but it was issued in the name of Mrs. Samuel Slater rather than that of Hannah Slater of Pawtucket, Rhode Island, thus legitimizing the invention by connecting it to Slater's husband.

The U.S. Patent and Trademark Office traditionally has recognized Mary Kies as the first American woman to obtain a patent in her own name. This patent was issued in 1809, for Kies's process of weaving straw with silk or thread. Although the issuance of this patent clearly opened the doors of the patent office to women, many subsequent contributions by women to technology in the form of inventions were still credited to men. This occurred partly because laws regarding women owning property (especially married women, who themselves were often considered property) were slow to change. In other instances, men simply stole and then capitalized on the ideas of women. For example, Ann Harned Manning developed a mowing machine that came to be known as the Manning Mowing Machine in about 1818. In May 1831, a patent for this machine was issued to William Manning, her husband. William Manning also obtained a patent on a clover cleaner that was reportedly developed by his wife.

Although there is no direct proof that William Manning stole and profited from the inventions of his wife, the case of Susan Hibbard does provide evidence of such an attempt. In 1876, Susan's husband, George, tried to obtain a patent on a household duster made from turkey feathers. At the same time, another man was trying to obtain a patent for the same invention. As a result of these competing claims, patent examiners questioned both men about "their" ideas for the feather duster and how it was constructed. Unable to sufficiently answer these questions, George Hibbard made it known that the feather duster for which he was seeking a patent actually was the idea of his wife, Susan. After speaking with Susan and finding her knowledge about the process to be convincing, the examiner issued the patent for the turkey feather duster in Susan Hibbard's name.

During the same year that Susan Hibbard was issued her patent for a turkey feather duster, the Centennial Exposition was held in Philadelphia, Pennsylvania. The exposition celebrated America's first one hundred years of existence as a nation, as well as its technological achievements. As plans were being laid for the celebration, a group of women leaders who strongly believed that the time had come for women to have the same rights as men and to be acknowledged alongside men for their contributions and value to society were beginning to make their voices heard. These women had raised most of the funds needed to hold the Centennial Exposition. Thus, they lobbied for their own space at the exhibition site for the purpose of promoting their cause. Included among these women were women's rights spokespersons Elizabeth Cady Stanton, Matilda Joslyn Gage, Susan B. Anthony, Sara Andrews Spencer, Lillie Devereaux Blake, and Phoebe Couzins.

In 1848, Stanton and others had written a document known as the Declaration of Rights and Sentiments. This declaration became the founding document of the American women's movement. The Declaration of Rights and Sentiments, which was modeled after the Declaration of Independence, was intended to inspire in women a sense of worth and equality with men and to encourage them to insist that they be given the same rights as men in suffrage, education, and ownership of property. The Declaration of Rights and Sentiments was adopted by the women attending a convention held in Seneca Falls, New York, in July 1848.

After much lobbying, Stanton and her followers were successful in getting approval to erect their own building, known as the Woman's Pavilion, at the Centennial. The building showcased the artistic and technological achievements of women. It also provided Stanton and her supporters with a venue from which they could present their views about the need for equal rights for women. In addition, Stanton and Gage prepared a document known as the Declaration of the Rights of Women, which they read at the opening festivities of the Centennial. In essence, the document stated that in the first one hundred years of American history, women had been denied equal status with men and thus had become subservient to men. The document also served as a plea for all citizens, including women, to be given equal citizenship rights under the law.

While the words of Stanton and Gage rallied the women outside the Woman's Pavilion to obtain equal recognition for their achievements, inside, the display of materials, tools, and machines developed by women reinforced the view that women had in fact made meaningful technological contributions to society. Among the more notable exhibits were maritime signal flares developed by Martha Coston in 1859; an improved sadiron developed by Mary Florence Potts (for which she received patents in 1870 and 1871); a washing machine developed by Margaret Plunkett Colvin; and a desk developed by Elizabeth Stiles. Almost 20 years would pass before women's technological contributions again would be prominently displayed at center stage, during the World's Columbian Exposition in Chicago.

In 1862, 14 years after the Seneca Falls Convention, Congress enacted the Morrill Act, which recognized the importance of education and courses of study related to agricultural and industrial arts. The act provided a means for states to obtain funds from the sale of public lands for the purpose of establishing colleges. Later amendments to this bill, in 1868 and 1890, provided additional funds for college expansion and encouraged greater educational opportunities for women, including courses that later evolved into home economics programs. Several colleges emerged specifically for women. Among them were Bryn Mawr, Mount Holyoke, Smith, Vassar, Barnard, Radcliffe, and Wellesley (schools that later came to be known as the "Seven Sisters"). In addition to courses in literature and the arts, these colleges began to offer rigorous programs in the sciences.

Although the Morrill Act provided a means for many women to obtain an education in scientific and technical areas, it did not ensure them equal opportunities for subsequent employment. Many colleges, businesses, and federal agencies had established policies that precluded (officially or unofficially) the hiring of women. Such policies often stemmed from the belief that women in the workplace were a distraction to men or that women would not remain loyal to their employment, favoring marriage and family over their work. Some universities had similar policies with regard to permitting women to enter certain programs of study. An example of this can be seen in the case of Florence Bascom, who wished to pursue doctoral studies in geology at Johns Hopkins University in Baltimore, Maryland. At the time, Johns Hopkins was one of the few schools offering studies in petrology, a new branch of geology that dealt with the origin and classification of rocks. Johns Hopkins did not at the time admit women; however, an exception was made for Bascom, who was granted permission to attend classes, provided that she remain seated behind a screen where she would not be seen by and distract the male students. In 1893, Bascom became the first woman to obtain a Ph.D. from Johns Hopkins; later she became a leading member of the faculty at Bryn Mawr College, where she formed a department offering a degree in geology.

The relegation of women scholars to the background was not a practice limited to the United States. Just after the twentieth century began, Lise Meitner, a physicist working in Berlin, was conducting experiments on radioactivity at the Kaiser Institute of Chemistry. Although permitted to practice her craft, Meitner, like Bascom, was pushed into the background; her work was permitted to occur only under the condition that she not enter laboratories where men were working. To accommodate this proviso, a separate laboratory was constructed for Meitner in the basement.

When women were fortunate enough to gain meaningful employment at universities, in business, or with the government, such employment often was conditional. The conditional employment was linked to the establishment's nepotism policies. Nepotism policies were developed as guidelines for working relationships between employees and members of their families who worked for the same facility. When nepotism policies were invoked as a result of marriage among coworkers, at most places of employment the women were dismissed and the men were permitted to remain at their jobs. For example, Joanne Simpson was employed as an assistant professor of meteorology at the University of Chicago in 1948, when she married William Malkus, also a member of the meteorology faculty. The day after the couple married, Joanne Simpson was discharged from the university. In other, less extreme cases, women were permitted to retain their positions and continue their work, but only if they did so at a greatly reduced salary or without any salary. Such was the case with both Gerty Cori and Maria Goeppert-Mayer, two women whose work was deemed of enough significance to be awarded Nobel Prizes.

With a few exceptions, tradition and societal pressures kept most women, even the most well educated, in the home. This status quo was maintained until the United States became involved in World War I. At this time in American history, the significant vacancies created in America's factories as men went off to war demanded that women be recruited to fill these positions. For many women, this was their first exposure to work involving machinery and other technological devices. Although many women excelled at factory work, their involvement in these undertakings was understood to be temporary, and they were expected to relinquish their jobs and return to full-time homemaking and child-rearing at the conclusion of the war.

The rush of women into the technological workplace during World War I was repeated on a larger scale from the late 1930s to the mid-1940s, as the United States became involved in World War II. Many women were again called to work in America's factories, to make products that supported the war effort. In addition, many women holding degrees in scientific and technical areas were recruited for work on special projects with the Office of Scientific Research and Development

(OSRD). This agency undertook many initiatives involved with the research and design of ordnance necessary to support the war. One of the major initiatives overseen by the OSRD was the Manhattan Project, the government program that ultimately led to the development of the atomic bomb. This endeavor involved the participation of women working in a variety of scientific areas, including chemistry, physics, geology, biology, and engineering. Included among these women were Maria Goeppert-Mayer, Chien-Shiung Wu, Edith Hinkley Quimby, and Leona Woods Libby.

Women recruited to support the war effort during World War II were for the most part expected to return home after the war, as were women in the aftermath of World War I. However, many of these women were reluctant to do so, electing instead to remain in the workplace on at least a part-time basis. This desire, in addition to the increased number of women pursuing education beyond the high school years, helped to refuel the women's rights movement. By the mid-1960s, this movement was gathering additional strength from the civil rights movement, which sought similar equality for members of minority groups (primarily African Americans and Latinos).

The Civil Rights Act of 1964 was passed by Congress to prevent discriminatory practices in education, housing, and employment on the basis of race, color, creed, and national origin. The act also established an Equal Employment Opportunity Commission (EEOC) to investigate reported violations of the act, which became effective in 1965. Many women were enraged by the failure of the Civil Rights Act to include gender among its protected categories. They banded together and sought to have Congress amend the act to provide women the same protections as other groups. Among the more active groups in this area was the National Organization for Women (NOW), founded by Betty Friedan in June 1966. To remedy the problem of women's exclusion, NOW stepped up the efforts to pass an Equal Rights Amendment (ERA), which was first introduced in Congress in 1923 but failed to meet the deadline for states' ratification in 1981. Their efforts drew enough attention to get Congress to amend the Civil Rights Act in 1972 to include Title IX, a provision forbidding gender discrimination. In addition, this amendment provided the EEOC greater powers of enforcement.

The enforcement powers granted to the EEOC opened doors for women to areas of education and employment that previously were closed. The effects of this act in technological areas were seen almost immediately as the college enrollments of women in fields such as architecture, science, and engineering increased. For example, for the academic year 1971 (the year immediately preceding passage of the Title IX amendment), only 400 of the 50,046 undergraduate degrees in all areas of engineering went to women. By contrast, in the 1976–1977 academic year (the year representing the first graduating class benefiting from the amendment), women obtained 2,218 of the 49,283 undergraduate degrees in engineering. In the field of architecture, women obtained 664 of the 5,570 undergraduate degrees in 1970–1971, but obtained 1,973 of the 9,222 degrees in this area in 1976–1977. Similar increases occurred in virtually all scientific disciplines.

Technology draws on scientific applications in such fields as architecture, engineering, mathematics, and other scientific disciplines (biology, chemistry, physics, and so on). As women increasingly have obtained higher educations and employment in these areas, the number of their technological contributions, as well as the significance of those contributions, also has increased. In addition to the women whose contributions to technology have been in the nature of practical inventions, other women, working in architecture, engineering, mathematics, and other scientific disciplines, also have made contributions to technology—just as diverse, and in many cases even more far-reaching—that clearly justify their inclusion in this work.

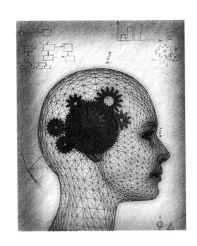

American Women
in Technology

Achievement Award
See **Society of Women Engineers (SWE)**

Acoustical Engineering

Acoustical engineering involves working with sound—specifically, its production, transmission, and effects. Much acoustical engineering research focuses on the development of techniques and materials for reducing or absorbing unwanted sound or for improving sound quality. Acoustical engineers research and develop sound transmitters and amplifiers, ranging from large speaker systems to miniature hearing aids.

Acoustical engineers are concerned with such tasks as reducing noise pollution levels; designing quieter buildings, auditoriums, offices, and machinery; and developing and selecting sound-absorbing or -deadening materials for use in furniture, flooring, walls, and ceilings. For example, acoustical engineers assist in the design and construction of noise-reducing baffle systems along highways. The baffles deflect sounds produced by fast-moving vehicles back onto the roadway to prevent disturbance to nearby residents. A similar concern involving elevated railroads was addressed by Mary Walton of New York City in the late 1800s. Although not trained as an engineer, Walton devised a means of using tar-coated boxes containing sand and cotton to absorb the vibrations that caused trains running on elevated tracks to be noisy. Another woman working in the area of acoustics is aerospace engineer Christine Darden. In this role, she experiments with how altering the design of jets (e.g., wing and nose shape) may eliminate the sonic booms that result when these aircraft reach supersonic speeds.

Improving sound quality is another concern of acoustical engineers. Recently, many concert halls, auditoriums, and movie theaters have been completely renovated to take advantage of advances in materials development resulting from acoustical engineering. Ceiling height, shape, and arrangement are important factors in improving sound quality. In addition, mechanical devices

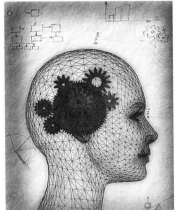

may be used to reposition portions of the walls and ceiling to produce a desired sound quality.

> **See also** Darden, Christine M.; Engineering; Railroads; Society of Women Engineers (SWE); Walton, Mary
> **References** Barnes-Svarney, Patricia, ed., *The New York Public Library Science Desk Reference* (1995); University of Hartford Engineering, "University of Hartford Engineering Acoustics," available at http://uhavax.hartford.edu/-celmer/acsprog1.html (cited 5 May 1998).

Aeronautical and Aerospace Engineering

Aeronautical and aerospace engineering involves the design, development, assembly, maintenance, and testing of commercial and military aircraft and spacecraft and of missiles. Areas of specialization within these fields focus on the structural design, instrumentation, and communication systems employed in helicopters, satellites, and rockets.

Research in aeronautical and aerospace engineering centers on noise abatement, aerodynamics, fuel efficiency, and materials strength and integrity. Aeronautical and aerospace engineers work with electrical engineers in developing complex navigational, guidance, communications, and other avionics systems. They assist mechanical engineers in designing engines suitable for various flight and atmospheric conditions.

1

Aeronautical and aerospace engineers also work with civil engineers in planning and designing airports, hangars, and other necessary housing and storage facilities.

Until the last third of the twentieth century, most of the women making contributions to the areas of aeronautics and aerospace were not trained as engineers. For example, although Mary E. L. Todd is credited with designing and displaying an airplane with collapsible wings as early as 1908, there is no evidence to suggest that she was trained as an aeronautical engineer. Similarly, the numerous women dubbed "Rosie the Riveter," who during World War II contributed their mechanical talents to the construction of airplanes designed for military use, were not formally trained as engineers.

Growth in the number of women receiving college training for aeronautical and aerospace engineering did not begin to take place until the 1970s. At that time, women obtained less than 1 percent of the bachelor's degrees in this discipline; no doctoral degrees were issued to women then. Ten years later, women's participation in aeronautical and aerospace engineering showed significant growth as the percentage of women obtaining bachelor's degrees in this field rose to almost 6 percent, while 2 percent of the master's degrees and 1 percent of the doctoral degrees went to women. The last decade of the twentieth century again marked significant change in the number of women pursuing studies in aeronautical and aerospace engineering. Between 1990 and 1994, the number of women obtaining bachelor's degrees in this area rose from 11.1 percent to 12.6 percent, respectively. The number of women pursuing advanced degrees in this area also increased, with the number of women obtaining Ph.D.s rising from only 1.6 percent in 1990 to 5 percent in 1994.

See also Berkowitz, Joan; Darden, Christine M.; Flügge-Lotz, Irmgard; Jet Propulsion Laboratory (JPL); Johnson, Barbara Crawford; Johnson, Katherine Coleman Goble; National Aeronautics and Space Administration (NASA); Ordnance; Resnik, Judith A.; Ride, Sally Kirsten; Rockwell, Mabel MacFerran; Ross, Mary G.; Widnall, Sheila
References Barnes-Svarney, Patricia, ed., *The New York Public Library Science Desk Reference* (1995); U.S. Department of Education, Office of Educational Research and Improvement, National Center for Education Statistics, *Chartbook of Degrees Conferred, 1969–70 to 1993–94* (December 1997); U.S. Department of Labor, Bureau of Labor Statistics, *Occupational Outlook Handbook, 1994–95,* Bulletin 2450 (1994).

Affirmative Action

The term *affirmative action* is used to describe a broad set of policies and programs designed to provide opportunities in education, employment, and housing to demographic groups commonly denied such opportunities by virtue of their race, ethnicity, gender, and social circumstance. The groups most affected by affirmative action policies and programs are women and minorities (African Americans, Hispanic Americans, Asian Americans, and Native Americans). Physically challenged individuals and veterans' groups also are affected by affirmative action policies.

Affirmative action programs began in the United States during the early 1960s, when President John F. Kennedy issued Executive Order 11246. This order required businesses having government contracts to create guidelines and a timetable for hiring minorities. Similar orders were later signed by Presidents Lyndon B. Johnson and Richard M. Nixon.

Affirmative action programs may be structured to accomplish specific objectives. For example, some programs establish quotas to ensure proportional representation in employment, assignment of federal and state contracts, college admissions, and other applicable areas. Other affirmative action policies encourage women and minority groups to apply for employment or small business contracts.

Although the women's rights movement was well under way in the United States by the late 1800s, affirmative action programs focusing on the rights of women did not begin to appear until the early days of the civil rights movement. During the 1960s, civil rights protests ignited a wave of women's movements. Women's organizations, known as women's rights groups, actively campaigned for legislation and strict enforcement of equal rights laws. President John F. Kennedy's Commission on the Status of Women, established in 1961, uncovered numerous cases of discrimination based entirely on gender. The findings of this commission ultimately resulted in a clause forbidding employment discrimination based on gender in Title VII of the Civil Rights Act of 1964. The Equal Opportunity Employment Commission (EEOC), a federal agency, was created to enforce the provisions of Title VII. Over time, the EEOC would be diligent in its enforcement of additional antidiscrimination legislation.

Affirmative action programs and equal rights legislation have had a profound effect on American women's lives over time. In 1972, there were about 12,000 women lawyers and 34,000 women physicians in the United States. In 1988, it was estimated that there were approximately 140,000 women lawyers and 108,000 women physicians. During the same period, the number of women pursuing careers in the many highly technical fields of engineering also grew significantly. In 1972, for example, women obtained 526, or 1 percent, of all the bachelor's degrees issued in engineering and engineering-related technology fields. By 1988, 12,134 bachelor's degrees, a number representing 13.7 percent of the total, were conferred upon women in engineering and engineering-related technology fields.

In recent years, affirmative action has been the center of much controversy. There are those who question affirmative action as a means of achieving nondiscrimination. Others believe that many affirmative action programs favor one group while penalizing others. In response to such beliefs, several municipalities, nationwide, have reversed or rescinded their affirmative action policies.

See also American Association of University Women (AAUW); Ancker-Johnson, Betsy; Association for Women in Science (AWIS); Nepotism Policies
References Franck, Irene M., and David M. Brownstone, *Women's World: A Timeline of Women in History* (1995); Ryan, Mary P., *Womanhood in America from Colonial Times to the Present* (1975); Sadker, Myra, and David Sadker, *Failing at Fairness: How Our Schools Cheat Girls* (1994); U.S. Department of Education, Office of Educational Research and Improvement, National Center for Education Statistics, *Chartbook of Degrees Conferred, 1969–70 to 1993–94* (December 1997).

Agricultural Engineering

Many contributions to agricultural technology have been made by individuals whose inventions arose through necessity. Such was the case for Anna Baldwin and Catherine Littlefield Greene. Baldwin developed and patented devices that advanced the dairy industry. Catherine Greene is associated with the development of the cotton gin. Although neither of these women were trained as engineers, their work influenced the concerns of contemporary agricultural engineers.

Agricultural engineering draws upon principles of engineering and technical specialties to design, develop, and test products and services for use by farmers, ranchers, and the agricultural industry. This unique field combines aspects of engineering, applied science, materials science, and architecture. For example, many agricultural engineers work to design effective and efficient arrangements of farm structures, including living, storage, and food-processing facilities. They may also design and develop computer-assisted programs that monitor and regulate the internal environment of such structures.

Another concern of agricultural engineers is the design of farm equipment, machinery, and water pumping and irrigation systems. In developing such equipment, agricultural engineers often work with engineers from other areas. For example, working with environmental and civil engineers, agricultural engineers must apply what is known about the biological and chemical nature of pollutants and the processes by which air, water, and wastes are transferred in order to develop systems for managing soil and water resources. Such systems may include those used for drainage, irrigation, and control of surface water and groundwater quality, as well as those that use soil and water resources, such as crop production, agricultural and municipal water supply, and waste management. In this work, agricultural engineers must be aware of potential environmental problems caused by the production of agricultural, industrial, and municipal wastes.

Generally, the number of people pursuing degrees in agricultural engineering is substantially lower than that in other areas of engineering.

However, the percentage of women obtaining degrees in this field did grow during the last thirty years of the twentieth century. In 1970, 1.3 percent of the bachelor's degrees issued in this field of study went to women; by 1994, this number had grown to just over 8 percent.

See also Agriculture; Baldwin, Anna; Civil Engineering; Environmental Engineering; Grandin, Temple; Greene, Catherine Littlefield; Jones, Amanda Theodosia; Manning, Ann Harned; Pinckney, Eliza Lucas; Strong, Harriet R.

References Barnes-Svarney, Patricia, ed., *The New York Public Library Science Desk Reference* (1995); Rossiter, Margaret W., *Women Scientists in America: Before Affirmative Action, 1940–1972* (1995); Stanley, Autumn, *Mothers and Daughters of Invention: Notes for a Revised History of Technology* (1993); U.S. Department of Education, Office of Educational Research and Improvement, National Center for Education Statistics, *Chartbook of Degrees Conferred, 1969–70 to 1993–94* (December 1997).

Agriculture

Agriculture is the application of science and technology to the cultivation of crops and raising of livestock. Most agriculture is practiced for the purpose of generating food for humans. However, agriculture also is practiced to produce food for animals and to produce products derived from plants and animals, such as textiles (woven fabrics), medicines, dyes, paints, and other industrial goods.

The formal practice of agriculture dates back about 10,000 years. Agriculture was practiced many years before Europeans colonized the Americas. After migrating to the New World, the European colonists combined their traditional agricultural practices with methods they learned from Native Americans to generate the foods and other materials they needed to sustain life.

Women have participated in and made significant contributions to agriculture in the United States since its earliest beginnings. They have worked alongside their husbands and children in farm fields and pastures as well as in the home, producing food and fashioning materials and objects of everyday life.

Sybilla Masters was one of the first to make a substantial contribution to agricultural technol-

ogy. In 1712, Masters and her husband, Thomas, traveled from their home in Philadelphia to London to secure a patent on a device that Sybilla had invented, which facilitated the cleaning and curing of Indian corn grown in the colonies. It also made use of a water wheel to grind the corn into meal. Four years later, while still in England, Thomas Masters obtained a second patent, for yet another invention by his wife. This patent was issued for a means of working and staining straw and the leaves of the palmetto tree to prepare these plant products for use in the making of hats and bonnets. This same process also was used to manufacture matting for furniture. Although the patents for both inventions were issued to Thomas Masters, Masters readily admitted in his patent applications that the ideas for the devices and processes had been developed by his wife, Sybilla. Custom at the time prevented married women from owning property, and Sybilla could not have obtained the patents in her own right.

Several years later, in the 1750s and 1760s, Eliza Lucas Pinckney, a resident of the Carolina colonies, developed a system for cultivating indigo (a plant valued for the blue dye derived from it) in the South. Pinckney selectively bred plants, using seeds she had imported from the West Indies, to develop a strain that thrived in the southern climate. She also developed a method of producing the highly desirable blue dye for which indigo is known. Prior to Pinckney's innovations, the indigo used in the colonies had to be imported from Europe. However, as a result of her efforts, this plant soon emerged as a major cash crop of the South.

About twenty years after Pinckney introduced indigo to the South, Hannah Wilkinson Slater developed an improved cotton thread for use in sewing. She was issued a patent for this invention in 1793, in the name of Mrs. Samuel Slater. The thread she developed later was widely used in the textile mills operated by her husband, Samuel, in Pawtuckett, Rhode Island.

Before people could process cotton into thread, the plant had to be grown and harvested. Much of the cotton growth in America took place in the southern colonies. The harvesting and processing of such cotton became mechanized largely through the development of the cotton gin. This mechanical device not only provided a means of harvesting cotton but also separated the fibers from the seeds in the process. In 1794, a patent for the device was issued to Eli Whitney (a former resident of Connecticut). However, evidence suggests that the idea for the cotton gin and an improvement that permitted the device to work came from Catherine Littlefield Greene of Georgia. Soon after the gin was developed, copies of the device emerged throughout the South. By the time a patent on the device was actually issued to Whitney, it was virtually worthless.

Shortly after the cotton gin emerged, several women in New England were gaining notoriety for processes they developed involving the production of hats from straw. In 1799, Betsey Metcalf, of Providence, Rhode Island, developed a new method for weaving bonnets using seven strands of straw. She also developed a means of bleaching the straw to produce a unique color. Although Metcalf's methods became widely used throughout New England, she elected not to patent her process because she did not want to furnish her name to the federal government, as would be required to obtain a patent.

About ten years after Metcalf developed her weaving process, Mary Kies, of South Killington, Connecticut, became the first American woman to be issued a patent in her own name (in 1809). Kies's patent was issued for a process of weaving straw hats, using silk or thread. The process was widely used until an improved straw-weaving process for hats was developed by Sophia Woodhouse Welles. Welles was issued a patent on her process in 1821.

In the 1830s, Cyrus McCormick was issued a patent for a harvesting machine known as a reaper. In his application for the patent, McCormick noted that his reaper improved upon ideas used in a slightly earlier machine known as the Manning Mowing Machine. The patent for this earlier creation was issued to William Manning only a short time before McCormick received his first patent on the reaper. However, the idea that led to the development of the Manning Mowing Machine is believed to have been provided by Manning's wife, Ann Harned Manning.

Forty-five years after the emergence of the Manning Mowing Machine and the McCormick reaper, Kansas native Iris Hobson obtained a patent for a potato digger.

Other women who contributed to the development of farm machinery include Minnesota natives Ann Trexler and Lucy Easton. Trexler was issued a patent on her machine, a Combined Plow and Harrow, in 1888. Easton received a patent on her Flaxseed Separating Machine, two years later. Only ten years later, yet another woman made a contribution to agricultural machinery when she patented a weeder. The patent on this machine was issued to Sarah E. Ball of Ritchey, Illinois, in 1910.

At about the same time that women in the Midwest were contributing to the development and improvement of farm machinery, Harriet Russell Strong of California devised a new irrigation system to provide water to her orchards. Strong's major crops were not the cotton, corn, and indigo commonly grown elsewhere in the country, but walnuts, citrus fruits, pomegranates, and pampas grass. To provide these crops with an adequate water supply in the semiarid region in which she lived, Strong developed an irrigation system that made use of a series of dams that controlled flooding and stored the water needed for her crops. This system was so well designed that it was copied by engineers and implemented for use by farmers as far away as Central America.

Not all of the contributions of women to agriculture dealt with the raising of plants or the development of products from plants. Women also have made contributions dealing with livestock, primarily in the dairy and meat industries. Among the early contributions in this area were those of Anna Baldwin of New Jersey. In the decade between the late 1860s and late 1870s, Baldwin was issued a total of five patents (one a reissue of an earlier patent) dealing with devices for use by dairy farmers. The first of these devices, an improved method of treating milk to obtain products such as pomade and butter, resulted in a patent in 1868. One year later, an improved milk separator and an improved milk cooler also were deemed worthy of patents. In 1871, Baldwin was reissued a patent for an improvement on her earlier milk cooler. Her most significant invention, however, was for an improved milking machine, for which she received a patent in 1879. This machine, called the Hygienic Glove Milker, made use of a hand pump and a glove-like structure that fit over the udders of the cow.

More recently, Colorado State University assistant professor of animal sciences Temple Grandin developed several devices for use in the livestock industry. Among these creations are new designs for corrals, passageways, and feeding lot facilities. In addition, Grandin also developed devices to make the treatment of livestock just prior to their slaughter a more humane process by developing ramps and other accessories to help eliminate fear and anxiety among the animals.

The collective contributions of women have significantly influenced the development of agriculture in the United States. In addition to the specific achievements described above, innovations are continually being made by women working in the related fields of agricultural engineering, animal husbandry, entomology, genetics, genetic engineering, and veterinary medicine. Such contributions are essential if the agricultural industry is to continue to meet the food and agricultural product needs of the growing global population.

See also Agricultural Engineering; Baldwin, Anna; Dickelman, Lizzie H.; Grandin, Temple; Greene, Catherine Littlefield; Kies, Mary; Manning, Ann Harned; Masters, Sybilla Righton; Metcalf, Betsey; Pinckney, Eliza Lucas; Slater, Hannah Wilkinson (Mrs. Samuel); Strong, Harriet R.; Welles, Sophia Woodhouse

References Andrews, Edmund L., "An Exhibit of Inventions By Women," in Patents, *New York Times* (20 January 1990); Graham, Judith, ed., *Current Biography Yearbook, 1994* (1994); Heinemann, Susan, *Timelines of American Women's History* (1996); Stanley, Autumn, *Mothers and Daughters of Invention: Notes for a Revised History of Technology* (1993); Van Vleck, Richard, "Early Cow Milking Machines," *Scientific Medical & Mechanical Antiques,* Issue 20 (1996); Vare, Ethlie Ann, and Greg Ptacek, *Mothers of Invention: From the Bra to the Bomb, Forgotten Women and Their Unforgettable Ideas* (1988).

Hattie Alexander developed treatments for influenzal meningitis in the late 1930s. (Corbis-Bettmann)

Alexander, Hattie Elizabeth (1901–1968)

Pediatrician and microbiologist Hattie Elizabeth Alexander is best known for her development of a serum that proved a successful treatment for influenzal meningitis, a bacterial disease that attacks the membranes surrounding the brain and spinal cord and that may result in death. Prior to Alexander's discovery, this disease was treated, with rare success, with a serum prepared from horses. Alexander learned that the Rockefeller Institute had developed a serum from rabbits that was successful in treating pneumonia. Working with immunochemist Michael Heidelberger, Alexander applied her laboratory experience and scientific knowledge to the development of a serum prepared from rabbits, for use in the treatment of influenzal meningitis. She reported her discovery in 1939, when she announced the first successful cure of this once-fatal disease.

Hattie Alexander was born in Baltimore,

Maryland, and attended that city's Goucher College, from which she graduated with a B.A. in 1923. She worked as a bacteriologist with the U.S. Public Health Service and the Maryland Public Health Service before entering the Johns Hopkins School of Medicine, from which she received her M.D. in 1930. Alexander then served two one-year internships in pediatrics—first at the Harriet Lane Home in Baltimore, then at the Babies' Hospital of the Columbia-Presbyterian Medical Center in New York City. It was while serving her second internship that Alexander developed an intense interest in influenzal meningitis.

Following her development of the rabbit serum in 1939, Alexander continued researching influenzal meningitis. She introduced antibiotics, including sulfa drugs, in combination with her rabbit serum as a treatment. Her insight accounted for a remarkable 90 percent reduction in fatalities resulting from the disease. As a result of this research, Alexander became the first to recognize that genetic mutations in the influenza bacillus accounted for its resistance to treatment with antibiotics. Although DNA research was then in its infancy, Alexander was able to alter the DNA of the influenza bacillus. This work provided a catalyst for further DNA research, including genetic research in viruses.

Alexander published more than 150 articles and was the recipient of many honors and awards. For her work on influenzal meningitis, she was presented with the E. Mead Johnson Award for Research in 1942. In 1961, she became the first woman to receive the Oscar B. Hunter Memorial Award of the American Therapeutic Society. She was also the first woman to be elected president of the American Pediatric Society, in 1964.

See also Antibiotics; Brown, Rachel Fuller; Elion, Gertrude Belle; Genetic Engineering; Hazen, Elizabeth Lee; Medicine/Medical Technology; Pharmacology
References McMurray, Emily M., ed., *Notable Twentieth-Century Scientists* (1995); Shearer, Benjamin F., and Barbara S. Shearer, eds., *Notable Women in the Life Sciences: A Biographical Dictionary* (1996); Sicherman, Barbara, and Carol Hurd Green, eds., *Notable American Women: The Modern Period* (1980); Stanley, Autumn, *Mothers and Daughters of Invention: Notes for a Revised History of Technology* (1993); Vare,

Ethlie Ann, and Greg Ptacek, *Mothers of Invention: From the Bra to the Bomb, Forgotten Women and Their Unforgettable Ideas* (1988).

Alexander, Lucy Maclay (n.d.)

Little is known about the life of Maryland native Lucy Maclay Alexander. However, in 1950, she became the first woman to receive the Distinguished Service Medal of the U.S. Department of Agriculture (USDA). The award was made in recognition of her scientific approach to the cooking of meat and poultry. Alexander developed her approach while working for the U.S. Bureau of Home Nutrition and Home Economics during World War II. She applied her unique cooking techniques to the less-than-choice cuts of meat that were then available to Americans.

See also Bevier, Isabel; Farmer, Fannie Merritt; Home Economics; Pennington, Mary Engle; Richards, Ellen Henrietta Swallow
References Read, Phyllis J., and Bernard L. Witlieb, *The Book of Women's Firsts* (1992).

Lucy Maclay Alexander was the first woman to be presented a Distinguished Service Medal of the U.S. Department of Agriculture in 1950. (Corbis/ Bettmann-UPI)

American Association for the Advancement of Science (AAAS)

The American Association for the Advancement of Science (AAAS) is the world's largest nonprofit professional scientific organization and represents all scientific disciplines. The primary objectives of the AAAS are to advance the progress of science and technology, to facilitate scientific cooperation, to improve the effectiveness of science in promoting human welfare, and to advance science awareness and education.

Founded in 1848, AAAS is among the oldest societies in the United States. It was the first organization to promote the development of science and engineering at the national level. National membership is about 135,000 with 296 scientific societies, professional organizations, and state and city academies. World membership exceeds 143,000. Astronomer Maria Mitchell became AAAS's first woman member in 1850. Mathematician Mina Spiegel Rees became the first woman president of AAAS in 1971. Other noted women who have served as president of AAAS include anthropologist Margaret Mead (1975–1976), astronomer (Eleanor) Margaret Burbidge (1981), and aeronautical engineer Sheila Widnall (1987).

AAAS sponsors many awards that recognize research, journalism, and the promotion of science and technology. Biochemist Gladys Anderson Emerson received the AAAS Certificate Award for her research on amino acids and vitamin E in 1959. Included among AAAS's many film and book publications is the weekly journal *Science,* which contains research reports, book reviews, editorials, and news.

See also Burbidge, (Eleanor) Margaret Peachey; Emerson, Gladys Anderson; Widnall, Sheila
References Franck, Irene M., and David M. Brownstone, *Women's World: A Timeline of Women in History* (1995); Heinemann, Sue, *Timelines of American Women's History* (1996); Maurer, Christine, and Tara E. Sheets, eds., *Encyclopedia of Associations* 33rd ed., vol. 1, part 1 (1998); American Association for the Advancement of Science available at http://www.aaas.org/aaas/geninfo.html/ (cited 11/27/98).

American Association of University Women (AAUW)

The American Association of University Women (AAUW) is a national advocacy group that promotes education and equity for women. The AAUW emphasizes ongoing and continued education for its college graduate membership through annual study and action programs on topics and issues of concern to women. Founded as the Association of Collegiate Alumni in 1881, the organization was originally formed to provide a forum for communication among women college graduates. It also promoted women's opportunities for higher education. In 1921, the organization merged with the Southern Association of College Women to form the current American Association of University Women. Today, the AAUW has a membership of approximately 160,000, with more than 1,600 chapters nationwide.

The AAUW publishes magazines, newsletters, booklets, and brochures containing articles on such issues as equity in education and the workplace and updates on legislation, child care, and family law. The organization funds an extensive program of postdoctoral fellowships and sponsors several awards, including the prestigious Achievement Award. Recipients of the AAUW Achievement Award include physician Helen Brooke Taussig, physicist Chien-Shiung Wu, biochemist Florence Barbara Seibert, and chemist Katherine Burr Blodgett.

See also Association for the Advancement of Women (AAW); Blodgett, Katherine Burr; Seibert, Florence Barbara; Taussig, Helen Brooke; Wu, Chien-Shiung
References Macdonald, Anne L., *Feminine Ingenuity: How Women Inventors Changed America* (1992); Maurer, Christine, and Tara E. Sheets, eds., *Encyclopedia of Associations: An Associations Unlimited Reference,* 33rd ed., vol. 1, part 1 (1998); Rossiter, Margaret W., *Women Scientists in America: Before Affirmative Action, 1940–1972* (1995); Sadker, Myra, and David Sadker, *Failing at Fairness: How Our Schools Cheat Girls* (1994); Weatherford, Doris, *American Women's History: An A to Z of People, Organizations, Issues, and Events* (1994); American Association of University Women, available at http://www.aauw.org (cited 29 July 1998).

American Chemical Society (ACS)

Founded in 1876, the American Chemical Society (ACS) is a scientific and educational organization composed of chemists and chemical engineers. With a membership of more than 150,000 professionals and more than 32 divisions, the ACS is the world's largest scientific organization. To accomplish its goals, the ACS conducts surveys, monitors legislation, provides programs for the physically challenged, sets graduate educational guidelines, and oversees employment opportunities for chemists and chemical engineers. The ACS also administers a number of funds, grants, and fellowships and sponsors numerous awards that are well known and highly regarded throughout the scientific and technological communities. Among these are the annual Francis P. Garvan–John M. Olin Medal, also known simply as the Garvan Medal, which honors distinguished service and achievement by women chemists. The first Garvan Medal was issued to chemist and educator Emma Perry Carr in 1937. Other notable women who received this award include Mary Engle Pennington (1940), Katherine Burr Blodgett (1951), Mary L. Caldwell (1960), Isabella Karle (1976), and Nobel laureates Gerty Cori (1948) and Gertrude Belle Elion (1968).

ACS publications focus on current developments in and evaluations of the fields of chemistry and chemical engineering, including those related to academics and industry; on experimental and theoretical research; and on the policies and activities of the ACS.

See also Blodgett, Katherine Burr; Caldwell, Mary Letitia; Carr, Emma Perry; Cori, Gerty Theresa Radnitz; Elion, Gertrude Belle; Francis P. Garvan–John M. Olin Medal; Nobel Prize; Pennington, Mary Engle
References American Chemical Society, *American Chemical Society Awards, 1998 Edition* (1998); Maurer, Christine, and Tara E. Sheets, eds., *Encyclopedia of Associations: An Associations Unlimited Reference*, 33rd ed., vol. 1, part 1 (1998); American Chemical Society, at http://www.acs.org (cited March 1999).

American Crystallographic Association (ACA)

The objective of this organization is to encourage and foster communication and interaction among chemists, biochemists, physicists, mineralogists, and metallurgists who through the application of X-ray, electron, and neutron diffraction, study the structure of matter at the atomic level. The organization also promotes the study of the arrangement of atoms and molecules in matter and the nature of the forces that control and result from these arrangements. Two renowned women crystallographers and past presidents of the ACA are Elizabeth Armstrong Wood (1957) and Isabella L. Karle (1976).

The ACA formed in 1949 through a merger of the American Society for X-Ray and Electron Diffraction (ASXRED) and the Crystallographic Society of America (CSA). Current membership in the ACA is approximately 2,300. Membership is open to individuals committed to the organization's interests and purposes who are sponsored by two regular members. Students also are encouraged to apply for membership. Included among the many benefits available to members is an employment clearinghouse for members and employers.

See also Crystallography; Karle, Isabella L.; Metals and Metallurgy; Richardson, Jane Shelby; Wood, Elizabeth Armstrong
References Bailey, Martha J., *American Women in Science: A Biographical Dictionary* (1994); Maurer, Christine, and Tara E. Sheets, eds., *Encyclopedia of Associations*, 33rd ed., vol. 1, parts 1–3 (1998); American Crystallographic Association, "About the ACA," available at http://www.hwi.buffalo.edu/ACA/Society-Info/history.html (cited 1 September 1998).

American Institute of Architects (AIA)

The American Institute of Architects (AIA) is a professional society whose members include licensed architects, graduate (unlicensed) architects, and retired architects. The organization is involved in various aspects of the building and construction industry, including designing public spaces, maintaining the nation's infrastructures, and developing affordable, well-designed housing. AIA fosters professionalism and accountability among its members through continuing education and training and promotes design excellence by influencing change within the industry.

AIA was established in 1857 in response to a need for standardization and minimum requirements in the profession. Today, AIA has a membership of more than 59,000. Louise Blanchard Bethune became AIA's first woman member in 1888. The following year, she was named a fellow.

AIA sponsors educational programs with architectural institutions, graduate students, and elementary and secondary schools. It also conducts professional development seminars, research programs, exhibitions, and competitions. AIA's Gold Medal Award and National Honor Award recognize achievements in design. Major publications of the AIA include the *American Institute of Architects AIArchitect* and *Architecture*, which feature information on products and services; book reviews; events calendars; and architectural design and technology articles.

See also Architecture; Barney, Nora Stanton Blatch; Bethune, Louise Blanchard; Hayden, Sophia Gregoria; Lin, Maya; Loftness, Vivian
References Maurer, Christine, and Tara E. Sheets, eds., *Encyclopedia of Associations,* 33rd ed., vol. 1, part 1 (1998); Wilkes, Joseph A., ed., *Encyclopedia of Architecture, Design, Engineering & Construction,* vol. 1 (1988); American Institute of Architects Public Affairs, at http://www.e-architect.com/media/inst_info/aiainfor.asp (cited 18 November 1998).

American Institute of Chemists (AIC)

Founded in 1923, the American Institute of Chemists (AIC) promotes and supports the advancement of chemists and chemical engineers in the United States. A primary focus of the AIC, whose membership numbers approximately 4,000, is to protect the public welfare by developing and monitoring high industry standards involving the production, use, and storage of chemicals. Among the awards sponsored by the AIC is its annual Chemical Pioneer Award. In 1975, Rachel Fuller Brown and Elizabeth Lee Hazen became the first women to receive this award, for their development of the antifungal antibiotic nystatin.

See also Brown, Rachel Fuller; Chemical Engineering; Chemical Pioneer Award; Hazen, Elizabeth Lee
References Franck, Irene M., and David M. Brownstone, *Women's World: A Timeline of Women in*

History (1995); Maurer, Christine, and Tara E. Sheets, eds., *Encyclopedia of Associations: An Associations Unlimited Reference,* 33rd ed., vol. 1, part 1 (1998); Read, Phyllis J., and Bernard L. Witlieb, *The Book of Women's Firsts* (1992).

American Institute of Electrical Engineers
See **Institute of Electrical and Electronics Engineers (IEEE)**

American Institute of Nutrition
See **American Society for Nutritional Sciences (ASNS)**

American Mathematical Society (AMS)

Founded in 1888, the American Mathematical Society (AMS) is a multinational organization of professional mathematicians and educators with a membership of approximately 30,000. AMS's goal is to promote mathematical research and scholarship through institutes, seminars, short courses, and symposia. The organization also seeks to increase awareness of the value of mathematics, and promotes excellence in mathematics education. In addition to employment information, member notices, and placement services, AMS publications include abstracts, journals, bulletins, and reviews of recent publications on a wide variety of topics in pure and applied mathematics.

Charlotte Agnes Scott, the first mathematics department chair at Bryn Mawr College, became the first woman vice president of the AMS in 1906. Seventy-six years later, in 1982, mathematician Julia Bowman Robinson became the first woman to be elected president of the AMS. Robinson also was the first woman mathematician elected into the National Academy of Sciences (NAS).

The AMS sponsors numerous awards recognizing outstanding achievement in mathematics. Other awards and prizes recognize outstanding mathematics research by undergraduate students and distinguished public service activities in support of mathematics. The organization also maintains an endowment fund to support mathematical memoirs.

See also Bernstein, Dorothy Lewis; Bryn Mawr College; National Academy of Sciences (NAS)
References Bailey, Martha J., *American Women in Science: A Biographical Dictionary* (1994); Franck, Irene M., and David M. Brownstone, *Women's World: A Timeline of Women in History* (1995); Goggins, Tim, American Mathematical Society, telephone interview with Leonard Bernstein (27 May 1998); Maurer, Christine, and Tara E. Sheets, eds., *Encyclopedia of Associations: An Associations Unlimited Reference,* 33rd ed., vol. 1, parts 1–3 (1998); American Mathematical Society, "American Mathematical Society Overview," available at http://www.ams.org/ams/ams-info.html (cited 26 May 1998).

American Society for Nutritional Sciences (ASNS)

The American Society for Nutritional Sciences (ASNS) is an organization of basic and clinical nutrition research scientists working in industry, government, and universities throughout the world. Its members study nutritional issues relating to humans and animals and promote education and training in nutritional research. ASNS investigates controversial nutritional claims and examines the effects of new technologies such as irradiation of meat and use of transgenic (genetically engineered) vegetables. The society also aids in the development of dietary guidelines.

ASNS was founded in 1928 as the American Institute of Nutrition. Among the women who have been affiliated with the ASNS was Grace Goldsmith (1904–1967), a physician and nutritionist noted for her work on diseases caused by vitamin deficiency. She became president of the organization in 1965.

See also Alexander, Lucy Maclay; Emerson, Gladys Anderson; Farmer, Fannie Merritt; Home Economics; Morgan, Agnes Fay; Richards, Ellen Henrietta Swallow
References Franck, Irene M., and David M. Brownstone, *Women's World: A Timeline of Women in History* (1995); Maurer, Christine, and Tara E. Sheets, eds., *Encyclopedia of Associations,* 33rd ed., vol. 1, part 2 (1998); Allison, Richard G., "About the American Society for Nutritional Sciences," available

at http://www.faseb.org/asns/about.html (cited 28 March 1998).

American Society of Civil Engineers (ASCE)

The American Society of Civil Engineers (ASCE) is a professional organization whose mission is to improve and enrich the quality of life by advancing the science and profession of civil engineering through education. To achieve its objectives, the society offers continuing education courses and technical specialty conferences. Publications of the ASCE include technical and professional books, journals, manuals, newsletters, and reports. The society also supports research of new civil engineering technology and materials.

Founded in 1852, the ASCE is the oldest professional engineering society in the United States. For the first 75 years, its membership was exclusively male. In 1876, Elizabeth Bragg, the first American woman to obtain an engineering degree, graduated in civil engineering from the University of California at Berkeley. However, although Bragg and other women were working as civil engineers, the ASCE did not admit its first woman member until 1927, when admittance was granted to Elsie Eaves. Some 55 years later, Eaves was elected an honorary member of the society—a form of recognition that granted her life membership with dues exemption.

Today, the ASCE has a worldwide membership of more than 120,000, including nearly 8,000 international members from 137 nations. The ASCE also has more than 15,000 student members in 224 chapters. The student chapters provide civil engineering students an opportunity to develop a relationship with the association through participation in field trips and engineering projects.

See also Barney, Nora Stanton Blatch; Cambra, Jessie G.; Eaves, Elsie; Environmental Engineering; Roebling, Emily Warren
References Kass-Simon, G., and Patricia Farnes, eds., *Women of Science: Righting the Record* (1990); Maurer, Christine, and Tara E. Sheets, eds., *Encyclopedia of Associations,* 33rd ed., vol. 1, part 1 (1998); American Society of Civil Engineers, California State Council, at http://www.asce-ca.org/abtasce.htm (cited 4 September 1998).

American Society of Heating, Refrigerating and Air-Conditioning Engineers (ASHRAE)

The American Society of Heating, Refrigerating and Air-Conditioning Engineers (ASHRAE) is an international organization dedicated to advancing the sciences of heating, ventilation, air conditioning, and refrigeration through its development of standards and uniform worldwide industry codes for testing and rating equipment. The ASHRAE was created in 1959 through a merger of the American Society of Heating and Ventilating Engineers (ASH&VE) and the American Society of Refrigerating Engineers (ASRE). The ASH&VE began in New York City in 1894; the ASRE also formed in New York City, in 1904. Mary Engle Pennington, who became known in 1917 for recommending standards for refrigerated railroad cars, became the first woman member of the ASRE in 1920.

Today, the ASHRAE has a membership of approximately 50,000, with chapters located around the world. The society's goal is to improve the quality of life through standards writing, continuing education, conferences, seminars, and publications. Its numerous research and technical programs are overseen by 90 technical committees organized in 11 sections.

See also Engineering; Pennington, Mary Engle
References Maurer, Christine, and Tara E. Sheets, eds., *Encyclopedia of Associations,* 33rd ed., vol. 1, parts 1–3 (1998); Stanley, Autumn, *Mothers and Daughters of Invention: Notes for a Revised History of Technology* (1993); American Society of Heating, Refrigerating and Air-Conditioning Engineers, "Bay Area Engineering Council," available at http://www/ashrae.org (cited 9 September 1998).

American Society of Mechanical Engineers (ASME)

The American Society of Mechanical Engineers (ASME) is a nonprofit educational and technical society composed of mechanical engineers and students enrolled in mechanical engineering programs. The organization was founded in 1880; it admitted its first woman member, Kate Gleason, in 1918. At the time of its founding, the main goals of the organization were to develop industry-wide standards and expertise in power and machinery resulting from the Industrial Revolution.

ASME has a worldwide membership of approximately 125,000, including 300 student chapters with 24,000 student members. It is the largest single organization devoted to research, development, and dissemination of information relating to mechanical engineering and professional development for mechanical engineers. Through its numerous professional publications, ASME reviews and presents abstracts on such topics as applied mechanics, biomechanical engineering, turbomachinery, solar energy, and acoustics.

ASME recognizes achievers in mechanical engineering through an awards program targeted at both professionals and students. Among these awards are the Hoover Medal, the Holley Medal, and the Charles T. Main Student Section Award. The Hoover Medal is awarded annually to recognize "great, unselfish, non-technical services by engineers to humanity." In 1966, industrial engineer Lillian Moller Gilbreth became the first woman recipient of this award; she remains the only woman so recognized. The Holley Medal honors an engineer whose work has contributed to the advancement of society. Donna Shirley, director of the Mars Exploration Program of NASA, was issued this award in 1998 and was the first woman to be so honored. In 1998, Virginia Tech student Angela S. Carr was awarded the Charles T. Main Student Section Award for her leadership role in an ASME student section.

See also Acoustical Engineering; Gleason, Kate; Industrial Engineering; Mechanical Engineering; Society of Women Engineers (SWE); Solar Technologies
References Maurer, Christine, and Tara E. Sheets, eds., *Encyclopedia of Associations: An Associations Unlimited Reference,* 33rd ed., vol. 1, part 1 (1998); Read, Phyllis J., and Bernard L. Witlieb, *The Book of Women's Firsts* (1992); American Society of Mechanical Engineers, available at http://www.coe.ttu.edu/me/asme.htm (cited 5 May 1998).

Ancker-Johnson, Betsy (b. 1929)

Betsy Ancker-Johnson is an internationally known solid state physicist with expertise in thermonuclear fusion, microwave electronics, and plasma semiconductors. Her reputation was built on her research and her managerial roles in both industry and government. As a researcher, Ancker-Johnson helped develop seven highly sophisticated inventions. Of these, three—a signal generator, an infrared optical detector-amplifier, and a detection-modulator for an optical communication system—were her sole creations. She received patents for these devices in 1966, 1974, and 1975, respectively. Ancker-Johnson is also named as a coinventor on patents issued for a probe (1967), a signal detector, a solid-state amplifier and phase detector (both 1969), and a fast-sequential switch (1974).

Ancker-Johnson began her physics studies at Wellesley College, from which she received her B.A. in 1949. She continued her studies at the University of Tübingen, in Germany. Unlike her undergraduate years at Wellesley, an all-female institution, Ancker-Johnson's graduate student experience was permeated by gender discrimination from classmates and faculty. Nevertheless, she received her Ph.D. in physics with highest honors in 1953.

After graduating, Ancker-Johnson found that gender was often an obstacle in procuring meaningful employment in her field. However, she did eventually obtain a position as a physicist at the Boeing Science Research Labs. Through her work at Boeing, she became an important research physicist, holding several patents by the late 1960s.

In the early 1970s, Ancker-Johnson's career changed focus. While still with Boeing, she sought management level work. In 1973, she was appointed assistant secretary for science and technology at the United States Department of Commerce. Ironically, the woman whose employment was once hindered by her gender received this appointment largely because she was a woman. One of Ancker-Johnson's greatest accomplishments as assistant secretary for science and technology was her development of a means to speed the patent process for corporations in-volved in genetic engineering that complied with National Institutes of Health (NIH) guidelines in their research with recombinant DNA. After leaving this position in 1977, Ancker-Johnson spent the next two years working as associate laboratory director for physical research at the Argonne National Laboratory.

Through her positions in government, Ancker-Johnson became a respected authority on energy research and development. In 1979, she again returned to industry, accepting a job as vice president for environmental affairs at the General Motors Corporation. With this position, Ancker-Johnson became the first woman to serve as a vice president in the automobile industry. She remained in this job until her retirement in 1992.

Ancker-Johnson is a fellow of the American Physical Society, the American Association for the Advancement of Science (AAAS), and the Institute of Electrical and Electronics Engineers (IEEE), which has cited her for contributions to the understanding of plasmas and development of government science policy. In 1975, she was elected to the National Academy of Engineering—the highest honor that can be awarded an engineer. Though retired, Ancker-Johnson still serves on many national and international committees on environmental problems.

See also Affirmative Action; Argonne National Laboratory; Dresselhaus, Mildred S.; Electrical and Electronics Engineering; Patent

References Gleasner, Diana C., *Breakthrough Women in Science* (1983); Kass-Simon, G., and Patricia Farnes, eds., *Women of Science: Righting the Record* (1990); Stanley, Autumn, *Mothers and Daughters of Invention: Notes for a Revised History of Technology* (1993); Torpie, Stephen L., et al., eds., *American Men and Women of Science*, 18th ed. (1992–1993) (1992)

Anderson, Elda Emma (1899–1961)

In 1945, the first atomic bomb was exploded in the New Mexico desert. Among the many scientists to witness the event was Elda Anderson, whose work on spectroscopy and neutron scattering aided in the building of the bomb and in the design of nuclear reactors. Years after carrying out this historic work, Anderson became a world leader in health physics, a science devoted to protecting people and the environment from the effects of radiation.

Elda Anderson was born and raised in Green Lake, Wisconsin. She attended Ripon College in a neighboring community, receiving her bachelor's degree in 1922. She then entered the University of Wisconsin at Madison with a graduate assistantship in physics and was awarded a master's degree in that field in 1924. After receiving this degree, Anderson began teaching mathematics, physics, and chemistry at the Estherville Junior College in Iowa.

In 1927, Anderson returned to Wisconsin to teach science at the Menasha High School. She then joined the faculty of Milwaukee Downer College, where she helped organize the physics department, served as a professor of physics, and eventually became department chair. In 1941, Anderson took a sabbatical leave from teaching and returned to the University of Wisconsin to obtain her Ph.D. The following year she became a staff member at the Office of Scientific Research and Development (OSRD) at Princeton University (working on a precursor to the Manhattan Project).

In 1943, the OSRD moved to the Los Alamos Scientific Laboratory in New Mexico. There Anderson's research centered on spectroscopy and neutron scattering, research that was vital to the development of the atomic bomb and to nuclear reactor design. Four years later, she returned to her position as professor and chair of the physics department at Milwaukee Downer College and also taught physics courses at Wisconsin State Teachers' College.

In 1949, Anderson became the first person to head education and training for the Health Physics Department at Oak Ridge National Laboratory in Tennessee. The goal of this new field was to devise ways to protect people and the environment from the harmful effects of radiation. She remained in this position for the duration of her career.

Anderson is credited with establishing the first master's degree program in health physics at Vanderbilt University in Nashville. She also orga-

nized training programs for military personnel, state and federal officers, and professors in the United States, Sweden, Belgium, and India. In 1955, she helped organize the Health Physics Society; she later served as its secretary-treasurer and was elected president in 1959. The following year, she helped establish the American Board of Health Physics, a group for which she later served as chair. This group helped develop professional standards for certification of those entering the health physics field.

Honors bestowed upon Anderson include her elections to Sigma Xi and Sigma Delta Epsilon and her being named a fellow of the American Association for the Advancement of Science (AAAS). Following her death in 1961, the Elda Anderson Memorial Scholarship fund was established in her honor by the Health Physics Society. The fund provides financial assistance to an outstanding young health physicist.

See also Eng, Patricia L.; Manhattan Project; Nuclear Physics; Office of Scientific Research and Development (OSRD); Safety Engineering; Spectroscopy

References "Elda Anderson, Pioneer of Health Physics in the Atomic Energy Program Dies at 61" [obituary], *Health Physics* (1961); "Elda E. Anderson" [obituary], *Physics Today* (July 1961); Sicherman, Barbara, and Carol Hurd Green, eds., *Notable American Women: The Modern Period* (1980); "Women in American History: Anderson, Elda Emma," in *Britannica Online,* available at http://women.eb.com/women/articles/Anderson_Elda_Emma.html (cited 26 August 1998).

Antibiotics

Antibiotics are chemical compounds produced by fungi and bacteria that inhibit the growth of or destroy microorganisms. The word *antibiotic* is derived from *antibiosis,* a term describing a competitive relationship between species in which one organism destroys another to preserve its own life. Antibiotics were once commercially prepared only from fungi and bacteria. However, developments in biotechnology and genetic engineering have made it possible to synthesize many of these compounds in the laboratory.

Some herbs have been used for their healing properties since ancient times. However, the age of antibiotics began in 1928, when the British bacteriologist Sir Alexander Fleming observed that the fungus *Penicillium notatum* prevented the growth of a type of bacteria he was studying. Fleming named the effective compound produced by the fungus *penicillin*. Although Fleming understood the bacteria-destroying properties of penicillin, he was unable to prepare a pure form of the compound for wide use by physicians. It was Howard Florey and Ernst Chain, working at Oxford University in England, who discovered a means of producing pure penicillin in 1940. During World War II, Gladys L. Hobby, a microbiologist at Charles Pfizer and Company, was among the first to clinically test penicillin. Today, penicillin, often called the "wonder drug," remains one of the most widely used antibiotics.

Antibiotics work in two main ways: by damaging the cell or disrupting cell processes. Antibiotics that damage cells usually affect cell wall formation or the cell membrane's ability to regulate the passage of materials into and out of the cell. Antibiotics that disrupt cell processes interfere with protein synthesis or disrupt cellular metabolism.

Since the discovery of penicillin, many other antibiotics have been identified. Included among these are: streptomycin (1944), bacitracin (1945), chloroamphenicol (1947), nystatin (1948), tetracyclines (1948–1954), and erythromycin (1952). Gladys Hobby is recognized as codiscoverer of terramycin (1950), a powerful antibiotic proven effective against more than 50 diseases. Hobby also worked on the development of streptomycin. Nystatin, the first effective antibiotic in the treatment of fungal infections was codiscovered and copatented (1957) by mycologist Elizabeth Lee Hazen and biochemist Rachel Fuller Brown.

See also Alexander, Hattie Elizabeth; Biotechnology; Brown, Rachel Fuller; Elion, Gertrude Belle; Genetic Engineering; Hazen, Elizabeth Lee; Hobby, Gladys Lounsbury; Patent
References Considine, Douglas M., ed., *Van Nostrand's Scientific Encyclopedia,* 5th ed. (1976); Macdonald, Anne L., *Feminine Ingenuity: Women and Invention in America* (1992); Shearer, Benjamin F., and Barbara S. Shearer, eds., *Notable Women in the Life Sciences: A Biographical Dictionary* (1996); Travers, Bridget, ed., *World of Scientific Discovery* (1994).

Apgar, Virginia (1909–1974)

Virginia Apgar, a native of Westfield, New Jersey, is noted for many pioneering achievements and medical firsts. She is, however, best known for the Apgar Score, a system for evaluating the physical condition of infants immediately after their birth. The Apgar Score, first presented in 1952, requires that five criteria—heart and respiration rate, muscle tone, reflex actions, and skin color—be observed and measured at 1 minute and again at 5 minutes after birth. A scale of 0 to 2 is assigned to each of the five factors, with a total score of 7 or higher being considered normal. Based upon the values obtained, the system can quickly identify an infant that is in need of special medical attention. Today, use of the Apgar Score is standard in hospitals worldwide.

Virginia Apgar received her bachelor's degree from Mount Holyoke College in 1929. She then entered Columbia University's College of Physicians and Surgeons as one of its few women students. She received her medical degree in 1933. Although she chose surgery as her specialty, gender discrimination from male surgeons led Apgar to direct her interest toward the new medical field of anesthesiology. She studied anesthesiology at the University of Wisconsin and at New York's Bellevue Hospital and in 1938 became only the fiftieth physician to be certified as an anesthesiologist by the American Board of Anesthesiology. After receiving this certification, Apgar was appointed director of the newly created division of anesthesiology at Columbia-Presbyterian Medical Center in New York, the first woman to receive such an appointment.

Apgar served as director of anesthesiology for 11 years. In 1949, she became a professor at Columbia University's College of Physicians and Surgeons, the first woman to hold such a position at this medical school. Later that year, Apgar resigned from this position to devote her skills to the applications of anesthesia during childbirth. Over the next 10 years, she participated in more than 17,000 births and developed an interest in infant mortality. To learn more about this subject, she enrolled in the public health program at Johns Hopkins University, from which she received a

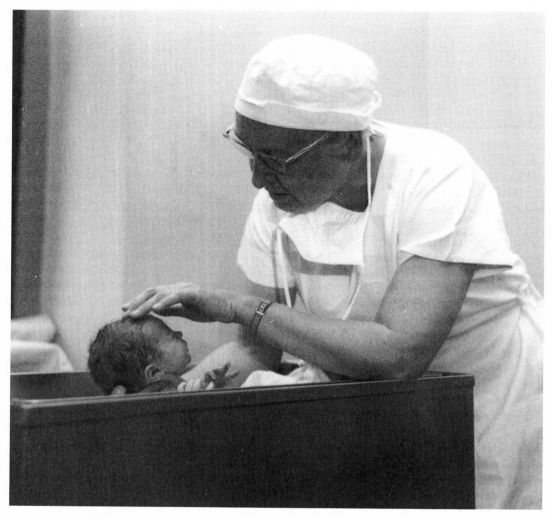

Virginia Apgar developed the Apgar score that is used to assess the health of newborn babies worldwide. (Elizabeth Wilcox Collection, Archives & Special Collections, Columbia University Health Sciences Division)

master's degree in 1959, at age 49. The same year, Apgar became director of research for the National Foundation–March of Dimes. In this position she studied, taught, lectured, and wrote articles about birth defects and prenatal care.

Apgar's work in medicine and research has had a lasting impact on American society and is credited with saving the lives of innumerable infants. For her work, Apgar received many prestigious awards, including the New York Infirmary's Elizabeth Blackwell Citation in 1960 and the Distinguished Service Award of the American Soci-ety of Anesthesiologists in 1961. In 1967, she was named Woman of the Year by the Federation of Women's Clubs of Westchester County, New York.

See also Baker, Sara Josephine; Medicine/Medical Technology; Taussig, Helen Brooke
References Bamberger, Werner, "Dr. Virginia Apgar Dies at 65; Devised Health Test for Infants" [obituary], *The New York Times Biographical Edition* (August 1974); Moritz, Charles, ed., *Current Biography, 1968* (1968); Shearer, Benjamin F., and Barbara S. Shearer, eds., *Notable Women in the Life Sciences: A Biographical Dictionary* (1996); Sicherman, Barbara, and Carol Hurd Green, eds., *Notable American Women: The Modern*

Period (1980); Stanley, Autumn, *Mothers and Daughters of Invention: Notes for a Revised History of Technology* (1993); Vare, Ethlie Ann, and Greg Ptacek, *Mothers of Invention: From the Bra to the Bomb, Forgotten Women and Their Unforgettable Ideas* (1988).

Architecture

Architecture is the application of science, art, and technology to the design and construction of buildings, memorials, and monuments. Traditionally, architecture has always made use of the concepts and principles of mathematics and physics, as it relates to strength, balance, and geometry. More recently, architects also have begun utilizing the principles of chemistry, as they make decisions concerning the appropriateness of different materials in the construction and aesthetic appearance of a structure.

Although architecture has traditionally been and continues to be a male-dominated field, women have made significant inroads into and contributions in this area. Although she was not trained as an architect, Harriet Irwin of Charlotte, North Carolina, designed a house for which she received a patent in 1869. Irwin's house featured a hexagonal design that limited wasted space, such as hallways and corners, and provided excellent ventilation and lighting through the calculated placement of windows. Noted architect of the time Calvert Vaux rebuked Irwin for attempting to be successful in a field he deemed inappropriate for women. However, Irwin's design did meet with success, becoming the model for several houses in the Charlotte area.

Less than twenty years after Harriet Irwin ventured into architecture, Louise Blanchard Bethune became the first American woman to practice as an architect. Louise Blanchard began her career as a drafter with an architectural firm in Buffalo, New York. After marrying another drafter, Robert Armore Bethune, she opened an architectural office in partnership with her husband. Louise personally designed a variety of buildings throughout the Buffalo area and became one of the first people to make use of steel framing and poured concrete in her designs. In 1888, she became the first woman to be admitted into the American Institute of Architects (AIA).

In 1890, Sophia Hayden became the first woman to obtain a degree in architecture from a four-year program when she graduated from the Massachusetts Institute of Technology (MIT). The next year, Hayden entered a competition for women architects that involved the design of a building that would be used at the World's Columbian Exposition in Chicago in 1893. Hayden's design was selected over those of twelve other women who had submitted plans for the construction of the Woman's Building (the structure that housed the technical creations of women). For her work, Hayden was awarded a $1,000 payment; she also won a gold medal for her design.

In 1911, Anna W. Keichline received her architectural degree from Cornell University's School of Architecture. She became New York's first registered woman architect. After receiving her degree, Keichline devoted her architectural attention to the inside of the home and obtained patents for kitchen designs that were based on time and efficiency studies.

Civil engineer Nora Stanton Blatch Barney began developing her interest in architecture in the 1920s. During this time, she worked as both an architect and a real estate developer in Connecticut. Eventually, her family moved into a house that Barney herself designed.

Frances Bateson Gabe began a home repair company shortly after World War II. This company, Batey's Building Repairs, purchased homes that were in disrepair, refurbished them, and sold them at a profit. Although this endeavor does not in and of itself constitute architectural work, Gabe's design of a "self-cleaning house," for which she was awarded a patent in 1984, does qualify as an architectural accomplishment. Gabe's house features almost 70 separate devices, including a combination dishwasher-cabinet, a system of adjustable floor joists, and furniture constructed of waterproof materials, designed to allow the home to be cleaned with the push of a few buttons, thus saving time and effort.

Vivian Loftness is a contemporary woman architect who has gained some notoriety in her field. Loftness currently is a Carnegie Mellon University professor and head of the department of architecture there. Over the last two decades, Loftness and her husband, Volker Hartkopf (also a professor of architecture), have developed a concept in architecture called Total Building Performance. This concept strives to unite concerns of architecture, art, engineering, and environmental sustainability in the development of new structures intended for use by people. In addition, Loftness also has developed housing units designed to take advantage of current technological advances, such as those in solar technology, to make buildings more energy efficient.

The work of architects is not limited to structures that will be directly used by people. Many architects have focused their talents on developing works of art that are classified as monuments and memorials. Such is the case with Maya Lin, who has developed such notable creations as the Vietnam Veterans Memorial, in Washington, D.C.; the Civil Rights Memorial in Montgomery, Alabama; and the Women's Table at Yale University, in New Haven, Connecticut (the school from which Lin received her architectural degree).

In the last quarter of the twentieth century, two major changes occurred in the field of architecture. The first is that more areas of specialty emerged; for example, environmental design, interior architecture, landscape architecture, and urban design and planning. The second is that the number of women participating in all areas of architecture increased dramatically. According to the National Center for Educational Statistics, women received only 5 percent of the 3,459 undergraduate degrees in architecture during the 1970–1971 school year. One decade later, women were receiving almost 17 percent of the 5,465 undergraduate degrees. Over the next decade, the proportion of undergraduate architectural degrees conferred on women rose to 27.2 percent. In the next four years (the most recent period for which data are available), this proportion rose to almost 30 percent.

See also American Institute of Architects (AIA); Barney, Nora Stanton Blatch; Bethune, Louise Blanchard; Gabe, Frances Bateson; Hayden, Sophia Gregoria; Irwin, Harriet; Keichline, Anna W.; Lin, Maya; Loftness, Vivian; Materials Engineering; Solar Technologies
References Ambrose, Susan A., et al., *Journeys of Women in Science and Engineering: No Universal Constants* (1997); Ashby, Ruth, and Deborah Gore Ohrn, eds., *Herstory: Women Who Changed the World* (1995); Macdonald, Anne L., *Feminine Ingenuity: How Women Inventors Changed America* (1992); McMurran, Kristan, "Frances Gabe's Self-Cleaning House Could Mean New Rights of Spring for Housewives," *People Weekly* (29 March 1982); U.S. Department of Education, Office of Educational Research and Improvement, National Center for Education Statistics, *Chartbook of Degrees Conferred, 1969–70 to 1993–94* (December 1997).

Argonne National Laboratory

Named after the famed World War I battle site, the Argonne National Laboratory is one of the largest energy-related research facilities in the United States. It is operated by the University of Chicago for the U.S. Department of Energy (DOE), and its primary research focus is nuclear and high-energy physics. The laboratory also conducts research in the application of alternative energy resources and synthetic fuels.

The Argonne National Laboratory was originally established in 1942 as the Metallurgical Laboratory at the University of Chicago. This name was used to mask the true nature of the work that was to be conducted at the laboratory, which was then part of the Manhattan Project, a top-secret World War II program to develop the first atomic bomb. Among the many women involved in this endeavor were Elda Emma Anderson, Maria Goeppert-Mayer, Edith Quimby, Chien-Shiung Wu, Helen Blair Bartlett, and Margaret Foster. The laboratory was moved to its present southwest Chicago location in 1946 and renamed the Argonne National Laboratory.

See also Anderson, Elda Emma; Atomic Energy Commission (AEC); Bartlett, Helen Blair; Butler, Margaret K.; Fink, Kathryn (Kay) Ferguson; Foster, Margaret; Goeppert-Mayer, Maria; Herzenberg, Caroline Littlejohn; Libby, Leona W.; Manhattan Project; Nuclear Physics; Office of Scientific Research and Development (OSRD); Ordnance; Quimby, Edith Hinkley; Way, Katharine; Wu, Chien-Shiung
References Groueff, Stephane, *The Manhattan Project: The Untold Story of the Making of the Atomic Bomb* (1967); Saari, Peggy, and Stephen Allison, eds.,

Scientists: The Lives and Works of 150 Scientists, vol. 3 (1996); Weatherford, Doris, *American Women's History: An A to Z of People, Organizations, Issues, and Events* (1994).

Askins, Barbara (n.d.)

When scientists at the National Aeronautics and Space Administration (NASA) needed to find a way to make photographic images of stars clearer and more visible, they assigned this project to research chemist Barbara Askins. While working at the Marshall Space Flight Center in Huntsville, Alabama, in the late 1970s, Askins created a new process for developing film containing star images. Her method involves the transfer of an unclear image from the original film to a new piece of film. The new film image, which is developed by a process in which radioactive materials are used, is called an *autoradiograph*. In addition to its use in the space sciences, this technique also has been found to have applications in other areas.

Long before she became a chemist for the Marshall Space Flight Center, Barbara Askins had other career plans. Askins began her college studies at the Middle Tennessee State College, where she planned to major in English; however, after filling one of her elective course slots with a chemistry course, she changed her major to chemistry. Askins did not complete her studies at college. Instead, she dropped out of college, married a former professor, and started a family. It was not until her children reached school age that Askins decided to return to college and complete her education. She did so at the University of Alabama in Huntsville, where she earned a B.S. degree in chemistry.

Askins worked briefly as a teacher of high school physics. While accompanying her students on a field trip to the Marshall Space Flight Center, she decided that she wanted to have a career that more actively involved her in science. She returned to the University of Alabama to obtain her master's degree in chemistry.

With her master's degree in hand, Askins applied to and was immediately hired by NASA. Her first assignment was to find a way to improve the quality of star photographs to make them useful to scientists. Askins worked on the problem for the next two years before coming up with the process and the new film that provided the solution, in 1976. To produce this film, she needed to find a chemical that would combine with the silver present in the original film without also combining with the film emulsion. She tried treating the original film with radioactive chemicals and then placing that film in contact with a second piece of film. In the process, the radioactivity from the original film exposed the new piece of film, while also transferring the original image from the first piece of film to the second. Unlike the original image, however, the transferred image was clear. This new technology not only benefited NASA and astronomy, it has since been used by biologists, who have found a way to use autoradiographs to study cells.

Askins received many accolades for the work that resulted in the autoradiograph. She was named as both the 1978 NASA Inventor of the Year and the 1978 National Inventor of the Year. She was the first woman to receive the latter award for work done by herself. The NASA award was accompanied by a bonus of $4,000 and a promotion from researcher to project manager. In her new post, Askins was assigned responsibilities that included developing plans for a space station. Since 1987, she has worked for the Office of Space Flight's Advanced Program Development Division, managing a project called the Assured Crew Return Vehicle. This vehicle will be based at the space station to provide astronauts with a means of returning to Earth if an injury occurs or if problems with the space station or a space shuttle necessitate such a return.

See also Astronomy; Blodgett, Katherine Burr; National Aeronautics and Space Administration (NASA); Space Exploration

References Jones, Stacy V., "Chemist Is Inventor of the Year," *New York Times* (27 January 1979); Macdonald, Anne L., *Feminine Ingenuity: How Women Inventors Changed America* (1992); Showell, Ellen H., and Fred M. B. Amram, *From Indian Corn to Outer Space: Women Invent in America* (1995); Stanley, Autumn, *Mothers and Daughters of Invention: Notes for a Revised History of Technology* (1993).

Association for the Advancement of Women (AAW)

Founded in 1873, the Association for the Advancement of Women (AAW) promoted the scholarship of women and their entrance into professional careers. During the association's early years, its membership consisted of women working in such fields as religion, education, medicine, astronomy, and geology. Astronomer Maria Mitchell, a founding member and later president of the AAW, and Emme Curtiss, mother of noted geologist Florence Bascom, were among the AAW members working to influence young women in those years.

In the early 1890s, several of AAW's charter members accepted positions with other organizations. New women's colleges were being founded (Bryn Mawr College, in 1885; Barnard College, in 1889; and Mount Holyoke and Radcliffe, in 1893), and state schools had begun to accept women. Both of these factors led to a decline in AAW's membership, resulting in its eventual collapse at the turn of the century. Despite its demise, the goals and objectives of AAW were realized when the American Association of University Women (AAUW) formed through a merger of the Association of Collegiate Alumni and the Southern Association of College Women in 1921.

See also Affirmative Action; American Association of University Women (AAUW); Barnard College; Bryn Mawr College; Mount Holyoke College
References Franck, Irene M., and David M. Brownstone, *Women's World: A Timeline of Women in History* (1995); Heinemann, Susan, *Timelines of American Women's History* (1996); Macdonald, Anne L., *Feminine Ingenuity: How Women Inventors Changed America* (1992); Shearer, Benjamin F., and Barbara S. Shearer, eds., *Notable Women in the Physical Sciences: A Biographical Dictionary* (1997); Weatherford, Doris, *American Women's History: An A to Z of People, Organizations, Issues, and Events* (1994).

Association for Women in Science (AWIS)

The Association for Women in Science (AWIS) is a nonprofit organization composed of professionals and students working in the life and physical sciences, mathematics, the social sciences, and engineering. Founded in 1971 as the Association of Women in Science, the organization changed its name in 1975 and broadened its membership to include men. The primary goal of the AWIS is to promote women's participation and advancement in the sciences.

The association currently has more than 6,000 members, more than 50 percent of whom hold doctorates in their fields. With more than 75 local chapters throughout the United States, the AWIS aids in networking among women scientists in many areas. The chapters also encourage and support the participation of women in science by sponsoring educational programs in schools and community-based mentoring initiatives nationwide. Many of these programs and projects are funded through scholarships and grants provided by organizations such as the U.S. Department of Energy (DOE), the National Aeronautics and Space Administration (NASA), the Alfred P. Sloan Foundation, and the National Science Foundation (NSF).

In addition to its scientific programs, the AWIS is actively involved in equal opportunity legislation for women and closely monitors events in this area. In 1971, seeking to remedy the limited representation of women at the National Institutes of Health (NIH), the AWIS filed a lawsuit against the NIH—a case that it won in 1978.

See also Affirmative Action; American Association of University Women (AAUW); Society of Women Engineers (SWE)
References Maurer, Christine, and Tara E. Sheets, eds., *Encyclopedia of Associations: An Associations Unlimited Reference,* 33rd ed., vol. 1, part 1 (1998); Association for Women in Science, "AWIS History," available at http://www.awis.org/htm/awis_history. html (cited 12 January 2000).

Astronomy

Astronomy, the study of the universe beyond Earth's atmosphere, is the oldest of all the sciences. Astronomy originated among prehistoric peoples who made observations of the sun, moon, stars, and planets (Mercury, Venus, Mars, Jupiter, and Saturn) visible with the unaided eye. Early civilizations recognized the regularity of motions of celestial bodies and used the movements of the sun and the moons as measurements of time. Others used astronomical observations as tools for navigation.

Records indicate that as early as the fourteenth century B.C., the Chinese developed a calendar, created a star catalog (of about 800 stars), and noted the occurrence of comets, meteors, large sunspots, and novae (exploding stars). Between 1800 and 400 B.C., the Babylonians and Assyrians calculated the length of a solar year and developed a lunar month based upon the 29.5 days the moon requires to undergo one complete cycle of its phases (the period from one full moon to the next). To some extent, these observations enabled early peoples to make predictions of such celestial events as lunar eclipses and solar eclipses. The Babylonians and the Egyptians also developed and constructed fairly accurate instruments to measure the passage of time, as evidenced by a fairly well preserved Egyptian sundial that dates back to the eighth century B.C.

Many early cultures treated astronomy as a religion. The Egyptians, Aztecs, Mayans, Greeks, and Romans were among the cultures that worshiped the sun and other celestial bodies. Astrology, which some consider a religion, was derived from the idea that an individual's fate and future is governed by the positions of the stars and other celestial bodies. It, too, probably had its beginnings with the Babylonians. The science of astronomy profited from astrology in that astrology requires an extensive knowledge of the motions of heavenly bodies. It also utilized charts and models displaying the positions and locations of these bodies in the sky. Methods of predicting future positions of these bodies also had to be developed. Though many famous astronomers, including Tycho Brahe and Johannes Kepler, did not believe in astrology, they were expected to prepare horoscopes as part of their daily tasks.

In 600 B.C., the Greek philosopher Thales proposed that the planet Earth was round. Others conceived of Earth as a rotating body. Aristotle (384–322 B.C.) explained how the moon went through its phases and why it appeared to change in appearance during the month. He also explained the basic concept of eclipses. Around 200 B.C., Eratosthenes, using simple geometry, successfully calculated Earth's diameter. Other Greek academicians developed methods of determining distances in space and calculated the relative distances of the sun and the moon from the Earth.

Around 140 A.D., Ptolemy compiled fourteen volumes on astronomy in which he developed a model showing Earth at the center of the universe. This model also showed all other celestial bodies revolving around Earth. Ptolemy's theories were considered valid and were accepted as true for the next thirteen centuries. During this expanse of time, only the Hindus and the Arabs, through their development of mathematical procedures and calculations, contributed to the science of astronomy.

In 1514, the Polish astronomer Nicolaus Copernicus (1473–1543) developed the heliocentric theory—a concept that held that Earth as well as the other planets revolve around the sun. Tycho Brahe (1546–1601) spent twenty years gathering data from observations of the heavens that were later used by Johannes Kepler (1571–1630) to formulate his laws of planetary motion. Kepler stated that all of the bodies in the solar system revolved around the sun at predictable speeds, in elliptical orbits. Meanwhile, in 1609, Galileo (1564–1642) built one of the first telescopes, with which he observed and discovered the moons of Jupiter, the phases of Venus, and the mountains and craters on the surface of Earth's moon. Sir Isaac Newton's (1643–1727) Laws of Motion provided evidence that explained Copernicus's theories and Kepler's Laws of Planetary Motion. In addition, Newton's findings marked the beginnings of the science of celestial mechanics.

In addition to Newton's studies of planetary motion, he also demonstrated that a prism (a pyramid-shaped piece of glass) could be used to separate white light into its component colors, producing a spectrum. The prism later became an essential component of the spectroscope (a device used to analyze the composition of light), which has become one of the most valuable tools in astronomy. This vital tool, which can be used to study the spectrum of a star, can reveal the star's temperature, its chemical composition, and its direction of motion. These data, in turn, can be used to ascertain the distance of the star from Earth, its size, and its approximate age.

Until about the mid-1700s, virtually all of the recorded discoveries in astronomy were attributed to men. However, women also made a significant contribution. Many of the earliest women to be recognized in the field began their work as assistants to husbands or other male relatives. Such was the case with Sir William and Caroline Herschel. In 1781, Sir William Herschel (1738–1822) discovered the existence of a new planet—Uranus—the first such discovery since ancient times. The evidence suggests that Sir William relied heavily on the assistance of his sister Caroline in the work that led to this discovery.

The spectroscope opened the door to the field of astrophysics, which is concerned with the composition of stars and galaxies. Sir William Huggins (1824–1910) was a pioneer in spectroscopic photography. He made the first spectroscopic observation of a nova in 1866. Although Huggins is considered one of the founders of astrophysics, it should be noted that his wife, Lady Huggins, not only assisted him in much of his work but also served as her husband's coauthor on ten scientific papers.

Astronomers turned their attention to the analysis and classification of stars in the mid- to late nineteenth century. It was at this time that women gained entry into the field. It was also during this time that many universities began to establish astronomical observatories. One of the pioneers in this area was Maria Mitchell, who by the late 1850s was recognized as America's first and only woman astronomer. In 1847, Mitchell observed and calculated the orbit of a new comet, which was later named Mitchell, in her honor. The following year, she became the first woman to be elected into the American Academy of Arts and Sciences. Mitchell later observed and recorded data relating to the surface features of Jupiter and Saturn. In the 1860s she developed an astronomy program at Vassar College in Poughkeepsie, New York, and became the first director of the college's observatory. During her tenure at Vassar College, Mitchell served as mentor and instructor to many other women who became significant figures in astronomy. In addition, in the 1870s, Mitchell cofounded the Association for the Advancement of Women (AAW). Despite all of these contributions, it has been reported that because Mitchell was a woman her salary was less than one-third of the $2,500 paid annually to the male professors of Vassar.

Just as Maria Mitchell was instrumental in introducing astronomy at Vassar, Sarah Frances Whiting (1847–1927) introduced astronomy courses at Wellesley College of Massachusetts. Whiting also was instrumental in securing the funds needed for the development of the Whitin Observatory at Wellesley.

Notable astrophysicists Mary Whitney (1847–1921) and Antonia Maury (1866–1952) were students of Mitchell, and Annie Jump Cannon (1863–1941), of Whiting. Whitney did studies on the orbits of minor planets (asteroids). Minor planets—for example, Ceres—differ from the nine major planets primarily in their sizes and in the place in which they revolve around the sun: a region called the asteroid belt, located between the orbits of Mars and Jupiter. Whitney also studied comets and variable stars (stars whose brightnesses appear to change in intensity).

Until the mid-1950s, most women who entered the field of astronomy were delegated those responsibilities that their male counterparts considered the "women's work" of astronomy. Such work included record keeping, cataloging, and data collecting based upon spectroscopic analyses of photographic plates. Antonia Maury worked at the Harvard Observatory between 1888 and 1896. In this job, Maury's major responsibilities included examining photographic plates of star spectra. As a result of her observations of almost 5,000 stars, an astute Maury was able to develop a system of star classification. This classification system directly related the width and sharpness of a star's spectral lines to the size and luminosity of that star.

The work of Annie Jump Cannon at the Harvard Observatory followed that done by Maury. Cannon simplified and perfected Maury's method of star classification. In addition, Cannon also discovered 277 variable stars and 5 new stars. She is credited with classifying more than one-quarter million stars during her tenure at Harvard. Cannon's work at the Harvard Observatory was of such significance that she was often referred to as the "census taker of the skies." Despite the significance of the work this accolade implies, Cannon was twice rejected as a candidate for membership in the exclusively male (at the time) National Academy of Sciences, primarily because of the presumed insignificance of any work done by a woman astronomer.

Henrietta Swann Leavitt (1868–1921) worked at the Harvard Observatory at about the same time as Cannon. She too was asked to analyze photographic plates of stars. Leavitt used these plates to determine the magnitude (brightness) of stars. She also studied variable stars and determined that there is a relationship between the length of a variable star's period of brightness and its magnitude. Leavitt recorded these data in a table known as the *Period Luminosity Relationship for Variable Stars*. In addition, Leavitt discovered 2,400 variable stars.

Charlotte Moore Sitterly was a spectroscopist who was an authority on the composition of the sun. Her major areas of research included the solar (sun's) spectra and atomic spectra. In 1933, she published tables identifying these spectra. Shortly thereafter, she used her observations of solar and atomic spectra to identify the presence of technetium, a newly discovered element, in the sun.

Another astrophysicist working at the Harvard Observatory was Cecilia Payne-Gaposchkin (1900–1979). Using photographic plates, she developed techniques for determining the magnitudes of stars. Payne-Gaposchkin also determined that most stars were composed of the gaseous elements hydrogen and helium. In 1956, Margaret Peachey Burbidge, together with her husband and two other astronomers, built on Payne-Gaposchkin's studies to develop a theory explaining how heavy metals form inside a star during its evolution. Burbidge also investigated the rotations of galaxies. In the 1980s, Vera

Cooper Rubin (1928–) used spectroscopic data to study the orbits of stars within galaxies. She also suggested that most of the universe is composed of dark matter—matter that cannot be detected using current technologies.

More recently, many technological advances in the fields of astronomy and astrophysics have been made thanks to the development of the radio telescope. The first such telescope was developed in 1931 by Karl Jansky. Such telescopes, which incorporate the use of huge parabolic dishes, are used to collect radio waves emitted from space. Among the many groups making use of this technology is SETI (the Search for Extraterrestrial Intelligence). Astrophysicist Jill Tarter cofounded the SETI Institute in 1984. In 1992, Tarter joined the newly developed SETI program of NASA. Tarter remains a leading authority in this area.

See also Askins, Barbara; Burbidge, (Eleanor) Margaret Peachey; Maury, Antonia; Payne-Gaposchkin, Cecilia; Rubin, Vera Cooper; Sitterly, Charlotte Moore; Space Exploration; Spectroscopy; Vassar College; Wellesley College; Whiting, Sarah Frances
References Abell, George, *Exploration of the Universe,* 2nd ed. (1969); Guernsey, Janet B., "The Lady Wanted to Purchase a Wheatstone Bridge: Sarah Frances Whiting and Her Successor," in *Making Contributions: An Historical Overview of Women's Role in Physics* (1984); Kass-Simon, G., and Patricia Farnes, eds., *Women of Science: Righting the Record* (1990); Kidwell, Peggy A., "Cecilia Payne-Gaposchkin: The Making of an Astrophysicist," in *Making Contributions: An Historical Overview of Women's Role in Physics* (1984); Lankford, John, and Rickey L. Slavings, "Gender and Science: Women in American Astronomy, 1859–1940," *Physics Today* 43:3 (March 1990); Moritz, Charles, ed., *Current Biography, 1962* (1962); "History of the SETI Institute," available at http://www.seti-inst.edu/general/seti-his.html (cited 14 January 2000).

Atomic Energy Commission (AEC)

Established by Congress in 1946, the Atomic Energy Commission (AEC) was a nonmilitary agency of the United States government with the responsibility of overseeing and regulating the production and use of atomic (nuclear) energy. Created after the development of the atomic bomb, the AEC at first focused primarily on military applications of nuclear energy. However, in

1954, the scope of the agency was broadened to include the development and application of nuclear energy by private industry. This redirection emphasized the production and refinement of nuclear materials; safety procedures to be used in the event of nuclear accidents; research in the fields of health and medicine; and applications of nuclear energy as a source of electricity.

In 1972, Dixy Lee Ray was appointed to the AEC. The following year, she was selected to chair the commission. Ray was the first woman to serve in this capacity. In 1975, after leaving the AEC, Ray served as governor of her home state of Washington. In 1974, Congress abolished the AEC, reassigning its responsibilities first to the Energy Research and Development Administration and later to the newly created Department of Energy (DOE). In 1975, the Nuclear Regulatory Commission (NRC) was formed to oversee the safe and efficient use of nuclear energy.

See also Argonne National Laboratory; Jackson, Shirley Ann; Manhattan Project; Nuclear Physics; Quimby, Edith Hinkley
References Heinemann, Susan, *Timelines of American Women's History* (1996); Nuclear Regulatory Commission, "NRC Short History," available at http://www.nrc.gov/SECY/smj/shorhis.htm (cited 3 March 1998).

Averell, Georgene Hopf (1876–1963)

Georgene Hopf Averell became well known as a New York doll maker during the first half of the twentieth century. Averell began her career in doll making after being hospitalized in Portland, Oregon, in 1910. While in the hospital, she is reported to have made a toy for a child who also was hospitalized; the happiness brought to the child by the toy was apparently the motive that drove her into the doll- and toy-making business, first in Seattle, later in Los Angeles, and then in New York.

The funding for Averell's New York toy and doll company, Georgene Novelties, Incorporated, was apparently provided by her husband James Paul Averell. The company became very successful during World War I, when Georgene Averell introduced a doll with an "unbreakable" head. Later, Averell is reported to have utilized mechanical doll parts developed by noted inventor Margaret E. Knight, permitting her dolls to walk and talk.

In 1918, the characters of Raggedy Ann and Raggedy Andy began to appear in children's stories fashioned by cartoonist John Gruelle. Averell's company quickly began producing and marketing these dolls, which today are collector's items. Among Averell's other notable dolls were the rag dolls she began producing during the Great Depression, which sold for $1 each. Several years later, in 1937, she began to produce the "Baby Georgene" doll, of which the company was soon producing more than 250,000 each year.

After retiring from the doll business, Georgene Averell moved to Santa Monica, California. She remained there until her death at the age of 87 in 1963.

See also Handler, Ruth; Knight, Margaret E.
References "Mrs. Averell, 87, Led Doll Concern: Founder of Company Here Dies on West Coast" [obituary], *New York Times* (28 August 1963); Stanley, Autumn, *Mothers and Daughters of Invention: Notes for a Revised History of Technology* (1993).

Baby Fae (1984–1984)

A fictitious name given to an infant girl who became the first recipient of an organ originating from an animal donor. In 1984, the heart of a seven-month-old female baboon was transplanted into the five-pound, two-week-old infant girl, who had been born with a malformed heart. To protect the identity of the child and her family, the child was given the pseudonym Baby Fae. The transplant surgery was performed by Leonard L. Bailey, a pediatric cardiologist, at the Loma Linda University Medical Center in Loma Linda, California. Following the delicate surgical procedure, Baby Fae survived 20 days, until her body rejected the transplanted heart, resulting in her death.

Bailey focused on animal-to-human transplants because no compatible human heart was available. Supporters of the procedure stessed that the use of animal organs for human transplant surgery might sustain a patient's life until an acceptable human donor was located. However, the transplant surgery sparked much controversy and gave rise to many procedural and ethical questions concerning the sacrifice of animals for scientific research and the use of animal organs in humans. Although ethical questions still remain, from a purely surgical, scientific, and technological standpoint much was learned from this precise and delicate procedure.

See also Biomedical Engineering; Biotechnology; Medicine/Medical Technology
References Dickson, Paul, *Timelines* (1991); Francis, Raymond L., *The Illustrated Almanac of Science, Technology, and Invention* (1997); Wallis, C. Rime, "Baby Fae Stuns the World," *Time,* vol. 124 (November 1984).

Baker, Sara Josephine (1873–1945)

Sara Josephine Baker is noted for her role in tracing the source of a typhoid fever outbreak in New York City around 1900 to a cook who came to be known as "Typhoid Mary." She is less known for her contributions to technology, which included her invention of a disposable infant eyedropper kit for inserting sterile silver nitrate solution into the eyes of infants following childbirth. The solution was used at the time to prevent congenital blindness. Baker also designed safer infant cloth-

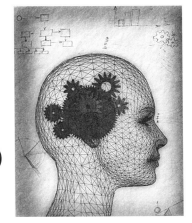

ing, patterns for which were made by the McCall Pattern Company. The Metropolitan Life Insurance Company thought the clothing important enough to buy 200,000 such patterns for distribution to its policyholders.

Sara Josephine Baker was born in Poughkeepsie, New York. In 1889, her father and brother died. This event prompted her to seek a career in medicine so that she could support her mother and sister. She entered New York Women's Medical College in 1894 and received her degree four years later, graduating second in her class. Baker interned at a clinic in the New England Hospital for Women and Children in Boston. She then moved to New York City, where she opened a private practice.

In 1901, Baker became a New York City medical inspector. Her assignment was to screen the city's immigrant population for contagious diseases, such as dysentery, smallpox, typhoid fever, and influenza. Her dedication and hard work eventually led to the discovery of the source of a typhoid fever outbreak that plagued the city. Baker identified a food service worker, Mary Mallon, as the source of the outbreak. Mallon, who came to be known as Typhoid Mary, worked as a cook in a Long Island restaurant. Baker's success in this endeavor led to her appointment as assistant health commissioner of New York City in 1907.

In 1908, the New York City Department of Health created a division of child hygiene. Baker

Sara Josephine Baker identified Mary Mallon ("Typhoid Mary") as the source of an epidemic in New York City. (Corbis/Bettmann-UPI)

left her position as assistant health commissioner to direct this agency. She thus became the first woman in the United States to hold an executive position in a health department. Among Baker's major accomplishments in her new post was making health reform and preventive medicine a responsibility of government. Milk stations were set up throughout the city where nurses examined infants and distributed free pasteurized milk. Baker also began training and licensing programs for midwives. On her instructions, nurses made home visits to examine newborns and to instruct mothers about nutrition and hygiene. Other nurses examined children at public schools, seeking evidence of contagious diseases. Baker also established the "Little Mothers' League," which trained young girls to care for their infant siblings while their mothers worked. She also is credited with establishing a foster care program for orphaned babies. From the onset of her work in child care and public health in 1907 until her retirement in 1923, Baker's initiatives

played a major role in lowering infant mortality rates in New York City from 111 per thousand to 66 per thousand.

In 1912, Baker helped establish the Federal Children's Bureau and Public Health Service (today's Department of Health and Human Services). Three years later, she accepted a position as an instructor of child hygiene at the New York University Medical School, with the understanding that she would be permitted to enroll in the school's public health program—a program traditionally closed to women. This agreement not only benefited Baker but also opened the door to other women. In 1917, Baker became the first woman in the United States to receive a Ph.D. in public health.

From 1922 to 1924, Baker served as a U.S. representative to the League of Nations' health committee. In addition to her work as an instructor and public health official, she also promoted awareness of public health concerns through her writing. She wrote five books and many professional articles. She was active in many professional organizations and served as president of two of them—the American Child Hygiene Association (1918) and the American Medical Women's Association (1935). She served as a consultant on child hygiene for the U.S. Public Health Service and the New York and New Jersey Departments of Health. After retiring from the New York City Department of Health, Baker became consulting director in maternity and child health for the Children's Bureau of the U.S. Department of Labor.

See also Apgar, Virginia; Demorest, Ellen Curtis; Taussig, Helen Brooke; Women's Rights
References Altman, Linda Jacobs, *Women Inventors: American Profiles* (1997); Bernstein, Leonard, Alan Winkler, and Linda Zierdt-Warshaw, *Multicultural Women of Science* (1996); Leavitt, Judith Walzer, *Typhoid Mary: Captive to the Public's Health* (1996); McMurray, Emily M., ed., *Notable Twentieth-Century Scientists* (1995); O'Hern, Elizabeth Moot, *Profiles of Pioneer Women Scientists* (1986); Vare, Ethlie Ann, and Greg Ptacek, *Mothers of Invention: From the Bra to the Bomb, Forgotten Women and Their Unforgettable Ideas* (1988).

Baldwin, Anna (n.d.)

Anna Baldwin is credited with developing four improved devices for use in the dairy industry. Although little is known about Anna Baldwin's life, it is known that she and her husband operated a dairy farm in Newark, New Jersey. Baldwin was granted a patent for her first device in 1868, an improved method of treating milk to obtain pomade—a scented ointment for dressing hair—and butter. One year later, she obtained her second and third patents for an improved milk separator and an improved milk cooler. The patent for her improved milk cooler was reissued in 1871.

In 1879, Baldwin was awarded a patent for her fourth dairy-related device, "an improved milking machine" called the Hygienic Glove Milker. The device, which fit over the udders like the fingers of a glove, differed from other models because it created suction to mimic the suckling of a calf through the use of a hand pump. Most earlier milking devices were mechanical and applied pressure, mimicking hand milking.

See also Agricultural Engineering; Agriculture; Greene, Catherine Littlefield; Patent
References Macdonald, Anne L., *Feminine Ingenuity: How Women Inventors Changed America* (1992); Stanley, Autumn, *Mothers and Daughters of Invention* (1993); Van Vleck, Richard, "Early Cow Milking Machines," *Scientific Medical & Mechanical Antiques,* no. 20 (1996), available at http://www.americanartifacts.com/smma/milker/milker.htm (cited 23 March 1998).

Barnard College

Barnard College is an independent liberal arts college for women that is affiliated with Columbia University. Although it was the last of the Seven Sister Colleges to be established, Barnard was a pioneer in providing young women the opportunity to pursue higher education. The college is named for its earliest and strongest advocate, Frederick A. P. Barnard, Columbia University's tenth president. Barnard admitted its first incoming class of 14 young women to a rented brownstone on Madison Avenue in 1889. At the time, the faculty consisted of six teachers. The college moved to its present location adjacent to Columbia University in 1898.

Since its beginnings, Barnard has issued degrees to nearly 30,000 students. The school's current president is Judith R. Shapiro, a former administrator at Bryn Mawr College. Barnard students enjoy a range of educational opportunities through the school's ties with Columbia University, the Juilliard School, the Manhattan School of Music, and the Jewish Theological Seminary of America. Many Barnard graduates continue their educations at the postgraduate level: According to the most recent edition of *Baccalaureate Origins of Doctorate Recipients,* published by Franklin and Marshall University, in the decade 1981–1990, the college had the fourth highest percentage of graduates pursuing Ph.D.'s in the sciences.

See also Seven College Conference
References Barnard College, *1997–1999 Catalogue* (1997–1998 edition); Weatherford, Doris, *American Women's History: An A to Z of People, Organizations, Issues, and Events* (1994); *Baccalaureate Origins of Doctorate Recipients,* 8th ed. (1998), available at http://www.fandm.edu/Departments/CollegeRelations/BacOrigins/bacorigins.html (cited 31 May 1998).

Barney, Nora Stanton Blatch (1883–1971)

Nora Stanton Blatch Barney is recognized as the first woman in the United States to receive a degree in civil engineering. She was also the first woman to be admitted into the American Society of Civil Engineers (ASCE). Although these accomplishments are themselves noteworthy, Barney also made significant contributions as an architect, real estate developer, writer, and women's rights activist.

Nora Stanton Blatch was born in Basingstoke, England, in 1883. While she was still a child, her family moved to the United States, settling in New York. There Blatch attended and graduated from the prestigious Horace Mann School before entering Cornell University in 1901. She received a degree in civil engineering with honors from Cornell in 1905 and immediately became a member, with junior status, in the American Society of Civil Engineers (ASCE).

While working toward her engineering degree, Blatch developed her skills by participating in a survey of New York State water resources. At the same time, Blatch, the granddaughter of famed women's rights activist Elizabeth Cady Stanton, became involved in women's rights issues. After graduating from Cornell, Barney spent the next three years working as a draftsperson for the American Bridge Company and then for the New York City Board of Water Supply. She then took graduate courses in mathematics and electricity at Columbia University.

In 1906, Blatch began work in the laboratory of Lee De Forest, the inventor of the radio vacuum tube and a pioneer in television. Blatch and De Forest married two years later. Over the objections of her husband, Nora Blatch continued working as an engineer and draftsperson throughout her marriage. The couple divorced in 1912, following the birth of their only child.

During and after her marriage to De Forest, Blatch remained active in women's rights issues—particularly in the women's suffrage movement. In 1916, when Blatch exceeded the age limit for junior status in the ASCE, the organization dropped her from its rolls. Blatch sued unsuccessfully for reinstatement. Despite this setback, she continued her work in engineering.

In 1919, Blatch married engineer Morgan Barney. The couple later had two children. Around this same time, Nora Blatch Barney began developing an interest in architecture. In 1923, at the age of 40, she began working as an architect and real estate developer in Greenwich, Connecticut. Soon after, Barney and her family moved into a house that she had designed.

In 1944, Barney achieved a certain notoriety as a writer with the publication of the pamphlet, "World Peace through a People's Parliament." The pamphlet called for a world government that was representative of the people as a means of achieving world peace and gaining women's rights. As a result of this writing and her membership in the Congress of American Women, Barney was investigated by the House Committee on Un-American Activities in 1950. Despite the investigation, Barney continued working to achieve women's rights and world peace. She also remained active as a real estate developer and architect, devoting much of her time to designing and building large estates until her death from a stroke in 1971.

See also American Society of Civil Engineers (ASCE); Bethune, Louise Blanchard; Cambra, Jessie G.; Civil Engineering; Gabe, Frances Bateson; Lin, Maya; Loftness, Vivian; Roebling, Emily Warren; Women's Rights
References Bailey, Martha J., *American Women in Science: A Biographical Dictionary* (1994); Litoff, Judy Barrett, and Judith McDonnell, *European Immigrant Women in the United States: A Biographical Dictionary* (1994); Read, Phyllis J., and Bernard L. Witlieb, *The Book of Women's Firsts* (1992); Sicherman, Barbara, and Carol Hurd Green, eds., *Notable American Women: The Modern Period* (1980); Stanley, Autumn, *Mothers and Daughters of Invention: Notes for a Revised History of Technology* (1993).

Bartlett, Helen Blair (1901–1969)

Helen Blair Bartlett was a mineralogist with a specialty in ceramics (clay-based materials such as enamel and porcelain). A significant property of ceramics is their resistance to electric current, due to which they make excellent insulators. During the early 1930s, Bartlett, who had earned a Ph.D. at Ohio State University in 1931, was employed as a ceramic scientist with the AC Spark Plug Division of the General Motors Corporation. Here she used her expertise in ceramics to develop insulating materials for use in the production of spark plugs. In addition to this work, Bartlett also is credited with having developed several products for which she received patents while employed at General Motors, the rights to which she assigned to the company.

Bartlett's application of ceramics to the making of automobile parts provides an excellent example of the types of contributions women have made to industry and technology. However, Bartlett played another important but far less known role in the applications of ceramic science. This role occurred when Bartlett was called away from her job at General Motors to work on a special ceramics-related research project being conducted at the Massachusetts Institute of Technology (MIT). The MIT project, one of the many that fell under the umbrella of the Manhattan

Project (the code name for America's secret project to develop the world's first atomic bomb), involved the development of a new material composed of a nonporous porcelain that would be used as one of the many internal components of the atomic bomb. Following her work on this project, Bartlett returned to General Motors, where she remained until her retirement in 1966.

See also Fink, Kathryn (Kay) Ferguson; Foster, Margaret; Goeppert-Mayer, Maria; Libby, Leona W.; Manhattan Project; Materials Engineering; Nuclear Physics; Ordnance; Way, Katharine; Wu, Chien-Shiung
References Kass-Simon, G., and Patricia Farnes, eds., *Women of Science: Righting the Record* (1990); Rossiter, Margaret W., *Women Scientists in America: Before Affirmative Action, 1940–1972* (1995).

Bath, Patricia (b. 1944)

In 1988, ophthalmologist and surgeon Patricia Bath became the first African American female physician to receive a patent for a medical device. Her invention, a Laser Cataract Surgery Device, is a specially designed laser-powered probe, irrigator, and aspirator, used to break apart and vaporize cataracts (cloudiness on the eye's lens, which obstructs vision). The device, which replaced earlier mechanical drills, earned Bath international acclaim. It also earned her additional patents in Canada (1992), Japan (1992), and several European countries (1995).

Bath was born in the Harlem section of New York City. She graduated from Hunter College with a bachelor's degree in 1964. Bath then attended Howard University in Washington, D.C., graduating four years later. During the next several years, she studied at Columbia University and New York University and completed an internship at Harlem Hospital.

Bath has long expressed her concern about the high rate of sight loss, especially among African Americans and the economically disadvantaged, due to cataracts and glaucoma, a disease in which pressure builds inside the eye. Committed to saving or restoring sight, Bath in 1974 cofounded the ophthalmology training center at King-Drew Medical Center, where she also served as chief of ophthalmology and associate professor of surgery,

ophthalmology, and community medicine. In 1975, she became the first African American female surgeon at UCLA's Jules Stein Eye Institute as well as the school's first African American woman associate professor of ophthalmology.

See also Baker, Sara Josephine; Blount (Griffin), Bessie J.; Bryant, Alice G.; Hyde, Ida Henrietta; Logan, Myra Adele; Medicine/Medical Technology; Patent; Rand, (Marie) Gertrude; Thompson, Mary H.
References Nazel, Joe, "Cataract Surgery Inventor . . ."; *Wave Community Newspapers* (14 February 1996); Stanley, Autumn, *Mothers and Daughters of Invention: Notes for a Revised History of Technology* (1993); Three Dimension Publishing, "Dr. Bath's Patent Drawing," in *TDP Newsletter for Young Inventors,* available at http://www.erols.com/tdpedu/patent.htm (cited 8 March 1998).

Beasley, Maria E. (ca. 1847–1904?)

Maria E. Beasley was a prolific inventor who held at least fifteen patents, most of which were related to cooperage (barrel making). In addition to her barrel-making machines and devices, Beasley was issued patents for at least three other machines. These included a machine that pasted shoe uppers (1882), a steam generator (1886), and an antiderailment mechanism for use on railroad cars (1898). Other inventions for which Beasley received multiple patents included life rafts (1880 and 1882) and hooping casks. These last two inventions were issued patents both in Britain and in the United States.

Maria Beasley (nee Kenny) was married to Samuel Beasley. The couple lived most of their lives in Philadelphia but in later years made their home in Chicago, Illinois.

Unlike many other women inventors, Maria Beasley profited greatly from her creations, receiving much of her income from oil and sugar refineries that used her barrel-making equipment. In addition, Beasley also displayed her machines at at least one major fair—the World Industrial and Cotton Centennial Exposition, held in New Orleans in 1884.

See also Blanchard, Helen Augusta; Knight, Margaret E.; S., Mary
Reference Stanley, Autumn, *Mothers and Daughters of Invention: Notes for a Revised History of Technology*

United States Patent [19]

Bath

[11] Patent Number: 4,744,360

[45] Date of Patent: May 17, 1988

[54] **APPARATUS FOR ABLATING AND REMOVING CATARACT LENSES**

[76] Inventor: **Patricia E. Bath,** 4554 Circle View Blvd., Los Angeles, Calif. 90024

[21] Appl. No.: **943,098**

[22] Filed: **Dec. 18, 1986**

[51] Int. Cl.⁴ A61B 17/36
[52] U.S. Cl. 128/303.1; 128/397; 604/20; 604/35; 604/43
[58] Field of Search 128/303.1, 395, 397, 128/398; 604/22, 20, 35, 43

[56] **References Cited**

U.S. PATENT DOCUMENTS

3,460,538	8/1969	Armstrong	128/303.1
3,971,382	7/1976	Kransov .	
3,982,541	9/1976	L'Esperance, Jr.	128/303.1
4,024,866	5/1977	Wallach	604/22
4,320,761	3/1982	Haddad	604/22
4,538,608	9/1985	L'Esperance, Jr.	128/395
4,580,559	4/1986	L'Esperance .	
4,583,539	4/1986	Karlin et al.	128/395

OTHER PUBLICATIONS

"Heatless Laser Etching" by John Free; Popular Science 12/83.
Serial No. 702,569 filed 2–19–85 to Gruen et al.

Primary Examiner—Lee S. Cohen
Assistant Examiner—David Shay
Attorney, Agent, or Firm—Cushman, Darby & Cushman

[57] **ABSTRACT**

A method and apparatus for removing cataracts in which a flexible line preferably 1 mm or less in diameter is inserted through an incision into the anterior chamber until its end is adjacent the cataract. Coherent radiation, preferably at a frequency between 193 and 351 nm, is coupled to the cataract by an optical fiber in the line. An irrigation sleeve provided about the fiber and an aspiration sleeve extending partially around the irrigation sleeve conduct irrigating liquid to and remove ablated material from the anterior chamber and form with the optical fiber the flexible line.

7 Claims, 1 Drawing Sheet

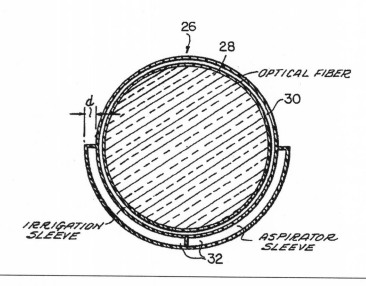

This is the patent drawing for ophthalmologist Patricia Bath's invention of a laser-powered probe that is used to vaporize cataracts. (USPTO)

(1993); Vare, Ethlie Ann, and Greg Ptacek, *Mothers of Invention: From the Bra to the Bomb, Forgotten Women and Their Unforgettable Ideas* (1988).

Benerito, Ruth Rogan (b. 1916)

With more than 50 patents to her name, textile chemist Ruth Benerito is one of the most prolific women inventors of the twentieth century. While employed at the Southern Regional Research Center of the U.S. Department of Agriculture (USDA), in New Orleans, Benerito developed the technology for chemically treating cotton and synthetic fabrics to make them crease-, water-, dust-, and oil-resistant. As a result, she is recognized as a pioneer in the development and treatment of wash-and-wear fabrics.

Benerito was born in New Orleans, Louisiana. She attended that city's Sophie Newcomb College, from which she received a B.S. in chemistry in 1935. She then attended Tulane University, also in New Orleans, earning her M.S. degree in physics in 1938. After receiving this degree, Benerito taught chemistry, first at Randolph-Macon Women's College and later at Tulane University. She then entered the University of Chicago, from which she received her Ph.D. in physical chemistry in 1948.

In 1953, Benerito joined the Southern Regional Research Center of the USDA as a physical chemist. Later she was promoted to head the Physical Chemical Research Group in the Natural Polymers Laboratory. She also was an adjunct professor at the Medical and Graduate School of Tulane University and a lecturer at the University of New Orleans. Benerito remained with the USDA for 30 years.

Benerito has received many awards in recognition of her achievements in the textile industry. In 1968, she received both the Federal Woman's Award and the Southern Chemist Award. Two years later she was awarded the Garvan Medal of the American Chemical Society (ACS) in 1970, an organization of which she is a member. Benerito also is a member of Iota Sigma Pi and of the American Association of Textile Chemists and Colorists and is a fellow of the American Institute of Chemists (AIC) and of the Association for the Advancement of Science (AAAS).

See also Agricultural Engineering; Agriculture; Federal Woman's Award; Fox, Sally; Francis P. Garvan–John M. Olin Medal; Kwolek, Stephanie Louise; Patent; Pinckney, Eliza Lucas; Sherman, Patsy O.; Tesoro, Giuliana Cavaglieri; Textiles
References Bailey, Martha J., *American Women in Science: A Biographical Dictionary* (1994); O'Neill, Lois Decker, *The Women's Book of Records and Achievements* (1979); Stanley, Autumn, *Mothers and Daughters of Invention: Notes for a Revised History of Technology* (1993); Torpie, Stephen L., et al., eds., *American Men and Women of Science,* 18th ed. (1992–1993), (1992).

Benjamin, Miriam E. (n.d.)

Miriam E. Benjamin was a Massachusetts schoolteacher during the late 1800s. Very little is known about the life of this woman who is recognized as the second female African American to be issued a U.S. patent. (The first was Sarah E. Goode, who received a patent in 1885 for a folding cabinet bed.) Benjamin was granted U.S. Patent No. 386,289 on 17 July 1888, for a gong and signal chair. The chair was designed for use in motels and hotels, where patrons could use it to signal attendants without leaving their seats. It was later adopted for use in the U.S. House of Representatives, where it provided those assembled a handy way of summoning pages.

See also Goode, Sarah E.; Patent
References Hine, Darlene Clark, Elsa Barkley Brown, and Rosalyn Terborg-Penn, eds., *Black Women in America: An Historical Encyclopedia,* vol. 1: *A–L* (1993); Smith, Jessie Carney, ed., *Black Firsts: 2,000 Years of Extraordinary Achievement* (1994); Stanley, Autumn, *Mothers and Daughters of Invention: Notes for a Revised History of Technology* (1993); Louisiana State University Libraries, Baton Rouge, "African American Inventors: Historical," in Faces of Science, African Americans in the Life Sciences, available at http://www.lib.lsu.edu/lib/chem/displays/women_inventors.html (cited 13 March 1998).

Berkowitz, Joan (b. 1931)

Joan Berkowitz is a physical chemist who has researched high-temperature oxidation of transition metals—most notably, alloys of molybdenum, tungsten, and zirconium. (Transition metals are those metals that have variable oxidation states or numbers [the charge on an ion or an atom]. They are commercially and technologically important metals located in Groups 3–11 in the Periodic Table of the Elements. Transition metals have similar properties; they are harder, more brittle, and have higher melting points than metals in Groups 1 and 2. Examples of transition metals include silver, copper, iron, and titanium.)

Berkowitz's research findings led to the use of these alloys in rockets and space vehicles. In addition to her research, Berkowitz also obtained a patent for applying special techniques to the manufacture of reusable molds of molybdenum and tungsten disilicides for casting iron and steel. These techniques have been used to provide oxidation resistance to metals used in space vehicles.

Joan Berkowitz was born in Brooklyn, New York. Following her graduation from high school, she attended Swarthmore College in Pennsylvania. While there, Berkowitz was elected to Phi Beta Kappa. She received a B.A. in chemistry in 1952. Seeking to continue her studies, Berkowitz applied to Princeton University; however, she was denied entry because Princeton did not accept women for graduate studies in chemistry. Berkowitz then enrolled at the University of Illinois at Urbana, from which she received her Ph.D. in physical chemistry in 1955. For the next two years, Berkowitz did postgraduate study at Yale University on a National Science Foundation (NSF) fellowship.

In 1959, Berkowitz took a position with A. D. Little, Inc., a management and technology consulting firm. It was here that Berkowitz conducted her research on oxidation in an attempt to identify alloys that retained tensile strength and hardness at extremely high temperatures. This work was important and timely because it occurred when the U.S. space program was developing. Berkowitz's research led to the development of improved radiation shields and the use of electrical fields to retard the high-temperature oxidation of metals and their alloys.

Berkowitz left A. D. Little to pursue research on hazardous wastes in the early 1970s. In 1975 she headed a research team that investigated alternatives to depositing hazardous wastes in landfills. This work contributed greatly to knowledge of the treatment of hazardous wastes and

continues to serve as an important point of reference. In recognition of this valuable work, Berkowitz was presented the Society of Women Engineers (SWE) Achievement Award in 1983.

See also Aeronautical and Aerospace Engineering; Eng, Patricia L.; Environmental Engineering; Metals and Metallurgy; Phi Beta Kappa Society
References Grinstein, Louise S., Rose K. Rose, and Miriam H. Rafailovich, eds., *Women in Chemistry and Physics: A Biobibliographic Sourcebook* (1993); James, Edward T., Janet Wilson James, and Paul S. Boyers, eds., *Notable American Women, 1607–1950: A Biographical Dictionary,* vol. 1 (A–F) (1971); Society of Women Engineers, "Achievement Award Recipients," available at http://www.swe.org/SWE/Awards/achiev.html (cited 31 May 1998).

Bernstein, Dorothy Lewis (1914–1988)

An applied mathematician and the first woman president of the Mathematical Association of America (MAA), Bernstein spent most of her professional career working as a college instructor and researcher. She made significant contributions to technology through her pioneering efforts to incorporate applied mathematics and computer science into the college mathematics curriculum. She also introduced computers and computer programming instruction into high school mathematics classrooms.

Dorothy Bernstein was born in Chicago, Illinois, and grew up in Milwaukee, Wisconsin. She entered the University of Wisconsin at Madison at age 16, where she majored in mathematics as a participant in an independant study program. In this program, Bernstein was not required to take any exams, nor was she assigned any grades. Instead, she received both a B.S. degree *(summa cum laude)* and a master's degree in mathematics, based on an oral examination and thesis, in 1934, at the young age of 20.

In 1935, Bernstein entered a doctoral program at Brown University on a scholarship. While working toward this degree, she experienced discrimination because she was a Jew and a woman. As a teaching fellow, her class included only three women. After being informed that male students would not want to be taught by a female instructor,

Bernstein was prohibited from teaching male students. In addition, she was made to submit to an examination for the Ph.D. that was several hours longer than that given male students seeking the same degree.

While working toward her Ph.D., Bernstein was cautioned that her gender and religion would be obstacles to securing employment. However, she achieved success both as an instructor and as a researcher at Mount Holyoke College (1937–1940); the University of California (1942); and the University of Rochester (1943–1959), where her research in affiliation with the Office of Naval Research (ONR) involved military applications of mathematical operations on computers.

After leaving Rochester, Bernstein became a full professor of mathematics at Goucher College, a position she held until her retirement in 1979. Following her retirement, she served as president of the MAA (1979–1981). Bernstein also is a member of the American Mathematical Society (AMS).

See also Computers/Computer Technology; Mathematical Association of America (MAA)
References Grinstein, Louise, and Paul J. Campbell, eds., *Women of Mathematics* (1987); McMurray, Emily M., ed., *Notable Twentieth-Century Scientists* (1995); "Dorothy Lewis Bernstein," in Biographies of Women Mathematicians, available at http://www.scottlan.edu/lriddle/women/bern.htm (cited 7 January 1998).

Bethune, Louise Blanchard (1856–1913)

The first American woman to practice as an architect, Bethune is credited with many achievements. She started her career as an apprentice drafter, drafting blueprints soon after her graduation from high school. At age 20, she accepted a job as drafter with an architectural firm in Buffalo, New York. There she studied in the firm's library, mastering many of the techniques used in drafting and architectural planning. It was also at this firm that she met and eventually married fellow drafter Robert Armour Bethune. In 1881, the couple opened an architectural office in Buffalo.

Louise Bethune designed a variety of structures, including a chapel, a brick factory, several storage facilities, and hotels. Among her most noted designs was a music store in Buffalo. The structure was one of the first in the country to make use of a steel frame and poured concrete slabs. Bethune also has been recognized for her design of school buildings. She is credited with having designed 18 schools in western New York state, including Lockport High School, construction of which began in 1890.

Through her work and her publications Bethune gained recognition as an accomplished architect. In 1888, she was elected to the American Institute of Architects (AIA), becoming the institute's first woman member. The following year she became the first woman fellow in the Western Association of Architects. In the public sphere, Bethune advocated for an architect licensing law and sought equal pay for women in the field. The school of architecture at the State University of New York (SUNY) in Buffalo was named in Bethune's honor.

See also American Institute of Architects (AIA); Architecture; Barney, Nora Stanton Blatch; Irwin, Harriet; Lin, Maya; Loftness, Vivian
References James, Edward T., Janet Wilson James, and Paul S. Boyers, eds., *Notable American Women, 1607–1950: A Biographical Dictionary,* vol. 1: (A–F) (1971); Read, Phyllis, J., and Bernard L. Witlieb, *The Book of Women's Firsts* (1992); Bois, Danuta, "Louise Blanchard Bethune," available at http://www.netsrq.com/%7Edbois/bethunel.html (cited 16 January 2000).

Bevier, Isabel (1860–1942)

Isabel Bevier was an early innovator in providing the home economics movement with a scientific basis. In 1908, Bevier instituted the first college laboratory for the study of nutrition and food chemistry. The use of a thermometer to check the temperature of cooking meat was one of the many technological advances Bevier introduced in the household science program that she organized at the University of Illinois at Urbana-Champaign.

Bevier was born on a farm near Plymouth, Ohio. In 1885, she received a Ph.B. from the College of Wooster in Ohio before accepting employment as a principal and teacher in a nearby high school. In 1888, Bevier was awarded a Ph.M. (master's degree) in Latin and German, also from the College of Wooster. Soon after, she became a professor of natural sciences at the Pennsylvania College for Women, in Pittsburgh. During the summers, she continued her education at the Case School of Applied Science in Cleveland and at Harvard and Wesleyan Universities in Massachusetts. She also studied at the Western Reserve University and with Ellen Swallow Richards at the Massachusetts Institute of Technology (MIT).

In 1898, Bevier served as a professor of chemistry at Lake Erie College in Painesville, Ohio. Two years later she was invited to create a new department in home economics at the University of Illinois at Urbana-Champaign. The department, named Household Science, involved the study of food, shelter, clothing, and institutional management. Bevier left her position in 1921 to serve as chair of the home economics department of the University of California at Los Angeles, but she returned to the University of Illinois in 1928, remaining a professor and director of home economics there until her retirement in 1930.

Bevier served as the second president of the American Home Economics Association, from 1910 to 1912. She was also a member of the American Chemical Society (ACS) and the American Public Health Association. Bevier was awarded honorary doctorates from both Iowa State and the College of Wooster. The home economics building at the University of Illinois was named in her honor.

See also Alexander, Lucy Maclay; American Society for Nutritional Sciences (ASNS); Farmer, Fannie Merritt; Home Economics; Morgan, Agnes Fay; Morrill Act of 1862; Richards, Ellen Henrietta Swallow
References Bailey, Martha J., *American Women in Science: A Biographical Dictionary* (1994); "Isabel Bevier, 82; Home Economist" [obituary], *New York Times* (18 March 1942); James, Edward T., Janet Wilson James, and Paul S. Boyers, eds., *Notable American Women, 1607–1950: A Biographical Dictionary,* vol. 1: (A–F) (1971); *Her Heritage: A Biographical Encyclopedia of Famous American Women,* available at http://www.plgrm.com/Heritage/women/B.HTM (8 August 1998); "Isabel Bevier," in A&E New Media, available at http://www.biography.com/cgi-bin/biomain.cgi (cited 8 August 1998).

Biomedical Engineering

Biomedical engineering, or bioengineering, applies the theories and principals of engineering and science to living systems and to medical and health-related issues. Biomedical engineering is an interdisciplinary field that combines knowledge in computer science, mechanics, electronics, physics, biology, chemistry, and medicine.

Many biomedical engineers work with surgeons, internists, orthopedists, and other medical specialists to develop and test devices used to replace or assist damaged or diseased organs. Examples of such engineered devices include the artificial heart, the pacemaker, the heart-lung machine, the dialysis machine, surgical lasers, and artificial limbs. Another biomedical specialty is the design and testing of computer and electronics equipment for use in hospital special care units. Such instruments may be used to detect and monitor electrical impulses emitted by the heart and brain or to analyze and regulate levels of hormones, enzymes, electrolytes, and blood constituents.

The National Aeronautics and Space Administration (NASA) employs biomedical engineers to assist in the development and testing of space habitats used by humans during space explorations. Electronic instrumentation is also required during space flights to monitor cabin pressure and levels of oxygen and carbon dioxide.

Other bioengineered instruments measure metabolic changes, or the effects of diet, gravity, and weightlessness on astronauts. Such instruments were used by astronauts Mae Jemison and Bonnie Dunbar to conduct tests to determine the physiological effects of negative pressure during space missions (e.g., calcium loss and a decrease in bone density).

See also Dunbar, Bonnie J.; Environmental Engineering; Estrin, Thelma; Jemison, Mae; Mack, Pauline Beery; National Aeronautics and Space Administration (NASA); Society of Women Engineers (SWE)
References Ambrose, Susan A., et al., *Journeys of Women in Science and Engineering: No Universal Constants* (1997); Barnes-Svarney, Patricia, ed., *The New York Public Library Science Desk Reference* (1995).

Biotechnology

Biotechnology involves the application of engineering and natural science principles to improve the quality of life. The use of bacteria in sewage treatment and in the production of foods such as yogurt, cheese, and sauerkraut are examples of biotechnology that have been practiced for hundreds of years. The use of yeast to make fermented beverages and to make bread rise also is an example of biotechnology.

Modern biotechnology draws upon and affects many disciplines, including genetics, immunology, medicine, plant science, and agriculture. New vaccines, hormones, antibiotics, and enzymes are the results of modern biotechnology, as are new cancer therapies, the development of frost- and disease-resistant plants, and nutritionally improved plants and animals that are used as food.

Much current biotechnology involves applications of recent advances in genetics—specifically, in genetic engineering. In genetic engineering, a DNA sequence that produces desirable characteristics is spliced with another DNA fragment to form a new molecule. The molecule resulting from the combination of parts of two different DNA molecules is called recombinant DNA. Another form of biotechnology involves the growth of plant or animal cells in the laboratory. Such research has led to the successful cloning of frogs, mice, and sheep and continues to be of interest to geneticists. Genetically engineered microorganisms are currently being used to break down environmentally harmful toxins and industrial wastes.

Advances in biotechnology have produced many new and useful techniques and products. They also have generated much concern. For example, many people question the ethics of experimenting with or altering genes and living things. People also have expressed concerns about the potential health effects of genetically altered food products. To ensure the safety of such products, federal agencies monitor and regulate biotechnology research in the United States.

See also Agricultural Engineering; Alexander, Hattie Elizabeth; Blackburn, Elizabeth Helen; Brown, Rachel Fuller; Elion, Gertrude Belle; Environmental Engineering; Genetic Engineering; Hazen, Elizabeth Lee; Industrial Engineering; Joullié, Madeleine M.; Krim, Mathilde Galland; Richardson, Jane Shelby
References Engelbert, Phillis, ed., *Science Fact Finder: The Natural World*, vol. 1 (1998); Parker, Sybil P., *McGraw-Hill Encyclopedia of Science and Technology*, 8th ed., vol. 2 (1997).

Blackburn, Elizabeth Helen (b. 1948)

In 1978, molecular biologist Elizabeth Helen Blackburn discovered the means by which chromosomes replicate themselves prior to cell division. This discovery shed new light on DNA and chromosome behavior. Applications of Blackburn's research might someday aid in preventing the replication of cancer cells.

Elizabeth Blackburn was born and educated in Australia. She received both her B.S. degree (1970) and her M.S. degree (1971) from the University of Melbourne. In 1976, she obtained a Ph.D. in molecular biology from Cambridge University in England. She then accepted a fellowship in biology at Yale University. It was at Yale that Blackburn began her studies of chromosomes.

In 1978, Blackburn accepted a position with the University of California at Berkeley. That same year, she discovered telomerase, an enzyme needed to preserve chromosome structure during replication. This research may help scientists develop effective means for combating cancer and certain fungal diseases. It may also help explain how early life forms evolved.

In 1993, Blackburn became the first woman to chair the department of microbiology and immunology at the University of California at San Francisco. She has been elected a foreign associate to the National Academy of Sciences (NAS) and has won the National Academy of Sciences Award in molecular biology. Blackburn is also a member of the Royal Society.

See also Biotechnology; Elion, Gertrude Belle; Genetic Engineering; Krim, Mathilde Galland; Stevens, Nettie Maria
References McMurray, Emily M., ed., *Notable Twentieth-Century Scientists* (1995); Saari, Peggy, ed., *Prominent Women of the 20th Century* (1996); UCSF Cancer Center, "Elizabeth H. Blackburn, Ph.D.," available at http://cc2.ucsf. edu/people/blackburn_elizabeth.html (cited 11 May 1998).

Blanchard, Helen Augusta (1840–1922)

Records detailing the life of Helen Augusta Blanchard, the recipient of at least 28 patents primarily related to sewing machine developments and attachments, are sketchy. However, it is known that Blanchard was born in Portland, Maine, in 1840; received her first patent for a sewing machine at age 33; obtained at least 27 others while living in the cities of Boston, Philadelphia, New York, and Portland; and died at age 82 in Providence, Rhode Island. The number of patents issued to Blanchard place her among the most prolific women inventors of the nineteenth and twentieth centuries.

Helen Blanchard received her first patent for a sewing machine in 1873 while living in Boston. This machine, known as the overseaming machine, was able to simultaneously sew and trim knitted fabrics. Today, a model of this machine is on display in the Smithsonian Institution's Museum of American History. Blanchard received an additional eight patents over the next three years, all issued in Boston. These patents were for sewing machines or improved methods or attachments related to sewing.

Patents issued to Blanchard suggest that she lived in Philadelphia between 1882 and 1883. While there, she received a patent for sewing machine needles and another for a spool case. Over the next 16 years, Blanchard received an additional eight patents from Boston, Philadelphia, and New York City. All but two—a pencil sharpener (1884) and a surgical needle (1894)—were related to sewing. From 1900 to 1901, she received another patent in Philadelphia and four more in Portland, Maine, all for sewing-related devices or processes. Her remaining four patents, dated between 1901 and 1915, were issued in Philadelphia.

Records indicate that Helen Blanchard achieved great wealth from her inventions. This is partly attributed to the success of the Blanchard Overseaming Company, which she founded in Philadelphia in 1876. Yet, despite her wealth and creativity, Blanchard is rarely recognized by the sewing machine industry for her achievements. Some evidence suggests that Blanchard invented zig-zag stitching and the sewing machine capable of carrying out this function. But the development of a commercial sewing machine that made use of zig-zag stitching is generally credited to the Singer Company, with comparable home machines being credited to Pfaff and Necchi. These machines actually might have been modified copies of the one developed by Blanchard, as they were not released for use by their respective companies until Blanchard's patent for her machine had expired.

See also Domestic Appliances; Invention/Inventors; Knight, Margaret E.; Patent; Textiles
References Macdonald, Anne L., *Feminine Ingenuity: How Women Inventors Changed America* (1992); Stanley, Autumn, *Mothers and Daughters of Invention: Notes for a Revised History of Technology* (1993); Lemelson-MIT Program, "Prolific Female Inventors of the Industrial Era," in Invention Dimension, available at http://web.mit.edu/invent/www/inventorsR-Z/whm2.html (cited 3 August 1998).

Blatch, Nora Stanton
See **Barney, Nora Stanton Blatch**

Blodgett, Katherine Burr (1898–1979)

Katherine Blodgett was a research physicist and industrial chemist who held six U.S. patents, the most notable of which was for development of a nonreflective or "invisible glass" that has important applications in cameras, telescopes, and other optical devices. Blodgett also developed a tool for measuring film thickness to within one-millionth of an inch, invented a smoke screen used by the military, improved the quality of the gas mask, and researched methods for deicing airplane wings.

Katherine Blodgett was born in Schenectady, New York. After her father's death, the family moved several times, eventually settling in New York City. Blodgett attended Bryn Mawr College in Pennsylvania, and graduated with a B.A. She then enrolled at the University of Chicago, where she received an M.S. in physics at age 19. Her master's thesis investigated the adhesion of gases

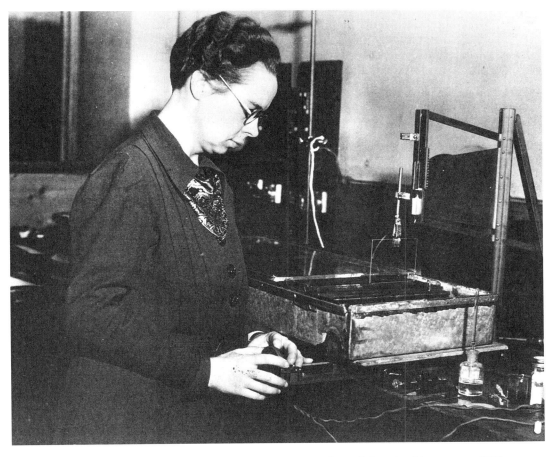

Katherine Burr Blodgett treats glass with a film to create her "nonreflective" glass. (Corbis/Bettmann-UPI)

to coconut charcoal, a study with application to improvements in the effectiveness of gas masks.

After receiving her master's degree, Blodgett returned to Schenectady and accepted a research position at the General Electric (GE) Research Laboratory; she was the first woman to hold a research position at GE. For the next six years, she worked with Nobel Prize–winning chemist Irving Langmuir and published papers with him detailing their work with electric currents. With the assistance of Langmuir, Blodgett later traveled to England to study physics with Nobel Prize–winning physicist Ernest Rutherford at the Cavendish Laboratory of Cambridge University. Blodgett received a Ph.D. in physics in 1926, becoming the first woman to be awarded this degree at Cambridge.

Blodgett returned to GE after receiving her doctorate. During the early 1930s she developed her film-thickness gauge. Her invention of nonreflective glass was announced in 1938. During World War II, Blodgett turned her research toward military efforts, developing a smoke screen and researching plane wing deicing. In 1947 she developed a weather balloon instrument that was used by the Army Signal Corps to measure upper atmosphere humidity.

In recognition for her work in chemistry, Blodgett received the 1945 Annual Achievement Award from the American Association of University Women (AAUW). Six years later, she received the Garvan Medal from the American Chemical Society (ACS). That same year she was honored in Boston's First Assembly of American Women of Achievement.

See also Bath, Patricia; Francis P. Garvan–John M. Olin Medal; Ochoa, Ellen; Patent; Rand, (Marie) Gertrude; Safety Engineering
References Bailey, Martha J., *American Women in Science: A Biographical Dictionary* (1994); Clark, Alfred E., "Dr. Katherine Burr Blodgett, 81, Developer of Nonreflecting Glass" [obituary], *New York Times* (13 October 1979); Macdonald, Anne L., *Feminine Ingenuity: How Women Inventors Changed America* (1992); McMurray, Emily M., ed., *Notable Twentieth-Century Scientists* (1995); Rothe, Anne, and Evelyn Lohr, eds., *Current Biography, 1952* (1952); Saari, Peggy, ed., *Prominent Women of the 20th Century* (1996); Shearer, Benjamin F., and Barbara S. Shearer, eds., *Notable Women in the Physical Sciences: A Biographical Dictionary* (1997).

Blount (Griffin), Bessie J. (ca. 1914–?)

Physical therapist Bessie J. Blount's contribution to technology arose from her desire to help the many World War II amputees who were her patients become more self-sufficient. She met this challenge in the 1940s when she invented an electrically powered feeding device that could be operated by individuals who had no use of their arms. Blount also invented a wash basin for use by patients following surgery.

Bessie Blount was born in Hickory, Virginia, around 1914. Little is known about Blount's youth; however, it is known that she attended the Union Junior College and the Panzer College of Physical Education, both of New Jersey. She later moved to Chicago, where she obtained additional training as a physical therapist.

Blount spent at least part of her career working with World War II soldiers at veterans' hospitals. Many of her patients had lost the use of their arms and/or legs as a result of war injuries. Blount believed that one of the best ways she could serve her patients was to help them gain as much independence and self-confidence as possible. In keeping with this belief, Blount (known as "Wonder Woman" by those with whom she worked) taught many of her patients to use their feet as they had once used their hands.

Blount developed a self-feeding device at the urging of a doctor with whom she worked. Com-plete development of the invention took Blount five years and cost her several thousand dollars. Once completed, the device, which was operated by biting on a switch, delivered bite-sized pieces of solid food to a mouthpiece, from which it could be eaten by the patient. The machine shut off after each portion was delivered, to prevent too much food from being taken in by the patient at one time. This regulating mechanism allowed patients to feed themselves from either a sitting or a prone position, with little risk of choking.

Blount received a patent for her device under the name Bessie J. Griffin, in 1951. However, the VA declined to authorize its use, claiming that they had nurses and aides to feed and care for veterans. Despite this setback, Blount believed her machine was important, and she contacted representatives of the government of France to see whether they might be interested in her invention. They were; and in 1952, Blount granted rights for use of her invention to France during a public ceremony held at the French Embassy. During the ceremony, Blount stated to the press that the event "proved a Black woman can invent something for the benefit of humankind."

See also Medicine/Medical Technology; Patent
References Stanley, Autumn, *Mothers and Daughters of Invention: Notes for a Revised History of Technology* (1993); Lemelson-MIT Program, "African-American Inventors of Our Times: Continued Successes, Improving Opportunities," available at http://web.mit.edu/inventorsA-H/AAweek4.html (cited 17 February 1999).

Boone, Sarah (n.d.)

Very little is known about the life of nineteenth-century African American inventor Sarah Boone. However, this New Haven, Connecticut, resident received a patent for an invention now present in most homes throughout the world—an ironing board. Boone's ironing board was not the first invented; however, her design was the first to include edges that were curved to correspond with the inner and outer sleeve seams. The patent for Boone's ironing board was issued by the U.S. Patent Office on 26 April 1892.

See also Patent; Patent and Trademark Office, U.S. (PTO)

References Hine, Darlene Clark, Elsa Barkley Brown, and Rosalyn Terborg-Penn, eds., *Black Women in America: An Historical Encyclopedia,* vol. 1: (A–L) (1993).

Bradberry, Henrietta M. (?–1979)

African American inventor Henrietta Mahim Bradberry was issued two patents during the time that the United States was involved in World War II. The first patent was issued to the Chicago native in 1943, for a domestic item called a "bed rack." This unusual invention was developed to provide a means of airing out clothes that had been recently worn to refresh them for use again, without rewashing. Bradberry's second invention, for which she was issued a patent in 1945, dealt with a mechanical device that one might not readily associate with a woman. This device, a "torpedo discharge means," was intended for use by naval attack vessels. Bradberry's device was essentially a system that used compressed air to provide the force needed to propel or discharge the torpedo below the surface of the water. Although Bradberry's invention was never adopted for use by the military, it is similar in some ways to the pneumatic system currently employed in some submarines.

See also Lamarr, Hedy; Mather, Sarah; Ordnance **References** Macdonald, Anne L., *Feminine Ingenuity: How Women Inventors Changed America* (1992); Sluby, Patricia Carter, "Black Women and Inventions," *Sage: A Scholarly Journal on Black Women,* vol. 6, no. 2 (Fall 1989); Stanley, Autumn, *Mothers and Daughters of Invention: Notes for a Revised History of Technology* (1993).

Bragg, Elizabeth
See **American Society of Civil Engineers (ASCE)**

Bramley, Jenny Rosenthal (1910–1997)

In 1929, at the age of 19, Jenny Rosenthal Bramley became the first woman in the United States to receive a Ph.D. in physics. Throughout her career as an industrial physicist Bramley continued to break new ground. In 1966 she became the second woman to be elected a fellow of the Institute of Electrical and Electronics Engineers (IEEE). The IEEE also granted Bramley a Fellow Award for her "achievement[s] in spectroscopy, optics, mathematical techniques, and their applications to the electron tubes, displays, and light sources to engineering." Numerous patents were issued to Bramley for her many inventions.

Jenny Rosenthal Bramley was born in Moscow, Russia. At age 16 she received her bachelor's degree in physics from the University of Paris. Only three years later she received a Ph.D. in physics from New York University. After receiving her Ph.D., Bramley began work as a researcher at Johns Hopkins University, under the direction of noted physicist Enrico Fermi; later, she became an assistant to Harold Urey. In 1953, Bramley began work as a physicist at the U.S. Army Signal Corps Engineering Laboratory in Belmar, New Jersey. She spent five years there directing a government project. At the same time, she also served as head of the mathematics department at Monmouth Junior College, and as an engineering and physics consultant for the Engineer Topographic Laboratories in Fort Belvoir, Virginia.

Bramley became a full-time consultant operating her own business in 1958. It was while working as a consultant that Bramley's reputation for applying physics principles to electrical engineering became known, resulting in her induction into the IEEE as a fellow. It was also during this period that Bramley obtained her 18 patents. One of these was for a lamp—the microwave pumped high efficiency lamp—used in laser technology. Bramley and her husband, Arthur, also received joint patents for their pioneering work in the area of electroluminescence. Electroluminescence is the property that causes a gas to emit light, or luminesce, when exposed to an electric current. Some solids (known as semiconductors) also possess this property. The Bramleys' patents in this area involved "applications of electroluminescence to solid state display and storage devices." The couple later licensed these patents to IBM. Among the practical applications of electroluminescence in solid state display devices today are light-emitting diodes (LEDs), common in digital watches, calculators, and similar electronic devices.

Jenny Bramley also developed applications for using alphanumerics (letters and numbers) to code and decode information represented pictorially. Bramley is recognized also for her research into the magnetic properties of subatomic particles and how these properties affect the location of these particles in an atom.

In addition to her induction as a fellow into the IEEE, Bramley received several other awards and honors throughout her career. At different times, Bramley served as chair of the North Virginia section of the IEEE and chair of the Washington chapter of the IEEE's Electron Devices Society. In 1984, the IEEE honored her with its Centennial Medal. The next year, the Interagency Committee on Women in Science and Engineering (WISE) presented Bramley with its Lifetime Achievement Award. In 1997, Bramley died at a health care facility in Lancaster, Pennsylvania.

See also Ancker-Johnson, Betsy; Computers/ Computer Technology; Electrical and Electronics Engineering; Institute of Electrical and Electronics Engineers (IEEE); Mathematics
References Kass-Simon, G., and Patricia Farnes, eds., *Women of Science: Righting the Record* (1990); Pankove, J. I., ed., *Electroluminescence* (1977); Schumacher, Sandy, Fellow Program Coordinator Awards/Fellow Activities, IEEE, e-mail correspondence with Alan Winkler (16 October 1998); Thornton, P. R., *The Physics of Electroluminescent Devices* (1967); American Physical Society, "Industrial and Applied Physics 1998: A Forum of the American Physical Society," available at http://www.aps.org/FIAP/feb98 /index.html (cited 17 June 1998); Institute of Electrical and Electronics Engineers (IEEE), "Jenny R. Bramley: Trailblazing Physicist," available at http:// spectrum.ieee.org/INST/obits.html (cited 17 June 1998); "Jenny Rosenthal Bramley," in the Engineering-Specific Career Advisory Problem-solving Environment, at http://www.ecn.purdue.edu/ESCAPE/ special/women/History/bramley.html (cited 7 June 1998).

Breedlove, Sarah
See **Walker, Madame C. J.**

Bridges

Historically, the design and construction of bridges has been the province primarily of men. However, two pioneering women of the nineteenth and twentieth centuries are known for their work in bridge design and construction: Emily Warren Roebling and Jesse Cambra.

Emily Roebling's contribution to bridge construction involved her work on New York's famous Brooklyn Bridge, a suspension bridge that joins the island of Manhattan with Brooklyn. The original contract for the construction of the Brooklyn Bridge was issued to John and Washington Roebling—Emily Roebling's father-in-law and husband, respectively. After John Roebling died in a construction accident and Washington Roebling became incapacitated as a result of injuries he suffered while working on the bridge, Emily Roebling was thrust into the position of construction engineer on the project. To prepare adequately for this role, Emily Roebling mastered the mathematics needed to calculate the curves formed by the free-hanging cables used in the bridge construction. In addition, she also researched materials strengths and wire cable construction. Knowledge of these elements was crucial, since this project was the first in which steel was used in the making of wire cables for a bridge. The concept of the steel wire cable was so unique that a sample cable later became a main display feature in Machinery Hall at the Centennial Exposition, held in Philadelphia in 1876. Under Emily Roebling's supervision, the construction of the Brooklyn Bridge was completed on schedule, in 1883.

Nearly one-half century after Emily Roebling contributed to the construction of the Brooklyn Bridge, Jessie Cambra became the first woman registered as a civil engineer in the state of California. Two years after obtaining her B.S. degree in civil engineering from the University of California at Berkeley in 1942, Cambra began employment with Alameda County in California. Her many responsibilities in this position included designing and supervising the development of much of California's highway system. In addition, Cambra also was responsible for the design of a bridge in which reinforced concrete was used.

In recent years, more women have become involved in the construction and design of bridges. Much of this increase may be attributed to legislation enacted by Congress in 1972, which strengthened the powers of the Equal Employment Opportunity Commission (created in 1964 under the Civil Rights Act). This increased power made it more difficult for employers (and others) to preclude women from entering fields of employment (or areas of study leading to such) previously dominated by men. The effects of this legislation appear to be reflected in the number of women receiving undergraduate degrees in civil engineering (the branch of engineering most closely related to highway and bridge design and construction). For example, according to the National Center for Education Statistics, during the 1970–1971 school year only 0.07 percent, or 52 of the 6,526 bachelor's degrees conferred in civil engineering, were issued to women. However, in the four-year period immediately following the strengthening of the Equal Employment Opportunity Commission (EEOC), this number increased to a dramatic 7 percent. By 1994–1995, the number of women receiving bachelor's degrees in civil engineering had grown to 19 percent (1,920 of the 9,927 degrees issued).

See also Cambra, Jessie G.; Civil Engineering; Roebling, Emily Warren

References McMurray, Emily M., ed., *Notable Twentieth-Century Scientists* (1995); Petroski, Henry, *Engineers of Dreams: Great Bridge Builders and the Spanning of America* (1995); U.S. Department of Education, Office of Educational Research and Improvement, National Center for Education Statistics, *Chartbook of Degrees Conferred, 1969–70 to 1993–94* (December 1997).

Brill, Yvonne Claeys (b. 1924)

Considered a pioneer in space exploration, aerospace engineer Yvonne Brill is most noted for developing rocket propulsion systems for geosynchronous communications satellites. Her most innovative invention, for which she holds a patent, is a single propellant hydrazine resistojet propulsion system. The advantages of such a system include reduced propellant requirements, which allow for increased payload and mission life. Although developed in 1970, this launch system is still in use today.

Yvonne Claeys Brill was born in Winnipeg, Canada. She received a bachelor's degree in mathematics from the University of Manitoba in 1945. After graduation, Brill worked for several companies in the aerospace industry, where she performed rocket and propellant research and became involved in missile designs. At the same time, she worked toward a master's degree in chemistry at the University of California, which she received in 1951. After receiving this degree, Brill married, moved from California to Connecticut, and worked for several companies before accepting a position as a senior engineer with RCA Astro-Electronics in 1966. It was while working for RCA Astro-Electronics that Brill developed the hydrazine/hydrazine resistojet thruster. For her work on this project, she received the company's Engineering Excellence Award.

Brill has worked on many space projects in addition to her rocket system. For example, she has been involved in programs connected with the Mars *Observer* and has studied the performances of the Scout, Delta, Atlas, and Titan launch rockets. She also served as director of the shuttle program's Solid Rocket Motor program at the National Aeronautics and Space Administration (NASA).

Yvonne Brill is now retired. She remains a fellow of both the American Institute of Aeronautics and Astronautics and the Society of Women Engineers (SWE). Her many honors and awards include the 1993 Resnik Challenger Medal (named for astronaut Judith Resnik, who was killed in the explosion of the space shuttle *Challenger* in 1986), the American Institute of Aeronautics National Capital Section Marvin C. Demler Award for Outstanding Service (1983), and the Society of Women Engineers (SWE) Achievement Award (1986).

See also Aeronautical and Aerospace Engineering; National Aeronautics and Space Administration (NASA); Patent; Space Exploration

References McMurray, Emily M., ed., *Notable Twentieth-Century Scientists* (1995); Parsons, Susan V., "1993 Resnik Challenger Medal Recipient: Yvonne C. Brill,"

SWE (September/October 1993); "Yvonne C. Brill, 1986 Achievement Award Winner," *U.S. Woman Engineer* (September/October 1986).

Brown, Marie Van Britton (n.d.)

A native of Jamaica, New York, Marie Van Britton Brown is an African American inventor who developed a security system for use in homes. The U.S. Patent and Trademark Office issued a joint patent (Patent No. 3,482,037) for this security system on 2 December 1969 to Marie Van Britton Brown and Albert L. Brown. Other security systems had been developed prior to Brown's system; however, unlike the more common hardwired systems that use modified switches on windows and doors to trigger a high-pitched tone when the system is armed and a circuit is opened, Brown's unique design makes use of video and audio components. The video component consists of a miniature camera and monitor that permits the home owner to observe a point of entry to view an individual seeking access. The monitor permits such viewing from any room in which it is installed. The audio component of Brown's system consists of microphones and speakers that permit dialogue between home owner and visitor. Brown also included in her design a door lock release, which allows a visitor entry when activated.

See also Blanchard, Helen Augusta; Cochran, Josephine G.; Eglin, Ellen F.; Gabe, Frances Bateson; Henry, Beulah L.; Joyner, Marjorie Stewart; Kenner, (Mary) Beatrice Davidson; Knight, Margaret E.; S., Mary

References Hine, Darlene Clark, Elsa Barkley Brown, and Rosalyn Terborg-Penn, eds., *Black Women in America: An Historical Encyclopedia*, vol. 1: (A–L) (1993); Stanley, Autumn, *Mothers and Daughters of Invention: Notes for a Revised History of Technology* (1993).

Brown, Mary Babnick
See **Ordnance**

Brown, Rachel Fuller (1898–1980)

The first antibiotic, penicillin, was discovered by Scottish bacteriologist Sir Alexander Fleming in 1928. By the 1940s, this antibiotic and others were proving extremely effective in treating illnesses caused by bacteria. However, it was not until the mid-1950s that nystatin, the first effective treatment for fungal infections, was developed. This development resulted from the collaborative work of biochemist Rachel Fuller Brown and mycologist Elizabeth Lee Hazen.

Rachel Fuller Brown was born in Springfield, Massachusetts. She spent her childhood in Missouri, then returned to Springfield as a teenager. After completing high school, Brown attended Mount Holyoke College, where she majored in history and chemistry and received a bachelor of arts degree in 1920. She then enrolled at the University of Chicago, where she obtained a master's degree in organic chemistry in 1921. For the next several years, Brown was a teacher of chemistry and physics; she also worked toward her Ph.D. in both chemistry and bacteriology, which she received from the University of Chicago in 1933.

After earning her Ph.D., Brown was employed as an assistant chemist with the New York State Department of Health. She spent her entire career at the health department, holding a variety of positions. One of Brown's first major projects at the department involved the development of a vaccine for use against the bacterium that causes pneumonia. The vaccine she helped develop remains in use today.

In 1948, Brown, who worked in Albany, began collaborating with fellow Department of Health scientist Elizabeth Hazen, who worked in New York City. Together the women sought to identify and isolate an antibiotic from soil bacteria that could be effectively used to treat fungal infections in humans. Soon after the collaboration began, Hazen obtained a soil sample from a farm in Virginia that contained a microorganism known as *Streptomyces noursei*. She sent the sample for analysis, via the U.S. mail, to Brown in Albany, who isolated two antifungal substances from the microorganism. One of these substances proved too toxic for use in humans; the other became the world's first effective antifungal treatment. Brown and Hazen named this compound nystatin, in honor of the *New York*

State Department of Health laboratories in which they worked.

Brown and Hazen presented their findings to the National Academy of Sciences (NAS) in 1950. By 1954, nystatin had been approved by the U.S. Food and Drug Administration (FDA). After receiving approval for the drug, Brown and Hazen enlisted the help of the Research Corporation (a nonprofit organization) in obtaining a patent for the new drug. They were issued Patent No. 2,797,183, on 25 June 1957. They then granted the rights for producing and marketing the drug to E. R. Squibb and Sons.

Nystatin has gained wide use since then in treating fungal infections of the skin, digestive system, and female reproductive system. The drug also has been used to treat Dutch elm disease, to fight mold growth in livestock feed, and to restore artwork damaged by molds. Sales of nystatin have generated more than $13 million in royalties for Brown and Hazen in addition to the money made by the pharmaceutical companies that have marketed the substance. However, Brown and Hazen chose not to profit personally from the drug's success and instead directed their royalties to the Research Corporation, which had helped them obtain their patent, to establish the Brown-Hazen Fund for medical research.

After discovering nystatin, Brown and Hazen continued their long-distance collaboration. Their work resulted in the discovery of the antibiotics capacidin and phalamycin. Brown retired from her position with the New York State Department of Health in 1968. At this time, she was granted the New York State Health Department's award for distinguished service. In 1975, she and Hazen became the first women recipients of the Chemical Pioneer Award of the American Institute of Chemists (AIC). They were also granted the Sara Benham Award of the Mycological Society of America. In addition, both Hazen and Brown were inducted into the National Inventor's Hall of Fame in 1994. They were the second and third women to receive this honor. The first was Nobel laureate Gertrude Belle Elion (1991), another woman who had devoted her life to the development of life-saving drugs.

See also Alexander, Hattie Elizabeth; Antibiotics; Chemical Pioneer Award; Elion, Gertrude Belle; Hazen, Elizabeth Lee; National Inventors' Hall of Fame

References Bailey, Martha J., *American Women in Science: A Biographical Dictionary* (1994); "Dr. Rachel F. Brown, 81, Chemist" [obituary], *New York Times* (16 January 1980); Muir, Hazel, *Larousse Dictionary of Scientists* (1994); Read, Phyllis J., and Bernard L. Witlieb, *The Book of Women's Firsts* (1992); Lemelson-MIT Program, "Elizabeth Lee Hazen and Rachel Fuller Brown: The Antifungal Drug Nystatin," in Invention Dimension, Inventor of the Week archives, available at http://web.mit.edu/www/inventorsA-H/ HazenBrown.html (cited 5 May 1998).

Bryant, Alice G. (1862?–1942)

Alice G. Bryant, inventor of widely used surgical instruments, was the first female physician in the United States to specialize in otolaryngology, the study of diseases and disorders of the ear, nose, and throat (ENT). In June 1914, she became one of the first two women to be inducted into the American College of Surgeons. Bryant practiced medicine at the New England Hospital for Women and Children and at the New England Deaconess.

In addition to practicing medicine, Bryant developed several medical inventions that advanced the practice of head and neck surgery and became standard instruments in both the clinic and the operating room. In her own office examinations, she made use of an electric control she had created that allowed her to maneuver equipment using her foot, thus keeping her hands free. Another instrument developed by Bryant was a tonsil tenaculum, an instrument used during the surgical removal of tonsils. She also designed a nasal polypus hook that was used for removing nasal polyps. Other surgical instruments designed by Bryant include tonsil separators, a tonsil snare cannula, and bone gripping forceps.

Bryant's inventive abilities may have been aided by the engineering courses she took in 1882–1883 at the Massachusetts Institute of Technology (MIT). She continued her education at Vassar College in Poughkeepsie, New York, where she earned an undergraduate degree in 1885. Following her graduation from Vassar, Bryant completed her medical degree at the Women's Medical College of New York in 1890.

Bryant was an active practitioner in her field. During her career, she authored and published more than seventy-five articles. She also pioneered the establishment of evening clinics to make medical services more convenient to the working people of Boston. She continued to hold evening clinics until she succumbed to illness and died in July 1942.

See also Medicine/Medical Technology; Thompson, Mary H.; Vallino, Lisa M., and Rozier, Betty M.
References "Dr. Alice G. Bryant, A Boston Physician: Ear, Nose and Throat Specialist Invented Surgery Instruments" [obituary], *New York Times* (27 July 1942); Stanley, Autumn, *Mothers and Daughters of Invention: Notes for a Revised History of Technology* (1993).

Bryn Mawr College

A private, nonsectarian facility, Bryn Mawr College was originally founded by the Quaker organization, the Society of Friends, to provide young Quaker women with a liberal arts education. The college, located in Bryn Mawr, Pennsylvania, was licensed by the state of Pennsylvania in 1880 and opened its doors in 1885. The college quickly established rigorous academic standards and acquired an excellent faculty. Charlotte Scott, professor of mathematics and department chair, taught at Bryn Mawr from 1885–1925. At the time, she was one of the few women in the world who held a Ph.D. in mathematics. Florence Bascom, one of the most notable geologists of her time, founded Bryn Mawr's geology department in 1898.

Under its original charter, Bryn Mawr gained its reputation as a school committed to community and social welfare. It provided course work and practical experience in social issues. By providing educational opportunities through summer programs, Bryn Mawr pioneered the expansion of academics to young upper- and working-class women.

Bryn Mawr was the first women's college in the United States to offer graduate degrees. Although the undergraduate division still accepts only women, Bryn Mawr's graduate school has been open to men since 1937. Today, the college issues degrees ranging from the bachelor of arts through the Ph.D. advanced programs in the sciences are offered in such fields as geophysics, biophysics, and biochemistry.

See also Seven College Conference
References Macdonald, Anne L., *Feminine Ingenuity: How Women Inventors Changed America* (1992); Weatherford, Doris, *American Women's History: An A to Z of People, Organizations, Issues, and Events* (1994).

Burbidge, (Eleanor) Margaret Peachey (b. 1919)

During the late 1970s, astronomer Margaret Burbidge served on a committee that advised the National Aeronautics and Space Administration (NASA) on space projects. Burbidge helped convince NASA to launch a telescope into space beyond Earth's atmosphere to provide clear, unobscured views of bodies in space. When NASA decided to build and launch the Hubble Space Telescope, they asked Burbidge to help design a "faint object" spectrograph that could be launched with the telescope. Once in space, the main mirror of the Hubble Space Telescope developed problems, but the spectrograph worked well, allowing Burbidge to record ultraviolet (UV) light from a distant quasar.

Margaret was born in Davenport, England. In 1939 she received a bachelor's degree in science with high honors from the University College of London (UCL). World War II was in progress when Margaret was working toward her Ph.D. at the same school. Thus, in addition to her research, she had to maintain observatory equipment and repair damage that occurred during the bombing of London. In spite of these added obligations, she received her Ph.D. in astrophysics in 1943 for her analyses of the amounts and kinds of elements present in distant stars.

In 1948, Margaret married Geoffrey Burbidge, another former astronomy student from UCL. The couple moved to the United States in 1951. Although she was prevented from working at some observatories because she was a woman, Margaret Burbidge was able to conduct research at several of the world's most prestigious observatories during the next several years. In 1957 she gained worldwide acclaim when she, her husband, and two other astronomers developed a theory to explain how heavy metals form inside stars as the latter evolve. For this work, the Burbidges were awarded the Warner Prize of the American Astronomical Society in 1959. Following this accomplishment, Margaret Burbidge turned her attention to the rotation of galaxies.

In 1962, Burbidge joined the chemistry faculty of the University of California at San Diego. Antinepotism policies at the school prevented her from working in the physics department because of her husband's employment there. However, these policies were later abolished, and Margaret Burbidge was made a full professor of astronomy (part of the physics department).

In 1972, Burbidge returned to England for one year to serve as director of the Royal Greenwich Observatory. She was the first woman to hold this prestigious position; however, she was denied the title of Astronomer Royal, which normally accompanied the position, because of her gender. That same year, she became a U.S. citizen. After returning to the United States, Burbidge became an active member of several professional organizations, holding key positions in two of them. From 1976 to 1978, she served as the first woman president of the American Astronomical Society. In 1981, she became president of the American Association for the Advancement of Science (AAAS).

Throughout her career, Margaret Burbidge made many significant contributions to astronomy. For these achievements she has been widely recognized by the scientific community both in the United States and in England. In 1964 she was elected a fellow of the Royal Society of London. Four years later she became a fellow of the American Academy of Arts and Sciences. In 1978, Burbidge became the first woman astronomer to be elected a fellow in the National Academy of Sciences (NAS). In addition, she was awarded the Catherine Wolfe Bruce Medal of the Astronomical Society of the Pacific in 1982, a National Medal of Science in 1985, and the Albert Einstein World Award of Science Medal in 1988.

See also American Association for the Advancement of Science (AAAS); Astronomy; Maury, Antonia; Spectroscopy
References Green, Timothy, "A Great Woman Astronomer Leaves England—Again," *Smithsonian*

(January 1974); McMurray, Emily M., ed., *Notable Twentieth-Century Scientists* (1995); Olsen, Kirstin, *Chronology of Women's History* (1994); Shearer, Benjamin F., and Barbara S. Shearer, eds., *Notable Women in the Physical Sciences: A Biographical Dictionary* (1997); Uglow, Jennifer, ed., *The International Dictionary of Women's Biography* (1982); Yount, Lisa, *Twentieth-Century Women Scientists* (1996).

Butler, Margaret K. (b. 1924)

Margaret Butler is a pioneer in the development of digital computers for scientific uses. She is currently senior computer scientist at the Argonne National Laboratory (ANL), where she conducts software research. Butler has been involved in specialties such as image-processing, information systems, computer-system performance, and the development of scientific and engineering applications for computers. In 1948, as a junior mathematician with the Naval Reactor Division of ANL, she worked on computations related to design studies of the prototype reactor for the *Nautilus* submarine.

Butler was born in Evansville, Indiana. She graduated from Indiana University in 1944 with an A.B. in mathematics. She then did postgraduate work with the U.S. Department of Agriculture (USDA) Graduate School in Washington, D.C. (1945), the University of Chicago (1949), and the University of Minnesota (1950). Butler worked as a statistician for the U.S. Bureau of Labor Statistics and the U.S. Air Force in Europe before she was hired at the ANL in 1948. She has since held various positions and served in many divisions of the ANL, while developing a vast knowledge of computers.

In 1960, she established and became director of the Argonne Code Center, which serves as a computer information and distribution exchange for nuclear reactor applications. In 1980, the center was renamed the National Energy Software Center and was given the responsibility of dealing with scientific and technical software developed for the Atomic Energy Commission (AEC) and the Department of Energy (DOE).

Butler is a member of the Computer Science Department Industrial Advisory Board of Bradley University in Peoria, Illinois. She also has served as a consultant for the Nuclear Energy Agency in Paris, France. She remains an active member of the Association for Computing Machinery, the American Nuclear Society, the Association for Women in Computers, and the Institute of Electrical and Electronics Engineers (IEEE) Computer Society. Her honors include the Award of Merit from the Chicago Association of Technological Societies (1988). In addition, Butler has written more than 100 research and development reports and a book titled *Careers for Women in Nuclear Science and Technology* (1992).

See also Argonne National Laboratory; Atomic Energy Commission (AEC); Computers/Computer Technology; Goldstine, Adele Katz; Hopper, Grace Murray; Mathematics; Nuclear Physics
References Butler, Margaret K., resume sent to Alan Winkler (10 September 1998); Litzenberg, Kathleen, ed., *Who's Who of American Women,* 18th ed. (1995); Stanley, Autumn, *Mothers and Daughters of Invention: Notes for a Revised History of Technology* (1993).

Butterick, Ellen (n.d.)

In the mid-1800s, Massachusetts native Ellen Butterick devised the idea of making patterns for men's clothing out of stiff paper. Butterick's original patterns were created for use by herself and for her husband, Ebenezer, who was a tailor. Ebenezer Butterick applied for and obtained a patent in his name for the development of the paper patterns produced by his wife (a practice that was not uncommon at the time, as women could not apply for patents in their own right). However, it was not until 1863, several years after the patent was obtained, that Ebenezer Butterick began marketing and profiting from the patterns created by his wife.

At first, Ebenezer Butterick sold the patented paper patterns from his home in Sterling, Massachusetts. Later he adopted the marketing method used with great success by another inventor of paper patterns, New Yorker Ellen Demorest. Demorest, who had developed thin paper patterns for use in dressmaking in the early 1850s, began a pattern sale business in 1860. After developing her patterns, Demorest had tried to obtain a patent for her invention but failed because a patent for the idea of paper patterns had already been issued to Ebenezer Butterick. Despite her inability to obtain a patent, Demorest profited from her creations by establishing the magazine *Mme. Demorest's Mirror of Fashions* with the help of her husband. A major selling point of the magazine was the copies of Demorest's patterns that were stapled inside each issue. Publication of *Mme. Demorest's Mirror of Fashions* began in 1860 and met with almost immediate success. The success of Demorest's publication likely led Ebenezer Butterick to begin marketing the Butterick patterns by a similar method. First, he introduced a magazine, the *Ladies' Quarterly of Broadway Fashions,* to showcase the Butterick patterns, which could be purchased via mail from a store that he had opened on Broadway in New York. Soon after establishing this magazine, he launched a monthly bulletin called the *Metropolitan.* In June 1873, Butterick developed a third magazine, which he called the *Delineator.* Like the earlier magazines, it was created to showcase Butterick fashions for which the patterns could be purchased by post. The sale of paper clothing patterns begun by the Buttericks and Ellen Demorest opened up a new and very profitable area within the clothing industry. Today, Butterick patterns continue to be a market leader in this area.

See also Blanchard, Helen Augusta; Demorest, Ellen Curtis; Fox, Sally; Invention/Inventors; Knight, Margaret E.; McCardell, Claire; Rodgers, Dorothy; Textiles
References Fuller, Edmund, *Tinkers and Genius: The Story of the Yankee Inventors* (1955); Macdonald, Anne L., *Feminine Ingenuity: How Women Inventors Changed America* (1992); Stanley, Autumn, *Mothers and Daughters of Invention: Notes for a Revised History of Technology* (1993); Vare, Ethlie Ann, and Greg Ptacek, *Mothers of Invention: From the Bra to the Bomb, Forgotten Women and Their Unforgettable Ideas* (1988); Butterick Company, "Our History," available at http://www.butterick.com/home/history.html (cited 28 July 1999).

Butterworth, Mary Peck (1686–1775)

Mary Peck Butterworth lived out her life in Rehoboth, Massachusetts. She was a gifted inventor who was unable to obtain a patent for her creation due to its illegality. Butterworth developed a method of counterfeiting the £5 notes in use in colonial America. She printed her counterfeit money by finding a way to transfer to paper an image that had been developed on muslin cloth—that was subsequently easily destroyed to eliminate evidence of her methods. Although an alleged accomplice testified at trial about how Butterworth made her money, authorities were unable to prosecute Butterworth due to the lack of physical evidence.

See also Textiles

References Read, Phyllis J., and Bernard L. Witlieb, *The Book of Women's Firsts* (1992); Vare, Ethlie Ann, and Greg Ptacek, *Mothers of Invention: From the Bra to the Bomb, Forgotten Women and Their Unforgettable Ideas* (1988).

Caldwell, Mary Letitia (1890–1972)

Mary Letitia Caldwell isolated the amylase enzymes and discovered their roles in the breakdown of carbohydrates into simple sugars in plants and animals. The methods Caldwell developed for obtaining pure enzymes have become the standard in laboratories throughout the United States and Europe. Pure enzymes have technological applications in fermentation, paper sizing, and in the production of some textiles and food products.

Caldwell was born in Bogota, Colombia, where her parents worked as missionaries. The family returned to the United States when Mary was ready to attend high school. After completing school, Caldwell attended and graduated from Western College for Women in Oxford, Ohio (1913). Western College was at that time the western outpost of Mount Holyoke College of Massachusetts; it is now part of Miami University of Ohio.

After receiving her bachelor's degree, Caldwell taught chemistry at Western for four years. She then resigned this position to accept a graduate fellowship in chemistry at Columbia University in New York City. Caldwell received a master's degree in 1919 and a Ph.D. in 1921. She then was appointed a university fellow, which allowed her to remain at Columbia. Caldwell remained at Columbia for thirty-eight years, serving as a teacher, a researcher, an academic adviser, and a departmental administrator. She was made full professor in 1948, becoming the only female professor in Columbia's chemistry department.

Caldwell retired from Columbia in 1959. The following year, she was awarded the Garvan Medal of the American Chemical Society (ACS). In addition, Caldwell was a fellow of the New York Academy of Sciences and the American Association for the Advancement of Science (AAAS). She also was a member of the ACS, the American Society of Biological Chemists, and the American Institute of Nutrition (AIN).

See also Carr, Emma Perry; Cori, Gerty Theresa Radnitz; Francis P. Garvan–John M. Olin Medal; Green, Arda Alden; Hahn, Dorothy Anna; Sherrill, Mary Lura; Textiles
References Daley, Marie M., "Mary Letitia Caldwell," in *American Chemists and Chemical Engineers* (1976);

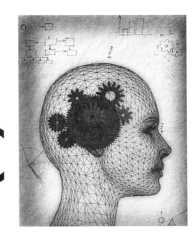

"Garvan Medal: Dr. Mary L. Caldwell," *Chemical and Engineering News* (18 April 1960); Grinstein, Louise S., Rose K. Rose, and Miriam H. Rafailovich, eds., *Women in Chemistry and Physics: A Biobibliographic Sourcebook* (1993); Shearer, Benjamin F., and Barbara S. Shearer, eds., *Notable Women in the Physical Sciences: A Biographical Dictionary* (1997); "Mary L. Caldwell of Columbia Dies" [obituary], *New York Times* (3 July 1972).

Cambra, Jessie G. (b. 1919)

Jessie G. Cambra is recognized as the first woman in California to become a registered engineer by passing the licensing examination. She is also acknowledged for her creative and innovative engineering and administrative abilities. Cambra led the development and supervision of much of California's transportation system. In this role, she was responsible for the designs of major road construction projects and a reinforced concrete bridge. Cambra also was a pioneer in the design of a computerized traffic signal system.

Jessie Cambra was born in Oakland, California, and attended the University of California at Berkeley, where she majored in engineering. She graduated in 1942, becoming the first woman to graduate from that university with a B.S. degree in civil engineering. After graduation, Cambra worked for an engineering firm as a field engineer and was soon promoted to assistant civil engineer. In 1944, she left industry to pursue what became a 36-year public service career in Alameda

County, California. After her first year, she was promoted to the position of civil engineer.

Cambra worked on the design of road and drainage systems. In 1947, she was invited to join the American Public Works Association and soon afterward, became its first woman director. Cambra quickly moved through the ranks, first as senior civil engineer, then as supervising civil engineer. In 1953, she was placed in charge of the engineering division of the Alameda County Road Department. In 1974, through successive promotions, Cambra was appointed deputy director of public works for the county.

For her work in civil engineering, Cambra has received many awards. In 1977, she received the Samuel A. Greeley Award for her achievements in public works. The following year she was ranked a top ten engineer by the American Public Works Association, and in 1979 she received the Achievement Award from the Society of Women Engineers (SWE). Cambra retired in 1980.

See also American Society of Civil Engineers (ASCE); Barney, Nora Stanton Blatch; Bridges; Civil Engineering; Eaves, Elsie; Roebling, Emily Warren
References McMurray, Emily M., ed., *Notable Twentieth-Century Scientists* (1995); Society of Women Engineers, "Achievement Award" (dated 9 February 1998), available at http://www.swe.org/SWE/Awards/achiev.htm (cited 5 May 1998).

Carr, Emma Perry (1880–1972)

Chemist Emma Perry Carr broke new ground when she introduced the use of ultraviolet (UV) spectroscopy (a means of using crystalline or quartz prisms or diffraction gratings rather than glass as a diffraction medium to study wavelengths in the ultraviolet region of the electromagnetic spectrum) in the United States. Using procedures developed in this technology, she and a joint student-faculty research team at Mount Holyoke College in Massachusetts were able to analyze the composition and structure of complex organic molecules that had been synthesized in the laboratory. UV spectroscopy presented greater insight into the energy relationships resulting from the different types of chemical bonds present in organic compounds. Robert Mulliken, winner of the 1966 Nobel Prize in chemistry, credited Carr's work in UV spectroscopy with helping him to build his molecular orbit theory, a mathematical means for describing the electron distribution within molecules.

Emma Carr was born in Holmesville, Ohio, in 1880. While she was still an infant, the Carr family moved to Coshocton, Ohio, where Emma was raised. After graduating from high school in 1898, she enrolled at Ohio State University in Columbus, where she studied chemistry for one year. Carr then transferred to Mount Holyoke College in South Hadley, Massachusetts. She remained at Mount Holyoke as a student for the next two years, while working as an assistant in the chemistry department there until 1904. Carr then transferred to the University of Chicago, where the following year she earned her B.S. in chemistry.

Carr was invited to become a member of the faculty at Mount Holyoke as an instructor of chemistry in 1905. She remained at the college until 1908, at which time she returned to the University of Chicago to pursue graduate studies. With the aid of the Mary E. Woolley Fellowship and the Lowenthal Fellowship, Carr pursued her doctoral studies. In 1910, she became the seventh woman awarded a Ph.D. in physical chemistry by the University of Chicago. Carr accepted an appointment at Mount Holyoke as an assistant professor of chemistry later that same year. By 1913, she was promoted to the position of full professor and head of the Department of Chemistry. By this time, Carr had earned a reputation as an excellent teacher, researcher, and administrator.

In 1919, Carr traveled to Belfast (Northern Ireland), where she did one year of postgraduate work to increase her understanding of the new field of UV spectroscopy and its applications. She then returned to Mount Holyoke, where she incorporated what she had learned in Ireland into the chemistry program at the college. Her reputation in this field grew, and in 1924 she was asked by the board of directors of the International Critical Tables (ICT) to serve with Victor Henri of the University of Zurich and Jean A. E. M. Becquerel of the College de France in Paris to prepare

In 1937, Emma Perry Carr of Mount Holyoke became the first woman to be awarded the Garvan Medal of the American Chemical Society. (Corbis/Bettmann-UPI)

a catalog of data and standards based on spectral research. The task was completed the following year. Carr returned to Europe again in 1925 to work with Victor Henri at the University of Zurich, once again focusing on UV spectroscopy.

In 1929, Carr was awarded the Alice Freeman Palmer Fellowship of the American Association of University Women (AAUW), which permitted her again to travel to Zurich and to spend another year studying with Henri. During this time, she investigated the techniques of far ultraviolet vacuum spectroscopy, a more accurate type of UV spectroscopy. Upon her return to the United States, Carr received a grant from the National Research Council and the Rockefeller Foundation. The grant provided funding for research using spectral analysis to investigate the structure of simple, unsaturated hydrocarbons. Carr's spectral studies required pure samples of organic

compounds; two of Carr's students, Dorothy Hahn and Mary Lura Sherrill, developed the techniques needed to prepare these compounds. Carr and her students then used UV spectroscopy to analyze the compounds and study the energy relationships that existed among their chemical bonds.

Throughout her career at Mount Holyoke, Carr served as both a role model and an inspiration to women in the sciences. The chemistry department she established at the college was recognized around the world as a model of excellence. Under Carr's tutelage, many successful graduates in chemistry emerged from Mount Holyoke, including noted chemists Dorothy Hahn and Mary Lura Sherrill.

Carr retired from her teaching and research position at Mount Holyoke in 1946. Throughout her career, she received many honors and awards for her groundbreaking work in UV spectroscopy and for her excellence as a teacher and mentor. She became the first recipient of the Garvan Medal of the American Chemical Society (ACS) in 1937. She was again recognized along with her former student Mary Lura Sherrill by the ACS in 1957, with the James Flack Norris Award of the Northeastern Section of that society. Carr was later honored by Mount Holyoke with an Alumnae Medal of Honor presented by the Mount Holyoke Alumnae Association, and in 1952, the college renamed its chemistry building the Carr Chemistry Laboratories in her honor. In addition to being elected to Phi Beta Kappa and Sigma Xi, Carr was awarded honorary doctoral degrees by Allegheny College, Russell Sage College, Hood College, and Mount Holyoke. Carr was elected a fellow of the American Physical Society (APS), and held memberships in the American Association for the Advancement of Science (AAAS), the American Optical Society, and the American Chemical Society (ACS).

See also Fenselau, Catherine Clarke; Francis P. Garvan–John M. Olin Medal; Hahn, Dorothy Anna; Herzenberg, Caroline Littlejohn; Mount Holyoke College; Sherrill, Mary Lura; Spectroscopy
References Bothamley, Jennifer, *Dictionary of Theories* (1993); "Dr. Emma P. Carr, 91, Chemist at Holyoke" [obituary], *New York Times* (8 January 1972); Grinstein,

Louise S., Rose K. Rose, and Miriam H. Rafailovich, eds., *Women in Chemistry and Physics: A Biobibliographic Sourcebook* (1993); Moritz, Charles, ed., *Current Biography, 1959* (1959); Roscher, Nina Matheny, "Women Chemists," *ChemTech* (December 1976); Sicherman, Barbara, and Carol Hurd Green, eds., *Notable American Women: The Modern Period* (1980).

Centennial Exposition

The first of America's world's fairs—the Centennial Exposition of 1876—was held in the city of Philadelphia, Pennsylvania, in celebration of the hundredth birthday of the United States. The Centennial Exposition celebrated the nation's history and achievements in such areas as horticulture, agriculture, and technology. To accomplish these goals, several major buildings were constructed for the Centennial Exposition. Among them were the Main Building, Memorial Hall, Horticultural Hall, Agricultural Hall, and Machinery Hall. In addition, the exposition also included the Women's Pavilion, a site that featured the artistic and technological achievements and contributions of women in America and that provided a forum in which women's rights advocates such as Elizabeth Cady Stanton, Susan B. Anthony, and Lucretia Mott could spread their messages to a large audience.

Machinery Hall, one of the most-frequented buildings of the fair, was the main structure in which the technological achievements of the United States were displayed. The building featured more than 10 acres of display area. Among its exhibits were a sample of the steel cable that John, Washington, and Emily Roebling intended to use in their construction of the Brooklyn Bridge (a project that was completed in 1883). Other exhibits included a telephone and the first typewriter. In addition, a featured attraction of this hall was a working Corliss Steam Engine.

The technological accomplishments of women of the era, as well as arts and crafts, were featured in the Women's Pavilion. Among the more than eighty exhibits on display were the technical inventions of more than fifty women who had received U.S. patents. Of these displays, more than half pertained to clothing and other items used daily by homemakers, reflecting the perceived role of women in society at the time. For example, the "Mrs. Potts's sadiron" (an archaic term used to describe heavy irons) was on display at the exposition; this was the first such iron featuring a wood handle and interchangeable bases. Another household device on exhibit was a washing machine developed by Margaret Plunkett Colvin.

Among the exhibits that did not focus on women's role as homemaker were Martha Coston's maritime signal flares. Coston received her first patent for these flares, which were used by ocean vessels as a means of signaling their location to others, in 1859. She was issued a second patent for improved signal flares in 1871. Coston, who made substantial profit from her invention, was so highly regarded for her work that she was again asked to display her invention at the Columbian Exposition held in Chicago in 1893.

Elizabeth Stiles won first prize at the exhibition for her development of what came to be known as the Stiles Desk. This versatile piece of furniture permitted use by two people at once and featured built-in inkwells, storage drawers, and trash receptacles. When folded, the unit had a depth of only about 18 inches; however, when opened, its depth increased to about 7 feet, providing its users ample working space. Another award-winning exhibit was a set of interlocking construction blocks presented by Mary Nolan. The blocks, which she called "Nolanum," were fireproof and relatively maintenance free.

One of the more unusual displays featured in Memorial Hall was a frozen butter sculpture created by artist Caroline Brooks. The unique aspect of this piece is that it was intended for use as a form over which plaster of Paris was to be poured and pressed, to form a mold. The butter would then be melted and drained out of the hardened plaster, forming a cast. This cast, in turn, provided a shell into which sculpting plaster could be poured and allowed to harden. The resulting hardened mold was then copied in marble to produce a new sculpture. At the time the piece was on display at the Exposition, Brooks was awaiting a patent for her unusual process.

Two other women artists who participated in

the Centennial Exposition festivities were Edmondia Lewis and noted artist Harriet Hosmer, both of whom displayed sculptures. In addition to being an artist, Harriet Hosmer also became an inventor who successfully obtained five patents, including one for a substance she developed that was known as faux marble.

Working behind the scenes, engineer Emma Allison also made a major contribution to the success of the event: Allison's responsibilities included monitoring the gauges and operating the steam-powered engines that supplied power to the displays in the Women's Pavilion.

The Centennial Exposition, a six-month extravaganza, was the first such event to highlight the contributions American women made to society both inside and outside the home. A similar event would not occur on such a large scale for another seventeen years.

See also Columbian Exposition; Colvin, Margaret Plunkett; Coston, Martha J.; Domestic Appliances; Potts, Mary Florence Webber; Roebling, Emily Warren; Women's Rights
References "The Centennial," *New York Times* (10 March 1876); Macdonald, Anne L., *Feminine Ingenuity: How Women Inventors Changed America* (1992); Olsen, Kirstin, *Chronology of Women's History* (1994); Stanley, Autumn, *Mothers and Daughters of Invention: Notes for a Revised History of Technology* (1993); Lemelson-MIT Program, "American Women Inventors Go Public: The Centennial Exhibition of 1876," available at http://web.mit.edu/invent/www/inventorsR-Z/whm1.html (cited 5 July 1999).

Chemical Engineering

Chemical engineering applies the principles of chemistry, mathematics, physics, and engineering to the production of chemicals and chemical products for industrial and consumer use. Chemical engineering focuses on processes that convert raw materials to useful products. Chemical engineers plan, design, and help in the construction of chemical plants and manufacturing equipment. They also research means by which chemicals and chemical products may be produced efficiently and economically and apply the results of their research findings to large-scale manufacturing operations.

Many chemical engineers are employed by cosmetics, petroleum products, food products, plastics, adhesives, explosives, fertilizers, pharmaceuticals, and ore-processing industries. They are also involved in environmental cleanup of chemical contaminants. Chemical engineers often work with environmental engineers to identify safe and efficient methods of transporting hazardous materials and disposing of byproducts of chemical processing. For example, Ivy Parker, a research chemist and engineer, pioneered studies on the causes and prevention of pipeline corrosion in the petroleum industry.

See also American Chemical Society (ACS); American Institute of Chemists (AIC); Environmental Engineering; Parker, Ivy; Society of Women Engineers (SWE); Textiles
References Barnes-Svarney, Patricia, ed., *The New York Public Library Science Desk Reference* (1995); Kass-Simon, G., and Patricia Farnes, eds., *Women of Science: Righting the Record* (1990); U.S. Department of Labor, Bureau of Labor Statistics, *Occupational Outlook Handbook, 1994–1995*, Bulletin 2450 (1994).

Chemical Pioneer Award

The American Institute of Chemists (AIC) presents its Chemical Pioneer Award annually to recognize chemists or chemical engineers for contributions to the advancement of chemical science and the chemical profession. The first women to receive the award were Rachel Fuller Brown and Elizabeth Hazen, who were recognized in 1975 for their development of the antifungal antibiotic nystatin. Other women who have been recipients of the Chemical Pioneer Award include Stephanie Kwolek, for her work with polymers, which led to the development of Kevlar (1980); and Edith Flanigen, for her development of molecular sieves used in petroleum refining (1991).

See also American Institute of Chemists (AIC); Brown, Rachel Fuller; Flanigen, Edith M.; Hazen, Elizabeth Lee; Kwolek, Stephanie Louise
References Read, Phyllis J., and Bernard L. Witlieb, *The Book of Women's Firsts* (1992); Torpie, Stephen L., et al., eds., *American Men and Women of Science*, 18th ed. (1992–1993) (1992).

Chilton, Annie H. (n.d.)

Little is known of the life and times of Annie H. Chilton, who designed and constructed a device not generally associated with women but that clearly reflects the needs and customs of the time in which she lived. Chilton developed a safety device called the Horse-Detacher and Brake. This device permitted the driver of a horse-drawn carriage to unfasten the carriage from the horse should an emergency arise. Chilton displayed a working model of her creation inside the Transportation Building at the Columbian Exposition, held in Chicago, Illinois, in 1893.

See also Columbian Exposition; Coston, Martha J.; Knight, Margaret E.
References Macdonald, Anne L., *Feminine Ingenuity: How Women Inventors Changed America* (1992).

Civil Engineering

Civil engineering, the oldest branch of engineering, involves the design, planning, and supervision of the construction of roads, bridges, tunnels, dams, harbors, canals, buildings, airports, and sewage systems. Civil engineering is important in city planning and urban renewal. Water resources, mining, transportation, and environmental projects are also areas that require the expertise of civil engineers.

Civil engineers are often called upon to provide surveys of potential construction sites. In this role, civil engineers may provide data on soil and rock characteristics and make recommendations before construction begins. They also work closely with architects, designers, and other engineers in meeting building and safety codes and in selecting appropriate building materials. Civil engineers must also understand the use and application of explosives and heavy power machinery, including bulldozers, cranes, earthmovers, and power shovels.

See also American Society of Civil Engineers (ASCE); Barney, Nora Stanton Blatch; Bethune, Louise Blanchard; Bridges; Cambra, Jessie G.; Environmental Engineering; Roebling, Emily Warren; Society of Women Engineers (SWE)
References Barnes-Svarney, Patricia, ed., *The New York Public Library Science Desk Reference* (1995); U.S. Department of Labor, Bureau of Labor Statistics, *Occupational Outlook Handbook, 1994–1995*, Bulletin 2450 (1994).

Clarke, Edith (1883–1959)

During the early 1900s, an increased electricity demand led to the development of large power systems. Electrical engineer Edith Clarke worked on constructing large power systems by integrating smaller systems. She also studied the movement of current through these systems to learn how they would function during power failures resulting from lightning strikes or short circuits. In her work, Clarke prepared charts and calculating instruments that were used by other engineers to predict events within the system. She received a patent for one such calculating device in 1925.

Edith Clarke was born on a farm in Howard County, Maryland. After graduating from the Briarley Hall boarding school, she attended Vassar College, from which she received an A.B. degree in mathematics and astronomy in 1908. Clarke then taught for three years before studying electrical engineering at the University of Wisconsin. While at Wisconsin, she also worked as a computing assistant with the American Telephone and Telegraph Company (AT&T). She left this job in 1918 to enroll at the Massachusetts Institute of Technology (MIT), to continue her study of electrical engineering. The next year, Clarke received the first M.S. degree in electrical engineering ever granted by MIT to a woman.

Following World War I, Clarke was unable to secure work in her field because men who had gone off to war were returning to the workforce. Thus, Clarke took teaching positions at various colleges for the next several years. In 1922, she was hired as an engineer in the Central Station Engineering Department of General Electric (GE). She remained with GE for the next 23 years. Here Clarke began working on electrical power systems. In addition to her calculating device, she also invented a method for regulating voltage in power transmission lines. GE was awarded a patent for this invention in 1927.

During her lifetime, Clarke authored or coauthored many technical articles on electrical engi-

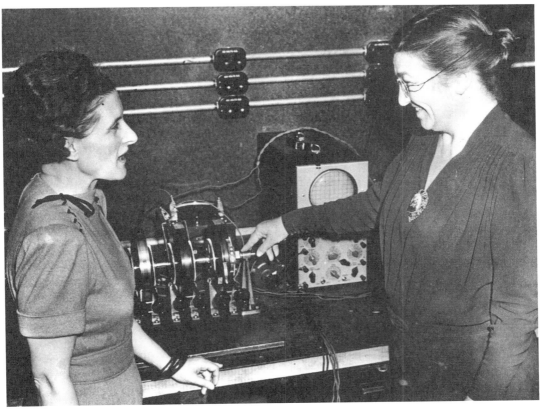

Vivian Kellems (left) and electrical engineer Edith Clarke (right) were two women holding early membership in the American Institute of Electrical Engineers. (Bettmann/Corbis)

neering. She is acknowledged as the first woman to present a technical paper to the American Institute of Electrical Engineers (AIEE), in 1926. Twenty-two years later, in 1948, she became the first woman elected a fellow of the AIEE, now the Institute for Electrical and Electronic Engineers (IEEE). She received the Society of Women Engineers' (SWE) Achievement Award in 1954.

See also Electrical and Electronics Engineering; Institute of Electrical and Electronics Engineers (IEEE); Lamme, Bertha; Patent

References Brittain, James E., "From Computer to Electrical Engineer: The Remarkable Career of Edith Clarke," *IEEE Transactions on Education* E28:4 (November 1985), pp. 184–189; McMurray, Emily M., ed., *Notable Twentieth-Century Scientists* (1995); Sicherman, Barbara, and Carol Hurd Green, eds., *Notable American Women: The Modern Period* (1980).

Cochran, Josephine G. (ca. 1842–?)

As indicated by a U.S. patent issued in 1886, Josephine Cochran was the inventor of the first powered dishwashing machine intended for commercial use. Cochran demonstrated her invention during the Columbian Exposition (Chicago World's Fair) of 1892–1893. At the time, the invention was already in use by most of the large restaurants at the fair, as well as some of Chicago's leading restaurants.

Little is known about the life of Josephine Cochran. However, it is known that she was born in Ohio around 1842. It is also known that Cochran received a second patent for a dishwasher in 1888 and an additional patent for a dish cleaner six years later. Cochran then made improvements to her first machine and began manufacturing the dishwashers. These improvements led to the use of her machines in many hotels across the country by 1908. Some of the larger models were powered by steam and could wash, scald, rinse, and dry between 5 and 20 dozen dishes of different sizes and shapes in about two minutes. Over time, the company she founded became one of the world's best-known appliance companies. KitchenAid, a familiar name in dishwashers and other domestic appliances, today manufactures a modern version of Cochran's early machine.

See also Columbian Exposition; Domestic Appliances; Invention/Inventors; Patent
References Macdonald, Anne L., *Feminine Ingenuity: How Women Inventors Changed America* (1992); Robertson, Patrick, ed., *The Book of Firsts* (1975); Stanley, Autumn, *Mothers and Daughters of Invention: Notes for a Revised History of Technology* (1993); Wiemann, Jeanne Madeline, *The Fair Women: The Story of the Woman's Building, World's Columbian Exposition, 1893* (1981); "History of the Dishwasher," in Whirlpool Homelife Network, at http://www2.whirlpool.com/html/homelife/cookin/cookdw5.htm (cited 15 July 1999).

Columbian Exposition

The first of America's world's fairs was held in Philadelphia in 1876, in celebration of the centennial of the United States. The Columbian Exposition of 1893 was America's second world's fair and was held in Jackson Park of Chicago from May through October. This exposition was intended to commemorate the four hundredth anniversary of Columbus's discovery of America. It also was intended to showcase the cultural and technological achievements of the United States. Construction of the fairgrounds cost more than $28 million and covered an area of approximately 686 acres. Estimates indicate that the fair was visited by more than 27 million people, most of whom paid admission fees of 25 cents (children) or 50 cents (adults) for the opportunity to explore the more than 65,000 exhibits. Additional fees were required to experience fair attractions such as theater performances, lectures, and rides on the Ferris wheel or in the hot-air balloons.

The buildings constructed for the Columbian Exposition were designed to represent individual states and territories, several other countries, and corporations. For example, the U.S. Government Building featured displays representing the various departments of the federal government; it also featured a California redwood tree. The Fisheries Building displayed numerous varieties of fish in fresh- and saltwater aquaria, and the Palace of Fine Arts (now the Chicago Museum of Science and Industry) displayed more than 8,000 paintings, sculptures, drawings, etchings, and decorative objets d'art from around the world. Within the Horticultural Building were eight greenhouses sheltering various natural environments in microcosm, including a Mexican desert and a Japanese garden. The Mines and Minerals Building demonstrated the mining techniques in use at the Kimberly Diamond mines; it also featured a silver statue of an actress and a replica of the Statue of Liberty that was made of salt. Railroad artifacts such as the first U.S. locomotive, models of English warships, a replica of an ocean liner, a Roman chariot, and the latest bicycles were the key attractions in the Transportation Building.

Among the many buildings showcasing the newest technological developments of the United States was Machinery Hall, which exhibited the Whitney cotton gin, the latest sewing machines, the world's largest conveyer belt, and the 43 steam engines that provided the electricity used throughout the fairgrounds. The Manufacture and Liberal Arts Building displayed Remington typewriters, Tiffany stained glass, the Yerkes telescope of the University of Chicago, and items of historical and artistic interest. The Agriculture Building housed weather stations; models of farm buildings, farm machinery, and animals; sculptures made of fruits and vegetables; and exhibits of tobaccos, cheeses, and beers.

The Electricity Building was among the most-frequented sites of the fair. In this building were a variety of lamps, elevators, fans, sewing machines, burglar alarms, stoves, washing machines, irons, a moving sidewalk, and a phonograph—all powered by electricity. Also on display in this building were the first seismograph; Edison's kinetoscope (a viewing machine for single moving pictures); the world's first elevated electric railway; and the Tower of Light, a display containing more than 18,000 incandescent bulbs.

Some achievements of women were featured in the many buildings covering the fairgrounds. However, most exhibits of women's achievements were presented at the Woman's Building, which also served as the headquarters for the Board of Lady Managers (the women responsible for the construction and administration of the building). Like the exhibits it contained, the physical structure of the Woman's Building was designed by a woman—Sophia G. Hayden of Boston. For her work on this project, Hayden reportedly was paid only about $1,000, a fraction of the $4,500 to $15,000 that the men who designed other fairgrounds buildings were paid. New York designer Candace Wheeler was the color director for the building and served as supervisor of all interior decorations. In addition, the building featured two murals painted by noted artist Mary Cassatt.

Among the exhibits featured in the Woman's Building were many items traditionally classified in the "women's domain," such as painted china, quilts, tablecloths, candlesticks, and paintings. However, the Woman's Building also featured a variety of technical and domestic inventions by women. For example, Caroline Wescott Romney demonstrated an iceless milk cooler and a heat-conserving dinner pail. The dishwasher for which Josephine Cochran had received a patent in 1886 was not only demonstrated within the walls of the Woman's Building but also was in use at most of the large restaurants throughout the fairgrounds. This invention was deemed sufficiently significant to win Cochran first prize at the Columbian Exposition.

Another technological achievement in use at the Woman's Building was the gravity elevator, invented by Harriet R. Tracy. Tracy's elevator was selected over one developed by a male inventor because it had automatic platforms that closed off the shaft—a safety feature intended to prevent a person riding the elevator from falling into the shaft and to keep away flames that could potentially rise into the elevator from the shaft. Tracy also displayed the rotary shuttle, lock- and chain-stitch sewing machine that contained a

lower bobbin capable of holding more than 1,000 yards of thread. Olivia P. Flynt displayed her "True Corset" or "Flynt Waist" invention—a ladies' undergarment that provided support for both the upper and lower body without restricting circulation, respiration, or movement. This corset won Flynt a bronze medal; she also secured many orders for the product. Martha J. Coston demonstrated her signal flares in the inventors' room of the Woman's Building.

Other displays at the Woman's Building included cartographic drawings and other illustrations by women geologists and botanists, such as those displayed by naturalist and scientific illustrator Anna Botsford Comstock. There also was an exhibit honoring noted astronomer Maria Mitchell. A water storage invention was demonstrated by Harriet Russell. Other scientific works included an archaeological display by Zelia Nuttall.

Many women were unable to ship their inventions to the exposition because of the expense. Others—among them Ellen Swallow Richards—elected to display their works alongside those of male inventors in other buildings. Richards's display involved a model kitchen that she had designed for maximum convenience and efficiency. Among the inventions making their public debut at the Columbian Exposition were several food products. For example, diet carbonated soda was first introduced at this fair, as was the hamburger. Other food items introduced at the fair included Cracker Jacks, Aunt Jemima Syrup, Cream of Wheat, Shredded Wheat, Pabst Beer, and Juicy Fruit gum.

The Columbian Exposition was deemed a success in amply demonstrating the progress America had made through technology. Many of its exhibits introduced and showcased the newly emerging engineering professions, and many highlighted the technological advances achieved by women in particular. The exposition also exerted a profound influence on later American art and architecture.

See also Agriculture; Architecture; Astronomy; Chilton, Annie H.; Cochran, Josephine G.; Coston, Martha J.; Hayden, Sophia Gregoria; Richards, Ellen Henrietta Swallow; Women's Rights

References Badger, Reid, *The Great American Fair* (1979); Macdonald, Anne L., *Feminine Ingenuity: How Women Inventors Changed America* (1992); Olsen, Kirstin, *Chronology of Women's History* (1994); Wiemann, Jeanne Madeline, *The Fair Women* (1981); Rose, Julie K., "World Columbian Exposition," (1996), available at http://xroads.virginia.edu/~MA96/WCE/title.html (cited 27 June 1999); Schulman, Bruce R., "Interactive Guide to the World's Columbian Exposition," available at http://users.vnet.net/schulman/ Columbian/columbian.html (cited 30 June 1999).

Colvin, Margaret Plunkett (1828–1894)

In 1871, Margaret Plunkett Colvin of Battle Creek, Michigan, was awarded a patent for a machine that is today found in most homes—a clothes washer. Colvin's washing machine, known as the Triumph Rotary Washer, was highly praised at the Philadelphia Centennial Exhibition of 1876; an improved version was later exhibited at the World's Columbian Exposition in Chicago in 1893. The washing machine developed by Margaret Colvin was manufactured and marketed by her husband, Ashley Colvin. In addition to that for the rotary washer, Margaret Colvin obtained three other patents for laundry-related devices described as "clothes-pounders"—two in 1878 and the third in 1881.

See also Centennial Exposition; Cochran, Josephine G.; Columbian Exposition; Eglin, Ellen F.; Potts, Mary Florence Webber
Reference Macdonald, Anne L., *Feminine Ingenuity: How Women Inventors Changed America* (1992); Stanley, Autumn, *Mothers and Daughters of Invention: Notes for a Revised History of Technology* (1993).

Colwell, Rita Rossi (b. 1934)

Microbiologist Rita Colwell is a leading authority in marine biotechnology and a pioneer in the use of computers to identify bacteria. In 1966, her research team at the University of Maryland Biotechnology Institute (UMBI) showed that *Vibrio cholerae,* the bacteria that cause cholera, live inside zooplankton (microscopic animals) present in estuaries—ecosystems formed where freshwater and saltwater meet. Using this knowledge, the team demonstrated that the incidence of cholera could be reduced by filtering water through several layers of cloth to remove zooplankton before using the water for drinking. This technology has important international implications, especially in developing nations, where people often must obtain their drinking water from untreated surface water sources. Colwell also has developed techniques for collecting medical, industrial, and aquacultural products from marine environments.

Rita Colwell was born in Beverly, Massachusetts. She attended Purdue University on a full scholarship, and received her B.S. in bacteriology there in 1956. Two years later, she received her M.S. in genetics, also from Purdue. In 1961, she received her doctoral degree in marine microbiology from the University of Washington at Seattle. She remained at the university, working as an associate professor, until 1964. She then taught at Georgetown University before accepting a post with the University of Maryland in 1972 as a professor of microbiology. She later served as both a professor and president of the UMBI until 1998, at which time she resigned to accept an appointment as director of the National Science Foundation (NSF). The appointment, which carries a six-year term, was made by President Bill Clinton in August 1998 and confirmed by the U.S. Senate.

Colwell has authored many books and technical articles and was involved in the production of the award-winning film *Invisible Seas*. She has earned many awards, including the Fisher Award from the American Association of Microbiologists (1985), the Gold Medal of the International Biotechnology Institute (1990), and the Civic Award from the State of Maryland (1990).

See also Biotechnology; Computers/Computer Technology; Genetic Engineering; National Science Foundation (NSF)
References Colwell, Rita, e-mail correspondence with Alan Winkler (28 February 1998); Dreifus, Claudia, "A Conversation with Rita Colwell, 'Always, Always, Going Against the Norm,'" *New York Times Biographical Service* (February 1999); McMurray, Emily M., ed., *Notable Twentieth-Century Scientists* (1995); Shearer, Benjamin F., and Barbara S. Shearer, eds., *Notable Women in the Life Sciences: A Biographical Dictionary* (1996); National Science Foundation, "Dr. Rita R. Colwell, Director

National Science Foundation," available at http://www.nsf.gov/od/lpa/forum/colwell/rrcbio.htm (cited 6 June 1999); University of Maryland Biotechnology Institute, Faculty, available at http://www.umbi.umd.edu (cited 24 March 1998).

Computers/Computer Technology

A computer is essentially a machine that is able to quickly process information, or data, by following a set of specially developed instructions called a program. The development of the computer was one of the most significant technological advances of the twentieth century. In fact, use of this machine has become so commonplace and has influenced so many aspects of society that the latter part of the twentieth century often has been described as the Computer Age.

The technologies involved in the development of computers draw from several areas of engineering, mathematics, and science. Perhaps more than in any other technological area, women have played vital roles in the emergence of computers and the computer industry since its beginnings. In addition, women have continued to make major contributions to this continually changing field.

The abacus, which has been in use for more than 2,000 years, is considered one of the earliest computing devices. In 1812, Charles Babbage, a professor of mathematics in England, designed a machine he called a "difference engine" to perform the long computations needed to produce mathematical tables. In 1833, seventeen-year-old Ada Byron, Countess of Lovelace, developed an interest in another of Babbage's computer machines. The countess, who was the daughter of poet Lord Byron, has been credited with devising a method for operating the computer constructed by Babbage, using punch cards.

The first computer to be produced in the United States was the ENIAC (electronic numerical integrator and computer). The ENIAC arose from a ballistics project that was being conducted on behalf of the U.S. Army at the University of Pennsylvania in Philadelphia. The project fell under the direction of Lieutenant Herman Goldstine, a former mathematics professor who

had been drafted into military service during World War II. Needing to find a way of quickly completing the many calculations required by the ballistics project, Goldstine sought the help of John Mauchly, who had built a machine called a differential analyzer, which used mechanical devices to make calculations. Working together, the two men developed the idea of modifying the machine to have it make calculations more quickly using electrical impulses. Thus, the idea of the ENIAC was born.

Goldstine and Mauchly, together with John Eckert (a mathematician and engineer), won approval from the U.S. Army to begin work on the ENIAC. A team was assembled, and construction of the massive machine commenced in July 1943. Construction was completed a little more than one year later, but there was a problem: Although the machine had been built, no one understood how to make it carry out the tasks for which it had been designed. To address this issue, six women who had recently obtained their degrees in mathematics were brought onto the project. The six women included: Elizabeth Snyder Holberton, Elizabeth Jennings, Kathleen McNulty, Marlyn Wescoff Meltzer, Frances Bilas Spence, and Ruth Lichterman Teitelbaum. These women, themselves known as "computers" because of their abilities to work with numbers, were provided the diagrams of all of the machine's components and were instructed to find a way to make it work. In time, the women did just that, and the nation's first computer was up and running. These women thus became the first computer programmers. In 1997, their achievement was recognized by Women in Technology International (WITI) through their induction into that organization's Hall of Fame.

Adele Katz Goldstine also was affiliated with the ENIAC project; however, her contributions are generally recognized as being less technological than those of the programmers. Goldstine, also a mathematician, was the wife of Lieutenant Herman Goldstine and was assigned the task of recruiting the women mathematicians for work on the ENIAC project. After the women hired for this task actually got the ENIAC to work, Goldstine

59

then developed the manual to accompany the computer system. The manual included detailed diagrams of all of the computer's components as well as instructions on how to make it perform certain tasks.

The ENIAC was an extremely large machine. Several years after its development, Eckert and Mauchly, who by now had their own company (known as Eckert-Mauchly), developed another computer, smaller in size than the first, but still quite large, known as the UNIVAC. When they began their company, Eckert and Mauchly hired some of the women who had worked on the ENIAC project. They also hired Grace Murray Hopper, a mathematician who had served in the U.S. Naval Reserves during World War II.

While with Eckert-Mauchly, Hopper worked on the UNIVAC as a computer programmer. Her role was to develop code that instructed the computer how to work. She later worked on many other projects with the company, trying to develop means of expediting the tedious and time-consuming tasks associated with computer programming. One of her time-saving innovations was the first practical computer compiler, a program that permitted codes to be stored magnetically on tape and accessed for retrieval when needed. In 1959, Hopper developed the computer innovation for which she is best known—the COBOL computer language. COBOL, an acronym for *common business-oriented language,* was the first computer language to use English in its instructions. Virtually anyone with some knowledge of programming would have been able to develop a working knowledge of COBOL.

Initially, computers were developed for military use. The early machines were extremely large, very expensive, and difficult to use. However, within a relatively brief period, several large corporations began to find ways of making these machines smaller, less expensive, and easier to use, while also developing software (packaged programs that could be installed on the computer to make it carry out specific applications) to make these machines useful in business. Such software included word processing programs, financial programs producing spreadsheets, and databases. These advances made computers useful to many large companies; however, the machines still remained too large and costly for general use by small companies and by individuals.

In 1948, John Bardeen, Walter H. Brattain, and William Shockley developed the transistor. This electronic component replaced the vacuum tubes that were used in the first computers. The transistors were approximately one one-hundredth of the weight and size of the vacuum tubes, were easier and cheaper to produce and to operate, and lasted longer. Transistors permitted the design of computers that were smaller, faster, and able to process greater amounts of information. In time, transistors, which are semiconductors made of silicon and germanium, became available on even smaller "silicon chips." These chips made use of printed circuitry that made it possible to fit the information carried in thousands of transistors on a single chip. In 1973, Patricia Wiener obtained a patent for a silicon computer chip that contained an entire memory system.

Chips such as the one developed by Patricia Wiener played a significant role in decreasing the size of computers. In addition, the incorporation of silicon chips into computers as a replacement for transistors made these machines easier to mass produce at a lower cost. Thus, many people who had been using computers in their offices were able to purchase similar systems for use at home. Despite this advancement, before the 1980s, the average person could not easily understand the operating system in use by most computers. Realizing this, Apple Computers began using small graphics called icons in their new Macintosh systems as a means of making these computers more "user-friendly." These icons were developed by Susan Kare, who was hired by Apple Computers to work as a graphic designer. The use of icons has since been adopted by most software manufacturers and has led to a rapid increase in the numbers of computers used in homes and schools.

Computer technology has made huge strides in many areas. In 1981, Martine Kempf modified her Apple computer to operate with voice-activated software that she developed for use by physically challenged individuals. This technology has since been adapted for use in operating rooms, where it permits microsurgeons to make hands-free magnification adjustments of their instruments. In addition, the voice-activated system also provides many physically challenged individuals the possibility of operating wheelchairs and automobiles by means of speech.

Many women have had successful careers in the computer industry through the formation of their own companies. For example, after leaving her position as a software developer for General Electric to raise a family, Sandra L. Kurtzig in 1972 decided to start her own computer company from her home. The company, ASK Computer Systems, designs software and is today generating millions of dollars in sales in this area. Lorraine Mecca, in 1979, also began her own company. Her company, Micro D, distributes the software it produces as well as computer peripherals—devices that permit computers to communicate with auxiliary apparatuses, such as printers, scanners, and modems.

Former nun Ann Piestrup used her technological skills to found the Learning Company in 1979. This company specializes in the production of educational software for children. Before forming her company, Piestrup obtained a Ph.D. in educational psychology from the University of California at Berkeley and also worked for a time as an elementary school teacher. The company she founded has become a leading producer and supplier of educational software for use by young children in the home, helping them to develop their knowledge and skills in areas such as spelling and mathematics.

See also Bernstein, Dorothy Lewis; Butler, Margaret K.; Colwell, Rita Rossi; Conway, Lynn Ann; Darden, Christine M.; Estrin, Thelma; Goldstine, Adele Katz; Granville, Evelyn Boyd; Harmon, Elise F.; Hoover, Erna Schneider; Hopper, Grace Murray; Kempf, Martine; Kurtzig, Sandra L. Brody; Richardson, Jane Shelby; Rogers, Marguerite M.; Shaw, Mary
References Hanauer, Mark, "A Friendly Frontier for Female Pioneers (Women in Computer and Software Industries)," *Fortune* (25 June 1984); Hogan, Kevin, "I Think, Therefore Icon," *Forbes* (13 September 1993); McCartney, Scott, *ENIAC: The Triumphs and Tragedies of the World's First Computer* (1999); Olsen, Kirstin, *Chronology of Women's History* (1994); "The Electronic 3 R's: Teaching on Home Computers (the Learning Company)," *Fortune* (24 January 1983).

Comstock Prize

The Comstock Prize is presented by the National Academy of Sciences (NAS) "to advance knowledge in electricity, magnetism, and radiant energy, by the giving of money prizes for important investigations or discoveries in those subjects." The prize was established in 1907 with resources provided by the Cyrus B. Comstock Fund (honoring engineer and surveyor Cyrus B. Comstock) and consists of an honorarium in the amount of $15,000 and a bronze medal. The award is presented every five years. Eligibility is limited to residents of North America. In 1963, Chinese American physicist Chien-Shiung Wu became the first woman to receive the Comstock Prize.

See also National Academy of Sciences (NAS); Wu, Chien-Shiung
References Claire, Walter, *The Book of Winners* (1979); Goldblum, Janice, National Academy of Sciences Archives, telephone interview with Leonard Bernstein, 20 May 1998; National Academy of Sciences, *A History of the First Half-Century of the National Academy of Sciences: 1863–1913* (1913); Read, Phyllis J., and Bernard L. Witlieb, *The Book of Women's Firsts* (1992); Siegman, Gita, ed., *Awards, Honors and Prizes,* Volume 1: *United States and Canada,* 10th ed. (1992).

Converse, Susan Taylor (n.d.)

Woburn, Massachusetts, native Susan Taylor Converse's invention in 1875 of what was called the Emancipation Suit of underwear literally created a sigh of relief among women. Prior to this development, women generally wore tight and restrictive corsets and other uncomfortable undergarments. These impractical garments made it difficult for women to work, play, and even breathe. It has even been reported that some women actually fainted due to the tightness of their corsets. Concern for women's health and well-being prompted feminists such as Susan Taylor Converse, as well as Sarah Strickland and others of Converse's predecessors, to try to create more comfortable undergarments for women.

Converse's idea, for which she received multiple patents in 1875, was actually an improvement of the Emancipation Union, a flannel undergarment that had been developed in 1868.

Converse's Emancipation Suit covered the body of the wearer from neck to ankles, and could be purchased in separate pieces (top and bottom) or as a one-piece unit. The two-piece set could be buttoned at the hips. The top half of the suit, designed to protect the breasts from the cramping and irritation often associated with tight-fitting corsets, was known as the Emancipation Waist. Women also could purchase the suit with either long or short sleeves and in cotton or linen. Another feature of the suit was that it provided sets of buttons at various locations that could be used to attach other articles of clothing, such as petticoats or skirts.

The Emancipation Suit developed by Converse was manufactured by George Frost & Co., and was displayed at the Centennial Exposition in Philadelphia in 1876. Unlike many other creations by women displayed at the exposition, Converse's garment was not on display in the Woman's Pavilion but in the regular, commercial exhibits. Converse received a twenty-five-cent royalty for each garment sold.

See also Crosby, Caresse; Demorest, Ellen Curtis; Miller, Elizabeth Smith; Rosenthal, Ida Cohen; Strickland, Sarah
References Macdonald, Anne L., *Feminine Ingenuity: How Women Inventors Changed America* (1992); Showell, Ellen H., and Fred M. B. Amram, *From Indian Corn to Outer Space: Women Invent in America* (1995); Stanley, Autumn, *Mothers and Daughters of Invention: Notes for a Revised History of Technology* (1993).

Conway, Lynn Ann (b. 1938)

Electrical engineer Lynn Ann Conway was a pioneer in computer technology and artificial intelligence. Conway simplified the design of large-scale integrated circuit systems and integrated computer chips (electronic configurations mounted on silicon chips), revolutionizing the computer industry.

Lynn Ann Conway was born in Mount Vernon, New York. She attended Columbia University and received her B.S. in electrical engineering there in 1962. Conway remained at Columbia, earning her M.S. in electrical engineering the following year. For the next 20 years, she worked as a researcher or senior staff engineer at several major electronics corporations, including IBM, Memorex, and Xerox. In 1983, she became chief scientist and assistant director of Strategic Computing at the Defense Advisory Research Projects Agency (DARPA). Two years later, she accepted a position as professor of electrical engineering and computer science at the University of Michigan's College of Engineering at Ann Arbor, a position she still holds.

In recognition of her contributions to the fields of electrical engineering and computer technology, Conway has received many honors and awards. In 1984, she was elected a fellow of the Institute for Electrical and Electronics Engineers (IEEE) and also received the IEEE Educational Activities Board's Major Educational Innovation Award. She was the 1984 recipient of the Harold Pender Award of the University of Pennsylvania and of the 1985 John Price Wetherill Medal of the Franklin Institute. In recognition of her participation on an advisory panel to the United States Air Force Scientific Advisory Board, Conway was presented the Meritorious Civilian Service Award by the U.S. Secretary of Defense in 1985. Five years later, she received the Achievement Award of the Society of Women Engineers (SWE).

See also Bernstein, Dorothy Lewis; Computers/Computer Technology; Electrical and Electronics Engineering; Estrin, Thelma; Goldstine, Adele Katz; Hopper, Grace Murray
References McMurray, Emily M., ed., *Notable Twentieth-Century Scientists* (1995); Saari, Peggy, and Stephen Allison, eds., *Scientists: The Lives and Works of 150 Scientists* (1996).

Conwell, Esther Marly (b. 1922)

Esther Marly Conwell is an internationally known solid state physicist who was a pioneer in the field of integrated optics and the use of polymers (long-chained molecules) as semiconductors in electronic devices. The nature of her work, for which she holds four patents, has led to improvements in the design and performance of radios, televisions, computers, artificial satellites, and other devices that use transistors or solar cells, both of which are semiconductor devices.

Conwell was born and raised in New York. She received an A.B. degree in physics from Brooklyn College in 1942, where she was elected to Phi Beta Kappa. She earned her master's degree in physics from the University of Rochester in 1945 and a Ph.D. in physics from the University of Chicago in 1948. After completing her education, Conwell taught physics at Brooklyn College for three years before joining Bell Telephone Laboratories to research semiconductors. She later worked at GTE Laboratories Research Center in Bayside, New York, as manager of both the electronic materials program and the physics department. Conwell remained at GTE until 1972. She then began work as the principal scientist at Xerox Corporation, and later at the Xerox Research Center in Webster, New York. She served as an adjunct professor of chemistry and associate director for the Center for Photoinduced Charge Transfer at the University of Rochester. She has been a member of the summer faculty of Stanford University and professor of physics at the Massachusetts Institute of Technology (MIT).

Conwell has been well recognized for her work. In 1960, she was presented the Achievement Award of the Society of Women Engineers (SWE). In 1980, she was elected into the National Academy of Engineering (NAE); ten years later, she was elected into the National Academy of Sciences (NAS). Conwell is only the second woman to have been elected into both of these organizations.

See also Conway, Lynn Ann; Electrical and Electronics Engineering; National Academy of Engineering (NAE); National Academy of Sciences (NAS); Phi Beta Kappa Society; Telecommunications
References Bailey, Martha J., *American Women in Science: A Biographical Dictionary* (1994); Kass-Simon, G., and Patricia Farnes, eds., *Women of Science: Righting the Record* (1990); McMurray, Emily M., ed., *Notable Twentieth-Century Scientists* (1995); Rossiter, Margaret W., *Women Scientists in America: Before Affirmative Action, 1940–1972* (1995).

Cori, Gerty Theresa Radnitz (1896–1957)

Much of what is today known about how the body obtains energy from food resulted from the pioneering work of Gerty Radnitz Cori and her husband, Carl Cori. In 1947, the couple was awarded a Nobel Prize in physiology/medicine for their discovery of the enzymes that enable the body to store and use carbohydrates and the description of how these processes occur. The Coris shared the Nobel Prize with Argentine scientist Bernardo A. Houssay, who determined the role of the pituitary gland in sugar metabolism. Gerty Cori became the first American woman, and only the third woman ever, to win a Nobel Prize in science. Later in her life, Gerty Cori built upon her discovery by proving that several glycogen storage diseases resulted from the absence of a particular kind of enzyme in the body.

Gerty was born in Prague, Czechoslovakia, into a fairly wealthy Jewish family. She was tutored at home until the age of ten and then attended a private finishing school for girls. The school prepared her for the accepted role of young women at that time, and did not stress the academic courses necessary for work in the sciences. At age 16, Gerty had already decided she wanted to attend medical school. In only two years, she studied on her own and mastered the Latin, physics, math, and chemistry required to take an entrance exam for medical school. Having passed the exam, she entered the Medical School of the German University of Prague in 1914. There, Gerty made two decisions that would affect the rest of her life: to pursue a career as a research biochemist and to marry fellow student Carl Ferdinand Cori.

In 1920, the same year that both received their M.D. degrees, Gerty and Carl married and moved to Vienna. Gerty took a position at a children's hospital in Vienna, where she researched congenital thyroid deficiency. Carl taught at the University of Graz and worked in the medical clinic at the University of Vienna. During the 1920s, Vienna, like many other cities in Europe, was suffering the effects of World War I. In addition, research positions for biochemists were limited,

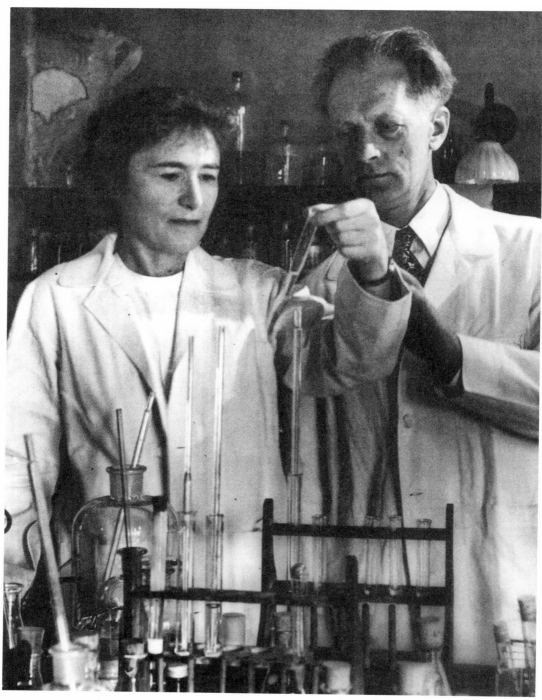

Gerty Radnitz Cori and her husband, Carl Cori, shared the 1947 Nobel Prize in physiology/medicine for their discovery of the enzymes used in carbohydrate metabolism. (Corbis-Bettmann-UPI)

and the Coris were forced to seek employment elsewhere.

In 1922, Carl Cori accepted a position in Buffalo at the New York State Institute for the Study of Malignant Diseases. (The institute is today known as the Roswell Memorial Park Institute.) Gerty followed Carl to the United States a few months later to work as an assistant pathologist at the same institution. With this move, the Coris entered into an employment pattern that would affect them for the remainder of their careers. The pattern involved Carl accepting an assignment at a research facility, and Gerty, whose ability was equal to Carl's, being offered a less prestigious position that offered less recognition and lower pay.

While working in Buffalo, the Coris devoted most of their time to the study of cancers and tumors and why they tended to store large amounts of glucose. This link between glucose and tumors revitalized an earlier interest the Coris had developed in carbohydrate metabolism following the discovery of insulin in 1921. A few years later, they were able to explain in general terms how the body derived energy from sugar metabolism. Their theory, which became known as the Cori cycle, explained how some glycogen contained in the body's muscles was converted to glucose (a sugar) to be "burned" for energy, and how the liver produced additional glycogen to be stored again in the muscles. With this explanation, physicians were better able to develop a clearer understanding of the disease known as diabetes melitis.

In 1928, six years after moving to the United States, Gerty and Carl Cori became naturalized U.S. citizens. The couple left Buffalo in 1931 to begin employment with the Washington University School of Medicine, in St. Louis, Missouri. Carl became chairman of the pharmacology department; Gerty was employed as a research associate professor of biochemistry. Both were actively engaged in carbohydrate research.

Four years after moving to St. Louis, the Coris discovered a new glucose compound, glucose-1-phosphate. This discovery allowed them to show that the breakdown of glycogen occurred in a se-

ries of steps. A short time later, the couple discovered phosphorylase, the enzyme that changes glycogen to glucose-1-phosphate. Once the Coris discovered and isolated these substances, they were able to produce glycogen in a test tube.

Gerty Cori remained an associate at the Washington University School of Medicine until 1946, when Carl became chairman of a newly formed department of biochemistry. Following his promotion, Carl appointed his wife to the position of full professor. Around the same time, the laboratory overseen by the Coris became the world's center for the study of enzyme reactions that drive biochemical processes in the body. Eight of the many scientists who worked at the lab, including the Coris, went on to win Nobel Prizes. These included Arthur Kornberg, Earl W. Sutherland, Edwin G. Krebs, Severo Ochoa, Christine R. de Duve, and Luis F. Leloir. The Coris were awarded their Nobel Prize in 1947.

A few weeks before the Coris left for Sweden to accept their Nobel Prize, Gerty was diagnosed with myelosclerosis, a rare and fatal bone marrow disease. As a result of the illness, her bone marrow was not producing red blood cells but was instead forming fibrous tissue. Despite the debilitating nature of her ailment, Gerty Cori lived another ten years after receiving the Nobel Prize and continued her research on enzyme-related disease—research that served as the foundation for the study of a number of genetic diseases. The same year the Coris were awarded the Nobel Prize, Gerty Cori became only the fourth woman to be elected a member of the National Academy of Sciences. The next year, Gerty Cori was awarded the Garvan Medal by the American Chemical Society (ACS). In 1952, she was appointed by President Harry S. Truman to serve on the board of the newly formed National Science Foundation (NSF).

See also Elion, Gertrude Belle; Francis P. Garvan–John M. Olin Medal; Frantz, Virginia Kneeland; Goeppert-Mayer, Maria; Levi-Montalcini, Rita; Medicine/Medical Technology; National Science Foundation (NSF); Nobel Prize; Yalow, Rosalyn Sussman

References Bailey, Martha J., *American Women in Science: A Biographical Dictionary* (1994); Litoff, Judy

Barrett, and Judith McDonnell, *European Immigrant Women in the United States: A Biographical Dictionary* (1994); McGrayne, Sharon B., *Nobel Prize Women in Science* (1992); McMurray, Emily M., ed., *Notable Twentieth-Century Scientists* (1995); Porter, Ray, ed., *The Biographical Dictionary of Science,* 2nd ed. (1994); Rothe, Anna, ed., *Current Biography, 1948* (1948); Sicherman, Barbara, and Carol Hurd Green, eds., *Notable American Women: The Modern Period* (1980); Yount, Lisa, *Contemporary Women Scientists* (1994).

Coston, Martha J. (1826–?)

Martha J. Coston was granted Patent No. 23,536 in 1859, and No. 115,935 in 1871, for the invention and subsequent improvement of Pyrotechnic Night Signals, a system of red, white, and green maritime signal flares. This technological advance in ship-to-shore and ship-to-ship communications replaced earlier signal flags, which were useless in fog and at night. In the event of a shipwreck, Coston's system of colored fireworks allowed rescuers to quickly locate and communicate with a disabled vessel. The invention helped save many people from drowning.

Martha was born in Baltimore, Maryland, and grew up in Philadelphia, Pennsylvania. At age 14, Martha met Benjamin Coston, an inventor. Two years later, the couple married. Benjamin died five years later, leaving his young widow (and their children) the notes, records, and descriptions of his unfinished inventions. Intrigued by her deceased husband's work and desperate to provide for her family, Martha Coston researched and perfected his ideas for signal flares and was ultimately granted patents for the inventions.

Coston sold her patent rights to the Union Congress for $20,000—half of what she had requested—and a contract to manufacture the flares. However, Coston believed she had received inadequate compensation for her invention because she was a woman. To secure additional finances, Coston applied for, and received, additional patents in France, England, Italy, Holland, Austria, and Sweden. She also sold the signal rights to maritime firms, yacht clubs, and the navies of several European countries. The importance of the signal flares was evidenced by the fact that they remained in use for nearly 100 years after their invention. Some believe the flares may have influenced the outcome of the Civil War.

See also Centennial Exposition; Columbian Exposition; Lamarr, Hedy; Ordnance; Patent
References Macdonald, Anne L., *Feminine Ingenuity: How Women Inventors Changed America* (1992); Vare, Ethlie Ann, and Greg Ptacek, *Women Inventors and Their Discoveries* (1993); Lemelson-MIT Program, "Martha J. Coston," in Invention Dimension, Inventor of the Week Archives, available at http://web.mit.edu/invent/www/inventorsA-H/coston.html (cited 14 December 1997).

Crosby, Caresse (1892–1970)

During the early 1900s, low-cut evening gowns for wear at social events were gaining in popularity among fashionable women. However, the necklines (front and back) were often cut in such a manner that the upper portion of the corset (an undergarment initially designed to reduce the girth of the waist) could be seen. This problem was solved by an industrious and inventive New York socialite named Mary Phelps Jacob (later, Caresse Crosby), who with the assistance of her maid Marie created a backless brassiere. The undergarment she designed was constructed of two silk handkerchiefs and a length of satin ribbon that were sewn together in a manner that separated and flattened the breasts, creating the desired "proper" look.

Mary Phelps Jacob was born into a wealthy family in New York in 1892. Her family roots can be traced back to Robert Fulton, inventor of the steamboat, and to Governor Bradford, the first governor of the Plymouth Colony. Although little is known of Jacob's early years, she was a child of privilege and attended private schools, took classes in dance, and received training in horseback riding.

It was while preparing for an evening's social event that Jacob encountered the corset problem and developed the idea for her backless brassiere. After learning of the garment and viewing it in a dressing room, many of Jacob's friends requested that a similar garment be made for them. This overwhelming response and popularity prompted Jacob to bring her idea to a patent attorney. The next year, in 1914, a patent for the invention was issued to Jacob.

After Jacob received her patent, she started a business in which she enlisted the services of her maid, obtained sewing machines, and hired girls to do the sewing. The business quickly produced several hundred backless brassieres, which Jacob began selling under the adopted and more glamorous name of Caresse. Although a number of the brassieres made by the company were purchased, the business eventually failed. Speculation as to the causes of its failure include poor advertising and the fact that the product itself may have been too far ahead of its time.

In 1915, Mary (Caresse) Jacob married Richard Rogers Peabody. Soon after her marriage, she decided to put her business interests aside. A few years later, Richard Peabody left home to serve in the military during World War I. When he returned from the war, he was suffering from serious problems with alcohol; the marriage ended shortly thereafter. During the brief period between her husband's return from the war and the end of their marriage, Caresse came upon a former acquaintance who was employed by the Warner Brothers Corset Company of Bridgeport, Connecticut. He convinced her to show her invention to his company. The Warner Brothers Corset Company liked what they saw and made an offer to purchase Peabody's patent rights to the invention for $1,500. Peabody readily accepted their offer, considering the dollar amount to be more than generous. It has since been estimated that the Warner Brothers Corset Company likely made a profit of about $15 million on the transaction.

In 1922, Caresse Peabody married poet and banker Harry Crosby, and together the couple founded a book publishing company, which printed works by Ezra Pound, James Joyce, Gertrude Stein, D. H. Lawrence, and other noted writers. Despite her earlier invention and her connections with the literary world, however, Caresse Crosby died in obscurity in 1970.

See also Converse, Susan Taylor; Demorest, Ellen Curtis; Handler, Ruth; Miller, Elizabeth Smith; Rosenthal, Ida Cohen; Strickland, Sarah

References "Caresse Crosby, Publisher, Dies: Former Editor of Black Sun Press in Paris Was 78" [obituary], *New York Times* (25 January 1970); Macdonald, Anne L., *Feminine Ingenuity: How Women Inventors Changed America* (1992); Pabst, Georgia, "Women Are Often Mothers of Invention," *Milwaukee Journal Sentinel* (6 April 1997); Baldwin, Deborah, "Caresse Crosby and the Brassiere," in Dead Inventors' Corner, Discovery Channel On-line, at http://discovery.com/...0522/inventors1.html (cited 11 July 1999); "Caresse Crosby," in Cosmic Baseball Association, available at http://www.clark.net/pub/cosmic/caresse8.html (cited 11 July 1999).

Crystallography

Crystallography is the study of the type and arrangement of atoms in a substance and the nature of the forces that control and result from these arrangements. The science of crystallography developed as a branch of mineralogy that emphasized geometric form, such as that occurring in quartz. Modern crystallography has become a separate science that deals with all crystalline matter.

The earliest recorded crystal studies, performed near the end of the sixteenth century, focused on crystalline shape and concluded that different substances have different characteristic shapes. By the end of the seventeenth century, crystallographers were studying crystal faces and their corresponding angles. Nearly a century later, it was determined that all crystals of a given substance have identical interfacial angles, regardless of their size. By the nineteenth century, a reflected beam of light and a mechanical device called a goniometer were being used to accurately measure the interfacial angles of crystals. Such measurements, combined with mathematical notations, led crystallographers to hypothesize that crystals were composed of tiny, invisible building blocks arranged in set patterns. About this same time, atomic theory and the concept of atoms as the building blocks of matter was gaining acceptance. Crystallographers drew upon this theory to begin speculating about the arrangement of atoms (atomic structure) in crystals.

In 1912, German physicist Max von Laue discovered that X rays are diffracted (spread out) by the three-dimensional atoms contained within crystals. For this discovery, von Laue was awarded the Nobel Prize in physics in 1914. Photographic plates and special cameras were later used to record the pattern of dots formed by the diffracted X rays, a science known as X-ray crystallography. Using this technology, it was soon concluded that each type of crystal has a unique diffraction pattern.

X-ray crystallography has become a powerful tool in chemistry, physics, metallurgy, and pharmacology. For example, Elizabeth Armstrong Wood performed research on crystal applications for optical devices at the Bell Labs in 1943. Her data were used in the development of lasers. British scientist Dorothy Crowfoot Hodgkin used X-ray crystallography to determine the molecular structure of the penicillin molecule and of vitamin B-12, groundbreaking research for which she was awarded the Nobel Prize in chemistry in 1964. Soon after this work was completed, scientists knew enough about the atomic structure of these molecules to begin synthesizing them in the laboratory.

In the early 1950s, British biologist Rosalind Franklin used X-ray crystallography to accurately record the structure of DNA. Scientists James Watson, Francis Crick, and Maurice Wilkins eventually applied Franklin's data to explain the structure of DNA, for which they shared the Nobel Prize in physiology/medicine in 1959. More recently, Isabella Karle has applied mathematical models to crystallographic studies of DNA and designed peptides. Karle's peptide research has broad applications in the field of pharmacology. For example, when a therapeutic drug is synthesized in the laboratory, its molecules can be structured so that the drug's beneficial properties are enhanced and its harmful side-effects reduced.

See also American Crystallographic Association (ACA); Karle, Isabella L.; Nobel Prize; Pharmacology; Richardson, Jane Shelby; Wood, Elizabeth Armstrong

References Bailey, Martha J., *American Women in Science: A Biographical Dictionary* (1994); Parker, Sybil P., *McGraw-Hill Encyclopedia of Science and Technology*, 8th ed., vol. 4 (1997); Schmittroth, Linda, Mary Reilly McCall, and Bridget Travers, eds., *Eureka!*, vol. 6 (1995); Shearer, Benjamin F., and Barbara S. Shearer, eds., *Notable Women in the Life Sciences: A Biographical Dictionary* (1996); Stanley, Autumn, *Mothers and Daughters of Invention: Notes for a Revised History of Technology* (1993).

Cunningham, Kate Richards O'Hare (1877–1948)

Kate Richards O'Hare Cunningham is best known for her activities involving the promotion of socialism and prison reform. For her socialist activities, Cunningham was charged, arrested, and sentenced to a term of five years imprisonment in 1919 under the nation's newly created Espionage Act. However, she served only one year in jail because socialist party activists were successful in getting her sentence commuted. Cunningham was later granted a full pardon by President Calvin Coolidge. While serving her year in jail, Cunningham authored two books: *Kate O'Hare's Prison Letters* (1919) and *In Prison* (1920). Ironically, this former inmate was later hired as the director of the California Penal System, where she sought to institute penal reform.

Kate Cunningham's involvement in technology preceded her socialist and prison reform activities. At the end of the nineteenth century, she was a machinist apprentice, in training under her father. During her apprenticeship, Cunningham was admitted to the International Order of Machinists in 1894. She was the first woman to be admitted as a member of this union.

See also Converse, Susan Taylor; Gleason, Kate; Knight, Margaret E.; Women's Rights
References Heinemann, Sue, *Timelines of American Women's History* (1996); Read, Phyllis J., and Bernard L. Witlieb, *The Book of Women's Firsts* (1992).

Darden, Christine M. (b. 1942)

Aerospace engineer and mathematician Christine Darden has devoted much of her career to the study of the environmental impact of supersonic transports (SSTs), airplanes that fly faster than the speed of sound. Planes flying at such speeds create a pressure wave in the air that causes a loud noise called a sonic boom when it reaches the ground. The energy contained within a sonic boom has enough intensity to shatter glass and damage structures.

In her work for the National Aeronautics and Space Administration (NASA), Darden has used mathematics to develop computer simulations that examine how altering aircraft design (primarily wing and nose shape) and speed might eliminate sonic booms. Concurrently, other NASA scientists built model SSTs with designs similar to Darden's computer models and tested them in high-speed wind tunnels. The results of both types of tests were nearly identical, although the computer simulations produced results more quickly and much less expensively. In 1979, Dar-

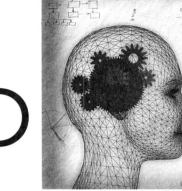

den's project on commercial SSTs was discontinued. However, she has conducted similar research on wing design for high-speed military aircraft.

Christine Darden was born in Monroe, North Carolina, in 1942. She received her bachelor's degree in mathematics from Hampton Institute in 1962 and a master's degree in mathematics from Virginia State College in 1967. While at Hampton, Darden's interests were not limited to the study of mathematics. She was also active in the civil rights movement. She participated in student sit-ins to help African Americans gain equal access at a lunch counter and participated in voter registration drives.

Darden began her work at NASA as a mathematician but later developed an interest in engineering. In 1983 she received a doctorate in mechanical engineering from George Washington University. She has since worked at NASA's Langley Research Center in Hampton, Virginia. For her work in aerospace engineering, Darden has received many awards. In 1985 she received the A. T. Weathers Technical Achievement Award from the National Technical Association. In 1989, 1991, and 1992 she was presented the Langley Research Center's Certificate of Outstanding Performance.

Christine Darden is an expert in aircraft design, especially as it relates to the speed of sound. (Associated Press/AP)

See also Acoustical Engineering; Aeronautical and Aerospace Engineering; Flügge-Lotz, Irmgard; National Aeronautics and Space Administration (NASA)

References Kessler, James H., et al., *Distinguished African American Scientists of the 20th Century* (1996); McMurray, Emily M., ed., *Notable Twentieth-Century Scientists* (1995); Van Sertima, Ivan, *Blacks in Science, Ancient and Modern* (1995).

Demorest, Ellen Curtis (1824–1898)

Noted for her imaginative and inventive talents, Ellen Demorest created accurate, mass-produced dress patterns on tissue paper for home dress-making. Demorest's husband, William, a dry goods merchant, began publishing a quarterly fashion magazine, *Mme. Demorest's Mirror of Fashions,* to promote Ellen's idea in 1860. A tissue-paper dressmaking pattern was stapled into each magazine. The popularity of the patterns spread rapidly, and in only four years, the magazine became a monthly publication, with sales of 60,000 copies per month. The success of this venture peaked in 1876, when 3 million patterns were sold.

Ellen was born and educated in Schuylerville, New York. While still in her teens, she developed an interest in fashion and an awareness of style. At age 18, her father helped her open a millinery shop. As her business flourished, Ellen moved her shop first to Philadelphia, Pennsylvania; then to Troy, New York; and finally to New York City. There she met William Demorest, whom she married in 1858.

By the mid-1860s, the Demorests were hiring skilled dress designers and models from England and France. With her successful pattern business and nationwide magazine sales, Ellen became a fashion leader. Her talents led to such inventions as a health corset, stocking suspenders, skirt supports, and a scaled-down hoop skirt. These and others of her inventions were exhibited at the Philadelphia Centennial Exposition in 1876.

In additional to her entrepreneurial talents, Demorest was also a supporter of women's rights and racial equality. She hired African Americans and whites to work side by side in her pattern business. She also encouraged women to seek employment opportunities as bookkeepers, typesetters, and telegraphers.

See also Blanchard, Helen Augusta; Fox, Sally; Invention/Inventors; Knight, Margaret E.; Textiles
References Macdonald, Anne L., *Feminine Ingenuity: How Women Inventors Changed America* (1992); Read, Phyllis J., and Bernard L. Witlieb, *The Book of Women's Firsts* (1992); Stanley, Autumn, *Mothers and Daughters of Invention: Notes for a Revised History of Technology* (1993); Vare, Ethlie Ann, and Greg Ptacek, *Mothers of Invention: From the Bra to the Bomb, Forgotten Women and Their Unforgettable Ideas* (1988).

Dick, Gladys Rowena Henry (1881–1963)

Gladys Dick and her husband, George Dick, made several significant contributions that led to the diagnosis, prevention, and treatment of scarlet fever. After more than ten years of research, in 1923, the Dicks proved that hemolytic streptococci bacteria caused scarlet fever. Following their discovery, the Dicks isolated a toxin produced by these bacteria from which they were able to develop a skin test (called the Dick test) that was used to detect an individual's susceptibility to the disease. Isolation of the toxin also allowed the Dicks to develop a vaccine to prevent the disease and an antitoxin to treat those who had the disease.

The Dicks were not alone in their research. The crippling effects and high mortality rate of scarlet fever prompted many researchers to investigate means of preventing or treating this disease. Some researchers had even begun their own production of toxin. Concerned about the purity and quality of these other toxins, the Dicks obtained, in 1924 and 1926, respectively, U.S. and British patents on their methods for producing the toxin and antitoxin. News of the patents sparked considerable controversy. The originality of the discovery was challenged, and questions were raised as to whether or not the development of the toxins and antitoxins could be considered an invention. In addition, medical communities in both the United States and Great Britain accused the Dicks of commercialism, claiming that patent rights were too restrictive, and thus limited research and standardization. To protect the quality and integrity of their invention, Gladys Dick filed and won a lawsuit against a pharmaceutical laboratory for patent infringement and improper toxin production.

Gladys Dick was born in Pawnee City, Nebraska, but later moved with her family to Lincoln. In 1900, she received a B.S. degree from the University of Nebraska. After receiving her degree,

Gladys wanted to attend medical school. However, discouragement from her mother and a lack of enthusiasm by most medical schools to accept female students led Dick to pursue a teaching career. After two years, however, her continued interest in medicine led her to apply to the Johns Hopkins University School of Medicine. Dick received her M.D. degree from the school in 1907.

Dick began her research into scarlet fever in 1911, while working at the Children's Memorial Hospital in Chicago. Three years later, she began working with her husband, conducting experiments to identify the cause of scarlet fever at the John R. McCormick Memorial Institute for Infectious Diseases in Chicago.

For their work on scarlet fever, the Dicks were nominated for a Nobel Prize in medicine in 1925. However, no prize in medicine was awarded that year. The following year, the Dicks were awarded the Mickle Prize of the University of Toronto for essential work in the field of practical therapeutics. In 1933, they received the Cameron Prize from the University of Edinburgh, also for work in practical therapeutics.

Gladys Dick remained at the John R. McCormick Memorial Institute for Infectious Diseases in Chicago until her retirement in 1953. Although she devoted most of her professional career to the study of scarlet fever, she also did research on polio. In addition, Dick was a founder of the Cradle Society in Evanston, Illinois. This society is reported to be the first professional children's adoption agency in the United States.

See also Alexander, Hattie Elizabeth; Elion, Gertrude Belle; Medicine/Medical Technology; Patent
References Bailey, Martha J., *American Women in Science: A Biographical Dictionary* (1994); Edmonson, Catherine M., *365 Women Who Made a Difference* (1996); Read, Phyllis J., and Bernard L. Witlieb, *The Book of Women's Firsts* (1992); Shearer, Benjamin F., and Barbara S. Shearer, eds., *Notable Women in the Life Sciences: A Biographical Dictionary* (1996); Sicherman, Barbara, and Carol Hurd Green, eds., *Notable American Women: The Modern Period* (1980).

Dickelman, Lizzie H. (n.d.)

Lizzie H. Dickelman, of Forest, Ohio, was the oldest of nine children. Dickelman worked with her father in his sheet metal business and, after his death in 1917, ran the family business alone. A few years later, in response to an appeal addressed to farmers nationwide by Herbert Hoover—who was at that time the War Food Administrator—urging crop conservation, Lizzie Dickelman developed drawings of a corncrib (a storage facility for corn), for which she later received a patent. Dickelman's corncrib provided a means for rain to drain off the corn, while allowing air to circulate around the corn stored in the crib. In addition to her patent for the corncrib, Dickelman also obtained patents for three other facilities for grain storage. The structures she developed found markets in the United States and abroad. Dickelman's agricultural creations were not exclusively related to the cultivation of plants; she also designed a brooder (a heated house for newly hatched chicks). Dickelman obtained a patent on her brooder in 1926, bringing her total number of patented inventions to five.

See also Agriculture; Grandin, Temple; Pennington, Mary Engle
References Macdonald, Anne L., *Feminine Ingenuity: How Women Inventors Changed America* (1992); Stanley, Autumn, *Mothers and Daughters of Invention: Notes for a Revised History of Technology* (1993).

Domestic Appliances

An appliance is a device or piece of equipment that is developed for a specific use. Gadgets developed for use in the home are called *domestic appliances*. Examples of domestic appliances include items for use in food preparation and cooking; washing machines and dryers; and devices designed to make housecleaning easier, such as improved garbage cans and vacuum cleaners. Until late in the twentieth century, most women did not enjoy careers outside the home. Instead, a woman's occupation often was described as "homemaker," a job that required her to remain at home and tend to the needs of the family by cooking, cleaning, sewing, washing clothes, and caring for children. It is no surprise that many domestic appliances designed to make these tasks easier or more efficient resulted from the creative genius of women.

Many women are credited with developing items related to food preparation and cooking. Such items range in levels of sophistication from the improved pastry fork for which African American inventor Ann Mangin was issued a patent in 1892 to more sophisticated electrical food-mixing appliances, such as the one home efficiency expert Lillian Moller Gilbreth has been credited with developing in the 1920s. The diversity of purpose and sophistication in these two inventions is a recurring trend among the many inventions of women related to food preparation. Other examples of such diversity are provided through the inventions of Mary Evard, Dicksie Spolard, Nancy Johnson, Madeline Turner, and Maria Kenny Beasley.

Mary Evard developed a new stove, which came to be called the "Reliance Cook Stove," around 1868. Evard's stove was unusual in that it was designed with moveable partitions that permitted the use of coal on one side while wood was burned on the other side. The simultaneous use of the two types of fuel allowed foods to be cooked at different temperatures on the different sides of the stove. In addition, the stove also featured moveable partitions within its oven section that made it possible to bake foods requiring a "dry baking" in one part of the oven, while foods better prepared through "moist baking" were prepared in another section.

Inventors Nancy Johnson and Madeline Turner are both noted for their developments of machines for use in processing food. Nancy Johnson (ca. 1795–1890), of Washington, D.C., is credited with developing the hand-cranked ice cream freezer, for which she was issued a patent in 1843. Almost half a century later, on 25 April 1916, Madeline Turner, of Oakland, California, was issued a patent for a fruit press.

Not all of the domestic appliances related to cooking are as mechanical as the inventions previously cited. For example, a device intended to provide the cook with a means of determining how much spaghetti to cook was developed by Dicksie Spolard of Fontana, California. The device essentially used a tape measure wrapped around a bundle of uncooked pasta as a guide for the number of servings represented by the bundle. Additionally, although not mechanical, cooking pots have proved essential to food preparation. Among the women who have made contributions in this area are Maria Beasley (ca. 1847–1904?), who also was known for her contributions to barrel making. Later, metallurgist Charlotte R. Manning of Meriden, Connecticut, developed a process of enameling metal hollowware. Manning was issued a patent on this process in 1907. Pots and pans coated with enamel are still popular today.

The development of products and devices intended to facilitate household cleanliness is another area in which women have made contributions. An early and simple development in this area was Susan Hibbard's duster made from discarded turkey feathers. Although Hibbard's husband tried to obtain the patent for this invention in his name, patent examiners discovered that it was in fact Susan who had created the implement and thus issued the patent to her, in 1876. Other developments in this area include a garbage can designed by Lillian Gilbreth, which featured a lid that was opened by stepping on a foot pedal (developed in the 1950s). This invention was originally designed for use by people with physical disabilities; however, it caught on with the general public and has become a common feature in many kitchens and bathrooms throughout the world. This style of garbage can also is common in doctors' offices and hospitals.

At the extreme end of inventions in the home-cleaning category is Frances Gabe's self-cleaning house. A working model of this house was constructed near Newburg, Oregon, in 1984. Gabe's home, for which she was issued multiple patents in 1984, features almost seventy separate devices that are intended to be entirely self-cleaning, thus eliminating the need for the home owner to do much more than push a few buttons to maintain a clean home. These devices include a self-cleaning tub and toilet, a kitchen cabinet that also serves as a dishwasher, and specially designed walls, floors, and furnishings that permit entire rooms to be washed and rinsed by a sprinkler-type system. Water then drains off the furnishings and onto the floors, which are angled slightly to carry away the water. Although Gabe has not yet found a buyer for her idea, she has enjoyed living in the home she developed, and has found that it fulfills the purpose for which it was designed.

Women have made notable contributions also in the development of devices related to laundering. Among the more prolific inventors in this area was Margaret P. Colvin, of Battle Creek, Michigan. In 1871, Colvin was issued a patent for a machine she called the "Triumph Rotary Washer." In 1876 and 1893, respectively, she displayed her creation at both the Centennial Exposition of Philadelphia and the Columbian Exposition of Chicago. Colvin also is credited with the development of other laundering devices, including three different laundry pounders.

In 1888, Ellen Eglin of Washington, D.C., sold her invention of an improved clothes wringer (a device attached to a washtub to help remove excess water from laundered clothing) for only $18. When she sold her device, Eglin had not bothered to apply for a patent for her creation, thus freeing the agent who purchased the device to make and market it as he wished, with no additional financial obligation to Eglin. When asked why she sold her creation so cheaply, Eglin often told people that she thought it unlikely that the device would become popular if it were known that it had been created by a black woman.

Until the era of wash-and-wear fabrics, ironing was an integral part of the laundering process. One of the most significant developments in this area (prior to the emergence of electric irons) resulted from the creative mind of Mary Webber Potts. In 1870, Potts developed an improved sadiron (a heavy, metal iron). At this time in history, irons were heated by placing them atop a stove. When heated, the metal portion of the device frequently burned the hands of the user. To address this problem, Potts developed a new wooden-handled iron that featured a base partially filled with plaster. The base made the iron lighter in weight and helped keep heat away from the user's hands. In addition, the handle was made to be easily removed from one iron and slipped onto either of the other two interchangeable bases (allowing two

irons to heat while the third was in use). Potts's iron was introduced to the public at the Centennial Exposition of Philadelphia, where it met with immediate success.

The appliances and domestic products discussed here represent but a fraction of those developed by women. Others include sewing machines and accessories, coffeemakers, dishwashers, and many items designed to assist in childrearing (such as disposable diapers, toys, and infant carriers). Although women today do not typically spend as much time in the home as did their forebears, they continue to develop new products that make the performance of household chores easier and more efficient.

See also Boone, Sarah; Centennial Exposition; Cochran, Josephine G.; Columbian Exposition; Colvin, Margaret Plunkett; Donovan, Marion; Eglin, Ellen F.; Frederick, Christine M.; Gabe, Frances Bateson; Gilbreth, Lillian Moller; Goode, Sarah E.; Henry, Beulah L.; Hibbard, Susan; Home Economics; Jones, Amanda Theodosia; Jones, Sarah E.; Keichline, Anna W.; Kenner, (Mary) Beatrice Davidson; Knight, Margaret E.; Low, Jeanie S.; Mangin, Anna; Moore, Ann; Morgan, Agnes Fay; Muller, Gertrude; Newman, Lyda; Potts, Mary Florence Webber; Proudfoot, Andrea H.; Richards, Ellen Henrietta Swallow; Russell, Lillian; S., Mary; Wells, Jane
References Macdonald, Anne L., *Feminine Ingenuity: How Women Inventors Changed America* (1992); Stanley, Autumn, *Mothers and Daughters of Invention: A Revised History of Technology* (1993); Vare, Ethlie Ann, and Greg Ptacek, *Mothers of Invention: From the Bra to the Bomb, Forgotten Women and Their Unforgettable Ideas* (1988).

Donovan, Marion (1917–1998)

Marion Donovan created a leakproof, reusable diaper cover that eventually led to the development of the disposable diaper. Frustrated by the frequent changes of baby clothing and bedding required because of leaking cloth diapers, Donovan used sections of shower curtain material to construct a diaper cover. In 1949, she changed her original design by substituting surplus nylon parachute cloth for the shower curtain material and plastic snaps in place of the safety pins used to hold the diaper cover together. The resulting product, called the Boater, soon sold at New York City's Saks Fifth Avenue, where it was a huge success with parents of young children. In 1951, Donovan sold her patent rights to the Boater for $1 million and began working to devise an absorbent paper diaper that could take the place of cloth.

As a child, Marion Donovan spent much of her after-school time at the Fort Wayne Lathe Works. The shop was owned by her father, Miles O'Brien and his twin brother, Richard, who coinvented the South Bend lathe used to make gears in automobiles. Later, Marion attended Rosemont College in Pennsylvania, where she majored in English literature. She graduated in 1939. Following graduation, Donovan worked for *Vogue* magazine in New York, as an assistant editor. She later moved to Westport, Connecticut, and began to raise a family. It was during this time that Donovan first had the idea that evolved into the Boater.

In 1958, Donovan received a degree in architecture from Yale University. She used her skills in this area to design her own home in Greenwich, Connecticut. However, the invention of practical devices remained Donovan's first love. In addition to the Boater, Donovan patented dozens of other inventions, including a specialized hanger that could hold up to 30 skirts or slacks in a compact space; a wire soap holder; and an elasticized zipper pull for women's dresses.

See also Baker, Sara Josephine; Patent
References Donovan, Christine, "Rash Idea: Marion Donovan Helped Put Cloth Diapers Behind Us," *People Weekly* (7 December 1998); "Marion Donovan, 81, Solver of the Damp-Diaper Problem" [obituary], *New York Times* (18 November 1998); Vare, Ethlie Ann, and Greg Ptacek, *Mothers of Invention: From the Bra to the Bomb, Forgotten Women and Their Unforgettable Ideas* (1988); Ward, Barbara, "The Mothers of Invention Deserve Credit," available at http://www.kentuckyconnect.com/heraldleader/news/030898/tlinvent.html (cited 2 February 1999).

Downs, Cornelia Mitchell (1892–1987)

Microbiologist Cornelia (Cora) Downs is internationally known for her development and perfection of a fluorescent antibody staining technique that is used as a diagnostic and research instrument for identifying viruses and bacteria. This rapid and inexpensive identification technique

(developed in 1959) changed the way pathologists worldwide identify disease-causing organisms. Cora Downs was also the first person to identify the cause of tularemia (rabbit fever)—an infectious viral disease transmitted by animals to humans. Her study of this disease provided insights into other infectious diseases passed by animals to humans, such as rickettsia, Rocky Mountain spotted fever, and "Q" fever.

Cornelia Downs was born in Wyandotte (a northern section of Kansas City), Kansas. She attended the University of Kansas in Lawrence, from which she received her A.B. (1915), her M.A. (1920), and her Ph.D. (1924). While a graduate student, Downs taught bacteriology at the university. She was hired as assistant professor in 1921 and promoted to associate professor in 1924 and to full professor in 1935 and remained at the school until her retirement in 1963. In addition to teaching, Downs worked for the Rockefeller Institute for Medical Research from 1939 to 1940 and served at the Army Bacteriological Laboratory at Fort Detrich, Maryland, during World War II.

In 1959, Downs was named a special fellow of the U. S. National Institutes of Health (NIH) at Oxford University in England. She was awarded the Citation for Distinguished Service in 1964—the highest honor given by the University of Kansas. In 1971, the Kansas Public Health Association presented Downs its Crumbine Medal. One year later, she was named Sommerfield Distinguished Professor of Bacteriology at the University of Kansas and was elected to honorary membership in the American Society of Microbiology. In 1975, Downs received the International Women's Year Award for Health Protection from the U.S. Department of Health, Education, and Welfare (HEW).

Downs was a member of the Society of American Bacteriologists, the Society of Immunologists, and the American Society of Pathologists and Bacteriologists. She also belonged to the American Association of University Professors, Phi Sigma, and Sigma Xi. Her portrait is displayed in the International Gallery of Medical Honor at the Russian Academy of Sciences in Moscow. In 1980, the annual graduate student award of the

Missouri Valley Section of the American Society for Microbiology was renamed in Downs's honor.

See also Antibiotics; Dick, Gladys Rowena Henry; Evans, Alice Catherine; Medicine/Medical Technology
References "Anthrax and Old Lace," *University of Kansas Alumni Magazine,* vol. 58, no. 8 (May 1960); Baldwin, Sara Mullin, and Robert Morton Baldwin, eds., "Cornelia Mitchell Downs," *Illustriana Kansas* (1933); "Cora Downs" [obituary], *Topeka Capital-Journal* (28 January 1987); Debus, Allen G., ed., *World Who's Who in Science* (1968); O'Hern, Elizabeth Moot, *Profiles of Pioneer Women Scientists* (1986); "Scientist Downs Leaves Legacy of Half a Century," *Kansas Alumni Magazine,* vol. 85, no. 5 (March 1987); Vare, Ethlie Ann, and Greg Ptacek, *Mothers of Invention: From the Bra to the Bomb, Forgotten Women and Their Unforgettable Ideas* (1988).

Dresselhaus, Mildred S. (b. 1930)

An eminent solid state physicist and a leader in developing opportunities for women in science and engineering, Dresselhaus is primarily a researcher; she is not involved with the practical applications of the materials she studies. However, others have used her research to advance technology.

Solid state physics deals with the physical properties of solids. Dresselhaus began her career in solid state physics during its infancy. She has devoted her career to the study of the electronic properties of metals and semimetals, particularly those classified as semiconductors and superconductors, and the effects of magnetic fields on these materials. Semiconductors are materials that have a limited ability to conduct electricity—such as silicon, gallium, and selenium. This property makes semiconductors useful in transistors and integrated circuits—the foundations of all electronic equipment. Superconductors are materials that can be made to carry an electric current indefinitely, without any resistance, when they are cooled to very low temperatures. Such materials will permit machinery to operate more efficiently and use less electricity. Applications of solid state physics include lasers, solar batteries, and radiation detectors. Solid state technology is also used in the communications, electronics, and aerospace industries.

Mildred Dresselhaus was born to an immigrant family in Brooklyn, New York. She attended Hunter High School in New York City before entering Hunter College, from which she received her bachelor's degree with honors in 1951. Dresselhaus then studied at Newnham, the women's college of Cambridge University in England, on a Fulbright Fellowship before receiving her master's degree from Radcliffe College in 1953. She obtained a Ph.D. in physics from the University of Chicago in 1958.

After receiving her Ph.D., Dresselhaus was accepted as a National Science Foundation (NSF) Fellow at Cornell University. In 1960, she accepted a research position at the Lincoln Laboratory of the Massachusetts Institute of Technology (MIT). Here, she researched the superconductivity of carbon-related materials, the work for which she is best known. In 1967, Dresselhaus became a visiting professor in MIT's Electrical Engineering Department. The next year, she became a full professor. She has since held positions at MIT as associate department head of electrical science and engineering, director of the Center of Materials Science and Engineering, and institute professor of electrical engineering and physics. She also has been a visiting professor at universities in Israel, Brazil, Venezuela, Germany, and Japan. In addition, she helped found the MIT Women's Forum in 1970, a group that helps women build careers and gain employment in science and engineering.

Dresselhaus is well recognized for her work as a physicist and with the MIT Women's Forum. In 1977, she received the Society of Women Engineers (SWE) Annual Achievement Award for her contributions in teaching and research. These achievements were also recognized in 1990, when President George Bush presented her with the National Medal of Science. In addition to her teaching and research, this award cited Dresselhaus's work in enhancing opportunities for women in science and engineering.

Dresselhaus has been an active member of numerous science organizations, including the National Research Council (NRC) and the National Science Foundation (NSF). In 1984, she served as president of the American Physical Society and treasurer of the National Academy of Sciences (NAS). In 1997, she was elected president of the American Association for the Advancement of Science (AAAS).

See also American Association for the Advancement of Science (AAAS); Bramley, Jenny Rosenthal; Computers/Computer Technology; Conwell, Esther Marly; Materials Engineering; Metals and Metallurgy; National Medal of Science; Spaeth, Mary
References Ambrose, Susan A., et al., *Journeys of Women in Science and Engineering: No Universal Constants* (1997); Jones, Edwin R., and Richard L. Childers, *Contemporary College Physics* (1993); Kass-Simon, G., and Patricia Farnes, eds., *Women of Science: Righting the Record* (1990); McMurray, Emily M., ed., *Notable Twentieth-Century Scientists* (1995); Nobel, Iris, *Contemporary Women Scientists of America* (1979); Veglahn, Nancy, *Women Scientists* (1992); Sirica, Coimbra, "Mildred S. Dresselhaus, 1997 AAAS President," *AAAS News & Notes* (29 November 1996), available at http://www.aaas.org/communications/inside17.htm (cited 12 March 1998).

Dunbar, Bonnie J. (b. 1949)

Bonnie J. Dunbar is a veteran of five space flights and has logged a total of 1,208 hours, or 50 days, in space. Dunbar became known to most people as an astronaut when she made her first flight into space, in 1985. However, her contributions to technology go well beyond her role as an astronaut. These contributions include her involvement in the development and production of the ceramic tiles that are used as the thermal protection system (heat shield) for NASA's space shuttles. In addition, Dunbar applied her knowledge of materials engineering to studies of calcium loss in bones under conditions of weightlessness, to determine how such loss affects the ability of bones to bear weight—research that falls into the engineering domain known as stress analysis. The results of her research have been examined by medical experts to determine their correlation to the disease known as osteoporosis.

Bonnie J. Dunbar was born on 3 March 1949, in Sunnyside, Washington. She grew up in the rural community of Outlook, Washington, where her family operated a cattle ranch. During their youth, Bonnie and her siblings had a daily bus ride of thirty minutes to reach the small country school they attended. Dunbar credits her interest in science and technology to this period of her life, when she first heard the story *The Angry Red Planet* in one of her grade-school classes.

Dunbar later attended the Sunnyside High School, from which she graduated in 1967. In high school, her interest in chemistry and physics was inspired by one of her science teachers. This teacher helped Dunbar realize that a career in engineering might prove beneficial to someone who wished to be involved in space exploration. Although Dunbar knew that she ultimately wanted to become an astronaut, she kept this desire to herself to avoid the criticism or embarrassment that were typical reactions in the 1960s to women who aspired to such "male-dominated" careers.

At the age of 18, Dunbar sent her first application to NASA for entry into its astronaut program. The reply she received informed her that she needed to obtain a college degree before she could even be considered a candidate for the astronaut program. Dunbar duly enrolled at the University of Washington, in 1967. While she was a student there, the university was awarded a research grant by NASA to conduct investigations related to the thermal protection system on the space shuttle NASA planned to develop. The research was headed by Jim Mueller, who chaired the ceramics engineering department of the University of Washington. Mueller shared with Dunbar some of the areas of research his group was working on, including the reentry heating profile for the yet-to-be-constructed space shuttle. This information convinced Dunbar to pursue studies in ceramics engineering. She earned her B.S. degree in this field in 1971.

After earning her bachelor's degree, Dunbar accepted a graduate fellowship in biomedical engineering at the Urbana-Champaign campus of the University of Illinois. However, she did not complete the program, due to the untimely death of her brother in the Vietnam War. Instead, she returned home to be near her family. While living at home, Dunbar obtained a job as a computer systems analyst with the Boeing Corporation in

Seattle. She worked in this position for two years, and then returned to the University of Washington on a NASA grant that involved studies on the space applications of high-energy-density batteries. Her work in this area led to a master's degree in ceramics engineering in 1975.

After completing her master's, Dunbar spent three months in Oxford, England, as a member of a research science exchange program. When she returned to the United States, she immediately found employment at the Rockwell International Space Division in Downey, California. There Dunbar resumed her work with thermal protection systems using ceramic tiles, which she had begun as a student of the University of Washington; however, now her efforts went beyond research and involved the production of ceramic tiles for an actual space shuttle.

While working at Rockwell, Dunbar again applied to the space program—this time in response to NASA's call for shuttle astronauts. Although she obtained an interview with NASA for this position, she was not selected for the astronaut program. She did, however, obtain an offer from NASA to work on their *Skylab* project. With encouragement from her supervisor at Rockwell, she accepted the position in 1978 and began work as a guidance and navigation engineer in Mission Control. Her primary duties in this position were to monitor and make needed adjustments to the orientation and navigation systems of the spacecraft, to keep it on course.

While working for NASA, Dunbar continued her education. She took night classes leading toward a doctoral degree at the University of Houston, and received her Ph.D. in mechanical/biomedical engineering in 1983. It was while working toward this degree that Dunbar did her important research on calcium loss and bone density, using rats as test subjects. This research became of interest both to NASA (who observed a loss of bone density in astronauts involved in space flights) and to the medical community (which was studying osteoporosis). At the same time, Dunbar applied once again to the astronaut program. This time she was accepted into the 1980 class, with the understanding that while

training for the program, she would also complete work toward her Ph.D.

After her astronaut training, Dunbar was scheduled for a flight. She trained for this flight for about eighteen months before going into space aboard the *Challenger,* during shuttle mission 61-A—a collaborative mission with Germany—in October 1985. Dunbar was the only woman on the mission. During this mission, the shuttle crew deployed the *Spacelab* (an orbiting research facility that had been built by the European Space Agency). Among Dunbar's primary responsibilities were to operate the *Spacelab* and to conduct more than seventy-five experiments. This mission lasted seven days (30 October–6 November).

In total, Dunbar has made five space flights. Her second trip into space, aboard *Columbia* (mission STS-32), occurred in 1990. This mission lasted almost 11 full days (9–20 January). During this flight, Dunbar's responsibilities included conducting experiments dealing with microgravity and echocardiology. In addition, the crew deployed a satellite and retrieved a research facility using the RMS (remote manipulator system)—the shuttle's robotic arm. Two years later, Dunbar made her third space flight. On this mission (25 June–9 July 1992), Dunbar served as the payload commander on *Columbia* (mission STS-50) during the almost 14-day flight.

Dunbar began her fourth space mission aboard *Atlantis* (STS-71) on 27 June 1995. This mission included the first of many dockings that would take place between U.S. space shuttles and the Russian space station *Mir.* During this historic flight, in which American astronauts exchanged places with Russian cosmonauts who had been living aboard the space station, Dunbar served as a mission specialist. In addition, the crew did medical evaluations on the Russian cosmonauts to determine the effects of weightlessness on bone density, cardiovascular function, and the immune system.

Dunbar's most recent mission occurred in 1998, aboard the *Endeavor* (STS-89). This eight-day flight also marked the eighth time a shuttle docked with the *Mir* space station. During the docking, the shuttle crew moved supplies it had brought from Earth into the space station for use by its inhabitants. On this mission, Bonnie Dunbar again served as a payload commander and also was responsible for conducting numerous technological and scientific experiments.

Through the years, Dunbar has garnered many prestigious awards. These include five NASA Space Flight Medals (one for each flight). In addition, she also has received from NASA: an Exceptional Service Medal (1988), an Outstanding Leadership Award (1993), an Exceptional Achievement Award (1996), and a Superior Accomplishment Award (1997). Dunbar also has been honored with numerous awards from other sources. Among the more significant of these are the 1993 *Design News* Engineering Achievement Award, the Resnik *Challenger* Medal of the Society of Women Engineers (SWE), and the Judith A. Resnik Award of the Institute of Electrical and Electronics Engineers (IEEE). Dunbar is a member of several professional societies, including the American Ceramic Society (ACS), the National Institute of Ceramic Engineers (NICE), and the American Association for the Advancement of Science (AAAS).

See also Bartlett, Helen Blair; Jemison, Mae; Lucid, Shannon Wells; Materials Engineering; National Aeronautics and Space Administration (NASA); Resnik, Judith A.; Ride, Sally Kirsten; Space Exploration

References Ambrose, Susan A., et al., *Journeys of Women in Science and Engineering: No Universal Constants* (1997); National Aeronautics and Space Administration, *Astronaut Fact Book* (1992); Sherr, Lynn, "Remembering Judy: The Five Women Who Trained with Judy Resnik Remember Her . . . and That Day," *Ms.* (June 1986); National Aeronautics and Aerospace Administration, "Biographical Data: Bonnie J. Dunbar," available at http://www.jsc.gov/Bios/htmlbios/dunbar.html (cited April 1998).

Earle, Sylvia (b. 1935)

One of the foremost marine biologists and oceanographers in the world, Sylvia Earle has contributed much to our understanding of the ocean environment and its inhabitants. This information has resulted largely from research conducted by Earle from ocean vessels or through diving. More recently, Earle's contributions have relied more heavily on technology through her roles in the development and use of submersibles that are specially designed for deep-sea exploration.

Sylvia Alice Earle was born in Gibbstown, New Jersey, in 1935. When Earle was a teenager, her family moved to the ocean community of Clearwater, Florida (located near the Gulf of Mexico). Here Earle completed her high school education at the age of 16. About this same time, Earle also took a scuba diving course—an experience that had a profound influence on the path her life has taken since.

Earle began her college education at St. Petersburg Junior College in Florida, but later transferred to Florida State University, where she majored in botany (the study of plants). She graduated with a B.S. degree in 1955. After receiving this degree, Earle enrolled in a master's program at Duke University in Durham, North Carolina. She completed this program in 1956, at which time she was awarded an M.A. in botany.

Over the next ten years, Earle worked for a time as a wildlife biologist for the U.S. Fish and Wildlife Service (FWS) and then taught college classes at St. Petersburg Junior College. She then joined the International Indian Ocean Expedition (a project sponsored by the National Science Foundation) for the purpose of exploring the plants and animals living in the Indian Ocean. Earle was the only woman of the sixty-member research team engaged in this exploration. Only two years later, in 1966, Earle was awarded a Ph.D. in botany by Duke University.

After receiving her Ph.D., Earle moved to Massachusetts, where she accepted a position as a researcher at the Radcliffe Institute. She remained in this position until 1969. The following year, Earle participated in an event that would become the first of her many notable achievements. That

year, she was appointed the project leader for an experiment in which a team of five women scientists were to spend two weeks in an enclosed underwater habitat known as *Tektite II*. The purpose of the venture was both to study marine life and to determine what effects living in a confined environment for a period of time might have on the physical and mental stamina of the inhabitants. The results of this research were of great interest to the National Aeronautics and Space Administration (NASA), as it was thought that the findings might serve as a prediction of how astronauts would fair under similar circumstances in space.

In 1979, Earle embarked on another major adventure when she participated in the testing of a new piece of diving equipment called the Jim suit, designed by British engineer Graham Hawkes. The Jim suit was a plastic and metal outfit that tethered its occupant to a submersible. While wearing this suit, Earle made a record-breaking dive of 1,250 feet (a record she still holds).

Following the "Jim-suit dive," Earle spent several years (1976–1980) researching the migration patterns of humpback whales, during the filming of a documentary. In addition, she coauthored the book *Exploring the Deep Frontier* in 1980. The next year, Earle entered into a partnership with Jim-suit designer Graham Hawkes to found Deep Ocean Technologies (DOT). The duo founded a second company, called Deep Ocean Engineering (DOE), in 1982. The primary aim of DOE is to de-

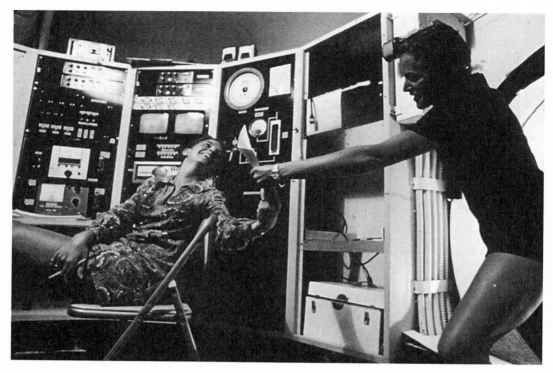

Sylvia Earle (right) is shown here inside an underwater research station. (UPI/Corbis-Bettmann)

sign and manufacture submersibles for use in deep-ocean exploration. These submersibles are quickly approaching depth capabilities of several miles. In addition to founding these companies, Earle also served as president and CEO of both companies until 1990, at which time she accepted the post of chief scientist at the National Oceanic and Atmospheric Administration (NOAA).

During Earle's tenure as chief scientist at NOAA, her two most important projects involved investigating the environmental damage that resulted from the *Exxon Valdez* oil spill that occurred in Prince William Sound in 1989 (the year before Earle began work at NOAA) and from the Kuwaiti oil spills at the conclusion of the Persian Gulf War. In 1992, Earle resigned from her post at NOAA, largely as a result of differences in opinion between herself and the administration. She did, however, remain with NOAA as an adviser to its administrator from 1992 to 1993. After leaving this position, Earle wrote her second book, *Sea Change,* which was published in 1995.

In addition to her numerous and varied career activities, Sylvia Earle has been an active member of many professional organizations and societies. She is a fellow of the American Association for the Advancement of Science (AAAS) and the Explorers' Club. In addition, she holds memberships in the International Phycological Society, the Phycological Society of America, the American Society of Ichthyologists and Herpetologists, and the Natural Resources Defense Council (NRDC).

Earle has received numerous honors and awards for her contributions to marine science and for her conservation activities. Among them are the Conservation Service Award of the California Academy of Sciences (1979), the Lowell Thomas Award of the Explorer's Club (1980), and the David Stone Medal of the New England Aquarium (1989). In addition, Earle was honored in 1998 by the United Nations with a listing in its Global 500 Roll of Honor for her "life-long commitment to deep-sea exploration."

See also Martinez, Lissa Ann; Mather, Sarah

References Bailey, Martha J., *American Women in Science, 1950 to the Present: A Biographical Dictionary* (1998); Breton, Mary Joy, *Women Pioneers for the Environment* (1998); Graham, Judith, ed., *Current Biography Yearbook, 1992* (1992); Holloway, Marguerite, "Profile: Sylvia A. Earle—Fire in Water," *Scientific American,* vol. 266, no. 4 (April 1992); Watkins, T. H., et al., "One Hundred Champions of Conservation," *Audubon,* vol. 100, no. 6 (November–December 1998).

Eaves, Elsie (1898–1983)

Civil engineer Elsie Eaves was known for her innovative methods of collecting, analyzing, and reporting statistics on the construction industry. After World War II, Eaves served as a manager in the Construction Economics Department of the *Engineering News-Record.* Her job was to analyze cost indexes and trends that served as standards for people who design, build, manufacture, service, and supply materials for construction projects. These statistics provided the first continuous inventory of construction at the planning stage.

Eaves was born in Idaho Springs, Colorado, and received her B.S. degree in civil engineering from the University of Colorado at Boulder in 1920. She later held positions at the U.S. Bureau of Public Roads, the Colorado State Highway Department, and the Denver and Rio Grande Railroad, before beginning work with the *Engineering News-Record* in 1927. In 1945, she became manager of *Business News,* a position she held until her retirement in 1963. Eaves then served as an adviser on housing costs to the National Commission on Urban Affairs, and to the International Executive Service Corps in Iran.

Among Eaves's honors was her admission into the American Society of Civil Engineers (ASCE) as its first woman member, in 1927. She was also the first woman admitted into the American Association of Cost Engineers (1957). In 1979, the ASCE also bestowed an honorary membership upon Eaves, a designation giving her all rights and privileges in the organization without payment of annual dues. She also was awarded the George Norlin Silver Medal, the highest award issued by the University of Colorado to alumni, in 1974.

See also American Society of Civil Engineers (ASCE); Barney, Nora Stanton Blatch; Cambra, Jessie G.; Civil Engineering; Roebling, Emily Warren

References Kass-Simon, G., and Patricia Farnes, eds., *Women of Science: Righting the Record* (1990); Read, Phyllis J., and Bernard L. Witlieb, *The Book of Women's Firsts* (1992); Bois, Danuta, "Elsie Eaves (1898–1983)," available at http://www.netsrq.com/~dbois/eaves.html (cited 20 June 1998).

Edwards, Helen Thom (b. 1936)

Helen Edwards was instrumental in the design and construction of the Tevatron—one of the world's first high-energy, superconducting particle accelerators. This accelerator produced high-energy collisions between subatomic particles called protons and antiprotons (protons with a negative charge), enabling scientists to study the nature of these particles and advance their knowledge in particle physics. Edwards's involvement in this project included work on superconducting magnetic production, radio frequency, power supplies, cryogenics, vacuum systems, lattice design, orbit theory, and radiation protection.

Helen Edwards was born in Detroit, Michigan, and attended primary school in a suburb of the city. She received her secondary education at a girls' high school near Washington, D.C. She then enrolled at Cornell University in Ithaca, New York, where she received her B.A. (1957), her M.S. (1963), and her Ph.D. (1966) in physics.

Edwards remained at the Cornell Laboratory for Nuclear Studies as a research associate for the next four years, working on the electron synchrotron (an accelerator that uses high energy to place electrons or other particles in circular orbits). In 1970, she accepted the position of associate head of the Booster Group at the Fermi National Accelerator Laboratory (or Fermilab) in Batavia, Illinois. She became head of the Accelerator Division at Fermilab in 1987, where she oversaw the completion of the Tevatron. In 1989, Edwards became head and associate director of the Superconduction Division of the Superconducting Super Collider (SSC), a laboratory that was to be built in Waxahachie, Texas. However, the project was later canceled due to budget cuts imposed by the U.S. Congress. In 1992, Edwards accepted her present position as guest scientist at Fermilab.

Helen Edwards is a fellow of the American Physics Society and a member of the National Academy of Engineering. For her work in accelerator design and construction, Edwards received the Ernest O. Lawrence Award from the U.S. Department of Energy (DOE) in 1986. In 1988, she was awarded a John D. and Catherine T. MacArthur Fellowship. The next year, she was given the National Medal of Technology.

> **See also** Eng, Patricia L.; Goeppert-Mayer, Maria; Jackson, Shirley Ann; National Medal of Technology; Nuclear Physics; Wu, Chien-Shiung
>
> **References** McMurray, Emily M., ed., *Notable Twentieth-Century Scientists* (1995); Shearer, Benjamin F., and Barbara S. Shearer, eds., *Notable Women in the Physical Sciences: A Biographical Dictionary* (1997); "Helen T. Edwards," in Virtual Museum of Virginia Tech, available at http://www.ee.vt.edu/~museum/women/helen/helen.html (cited 19 November 1998); University of California at Los Angeles, Department of Physics, "Edwards, Helen T.," in Contributions of 20th Century Women to Physics, available at http://www.physics.ucla.edu/~cwp (cited 19 November 1998).

Eglin, Ellen F. (n.d.)

Among the many episodes of women's inventions being patented by men is that of African American inventor Ellen F. Eglin. Eglin was a native of Washington, D.C., who invented a clothes wringer. Eglin did not obtain a patent for her wringer but instead sold her invention to an agent for $18 in 1888. The agent is believed to have profited greatly from the device. When Eglin was asked why she sold her invention, she stated that she believed that whites would not buy the product if it became known that the wringer was patented by a Negro.

> **See also** Blount (Griffin), Bessie J.; Colvin, Margaret Plunkett; Greene, Catherine Littlefield; Hibbard, Susan; Masters, Sybilla Righton
>
> **References** Macdonald, Anne L., *Feminine Ingenuity: How Women Inventors Changed America* (1992); Salerno, Heather, "Mothers of Invention: Though Unsung and Ignored, Women Have Pushed Technology's Frontiers," *Washington Post* (12 March 1997); Smith, Jessie Carney, ed., *Black Firsts: 2,000 Years of Extraordinary Achievement* (1994); Stanley, Autumn, *Mothers and Daughters of Invention: Notes for a Revised History of Technology* (1993).

Eldering, Grace (1900–1989)

In 1932, microbiologist Grace Eldering, working with bacteriologist Pearl Kendrick, helped show that the *Bordetella pertussis* bacterium, which was discovered in 1906, was the agent responsible for pertussis (whooping cough). Later that year, after conducting extensive field investigations on pertussis, the pair developed a successful vaccine for prevention of this disease. They later combined their vaccine with a diphtheria vaccine and the tetanus toxoid (a nontoxic substance produced by treating a toxin with chemicals) to create the world's first DPT vaccine.

Grace Eldering was born in Hysham, Montana, in 1900. She was awarded a B.A. in 1927 from the University of Montana, after completing a program in biology and chemistry. In the fall of the following year, she began work as a microbiologist at the Michigan State Department of Health Laboratories in Lansing. She was transferred to the Grand Rapids laboratory in 1932, at which time she met and began working with Pearl Kendrick. The two women began focusing their attention on pertussis, an illness that was claiming the lives of as many as 6,000 American children each year and many thousands more worldwide. Later that same year, they developed what became the world's first successful vaccine for preventing this disease.

Within seven years of its development, the vaccine prepared by Kendrick and Eldering was ready for commercial production. In 1940, the Michigan State Department of Health began producing and distributing the vaccine. It quickly decreased the incidence of pertussis by one-half. Around this same time, Eldering enrolled at Johns Hopkins University to pursue graduate studies. She received her Sc.D. in immunology in 1941. Ten years later, Eldering assumed Kendrick's position as director of the Grand Rapids Laboratory when Kendrick retired and accepted a position as a lecturer at the University of Michigan. Eldering remained director of the laboratory until her retirement in 1969.

Eldering was an active member of the American Public Health Association and the American Board of Bacteriologists. She also served one term as president of the Michigan Branch of the American Society for Microbiology. For their work in developing the pertussis vaccine, both Eldering and Kendrick were inducted into the Historical Honors Division of the Michigan Women's Hall of Fame in 1983. Eldering died five years later.

See also Alexander, Hattie Elizabeth; Baker, Sara Josephine; Dick, Gladys Rowena Henry; Elion, Gertrude Belle; Evans, Alice Catherine; Kendrick, Pearl Luella; Williams, Anna Wessels

References O'Hern, Elizabeth Moot, *Profiles of Pioneer Women Scientists* (1986); Stanley, Autumn, *Mothers and Daughters of Invention: Notes for a Revised History of Technology* (1993); Greater Grand Rapids Women's History Council, "Dr. Pearl Kendrick, Dr. Grace Eldering," available at http://www2.gvsu.edu/ ~whc/ge.htm (cited 20 March 1999); Michigan Digital Historical Initiative (MDHI), "Eldering, Grace (1900–1989)," available at http://www.si.umich.edu/ HCHS/HCHS-GUIDE/hchs.source243.html (cited 22 March 1999).

Electrical and Electronics Engineering

Of all branches of engineering, electrical engineering has the greatest number of practitioners; it is therefore the largest of the main branches of engineering. Electrical engineering involves the design, development, production, and testing of electrical equipment and electronic devices. Electrical equipment includes power generators, transformers, and transmitters such as those used by electric utility companies and power stations. It also includes motors, controls, wiring and lighting devices, and switches such as those used in buildings, automobiles, aircraft, and ships. Electronic equipment includes computer hardware and systems used in guidance, navigation, detection, monitoring, and communication.

Engineers who specialize in electronic devices are known as electronics engineers. These engineers design, produce, and test communication and weather satellites, computers, and industrial robots such as those used on assembly lines. They also are involved with the design and programming of medical and scientific instruments and monitoring devices; missile guidance, con-

trol, and navigation systems; and special devices used by the military.

See also Ancker-Johnson, Betsy; Clarke, Edith; Engineering; Estrin, Thelma; Society of Women Engineers (SWE)

References Barnes-Svarney, Patricia, ed., *The New York Public Library Science Desk Reference* (1995); U.S Department of Labor, Bureau of Labor Statistics, *Occupational Outlook Handbook, 1994–1995*, Bulletin 2450 (1994).

Elion, Gertrude Belle (1918–1999)

Gertrude Belle Elion enjoyed a successful career developing life-saving drugs. Her successes in this area are illustrated by the 45 patents on which her name appears, her induction into the National Inventor's Hall of Fame, and a Nobel Prize. Elion shared the Nobel Prize in physiology/medicine in 1988 with her colleague George Hitchings and British pharmacologist Sir James W. Black. Elion and Hitchings received the prize for their lifetime of contributions to pharmacology and medicine. These contributions included the development of medications that have proved helpful in treating diseases such as leukemia, malaria, herpes, and gout.

Gertrude Elion was born and raised in New York City. After completing high school, she entered Hunter College (then an all-women's institution) at the age of only 15. At about this same time, Elion witnessed the pain and suffering of her grandfather, who was dying of stomach cancer. She has identified this event as the primary influence on her decision to pursue a career in science, and more specifically, in a field that would help eradicate the dreaded disease from which her grandfather died.

Elion graduated from Hunter College *summa cum laude* with a B.A. in chemistry in 1937. At this time, the United States was in the midst of the severe economic downturn now called the Great Depression. Elion quickly discovered that obtaining a full-time job as a woman chemist was nearly impossible. She was, however, successful in obtaining various part-time jobs, which allowed her to earn the money she needed to pay for graduate school.

Gertrude Elion shared the 1988 Nobel Prize in physiology/medicine for her life's work developing life-saving drugs. (Corbis-Bettmann/UPI)

Elion attended graduate school at New York University, devoting evenings and weekends on research toward her degree. At the same time, she worked as a substitute teacher of high school science. She was awarded a master of science degree in chemistry in 1941, the same year the United States became embroiled in World War II. Because of the war, millions of men from all professions were called into military service. This resulted in vacancies in many jobs that were once unavailable to women. This situation helped Elion obtain a full-time position as an analyst in food chemistry with the Quaker Maid Company in 1942. The following year, Elion left this position to work as a research assistant in organic chemistry with Johnson & Johnson (J&J). After only six months, J&J canceled the project on which Elion was working. She was again unemployed.

Soon after losing her job with J&J, Elion was hired by the Burroughs-Wellcome pharmaceutical company (now Glaxo-Wellcome). Her job was as a research assistant to George Hitchings. At Hitchings's request, Elion immediately began work on the synthesis and testing of purine compounds (one of the compounds present in DNA). She was specifically seeking to identify compounds called antimetabolites that interfered with the nucleic acid metabolism of cancer cells without affecting healthy cells.

By the early 1950s, Elion began to see promising results in one of the compounds she developed to treat some forms of leukemia. Though it was not 100 percent effective, Elion and Hitchings discovered that their new compound, 6-mercaptopurine (6-MP), when combined with other drugs and radiation treatment, increased the likelihood that patients with leukemia could be cured of the disease.

The creation of 6-MP marked the first of many successful collaborations between Elion and Hitchings in the development of new drugs. However, the greatest contribution of this research team to pharmacology may be the methods they used to develop new drugs rather than the actual drugs that resulted from their work. Prior to the work of Hitchings and Elion, new drugs were developed largely as a result of trial and error. This method involved treating a sick organism with a specific compound to see if it helped eradicate disease. If it did not, another compound was tried; the process was repeated until a successful result was obtained. In their work, Hitchings and Elion investigated the chemical composition and metabolic mechanisms of diseased cells. They then used their knowledge of chemistry to develop substances that would interrupt the metabolic processes of diseased cells without harming healthy cells. These methods of study, which are still used today, revolutionized the way new drugs were developed. In fact, two years after Elion's retirement in 1983, researchers whom she and Hitchings had trained were using these methods to develop azidothymidine (AZT) —the first drug used to treat AIDS.

Soon after the development of 6-MP, it was determined that a derivative (chemical relative) of this compound, called 6-thioguanine, which was initially developed to treat leukemia, suppressed the immune system. This property led to the use of the compound as an antirejection drug in kidney transplants involving unrelated donors and recipients. More than 40 years later, this drug continues to be used for this purpose.

While working with Hitchings at Boroughs-Wellcome, Elion received several promotions. These promotions involved her movement from the position of biochemist to senior research biochemist and then to assistant to the director of the chemotherapy division. She later became the director for chemotherapy, and in 1967, the head of the Department of Experimental Therapy. In time, this department expanded to include sections for research in chemistry, enzymology, pharmacology, immunology, and virology.

In 1969, Elion received a report that one of the compounds she created reacted in such a way with the DNA of a virus that it caused the virus to destroy itself. This compound proved effective in treating two different varieties of the herpes virus. For the next four years, Elion and her research team devoted their time to the development of what would become the first antiviral medication—acyclovir. Acyclovir is used in the treatment of chicken pox, shingles, genital herpes, herpes encephalitis, and other herpes infections.

Elion retired from her position with Boroughs-Wellcome in 1983 but retained an office at the company, from which she continued to work as a consultant for several years. Five years after her retirement, Elion learned she and George Hitchings had been selected to receive the 1988 Nobel Prize in physiology/medicine. Her selection for this prestigious award was in many ways unusual because it rarely goes to a woman, and even more rarely goes to an individual who lacks a doctoral degree and does not work for a nonprofit institution.

The Nobel Prize is the highest award that can be bestowed upon a scientist. However, it was not the first or only award granted to Gertrude Elion during her research career. In 1968, she received the Garvan Medal, an annual award presented to a female chemist by the American Chemical Society (ACS). In 1989, she was elected into the National Academy of Sciences (NAS). Two years later, in 1991, Elion became the first woman inducted into the National Inventors' Hall of Fame. The same year, she also received the National Medal of Science from President George Bush, was inducted into the National Women's Hall of Fame, and became a fellow of the American Academy of Pharmaceutical Scientists. After receiving the Nobel Prize, Elion was also awarded at least 20 honorary doctoral degrees.

Although long retired, Elion remained active in science and medicine until her death in 1999. She served as an instructor at Duke University and as a mentor to medical students from Duke University Medical Center in Durham, North Carolina. She was an adviser to the National Cancer Institute, the American Cancer Society (ACS), and the tropical disease research division of the World Health Organization (WHO). Elion also spent much of her time writing, traveling, and lecturing to a wide range of audiences. She published more than 225 scientific articles and contributed many chapters to books.

See also Blackburn, Elizabeth Helen; Francis P. Garvan–John M. Olin Medal; Genetic Engineering; Lemelson-MIT Program; Medicine/Medical

Technology; National Inventors' Hall of Fame; National Medal of Science; National Women's Hall of Fame; Nobel Prize; Pharmacology

References Altman, Lawrence K., "Gertrude Elion, Drug Developer, Dies at 81," [obituary] *New York Times* (23 February 1999); Ambrose, Susan A., et al., *Journeys of Women in Science and Engineering: No Universal Constants* (1997); Bailey, Martha J., *American Women in Science: A Biographical Dictionary* (1994); Graham, Judith, ed., *Current Biography Yearbook 1995* (1995); McGrayne, Sharon B., *Nobel Prize Women in Science* (1992); Oliver, Myrna, "Gertrude Elion: Nobel-Winning Scientist," [obituary] *Los Angeles Times* (23 February 1999); Simmons, John, *The Scientific 100: A Ranking of the Most Influential Scientists, Past and Present* (1996); "Gertrude B. Elion" (Interview, 6 March 1991), in Hall of Science and Exploration, available at http://www.achievement.org.autodoc/page/eli0int (cited 12 April 1998).

Emerson, Gladys Anderson (1903–1984)

Biochemist and nutritionist Gladys Emerson's studies on vitamins and nutrients advanced our understanding of the relationship between nutrition and disease. Emerson's earliest studies involved vitamin E, which she successfully isolated in a pure, crystalline form in 1933. This accomplishment allowed other scientists to determine the vitamin's chemical structure, paving the way for its synthetic production. Emerson's later research focused on establishing the roles of vitamin E, the B-complex vitamins, and amino acids in the body.

Emerson was born in Caldwell, Kansas, attended elementary school in Fort Worth, Texas, and graduated from high school in El Reno, Oklahoma. In 1925, she graduated from Oklahoma College for Women with an A.B. degree in history and English and a B.S. in physics and chemistry. Following her graduation, Emerson was offered assistantships in both chemistry and history. She chose history as her major and received her M.A. one year later. Emerson taught history for a short time at a junior high school before accepting a fellowship to study nutrition and biochemistry at the University of California at Berkeley. She completed her fellowship, receiving a Ph.D. in animal nutrition and biochemistry in 1932.

After receiving her Ph.D., Emerson completed

one year of postgraduate work at the University of Göttingen, in Germany. She returned to the United States in 1933 and began work as a research associate at the Institute of Experimental Biology of the University of California at Berkeley. It was here that Emerson became the first person to isolate vitamin E. She later conducted experiments that showed that depriving rabbits of this vitamin disrupted the functioning of their muscles, resulting in a condition similar to muscular dystrophy in humans.

In 1942, Emerson left the Institute to head the department of animal nutrition at the Merck Institute for Therapeutic Research in Rahway, New Jersey. She remained at Merck until 1956, while also conducting research with other organizations. One of these organizations was the U. S. Office of Scientific Research and Development (OSRD), for which she conducted war-related studies in nutrition. Emerson was presented a government citation for this work. From 1950 to 1953, Emerson also served as a research associate, investigating the relationship between diet and cancer at the Sloan-Kettering Institute for Cancer Research in New York City. When Emerson returned to Merck on a full-time basis, one of her major research projects involved the B-complex vitamins and their role in the body. Her research showed that a lack of these vitamins in monkeys led to the development of arteriosclerosis (a thickening and hardening of the arterial walls).

Emerson left Merck in 1956 to accept the posts of professor of nutrition and chair of the department of home economics at the University of California at Los Angeles (UCLA). Six years later, she was made vice-chair of the school's department of public health, while remaining as a professor of nutrition. She retained both positions at the school until her retirement in 1970.

While she was at UCLA, President Richard M. Nixon appointed Emerson vice president of the Panel on the Provision of Food as it Affects the Consumer during the White House Conference on Food, Nutrition, and Health in 1969. The next year, she testified at hearings about vitamin and mineral supplements and food additives before the U.S. Food and Drug Administration (FDA).

The results of these hearings were used to establish the USDA's recommended daily allowances for various vitamins and nutrients (information now required on all food labels).

After her retirement, Emerson remained active in organizations devoted to nutritional studies. She served for a time as associate editor of the journal *Nutrition*. In 1979, she worked with the Southern California Committee of the World Health Organization (WHO) and the California State Nutrition Council as a member of that organization's board. At the same time, she also served as a board member of the Nutritional Programs Committee's Meals for Millions project and on the planning committee for the International Year of the Child. For her work in nutrition, Emerson was chosen by the American Chemical Society (ACS) as the recipient of the Garvan Medal in 1952.

Throughout her life, Emerson encouraged other women to pursue education and careers in science. She was an active member in the Iota Sigma Pi (ISP) chemistry sorority and served two terms as that group's national vice president (1945 to 1951) and two terms as its national president (1951 to 1957). In 1966, she was elected ISP's tenth honorary member. Other women with this status in the organization include Agnes Fay Morgan, Nobel Prize–winning chemist Dorothy Crowfoot Hodgkin, and Gertrude E. Perlman. Emerson also served as national president of Delta Omega (1971–1972). To encourage other women to pursue careers in the sciences, Emerson established the Emerson Scholarship fund, which is administered by ISP.

See also Francis P. Garvan–John M. Olin Medal; Morgan, Agnes Fay

References Bailey, Martha J., *American Women in Science: A Biographical Dictionary* (1994); "Emerson Scholarships Announced for '87," *ISP News* (the national newsletter of Iota Sigma Pi) (1986); Haber, Louis, *Women Pioneers of Science* (1979); McMurray, Emily M., ed., *Notable Twentieth-Century Scientists* (1995); Sawrey, Barbara, Vice Chair for Education, Department of Chemistry and Biochemistry, University of California at San Diego, e-mail correspondence with Alan Winkler, 16 March 1998; Uglow, Jennifer S., ed., *The International Dictionary of Women's Biography* (1982).

Eng, Patricia L. (b. 1955)

As chief of the Transportation and Storage Inspection Section of the Nuclear Regulatory Commission (NRC), Patricia Eng uses her expertise in radiation and containment of spent nuclear fuel to safeguard the public from the potential dangers of radiation derived from nuclear power plants. In her work, Eng is responsible for overseeing testing, maintenance, operations, and safety at the nation's nuclear power plants. She also personally developed the procedures the NRC follows in its inspections of pumps and valves on safety systems as well as the inspection and handling of spent fuels being placed in storage.

Patricia Eng was born in Oak Park, Illinois, in 1955. At an early age, she had ambitions of someday becoming a ballerina. Her interest in dance and motion along with the influence of a grammar school teacher led to Eng's early decision to study physics when she reached high school. She did just that and decided to pursue further studies in science when she completed high school.

After graduating from the New Trier High School in Northfield, Illinois, Eng enrolled at Smith College in Northampton, Massachusetts, in 1972. However, once enrolled, she found the physics program at Smith to be very small and not challenging enough. After completing her freshman year at Smith, Eng transferred to the University of Illinois at Urbana-Champaign, because at the time, they had what was considered the best physics department in the country. During her junior year at the university, Eng determined she did not wish to pursue a graduate degree in physics. This decision resulted in her changing her major from physics to engineering, since jobs were more readily available to engineers who did not hold a Ph. D. As a result of this change in majors, in 1976 Eng became the first person at the University of Illinois to be awarded a bachelor of science degree in nuclear engineering, a new undergraduate program offered at the University of Illinois. Nationwide, only 418 bachelor's degrees were issued in this field, and only 12 of those to women, including Eng.

Following graduation, Eng began her engineering career at a research and development facility for Westinghouse Hartford in Richland, Washington. During the four years that she was with this company, she developed the expertise for which she is most known—radiation shielding. This technology involves the development and installation of materials designed to protect people and the environment from the harmful effects of radiation in use at nuclear power plants.

At Westinghouse Hartford, Eng worked on the development of materials that would serve as radiation shields for a nuclear reactor prototype. While with the company, she also was placed in a two-year training program that provided her an opportunity to gain valuable work experience in several other areas within the company, including its chemical laboratory, computer analysis laboratories, and nuclear plant construction site. In 1980, when the construction phase of her training ended and her training in program systems was scheduled to begin, Eng decided to leave Westinghouse Hartford in pursuit of work she believed would be of greater interest to her.

Eng spent the next two years doing technical work in a variety of areas. She then accepted a position at Garrett AiResearch in Torrance, California. While working for Garrett AiResearch, her job responsibilities included testing the performance of new machine designs; she also took and passed the exam required to become a registered mechanical engineer in 1982. The following year, Eng left Garrett AiResearch to join the staff of the NRC in Glen Ellyn, Illinois, as a nuclear reactor inspector. With this position, she became the first woman reactor inspector in that region's Division of Reactor Safety. It was while working with the Glen Ellyn office of the NRC that Eng also developed and wrote the procedures the NRC now uses in its inspections of the valves and pumps used in the safety systems of nuclear reactors.

In 1986, Eng received a promotion with the NRC when she became its resident inspector at the Zion Nuclear Power Plant (located 40 miles north of Chicago, Illinois). Here, she reviewed and supervised plant maintenance and safety operations to ensure that all components of the plant remained in good working order and in compliance with federal regulations governing such plants. During the first year she worked at the Zion Nuclear Power Plant, Eng received the NRC's Meritorious Service Award for Resident Inspector Excellence. She was the first woman to be so honored. Two years later, her work in nuclear engineering was recognized by the Society of Women Engineers (SWE), when that organization presented Eng its Distinguished New Engineer Award.

In 1990, Eng was promoted by the NRC to the position of project manager. Her responsibilities in this position included reviewing and evaluating the operational activities of nuclear power plants. In 1992, Eng was again promoted, when she became the technical assistant to NRC Commissioner E. Gail dePlanque (the first woman to serve as Commissioner of the NRC). In this position, Eng's responsibilities included advising the commissioner about NRC policies, programs, activities, and related issues. Later that same year, Eng assumed a position as senior operations engineer for the Human Factors Assessment Branch of the NRC. Her role in this post was to investigate the role of human performance in the operation of nuclear power plants.

Eng remained with the Human Factors Assessment Branch for two years, before assuming her current post as chief of the Transportation and Storage Safety Section of the Spent Fuel Project Office (SFPO) in 1994. In this position, Eng's responsibilities include creating and implementing a program to ensure the safe containment, storage, and transportation of radioactive materials. In this role, she again uses her expertise in radiation shielding to make sure that containers designed to hold radioactive wastes are composed of materials that will adequately protect people and the environment from radiation.

In addition to her work, Eng has been an active member of the SWE since she was in college and has since been involved with that group at the local, regional, and national levels. In the early 1990s, she was responsible for conducting the first statistically valid national survey of women and men engineers for SWE as a means of gathering data regarding their work and their attitudes toward their profession. Because of her work on this survey, she was called upon in 1994 to testify as an expert witness before the House Subcommittee on Energy about careers for women in the various fields of science and technology. Two years later, she was elected a fellow of the SWE. In addition to her work with the SWE, Eng also is active in several other professional organizations, including the American Society of Mechanical Engineers (ASME), the American Association of University Women (AAUW), and the Institute of Electrical and Electronics Engineers (IEEE).

See also Anderson, Elda Emma; Atomic Energy Commission (AEC); Jackson, Shirley Ann; Nuclear Physics; Pressman, Ada I.; Safety Engineering
References Ambrose, Susan A., et al., *Journeys of Women in Science and Engineering: No Universal Constants* (1997); Eng, Patricia L., e-mail interview and correspondence with Alan Winkler (1 July 1999); U.S. Department of Education, Office of Educational Research and Improvement, National Center for Education Statistics, *Chartbook of Degrees Conferred, 1969–70 to 1993–94* (December 1997); National Academy of Engineering, "Featured Engineer Profile: Patricia L. Eng, P.E.," available at http://www.nae.edu/ nae/cwe.nsf/2064al . . .abbc5f4730e8852566770058efa5 ?OpenDocument (cited 22 June 1999).

Engineering

Engineering draws upon and applies the theories and principles of science and mathematics to the efficient and economic solutions of practical technical problems. Engineering is a bond that unites invention, discovery, and its useful applications in the design of machines, the research and development of products, and the creation of systems to manage and monitor complex technical and industrial processes. In addition, engineers are involved in the planning, design, and construction of buildings, roads, tunnels, bridges, dams, and rapid transit systems. Engineers also are involved in the design and development of the smallest miniature electronic circuits and other technical devices used in computers, space travel, and medicine.

Engineers are often called upon to design machinery and equipment for use in the manufacture of goods and products for industrial and home use. They are involved in testing, installation, repairs, and upgrading. They also create models that provide time and cost estimates needed to determine efficiency and economic considerations important to industry. To provide certain types of data where time, space, materials, and cost are factors, engineers often use computers to simulate and test machine or systems operations. Computers also are used to produce and analyze designs. Research and development departments of major industrial corporations utilize the skills, expertise, and creativity of engineers to develop, design, and test virtually all products.

Solutions to problems that require the expertise of engineers often require engineers from several specialties. Electrical, acoustical, mechanical, civil, chemical, and petroleum engineering are just a few of the 25 recognized fields of engineering. Within each of these fields, there may also be further subdivisions. For example, subdivisions of civil engineering include environmental and structural engineering. Most engineers are specialists in one field, but are knowledgeable in other fields as well. Engineers often consult with and work together with other engineers along with specialists in other technical, scientific, or business fields. In addition, engineers within a specialty area may elect to specialize within a particular industry. For example, electrical or acoustical engineers may choose to apply their knowledge in the automobile industry.

With a few notable early exceptions such as Kate Gleason, Mary Engle Pennington, Bertha Lamme, and Edith Clarke, engineering throughout most of the twentieth century was a field largely restricted to men. This circumstance began to change in the last quarter of the century largely as a result of the implementation of affirmative action policies that were initiated by the federal government in 1972 under Title IX. Just prior to affirmative action, in 1970, less than 1 percent of all bachelor's degrees issued in engineering or engineering-related technologies were issued to women. By 1980, only two years after the first class to have benefited from affirmative action policies would have graduated, the percentage of women receiving bachelor's degrees in engineering and engineering-related technolo-

gies rose to 9.29 percent; by the middle of the next decade this number rose to 15.64 percent. In addition to affirmative action policies, the efforts of organizations such as the Society of Women Engineers (SWE), along with annual celebrations such as National Engineers Week and National Women's History Month also have helped promote the field of engineering to women.

See also Acoustical Engineering; Aeronautical and Aerospace Engineering; Affirmative Action; Agricultural Engineering; Barney, Nora Stanton Blatch; Biomedical Engineering; Cambra, Jessie G.; Chemical Engineering; Civil Engineering; Clarke, Edith; Computers/Computer Technology; Darden, Christine M.; Eaves, Elsie; Electrical and Electronics Engineering; Environmental Engineering; Gleason, Kate; Industrial Engineering; Jackson, Shirley Ann; Lamme, Bertha; Martinez, Lissa Ann; Materials Engineering; Mechanical Engineering; National Engineers Week; National Women's History Month; Pennington, Mary Engle; Petroleum Engineering; Safety Engineering; Shirley, Donna; Society of Women Engineers (SWE); Widnall, Sheila

References Barnes-Svarney, Patricia, ed., *The New York Public Library Science Desk Reference* (1995); U.S. Department of Education, Office of Educational Research and Improvement, National Center for Education Statistics, *Chartbook of Degrees Conferred, 1969–70 to 1993–94* (December 1997); U.S. Department of Labor, Bureau of Labor Statistics, *Occupational Outlook Handbook, 1994–1995 Ed.,* Bulletin 2450 (1994).

Enrico Fermi Award

The Enrico Fermi Award is one of the oldest and most prestigious technical awards that can be granted to a scientist, engineer, or science policy maker. The award was established jointly by President Dwight D. Eisenhower and the Atomic Energy Commission (AEC) in 1956, in honor of Italian physicist Enrico Fermi—the scientist who headed the Manhattan Project at the University of Chicago and achieved the first controlled, self-sustaining nuclear reaction. This achievement enabled the United States to develop the atomic bombs that brought an end to World War II.

The Enrico Fermi Award is presented annually to recognize an individual who has made significant contributions to the development, use, or control of nuclear energy. Recipients of the award, which is presented by the president of the United States and administered by the U.S. Department of Energy (DOE), are given a gold medal and $100,000 ($200,000, if the award is to be shared by more than one scientist). Recipients also receive a citation signed by both the president and the secretary of energy.

Austrian physicist Lise Meitner in 1966 became the first woman to be presented the Enrico Fermi Award. Meitner was recognized for her "pioneering research in naturally occurring radioactivities and extensive experimental studies leading to the discovery of fission." The only other woman who has received the award is American geneticist Liane B. Russell, who was honored in 1993. Russell's citation acknowledged her contributions to radiation biology and genetics, including "knowledge of the effects of radiation on the developing embryo and fetus." Russell's work in this area has important implications for the study of mammalian mutations and for genetic risk assessment.

See also Atomic Energy Commission (AEC); Manhattan Project
References Bernstein, Leonard, Alan Winkler, and Linda Zierdt-Warshaw, *Multicultural Women of Science* (1996); International Congress of Distinguished Awards, available at http://icda.org/news/newsvol3F.html (cited 26 January 1999); U.S. Department of Energy, "Enrico Fermi Award Recipients," available at http://webster.er.doe.gov/Fermi/RECIPIENTS.html (cited 24 January 1999).

Environmental Engineering

Environmental engineering is one of the newest branches of engineering. The main concerns of this field are detecting, monitoring, preventing, and controlling disruptive and destructive natural events (e.g., earthquakes, floods, and severe storms) as well as minimizing nuisances resulting from the activities of humans (e.g., noise pollution).

Environmental engineers often are called upon to conduct or assess environmental impact studies to determine potential effects resulting from mining operations, large-scale agricultural practices, movement of hazardous materials along newly proposed routes, power plant construction, or the diversion of natural waterways. They also assess the damage to natural resources, including wildlife, that results from oil spills, forest fires, and the disposal of hazardous wastes. In conducting their work, environmental engineers often work with engineers and specialists from many other fields. For example, environmental engineers work with mining engineers to determine the least harmful effects of mining operations, including the use of mercury to extract gold from soils and sediments. They work with chemical engineers in matters of hazardous waste disposal. Environmental engineers also assist civil engineers in the planning and construction of roads, bridges, tunnels, rapid transit systems, and waste disposal and water supply projects.

In recent years, many women have become involved in various aspects of environmental engineering. For example, Hispanic American ocean engineer Lissa Martinez works to develop pollution-control devices for use on boats and ships as a means of reducing harmful discharges into the ocean. Ellen Silbergeld, a researcher and noted environmental engineer, was instrumental in the phasing-out of leaded gasoline. She also was a force in the changing of fast-food packaging material from styrofoam (a nonbiodegradable substance) to paper (a biodegradable and recyclable substance).

See also Ancker-Johnson, Betsy; Berkowitz, Joan; Darden, Christine M.; Engineering; Richards, Ellen Henrietta Swallow; Silbergeld, Ellen Kovner; Society of Women Engineers (SWE); Walton, Mary
References Barnes-Svarney Patricia, ed., *The New York Public Library Science Desk Reference* (1995); Kass-Simon, G., and Patricia Farnes, eds., *Women of Science: Righting the Record* (1990); U.S. Department of Labor, Bureau of Labor Statistics, *Occupational Outlook Handbook, 1994–1995*, Bulletin 2450 (1994).

Estrin, Thelma (b. 1924)

Thelma Estrin pioneered the use of computers and technology in medical research, a field known as biomedical engineering. Much of Estrin's work involved applying computer technology to brain research. Estrin developed techniques for using computers to measure the brain's electrical impulses. These techniques provide information on how the brains of humans and animals process information. Other programs developed by Estrin have assisted neuroscientists and neurosurgeons in mapping regions of the brain for treating certain disorders.

Thelma Estrin was born in New York City and attended Brooklyn's Abraham Lincoln High School. She married before she turned 18, and with the outbreak of World War II, her husband joined the military. In need of a job, and with factory workers in demand, Estrin took a position assembling test equipment and repairing radios. In the evenings, she attended engineering classes at the City College of New York (CCNY).

In 1945, Estrin and her husband moved to Madison, Wisconsin. There, both entered the undergraduate engineering program of the University of Wisconsin. Estrin earned her B.S. in electrical engineering in 1948. The following year, she earned her master's degree in electrical engineering, also at Wisconsin. In 1951, the University of Wisconsin awarded Estrin a Ph.D. in electrical engineering.

Following graduation, Estrin and her husband worked briefly at the Institute for Advanced Studies (IAS) at Princeton University. Thelma then took a position at the Neurological Institute of Columbia Presbyterian Hospital in New York City, where she began using computers to study the electrical impulses in the brain. As a result of this research, she was hired as an engineer by the Brain Research Institute of UCLA Medical School. While there, she and an associate designed and founded the Data Processing Laboratory, the nation's first computer facility for brain research. Estrin became project director and remained at the facility until 1980. She then accepted an appointment as full professor in the Computer Science Department at UCLA. In 1982, Estrin took a two-year leave from UCLA to serve as director of the Division of Electrical, Computing, and Systems Engineering for the National Science Foundation (NSF).

Estrin retired from UCLA in 1991, but remains with the school as a professor emeritus. For her professional accomplishments and achievements in biomedical research, Estrin was elected a fellow of the Institute for Electrical and Electronics Engineers (IEEE), the American Association for the Advancement of Science (AAAS), and the Society of Women Engineers (SWE). She also was the first woman to be certified as a clinical engineer. Estrin served as executive vice president of the IEEE and in 1984 was awarded its Centennial Medal. She has also served as president of the Biomedical Engineering Society.

Estrin has long been a proponent of women's rights and has devoted much of her time working to get women into leadership roles and into engineering fields.

See also Biomedical Engineering; Biotechnology; Computers/Computer Technology; Richardson, Jane Shelby

References McMurray, Emily M., ed., *Notable Twentieth-Century Scientists* (1995); Stanley, Autumn, *Mothers and Daughters of Invention: Notes for a Revised History of Technology* (1993); University of California at Los Angeles, UCLA Computer Science Department, "Thelma Estrin, Professor-in-Residence," available at http://www.cs.ucla.edu/csd/people/faculty_pages/testrin.html (cited 23 January 2000).

Evans, Alice Catherine (1881–1975)

Bacteriologist Alice Evans gained recognition when she discovered that humans could develop undulant fever (also known as Malta fever, or brucellosis) from contact with seemingly healthy farm animals that were infected with the bacteria that cause the disease. At the time, undulant fever was difficult to diagnose in humans because its symptoms resembled those of influenza, typhoid fever, tuberculosis, malaria, and rheumatism. Evans showed that the bacterium that causes undulant fever, *Micrococcus melitensis,* was closely related to another bacterium, *Bacillus abortus,* which caused abortions in cows and undulant fever in humans. Evans realized that *Bacillus abortus* commonly lived in the udders of cows. To avoid infection in humans, she recommended requiring that milk be pasteurized prior to sale. Today's practice of pasteurizing milk resulted largely from Evans's recommendations.

Alice Evans was born in Neath, Pennsylvania. She attended the local primary school and later the Susquehanna Institute at Towanda, Pennsylvania. Unable to afford college tuition, Evans worked as a grade school teacher for four years. She then enrolled in a tuition-free nature study course for teachers at Cornell University's College of Agriculture, in Ithaca, New York. She remained at Cornell, graduating with a B.S. degree in agriculture in 1909 and a scholarship to the College of Agriculture at the University of Wisconsin in Madison; Evans was the first woman awarded this scholarship. One year later, she graduated with an M.S. in bacteriology.

After receiving her M.S. degree, Evans worked in the Dairy Division of the Bureau of Animal Industry of the U.S. Department of Agriculture (USDA) in Madison. Here she investigated bacteria found in milk and cheese. Three years later she transferred to the Washington, D.C., office, becoming the first woman permanently assigned to the Dairy Division.

In 1917, Evans presented her findings on undulant fever to the Society of American Bacteriologists. The society members were skeptical about accepting the findings of a woman, especially one holding only a master's degree. The next year, Evans took a position as an assistant bacteriologist at the U. S. Public Health Service, where she began to study meningitis. By 1920, scientists worldwide had confirmed her 1917 conclusions regarding undulant fever transmission. Ironically, Evans contracted the disease in 1922 and was affected by it for the rest of her life.

From 1925 to 1931, Evans served on the National Research Council's Committee on Infectious Abortion. In 1928, she was elected as the first woman president of the Society of American Bacteriologists (now the American Society for Microbiology), largely as a result of her work on undulant fever. Around this same time, the dairy industry instituted the practice of milk pasteurization recommended by Evans.

In the 1930s, Evans represented the United States as a delegate to the First International Congress of Bacteriology in Paris. She attended the second Congress in London six years later. Evans was presented an honorary M.D. degree from the Women's Medical College in Pennsylvania in

1934. Two years later, she received an honorary Sc.D. degree from Wilson College. Evans continued her professional career with the U. S. Public Health Service (now the National Institutes of Health), where her research focused on immunity against streptococcal infections. She retired as a senior bacteriologist in 1945. The same year, she was made honorary president of the Inter-American Committee on Brucellosis.

See also Alexander, Hattie Elizabeth; Baker, Sara Josephine; Baldwin, Anna; Dick, Gladys Rowena Henry; Downs, Cornelia Mitchell; Eldering, Grace; Hamilton, Alice; Kendrick, Pearl Luella; Williams, Anna Wessels
References Bailey, Martha J., *American Women in Science: A Biographical Dictionary* (1994); McMurray, Emily M., ed., *Notable Twentieth-Century Scientists*, vol. 1 (1995); O'Hern, Elizabeth Moot, *Profiles of Pioneer Women Scientists* (1986); Porter, Ray, ed., *The Biographical Dictionary of Science*, 2nd ed. (1994); Rothe, Anna, ed., *Current Biography, 1944* (1944); Shearer, Benjamin F., and Barbara S. Shearer, eds., *Notable Women in the Life Sciences: A Biographical Dictionary* (1996); Vare, Ethlie Ann, and Greg Ptacek, *Mothers of Invention: From the Bra to the Bomb, Forgotten Women and Their Unforgettable Ideas* (1988); Bois, Danuta, "Alice Catherine Evans," available at http://www.netsrq.com/~dbois/evans-a.html (cited 14 April 1998).

Evard, Mary (n.d.)

In the mid- and late nineteenth century, the majority of women spent most of their time working in the home and attending to the needs of their families. Thus, it is not surprising that most inventions developed by American women during this period in history were associated with the "women's work" of the time—cooking, cleaning, sewing, and child rearing. Such was the case with Mary Evard, who in the late 1860s developed three inventions related to cooking: a toaster, an improved boiling apparatus, and a stove that featured the capability of being divided into sections that could perform different cooking tasks through the movement of partitions. Evard obtained patents for all three inventions in 1868.

Evard was a skilled milliner in addition to being a homemaker. After conceiving the idea for her improved stove, Evard had a model of her invention made for the purpose of demonstrating it at a fair being held in St. Louis. Partitions in the stove, which allowed it to simultaneously burn both coal and wood, made the stove truly unique, with a capability of providing different cooking temperatures on the two sides. In addition, Evard also divided the front and back sections of the stove to allow one area to provide moist heat for the cooking of foods such as meats, while the other area provided the dry heat desired for baking.

The response to Evard's stove at the fair was extremely positive. As soon as she had a patent in hand, Evard and her husband began to manufacture and sell her invention, which they called the "Reliance Cook Stove." Initial sales of Evard's stove were promising; however, competitive products soon emerged, causing the Evards to cease manufacturing their stove.

> **See also** Cochran, Josephine G.; Frederick, Christine M.; Jones, Amanda Theodosia; Telkes, Maria
> **References** Heinemann, Susan, *Timelines of American Women's History* (1996); Macdonald, Anne L., *Feminine Ingenuity: How Women Inventors Changed America* (1992); Stanley, Autumn, *Mothers and Daughters of Invention: Notes for a Revised History of Technology* (1993).

Everson, Carrie Jane (1842–1914)

Much of today's mining separation technology is based on an oil flotation process developed by Carrie Everson, for which she received a patent in 1886. Everson's idea involved agitating a mixture of cottonseed oil, water, and sulfuric acid to separate flakes of precious metals from waste matter. During the agitation process, the lighter dross (waste material) was attracted to the cottonseed oil that floated to the top of the mixture, while the heavier metallic flakes of precious metal (gold, silver, copper, or whatever) sank to the bottom. The process, designed for use with low-grade ore, made many abandoned mines profitable and productive.

Carrie was born near Sharon, Massachusetts. In 1851, she moved to Springfield, Illinois, where she was educated. In 1864, she married physician William Everson. The Eversons moved to Denver, Colorado, in the late 1870s to salvage a mining investment that had gone bad. It was there that Carrie Everson began experimenting with her oil flotation process. Although her process proved successful and worthy of a patent, it was deemed unnecessary at the time because the most sought-after precious metals could still be obtained through regular mining practices. Despite this fact, Everson continued working on her ideas and eventually went into partnership with chemist Charles B. Hebron. Together they revised her earlier process, leading to the issue of another patent in 1892.

By 1912, the previously abundant supply of high-grade ores had begun to diminish, and miners began using Everson's oil separation methods. However, by this time both of Everson's patents had expired. Additionally, the success of the flotation process attracted outside mining interests, which claimed to own all rights to the flotation process. A lawsuit followed, and for unknown reasons, Everson never challenged the suit. Eventually, the courts ruled in favor of the outside mining interests. As a result, Everson never earned any money from her invention.

> **See also** Metals and Metallurgy; Patent
> **References** Altman, Linda Jacobs, *Women Inventors: American Profiles* (1997); Vare, Ethlie Ann, and Greg Ptacek, *Mothers of Invention: From the Bra to the Bomb, Forgotten Women and Their Unforgettable Ideas* (1988); Mouat, Jeremy, "The Development of the Flotation Process: Technological Change and the Genesis of Modern Mining, 1898–1911," available at http://www.athabascau.ca/html/staff/academic/mouat/article.htm (cited 31 August 1998).

Farmer, Fannie Merritt (1857–1915)

Fannie Merritt Farmer may be best known for the candy shops that bear her name; however, her cookbook, the *Boston Cooking School Cook Book,* published in 1896, established her as a pioneer in applying technology and science to nutrition. In this book, Farmer became the first person to use exact measurements for ingredients in food recipes. Before this, recipes called for a "pinch" of this, a "lump" of that, or a "handful" of something else. Farmer's precise measurements assured that food would have the same taste, color, and consistency each time it was prepared. This book, which is today called *The Fanny Farmer Cookbook,* has sold more than four million copies in several languages.

Fannie Farmer lived most of her life in Boston, Massachusetts. Paralysis in a leg during her teenage years caused her to drop out of school. She later worked as a mother's helper before enrolling at the Boston Cooking School. Farmer did so well at the school that she eventually became its principal. She later resigned that post to open her own cooking school, Miss Farmer's School of Cookery.

Farmer became very interested in the role of nutrition in maintaining good health. She lectured often and wrote many articles on this subject, including her second cookbook, *Food and Cookery for the Sick and Convalescent,* in 1904. Farmer used her expertise on nutrition for the

Fannie Farmer (right) standardized recipes when she introduced measurements in the preparation of foods. (Bettmann/ Corbis)

sick to train hospital dietitians. She also aided Elliott P. Joslin, a pioneer in the study of diabetes, in his research. Farmer's knowledge of nutrition and illness was so well respected that she was invited to lecture at the Harvard Medical School; she was the first woman given this opportunity.

See also American Society for Nutritional Sciences (ASNS); Bevier, Isabel; Home Economics; Morgan, Agnes Fay; Morrill Act of 1862; Richards, Ellen Henrietta Swallow; Stanley, Louise
References Ashby, Ruth, and Deborah Gore Ohrn, eds., *Herstory: Women Who Changed the World* (1995); Bernikow, Louise, *The American Women's Almanac* (1997); Vare, Ethlie Ann, and Greg Ptacek, *Mothers of Invention: From the Bra to the Bomb, Forgotten Women and Their Unforgettable Ideas* (1988); Vare, Ethlie Ann, and Greg Ptacek, *Women Inventors and Their Discoveries* (1993).

Federal Woman's Award

The Federal Woman's Award was created by the U.S. government in 1961 to acknowledge women for outstanding government service. Astronomer Charlotte Moore Sitterly was among the first six women to receive the award the first year it was presented. The following year, organic chemist Allene Jeanes was presented with the award for her research involving the carbohydrate known as dextran. In 1968, textile chemist Ruth Rogan Benerito was honored by the government. Margaret Pittman was presented a Federal Woman's Award in 1970 for her efforts involving standardization of various medical vaccines. Among the other women working in science and technology to receive this award was physicist Marguerite Rogers, who contributed to the design and development of weapons systems for the U.S. Navy. Rogers was presented with the Federal Woman's Award in 1976.

See also Benerito, Ruth Rogan; Jeanes, Allene Rosalind; National Medal of Science; National Medal of Technology; Pittman, Margaret; Rogers, Marguerite M.; Sitterly, Charlotte Moore
References Moritz, Charles, ed., *Current Biography, 1962* (1962); "Rogers Led the Way for Women—Devoted Her Life to Science," *China Lake Rocketeer* (17 March 1989).

Fenselau, Catherine Clarke (b. 1939)

Catherine Fenselau pioneered the use of mass spectrometry (also called mass spectroscopy) in biomedical studies. Mass spectrometry is a method of separating ionized atoms or molecules according to their masses and electrical charges. It is used to analyze and identify elements, isotopes, and molecules present in compounds. Much of Fenselau's research has focused on identifying chemical interactions related to pharmacology, biochemistry, and medicine. Specifically, she has done extensive work on identifying how certain anticancer drugs bring about changes in the body and how drugs and proteins in the body interact to allow patients to develop drug resistance. Fenselau also has worked as an educator and as a promoter of the work of women in science.

Catherine Fenselau was born Catherine Clarke in York, Nebraska. She began her college studies in chemistry at Bryn Mawr College in Pennsylvania, where she spent summers doing research related to her field of study. She graduated *magna cum laude* with an A.B. in chemistry in 1961. Clarke next attended Stanford University in California, from which she received her Ph.D. in chemistry with a specialty in mass spectrometry in 1965. That same year, she married Allan H. Fenselau, also a scientist.

Between 1965 and 1967, Catherine Fenselau served as a postdoctoral fellow at Berkeley and at the Space Science Laboratory of the National Aeronautics and Space Administration (NASA). At NASA, she worked on the Lunar Landing Project, where she developed techniques for using mass spectrometry to locate biochemical markers (evidence of chemicals present in living things) in moon rocks.

In 1967, Fenselau joined the Department of Pharmacology of the Johns Hopkins University Medical School, where she established biomedical mass spectrometry as a new area of study. With this position, Fenselau became the first person trained in mass spectroscopy to be appointed to the faculty of a U.S. medical school. Over the next twenty years, she rose in position from instructor

(1967) to assistant professor (1969), associate professor (1973), and full professor (1982).

At Johns Hopkins, much of Fenselau's research centered on the body's reaction to certain anti-cancer drugs. Information from this research enabled oncologists to determine the effectiveness of antitumor agents in the body and also aided in the design of new drugs. In addition, Fenselau founded the journal, *Biomedical and Environmental Mass Spectrometry* in 1973 and served as that publication's editor in chief until 1989.

Fenselau left Johns Hopkins in 1987 to serve as a professor and chair of the Department of Chemistry and Biochemistry at the University of Maryland, Baltimore County (UMBC). She is the first woman to serve in this department on a permanent basis. In 1990, she also became an associate editor of *Analytical Chemistry.* In 1995, Fenselau became interim dean of the graduate school and associate vice president for research at UMBC. In 1999, she moved to the university's College Park campus, where she serves as an educator, continues her research on acquired drug resistance, and also serves on a research team that is developing a mass spectrometry system for use in identifying airborne microorganisms. This work is expected to benefit environmental scientists as well as medicine and defense.

Fenselau has been active in several professional organizations and continues to serve on the editorial boards of many journals. In 1984, she served as president of the American Society for Mass Spectrometry (ASMS). In addition, Fenselau has been recognized for her work through various honors and awards. The National Institutes of Health (NIH) presented her with a Research Career Development Award in 1972. In 1985, her work involving the use of mass spectrometry on biochemicals earned her a Garvan Medal from the American Chemical Society (ACS). She was again honored by this organization in 1989 with its Maryland Chemist Award. One year later, she was named Distinguished University Scholar by the University of Maryland. In 1992, the NIH presented Fenselau its Merit Award; the following year, she received the Pittsburgh Spectroscopy Award.

See also Biotechnology; Elion, Gertrude Belle; Francis P. Garvan–John M. Olin Medal; Hahn, Dorothy Anna; Hollinshead, Ariel; National Aeronautics and Space Administration (NASA); Pharmacology; Sherrill, Mary Lura; Space Exploration; Spectroscopy

References American Chemical Society, "1985 Garvan Medal" [pamphlet prepared for presentation ceremony of Garvan Medal to Catherine Fenselau, 1985]; Fenselau, Catherine, biographical information sent to Alan Winkler (31 March 1999); McQueen, Camille Peplowski, and Margaret Cavanaugh, "Fenselau Addresses Women Chemists," *Women Chemists Newsletter* (July 1985); Shearer, Benjamin F., and Barbara S. Shearer, eds., *Notable Women in the Physical Sciences: A Biographical Dictionary* (1997).

Fieser, Mary Peters (1909–1997)

Mary Fieser was an internationally known organic chemist and researcher who developed a method for quickly synthesizing large amounts of vitamin K. With her husband, she also helped develop techniques for synthesizing lapinone (an antimalarial drug), cortisone (a steroid), and carcinogenic chemicals used in medical research. Both Fiesers were also prolific writers of texts and technical articles.

Mary Fieser was born in Atchison, Kansas, but grew up in Harrisburg, Pennsylvania, where her father was employed as an English professor at Midland College (now Carnegie Mellon University). She attended a private girls' school and then entered Bryn Mawr College as a premedical major. Influenced by Louis F. Fieser, a chemistry instructor whom she later married, Mary Fieser changed her major to chemistry. She received a B.A. in 1930. Six years later, she received a master's degree in organic chemistry from Radcliffe College. Believing that she would have greater access to research by joining her husband's research group at Harvard, Fieser chose not to pursue a Ph.D.

While working in her husband's laboratory, Mary Fieser received no payment from Harvard for her work. After 29 years, the college did honor her with the title of Research Fellow in Chemistry. She and her husband were later honored when a renovated organic chemistry teaching laboratory was dedicated to them. In 1971, the American Chemical Society (ACS) recognized Fieser by awarding her a Garvan Medal for her contributions to research, writing, teaching, and inspiration to chemistry students.

See also Elion, Gertrude Belle; Emerson, Gladys Anderson; Francis P. Garvan–John M. Olin Medal
References "Mary Fieser, Researcher, Writer in Organic Chemistry, Dies at Age 87" [obituary], *Harvard Gazette* (27 March 1997); McMurray, Emily M., ed., *Notable Twentieth-Century Scientists* (1995); O'Neill, Lois Decker, *The Women's Book of Records and Achievements* (1979); Shearer, Benjamin F., and Barbara S. Shearer, eds., *Notable Women in the Physical Sciences: A Biographical Dictionary* (1997); American Chemical Society, "Chemical & Engineering News' Top 75: Mary Fieser," *Chemical & Engineering News,* available at http://www.pubs.acs.org/hotartcl/cenear/980112/top.html (cited 18 August 1998); "Mary Fieser, Researcher, Writer in Organic Chemistry, Dies at Age 87," also available at http://www.news.harvard.edu/hno.subpages/ gazette.march.27html#gen5 (cited 18 August 1998).

Fink, Kathryn (Kay) Ferguson (b. 1917)

Soon after receiving her B.A. degree in biochemistry at the University of Iowa in 1938, Kathryn Ferguson Fink accepted a position as research technician at the Mayo Institute of Experimental Medicine in Rochester, Minnesota. The next year she became an Atomic Energy Commission (now the NRC, or Nuclear Regulatory Commission) fellow at the University of Rochester. After completing her fellowship with the Atomic Energy Commission (AEC) in 1942, Fink became a research associate, working on the Manhattan Project (the secret project concerned with the development of the world's first atomic bomb). She remained with this project until 1947; while there, she earned her doctoral degree (1943).

One of the major concerns of those involved in the development of the atomic bomb was how the radiation resulting from the detonation of this device might affect living things over time. The biological effects of radiation became one of Kathryn Fink's most important areas of research, a field in which she was a pioneer.

Fink left the Manhattan Project in 1947 (two years after the end of World War II) and accepted a position as associate clinical professor of biophysics at the School of Medicine of the Univer-

sity of California at Los Angeles (UCLA). From the time she began her association with UCLA until 1961, Fink also served as a research biologist with the Veterans Administration (VA) Hospital in Long Beach, California. While at UCLA, Fink received several promotions, advancing in position to assistant dean by 1976.

See also Atomic Energy Commission (AEC); Goeppert-Mayer, Maria; Koshland, Marian Elliot; Libby, Leona W.; Manhattan Project; Nuclear Physics; Office of Scientific Research and Development (OSRD); Ordnance; Quimby, Edith Hinkley; Way, Katharine; Wu, Chien-Shiung
References Bailey, Martha J., *American Women in Science: A Biographical Dictionary* (1994); Debus, A. G. ed., *World Who's Who in Science,* 1st ed. (1968); Jaques Cattell Press, ed., *American Men and Women of Science,* 12th ed. (1972); Jaques Cattell Press, ed., *American Men and Women of Science,* 17th ed. (1990).

Fitzroy, Nancy D. (b. 1927)

Engineer Nancy D. Fitzroy devoted her career to researching the properties of materials—particularly heat transfer and fluid flow. Her work in thermal engineering resulted in at least two inventions: a thermal chip that measures temperature in integrated circuits and a thermal protection system for radar antennae. This second invention is used by the U.S. Department of Defense (DoD) in their early warning system (now the North Warning System), a long-range radar network developed to provide the United States and Canada with warning of an air attack from the north.

Nancy Fitzroy was born in Pittsfield, Massachusetts. In 1949, she received a B.S. degree in chemical engineering from Rensselaer Polytechnic Institute (RPI) of Troy, New York. In 1950, she began her engineering career at the Knolls Atomic Power Laboratory, where she investigated heat surface transfers in nuclear reactor cores. In 1952, she became a project engineer at the Hermes Missile Project, but after one year resigned this position for a similar post with General Electric (GE). Fitzroy remained with GE for ten years. While there, she authored a book about heat transfer and fluid flow for the company and served as a lecturer for advanced engineering courses.

In 1963, Fitzroy began work as a heat transfer engineer at Advanced Technological Laboratories. Two years later, she moved into their Research and Development Center as a consultant and at the same time began to serve as a research committee adviser to the National Science Foundation (NSF). She left her job at Advanced Technological Laboratories to become an independent consultant (1987).

Fitzroy has been active in several professional organizations and is well recognized for her work. The Society of Women Engineers (SWE) presented her its achievement award for her work on heat transfer and fluid flow in 1972. Three years later, she was awarded the Demers Medal by RPI. In 1980, the American Society of Mechanical Engineers (ASME) presented Fitzroy its Centennial Medallion. Fitzroy later served as president of this organization (1985–1987). In 1984, she received a second achievement award, this one from the Federation of Professional Women. Fitzroy achieved one of the highest honors that can be bestowed upon an engineer in 1995 when she was elected into the National Academy of Engineering for "contributions to technology in heat transfer and for serving as a mentor for women in engineering."

See also American Society of Mechanical Engineers (ASME); Jackson, Shirley Ann; Materials Engineering; National Academy of Engineering (NAE); National Science Foundation (NSF); Society of Women Engineers (SWE)

References McMurray, Emily M., ed., *Notable Twentieth-Century Scientists,* vol. 2: (F–K) (1995); National Academy of Engineering, "National Academy of Engineering Elects 77 Members and 8 Foreign Associates," press release dated 9 February 1995, available at http://www.nas.edu (cited 18 March 1999).

Flanigen, Edith M. (b. 1929)

Chemist Edith Flanigen helped develop more than 200 compounds, primarily for use as "molecular sieves"—crystalline compounds with molecule-sized pores that are used to filter and separate parts of a mixture. Flanigen's most important invention was zeolite, a crystal compound used as a molecular sieve in petroleum refining and as a catalyst (a substance that speeds a

chemical reaction without itself being affected). Use of such sieves has made gasoline and jet fuel production more efficient, cleaner, and safer. With a coworker, Flanigen also developed a process for making synthetic emeralds.

Edith Flanigen was born in Buffalo, New York. She became interested in chemistry while attending the Holy Angels Academy, a Catholic High School in Buffalo. She continued her study of chemistry at D'Youville College in Buffalo, graduating *magna cum laude,* as valedictorian and class president, with a B.A. in 1950. Two years later, Flanigen received an M.S. degree in inorganic physical chemistry from Syracuse University.

Flanigen began her career with Union Carbide in Tonawanda, New York. Her initial assignment involved work with silicates (compounds of silicon and oxygen). In 1956, she joined the molecular sieve group; she became senior research chemist in 1960, research associate in 1962, senior research associate in 1967, and senior research scientist one year later. In 1973, she was promoted to senior corporate research fellow and became the first woman to hold this position.

During the 1980s, Flanigen's research group created the zeolite compound sieves, for which they applied for more than 30 patents by 1985. In 1988, Union Carbide and Allied Signal embarked on a joint venture (UOP), for which Flanigen served as senior research fellow. By the time she retired in 1994, Flanigen had obtained 102 patents for her sieves, which were being used in the petroleum industry, for water purification, and in environmental cleanup projects.

In 1983, the International Zeolite Association presented Flanigen the Donald Wesley Breck Award for her work on molecular sieves. The same year, D'Youville College awarded her an honorary doctorate of science. She received the National Honorary Member Award from Iota Sigma Pi in 1986 and its Award for Professional Excellence in 1993. The American Institute of Chemists (AIC) presented Flanigen its Chemical Pioneer Award in 1991. The next year, Flanigen received one of the highest honors in applied chemistry when the American Chemical Society (ACS) gave her its Perkins Medal; they honored

Flanigen again in 1993, with a Garvan Medal. In 1994, Flanigen received the Outstanding Lifetime Contributions and Achievements in the Field of Zeolites award from the International Zeolite Association.

See also Chemical Engineering; Chemical Pioneer Award; Environmental Engineering; Francis P. Garvan–John M. Olin Medal; Gardner, Julia Anna; Parker, Ivy; Patent; Petroleum Engineering
References Buderi, Robert, "The Case of the Catalytic Chemist," *Business Week* (18 January 1993); Stinsin, Stephen, "Edith M. Flanigen Wins Perkin Medal," *Chemical and Engineering News* (9 March 1992); Torpie, Stephen L., et al., eds., *American Men and Women of Science*, 18th ed. (1992–1993) (1992); Chemical Heritage Foundation, "Edith M. Flanigen," available at http://www.chemheritage.org/perkin/Flanigen/flanigen.html (cited 22 May 1999); Federal Highway Administration, "Women in Transportation-Chemical Engineering," available at http://www.fhwa.dot.gov/wit/chem.html (cited 25 March 1999).

Flügge-Lotz, Irmgard (1903–1974)

Irmgard Flügge-Lotz is known internationally for her pioneering work in aeronautical engineering and design. In 1931, she formulated an equation to measure the lift force on an airplane's wings, regardless of their shape. However, she is best known for her work in flight control. This work led to the development of the first automatic "on and off" controls for maneuvering aircraft.

Irmgard Lotz was born in Hameln, Germany. After graduating from high school in 1923, she entered the Technische Hochschule (Technical University) of Hannover to study applied mathematics and engineering. In 1927, she received an engineering degree. She was awarded a doctorate in engineering from the same university two years later.

Lotz's first professional position was as a junior research engineer at the Aerodynamische Versuchsanstalt (AVA), in Göttingen, Germany. When she began this job, she spent about half her time doing clerical work. However, her clerical assignments ended after she developed the equation, today known as the Lotz method, for determining the lift distribution on airplane wings in 1931. The importance of this work, which is still in use, earned Lotz a promotion to the position of supervisor of an engineering group that was studying theoretical aerodynamics. In 1938, Lotz married Wilhelm Flügge, a civil engineer she met at AVA. That same year both accepted positions at Deutsche Versuchsanstalt für Luftfahrt (DVL), a government research institute concerned with aerodynamics. Here, Flügge-Lotz worked as a consultant on problems of navigation and aerodynamics. It was at this time that she also began her research into flight control, which resulted in the development of the theory of discontinuous control systems. These systems make use of "on and off" impulses (much like today's computers) to direct equipment to respond in a certain manner, making automatic flight possible. Planes traveling at jet speeds could not function without such systems.

In 1947, Flügge-Lotz and her husband joined the French National Office for Aeronautical Research (ONERA) in Paris. However, they remained there only one year, deciding to accept positions with Stanford University in the United States. At Stanford, Flügge-Lotz worked as a lecturer and a research supervisor in engineering, and her husband obtained the post of professor of engineering. While working to establish new graduate programs and seminars in mathematical aerodynamics and hydrodynamics and in fluid mechanics, Flügge-Lotz continued her own research on flight control.

In 1954, the year after publishing her first book, *Discontinuous Automatic Control,* Flügge-Lotz became a U.S. citizen. Six years later, she was invited to serve as a U.S. delegate to the First Congress of the International Federation of Automatic Control in Moscow. This achievement, combined with the success of her book, resulted in Flügge-Lotz's promotion to full professor of engineering mechanics and of aeronautics and astronautics, and she became the first woman professor of engineering at Stanford.

Flügge-Lotz retired from Stanford and published her second book in 1968. Upon her retirement, Stanford named her professor emerita of applied mechanics and of aeronautics and astronautics, in recognition of her work there. Two years later, she was presented the Achievement Award of the Society of Women Engineers (SWE) and became the first woman to be elected a fellow of the American Institute of Aeronautics and Astronautics (AIAA). In 1971, she was again honored when she became the first woman asked to give the prestigious von Karman Lecture before the AIAA.

See also Aeronautical and Aerospace Engineering; Darden, Christine M.; National Aeronautics and Space Administration (NASA)
References Bailey, Martha J., *American Women in Science: A Biographical Dictionary* (1994); McMurray, Emily M., ed., *Notable Twentieth-Century Scientists,* vol. 2: (F–K) (1995); Sicherman, Barbara, and Carol Hurd Green, eds., *Notable American Women: The Modern Period* (1980); Vare, Ethlie Ann, and Greg Ptacek, *Mothers of Invention: From the Bra to the Bomb, Forgotten Women and Their Unforgettable Ideas* (1988); Cooper, Julie, and Maria Banderas, "Irmgard Flügge-Lotz," available at http://www.scottlan.edu/Iriddle/women/lotz.htm (cited 14 April 1998).

Foster, Margaret (1895–1970)

Geochemist Margaret Foster worked as an analyst with the United States Geological Survey (USGS) in Washington, D.C., in 1918. As a chemist trained in water resources, Foster researched ways to identify and measure trace materials in water. During World War II, Foster was called upon to work on the Manhattan Project, a secret program established to develop the world's first atomic bomb. On this project, Foster's job was to apply her knowledge of chemistry to developing a method of separating the radioactive element thorium (Th) from the radioactive element uranium (U). The use of such radioactive elements was crucial to the atomic bomb project.

See also Bartlett, Helen Blair; Fink, Kathryn (Kay) Ferguson; Goeppert-Mayer, Maria; Koshland, Marian Elliot; Libby, Leona W.; Manhattan Project; Nuclear Physics; Ordnance; Way, Katharine; Wu, Chien-Shiung
References Kass-Simon, G., and Patricia Farnes, eds., *Women of Science: Righting the Record* (1990); Rossiter, Margaret W., *Women Scientists in America: before Affirmative Action 1940–1972* (1995).

Fowler, Joanna S. (b. 1942)

Organic chemist Joanna Fowler has significantly contributed to our understanding of the bio-

chemical processes associated with addictions and with aging. Fowler devised a method of attaching radioactive isotopes to molecules (a process known as labeling or tagging) so that the molecules' movement can be tracked using positron emission tomography (PET). PET is an imaging technology that allows physicians to locate and observe metabolic processes by tracing the location and concentration of tagged molecules as they are metabolized in the brain or other parts of the body. One short-lived radioisotope Fowler helped develop mimics glucose and is used in PET centers worldwide to study neurological and psychiatric diseases and to diagnose lung and colon cancers and cardiac diseases. Fowler has received eight patents for radiolabeling procedures.

Fowler was born in Miami, Florida, and attended primary and secondary school in South Miami. She majored in chemistry at the University of South Florida in Tampa and received a B.A. in 1964. She began her graduate studies at the University of Colorado in Boulder and was awarded her Ph.D. in chemistry in 1968. Fowler then spent a year at the University of East Anglia in Norwich, England, as a senior research associate. In 1969, she joined the staff at Brookhaven National Laboratories in Upton, New York, where she is currently senior chemist. One study Fowler has conducted at Brookhaven involves the relationship between smoking and Parkinson's disease.

Fowler was given the Jacob Javits Investigator Award in the Neurosciences in 1986 and in 1992; she shared both awards with senior chemist Alfred Wolf. In 1988, the American Chemical Society (ACS) honored her with the Esselen Award for Chemistry in the Public Interest. She received Brookhaven National Laboratories' R&D Award in 1994, and the Paul Abersold Award from the Society of Nuclear Medicine in 1997. That same year, the Department of Energy (DOE) gave Fowler the E. O. Lawrence Memorial Award, for her work with atomic energy. In addition, Fowler accepted the Biological & Environmental Research 50 Program Recognition Award for Exceptional Service from the DOE and the National Research Council (NRC). In 1998, the American

Chemical Society awarded Fowler the Francis P. Garvan–John M. Olin Medal.

See also Cori, Gerty Theresa Radnitz; Francis P. Garvan–John M. Olin Medal; Frantz, Virginia Kneeland; Nuclear Physics; Patent; Pert, Candace Bebe; Pharmacology; Radioimmunoassay (RIA); Yalow, Rosalyn Sussman

References Belford, Marsha, "Joanna Fowler Wins DOE's Lawrence Award," *Brookhaven Bulletin* (30 October 1998); Fowler, Joanna S., e-mail correspondence with Alan Winkler, 24 November 1998; Greenberg, Diane, "Joanna Fowler Wins DOE's Lawrence Award," *Brookhaven Bulletin* 52:42 (30 October 1998); Scheff, Lynn, and Virginia Dunleavy, "Winners: Scientist Joanna Fowler," *Newsday* (15 November 1998); Torpie, Stephen L., et al., eds., *American Men and Women of Science,* 18th ed. (1992–1993) (1992).

Fox, Sally (b. 1956)

Sally Fox is known for her development of naturally colored cotton fibers that are free of bleach residues, chemical dyes, and pesticides. Fox produced these colored cotton fibers by applying principles of genetics to the selection and planting of brown cotton seeds and then hand-spinning the delicate cotton fibers into a unique yarn.

Sally Fox was born in Menlo Park, California. As a child, she enjoyed hand-spinning fibers into yarn and then weaving the yarn into cloth. Fox earned a bachelor's degree in biology in 1982. Soon after, she took a job that involved researching the resistance of cotton seeds to insects. During her studies, she came upon some brown seeds. Fascinated by the natural brown color of their cotton, Fox attempted to cultivate the seeds. After several years, she was successful in obtaining short brown cotton fibers. Fox selected seeds from those plants with the strongest colors and longest fibers (suitable for machine spinning). After many generations, she successfully grew plants that yielded longer cotton fibers in assorted natural colors, including varying shades of brown, red, and green. Fox received a patent for her fibers, which she called FoxFibre®.

Fox opened a mail order business selling her natural fibers to hand-spinning hobbyists. As the business grew, she started her own company, Natural Cotton Colours, Inc. During the late 1980s, a Japanese textile mill purchased her products for use in making towels. By 1991, Fox began selling cotton in large quantities to denim manufacturer Levi Strauss. Today, she continues experimenting with new colors. Because FoxFibre® is fire resistant, Fox also is using her fibers to develop children's clothing.

See also Agricultural Engineering; Benerito, Ruth Rogan; Genetic Engineering; Pinckney, Eliza Lucas; Textiles

References Saari, Peggy, ed., *Prominent Women of the 20th Century* (1996); Saari, Peggy, ed., *Scientists: The Lives and Works of 150 Scientists* (1996).

Francis P. Garvan– John M. Olin Medal

Formerly called the Garvan Medal, the Francis P. Garvan–John M. Olin Medal is an annual award of the American Chemical Society (ACS) that acknowledges distinguished service and achievement by a woman chemist who is a citizen of the United States. The award consists of a $5,000 cash prize, an engraved gold medal, a bronze duplicate of the medal, and a travel allowance of $1,000 to attend the award ceremony. For the years 1979–1983, the award was sponsored by W. R. Grace & Company. Since 1984, the Francis P. Garvan–John M. Olin Medal has been sponsored by the Olin Corporation, a company that manufactures chemicals, aerospace hardware, and munitions. The award was initially established in 1936 through a donation from Francis P. Garvan, and the first award was presented to Emma P. Carr in 1937. Insufficient funds made it impossible to issue the award annually during its early years. Thus, no award was issued in 1938, 1939, 1941, and from 1943 through 1945. A list of medal winners appears in Table A.1 in the appendix.

See also American Chemical Society (ACS); Carr, Emma Perry; Chemical Engineering

References American Chemical Society, "1985 Garvan Medal: Catherine C. Fenselau" (1985); Claire, Walter, *The Book of Winners* (1979); Siegman, Gita, ed., *Awards, Honors, and Prizes, Volume 1—United States and Canada,* 10th ed. (1992); Stuart, Sandra Lee, ed., *Who Won What When: The Record Book of Winners* (1980).

Frantz, Virginia Kneeland (1896–1967)

Virginia Frantz is recognized for her studies on the pathology of tumors of the pancreas, thyroid, and breast. In 1935, she became the first person to describe insulin-secreting tumors of the pancreas. During the 1940s, she became one of the first people to use radioactive iodine to detect and treat thyroid cancer.

Frantz was born in New York City. In 1914, she entered Bryn Mawr College as a chemistry major and graduated first in her class four years later. Encouraged to study medicine by the president of Bryn Mawr, Frantz entered the College of Physicians and Surgeons of Columbia University in New York City. She was second in her class when she received her M.D. degree in 1922 and became the first woman accepted as a surgical intern at New York's Columbia Presbyterian Hospital. Frantz remained at Columbia Presbyterian, serving as assistant surgeon in the outpatient department from 1924 to 1927. She then moved to the Surgical Pathology Department. Frantz also taught surgery at the College of Physicians and Surgeons, where she became a full professor in 1951. She retired in 1962, but retained an office at the Columbia-Presbyterian Medical Center, where she served as a surgical consultant.

During World War II, Frantz worked at the Office of Scientific Research and Development (OSRD). While there, she developed a gauze-like substance that could be placed directly into a wound to control bleeding. The substance was later absorbed by the body during the healing process. In 1948, Frantz received the Army-Navy Certificate of Appreciation for Civilian Service for this invention. The next year, and again in 1950, she was elected president of the New York Pathological Society. In 1957, she was honored with the Elizabeth Blackwell Award for distinguished service in medicine by the New York Infirmary. Two years later, she wrote the *Armed Forces Atlas of Tumor Pathology*, which remains a standard reference book on the subject. In 1961, Frantz became the first woman president of the American Thyroid Association. The following year, she was awarded the Janeway Medal of the American Radium Society.

See also Cori, Gerty Theresa Radnitz; Fowler, Joanna S.; Medicine/Medical Technology; Radioimmunoassay (RIA); Yalow, Rosalyn Sussman
References Sicherman, Barbara, and Carol Hurd Green, eds., *Notable American Women: The Modern Period* (1980); Stanley, Autumn, *Mothers and Daughters of Invention: Notes for a Revised History of Technology* (1993); "Virginia Frantz, Teacher, Is Dead" [obituary], *New York Times* (24 August 1967).

Frederick, Christine M. (1883–1970)

Christine Frederick is recognized for her contributions in the field of home economics. Her most noted innovation was the establishment of a household equipment and appliance testing facility in her home. Research she conducted in this setting was instrumental in standardizing the height of sinks, countertops, and other working surfaces.

Christine was born in Boston, Massachusetts. Shortly after her birth, her parents separated and Christine's mother took her to live with an aunt in Russia. They returned to the United States in 1890, settling with family in St. Louis, Missouri. Several years later, Christine's mother married Wyatt MacGaffey and the family moved to Chicago. Christine attended Chicago's public schools, graduating from Northwest Division High School in 1901. The following year, she entered Northwestern University. She was elected to Phi Beta Kappa and received her B.S. degree in 1906.

Christine McGaffey (the spelling she preferred) married business executive Justus George Frederick in 1907. Three years later, they moved to a home in Greenlawn, Long Island, New York. As her family grew, Christine Frederick's interests turned to improving home efficiency. She converted several rooms in her home into a laboratory facility—the Applecroft Home Experiment Station, where she tested home appliances, utensils, and other home products. In time, manufacturers sent products to her for testing, evaluation, and promotion. She also prepared food charts, recipes, and manuals on domestic products and home efficiency.

As Frederick's reputation grew, so did demand for her expertise. She was named household editor for *Ladies Home Journal* in 1912. One of her articles, *Household Engineering: Scientific Management in the Home* (1915), was made into a book and used as a model for standardizing work practices in offices and factories. It also was used as a home economics text in colleges.

Frederick was an advocate for consumerism and worked to maintain reliability of familiar products and to promote training in purchasing. She also was one of the first to conduct surveys on the purchasing habits of women and to interpret these patterns for manufacturers and marketing and advertising agencies. During the 1920s and 1930s, Frederick wrote, gave radio talks, and lectured in the United States and abroad. During the 1940s, she developed an interior design and decorating practice, at which she remained until her retirement in 1957.

See also Cochran, Josephine G.; Columbian Exposition; Domestic Appliances; Gabe, Frances Bateson; Gilbreth, Lillian Moller; Home Economics; Morgan, Agnes Fay; Richards, Ellen Henrietta Swallow; Stanley, Louise
References Bailey, Martha J., *American Women in Science: A Biographical Dictionary* (1994); Sicherman, Barbara, and Carol Hurd Green, eds., *Notable American Women: The Modern Period* (1980); Stanley, Autumn, *Mothers and Daughters of Invention: Notes for a Revised History of Technology* (1993).

Free, Helen Murray (b. 1923)

In the course of her career, Helen Murray Free was awarded seven patents for various improvements in laboratory techniques and clinical laboratory tests. She developed new, more reliable chemical reagents and procedures for use in urinalysis, blood chemistry, histology (tissue study), and cytology (cell study). Her innovations in laboratory instrumentation, reagents, and procedures have since become the standards in clinical laboratories worldwide.

Helen was born in Pittsburgh, Pennsylvania. She attended Poland Seminary High School in Ohio before entering the College of Wooster (in Ohio), from which she received a B.S. degree with honors in chemistry in 1944. After graduation, she took a position as a chemist at Miles Laboratories in Elkhart, Indiana. She later held positions as research chemist, new products manager,

director of clinical laboratory reagents, and director of marketing services of the research products division. Although she retired from Miles Laboratory in 1982, she continued to serve as a consultant in their diagnostic division.

Helen developed many of her groundbreaking methods and techniques in medical laboratory technology and coauthored books and articles in the field while working at Miles Laboratories. She also met, collaborated with, and eventually married biochemist Alfred Free. While at Miles, Helen Free also obtained her M.A. degree in laboratory management and health care administration from Central Michigan University in Mount Pleasant, Michigan.

Helen Free has been the recipient of many honors and awards. In 1967, she and her husband shared the Honor Scroll of the Chicago chapter of the American Institute of Chemists (AIC). She received a Professional Achievement Award from the American Society of Medical Technologists (ASMT) in 1976. The American Chemical Society (ACS) has granted Free three separate awards: its Garvan Medal (1980); the Service Award (granted by the St. Joseph Valley Section in 1981); and the Mosher Award, which she shared with her husband (granted by the Santa Clara Valley Section in 1983). Additionally, Free was named YMCA Woman of the Year and the first recipient of the Helen M. Free Public Outreach Award, both in 1993.

Free served as president of the American Association for Clinical Chemistry (AACC) in 1990. In 1993, she became the third woman president of the ACS. Free was a fellow of both the American Institute of Chemists and the American Association for the Advancement of Sciences (AAAS). She is also a member of Iota Sigma Pi.

See also American Chemical Society (ACS); Francis P. Garvan–John M. Olin Medal; Medicine/Medical Technology; Patent
References Grinstein, Louise S., Rose K. Rose, and Miriam Rafailovich, eds., *Women in Chemistry and Physics: A Biobibliographic Sourcebook* (1993); Shearer, Benjamin F., and Barbara S. Shearer, eds., *Notable Women in the Physical Sciences: A Biographical Dictionary* (1997); *Chemical & Engineering News* (12 January 1998), available at http://pubs.acs.org/hotartcl/cenear/980112/society.html (cited 30 September 1998).

French, Elizabeth J. (1821–1900)

Noted for developing and using electrotherapeutic appliances (devices that deliver electric current) to areas of the body for the purpose of treating a variety of disorders, Elizabeth French received a patent for her first such device in 1875. While the electrotherapeutic device might be applied to virtually any part of the body, French's area of specialization was what was termed "nervous headache" or cranial depression. She displayed her electrical devices at the Centennial Exposition that was held in Philadelphia in 1876. French developed an interest in the use of electricity as a means of treating disorders early in her medical career. Her interest in this area was heightened by her study of the works of Austrian physician Franz Anton Mesmer, who was most noted for his work with hypnotism (mesmerism). Mesmer also was a strong proponent of the belief that a mysterious fluid that had a strong magnetic influence pervaded the human body.

French's use of the electrotherapeutic appliance for treating headache called for administering an unspecified amount of electric current, generally described as an amount short of that which might cause pain, for several minutes. The electrical impulses were delivered using a rubberized cup applied to the base of the brain, while a second electrode was held between the palms of the hands of the patient.

French's professional work was not limited to seeing patients who came to her clinic for treatment. She also conducted instructional sessions in the use of the electrotherapeutic appliances for patients, who in turn would themselves become trained practitioners. She also published a work titled *A New Path in Electrical Therapeutics* in 1873. While French's appliance raised more questions than it answered, it did display the creativity and ingenuity that often is perceived to be the precursor of meaningful invention. In fact, some physicians and medical researchers are currently investigating the therapeutic value of electrical devices.

See also Bryant, Alice G.; Thompson, Mary H.; Vallino, Lisa M., and Rozier, Betty M.
References Macdonald, Anne L., *Feminine Ingenuity:*

How Women Inventors Changed America (1992); Stanley, Autumn, *Mothers and Daughters of Invention: Notes for a Revised History of Technology* (1993); Vare, Ethlie Ann, and Greg Ptacek, *Mothers of Invention: From the Bra to the Bomb, Forgotten Women and Their Unforgettable Ideas* (1988).

Friend, Charlotte (1921–1987)

When microbiologist and virologist Charlotte Friend used an electron microscope to discover and photograph a virus that caused leukemia in mice, she provided new insight into a possible cause of cancer. This virus, called the Friend virus, has proved an important tool in the study of the relationship between animal cancers and viruses. In 1957, Friend developed the first successful vaccine to prevent mice from developing a virus-induced leukemia. In 1972, she discovered a method for altering a leukemia cell from a mouse in a test tube so that it behaved like a normal cell. Although there is no proof that viruses cause cancer in humans, Friend's research has provided new avenues of study about cancer causes and treatments.

Friend was born and raised in New York City, where she attended Hunter College High School. After high school, she attended Hunter College, and received her B.A. in 1944. She then enlisted in the women's unit of the U.S. Navy (WAVES), where she was placed in charge of a chemical pathology laboratory at the U.S. Naval Hospital in Shoemaker, California. After World War II, Friend entered graduate school at Yale University. She obtained a Ph. D. there in bacteriology in 1950.

After receiving her doctorate, Friend joined the Sloan-Kettering Institute for Cancer Research in New York City. In 1952, she became an associate professor of microbiology in a joint program conducted by Sloan-Kettering and Cornell University. In 1966, Friend left Sloan-Kettering to become a professor and director of the Center for Experimental Biology at Mt. Sinai School of Medicine. She remained at this school, where she was instrumental in shaping the educational and research philosophy, until her death in 1987.

Among Friend's many honors and awards were the Alfred P. Sloan Award in 1954, 1957, and 1962; the American Cancer Society Award

(1962); the Hunter College Presidential Medal Centennial Award (1970); and the National Institutes of Health (NIH) Virus-Cancer Progress Award (1974). Friend also was elected into the Hunter College Hall of Fame in 1970. She held memberships in the National Academy of Sciences (NAS), the American Association of Hematology, the American Association of Immunology, and the American Association of Cancer Research and became president of the last in 1976. Two years later, she became the first woman president of the New York Academy of Sciences.

See also Elion, Gertrude Belle; Hollinshead, Ariel; Logan, Myra Adele; Yalow, Rosalyn Sussman
References McMurray, Emily M., ed., *Notable Twentieth-Century Scientists* (1995); Nobel, Iris, *Contemporary Women Scientists of America* (1979); Schmeck, Harold M. Jr., "Charlotte Friend Dies at 65; Researched Cancer Viruses" [obituary], *New York Times* (16 January 1987); Shearer, Benjamin F., and Barbara S. Shearer, eds., *Notable Women in the Physical Sciences: A Biographical Dictionary* (1997); Stanley, Autumn, *Mothers and Daughters of Invention: Notes for a Revised History of Technology* (1993).

Gabe, Frances Bateson (b. 1915)

It takes a one-of-a-kind woman to design a one-of-a-kind house—and Frances Gabe fits the bill. This builder-artist-musician patented her design for a "Self-Cleaning Building Construction" in 1984, although she first conceived of the idea in 1956. The patent issued to Gabe was the first patent ever issued in this category.

Frances Arnholtz was born in 1915 in Boise, Idaho. Her father, Fred Arnholtz, was an architect and building contractor who often had his daughter accompany him to the construction sites at which he worked. While visiting these sites, young Frances absorbed the rudiments of the plumbing, carpentry, and electrical trades that she would someday use to operate her own construction business as well as in the design of her self-cleaning house. Throughout her childhood, Arnholtz got along well with her father; however, the same cannot be said for the relationship she had with her stepmother. Because of difficulties between Frances and her stepmother, Arnholtz left home while still a teenager. At the age of fourteen, she enrolled at the Girls' Polytechnic College in Portland, Oregon. Only two years later, she graduated, having completed what was typically a four-year program.

Arnholtz later married an electrical engineer named Bateson, with whom she had two children. In the mid-1940s, the family was suffering financially because her husband was unable to find employment. To provide an income, Frances Bateson established and managed her own business—Batey's Building Repairs—at which both she and her husband worked. While operating the business, Frances Bateson drew on the construction knowledge she had acquired as a child to purchase older homes for the purpose of rehabilitating and reselling them. The company was successful and remained in operation for more than forty years.

Frances Bateson was a woman who readily accepted challenge and never yielded to adversity. Over the years she faced serious physical problems, including a broken back and the unexplained temporary loss of her sight after the birth of her first child. In addition, Bateson's relation-

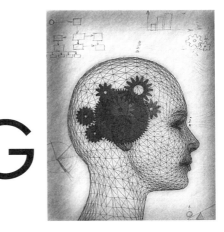

ship with her husband faltered and the couple divorced. Despite these challenges, Bateson continued to manage her company, raise her two children, and pursue her artistic and musical interests.

The idea for a self-cleaning house first came to Bateson in the mid-1950s as she considered how much she disliked the repetitiveness and time-consuming nature of housework. Bateson finally obtained a patent on her house in 1984, under the name Gabe. She devised this name from the initials of her middle and former last names, because her husband was embarrassed by the idea of her self-cleaning home. When the patent was issued, the "Self-cleaning Building Structure" Gabe had designed included almost seventy devices that were designed to save time, run economically, and provide a thorough cleaning to the home.

Among the many devices included in Gabe's design are a self-cleaning sink, tub, and toilet. Dishes are washed and stored in a unit that serves as a combination dishwasher and cabinet, thus eliminating the need to move clean dishes from one location to another. When the home is built, the floors, walls, and ceiling of each room are sprayed with a liquid resin that hardens to form a waterproof barrier on these surfaces. In addition, all furniture is constructed of waterproof base materials that are then covered by waterproof fabrics that Gabe herself has designed. This combination of materials permits each room to be closed off and washed by a rotating ceiling fixture that sprays soapy water, and then clean rinse water, over the entire room and its contents. For drainage, Gabe developed a system of adjustable floor joists (supports) that permit the flooring to be sloped so that water will drain off. The adjustability of the joists also permits leveling adjustments to be made to the flooring as the house settles over time.

In 1984 (the same year she obtained her patent), Gabe was asked by the Inventors' Council of Oregon to build a prototype of her design. She selected a site in Newberg, Oregon, and began the construction of her house with periodic assistance from friends. The outside of the house was constructed of cinder blocks because of its low cost, low maintenance, and its added advantage of being termite-proof. When construction of the house was completed, Gabe noted that the structure cost only $15,000 to build, although she noted that a similar dwelling would likely cost the average home buyer about $50,000.

Gabe moved into her home when construction was completed. Many people have visited the home and shown interest in its low cost and maintenance-free features. Gabe has noted that the home has appealed to the elderly, those who are physically challenged, and many working couples who are pressed for time. However, despite this widespread interest, Gabe has not yet found a buyer for the rights to the design of the house. Today, she continues to live and work in the dwelling, which has a studio where she creates the artwork from which she now earns her living.

See also Architecture; Cochran, Josephine G.; Colvin, Margaret Plunkett; Domestic Appliances; Gilbreth, Lillian Moller; Irwin, Harriet; Keichline, Anna W.; Loftness, Vivian
References Macdonald, Anne L., *Feminine Ingenuity: How Women Inventors Changed America* (1992); McMurran, Kristan, "Frances Gabe's Self-Cleaning House Could Mean New Rights of Spring for Housewives," *People Weekly* (29 March 1982); Stanley, Autumn, *Mothers and Daughters of Invention: Notes for a Revised History of Technology* (1993); Lemelson-MIT Program, "Frances Gabe: The Self-Cleaning House," available at http://web.mit.edu/invent/inventorsA-H/gabe.html (cited 4 July 1999).

Galloway, Betty (b. 1958)

Betty Galloway of Georgetown, South Carolina, was a child of only ten when she was issued her first patent. The patent (no. 3,395,481) was issued in 1968 for a bubble-making toy. Galloway's achievement shows that the creative spirit is not solely an adult venture and places her in the company of America's youngest patented inventors.

See also Low, Jeanie S.
References Vare, Ethlie Ann, and Greg Ptacek, *Mothers of Invention: From the Bra to the Bomb, Forgotten Women and Their Unforgettable Ideas* (1988).

Gardner, Julia Anna (1882–1960)

Paleontologist Julia Anna Gardner devoted most of her career to the study of mollusk fossils and their distribution throughout the world. Although such research generally falls into the realm of pure science, data gathered by Gardner have found technological applications. For example, petroleum geologists have successfully used Gardner's data of the geographic origin, composition, and distribution of sedimentary rock strata to locate petroleum deposits in Texas and the southern Caribbean. A more unusual application of Gardner's knowledge of mollusks proved useful to the military during World War II. In this case, by analyzing seashells contained in the sand ballasts of Japanese balloons that were being used to deploy bombs, Gardner could identify the beaches in Japan from which the balloons had been launched.

Julia Gardner was born in Chamberlain, South Dakota. Using money received through an inheritance, Gardner attended Bryn Mawr College. While there, she was encouraged by geology educator Florence Bascom to pursue studies in geology and paleontology. Gardner followed this suggestion and received her bachelor's degree in geology in 1905. She later returned to Bryn Mawr for graduate work and was awarded a master's degree in geology in 1907. She then entered Johns Hopkins University, and in 1911, she received a Ph.D. in geology and paleontology. She also received an offer of employment as a teacher and research assistant at Johns Hopkins, a position she held until 1917.

When World War I broke out, Gardner went to Europe to serve as a Red Cross volunteer. After the war, she remained in France, working with the American Friends Committee. In 1920, Gardner returned to the United States to work as an associate geologist with the United States Geological Survey (USGS). Her primary assignment was to prepare geological maps of the lower Rio Grande of Texas. Her data were later used by petroleum geologists to locate oil deposits in the region.

Gardner again became involved in the war effort during World War II. She joined the Military Geology Unit (MGU) of the USGS, a unit under the auspices of the U.S. Army Corps of Engineers. Gardner's primary responsibilities within the MGU involved making maps and analyzing maps and aerial photographs for strategic and tactical information about the movement of Japanese troops. It was during this time that Gardner used her knowledge of mollusks to identify beaches being used by the Japanese as launch sites for bomb-carrying hot air balloons.

Gardner retired from the USGS in 1952. Later that year, she was honored with a Distinguished Service Award by the Department of the Interior for her USGS service. Following her retirement, Gardner continued working with the USGS as a contracted employee. She also served as president of the Paleontological Society (1952) and was elected in 1953 as a vice president of the Geological Society of America. Gardner remained active in her geologic studies and collaborated on a book about invertebrate paleontology until 1954, when she suffered a cerebral hemorrhage. Although she survived this incident, she remained in poor health until her death of a stroke in 1960.

See also Parker, Ivy; Petroleum Engineering
References Kass-Simon, G., and Patricia Farnes, eds., *Women of Science: Righting the Record* (1990); McMurray, Emily M., ed., *Notable Twentieth-Century Scientists,* vol. 2: (F–K) (1995); Sicherman, Barbara, and Carol Hurd Green, eds., *Notable American Women: The Modern Period* (1980).

Garvan Medal
See **Francis P. Garvan–John M. Olin Medal**

Genetic Engineering

Genetic engineering, or biotechnical engineering, is a technological field in which biochemical techniques are used to manipulate or modify genes. Many procedures and techniques are used in genetic engineering; however, the most common involves use of recombinant DNA (deoxyribonucleic acid). Recombinant DNA comprises various bits of DNA—the protein molecule that carries genetic information from cell to cell or parent to offspring—from different organisms. An enzyme serves as the "glue" that holds the DNA pieces together. The processes involved in this type of genetic engineering include adding new genes to DNA, removing genes from DNA, or altering part of a gene.

Genetic engineering principles together with advanced recombinant DNA techniques have been successfully used in medicine, industry, and agriculture. One of the first significant medical achievements occurred in the mid-1970s, when a gene for human insulin was inserted into the DNA of a bacterial cell, an action that drove the bacterial cell to make human insulin. Insulin is a hormone that regulates the amount of glucose in the blood. If the body cannot produce insulin in sufficient quanities, the condition known as diabetes mellitus results. Treatment for this condition often involves daily injections of insulin. Such insulin was once provided only by animals such as pigs and cows. However, some diabetics become immune to or develop allergies to animal insulin. Bacteria-produced human insulin does not cause allergic or other undesirable reactions and is quick and inexpensive to produce using recombinant DNA techniques. Other proteins have been developed by means of genetic engineering to treat growth and developmental deficiencies, hemophilia, cancers, and multiple sclerosis.

Genetic engineering also is applied to agriculture. Methods are being investigated to produce low-cholesterol eggs. Genetic engineering techniques also are being explored to stimulate increased milk and meat production in cows and to develop disease- and weather-resistant livestock. Genetic engineering also has been applied to pest insects as a means of reducing their potential damage to crops. A pioneer in this area is entomologist Marjorie Ann Hoy. Specifically, her research has focused on increasing the efficiency of insect pest predators while also developing plants that have increased pest resistance. Cloning in plants has already produced disease-, insect-, and frost-resistant varieties.

Genetic engineering has industrial applications. For example, genetically engineered bacteria are used in sewage treatment facilities to break down harmful toxins, oils resulting from spills, and other industrial wastes. Many methods and techniques of genetic engineering have applications beyond those currently in use. However, some people question the ethics and morality of experimentally altering genes and organisms. One concern is that genetic engineering may one day be used on humans. Several countries have passed legislation barring the use of genetic information for insurance and employment purposes. In the United States, the Recombinant DNA Advisory Committee of the National Institutes of Health (NIH) currently rules on what types of experiments are permitted in genetic engineering research. Several states also have introduced legislation regulating genetics testing laboratories.

See also Alexander, Hattie Elizabeth; Biotechnology; Krim, Mathilde Galland

References Bains, William, *Biotechnology from A to Z* (1998); Barnes-Svarney, Patricia, ed., *The New York Public Library Science Desk Reference* (1995); Parker, Sybil P., *McGraw-Hill Encyclopedia of Science and Technology,* 8th ed., vol. 7 (1997); Stanley, Autumn, *Mothers and Daughters of Invention: Notes for a Revised History of Technology* (1993).

Gilbreth, Lillian Moller (1878–1972)

Cheaper by the Dozen mother, Lillian Moller Gilbreth, may have been America's first "supermom." In an era when women typically did not work outside the home, Gilbreth successfully raised twelve children while pursuing a brilliant career that introduced revolutionary concepts of time and motion management (industrial psychology) and design into engineering.

Lillian Moller was the eldest of the eight surviving children (three boys and five girls) of William and Annie Moller, a prominent family of Oakland, California. Lillian was often described as a shy and studious child whose interests leaned toward music and poetry. She was tutored at home until the age of nine, after which she attended the local public elementary and high schools. Although the Moller family was considered well-to-do, Lillian, as the eldest daughter, shouldered a large share of the responsibility for raising her younger siblings because her mother was frequently either ill or pregnant.

After completing her high school education, Lillian attended the University of California at Berkeley. She graduated in 1900, with a bachelor's degree in literature, and simultaneously was honored through her selection as the first woman to serve as a commencement speaker. Moller then lived in New York City for a short interval while pursuing a master's degree from Columbia University; however, she had difficulty adjusting to being away from home, and she soon returned to California to continue her studies at her alma mater. She received a master's degree in English in 1902.

Moller began studies toward a doctoral degree, but soon abandoned this endeavor to travel to Europe. There she met thirty-five-year-old Frank Bunker Gilbreth of Maine. Gilbreth was an established building contractor, who had become known for "speed building," a process in which he used managerial and technological methods to speed on-site construction. Moller and Gilbreth married in 1904 and moved to New York.

From the moment they married, the Gilbreth partnership revolved around both family and business. At home, Lillian Gilbreth more than fulfilled her role as a mother, raising twelve children. While the children were young, Lillian's role as Frank's business partner focused primarily on editing Frank's articles prior to their publication.

In the years between 1910 and 1920, Frank Gilbreth left the construction business to be-

In 1954, industrial psychologist and engineer Lillian Gilbreth became the first woman to receive the engineering industry's Washington Award. (Corbis/Bettmann-UPI)

come a management consultant in Providence, Rhode Island. In this position, he focused his work on finding the industrial applications of his ideas regarding time and motion. During this period, Frank and Lillian opened a motion study laboratory in their home, where they also lectured and taught classes on the subject. In addition, Lillian's mother moved in with the Gilbreth family to assist in the care of the children while Lillian worked and attended classes at nearby Brown University. Lillian Moller Gilbreth was issued a Ph.D. in psychology from Brown University in 1915.

While working toward her Ph.D., Gilbreth wrote her first book, *The Psychology of Management,* which was published in 1914. Much of the information contained in the book resulted from the research she had conducted while working on her doctoral thesis. The book immediately won great praise and became one of the most significant works on the history of engineering thought because it factored human characteristics and abilities into the process of scientific management. In addition, the ideas presented in the publication formed the basis for much of today's management theory.

The family moved to Montclair, New Jersey, shortly after Lillian obtained her Ph.D. Here the Gilbreths opened a new firm, Gilbreth, Inc. The couple worked together until Frank's death in 1924. By the time of Frank's death, they had coauthored five books on motion studies. Lillian took over the business after her husband's death. Initially, she encountered resistance from factory clients who were unsure of her abilities, despite the fact that when compared to her husband, it was Lillian who held the more significant academic credentials. After a slow start, during which she struggled financially, Lillian slowly established credibility in the business world through her lectures and the courses she continued to offer in her home laboratory.

Lillian also began acting as a consultant to university departments of home economics. In time, she became widely recognized among home economists for her work, especially those wishing to apply her business methods to the management of the home. Research Gilbreth conducted in this area was reported in two books, *The Home-Maker and Her Job,* which was published in 1927, and a much later publication, *Management in the Home* (1954).

Gilbreth served as a lecturer at Purdue University from 1924 through 1935, before joining the faculty as a professor of management at their School of Mechanical Engineering. During her tenure at Purdue, she established a motion study laboratory and served as a consultant on careers for women. In addition, her earlier interest in designing usable home and work spaces for the physically challenged, which became evident in a book titled *Motion Study for the Handicapped* that she coauthored with Frank in 1920, led to an affiliation with the Institute of Rehabilitation Medicine at the New York University Medical Center. Here Gilbreth created an ergonomically designed model kitchen for use by persons with disabilities. As part of this design, she developed special equipment and routines to enable physically challenged persons to be more self-sufficient and lead more independent lives. Among the devices credited to Gilbreth were her patented trash can, the lid of which could be opened by stepping on a pedal at the base, and an electric food (processing) machine. Variations of the trash can she designed continue to be found in many homes and medical facilities today.

The kitchen designed by Gilbreth for New York University became an internationally known training center for rehabilitation of people with disabilities. In addition, Gilbreth's opinions re-

garding new appliances for the home were widely sought after. Throughout the 1930s and 1940s, few household appliances reached market without her review.

In 1941, Gilbreth accepted a post as head of the Department of Personnel Relations at the Newark School of Engineering. She also served concurrently as a visiting professor of management at the University of Wisconsin at Madison in 1955.

Despite her demanding professional schedule, Gilbreth also participated in various community activities. She often performed volunteer services for causes and interests outside her business and educational circles. For example, Gilbreth maintained affiliations with the Girl Scouts of America, local churches and libraries, and organizations dealing with meeting the needs of the physically challenged. During the Great Depression (1930s), she served as a member of the President's Emergency Committee for Unemployment Relief. During World War II, she acted as an educational adviser to the Office of War Information. Later, in 1951, she was a member of the Civil Defense Advisory Commission.

A listing of the honors bestowed upon Gilbreth serves as testimony to the progression of her acceptance within her profession. In 1921, she was made an honorary member of the Society of Industrial Engineers (honorary because the society did not admit women to its ranks). In 1931, this same society created the Gilbreth Medal, named for her husband, Frank, and bestowed the first award on Lillian. She was presented the Hoover Medal for Distinguished Public Service in engineering by the American Society of Mechanical Engineers (ASME) in 1966. Before her death in 1972, Gilbreth also had been awarded more than twenty honorary degrees in engineering and commendations from numerous professional groups. In addition, a fellowship was created in her name by the Society of Women Engineers (SWE), an organization in which Gilbreth was acknowledged as the first member.

What made Lillian Gilbreth unique in the field of time-motion studies was her focus on the worker as an individual. During a time when management often punished workers for not fitting the production model, and in contrast to her husband's focus almost exclusively on the physiological aspects of time-motion study, Lillian espoused the concepts of psychology to integrate the mental abilities of workers with production methods. She strongly believed that the happiness, comfort, safety, and general well-being of the employee was an area that could be improved upon to positively affect the bottom line, and she spent a good part of her career trying to convince industry management to join in her beliefs. Her focus on employee feelings, behavior, motivation, and attitudes was decades ahead of its time. Not until the 1960s did sensitivity training in management come into vogue.

Much of the resistance Gilbreth experienced from her colleagues resulted from their beliefs that she placed too much emphasis on the worker and work environment and too little on time and profits. However, over time, she slowly changed many of these beliefs. Gilbreth continued to research and to lecture well into her eighties. She died in 1972, after suffering a stroke.

See also Blount (Griffin), Bessie J.; Domestic Appliances; Frederick, Christine M.; Gabe, Frances Bateson; Keichline, Anna W.; Kenner, (Mary) Beatrice Davidson; Loftness, Vivian
References "Dr. Gilbreth, Engineer, Mother of Dozen," Obituary reproduced in *The New York Times Biographical Edition* (1972); Kass-Simon, G., and Patricia Farnes, *Women of Science: Righting the Record* (1990); Stanley, Autumn, *Mothers and Daughters of Invention: Notes for a Revised History of Technology* (1993).

Gleason, Kate (1865–1933)

Kate Gleason made significant contributions in a variety of areas, including the gear industry, the building industry, and the banking industry. Gleason gained recognition from prominent inventors such as Thomas Alva Edison and Henry Ford for her contributions to the invention of a machine that produced beveled gears quickly and cheaply. Although Gleason became famous for the design of this machine, she credited her father with the idea on which the Gleason bevel-gear planer was based. Despite this admission,

Kate Gleason became the first woman admitted to the Verein Deutscher Ingenieure (Association of German Engineers) in 1913. In 1914, she was again rewarded for designing the bevel-gear planer by becoming the first woman to be awarded membership to the American Society of Mechanical Engineers (ASME). Gleason later represented ASME at the World Power Conference in Germany, in 1930.

Born in Rochester, New York, Kate Gleason began helping out in her father's tool-making business when she was only 11. In 1884, she became the first woman to enter Cornell University's engineering program; however, she left Cornell to help save her father's struggling business. Gleason returned to Cornell in 1888, only to leave once again, this time to represent her father's company on a national sales tour. In 1893, she expanded this market by traveling and selling gears throughout Europe. Gleason's successful sales efforts eventually made her father's business one of the foremost gearing companies worldwide.

Gleason left her father's business in 1913 and took over the bankrupt Ingle Machine Company of East Rochester. By 1915, her efforts led the company from a $140,000 debt to more than $1 million profit. The next year, Gleason became the first woman elected to both the Rochester Chamber of Commerce and the Rochester Engineering Society. Two years later, she became the first woman president of a national bank when she took over the National Bank of East Rochester.

In 1921, Gleason developed a method for pouring concrete that could be used in housing construction. Gleason used this method in the construction of low-cost homes. This successful venture led to her becoming the first woman member of the American Concrete Institute and also served as a construction model for future suburban communities.

At the time of her death in 1933, Gleason left an estate of more than $1 million to the Rochester Institute of Technology (RIT), a school she had attended on a part-time basis years earlier.

See also American Society of Mechanical Engineers (ASME); Cambra, Jessie G.; Civil Engineering; Mechanical Engineering

References Kass-Simon, G., and Patricia Farnes, eds., *Women of Science: Righting the Record* (1990); Olsen, Kirstin, *Chronology of Women's History* (1994); Bartels, Nancy, "The First Lady of Gearing," available at http://www.geartechnology.com/mag/gt-kg.htm. (cited 20 June 1998); "Kate Gleason," in *Britannica Online,* at http://women.eb.com/women/articles/Gleason_Kate. html. (cited 20 June 1998); "Kate Gleason," available at http://www.netsrq.com:80/-dbois/gleason.html (cited 20 June 1998); LeBold, William K., and Dona J. LeBold, "Women Engineers: A Historical Perspective," available at http://www.asee.org/pubs3/html/women_engi-neers.htm (cited 20 June 1998).

Goeppert-Mayer, Maria
(1906–1972)

Maria Goeppert-Mayer became an expert in the field of quantum mechanics, a scientific discipline the purpose of which is to define and explain the behavior of subatomic particles. For her work in this area, Goeppert-Mayer became the second woman to be awarded a Nobel Prize for physics, in 1963. She was awarded the prize for her discoveries concerning nuclear shell structure, the arrangement of the particles that make up the nucleus of an atom. Goeppert-Mayer's theory holds that the protons and neutrons in the atomic nucleus move in orbits, just as electrons move in orbits outside the nucleus. In addition, her theory suggests that within these orbits, neutrons pair with protons in a predictable pattern. Once paired, the units spin, much like Earth spins on its axis, while also revolving in their orbits inside the nucleus—a concept known as spin-orbit coupling. While working on this research, Goeppert-Mayer observed that the presence of unpaired neutrons in the nucleus seemed to correlate with whether or not an atom was likely to give off nuclear particles (neutrons), a process known as radioactivity. Thus, her work is used to help predict which isotopes (forms of the same element having different atomic weights) of a substance are most likely to be unstable.

Maria Goeppert was born in Kattowitz, in the region of Germany known as Upper Silesia (today, Katowice, in Poland). Both of Goeppert's parents were well educated and encouraged their daughter to excel in her studies. Her father was a professor of pediatrics at the University of Göttingen, and her mother was a former teacher. Goeppert attended public schools until age 15, when she entered a private school to prepare her for the qualifying exams required for entrance into the university. After passing these exams, in 1924, Goeppert enrolled at the University of Göttingen as a mathematics major.

The area of physics known as quantum mechanics was then in its infancy. Influenced by the work being done at the University of Göttingen by Max Born and James Franck, Goeppert changed her major to physics. In 1928, four years after beginning her university studies, Goeppert was awarded a fellowship by the German government to study in England. She attended Cambridge University for one semester, studying physics and English. The following year, she returned to Göttingen to continue her studies in physics. That same year, she also met American chemist Joseph E. Mayer. The couple married in 1930, only a short time before Maria was awarded her Ph.D. in physics.

Soon after Maria Goeppert-Mayer received her Ph.D., Joseph Mayer accepted a position in the physics department at Johns Hopkins University in Baltimore, and the Mayers moved to the United States. Although qualified to hold a university position, Maria Goeppert-Mayer was unable to obtain one at Johns Hopkins because of nepotism policies that prohibited the simultaneous employment of both husband and wife. However, the university did permit her to perform research in their laboratories, on an informal basis and without pay.

During the summers, Goeppert-Mayer returned to her homeland. There she collaborated with her former instructor and mentor Max Born on beta decay, a process in which high-speed particles are emitted from the nuclei of radioactive elements. This work resulted in the joint publication of several articles by Born and Goeppert-Mayer. It also provided a basis for the research for which Goeppert-Mayer would later become known.

In 1939, Joseph Mayer left Johns Hopkins and accepted a position as an associate professor of chemistry at Columbia University in New York. At

Maria Goeppert-Mayer shared the 1963 Nobel Prize in physics for her research on the structure of the atomic nucleus. (Corbis/Betmann-UPI)

the same time, Columbia granted Goeppert-Mayer an opportunity to lecture within the chemistry department, with the understanding that her husband's employment prohibited her from being paid for this work. In addition, she would not be provided either a title or an office. During this same period, Goeppert-Mayer also lectured at Sarah Lawrence College in Bronxville, New York.

In the early 1940s, Goeppert-Mayer was invited (unofficially) to become a member of the research team that was secretly working on the Manhattan Project—the code name for the U.S. government–sponsored effort to construct an atomic bomb. This research team was housed at Columbia University and worked under the direction of physicist Harold Urey. Goeppert-Mayer's role in this project involved uranium isotope separation.

In 1946, the Mayers moved to Illinois, when they were both offered positions at the University of Chicago. Joseph was to work at the university's Institute of Nuclear Studies, with such notable physicists as Enrico Fermi, Harold Urey, and Edward Teller. Maria also was given an opportunity to work at the university, once again without pay; however, she was granted an office and other university benefits. In time, Goeppert-Mayer's talents and expertise in the fields of physics and mathematics became well recognized. As a result, she was offered a part-time position as a senior physicist at the Argonne National Laboratory. It was while working here that Goeppert-Mayer's research emphasis began to focus on nuclear physics.

While working at the Argonne National Laboratory, Goeppert-Mayer also began collaborating with Edward Teller on research involving the origin of the elements (Teller later abandoned this effort). Goeppert-Mayer began to examine why some isotopes occur more commonly in nature than others. While conducting her studies, she observed a pattern emerging among the numbers of protons and neutrons present in the nuclei of stable (nonradioactive) elements. From this pattern, she deduced that in stable nuclei these atomic particles orbited in layers within the nucleus, although she could not at the time explain the reasons for this phenomenon. In collaboration with other scientists, including Enrico Fermi and Hans Jensen, Goeppert-Mayer eventually arrived at a theory of motion of atomic particles—the theory of spin-orbit coupling. She published these findings in several papers in 1950, and in a book she coauthored with Jensen five years later.

Over the next several years, Goeppert-Mayer's ideas regarding the shell model and spin-orbit coupling gradually were accepted by the larger scientific community. In 1959, she was offered a full professorship, at full pay, by the University of California at San Diego. Her husband also was offered a position at the same university. Within only a few weeks of the Mayers' arrival in California, Maria suffered a stroke that resulted in the paralysis of her left arm as well as slurred speech. Despite the limitations these problems imposed, she continued to teach and carry out her research.

In 1963, Goeppert-Mayer shared the Nobel Prize in physics with her collaborator Hans Jensen, and with physicist Eugene P. Wigner of Princeton University for an unrelated research project in another area of physics. In addition to the Nobel Prize, Goeppert-Mayer received recognition in the form of honorary degrees from several institutions, including Smith, Mount Holyoke, and Russell Sage. She also was elected into the National Academy of Sciences (NAS), the American Academy of Arts and Sciences (AAAS), Sigma Xi, and the American Physical Society (APS). This last organization later created the Maria Goeppert-Mayer Award—an annual award that recognizes the achievements of a female physicist—to commemorate Goeppert-Mayer's achievements.

See also Argonne National Laboratory; Elion, Gertrude Belle; Jackson, Shirley Ann; Levi-Montalcini, Rita; Manhattan Project; Nepotism Policies; Nobel Prize; Nuclear Physics; Quimby, Edith Hinkley; Way, Katharine; Wu, Chien-Shiung; Yallow, Rosalyn Sussman

References Grinstein, Louise S., Rose K. Rose, and Miriam H. Rafailovich, eds., *Women in Chemistry and Physics: A Biobibliographic Sourcebook* (1993); "Hypatia's Sisters: Biographies of Women Scientists Past and Present," Women in Science Class, Women Studies Program, University of Washington (Summer 1975); Kass-Simon G., and Patricia Farnes, eds., *Women of Science: Righting the Record* (1990); "Maria Goeppert-Mayer," [obituary] *New York Times* (22 February 1972); Moritz, Charles, ed., *Current Biography, 1964* (1964).

Goldsmith, Grace
See **American Society for Nutritional Sciences (ASNS)**

Goldstine, Adele Katz (b. 1920)

Mathematician Adele Katz Goldstine was one of the women involved in the development of ENIAC—the first computer made in the United States. At the time this computer was being developed, Adele Goldstine was married to Lieutenant Herman Goldstine, a mathematics professor at the University of Michigan who had been drafted for military service. Lieutenant Goldstine was placed in charge of a ballistics program at the University of Pennsylvania, a program that later evolved into the development of ENIAC.

Adele Katz Goldstine was put to work in the program headed by her husband. Her initial responsibility was to recruit women who were graduating from college with mathematics degrees to work for the military (in civil service positions), performing the calculations needed for ballistics work. In time, the women she recruited were assigned the task of programming ENIAC; thus, they became the nation's first computer programmers.

Although Adele Goldstine did not serve as a programmer of the ENIAC, she did make a vital contribution to the project. In addition to her role in finding the women to program this computer system, Goldstine authored the manual for the computer. The manual not only described how this machine worked but also included technical descriptions of all of the components used in its construction.

> **See also** Computers/Computer Technology; Hopper, Grace Murray; Kempf, Martine; Kurtzig, Sandra L. Brody; Mathematics; Ordnance
>
> **References** McCartney, Scott, *ENIAC: The Triumphs and Tragedies of the World's First Computer* (1999); Stanley, Autumn, *Mothers and Daughters of Invention: Notes for a Revised History of Technology* (1993).

Good, Mary Lowe (b. 1931)

Mary Good is recognized for her accomplishments as an industrial research chemist, educator, and adviser on matters of science and technology to U.S. Presidents Jimmy Carter, Ronald Reagan, and George Bush. Her research and expertise in catalysis (a process that uses a substance to increase the rate of a chemical reaction without itself entering into the reaction) increased understanding of the usefulness of the rare metal ruthenium in petroleum and petrochemical processing.

Mary Good was born in Grapevine, Texas. In 1943, her family moved to Arkansas, where she attended high school. Good later entered the Arkansas State Teachers' College in Conway (now the University of Central Arkansas) to study home economics. Encouraged by her freshman chemistry instructor, Good changed her major to chemistry, earning a B.S. degree in 1950. She then accepted a fellowship to the University of Arkansas at Fayetteville, where she double-majored in inorganic chemistry and radiochemistry (a branch of chemistry dealing with radioactive isotopes). She received her master's degree in 1953 and her Ph.D. in 1955.

In 1954, Good worked as an instructor of chemistry and as director of the radiochemistry laboratory at Louisiana State University (LSU) in Baton Rouge. She advanced in position to assistant professor and in 1958 moved to the newly founded LSU campus in New Orleans. Here she developed a radiochemical research course, designed a laboratory, and wrote the text for an undergraduate laboratory program. While at LSU, Good used infrared and Mössbauer spectroscopy (a technique that uses gamma ray absorption and emission to determine the composition of solid samples) to research and develop effective separation procedures and techniques for synthesizing complex metals. She also conducted research that led to the development of long-lasting antifouling coatings to protect ships from barnacles. In 1967, Good was made full professor; in 1974, she was named Boyd Professor of Chemistry. In 1978, Good returned to the Baton Rouge campus of LSU as Boyd Professor of Materials Science in the Division of Engineering Research.

Good left teaching and moved to Des Plaines, Illinois, in 1980 to become vice president and director of research for Universal Oil Products (UOP). Good's title and responsibilities changed as the company expanded through mergers. In 1985, she became president of the engineered materials research division of Allied Signal, Inc. Three years later, she was named senior vice president for technology for Allied Signal in Morristown, New Jersey.

Good has served on advisory panels for the Chemistry Division of the National Science Foundation (NSF), the Oak Ridge Associated Universities, and the Industrial Research Institute. In 1991, she became a member of the Council of Advisors on Science and Technology. This led to her appointment as undersecretary of technology at the U.S. Department of Commerce in 1993.

Good has received many honors and awards, including the Agnes Fay Morgan Research Award from Iota Sigma Pi (1969); the Garvan Medal from the American Chemical Society (ACS) (1973); and the American Institute of Chemistry's Gold Medal (1983). In 1987, she became the second woman elected president of the ACS. The following year, she was given the Delmer S. Fahrney Medal by the Franklin Institute. In 1991, she was awarded the Industrial Research Institute Medal for her work on the President's Council of Advisors for Science and Technology. The next year, Good received the NSF's Distinguished Public Service Award, the American Association for the Advancement of Science (AAAS) Award, and the Albert Fox Demers Medal Award from Rensselaer Polytechnic Institute.

See also American Chemical Society (ACS); Flanigen, Edith M.; Francis P. Garvan–John M. Olin Medal; Metals and Metallurgy; Morgan, Agnes Fay; National Science Foundation (NSF); Parker, Ivy; Petroleum Engineering; Spectroscopy

References Grinstein, Louise S., Rose K. Rose, and Miriam Rafailovich, eds., *Women in Chemistry and Physics: A Biobibliographic Sourcebook* (1993); McMurray, Emily M., ed., *Notable Twentieth-Century Scientists,* vol. 2: (F–K) (1995); "The Leaders of Science: The Readers of *The Scientist,*" *The Scientist,* available at http://www. thescientist.library.upenn.edu/yr1996/sept/ leaders_960930.html (cited 28 August 1998); Long, Janice R., "Mary Lowe Good To Receive 1997 Priestley Medal," *Chemical and Engineering News,* available at http://pubs.acs.org/hotartcl/cenear/960513/medal.html (cited 28 August 1998).

Goode, Sarah E. (n.d.)

Sarah E. Goode is recognized by the U.S. Patent and Trademark Office as the first African American woman inventor to be granted a U.S. patent. Goode received Patent No. 322,177 on 14 July 1885, for a piece of furniture known as a folding cabinet bed. The bed was designed to perform a function similar to that of today's sofabed. At the time the patent was issued, Goode owned and operated a furniture store in Chicago. Little else is known about the life of this early woman inventor.

See also Benjamin, Miriam E.; Invention/Inventors; Kies, Mary; Patent; Patent and Trademark Office, U.S. (PTO)

References Hine, Darlene Clarke, Elsa Barkley Brown, and Rosalyn Terborg-Penn, eds., *Black Women in America: An Historical Encyclopedia,* vol. 1: (A–L) (1993); Smith, Jessie Carney, ed., *Black Firsts: 2,000 Years of Extraordinary Achievement* (1994); U.S. Patent and Trademark Office, *A Quest for Excellence* (1994).

Graham, Bette Nesmith (1924–1980)

Texan Bette Graham turned an occupational shortcoming into a multimillion-dollar industry by inventing Liquid Paper®, a correction fluid for use by typists. Graham, a high school dropout, worked as a secretary, even though she had poor typing skills. She could not adapt to the light touch needed to use the then newly developed electric typewriters. In addition, the typewriters used a carbon-film ribbon, making ordinary erasers and ink eradicator an ineffective and messy way to correct errors. Graham, who had done some art work, decided to try using white tempera paint to cover her typing mistakes. She kept her "correction fluid," which she called "Mistake Out," a secret for more than four years. Then, secretaries with whom she worked learned of her correction fluid and began purchasing the product for their own use.

In 1956, Graham coined the name Liquid Paper® and began to market the product. By the end of 1957, she was using her kitchen and garage to prepare the 100 bottles she was selling each month. Graham improved the formula by making it thicker and faster drying. She gradually expanded her operation and, by the end of the 1960s, was grossing more than $1 million each year from domestic sales. In 1968, Graham moved her company to new headquarters and, using automated machinery, was able to produce 60 bottles per minute. Within two years, she was selling up to 5 million bottles each year.

Graham resigned from the Liquid Paper Corporation in 1976. The company was purchased by the Gillette Corporation for 47.5 million dollars in 1979. Graham died in 1980, leaving a fortune of more than $50 million to be shared among her son and several philanthropic foundations.

See also Invention/Inventors

References Altman, Linda Jacobs, *Women Inventors: American Profiles* (1997); Macdonald, Anne L., *Feminine Ingenuity: How Women Inventors Changed America* (1992); O'Neill, Lois Decker, *The Women's Book of Records and Achievements* (1979); Vare, Ethlie Ann, and Greg Ptacek, *Mothers of Invention: From the Bra to the Bomb, Forgotten Women and Their Unforgettable Ideas* (1988); Lemelson-MIT Program, "Bette Nesmith Graham (1924–1980): Liquid Paper," available at http://web.mit.edu/invent/www/inventorsA-H/ nesmith.html (cited 21 October 1998); Ward, Barbara, "The Mothers of Invention Deserve Credit," available at http://www.kentuckyconnect.com/heraldleader/news/ 030898/t1invent.shtml (cited 21 October 1998).

Grandin, Temple (b. 1947)

Temple Grandin's need to understand herself led her to develop an expertise in animal psychology and behavior as well as achieve worldwide success through the invention of devices designed to assist in the care, handling, and eventual slaughter of livestock. At age two, Grandin was diagnosed with autism, a genetic disorder that results from a lack of total development of certain areas of the brain. The disorder prevents the brain from correctly interpreting or responding to signals it receives from one or more of the five senses (sight, touch, taste, smell, and hearing). People who have autism often are overwhelmed by the intensity of the information received from their senses and are unable to concentrate or focus their thoughts. This inability results in anxiety and fear. The autistic often obtain relief from this anxiety and fear by detaching themselves mentally from their environment—that is, by ignoring the happenings in their surroundings and retreating into nonresponsiveness. Although autism does not necessarily affect intellectual ability, the mechanisms by which autistic individuals think and process sensory information are generally different from the ways in which those who do not have this condition process information.

Temple Grandin first began to think that a relationship existed between her autism and the behavior she observed in some animals while she was on a visit to a relative's ranch at the age of 16. She observed that prior to slaughter, livestock handled in a device called a "squeeze chute" became calm. A squeeze chute is a mechanical device that physically restrains an animal and blocks its access to sights and sounds that may frighten it. Curious about the calming effect the device had on the animals she observed, Temple, with her aunt's assistance, tried the device on herself. She quickly observed that the physical pressure exerted by the device as well as the decrease in her awareness of certain external stimuli had a calming effect on her.

Grandin was so impressed by her positive responses to the experience she had with the squeeze chute, that she went on to develop a similar machine for herself. Grandin, who holds degrees in both psychology and animal science, has written many articles about her experiences with autism. After she reported her experiences with the squeeze machine that she developed for her own use, the design was adopted for use at several sensory integration clinics (facilities specializing in the treatment of autistic individuals) throughout the United States. The device in use at these clinics provides the user the ability to regulate the amount of pressure exerted by the machine, thus placing that individual in control of how much stimulus they receive from the environment. Grandin reported that the device enhanced her social and emotional adjustment, enabling her to succeed in her pursuit of higher education.

Temple Grandin studied psychology at Franklin Pierce College, graduating with a B.A. degree in this area in 1970. She then continued her education and received an M.S. from Arizona State University (1979) and a Ph.D. from the University of Illinois (1989), both in animal sciences. As Grandin pursued her college studies, she continued to analyze her own reactions to external stimuli and use what she learned to overcome her weaknesses. She also applied her strengths—her ability to focus, think logically, and make keen observations—to succeed in the academic environment. Through her studies in both psychology and animal sciences, Grandin also became more aware of the similarities that exist between the thought processes of people with autism and the behaviors she observed in animals. This led her to focus her studies on animal behavior.

Grandin has devoted her career and her life to increasing awareness in the care and humane treatment of livestock animals. She has designed and developed many devices for use by the livestock industry, all of which are intended to ease the fear and pain of livestock prior to their slaughter. Her developments include corral systems with covered alleyways, veterinary facilities for feed lots, improved handling chutes, and a device she calls the "Staircase to Heaven." This last device is used by slaughterhouses to guide the animals to the place where their slaughter will occur, while allowing the animals to touch nose to rump, as they would in nature. At the same time, each of the animals is contained within a harness that supports the animal's underbelly and chest. The harness blocks the animal's vision to prevent it from being startled on its journey and holds the animal securely during the slaughter process.

More than one-third of the meat-processing plants in the United States now use this equipment. In addition, livestock facilities located in the United States, Canada, Europe, Mexico, Australia, New Zealand, and other countries have been designed by Grandin.

Grandin currently works as an assistant professor at Colorado State University, where she teaches courses dealing with livestock behavior and facility design. She has authored more than 300 articles for scientific journals and livestock periodicals on the subjects of animal welfare, animal handling, and facility design. She is coauthor of the book *Thinking in Pictures: And Other Reports from My Life with Autism,* which was published in 1993. Grandin also is the author of *Emergence: Labeled Autistic* (1986) and *Animal Welfare and Meat Science* (1999). Her first book is her autobiography and focuses, as does her second book, on her experiences and thoughts about autism.

Grandin's other career-related activities include service as a consultant to the meat industry, through which she provides information on efficient ways to raise livestock while treating the animals humanely. For her work in this area, Grandin was presented the Livestock Conservation Institute's Award for Meritorious Service in 1984; the Innovator's Award for Technology from the meat industry in 1993; and the Industry Innovator Award from *Meat Marketing and Technology Magazine* in 1994. In addition, both for her work in animal science and for her studies and writings on autism, Grandin was presented a Distinguished Alumni Award from Franklin Pierce College in 1989.

See also Agricultural Engineering; Agriculture; Baldwin, Anna; Dickelman, Lizzie H.
References Ambrose, Susan A., et al., *Journeys of Women in Science and Engineering: No Universal Constants* (1997); Graham, Judith, ed., *Current Biography Yearbook, 1994* (1994); University of Arkansas, Fayetteville, "Dr. Temple Grandin Visits Department," *Animal Sciences,* newsletter of the Department of Animal Sciences at the University of Arkansas (Spring 1998).

Granville, Evelyn Boyd (b. 1924)

Mathematician Evelyn Boyd Granville was involved with the U.S. space program during its infancy. In this work, she developed computer programs that were used for trajectory analysis during both the *Mercury* and the *Apollo* projects —projects that placed the first Americans in space and the first astronauts on the moon. Granville also has served as a consultant to ordnance engineers and as a mathematics instructor at various levels, from elementary school to college.

Evelyn Boyd was born in Washington, D.C. She attended that city's Dunbar High School—a segregated African American school known for its high academic standards—and graduated as valedictorian. Boyd received a partial scholarship and enrolled at Smith College in Northampton, Massachusetts, where she majored in mathematics and physics. During the summers, she worked as a mathematician at the National Bureau of Standards (now the National Institute of Standards and Technology) to help finance her education. In 1945, Boyd graduated from Smith College *summa cum laude* and was elected to Phi Beta Kappa.

Boyd pursued graduate work at Yale University, graduating in 1946 with an M.A. in mathematics and physics. She remained at Yale on a Julius Rosenwald Fellowship, followed by an Atomic Energy Commission (AEC) Predoctoral Fellowship. In 1949, she was inducted into the scientific honor society Sigma Xi and awarded a Ph.D. in mathematics, becoming one of the first African American women to hold a doctoral degree in that field (the other was Marjorie Lee Brown, who obtained her Ph.D. from the University of Michigan).

After one year of postgraduate work at New York University's Institute of Mathematics and Science, Boyd became an assistant professor of mathematics at Fisk University in Nashville, Tennessee. She remained there two years and then returned to Washington, D.C., to work as an applied mathematician for the National Bureau of Standards. The division in which she worked later became the Diamond Ordnance Fuse Laboratories of the U.S. Army. In this job, Boyd applied mathematical formulae to problems involving missile fuses (devices responsible for detonating missiles).

In 1956, Boyd's career focus shifted from military ordnances to spacecraft when she accepted a job as a mathematician with IBM. At IBM, Boyd used computers to make trajectory analyses and orbit computations for the *Vanguard* and *Mercury* space probes. In 1960, Boyd married and moved to Los Angeles. Here she worked on orbit computations for the Computation and Data Reduction Center of the U.S. Space Technology Laboratories. In 1962, she joined the Space and Information Systems Division of the North American Aviation Company (NAA). Her job was to provide engineers working on the *Apollo* space missions with technical support in trajectory and orbit computations and celestial mechanics. The next year, Boyd returned to IBM, where she did work similar to that she had done at NAA.

Boyd divorced in 1967. That same year, she returned to teaching. She accepted a position at the California State University in Los Angeles (CSULA), where she trained future mathematics teachers. While at CSULA, Boyd also directed an after-school tutorial program in mathematics for elementary school children.

In 1970, Boyd married real estate broker Edward V. Granville. The couple remained at their jobs in Los Angeles until 1984, when they retired and moved to Texas. Evelyn Boyd Granville's retirement was short lived. Within one year, she was again teaching—now mathematics and computer science—at Texas College in Tyler. She remained in this position until 1988. Two years later, she was appointed to the Sam A. Lindsey Chair at the University of Texas in Tyler.

In addition to her work in government, industry, and education, Granville wrote a textbook, *Theory and Application of Mathematics for Teachers,* in 1975. In 1989, Smith College awarded Granville an honorary doctorate. She was the first African American woman mathematician to be so honored by an institution of higher learning in the United States. Granville is active in many professional organizations and has served on the boards of the National Council of Teachers of Mathematics (NCTM) and the American Association of University Women (AAUW).

See also American Association of University Women (AAUW); Bernstein, Dorothy Lewis; Brill, Yvonne Claeys; Butler, Margaret K; Computers/Computer Technology; Goldstine, Adele Katz; Herzenberg, Caroline Littlejohn; Hopper, Grace Murray; Johnson, Barbara Crawford; Johnson, Katherine Coleman Goble; Mathematics; National Aeronautics and Space Administration (NASA); National Institute of Standards and Technology (NIST); Ordnance; Space Exploration

References Granville, Evelyn Boyd, "My Life as a Mathematician," *SAGE: A Scholarly Journal on Black Women,* vol. 6, no. 2 (Fall 1989); Grinstein, Louise S., and Paul J. Campbell, eds., *Women of Mathematics: A Biobibliographic Sourcebook* (1987); Hine, Darlene Clark, Elsa Barkley Brown, and Rosalyn Terborg-Penn, eds., *Black Women in America: An Historical Encyclopedia,* vol. 1: (A–L) (1993); Kenschaft, Patricia C., "Black Women in Mathematics in the United States," *American Mathematical Monthly* (October 1981); McMurray, Emily M., ed., *Notable Twentieth-Century Scientists,* vol. 2: (F–K) (1995).

Green, Arda Alden (1899–1958)

Biochemist Arda Green made substantial contributions to the study of enzymes and blood chemistry. She developed methods of isolating, crystallizing, and obtaining pure samples of proteins present in blood for use in biological and immunological studies. The technologies she developed later influenced the work of Nobel Prize–winning biochemists Severo Ochoa (RNA synthesis), Arthur Kornberg (DNA synthesis), and Gerty and Carl Cori (mechanisms involved in polysaccharide synthesis). In addition, her work provided insights into the enzyme-substrate reactions responsible for bioluminescence (the ability of a living organism to produce light) in fireflies.

Green was born in Prospect, Pennsylvania. She graduated from the University of California at Berkeley in 1921 with an A.B. in chemistry and philosophy and returned to UC–Berkeley to study medicine. In 1924, she interrupted her studies for one year to conduct research on hemoglobin (the iron-carrying compound in red blood cells) at Harvard University Medical School. She then returned to UC–Berkeley on a fellowship. In 1925, Green transferred to the medical school of Johns

Hopkins University. She received her medical degree in 1927.

After receiving her M.D., Green returned to Harvard as a National Research Council (NRC) fellow. There she continued the hemoglobin studies she had begun earlier. Green developed techniques for purifying hemoglobin (that is, obtaining samples not mixed with other substances)—techniques that later enabled Linus Pauling to describe the structure of hemoglobin. Green also developed methods for isolating angiotensin from blood. This substance helps regulate blood pressure and kidney function and maintains the body's sodium and water balance. In addition, she performed immunological studies on the prevention of measles. Green's fellowship ended in 1929, but she remained at Harvard for the next twelve years.

In 1941, Green moved to St. Louis to work as a research associate in pharmacology at Washington University. There she researched muscle proteins and developed methods of purifying and crystallizing rabbit aldolase, an enzyme that helps convert fructose (a sugar) into energy needed for muscle activity. She also developed a method for isolating the crystalline enzyme phosphorylase. This enzyme was later used by Gerty and Carl Cori in their Nobel Prize–winning research on polysaccharide synthesis. Techniques and standards Green developed for obtaining pure samples of enzymes also influenced the work of biochemists Severo Ochoa and Arthur Kornberg in their research on the synthesis of RNA and DNA, respectively.

In 1945, Green began work at the Cleveland Clinic, where she conducted research on substances present in blood serum. Her research team discovered serotonin, a substance in blood that constricts blood vessels. Serotonin has since been found to regulate many activities of the central nervous system.

Green returned to Maryland in 1953, after accepting a position at the McCollum-Pratt Institute of Johns Hopkins University. There she began studies of bioluminescence. In 1956, she discovered and crystallized luciferase—the enzyme that triggers light-production in fireflies. In

Baltimore, Green also served as a consultant biochemist to the pediatrics department of Baltimore's Sinai Hospital. She continued working until her death in 1958. That same year, the American Chemical Society (ACS) posthumously presented her the Garvan Medal for her many accomplishments in chemistry.

See also Biotechnology; Caldwell, Mary Letitia; Cori, Gerty Theresa Radnitz; Francis P. Garvan–John M. Olin Medal; Pharmacology; Medicine/Medical Technology

References "Arda A. Green: [obituary], *Chemical and Engineering News* (17 February 1958); Colowick, Sidney P., "Arda Alden Green, Protein Chemist," *Science* 128 (5 September 1958); O'Neill, Lois Decker, *The Women's Book of Records and Achievements* (1979); Shearer, Benjamin F., and Barbara S. Shearer, eds., *Notable Women in the Physical Sciences: A Biographical Dictionary* (1997).

Greene, Catherine Littlefield (1755–1814)

Eli Whitney is generally recognized as the inventor of the cotton gin; he received a patent for the device in 1794. However, some question exists about the role Catherine Littlefield Greene played in the development of this agricultural machine. Some accounts credit Greene with conceiving the idea for the cotton gin, with Whitney serving primarily as model maker. Others suggest that Whitney invented the gin, but that Greene assisted him by solving a crucial problem that led to the machine's success. Still other accounts do not recognize any involvement of Greene in the invention of the machine.

Catherine Littlefield Greene was born in Rhode Island. She later settled on a Georgia estate that was awarded to her husband, Revolutionary War hero Nathaniel Greene, following the war. In 1792, Greene met Whitney, who had been hired as a tutor for a neighboring family. However, after the tutoring job fell through, Greene suggested that Whitney, who had displayed mechanical creativity and inventiveness in the construction of an embroidery frame, remain in the area to design a machine that would remove seeds from short-staple cotton.

Whitney worked in a basement room on the Greene estate, with tools and other materials pro-

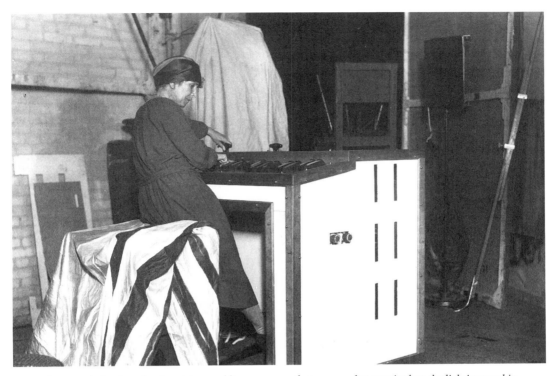

Mary Greenewalt developed a rheostat resembling an organ that was used to manipulate the lighting used in theater productions. (Bettmann/Corbis)

vided by Greene. After six months, he unveiled the cotton gin. However, when the device failed to operate as intended, Greene, it is alleged, suggested a redesign of the separating brushes. Success was thus achieved.

Greene prematurely began promoting and publicizing the machine and its design. As a result, many copies of the cotton gin appeared long before a patent for the device was issued. Although many cotton growers became wealthy through the use of the cotton gin, neither Greene nor Whitney profited from the invention. In fact, Greene went bankrupt trying to establish the rights to the cotton gin, which culminated in the issuance of the 1794 patent to Eli Whitney.

See also Agricultural Engineering; Baldwin, Anna; Industrial Engineering; Invention/Inventors; Patent
References James, Edward T., Janet Wilson James, and Paul S. Boyers, eds., *Notable American Women: A Biographical Dictionary (1607–1950)*, vol. 2: (G–O) (1971); Macdonald, Anne L., *Feminine Ingenuity: How Women Inventors Changed America* (1992); Ogilvie,

Marilyn, *Women in Science Antiquity through the Nineteenth Century: A Biographical Dictionary with Annotated Bibliography* (1986); Stanley, Autumn, *Mothers and Daughters of Invention: Notes for a Revised History of Technology* (1993); Vare, Ethlie Ann, and Greg Ptacek, *Mothers of Invention: From the Bra to the Bomb, Forgotten Women and Their Unforgettable Ideas* (1988).

Greenewalt, Mary E. H. (1871–?)

Artist and inventor Mary E. H. Greenewalt changed the way people experience theatrical productions when she developed an invention that combined mathematics, light, and color to enhance the visual effectiveness of drama. To achieve the desired effects, Greenewalt invented and patented a rheostat, a device similar to a household light dimmer, capable of altering the color and intensity of light produced by incandescent bulbs at any given moment during a production. The rheostat, with its series of switches, resembled a piano keyboard. Greenewalt lectured on her theories of color, light, pulse, and rhythm and wrote articles on the subject. In 1916, she described her invention before a national convention of the Illuminating Engineering Society of North America.

Greenewalt was born in Beirut, Syria, where her father served as U.S. consulate. In 1893, she won a gold medal for a piano performance at the Philadelphia Musical Academy, where she studied. She then toured as a soloist with the Pittsburgh and Philadelphia symphony orchestras and also gave private recitals. Between 1919 and 1920, she also recorded several of Chopin's works for Columbia Records.

See also Illuminating Engineering Society of North America (IESNA); Patent
References Vare, Ethlie Ann, and Greg Ptacek, *Mothers of Invention: From the Bra to the Bomb, Forgotten Women and Their Unforgettable Ideas* (1988).

Greneker, Lillian (1895–1990)

Businesswoman and inventor Lillian Greneker made an important contribution to the U.S. Navy at the start of World War II with her development of the "Pullcord," a means for removing the inner mold around which a vulcanized rubber object had been formed, without damaging the rubber. This development came about some time after the Navy hired the U.S. Rubber Company to construct rubber fuel tanks for their submarines and fighter planes. Engineers at U.S. Rubber at first tried to construct the tanks by covering a wooden mold with sheets of vulcanized rubber that were secured in place with glue. However, when the rubber hardened into its desired shape, the engineers could not figure out how to remove the inner wooden mold while keeping the rubber intact. The engineers thought a paper mold might be the solution to their problem, so they decided to call upon Lillian Greneker, an inventor who had also become well known for her knowledge of paper.

Lillian Greneker owned and operated the Greneker Corporation, a mannequin manufacturing company, in Pleasantville, New York. When she was contacted by representatives from the

U.S. Rubber Company, Greneker suggested that they use plaster rather than wood or paper as the mold substance. However, company engineers who had already considered plaster as a substitute mold medium dismissed this idea and told Greneker the substance was unsuitable for the mold because it presented the same problems as the wood—it could not be removed once the rubber hardened around it. Refusing to give up on her idea so easily, Greneker enlisted assistance from a plaster birdbath maker and conducted her own experiments using the hollow appendages of mannequins she had in her shop as a model for the rubber coating.

Greneker and her assistant decided to fill one of the mannequin appendages with plaster. Greneker then inserted a rope into the liquid plaster in a coiling fashion and left a length of rope extending beyond the top of the mannequin form. She then waited for the plaster to harden inside the form. Once hardened, Greneker and her assistant pulled on the rope. This action caused the plaster inside the form to break into small pieces. The pieces were then removed through an opening that had been left in the form. Greneker's experiment was a success.

Greneker took her idea back to the U.S. Rubber Company and demonstrated the process. To the amazement of the company's engineers, it worked perfectly. In addition to receiving the thanks of the company for solving their problem, the Greneker Corporation also was awarded a contract to help the U.S. Rubber Company manufacture the fuel tanks. Greneker employees worked around the clock on the project, producing five fuel tanks each day. While manufacturing the fuel tanks, Greneker continued to devise methods for improving her idea and applying it to other products. This led to her receipt of three different patents on the invention, which she called a "destructible form." Between the years of 1937 and 1945, Greneker, who had always been a prolific inventor, was issued a total of fifteen patents.

One of the inventions for which she received a patent was for an unusual apparatus she called Fingertips. Fingertips were small covers that fit over the ends of the fingers, to which different

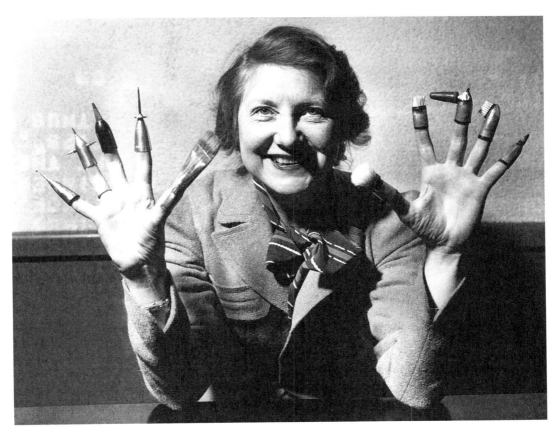

Lillian Greneker demonstrates her "fingertips," miniaturized tools that fit over the tips of the fingers. (Bettmann/ Corbis)

tools, such as a screwdriver or a paintbrush, had been attached. The devices were intended to help people do work that made use of such tools more easily. Although Greneker never profited from the Fingertips idea, she believed in the product and kept improving on her invention. As a result of her improvements, she was issued a second patent for the tools in 1980, at the age of 85.

See also Bradberry, Henrietta M.; Kenner, (Mary) Beatrice Davidson; Knight, Margaret E.; Ordnance

References Cook, Joan, "L. L. Greneker, 95: Made Mannequins with Movable Parts" [obituary], *New York Times* (6 February 1990); Macdonald, Anne L., *Feminine Ingenuity: How Women Inventors Changed America* (1992); Showell, Ellen H., and Fred M. B. Amram, *From Indian Corn to Outer Space: Women Invent in America* (1995).

Griffin, Bessie J.
See **Blount (Griffin), Bessie J.**

Hahn, Dorothy Anna (1876–1950)

Dorothy Hahn and Emma Carr were the first Americans to use ultraviolet (UV) spectroscopy to determine the structure of organic molecules. Working together at Mount Holyoke College, Dorothy Hahn prepared and purified organic compounds for study; Carr later analyzed these compounds. In addition, Hahn discovered that hydantoins—organic compounds similar to vitamin B-1—have a ring structure. She also was the first to describe in English the role of electrons in chemical valence, a task accomplished one year before Nobel laureates Gilbert Lewis and Irving Langmuir put their valence theories into print.

Hahn was born in Philadelphia, Pennsylvania. She entered Bryn Mawr College in 1895 and received her A.B. degree in chemistry and biology in 1899. Hahn then worked as a professor of chemistry and biology at the Pennsylvania College for Women (later Chatham College) in Pittsburgh, where she remained until 1906. She also served as professor of biology at Kindergarten College in Pittsburgh from 1904 to 1906. From 1906 to 1907 Hahn began graduate work in organic chemistry at the University of Leipzig in Germany. She then returned to Bryn Mawr for an additional year of study.

In 1908, Hahn was invited to join the staff at Mount Holyoke College as an instructor of organic chemistry. She advanced to associate professor by 1914 and in 1915 left Mount Holyoke to pursue a doctorate at Yale University on a fellowship from the American Association of University Women (AAUW). She was awarded a Ph.D. in 1916. She then returned to Mount Holyoke as a full professor of organic chemistry, where she remained until her retirement in 1941. Between 1917 and 1918, Hahn also did industrial research with coal tar products at the Barnett Company.

Hahn published many articles in the *Journal of the American Chemical Society*. She coauthored *Theories of Organic Chemistry* and contributed much of the research for *A Dictionary of Chemical Solubilities: Inorganic*. Hahn did much to foster scientific education among the women attending Mount Holyoke. Her former students established the Dorothy Hahn Memorial Fund in

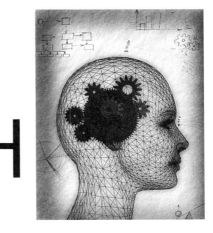

her honor to furnish a seminar room located in the chemistry building at Mount Holyoke.

> **See also** American Association of University Women (AAUW); Carr, Emma Perry; Sherrill, Mary Lura; Spectroscopy
>
> **References** James, Edward T., Janet Wilson James, and Paul S. Boyer, eds., *Notable American Women: A Biographical Dictionary (1607–1950),* vol. 2: (G–O) (1971); Miles, Wyndham D., ed., *American Chemists and Chemical Engineers* (1976); Shearer, Benjamin F., and Barbara S. Shearer, eds., *Notable Women in the Physical Sciences: A Biographical Dictionary* (1997).

Hall, Julia Brainerd (1858–1925)

When Charles Martin Hall was issued patents in 1889 for developing the electrolytic process for manufacturing aluminum, his older sister Julia Brainerd Hall should have been cited as coinventor. Julia assisted Charles in the experiments that led to the invention, helped design the laboratory in which Charles worked, and maintained accurate records of all documents associated with the process. Julia Hall was also instrumental in the campaign to produce and market aluminum—a campaign that led to the founding of the Pittsburgh Reduction Company (later known as the Aluminum Company of America, or Alcoa).

Julia Hall was born in the British West Indies. At the time of Julia's birth, her parents were missionaries. Later the family returned to the United States, to Ohio, to raise their children. Each of the children later attended and graduated from

Oberlin College. At Oberlin, both Julia and Charles took courses in chemistry, geology, and mathematics. By the time of their graduations, Julia had more science credits than her brother; however, as was the school's custom, she was awarded a diploma in the "literary course for ladies" (1881), while he was awarded a bachelor's degree in science (1885).

After college, Julia became caretaker for her younger siblings and ailing mother. She also spent much time working with Charles in his laboratory, which was on the family's property. She advised him about materials and procedures to use in his work. She helped Charles make his own batteries. She recorded each step of the inventive process, including the dates and technical details, and kept records of all Charles's correspondence. Julia also aided Charles in finding financial backing for the project.

In July 1886, Julia encouraged Charles to patent his process. However, a French inventor named Heroult had filed a patent application seeking rights to the same process in May of the same year. (Heroult already had a patent for the process in France.) The dual applications culminated in a patent interference case between Charles Hall and Heroult.

Using the notes she had taken while assisting Charles with his experiments, Julia Hall developed a six-page document titled "History of C. M. Hall's Aluminum Invention." This document, along with eyewitness testimony about the development of the process, helped Charles win the case and obtain his patents. Following this legal battle, Julia helped Charles establish the Pittsburgh Reduction Company. Both Halls received annual incomes from stocks in the company; however, by the time of his death in 1914, Charles's yearly income was $170,000, while Julia's was a mere $8,000. Although Julia Hall received some financial remuneration, she never received adequate recognition for her contributions to the development or the success of the process.

See also Metals and Metallurgy; Patent
References Kass-Simon, G., and Patricia Farnes, eds., *Women of Science: Righting the Record* (1990);

Vare, Ethlie Ann, and Greg Ptacek, *Mothers of Invention: From the Bra to the Bomb, Forgotten Women and Their Unforgettable Ideas* (1988).

Hamilton, Alice (1869–1970)

Alice Hamilton was a physician, pathologist, and bacteriologist. Her technical contributions stem from her pioneering research on health hazards linked to certain types of employment—particularly hazards facing workers in the mining, paint, dye-making, explosives, rayon, and rubber industries. By identifying the toxic substances in factories and mines, Hamilton helped build awareness of the health hazards faced by many workers. Her findings led to the passage of workers' compensation laws and legislation requiring the improvement of hazardous working conditions.

Alice Hamilton was born in New York City and grew up in Fort Wayne, Indiana, where she and her sisters were home schooled. In 1893, she received her medical degree from the University of Michigan at Ann Arbor. While completing internships at the Hospital for Women and Children in Minneapolis and the New England Hospital for Women and Children near Boston, Hamilton became interested in bacteriology. To increase her knowledge in this area, she took courses in bacteriology and pathology at the universities of Leipzig and Munich in Germany. She returned to the United States in 1896 and continued her studies at Johns Hopkins University in Baltimore.

In 1897, Hamilton accepted the position of professor of pathology at the Women's Medical School of Northwestern University in Chicago. When the school closed two years later, she studied briefly at the Pasteur Institute in Paris before accepting another teaching position as professor of pathology at the Memorial Institute for Infectious Diseases in Chicago, in 1902. At this time, Chicago was plagued by a typhoid fever epidemic. Through investigation and research, Hamilton showed a connection between improper sewage disposal in the city and the spread of typhoid by flies, a discovery that prompted the city's health department to undertake the appropriate measures to combat the epidemic.

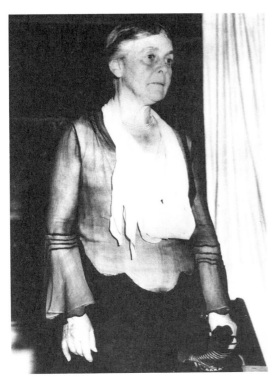

Alice Hamilton conducted groundbreaking research into health hazards present in the workplace in the late 1870s. (Corbis/Bettmann-UPI)

While in Chicago, Hamilton met Jane Addams, a woman dedicated to social reform (for which Addams became the first woman to win the Nobel Peace Prize, in 1931). Addams invited Hamilton to stay at Hull House, a settlement house cofounded by Addams in 1889 to help Chicago's poor. Hamilton called Hull House home until 1919, and while there, started medical education classes and formed the first well-baby clinic. At the same time, becoming familiar with the living conditions of the people she served, Hamilton also became aware of the unhealthy and unsafe work environments faced by many in the factories and mines.

In 1910, Hamilton became director of the Occupational Disease Commission, a new department created by the governor of Illinois. It was the first such commission in the United States. The investigations and recommendations of this commission resulted in workmen's compensa-

tion laws being passed in Illinois. For the first time, workers would receive compensation for job-related health impairment or injuries. In 1911, the U.S. commissioner of labor invited Hamilton to accept a similar position within the Department of Commerce. She served in this unsalaried post from 1911 to 1921, investigating the potential health hazards associated with exposure to lead, arsenic, mercury, radium, and organic solvents.

Hamilton became well known for her research of occupational illnesses. In 1919, she was invited to join the faculty of the Harvard University Medical School, as an assistant professor in the new field of industrial medicine. She became the first woman faculty member at the school. Hamilton remained in this position on a part-time basis until her retirement in 1935, when she was made assistant professor emerita of the Harvard Medical School.

In addition to her work to improve health conditions in industry, Hamilton, along with Jane Addams and others, was involved in the world peace movement. She traveled throughout the United States and Europe, encouraging an end to wars. From 1924 to 1930, she served on the League of Nations Health Committee. Later, she published the books *Industrial Poisons in the United States* (1925) and *Industrial Toxicology* (1934). Her extensive research into the effects of toxins focused national attention on tetraethyl lead (leaded gasoline) in 1925 and on radium in 1928. After retiring from Harvard, Hamilton served as a consultant to the U.S. Labor Department (Division of Labor Standards). In 1943, she published her autobiography, *Exploring the Dangerous Trades*.

Alice Hamilton belonged to several professional and social organizations. Among them were the American Association for the Advancement of Science (AAAS), the National Women's Trade League, the American Association of University Women (AAUW), and the National Consumers League, of which she served as president from 1944 to 1949. For her work, she was granted honorary degrees by many of the nation's leading colleges and universities, including Mount

Holyoke, Smith, Tulane, and the universities of Rochester and Michigan. Hamilton also received other honors and awards: In 1947, she became the first woman to receive the Lasker Award—considered the most prestigious award in the field of public health—from the U.S. Public Health Association, for her work in occupational disease prevention. In addition, for her work both in medicine and as a social reformer, Hamilton was inducted into the National Women's Hall of Fame in 1973.

> **See also** American Association of University Women (AAUW); Anderson, Elda Emma; Baker, Sara Josephine; Environmental Engineering; National Women's Hall of Fame; Safety Engineering; Textiles; Walton, Mary
> **References** Bailey, Martha J., *American Women in Science: A Biographical Dictionary* (1994); Edmonson, Catherine M., *365 Women Who Made a Difference* (1996); Kass-Simon, G., and Patricia Farnes, eds., *Women of Science: Righting the Record* (1990); McMurray, Emily M., ed., *Notable Twentieth-Century Scientists,* vol. 2: (F–K) (1995); Rothe, Anna, ed., *Current Biography, 1946* (1947); Yount, Lisa, *Twentieth-Century Women Scientists* (1996); Bois, Danuta, "Distinguished Women of Past and Present: Alice Hamilton," available at http://www.netsrq.com/~dbois/hamilton-a.html (cited 7 June 1998).

Handler, Ruth (1917–?)

The inventions of Ruth Handler have impacted the lives of countless young girls as well as mature women. Handler is the creator of what may be the world's most well known doll—Barbie®. Handler conceived the idea for Barbie in 1956. Nineteen years later, she developed and began marketing her second invention—a prosthetic breast for use by women who had lost a breast to cancer. The Nearly Me® artificial breast became the first realistic prosthetic available to breast cancer survivors.

After graduating from high school, Ruth attended the University of Denver and married her high school sweetheart, Elliot Handler. Later the Handlers moved to California, where Ruth took courses in business education at the University of California at Los Angeles (UCLA). From 1937 to 1941, Ruth worked for Paramount Studios in Los Angeles. She left this job when she became pregnant with her daughter and spent the next three

Ruth Handler invented both the Barbie® doll and a prosthetic breast for use following a mastectomy. (Corbis-Bettmann)

years at home, during which time she also had her son Ken.

In 1944, Elliot Handler and Harold "Matt" Matson started a new business called Mattel®. Initially the company produced and sold picture frames made from lucite; however, a ban on the use of plastics during World War II led the pair to begin making their products from wood. In addition to picture frames, the Mattel Company, of which Ruth had become an integral part, began making wood furniture for doll houses, and later, a variety of children's toys.

In 1956, while observing her daughter playing with paper dolls, Ruth developed the idea for what would come to be known as the Barbie doll. Although people were skeptical about the need for a doll with grownup features, by 1959 Barbie® made her debut and was ready for mass production. The doll (and its accessories) boosted company sales by $500 million in its first ten years. (It continues to be a sales success today.) During the same period, Ruth moved up the corporate ladder to become cochair of the company's board of directors.

In 1970, Ruth was diagnosed with breast cancer and had to have her left breast removed. The psychological trauma she suffered as a result of this loss and other factors led her to resign her position with Mattel®. To try to regain some of her feelings of femininity, she began seeking a prosthetic to be worn in place of her missing breast. However, she found those available unsatisfactory. To solve the problem, she contacted a prosthetic designer named Peyton Massey and asked him to create a prosthesis as she believed it should be made.

Ruth Handler and Peyton Massey began working together. Soon Handler had hired a small staff that included chemists, engineers, and physicians. The results of this collaboration led to Nearly Me® prosthetic breasts—the first such creations to be produced in definite right and left versions, to have the structure and shape of real breasts, and to be adaptable to wear with a regular brassiere. The prosthesis was made from a silicone gel covered by polyurethane.

Nearly Me® quickly expanded, and a factory was set up in West Los Angeles. The company manufactured prosthetics (left and right) in 30 sizes. It also began making swimsuits and other products for women who had had mastectomies. To aid in fitting its customers, Ruth hired women who had had a mastectomy and thus were aware of the needs and concerns of potential customers. She oversaw all aspects of the company until 1991, when she sold it to a subsidiary of the Kimberly Clark Corporation and retired to her beach home in California.

For her achievements as a businesswoman and inventor, Ruth Handler has received several awards and honors. She was presented the Outstanding Business Woman Award by the National Association of Accountants in 1961. In 1968, the *Los Angeles Times* named her its Woman of the Year in Business. Four years later, she was presented the Brotherhood Award of the National Conference of Christians and Jews.

See also Blount (Griffin), Bessie J.; Donovan, Marion; Henry, Beulah L.
References Macdonald, Anne L., *Feminine Ingenuity: How Women Inventors Changed America* (1992); Stanley, Autumn, *Mothers and Daughters of Invention: Notes for a Revised History of Technology* (1993), Vare, Ethlie Ann, and Greg Ptacek, *Women Inventors and Their Discoveries*, with a Foreword by Ruth Handler (1993).

Harmon, Elise F. (1909–1985)

Elise F. Harmon might be considered a World War II hero for her development of improved brushes for aircraft generators that did not disintegrate when the aircraft flew at altitudes greater than 15,000 feet. Harmon was a pioneer in the development and miniaturization of printed circuitry—an innovation that led to advances in missiles, space exploration, and computer research. In 1953, while working for Aerovox Corporation, she received a patent for a process of constructing a printed circuit by using a hot die stamp to infuse silver conductors onto polymerized substances. Three years later, she was honored with the Achievement Award of the Society of Women Engineers (SWE) for her innovations with printed circuits.

Elise Harmon was born and raised in Texas. She graduated with a B.S. degree in 1931 from North Texas State Teachers' College and then began a teaching career, while taking graduate summer courses at the University of Texas at Austin from 1933 through 1940. She later took graduate courses in engineering at George Washington University and chemistry courses at the University of Maryland. From 1938 to 1942, Harmon worked as a chemist for Standard Oil Company. She then worked for the Army Ordnance Center in St. Louis, Missouri, in 1942. It was here that she became interested in engineering.

In 1945, Harmon worked at the Aircraft and Electrical Division of the Naval Research Laboratory, where she tested the chemical properties of electrical equipment. Three years later, while working at the Ordnance Division of the National

Bureau of Standards (now the National Institute of Standards and Technology), she became interested in printed circuits. For the next 20 years, Harmon served as senior engineer in charge of computer development at American Bosch Arma Corporation and as a staff chief engineer and senior technical specialist at Autonetics in Anaheim, California. She left this last position in 1969 to start her own company. Harmon holds many patents, including one for stretching fabric and another for an injection-printing machine. She is also a member of the American Chemical Society (ACS), the Texas Academy of Sciences, and the Institute of Radio Engineers.

See also Aeronautical and Aerospace Engineering; Computers/Computer Technology; Electrical and Electronics Engineering; Ordnance; Textiles
References McMurray, Emily M., ed., *Notable Twentieth-Century Scientists,* vol. 2 (F–K) (1995); Stanley, Autumn, *Mothers and Daughters of Invention: Notes for a Revised History of Technology* (1993); Society of Women Engineers, "Elise F. Harmon," available at http://www. swe.org/SWE/Awards/achieve3.htm (cited 19 January 2000).

Hayden, Sophia Gregoria (1868–1953)

Sophia Hayden is the architect whose impeccable designs and watercolor renderings of buildings earned her first prize in the competition for the design of the Woman's Building that was to be constructed as one of the main attractions at the Columbian Exposition held in Chicago in 1893. Hayden also holds the distinctions of being the first woman admitted into the architectural program at the Massachusetts Institute of Technology (MIT) and the first woman to graduate from this program.

Sophia Hayden was born in Santiago, Chile, in 1868, to a South American mother and a North American father. When she was six years old, Sophia was sent by her parents to live with her paternal grandparents in the Jamaica Plain section of Boston. There Sophia attended public schools, eventually graduating from West Roxbury High School in 1886. In the fall of that same year, she became the first woman to be admitted

into the architectural program at MIT. She received her bachelor of architecture degree with honors in 1890. After her graduation, Hayden's gender impeded her ability to find employment as an architect. Unable to practice her craft, she instead accepted a position as a teacher of mechanical drawing at a high school in Boston.

By 1891, plans were already under way for the World's Columbian Exposition—the second world's fair to be held in the United States. (The first, the Centennial Exposition, was held in Philadelphia seventeen years earlier.) The Columbian Exposition slated to be held in Chicago's Jackson Park in 1893 had two goals: to celebrate the four hundredth anniversary of Columbus's discovery of America and to showcase the cultural and technological achievements of the United States. To prepare for the Columbian Exposition, the Board of Lady Managers, a group of women whose responsibility it was to develop plans for the design and construction of the Woman's Building (a pavilion dedicated to the achievements of women) and to arrange for the exhibits to be showcased there, extended an invitation in 1891 to women architects to submit designs for the structure. Sophia Hayden entered the competition with a design she had based on the architectural style of the Italian Renaissance. Of the thirteen submissions received by the Board of Lady Managers, Hayden's entry was selected as the winning design, an achievement for which she received about $1,000. This amount represented significantly less (one-third to one-tenth) than the sum awarded to male architects whose building designs had been selected for construction at the Exposition.

Construction of the Woman's Building was completed in 1892. Throughout the period of the building's construction, the Board of Lady Managers continuously pressured Hayden to incorporate the materials and designs of other women artists into her design, even when these designs and materials did not fit the overall scheme of the building. In addition, Hayden often was subjected to verbal abuse and innuendo from male architects working on other structures in the fairgrounds. In spite of all this adversity, Hayden was ultimately awarded a gold medal for her work by Daniel Burnham, the chief of construction at the Exposition. She also received a gold medal from the Board of Lady Managers.

The design and construction of the Woman's Building became the highlight of Hayden's career. It was the only building she designed that was ever actually constructed. Ironically, her building, like most of the others constructed for the fair, was torn down at the conclusion of the Exposition. In 1894, Hayden submitted completed plans for a memorial building dedicated to the work of women; however, construction of this building never came to fruition. In 1901, Hayden married artist William Blackstone Bennet and retired from architecture. She spent the remainder of her life in Winthrop, Massachusetts, until her death from a stroke in 1953.

> **See also** Architecture; Barney, Nora Stanton Blatch; Bethune, Louise Blanchard; Columbian Exposition; Lin, Maya; Loftness, Vivian; Morgan, Julia
> **References** Ashby, Ruth, and Deborah Gore Ohrn, eds., *Herstory: Women Who Changed the World* (1995); Badger, Reid, *The Great American Fair* (1979); Heinemann, Susan, *The New York Public Library Amazing Women in American History: A Book of Answers for Kids* (1998); Wiemann, Jeanne Madeline, *The Fair Women: The Story of the Woman's Building, World's Columbian Exposition, 1893* (1981); Massachusetts Institute of Technology, "Sophia Hayden Bennett," available at http://w3.mit.edu/museum/chicago/bennett.html (cited 30 June 1999).

Hazen, Elizabeth Lee (1885–1975)

In 1948, microbiologist Elizabeth Hazen and biochemist Rachel Brown began a long-distance collaboration to find an antibiotic for the treatment of fungal infections in humans. Months later, the pair discovered the world's first successful antifungal medication. Hazen and Brown named the drug nystatin, in honor of the *New York State* Department of Health, which employed them both. Nystatin earned Hazen and Brown worldwide notoriety. After this success, the women continued working together to find new medicines derived from microorganisms. Their ongoing collaboration resulted in the discovery of two more antibiotics—phalamycin and capacidin.

Elizabeth Hazen was born in rural Mississippi. She was raised by relatives, following the death of her parents when she was three. After completing secondary school, Hazen enrolled at the Mississippi University for Women. She graduated in 1910 with a bachelor's degree in science. For the next seven years, Hazen worked as a teacher while she pursued a master's degree in science at Columbia University. She received this degree in 1917.

Around the time she received her master's degree, the United States became involved in World War I. Hazen obtained work as a diagnostic laboratory technician studying human fungal infections for the U.S. Army. When the war ended, Hazen became one of the first women doctoral candidates at Columbia University; she also worked in Columbia's research laboratories. She received her Ph.D. in microbiology in 1927, at the age of 42.

For the next few years, Hazen taught at the College of Physicans and Surgeons in New York. In 1931, she then took a research position with the New York State Department of Health. Seventeen years later, Hazen, who worked in New York City, began her collaboration with Rachel Brown, who worked at the department's laboratories in Albany, in a search for an antibiotic substance that could be successfully used to treat fungal infections. Based on the studies Hazen made of fungal infections during the war, the pair focused their research on soil bacteria. Soon after the collaboration began, Hazen sent Brown soil samples from a farm in Virginia that contained bacteria known as *Streptomyces noursei*. Brown isolated two antibiotics from this bacterium, one of which proved effective in treating fungal infections in mice. Hazen and Brown reported their findings to the National Academy of Sciences (NAS) in 1950. Following further tests, they applied to the U.S. Food and Drug Administration (FDA) for approval of nystatin. The drug was approved in 1954.

After receiving FDA approval of nystatin, Hazen and Brown contacted the nonprofit group known as the Research Corporation for help in obtaining a patent for their medication. The patent was issued in 1957. Hazen and Brown then licensed the rights to produce nystatin to the pharmaceutical company E. R. Squibb and Sons, in return for a royalty on sales.

Hazen and Brown arranged for royalties to go to a new fund for medical research, which they established under the administration of the Research Corporation. The profits that accumulated in the Brown-Hazen Fund from sales of nystatin were substantial: during their lifetimes, totaling more than $13 million.

Hazen remained with the New York State Department of Health until 1960. During her last two years there, she also worked as an associate professor at Albany State College. After her retirement from the Department of Health, she worked as guest investigator in the Mycology Laboratories of Columbia University in New York City. She remained with the school until 1973.

For her achievements in science and technology, Elizabeth Hazen received many awards. In 1955, the same year she coauthored the book *Laboratory Identification of Pathogenic Fungi Simplified,* Hazen shared the Squibb Award in Chemotherapy with Rachel Brown. In 1968, the New York State Health Department granted Hazen its Distinguished Service Award. In 1975, a few months before Hazen's death, she and Brown together became the first women to receive the Chemical Pioneer Award of the American Institute of Chemists (AIC). The pair was also granted the Sara Benham Award of the Mycological Society of America. More recently, in 1994, Hazen and Brown became only the second and third women to be inducted into the National Inventors' Hall of Fame.

See also Alexander, Hattie Elizabeth; Antibiotics; Brown, Rachel Fuller; Chemical Pioneer Award; Dick, Gladys Rowena Henry; Eldering, Grace; Elion, Gertrude Belle; Hollinshead, Ariel; Kendrick, Pearl Luella; National Inventors' Hall of Fame; Pearce, Louise; Pharmacology

References Bailey, Martha J., *American Women in Science: A Biographical Dictionary* (1994); Muir, Hazel, *Larousse Dictionary of Scientists* (1994); Stanley, Autumn, *Mothers and Daughters of Invention: Notes for a Revised History of Technology* (1993); Lemelson-MIT Program, "Elizabeth Lee Hazen and Rachel Fuller Brown: The Antifungal Drug Nystatin," in Invention Dimension's Inventor of the Week archives, available at http://web.mit.edu/invent/www/inventorsA-H/HazenBrown.html (cited 5 May 1988).

Henry, Beulah L. (1887–?)

Beulah Henry was one of the most prolific women inventors of the first half of the twentieth century. She earned her first patent, for an ice cream freezer, in 1912. Over the next 58 years, she received at least 48 additional patents, in four different countries. She is believed to have developed more than 100 different inventions in such diverse areas as fashion, domestic appliances, business machines, children's toys, and personal hygiene. Because of the quantity and diversity of her inventions, Henry often was called "Lady Edison."

Beulah Henry was born in Raleigh, North Carolina, in 1887 and was a descendant of American patriot Patrick Henry. Little is known of her early life. It is known that beginning in 1909, she for a time attended the Presbyterian College (which later became Queens College) and Elizabeth College, both in Charlotte, North Carolina. It also is known that Henry never married and spent much of her adult life living in various hotels in New York City.

Henry was awarded her first patent in 1912. The following year, she received her second and third patents, for a handbag and parasol, both with detachable snap-on covers in various colors. At the time these three patents were issued, Henry's patent applications indicated that she still resided in Charlotte, the city where she attended college.

Henry did not apply for her next patent, for a spring-limbed doll, until 1922. By the time a patent was issued for this doll in 1925, Henry was living in New York City, where a second patent for her parasol had been issued to the Henry Umbrella and Parasol Company of New York City, a company of which Henry was president. Henry's parasol was featured in the windows of Lord and Taylor's department stores and, by some accounts, earned her at least $50,000. Henry continued to work as an inventor through the 1920s. Her success is evidenced by the fact that by 1929, she had founded and was serving as president of a second company, the B. L. Henry Company of New York.

In 1929, Henry received a patent for a doll-shaped sponge for use by children while bathing.

Beulah Henry, one of the most prolific women inventors, is shown here with her Miss Illusion doll. (Corbis-Bettmann)

The sponges, called Dolly Dips, held a bar of soap inside, secured by a snap. An adult version of the sponge, called the Latho, also was developed by Henry. In addition to the sponges, Henry is reported to have also developed the machine that made production of the sponges possible.

In the 1930s, many of the patents issued to Henry were related to machines—specifically sewing machines and typewriters. Among these were a 1930 patent for an invention called the protograph, which allowed a typist to make an original and four copies of a document without the use of carbon paper. Other patents received by Henry during this period were for a double-chain-stitch sewing machine (1936) and a feeding and aligning device for typewriters. In addition, Henry received a patent in 1935 for a doll called Miss Illusion, whose eyes could open and close and could be changed in color from brown to blue with the push of a button.

During the 1940s, most of the patents issued to Henry again dealt with inventions related to sewing machines and typewriters. Many of these inventions were developed for companies that had hired Henry to create products for them. In the 1950s, Henry again developed several products for children. These included a toy cow that actually dispensed milk (1951) and a toy animal with moving mouth parts that simulated eating (1953). In addition, she invented and was issued patents for continuously attached envelopes (1952), a can opener (1956), and a method for forming a lock stitch (1959). In 1962, Henry obtained two patents: one for direct and return mail envelopes, and a second for a baster oven.

The patents issued for many of Henry's inventions were issued in her own name or in the names of one of her two companies. It is likely that many other inventions created by Henry were issued to companies that had hired her to develop products for them. In either case, Henry, unlike many other early women inventors, profited from her inventions and was able to support herself with the income they generated. Henry also devoted time to activities such as painting watercolors and writing. She held memberships in the Museum of Natural History, the Audubon Society, and the League for Animals.

See also Averell, Georgene Hopf; Baldwin, Anna; Blanchard, Helen Augusta; Blount (Griffin), Bessie J.; Columbian Exposition; Domestic Appliances; Donovan, Marion; Gilbreth, Lillian Moller; Graham, Bette Nesmith; Handler, Ruth; Johnson, Nancy M.; Kenner, (Mary) Beatrice Davidson; Knight, Margaret E.; S., Mary

References Fowler, Elizabeth M., "Beulah Louise Henry Has Been Called 'Lady Edison,'" *New York Times* (27 January 1962); Jones, Stacy V., "Inventive Woman Patents 2-Way Envelope: A Single Unit Serves for Mailing and Also Returning," *New York Times* (27 January 1962); Macdonald, Anne L., *Feminine Ingenuity: How Women Inventors Changed America* (1992); Stanley, Autumn, *Mothers and Daughters of Invention: Notes for a Revised History of Technology* (1993); Lemelson-MIT Program, "Prolific Female Inventors of the Industrial Era," in Invention Dimension's Inventor of the Week archives, available at http://web.mit.edu/invent/www/inventorsR-Z/whm2.html (cited 19 May 1999).

Herzenberg, Caroline Littlejohn (b. 1932)

Caroline Herzenberg is best known for her work in fluids engineering and space physics and her writings on women's contributions to science. Herzenberg used Mössbauer spectrometry—a technology based on gamma ray absorption and emission—to determine the composition of lunar soil and rock samples obtained by the crew of *Apollo 11*. Herzenberg also developed analytic instruments for studying fossil fuels, particularly coal. In addition to her technological achievements, Herzenberg authored the best-selling book *Women Scientists from Antiquity to the Present,* a text that details the history of women in science.

Caroline Herzenberg was born in East Orange, New Jersey, and grew up in Oklahoma City. Using scholarship money she received through a Westinghouse Science Talent Search award during her senior year of high school, Herzenberg was able to attend the Massachusetts Institute of Technology (MIT). In 1953, she graduated with a B.S. degree in physics from MIT. She then went to the University of Chicago, where she received both her M.S. (1955) and her Ph.D. (1958) in physics.

Herzenberg began her career as a research associate at the Enrico Fermi Institute for Nuclear Studies at the University of Chicago. She next worked at the Argonne National Laboratory in Illinois, where she studied the Mössbauer effect. In 1961, she was appointed assistant professor of physics at the Illinois Institute of Technology (IIT); she remained there for the next six years, doing research that used Mössbauer spectrometry to analyze rocks and minerals. In 1970, she was appointed senior physicist. For the next several years, Herzenberg served as a visiting associate professor of physics at the University of Illinois Medical Center in Chicago and as a lecturer at California State University. She returned to the Argonne Laboratory in 1977.

In 1989, Herzenberg became the first woman scientist elected to the Chicago Women's Hall of Fame, and a fellow of the American Physical Society (APS). The next year, she became a fellow of the American Association for the Advancement of Science (AAAS). Herzenberg is also active in Sigma Xi, the Federation of American Scientists, and the Association for Women in Science (AWIS), serving as president of the last from 1988 to 1989. In 1996, she was named a fellow of the AWIS.

See also Argonne National Laboratory; Brill, Yvonne Claeys; Gardner, Julia Anna; Good, Mary Lowe; National Aeronautics and Space Administration (NASA); Space Exploration; Spectroscopy

References Grinstein, Louise S., Rose K. Rose, and Miriam H. Rafailovich, eds., *Women in Chemistry and Physics: A Biobibliographic Sourcebook* (1993); McMurray, Emily M., ed., *Notable Twentieth-Century Scientists,* vol. 2: (F–K) (1995); Muir, Hazel, ed., *Larousse Dictionary of Scientists* (1994); Herzenberg, Caroline L., "Welcome to My Web Site!," at http://enter-act.com/~cherzenb (cited 22 October 1998); "Herzenberg, Caroline Stuart Littlejohn," in *Contributions of 20th Century Women to Physics,* available at http://www.physics.ucla.edu/~cwp (cited 22 October 1998).

Hibbard, Susan (n.d.)

In 1876, U.S. Patent No. 177,939 was issued to Susan Hibbard for a feather duster created from the wing and tail feathers of turkeys. The technological importance of Hibbard's invention is relatively little, but the events that surrounded her recognition as this creation's inventor are significant. Susan Hibbard's husband, George, applied for a patent for the feather duster. However, during the patent application process, the creation of the invention was challenged by a third party, resulting in a patent interference suit. To clarify who had actually developed the feather duster, George Hibbard was called before the patent examiners to testify about his role in the creation of the product. During this investigation, George Hibbard revealed to the examiners that the "idea" for the feather duster did not originate with him but rather with his wife, Susan. As the inquiry continued, records kept by Susan regarding the various attempts she had made to develop a working feather duster provided sufficient evidence to the examiners that she had in fact created the feather duster, and had done so earlier than the individual who had initiated the interference suit. The patent examiners thus approved and issued a patent for the invention in Susan Hibbard's name.

> **See also** Boone, Sarah; Domestic Appliances; Kies, Mary; Mangin, Anna; Masters, Sybilla Righton; Patent
> **References** Macdonald, Anne L., *Feminine Ingenuity: How Women Inventors Changed America* (1992); WGBH, "The American Experience: Forgotten Inventors," in PBS Online, available at http://www.pbs.org/wgbh/pages/amex/technology/forgotteninv.html (cited 9 June 1999).

Hicks, Beatrice Alice (1919–1979)

Beatrice Hicks is noted for her contributions to engineering and aerospace technology, particularly the design of environmental sensors used in airplanes, rockets, and missiles. The sensors were used to monitor cabin pressure and density, speed, and fuel flow (liquid and gas). An environmental density sensor, for which Hicks received a patent in 1962, was used in the *Saturn V* rockets that launched the *Apollo* spacecraft on missions to the moon.

Beatrice Hicks was born in Orange, New Jersey. At an early age she demonstrated an aptitude in mathematics and the physical sciences and an interest in engineering. Hicks graduated from Orange High School in 1935 and entered Newark College of Engineering (now the New Jersey Institute of Technology, or NJIT). She received a B.S. in chemical engineering in 1939 and remained at the school as a research assistant for three additional years.

As men were called to active duty during World War II, their departures provided job opportunities for women in science and engineering. Hicks accepted a position as a technician with Western Electric (a branch of Bell Telephone) in 1942. There she developed technology used for long-distance dialing and a crystal oscillator (a device that generates radio frequencies) for use in aircraft communications. At this time, she also began taking graduate courses in electrical engineering at Columbia University.

Hicks left Western Electric to pursue consulting opportunities in 1945. When her father died the next year, she took over the family business, first as chief engineer and later as vice president. This business, the Newark Controls Company, manufactured electrical heat monitoring and control equipment and environmental sensing devices. It was here that Hicks worked on the design and development of the environmental sensors for which she is known. While running the business, Hicks also earned a master's degree in physics from Stevens Institute of Technology, in Hoboken (1949).

Through her work, Hicks became keenly aware of the underrepresentation of women in the sciences and of the failure of schools to encourage women to enter the engineering professions. To address these concerns, she cofounded and became the first president (1950–1953) of the Society of Women Engineers (SWE), an organization that encourages women to enter engineering fields and that disseminates information about the achievements of women engineers.

In recognition of her achievements and contributions to engineering and business, *Mademoiselle* magazine named Hicks Outstanding

Woman of the Year in Business in 1952. Hobart and William Smith College conferred an honorary Sc.D. on Hicks in 1958. In 1963, the SWE presented her its Achievement Award. The following year, Hicks was named director of the First International Conference on Women Engineers and Scientists. In 1965, Hicks was awarded an honorary doctorate of engineering by Rensselaer Polytechnic Institute (RPI), the first woman to be so honored. She later received honorary doctoral degrees from Stevens Institute of Technology and Worcester Polytechnic Institute, both in 1978. In addition, Hicks held memberships in the American Society of Mechanical Engineers (ASME) and the Institute of Electrical and Electronics Engineers (IEEE).

See also Aeronautical and Aerospace Engineering; Darden, Christine M.; Flügge-Lotz, Irmgard; Hoover, Erna Schneider; Ordnance; Society of Women Engineers (SWE); Space Exploration

References Bailey, Martha J., *American Women in Science: A Biographical Dictionary* (1994); Burstyn, Joan N., ed., *Past and Promise: Lives of New Jersey Women* (1990); Stanley, Autumn, *Mothers and Daughters of Invention: Notes for a Revised History of Technology* (1993).

Hobby, Gladys Lounsbury (1910–1993)

In 1945, Sir Alexander Fleming shared the Nobel Prize in physiology/medicine with Australian physiologist Howard Walter Florey and German biochemist Ernst Boris Chain. Fleming received the prize for his discovery of penicillin; Florey and Chain shared the prize for their production and preliminary tests of the antibiotic on several patients. Despite the accomplishments of these scientists, Florey and Chain were not able to develop therapeutic-grade penicillin in large enough quantities to effect recovery in all patients. A breakthrough in this area was made by microbiologists Gladys Hobby, Martin Henry Dawson, and biochemist Karl Meyer, who cured a patient suffering from bacterial endocarditis (an inflammation of the heart) through treatment with a penicillin injection in 1940. Additionally, this team, working with other researchers, devel-

oped the technology necessary to produce sufficient quantities of therapeutic-quality penicillin in the United States.

Gladys Hobby was born in the Washington Heights section of New York City. She graduated from Vassar College with an A.B. in 1931. She received an M.S. (1932) and a Ph.D. (1935), both in bacteriology, from the College of Physicians and Surgeons (P&S) at Columbia University in New York. After receiving her advanced degrees, Hobby remained at P&S to research the effectiveness of various drugs in eliminating hemolytic streptococci (bacteria that disrupt the function of blood cells). Her treatments involved using gold salts, sulfonamide, and in 1940, penicillin.

Hobby accepted a position as a microbiologist with the Pfizer Corporation in 1944. She eventually became scientific director of Pfizer's Infectious Diseases Research Institute. At Pfizer, Hobby aided in the development of viomycin, streptomycin, and several other broad spectrum antibiotics. She also codiscovered the antibiotic Terramycin® in 1950 and organized a worldwide program to evaluate the drug's effectiveness.

In 1959, Hobby left Pfizer to serve as chief of the Veterans Administration (VA) Special Research Laboratory for the Study of Chronic Infectious Diseases. Her investigations involved antimicrobial drug treatments for tuberculosis, pneumonia, and rheumatic (autoimmune) diseases. Hobby remained with the VA for 18 years, while also serving as a clinical instructor and assistant professor of public health at Cornell's Medical College in New York.

Hobby was a prolific writer who contributed hundreds of articles to professional journals and books, detailing her research on antibiotics. She also served on the editorial boards of several professional publications and held the post of editor in chief with the journal *Antimicrobial Agents and Chemotherapy.* Hobby also held memberships in several professional organizations, including the American Academy of Microbiology, the American Society for Microbiology, the American Thoracic Society, the New York State Academy of Medicine, the New York Academy of Sciences, the American Public Health Association, and the American Association for the Advancement of Science (AAAS). Hobby was elected to key positions in several and served a term as president of the New York Lung Association (1963–1965). Hobby also received many awards for her work and achievements. Among them were a 1950 Merit Award in Science from *Mademoiselle* magazine and the 1983 Trudeau Medal from the New York Lung Association for outstanding service in improving community health and in the fight against tuberculosis and other lung diseases.

See also Alexander, Hattie Elizabeth; Antibiotics; Biotechnology; Brown, Rachel Fuller; Elion, Gertrude Belle; Hazen, Elizabeth Lee; Nobel Prize
References Hobby, Gladys L., *Penicillin: Meeting the Challenge* (1985); O'Hern, Elizabeth Moot, *Profiles of Pioneer Women Scientists* (1986); Stanley, Autumn, *Mothers and Daughters of Invention: Notes for a Revised History of Technology* (1993); Torpie, Stephen L., et al., eds., *American Men and Women of Science*, 18th ed. (1992–1993) (1992); Vare, Ethlie Ann, and Greg Ptacek, *Mothers of Invention: From the Bra to the Bomb, Forgotten Women and Their Unforgettable Ideas* (1988); "Women's History Month," available at http://pafb. af.mil/deomi/whm96.htm (cited 19 May 1998).

Hollinshead, Ariel (b. 1929)

Ariel Hollinshead is known for her work in pharmacology, virology, and oncology. By demonstrating the relationship of certain viruses to cancers, she made breakthrough discoveries in the use of drugs and vaccines in chemotherapy and immunotherapy treatments of viral diseases and cancers. Among her greatest achievements in this area was her identification and isolation of certain tumor-associated antigens (TAA), foreign substances in the body that trigger the immune system to stimulate the production of antibodies. This achievement led to the development of several vaccines for treating various types of cancer.

Ariel Hollinshead was born in Allentown, Pennsylvania, in 1929. Her reading of Paul De Kruif's book *Microbe Hunters* at age 15 inspired her later to pursue a career in science. After graduating as valedictorian from Bethel Park High School, Hollinshead entered Swarthmore College. However, she left one year later to attend Ohio University in Athens. At Ohio University, Hollinshead worked as a laboratory assistant, majored in zoology, and graduated with an A.B. in 1951. She then attended George Washington University in Washington, D.C., from which she received an M.A. in 1955 and a Ph.D. in pharmacology two years later.

In 1958, Hollinshead worked as a postdoctoral fellow and assistant professor of virology and epidemiology at Baylor University Medical Center in Houston, Texas. The following year she moved back to Washington, D.C., to join her new husband, attorney Montgomery K. Hyun. She accepted an assistant professorship in pharmacology at George Washington University Medical Center. In 1961, she was appointed assistant professor of medicine, and in 1964 she was promoted to associate professor.

Around this time, Hollinshead set up and directed the Laboratory for Virus and Cancer Research. Hollinshead's work in cancer research led to the development and use of vaccines as a method of immunotherapy. She developed techniques for causing the immune systems of cancer patients to recognize cancer cells in the body as alien, thereby triggering the immune system to attack and destroy these cells. She also devised means for testing antibodies in cancer patients. These methods allowed Hollinshead to show that immunotherapy or immunochemotherapy that made use of vaccines she developed protected some lung cancer patients up to fifteen years following their use.

Hollinshead became a full professor of medicine at George Washington University in 1974. Over the years, she expanded her research to include ovarian cancer, and in 1983, she developed a vaccine for use in ovarian cancer patients who had undergone surgery to remove advanced tumors. This vaccine later received approval for use from the U.S. Food and Drug Administration (FDA).

More recently, Hollinshead's research has been in the area of breast cancer. In 1994, she devised a sensitivity test for drugs used in the treatment of breast cancer. Four years later, she patented a new method for treatment of HIV/AIDS that makes use of a vaccine-drug combination. In addition to her work as an educator and researcher, Hollinshead has written or coauthored more than 260 papers that describe her research work and clinical experiments.

Ariel Hollinshead has been well recognized for her contributions to medicine. In 1976, she was chosen Medical Woman of the Year by the Joint Board of American Medical Colleges, awarded the Alumni Association Certificate of Merit from Ohio University, and presented the Marion Spencer Fay National Board Award for Women in Medicine from the Medical College of Pennsylvania (now Allegheny University for the Health Care Sciences). The next year, she became the first woman appointed to chair the Review Board of Oncology for the Veterans Administration (VA); she also was awarded an honorary doctor of science degree by Ohio University. In 1985 and again in 1996, the Society of Experimental Biology and Medicine (SEBM) presented Hollinshead with its Distinguished Scientist Award.

Hollinshead has served on committees and advisory boards of the National Cancer Institute (NCI), the National Institutes of Health (NIH), the National Academy of Sciences (NAS), the U.S. Department of Agriculture (USDA), the Food and Drug Administration (FDA), and the National Aeronautics and Space Administration (NASA). She also belongs to numerous professional organizations, including the American Association for the Advancement of Science (AAAS), the New York Academy of Sciences, Sigma Xi (a scientific research society), the American Society of Clinical Oncology (ASCO), and the American Association for Cancer Research (AACR). From 1980–1981, Hollinshead served as president of the Washington, D.C., chapter of SEBM. In addition, she is an outspoken proponent of women in the sciences and helped to establish Professional Opportunities for Women in Science, an organization that helps train women for part-time work in science. She joined the Graduate Women in Science/Sigma Delta Epsilon in 1961 and served as its president in 1968–1969 and again in 1985–1986. She also serves as a mentor for Women in Cancer Research (WICR), a program within the AACR.

See also Blackburn, Elizabeth Helen; Dick, Gladys Rowena Henry; Downs, Cornelia Mitchell; Eldering, Grace; Elion, Gertrude Belle; Fenselau, Catherine Clarke; Frantz, Virginia Kneeland; Friend, Charlotte; Kendrick, Pearl Luella; Logan, Myra Adele; Williams, Anna Wessels

References Hollinshead, Ariel C., Resume, e-mail communication with Alan Winkler (21 March 1999); Shearer, Benjamin F., and Barbara S. Shearer, eds., *Notable Women in the Life Sciences: A Biographical Dictionary* (1996); Stanley, Autumn, *Mothers and Daughters of Invention: Notes for a Revised History of Technology* (1993).

Home Economics

Home economics (also called domestic science, human ecology, or family studies) includes a broad cluster of interrelated subjects designed to strengthen and improve the quality of the home and family living through training and education. In addition, home economics provides families with information about home products and family services. Personal issues and family concerns contributed to the early development and growth of the home economics movement in the United States around the mid-1700s. Social and political changes, along with advances in science, medicine, education, and health also contributed to its development.

Before 1750, sewing, cooking, and homemaking skills were exclusively taught in the home (passed from mother to daughter), where they were governed by tradition and pride. During the early nineteenth century, educator and women's rights advocate Emma Willard pioneered "women's education" outside the home at the Troy Female Seminary in New York. The pre–Civil War period (beginning around 1830) witnessed the next surge in the development of home economics. Public schools emerged, the immigrant population increased, and school curricula expanded to include teachings of "home art" subjects such as cooking, dress, and manners. A decade later, educator and family advocate Catherine Beecher (sister of Harriet Beecher Stowe) published books on household problems and management. Beecher's works greatly influenced the acceptance of the home economics curriculum in girls' schools across the United States. She envisioned a home where students could practice housekeeping under the guidance of a teacher. This vision later became a reality when college home economics courses were, in fact, conducted in household settings.

The Morrill Act of 1862 was likely the greatest single influence in support of home economics as a science and a recognized program of study. The Morrill Act created land-grant colleges that encouraged the development of home economics programs by emphasizing a practical education focused on cooking, sewing, and other "household arts." Similar land-grant legislation supporting and extending the 1862 Act was passed in 1868 and 1890.

As cities grew, so did school enrollments and educational and career opportunities for women. Schools undertook greater responsibilities and broadened their curricula to include home economics. Women's associations began to promote specialized home economics courses teaching specific skills and scientific understandings. For example, the Women's Educational Association in Boston sponsored a cooking school. Fannie Farmer, a pioneer in the technology of cooking and home economics, attended and later administered the program at one of these schools. Her books, which emphasized nutrition and the precise use of measurement in preparing foods, strengthened the development of home economics as a science.

As the nutritional benefits of vitamins and minerals were being investigated, so too were issues concerning food selection, sanitation, handling, storage, and preparation. To address these concerns, Congress authorized the U.S. Department of Agriculture (USDA) to conduct nutritional research in 1894. Chemist Ellen Henrietta Swallow Richards, a pioneer in the home economics movement and the founder of the first school lunch program in Boston, served as a consultant to the USDA and assisted in the preparation of bulletins on nutrition. In 1899, Richards helped organize a series of conferences in Lake Placid, New York. The conferences, which became annual events, were attended by educators, schol-

ars, and scientists for the purpose of developing home economics courses for public schools, colleges, and women's associations. The American Home Economics Association evolved from the Lake Placid conferences, with Richards serving as its president from 1908 to 1910. Suggestions resulting from these conferences and recommendations made by the American Home Economics Association led to the passage of federal legislation—the Smith-Lever Act (1914), the Smith-Hughes Act (1917), the Purnell Act (1925), the George Reed Act (1929), and the George-Ellgey Act (1937)—that provided funds for the continued development of home economics education for women.

The home economics movement, which originated from concerns about clean food and water, has developed into a vital part of American life. Advances in science and technology, linked to changing gender roles and economic and social change, gradually have broadened the scope of this field of study. Modern home economics still incorporates such fields of study as child development, child care, family relationships, textiles, clothing, home furnishings, and interior design; but it also links the domestic sphere with the larger society, seeking to strengthen and support the home through action in the public arena (e.g., assisting in the development and support of legislation affecting the home and family).

See also Alexander, Lucy Maclay; American Society for Nutritional Sciences (ASNS); Baker, Sara Josephine; Benjamin, Miriam E.; Bevier, Isabel; Blanchard, Helen Augusta; Boone, Sarah; Cochran, Josephine G.; Demorest, Ellen Curtis; Domestic Appliances; Donovan, Marion; Emerson, Gladys Anderson; Evans, Alice Catherine; Farmer, Fannie Merritt; Fieser, Mary Peters; Fox, Sally; Gabe, Frances Bateson; Hibbard, Susan; Jones, Amanda Theodosia; Joyner, Marjorie Stewart; Kenner, (Mary) Beatrice Davidson; Kies, Mary; Mangin, Anna; Masters, Sybilla Righton; Metcalf, Betsey; Morrill Act of 1862; Newman, Lyda; Richards, Ellen Henrietta Swallow; Sherman, Patsy O.; Stanley, Louise; Waltz, Hazel Hook; Welles, Sophia Woodhouse

References Bailey, Martha J., *American Women in Science: A Biographical Dictionary* (1994); Franck, Irene M., and David M. Brownstone, *Women's World: A Timeline of Women in History* (1995); Macdonald, Anne L., *Feminine Ingenuity: How Women Inventors Changed America* (1992); Stanley, Autumn, *Mothers and Daughters of Invention: Notes for a Revised History of*

Technology (1993); Weatherford, Doris, *American Women's History: An A to Z of People, Organizations, Issues, and Events* (1994); Zophy, Angela Howard, ed., *Handbook of American Women's History* (1990).

Hoobler, Icie
See **Macy-Hoobler, Icie Gertrude**

Hooper, Mary Carpenter (n.d.)

Mary Carpenter Hooper was a prolific inventor who developed most of her devices during the latter part of the nineteenth century. Among her many inventions were self-threading and self-setting sewing machine needles designed for use by the textile industry. The self-threading needles were an improvement over earlier sewing machine needles because they increased productivity among sewing machine operators by reducing the need to constantly adjust or rethread the machines. Carpenter also patented an ironing and fluting machine (fluting is a decoration of long, rounded grooves) as well as a sewing machine and arm and an improvement to sewing machine feeding mechanisms.

One of Carpenter's most successful inventions was a straw-braiding and -sewing machine for use in making hats. This machine provided milliners a means of sewing an entire hat, from crown to brim, without removing the hat from the machine. This time-saving machine was widely used throughout the hat-making industry.

Not all of Carpenter's inventions were industrial. She also is credited with the design of an improved mop wringer, a device for numbering houses, and a canopy for bedsteads.

> **See also** Blanchard, Helen Augusta; Kies, Mary; Knight, Margaret E.; Masters, Sybilla Righton; Metcalf, Betsey; Rodgers, Dorothy; Welles, Sophia Woodhouse
> **References** Macdonald, Anne L., *Feminine Ingenuity: How Women Inventors Changed America* (1992); Stanley, Autumn, *Mothers and Daughters of Invention: Notes for a Revised History of Technology* (1993).

Hoover, Erna Schneider (b. 1926)

The latter part of the last millennium has often been referred to as the "information age." Without devices such as the electronic telephone switching system developed by New Jersey native Erna Schneider Hoover, it is unlikely that the technological developments characteristic of this age, particularly those devices dependent upon telephone lines, could have occurred. In 1971, Erna Hoover became one of the first women in the United States to receive a software patent when she was issued patent No. 3,623,007 for a computerized telephone switching system. The system was developed to regulate the number of incoming telephone calls that could be accepted at any given time, as a means of preventing call overload. Prior to the system's development, most businesses made use of hardwired or mechanical switching systems that were unable to deal with many incoming calls at the same time.

During her college years, Hoover studied in diverse areas. She attended Wellesley College, from which she graduated with honors and a B.A. in medieval history in 1948. Several years later, she received a Ph.D. in the philosophy and foundations of mathematics, from Yale University. After graduating from Yale, Hoover accepted a position at Swarthmore College, teaching philosophy. However, she resigned this position to relocate to New Jersey when her husband got a job there. Once in New Jersey, Hoover accepted a position with Bell Laboratories. When Hoover joined Bell, the company was seeking a way to improve the ability of their offices to accept a greater number of incoming calls. Hoover developed the initial design for her switching system while she was in the hospital, recuperating from childbirth.

After a patent was issued on her switching system, Hoover was promoted and became the first woman to head a technical department at Bell Laboratories. While working in this new department, Hoover went on to develop computer programs designed to ensure that outdoor telephone lines remained in good working order.

Hoover retired from Bell Laboratories in 1983. Since her retirement, she has devoted much of her time to publicizing the importance of education to school-aged children. In this work, Hoover has shown a particular concern with lack of female representation in science, technology, and math. To address these concerns, Hoover, with sponsorship from the American Association of University Women (AAUW) and the Girl Scouts of America, helped develop an Expanding Your Horizons conference. The conference was held in Montclair, New Jersey, in 1994. The Expanding Your Horizons program began in 1976, at Mills College in California (under sponsorship of the Math/Network Society). Its goal is to bring together middle- and high-school-aged girls with women who have successful careers in science, technology, and mathematics. During the conferences, the girls are not only provided opportunities to meet women who have achieved successs in technical fields but also to develop their own means of using technology to solve practical problems under the direction of these mentors. Hoover served on the Board of Higher Education for the State of New Jersey and as a trustee for Trenton State College from 1977 through 1989.

See also American Association of University Women (AAUW); Computers/Computer Technology; Hicks, Beatrice Alice; Hopper, Grace Murray; Kempf, Martine; Kurtzig, Sandra L. Brody; Telecommunications
References Dietz, Jean Pinanski, "The Medievalist Who Helps Make Telephones Work," *Wellesley* (Spring 1990); Macdonald, Anne L., *Feminine Ingenuity: How Women Inventors Changed America* (1992); Perl, Teri, *Women and Numbers: Lives of Women Mathematicians* (1993); Salerno, Heather, "Mothers of Invention: Though Unsung and Ignored, Women Have Pushed Technology's Frontiers," *Washington Post* (12 March 1997); Showell, Ellen H., and Fred M. B. Amram, *From Indian Corn to Outer Space: Women Invent in America* (1995); Lemelson-MIT Program, "Erna Schneider Hoover: Computerized Telephone Switching System," in Invention Dimension's Inventor of the Week archives, available at http://web.mit.edu/invent/www/inventorsA-H/hoover.html (cited 16 June 1999).

Hopper, Grace Murray (1906–1992)

The computer is one of the most significant technological advances of the twentieth century. At the forefront of this technology was mathematician and physicist Grace Murray Hopper. Hopper's contributions to computer programming—the use of codes to instruct computers how to work—improved the performance of these machines and made them more useful.

Grace was born and raised in New York City. As a child, she was very curious about how mechanical things worked; perhaps for this reason she later pursued studies in physics and mathematics. She attended Vassar College, where she was elected to Phi Beta Kappa and received her B.A. in both math and physics in 1928. She continued her studies at Yale University, where she received her master's degree (1930) and her Ph.D. (1934). The year she received her master's degree, she also married Vincent Foster Hopper.

After graduating from Yale, Grace Hopper accepted a position at Vassar as an associate professor of mathematics. She remained at Vassar until 1943, when she took a leave of absence to enlist in the U.S. Naval Reserves. After completing her initial training at the rank of lieutenant, Hopper was assigned to the Navy's Bureau of Ordnance Computation Project at the Cruft Laboratory of Harvard University. It was here that Hopper was introduced to computers.

The computer Hopper first worked on was the Mark I. This computer, which Hopper described as "an impressive beast . . . fifty-one feet long, eight feet high, and five feet deep," was essentially a giant calculator. She soon mastered this computer, and later, its successors the Mark II and Mark III. During this time, she also coined the term *computer bug,* when in an attempt to get the Mark I to work, she removed a moth from inside the machine.

In 1946, the year after her husband was killed in the war, Hopper was placed on inactive duty with the Navy. She resigned her position at Vassar College to become a research fellow at Harvard's Computation Laboratory, where she remained until 1949. Hopper then took a job as a senior mathematician with the Eckert-Mauchly Computer Corporation. She remained with Eckert-Mauchly (which eventually became the Sperry Corporation) until her retirement in 1971. From 1967 through 1971 she also was on active duty with the Navy.

While at Eckert-Mauchly, Hopper worked at making computers friendlier to the people programming them and using them. She had programmers begin using shared libraries of code to

Grace Murray Hopper was a pioneer in the workings of computers and computer languages. (Corbis)

reduce their need to rekey information over and over. This procedure made programming less tedious and reduced errors resulting from inaccurately keyed codes. Next, Hopper developed a program that could translate symbolic math codes into machine language a computer could interpret. She also developed the world's first compiler, a device that allows codes to be stored on magnetic tape from which they can be accessed and retrieved when needed.

Hopper's most notable contribution to computer technology occurred in 1959, when she developed the COBOL (Common Business Oriented Language) computer language—the first computer language using English in its programming. This breakthrough permitted nonexperts to more easily develop programming skills and led to greater standardization in computer software.

Hopper's achievements are not limited to her accomplishments in private industry. During her first 15 years at Eckert-Mauchly, she remained a member of the U.S. Naval Reserves. She retired from the Navy in 1966 with the rank of commander, but was asked to return months later to help standardize the Navy's computer programming language, to enable different computers to "talk" with each other. In 1973, Hopper was promoted to captain. Ten years later, while serving as adviser to the commander of the Naval Data Automation Command, Hopper was promoted to commodore. With this promotion, Hopper, at age 76, became the oldest officer on active duty in the U.S. armed services. Two years later, in 1985, she was promoted to rear admiral, the first woman ever to hold this rank.

Hopper retired from the Navy a second time in 1986, at the age of 81. Following her retirement, she worked as a consultant for Digital Equipment Corporation (DEC). She remained in this position until her death in January 1992.

Hopper received many honors and awards for the work she did in her corporate and military careers. In 1962, she was elected into the Institute of Electrical and Electronics Engineers (IEEE). The next year she was elected into the American Association for the Advancement of Science (AAAS). In 1969, the Data Processing Management Association awarded Hopper its first Man-of-the-Year Award. She was named a distinguished fellow of the British Computer Society in 1973, becoming both the first American and the first woman to receive this honor. In 1984, Hopper was inducted into the Engineering and Science Hall of Fame. Three years later, the U.S. Navy presented Hopper with its Distinguished Service Medal. In 1991, she was presented the National Medal of Technology by President George Bush. Hopper also has received more than 30 honorary doctorates from American colleges and universities.

Hopper dedicated much of her time to the training of young people and was a highly sought-after speaker. In view of her dedication to the younger generation, the year Hopper retired the Sperry Corporation established an annual award in her name, to honor young computer professionals. After Hopper's death in 1992, the U.S. Navy bestowed an additional honor on her: the christening of a new ship in her name. The USS *Hopper* is the first warship since World War II to be named after a female member of the Navy. In 1994, Hopper was posthumously inducted into the National Women's Hall of Fame in Seneca Falls, New York.

See also Bernstein, Dorothy Lewis; Butler, Margaret K.; Computers/Computer Technology; Estrin, Thelma; Goldstine, Adele Katz; Hicks, Beatrice Alice; Hoover, Erna Schneider; Kempf, Martine; Kurtzig, Sandra L. Brody; National Medal of Technology; National Women's Hall of Fame; Ordnance

References Bailey, Martha J., *American Women in Science: A Biographical Dictionary* (1994); Felder, Deborah G., *The 100 Most Influential Women of All Time: A Ranking Past and Present* (1996); Hellemans, Alexander, and Bryan Bunch, *The Timetables of Science* (1988); Read, Phyllis J., and Bernard L. Witlieb, *The Book of Women's Firsts* (1992); Sherrow, Victoria, *Women and the Military* (1996); Showell, Ellen H., and Fred M. B. Amram, *From Indian Corn to Outer Space: Women Invent in America* (1995); National Women's Hall of Fame, "Grace Hopper (1906–1992)," available at http://www.greatwomen.org/hopper.htm (cited 1 April 2000); U.S. Navy, "Tribute to Grace Murray Hopper," available at http://www.navsea.navy.mil.hopper_grace. html#time (cited 20 January 1999); Yale University, "Grace Murray Hopper," in the Grace Hopper Celebration of Women in Computing 1994 conference proceedings, available at http://www.cs.yale.edu/utap/ Files/hopper-story.html (cited 20 January 1999).

Hosmer, Harriet (1830–1908)

Watertown, Massachusetts, native Harriet Hosmer became a well-known sculptor in the mid-nineteenth century. However, her life's work was not limited to the world of art. From the late 1870s until her death in 1908, Hosmer turned her attention from sculpting to inventing. The results earned her a total of five patents (three in Great Britain and two in the United States).

Harriet Hosmer was born on 6 October 1830. An only child, she was encouraged by her parents to pursue a variety of interests at an early age, including drawing and tinkering with mechanical objects. Once grown, Hosmer studied art (drawing and modeling) in Boston. She then returned briefly to her parent's home in Lenox, Massachusetts, where her father built a studio onto the family home.

In 1852, Hosmer traveled to Rome to study under noted English sculptor John Gibson. Within a few years, she had produced several sculptures of her own that had earned her great attention in Europe. Among these was a statue called "Puck," copies of which sold for as much as $1,000 each to such notable people as the Duke of Hamilton and the Prince of Wales. In total, Hosmer reportedly made $30,000 from sales of these pieces. Several years later, Hosmer was called upon by representatives from the state of Missouri to create a statue of that state's former Senator Benton. The statue was unveiled with great acclaim at Lafayette Park in Saint Louis, in 1868. In the mid-1870s, Hosmer was commissioned by the Board of Lady Managers of the Centennial Exposition of Philadelphia to create a sculpture for the Woman's Pavilion. Her work went on display at the Centennial's opening in 1876.

Hosmer lived in Rome throughout much of the 1870s. It was late during this decade that she began to turn her attention away from sculpting and toward inventing. She obtained her first patent for a device known as "motive power" in Great Britain in 1878. In 1880 and again in 1881, Hosmer was issued two additional patents in Great Britain for related inventions. At the same time that Hosmer was obtaining patents in Great Britain, she also was successful in obtaining two U.S. patents. The first of these, which was for a process of making artificial or "faux" marble, is the invention Hosmer is most often associated with. This patent was issued in 1879. She later received another U.S. patent, for a device that could be used by musicians to turn the pages of their musical scores.

The process by which Hosmer created her marble suggests that she had some understanding of the scientific principles relating to geology. Hosmer's process began with a piece of common limestone (a sedimentary rock). To develop a product that resembled marble (a metamorphic rock that is natually formed when limestone is subjected to great heat and pressure), Hosmer placed the limestone in an environment where it was subjected to pressure and moist heat. The "faux" marble produced through this process was used in interior architectural design.

By the mid-1890s, Hosmer was again living in the United States. Although she was still devoting much of her time to inventing, she completed a number of commissioned sculptures during this period. In 1893, a statue of Spain's Queen Isabella I created by Hosmer was displayed at the World's Columbian Exposition held in Chicago. The following year, a similar statue was purchased by the city of San Francisco.

Hosmer spent her final years in the town where she had been born. During this period she revisited her earlier interests in motive power, conducting various experiments with electromagnetic motors in an attempt to create a perpetual motion machine. Hosmer continued to work on this device until her death in Watertown, Massachusetts, in 1908.

See also Architecture; Centennial Exposition; Columbian Exposition; Knight, Margaret E.; Materials Engineering

References Macdonald, Anne L., *Feminine Ingenuity: How Women Inventors Changed America* (1992); "Miss Harriet Hosmer Dead: Sculptress Modeled a Notable 'Puck,' of Which 30 Copies Were Made" [obituary], *New York Times* (22 February 1908); Olsen, Kirstin, *Chronology of Women's History* (1994); Stanley, Autumn, *Mothers and Daughters of Invention: Notes for a Revised History of Technology* (1993).

Hyde, Ida Henrietta (1857–1945)

Ida Henrietta Hyde's major contribution to technology was her invention of a microelectrode that is used for intracellular study. This instrument can deliver either electrical or chemical stimuli to a single cell and record the electrical activity within that cell. Much of what is now known about muscle and nerve function is attributed to the use of this tool.

Ida Henrietta Hyde was born in Davenport, Iowa. She received her B.S. from Cornell University in 1891, at age 34. She then enrolled at Bryn Mawr College to study physiology. Much of her research focused on the structure and workings of the nervous and respiratory systems of horseshoe crabs, grasshoppers, and skates. In 1893, Hyde was awarded a fellowship by the Association of Collegiate Alumnae for Study in Foreign Universities. The next year, she entered the University of Heidelberg. In 1896, Hyde became the first woman granted a Ph.D. by the University of Heidelberg (or any German university). She received this degree with the special tribute of *multa cum laude superavit*, "with greater than high honors," because of the university's reluctance to attribute "highest honors" to a woman.

After receiving her Ph.D., Hyde did postgraduate research at Heidelberg's marine biological laboratories, at the Naples Marine Station. She also spent one year at the University of Bern before returning to the United States. Between 1896 and 1897, Hyde was a research fellow at Radcliffe College, working with physiologist William Townsend Porter of the Harvard Medical School. Hyde was the first woman to conduct research at Harvard. The next year, in 1898, she accepted a position as associate professor of physiology at the University of Kansas.

In 1902, Hyde was elected into the American Physiological Society, the first woman to receive this honor. Three years later, she became full professor and chair of the physiology department at the University of Kansas. She remained in this position until her retirement in 1920.

Ida Hyde was a supporter of educational opportunities for women. In 1896, she helped create an organization that funded a Women's Table at the Naples Zoological Station. Among the first women to take advantage of this opportunity was Florence Peebles. Hyde also endowed scholarships that enabled women students of science to pursue their studies at Cornell University and the University of Kansas. In addition, Hyde established the Ida H. Hyde Women's International Fellowship of the American Association of University Women (AAUW) through a donation of $25,000.

See also American Association of University Women (AAUW); Biotechnology; Levi-Montalcini, Rita; Pool, Judith Graham

References Bailey, Martha J., *American Women in Science: A Biographical Dictionary* (1994); James, Edward T., Janet Wilson James, and Paul S. Boyers, eds., *Notable American Women: A Biographical Dictionary (1607–1950),* vol 2: (G–O) (1971); Kass-Simon, G., and Patricia Farnes, eds., *Women of Science: Righting the Record* (1990); Ogilvie, Marilyn, *Women in Science Antiquity through the Nineteenth Century: A Biographical Dictionary with Annotated Bibliography* (1986); San Jose State University, "Ida Hyde," available at http://www.sjsu.edu/depts/Museum/hyd.html (cited 22 June 1998); Woods Hole Marine Biological Laboratory (MBL), "Women of Science at MBL: Ida H. Hyde (1857–1945)," available at http://www.mbl.edu/html/WOMEN/hyde.html (cited 22 June 1998).

Illuminating Engineering Society of North America (IESNA)

The Illuminating Engineering Society of North America (IESNA) maintains standards on state-of-the-art technology and research in the lighting industry. IESNA's standards and publications dictate interior and exterior lighting requirements for marine lighting, stage and theatrical lighting, and solar lighting. They also provide standards for lighting measurement, testing, and efficiency.

IESNA was founded in 1906. Ten years after its founding, Mary Greenewalt, inventor of the rheostat, was invited to a national convention of the organization to describe the workings of her invention to society members. The society admitted its first woman fellow, prominent ophthalmology and physiological optics researcher Gertrude Rand, in 1952. Today, IESNA has more than 10,000 members. They include men and women who are consulting, lighting, and electrical engineers; manufacturers; utility personnel; architects; interior designers; lighting professionals; educators; and students. The organization provides assistance with technical concerns, and sponsors technical and research committees through its regional and local symposia, workshops, exhibitions, and design competitions. The society also offers several awards to recognize outstanding professionals in the field. *Lighting Handbook,* IESNA's leading publication, is considered the definitive source on lighting and complex design problems.

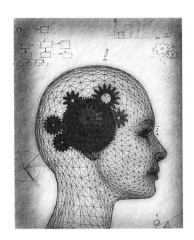

> **See also** Engineering; Greenewalt, Mary E. H.; Rand, (Marie) Gertrude
> **References** Bailey, Martha J., *American Women in Science: A Biographical Dictionary* (1994); Maurer, Christine, and Tara E. Sheets, eds., *Encyclopedia of Associations: An Associations Unlimited Reference,* 33rd ed., vol. 1, parts 1–3 (1998); Illuminating Engineering Society of North America, available at http://www.iesna.org (cited 1 February 2000).

Industrial Engineering

Industrial engineering bridges the gap between management and operations by focusing on productivity and the management of resources. Unlike other engineering professionals, whose concerns are products and processes, industrial engineers focus on quality control. They analyze and determine the most effective and efficient ways to utilize machines, materials, data, energy, and personnel. To prepare themselves to accomplish these tasks, industrial engineers often obtain an education in personnel management, economics, and psychology. A pioneer in this area was Lillian Moller Gilbreth, who combined her knowledge of psychology and time-motion studies to improve productivity in the workplace. Gilbreth conducted much of her work in this area during the 1930s and 1940s; however, it was not until the 1960s that many of the ideas she advocated were accepted. Many industrial engineers move into management positions, since this area is a natural extension of their on-the-job responsibilities.

Industrial engineers are often involved in plant site selection as it relates to the effective and economically efficient movement of raw materials and finished products. They also develop training programs, assist in employee evaluations, help set performance standards, and decide employee wages and benefits. In this work, industrial engineers often use computer-generated mathematical models and data processing systems to simulate all aspects of production, including cost efficiency, inventory control, scheduling, and management. They also analyze and assess the effects that proposed changes may have on productivity. One woman who has used her knowledge of computers to help businesses function more efficiently is Sandra L. Kurtzig. Her company, ASK Computer Systems, was initially founded with the idea of developing software packages to help businesses monitor personnel data as well as track inventory. Kurtzig also developed software that permitted improved communication among computers using different operating systems. Later, Kutzig and her son opened a second company that assisted small businesses with human resource management solutions in such areas as health insurance and employee benefits.

See also Engineering; Gilbreth, Lillian Moller; Kurtzig, Sandra L. Brody
References Barnes-Svarney, Patricia, ed., *The New York Public Library Science Desk Reference* (1995); Stanley, Autumn, *Mothers and Daughters of Invention: Notes for a Revised History of Technology* (1993); U.S. Department of Labor, Bureau of Labor Statistics, *Occupational Outlook Handbook,* 1994–1995 ed., Bulletin 2450 (1994).

Institute of Electrical and Electronics Engineers (IEEE)

The Institute of Electrical and Electronics Engineers (IEEE) is an international engineering organization dedicated to the promotion and application of engineering processes related to electricity, electronics, and information technologies (involving radio, television, telephones, and computers, among other devices). The IEEE was incorporated on 1 January 1963, through a merger of the American Institute of Electrical Engineers (AIEE), which was incorporated in 1884, and the Institute of Radio Engineers (IRE), which was incorporated in 1912.

The IEEE has a membership of nearly 275,000; the membership includes engineers, scientists working in electrical or electronics engineering, and about 50,000 students. Women have long been included in the membership of the IEEE and its predecessor organizations. For example, Edith Clarke became the AIEE's first woman fellow in 1948. Jenny Bramley became the second woman to achieve this honor twenty-two years later, when she was made a fellow of what is now known as the IEEE. In 1984, Bramley also was awarded the association's Centennial Medal, as was Thelma Estrin. Other notable women who have been elected fellows of the IEEE include Thelma Estrin, Betsy Ancker-Johnson, Harriet B. Rigas, Margaret K. Butler, Lynn Ann Conway, Grace Murray Hopper, Yvonne Claeys Brill, and Judith A. Resnik.

The IEEE sponsors an extensive awards program that recognizes individuals who have made contributions in various areas of electrical, electronics, and information technologies. The Judith A. Resnik Award (established in honor of astronaut Judith Resnik, who was killed along with her crew members in the explosion of the *Challenger* space shuttle in 1986) recognizes outstanding contributions to space engineering. Astronaut Bonnie J. Dunbar was presented this award for her contributions to the processing and development of electronics materials in space in 1993. The Emanuel R. Piore Award recognizes achievement in information processing as it relates to computer sciences. In 1988, Grace Murray Hopper (the inventor of the COBOL computer language) was the recipient of this award, which includes a bronze medal, certificate, and cash prize. That same year, Harriet B. Rigas was the recipient of the Meritorious Award; and later, in 1989, she was posthumously honored with the Rare Fellow Award. In addition, the IEEE has established a Harriet B. Rigas Award, which is presented annually to an outstanding woman educator in electrical and electronics engineering.

See also Ancker-Johnson, Betsy; Brill, Yvonne Claeys; Bramley, Jenny Rosenthal; Butler, Margaret K.; Clarke, Edith; Conway, Lynn Ann; Dunbar, Bonnie J.; Estrin, Thelma; Harmon, Elise F.; Hopper, Grace Murray; Rigas, Harriet B.; Resnik, Judith A.
References Maurer, Christine, and Tara E. Sheets, eds., *Encyclopedia of Associations,* 34th ed., vol. 1, parts 1–6 (1999); Institute of Electrical and Electronics Engineers (IEEE), "About the IEEE," available at http://www.ieee.org/about (cited 5 May 1999); Institute of Electrical and Electronics Engineers (IEEE), "IEEE Awards Program," available at http://www.ieee.org/about/awards (cited 5 May 1999).

Invention/Inventors

An invention is any new device, product, or process developed by a person or group of people. Inventions include such things as machinery, tools, utensils, and other devices, as well as new methods of carrying out tasks. For example, the cotton gin is a piece of machinery that was developed in the 1790s to separate the seeds of cotton from the fibers. The credit for the development of this invention generally is given to Eli Whitney, who received a patent for it in 1794; however, much evidence suggests that Catherine Littlefield Greene also was involved in the development of the cotton gin. The pastry fork developed by African American Anna Mangin in the late 1800s is an example of a utensil, or tool, that is an invention. Processes that are considered inventions include such things as new breeding techniques for plants or animals as well as new methods of weaving, coloring cloth, and cooking or preparing foods.

The people who develop new devices, products, or processes are called inventors. Throughout American history both men and women have developed a great number of inventions. However, until 1809, when Mary Kies received the first patent ever issued to a woman in the United States, women's contributions in this area went virtually unnoticed. A patent is a document or grant issued by the government that recognizes an inventor as the creator of a device or process and provides this individual (or sometimes corporation) the right to exclude others from producing, selling, or using their invention without due compensation for a stipulated period of time. In the United States, patents have been issued by the federal government since 1790, when the Congress passed the nation's first patent act.

Although the Patent Act of 1790 did not expressly exclude women from obtaining patents, many women did not apply for such protection. Thus, their contributions to the inventive process went virtually unnoticed. When the first patent act was passed, many states had laws prohibiting women, especially married women, from owning property in their own names. As a result of such laws, when creations developed by women were patented, the patents often were issued in the name of a husband or other male family member. In such cases, a man was erroneously credited with developing the invention. An example was what occurred in 1868 when John D. Jones obtained a patent for a device that was invented by his wife, Sarah. At the time of this invention, state law in Pennsylvania forbade women to own property. Thus, the patent for an "improved sieve for straining hot food" that was developed by Sarah Jones was issued to John D. Jones. More than 150 years earlier, in 1715, Thomas Masters obtained a patent in England for "a process of cleaning and curing Indian corn" that was developed by his wife, Sybilla. Masters also was granted other patents in England for his wife's creations.

Not all cases of men receiving credit for inventions by women resulted from legal restrictions. In some cases, men sought patents on creations that they in fact had nothing to do with, taking advantage of a woman inventor's lack of knowledge of patent laws, or of loopholes that existed in the patent structure. For example, in the 1870s, George Hibbard attempted to obtain a patent for a turkey-feather duster that his wife, Susan, had developed. At the same time, another man also was trying to obtain a patent on the same invention. During the infringement inquiry that resulted from these competing claims, astute patent examiners discovered that neither man was responsible for the creation; instead, it became apparent that George Hibbard's wife, Susan, was actually the true inventor. As a result of these findings, the examiners issued patent No. 177,939 in Susan Hibbard's name. Undoubtedly, many other men who pursued patents in a similar manner were successful in their quests.

Some women elected not to seek patents for their work because they did not want to draw attention to themselves, were intimidated by the patent process, or believed that existing prejudices against women or persons of color would prevent their inventions from enjoying success. An example of a woman who chose not to obtain a patent because she did not want to draw attention to herself or gain notoriety is Betsey Metcalf. During the last decade of the 1700s, Metcalf developed a weaving method that became extremely popular throughout New England. However, when she was asked why she chose not to patent the process, she indicated that she preferred to remain anonymous and protect her privacy. African American inventor Ellen F. Eglin invented a clothes wringer in the late 1880s for which she did not pursue a patent. She instead sold her invention to an agent for a small amount of money, believing that whites would not purchase her product if they discovered it had been patented by a Negro.

Although history provides many examples of women who did not receive recognition for their inventions, many other women have been recognized. Much of this recognition has resulted from research into patent records. However, while the number of women receiving recognition for their inventions through the patent process has increased over time, women today still receive only a small number of patents, compared to men. In fact, some estimates indicate that as recently as 1990, only about 5 percent of all patents issued in the United States went to women.

See also Centennial Exposition; Columbian Exposition; Domestic Appliances; Genetic Engineering; Medicine/Medical Technology; National Institute of Standards and Technology (NIST); National Inventor's Hall of Fame; Patent Act of 1790; Patent and Trademark Office, U.S. (PTO); Textiles; Women's Rights

References Hine, Darlene Clark, Elsa Barkley Brown, and Rosalyn Terborg-Penn, eds., *Black Women in America: An Historical Encyclopedia,* vol. 1: (A–L) (1993); Macdonald, Anne L., *Feminine Ingenuity: How Women Inventors Changed America* (1992); Office of the Federal Register, National Archives and Records Administration, *The United States Government Manual 1997/98* (1997); Sluby, Patricia Carter, "Black Women and Inventions," *SAGE: A Scholarly Journal on Black Women,* vol. 6, no. 2 (Fall 1989); Stanley, Autumn, *Mothers and Daughters of Invention: Notes for a Revised History of Technology* (1993); U.S. Patent and Trademark Office, *A Quest for Excellence* (1994); National Patent Association, "A Brief History of the U.S. Patent," available at http://www.national patent.com.history.html (cited 4 July 1999).

Irwin, Harriet (?–1897)

Harriet Irwin became the first woman to receive a patent for the design of a house when she was awarded U.S. Patent No. 94,116, under the title "Improvement in the Construction of Houses," in 1869. Following the devastation resulting from the Civil War, Irwin's hometown of Charlotte, North Carolina, became a town of opportunity. Although she never had received any formal training in architecture or construction, Irwin conceived of and developed plans for a hexagonal house. The design later became very popular in the Charlotte area.

Harriet Irwin (nee Morrison) was the third child of Robert Hall Morrison. As a young girl in Charlotte, North Carolina, Harriet was given what was considered a proper Southern upbringing. Although encumbered by prevalent societal norms and gender discrimination, she was nonetheless strongly influenced by the presence and encouragement of her father, a minister and the founder and first president of Davidson College. Harriet was a frail child with many health problems. Because of her delicate health, she was somewhat inactive and was home-schooled. To compensate for her lack of physical activity, she became a voracious reader.

As Harriet grew older, her health problems gradually subsided enough to permit her to attend the Moravian Church's Institute for Female Education, in Salem, North Carolina. There she excelled in her schoolwork. She began to write articles, several of which were published in magazines and newspapers.

When Harriet was 20, she married James Irwin, a prosperous cotton manufacturer. Settling at first in Alabama, where James had his business, the couple soon returned to Charlotte when Harriet's health problems flared up again. Gradually, Harriet settled into the routine of homemaker and mother. She gave birth to nine children, four of whom died in infancy.

At the age of 40, Harriet Irwin realized there was an opportunity in housing construction in Charlotte as a result of the destruction caused by the Civil War. It was at this time that she developed plans for the construction of a house that had an unusual, hexagonal shape. Calvert Vaux, a noted architect of the time, advised Irwin to give up the notion that she could be successful in the architectural and construction field—a vocation deemed inappropriate for women and typically reserved for men. Nonetheless, Irwin, refusing to be dissuaded, applied for a patent under the name H. I. Irwin, possibly to conceal the fact that she was a woman. (A similar tactic was used by Mary Engle Pennington in the early 1900s when she sought employment with the U.S. Department of Agriculture.)

Having spent the previous two decades as a homemaker, Irwin considered herself knowledgeable about what constituted a comfortable home. During this period of rebuilding, the "new Southerners" desired homes that were less grandiose and more intimate than those of their predecessors. Recognizing this desire, Harriet designed a home in which hallways and foyers were minimized and the number of corners was reduced (an effort to eliminate wasted spaces that

would serve no purpose other than to gather dust). In addition, her hexagonal design featured window placements that ensured adequate light and ventilation.

After receiving the patent for her design, the Irwins built Harriet's house. One year later, her husband and her brother opened the General Land Company to market and build the design. Harriet Irwin lived in her hexagonal home until her death in 1897. During this time, she also saw her design gain in popularity. The house constructed by the Irwins stood until 1963, when it was demolished for new development.

See also Architecture; Barney, Nora Stanton Blatch; Bethune, Louise Blanchard; Gabe, Frances Bateson; Keichline, Anna W.; Loftness, Vivian; Morgan, Julia
References Macdonald, Anne L., *Feminine Ingenuity: How Women Inventors Changed America* (1992); Stanley, Autumn, *Mothers and Daughters of Invention: Notes for a Revised History of Technology* (1993).

Jackson, Shirley Ann (b. 1946)

Shirley Jackson is a leading theoretical physicist specializing in particle physics. Much of her research has focused on identifying the existence of subatomic particles and the forces that hold them together. Jackson also has conducted research on semiconductors, the findings of which have been applied to advanced communication systems. In addition to her technical work, Jackson has broken color and gender barriers in several other areas. She is the first African American woman to be awarded a Ph.D. in physics from the Massachusetts Institute of Technology (MIT). She also was the first African American to chair the U.S. Nuclear Regulatory Commission (NRC). In 1999, she became the first African American woman to serve as president of a major research institute (Rensselaer Polytechnic Institute).

Born and raised in Washington, D.C., Shirley Jackson attended that city's segregated Roosevelt High School, where she was placed in accelerated programs in mathematics and science. Jackson graduated as valedictorian in 1964 and entered MIT to study theoretical physics. Her education was largely funded through scholarships granted by the Martin Marietta Aircraft Company and the Prince Hall Masons. She received her B.S. in 1968.

Jackson chose to remain at MIT for her graduate studies, hoping to encourage other African Americans to attend the school. Her graduate education was made possible through various scholarships, fellowships, and grants, including a National Science Foundation (NSF) Traineeship (1968–1971), a Ford Advanced Study Fellowship (1971–1973), and the Martin Marietta Aircraft Company Fellowship (1972–1973). In 1973, Jackson completed her graduate studies and received her Ph.D. in theoretical elementary particle physics.

During the mid-1970s, Jackson worked in research at prominent physics laboratories in the United States and Europe. She was a research associate at the Fermi National Accelerator Laboratory in Batavia, Illinois, and a visiting scientist at the European Center for Nuclear Research in Switzerland. From 1976 to 1977, Jackson lectured in physics at the Stanford Linear Accelerator Cen-

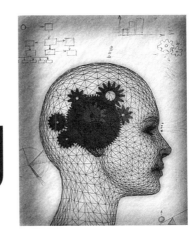

ter and served as a visiting scientist at the Aspen Center for Physics, in Colorado. Also in 1976, she began a fifteen-year association with the AT&T Bell Laboratories in Murray Hill, New Jersey, where she conducted studies in theoretical physics, solid state and quantum physics, and optical physics.

While working for AT&T, Jackson was appointed to New Jersey's Commission on Science and Technology. The appointment was made by New Jersey Governor Thomas Kean in 1985. Jackson remained a member of the commission until 1994. From 1991 to 1995, Jackson was employed as a professor of physics at Rutgers University in Piscataway, New Jersey, and simultaneously as a consultant on semiconductors at Bell Laboratories.

In 1995, Jackson made history when she was nominated by President Bill Clinton to serve as chair of the Nuclear Regulatory Commission (NRC), the organization charged with the responsibility of regulating and monitoring the use of nuclear materials and technology. Jackson was sworn into office on 2 May 1995, becoming the first African American to hold this post. In only a short time, Jackson made her presence felt when she began closing down nuclear power facilities that were not in compliance with NRC standards. In December 1998, Rensselaer Polytechnic Institute (RPI) in Troy, New York, selected Jackson to become its new president in July 1999, at the conclusion of her NRC term. Jackson is the first African American woman to head a research institution.

Shirley Ann Jackson, a particle physicist, was the first African American to chair the Nuclear Regulatory Commission. (Associated Press/AP)

For her contributions to particle physics research, Jackson has been granted several honorary doctorates. In 1990, New Jersey Governor Jim Florio presented her the Thomas Alva Edison Science Award. She received the New Jersey Governor's Award in Science in 1993. She is a fellow of the American Academy of Arts and Sciences (AAAS) and the American Physical Society. In addition, she has served on the boards of directors of many public service groups, advisory panels, and research councils. In 1997, she was elected chair of the newly formed International Nuclear Regulators' Association. The next year, she was inducted into the National Women's Hall of Fame for her contributions to science, education, and public service.

See also Ancker-Johnson, Betsy; Anderson, Elda Emma; Argonne National Laboratory; Atomic Energy Commission (AEC); Bramley, Jenny Rosenthal; Conwell, Esther Marly; Dresselhaus, Mildred S.; Fitzroy, Nancy D.; Goeppert-Mayer, Maria; Hoover, Erna Schneider; National Women's Hall of Fame; Nuclear Physics; Ochoa, Ellen; Wu, Chien-Shiung
References Arenson, Karen W., "Rensselaer Polytech-

nic Picks New President," *New York Times* (12 December 1998); Bernstein, Leonard, Alan Winkler, and Linda Zierdt-Warshaw, *Multicultural Women of Science* (1996); McMurray, Emily M., ed., *Notable Twentieth-Century Scientists,* vol. 2: (F–K) (1995); Smith, Jessie Carney, ed., *Notable Black American Women* (1992); Smith, Jessie Carney, and Nikki Giovanni, eds., *Black Heroes of the 20th Century* (1998).

Jacobs, Mary Phelps
See **Crosby, Caresse**

Jeanes, Allene Rosalind (1906–1995)

Organic chemist Allene Jeanes is recognized for her research on the biochemistry of carbohydrates (starches)—specifically, polysaccharides resulting from the fermentation of sugars by certain bacteria. In the course of her career, Jeanes received ten patents. In 1950, her research on carbohydrates called dextrans led to the development of a blood plasma substitute that was used during the Korean War. She also developed chemical techniques for analyzing carbohydrate structures and their degradation (breakdown) products and derivatives.

Jeanes was born in Waco, Texas. After graduating from Waco High School in 1924 with honors, she entered Baylor University, where she was employed part time as a laboratory assistant while working toward her bachelor's degree. In 1928, she received her B.A. *summa cum laude,* with departmental honors. The next year, Jeanes was awarded an M.A. in organic chemistry from the University of California at Berkeley. After receiving this degree, Jeanes worked briefly as a teacher of high school mathematics before accepting a position as head of the science department at Athens College in Alabama. She also taught biology, chemistry, and physics for five years. Jeanes then took a position as an instructor of chemistry, while working toward her Ph.D. at the University of Illinois in Urbana.

In 1938, Jeanes was awarded a Ph.D. in organic chemistry. She then accepted a laboratory position with the National Institutes of Health (NIH) on a Corn Industry Research Foundation fellowship. It was here that she began her work on dextran, a glucose polymer similar to starch and cellulose. Jeanes also developed xanthan gum, a polysaccharide (a substance composed of many sugars, including glucose and mannose) that is commonly used as a thickening and emulsifying agent in food products such as ice cream and salad dressings. From 1940 to 1941, Jeanes continued her research on carbohydrates while working at the National Bureau of Standards (now the National Institute of Standards and Technology) near Washington, D.C. She then returned to Illinois to begin work at the newly opened Northern Regional Research Laboratory (NRRL) of the U.S. Department of Agriculture (USDA), in Peoria. She remained at the NRRL until her retirement in 1976.

Throughout her career, Jeanes was active in a number of organizations, including the American Chemical Society, Sigma Xi, and Iota Sigma Pi. In 1953, Jeanes was granted the USDA's highest award—the Distinguished Service Award—for her work on dextrans, becoming the first woman in the USDA to be so honored. She was honored in 1956 with a Garvan Medal by the American Chemical Society (ACS) and a Distinguished Service Award granted by the USDA to the NRRL Dextran Team. In 1962, Jeanes received the Federal Woman's Award from the U.S. Civil Service Commission. In 1968, the USDA rewarded Jeanes and her Biopolymer Research Team with the Superior Service Award for their work with xanthan gum. That same year, Baylor University honored her with its Outstanding Alumna Award.

See also Agriculture; American Chemical Society (ACS); Biomedical Engineering; Federal Woman's Award; Fieser, Mary Peters; Francis P. Garvan–John M. Olin Medal; National Institute of Standards and Technology (NIST); Patent
References "Allene R. Jeanes," *Chemical and Engineering News* (23 April 1956); Shearer, Benjamin F., and Barbara S. Shearer, eds., *Notable Women in the Physical Sciences: A Biographical Dictionary* (1997); Stanley, Autumn, *Mothers and Daughters of Invention: Notes for a Revised History of Technology* (1993); "Allene R. Jeanes," in Iowa State University Archives of Women in Science and Engineering, available at http://www.lib.iastate.edu/spcl/wise/aids/jeanes.html (cited 19 January 2000).

Jemison, Mae (b. 1956)

Mae Jemison is a physician, chemical engineer, educator, and entrepreneur. On the morning of 12 September 1992, she also became the first African American woman to participate in America's space program when she journeyed into space aboard the shuttle *Endeavor*. One goal of this eight-day mission was to launch a space laboratory for Japan. Jemison's job was to perform experiments to determine the effects of zero gravity on humans and other animals.

Mae Jemison was born in Decatur, Alabama, in 1956. When she was three years old, her family moved to Chicago, Illinois, where Mae was raised and attended school. At an early age, she became interested in astronomy and space exploration. She was further inspired by the successful moon flight of *Apollo 11*. In 1973, Jemison graduated from Morgan Park High School with honors and multiple scholarship offers: a National Achievement Scholarship from Stanford University, a scholarship from the Massachusetts Institute of Technology (MIT), and an AT&T Bell Laboratories scholarship.

Jemison elected to attend Stanford University, in Palo Alto, California, and began her freshman year at only 16 years of age. She majored in chemical engineering and African and Afro-American studies, and graduated in 1977 with both a B.S. and a B.A. degree. She then entered Cornell University Medical School in New York. While at Cornell, she became a member of the National Student Medical Association. Her participation in this group allowed her to complete some of her studies in Cuba. In addition, the International Traveler's Institute for Health Studies provided funds for her to travel to Kenya, Africa, where she worked with the African Medical and Research Foundation, and to Thailand, where she worked at a refugee camp for Cambodians.

Jemison received her M.D. degree in 1981. After completing her internship at the University of Southern California Medical Center in Los Angeles in 1982, she worked briefly as a general practitioner in Los Angeles and then returned to Africa as a medical officer with the Peace Corps. In this role, Jemison worked in eastern Africa's Sierra

In 1992, physician and chemical engineer Mae Jemison became the first African American woman to travel into space. (UPI/Corbis-Bettmann)

Leone region, and in Liberia, in west Africa. Her responsibilities included managing personnel and laboratory facilities, teaching and developing curricula, and developing health and safety protocols for volunteers. In addition, she worked with the National Institutes of Health (NIH) and the Centers for Disease Control (CDC) on research involving a hepatitis B vaccine and parasitic diseases.

Jemison returned to the United States in 1985 and took a job as a general practitioner with a health maintenance organization (HMO). This same year, she applied to the National Aeronautics and Space Administration (NASA) for admission to the space program. She also took night classes in engineering at the University of California in Los Angeles (UCLA). In January 1986, the explosion of the space shuttle *Challenger,* which resulted in the deaths of all crew members, brought NASA's shuttle program to a halt. Despite this tragedy and setback, Jemison remained firm in her decision to become an astronaut, and she reapplied to NASA in October of that year. Within six months she was notified that NASA had selected her to train for the shuttle program. Jemison, who was one of fifteen candidates selected from a list of approximately 2,000 applicants, became the first African American woman to achieve this status. Upon completion of her training in 1988, Jemison was named science mission specialist. On her 1992 shuttle flight, her job was to perform scientific experiments to determine the effects of space on astronauts during a shuttle mission. These experiments dealt with the use of biofeedback to alleviate symptoms of motion sickness; the loss of calcium in bones that occurs in space; and the effects of weightlessness on frog development.

In 1993, Jemison resigned from NASA. She practiced medicine briefly, before founding her own company—the Jemison Group—in Houston, Texas. The Jemison Group seeks ways to use technology to improve health care in developing nations, such as those in west Africa. One project of the company is a telecommunications system that uses space satellites to allow doctors to speak with patients living in developing nations. Jemison also strives to promote science and technology as fields accessible to women and minorities.

Mae Jemison has received numerous awards for her work in science, technology, and the astronaut program, as well as for her work in encouraging women and minorities to pursue their interests. Among them are the *Essence* Science and Technology Award (1988), Gamma Sigma Gamma's Woman of the Year award (1989), and the *Ebony* Black Achievement Award (1992). In 1992, an alternative public school in Detroit, Michigan, was named the Mae C. Jemison Academy in her honor. The following year, Jemison was inducted into the National Women's Hall of Fame.

See also Dunbar, Bonnie J.; Mack, Pauline Beery; National Aeronautics and Space Administration (NASA); National Women's Hall of Fame; Ochoa, Ellen; Resnik, Judith A.; Ride, Sally Kirsten; Space Exploration; Telecommunications
References Altman, Susan, *The Encyclopedia of African American Heritage* (1997); Bernstein, Leonard, Alan Winkler, and Linda Zierdt-Warshaw, *Multicultural Women of Science* (1996); Graham, Judith, ed., *Current Biography 1993* (1993); Kessler, James H., et al., *Distinguished African American Scientists of the 20th Century* (1996); Smith, Jessie Carney, and Nikki Giovanni, eds., *Black Heroes of the 20th Century* (1998); National Women's Hall of Fame, available at http://www.greatwomen.org (cited 29 April 1999).

Jet Propulsion Laboratory (JPL)

Established in 1936 as a site for pioneering rocket research, the Jet Propulsion Laboratory (JPL) is a federally funded research facility for the design and development of unmanned spacecraft. JPL is managed for the National Aeronautics and Space Administration (NASA) by the California Institute of Technology and is located in Pasadena, California. It is the major U.S. center and world leader in the manufacture and guidance of robotic spacecraft.

Early research conducted by JPL involved "strap-on" rockets designed to provide added thrust capabilities on overloaded military aircraft on shortened runways. With the outbreak of World War II, the U.S. military demand for rockets increased in response to the German rocket program. Using missiles, JPL initiated experiments to study aerodynamics, propellants, navigation, guidance, and communication systems.

JPL's research and development in the technologies of navigation, guidance, and control systems eventually led to the first successful unmanned U.S. space mission, in 1958. That year, a Juno 1 rocket was used to launch *Explorer 1,* the first American satellite, into orbit.

In 1958, NASA was created, and the management of JPL was transferred from the military to the space agency. Today, although JPL no longer researches jet propulsion, it retains its name. In the 1960s, JPL began to focus its vast experience and resources on the manufacture of robotic spacecraft specifically for space exploration. The following list includes some major accomplishments of JPL:

- 1960s *Ranger* and *Surveyor* missions to the moon
- 1970s *Mariner* missions to Mercury, Venus, and Mars
- 1975 *Viking* mission to search for life on Mars
- 1977 *Voyager I* flyby of the planets Jupiter (1979) and Saturn (1980–1981); *Voyager II* flyby of the planets Uranus (1986) and Neptune (1989)
- 1989–1990 *Magellan* studies the cloud cover and surface features of Venus
- 1995 *Galileo* probes the atmosphere of Jupiter
- 1997 *Sojourner* is sent to explore the surface of Mars

See also Aeronautical and Aerospace Engineering; Berkowitz, Joan; Brill, Yvonne Claeys; Burbidge, (Eleanor) Margaret Peachey; Johnson, Barbara Crawford; Johnson, Katherine Coleman Goble; National Aeronautics and Space Administration (NASA); Shirley, Donna; Space Exploration
References Harris, Ian, "JPL: Open Day 1998," *Spaceflight* (1998); Koppes, Clayton R., *JPL and the American Space Program: A History of the Jet Propulsion Laboratory 1936–1976* (1982); Jet Propulsion Laboratory, National Aeronautics and Space Administration, California Institute of Technology, available at http://www.jplnasa.gov.

Johnson, Barbara Crawford (b. 1925)

Aerospace engineer Barbara Johnson is credited with creating, supervising, and analyzing the performance of a backup guidance system for the reentry phase of the *Apollo* spacecraft. The Entry Monitor System, or EMS, was a graphic display on which *Apollo* astronauts could rely to direct their spacecraft during its reentry into Earth's atmosphere at an angle not too shallow to cause overheating or too deep to cause unbearable gravitational forces. Today, such graphic displays are used in most spacecraft, in aircraft, and in some automobiles. Johnson was also involved in the design and development of managed systems engineering related to lunar landings, *Skylab, Apollo-Soyuz,* and the flights of the various shuttles/orbiters operated by NASA.

Barbara Johnson received her B.S.E. in 1946 from the University of Illinois (Champaign-Urbana). She was the first woman to earn a B.S. in engineering from the university. Following her graduation, she accepted a position at Rockwell International Space Division in California, eventually becoming the project leader responsible for supervising the design and performance of the Hound Dog air-to-ground missile used by the B-52 bomber. By 1961, Johnson was supervising the Entry Trajectories Program at Rockwell and developing the EMS system. In 1968, she became Engineering Systems Manager for Command and Service Module Programs for the Rockwell Space Division, which included work on *Apollo, Skylab,* and the *Apollo-Soyuz* Test Project (ASTP). By 1973, she was appointed Manager of Mission Requirements and Integration for the Rockwell Space Systems Group, a position she held until her retirement in 1984.

In 1971, Johnson was presented the University of Illinois Mothers' Association Medallion of Honor. Three years later she was awarded their Distinguished Alumni Merit Award, and that same year she was presented the Achievement Award of the Society of Women Engineers (SWE). In 1976, she received the Outstanding Engineer Merit Award from the Institute for the Advancement of Engineering (IAE) and the Dirk

Brower Award from the American Astronautical Society. She also was presented a medallion for exceptional achievements by Christopher Craft, director of the Johnson Space Center. Johnson is a fellow of the IAE, a senior member of the SWE, and a member of the American Institute of Aeronautics and Astronautics (AIAA).

See also Aeronautical and Aerospace Engineering; Johnson, Katherine Coleman Goble; National Aeronautics and Space Administration (NASA); Ordnance; Space Exploration
References McMurray, Emily M., ed., *Notable Twentieth-Century Scientists*, vol. 2: (F–K) (1995); Vare, Ethlie Ann, and Greg Ptacek, *Mothers of Invention: From the Bra to the Bomb, Forgotten Women and Their Unforgettable Ideas* (1988); "Barbara Crawford Johnson," Society of Women Engineers Achievement Award, available at http://swe.org/SWE/Awards/achiev.html (cited 12 November 1998).

Johnson, Katherine Coleman Goble (b. 1918)

Research mathematician and scientist Katherine Johnson's work in aerospace technology helped make possible the space missions of astronauts Alan Shephard, John Glenn, and Neil Armstrong. Johnson's mathematical calculations contributed to the development of navigational procedures for accurately tracking spacecraft trajectories. By investigating the complexities of interplanetary orbits, Johnson provided early astronauts with emergency navigational maps and charts. She also was involved with the Earth Resources Satellite, which is used to locate underground deposits of minerals and other valuable resources.

Katherine Johnson was born in White Sulphur Springs, West Virginia. Although White Sulfur Springs remained their home, Katherine's father moved the family to Institute, West Virginia, at the beginning of each school year because he believed the school system there provided better educational opportunities for African American children than that in their hometown. In 1937, Johnson graduated from West Virginia State College *summa cum laude* with a B.S. in education. She then taught French and math while doing graduate work in math and physics at West Virginia University.

In 1953, Johnson was hired as a mathematician at NASA's Langley Research Center in Hampton, Virginia. She advanced from projects involving the B-17 bomber to those involving the analysis of data gathered during the *Apollo* moon missions. In 1967 and again in 1970, Johnson and her colleagues on the Lunar Spacecraft and Operations Team won NASA's Group Achievement Award. Special achievement awards were also presented to Johnson in 1970, 1980, and 1985. After retiring from the Langley Research Center, Johnson participated in a television documentary on math sponsored by the U. S. Department of Education.

See also Aeronautical and Aerospace Engineering; Brill, Yvonne Clayes; Computers/Computer Technology; Darden, Christine M.; Granville, Evelyn Boyd; Johnson, Barbara Crawford; Mathematics; National Aeronautics and Space Administration (NASA); Ordnance; Space Exploration
References McMurray, Emily M., ed., *Notable Twentieth-Century Scientists* (1995); Plaski, Harry A., and James Williams, eds., *The Negro Almanac: A Reference Work on the Afro-American* (1983); Sammons, Vivian Ovelton, *Blacks in Science and Medicine* (1990); U.S. Department of Energy (DOE/ OPA-0035), *Black Contributors to Science and Technology* (1979); Winston, Bonnie V., "Black History: Virginia Profiles Katherine Johnson," Richmond Newspaper, Inc., available at http://www.gatewayva.com/ pages/bhistory/1997/john.html (cited 10 November 1998).

Johnson, Nancy M. (ca. 1795–1890)

Nancy M. Johnson was a resident of Washington, D.C., when she obtained a patent for her hand-cranked ice cream maker in 1843. Johnson's ice cream maker consisted of a wooden bucket that held crushed ice that had been salted. A covered can with a dasher that mixed the ingredients sat inside the wooden bucket. This inner container was then rotated by turning a hand crank. Before Johnson's ice cream maker was developed, the making of ice cream was a lengthy process that involved the continual stirring of ingredients with a spoon. After receiving her patent, Johnson sold the rights to her machine for the then large sum of $1,500. Ice cream makers sold today for use in the home continue to share many similarities with the device developed by Johnson.

See also Baldwin, Anna; Domestic Appliances; Gilbreth, Lillian Moller; Henry, Beulah L.; Jones, Amanda Theodosia
References Macdonald, Anne L., *Feminine Ingenuity: How Women Inventors Changed America* (1992); Stanley, Autumn, *Mothers and Daughters of Invention: Notes for a Revised History of Technology* (1993).

Jones, Amanda Theodosia (1835–1914)

Amanda Jones's 1873 invention of a vacuum-canning process to preserve food laid the groundwork for a billion-dollar industry that affected the lives and dietary habits of people worldwide. Despite this fact, Jones never acquired fame or fortune from her work: canning was practiced long before Jones developed her process. However, unlike earlier methods, Jones's canning process did not require food to be cooked at high temperatures—a practice that caused foods to lose flavor, texture, and nutritional value.

Amanda Jones was born into a family of 12 children in East Bloomfield, New York. She attended classes at East Aurora Academy in New York, and by the age of 15 was teaching at a country school. During the summers, Jones continued her high school studies; however, ill health forced her to abandon school and teaching and turn to writing poetry. In 1872, with the aid of a relative, Professor LeRoy C. Cooley, she invented a vacuum-canning process for which she later received seven patents. She also tried—unsuccessfully—to establish a canning company.

Jones's experiments with food canning helped her develop mechanical skills. In 1880, she developed and patented an oil burner that could safely use crude oil as a fuel. The device revolutionized the shipping industry, which could now substitute oil for coal on its ships. However, unable to secure financing for production of the burner, Jones had to abandon this project. In 1890, she again turned to her canning invention. This time she established the Women's Canning and Preserving Company of Chicago—a company composed solely of women workers and stockholders. The enterprise did well, but Jones lost control

of the company after three years (the company itself remained in existence for the next 31 years). Despite this setback, Jones continued her canning experiments and received four more patents between 1903 and 1906. She later became a writer and spiritualist.

See also Domestic Appliances; Home Economics; Invention/Inventors; Patent
References Altman, Linda Jacobs, *Women Inventors: American Profiles* (1997); James, Edward T., Janet Wilson James, and Paul S. Boyers, eds., *Notable American Women: A Biographical Dictionary (1607–1950)*, vol. 2: (G–O) (1971); Macdonald, Anne L., *Feminine Ingenuity: How Women Inventors Changed America* (1992); Stanley, Autumn, *Mothers and Daughters of Invention: Notes for a Revised History of Technology* (1993); Vare, Ethlie Ann, and Greg Ptacek, *Mothers of Invention: From the Bra to the Bomb, Forgotten Women and Their Unforgettable Ideas* (1988).

Jones, El Dorado (1860/1861?–1932)

At various times, El Dorado Jones worked as a schoolteacher, an insurance salesperson, and an inventor. Her career as an inventor emerged from her interest in making objects from metal and led her to develop small electric irons suitable for travel, an accompanying ironing board, and later, a collapsible hat rack and an exhaust attachment for airplanes that was designed to muffle the noise of the engines.

El Dorado Jones was a native of Moline, Illinois. While living in that state in the late 1800s, Jones abandoned her somewhat lucrative position as an insurance salesperson to pursue a career as an inventor. She was successful in this venture and at one point owned and operated a factory that manufactured the products she invented. Having a keen dislike and distrust of men, Jones hired only women older than 40 to work in her factory. Several times she received offers for the purchase of her company, but she consistently refused to sell.

In 1917, Jones finally abandoned her company and moved to New York City. She hoped to obtain funding to begin producing an airplane exhaust system she had developed; however, she was unsuccessful in this venture, possibly because of her antimale views. By the time of her death in November 1932, the 71-year-old former inventor, who had once enjoyed a lifestyle supported by a lucrative business, was impoverished. She had exhausted her own resources and was subsisting in a small East Side tenement apartment with aid from the city.

See also Darden, Christine L.; Domestic Appliances; Metals and Metallurgy; Potts, Mary Florence Webber; Todd, E. L.
References Macdonald, Anne L., *Feminine Ingenuity: How Women Inventors Changed America* (1992); "Woman Inventor Dies in Poverty: El Dorado Jones Spent Recent Years Seeking Backing for Airplane Muffler" [obituary], *New York Times* (27 November 1932).

Jones, Sarah E. (1829–1884)

The Patent Act of 1790 permitted women to obtain patents; however, many state laws forbade women to own property. This dilemma resulted either in many women inventors not patenting their inventions or in their obtaining patents in the name of a male relative. The latter was the case for an improved sieve for straining hot food, invented by Pennsylvania native Sarah E. Jones. Jones believed a larger version of her food straining device would be adequate for the commercial preparation of fruit spreads and other condiments. On 11 August 1868, U.S. Patent No. 80,966 was issued for the device to Sarah's husband, John D. Jones, a shoe merchant in Jersey City, New Jersey. Little else is known about the life of this early woman inventor.

See also Bevier, Isabel; Eglin, Ellen F.; Farmer, Fannie Merritt; Hibbard, Susan; Home Economics; Jones, Amanda Theodosia; Masters, Sybilla Righton; Richards, Ellen Henrietta Swallow
Reference Burstyn, Joan N., ed., *Past and Promise: Lives of New Jersey Women* (1990).

Joullié, Madeleine M. (b. 1927)

Madeleine Joullié is an organic chemist who has isolated natural substances effective in eliminating viruses and parasites and then synthesized these substances in the laboratory. In this work, she has developed fungal substances that are used in the treatment of cancer and diseases caused by protozoans. In addition, her research team has synthesized an interferon inducer known as tilorone in 1976. Interferons are proteins with low molecular weights that are produced by the body to combat cancers and a variety of viral infections.

Joullié was born in Paris and grew up in Rio de Janeiro, Brazil. She attended Simmons College in Boston, graduating with a B.S. in chemistry in 1949. She next attended the University of Pennsylvania, from which she received an M.S. degree (1950) and a Ph.D. (1953). Joullié remained at the University of Pennsylvania as an instructor of organic chemistry. She also established a research group that conducts experiments in organic chemistry. The focus of many of these experiments involves isolating antitumor and antiviral agents from plants and marine organisms for the purpose of synthesizing the agents in the laboratory. Her group has successfully synthesized substances that inhibit the growth of certain blood vessels. This action effectively reduces blood flow and the transport of nutrients to cancerous cells.

Madeleine Joullié has been well recognized for her work. In 1972 she became the first woman to receive the Philadelphia Section Award of the American Chemical Society (ACS); six years later, she was awarded its Garvan Medal for her contributions as a teacher and developer of research personnel and her accomplishments in chemistry. In 1984, Joullié received the American Cyanamid Faculty Award from the University of Pennsylvania. The next year, she was presented the Scroll Award of the American Institute of Chemists (AIC). In 1991, she received the Linback Award for Distinguished Teaching from the University of Pennsylvania's Philadelphia Section of the Association of Women in Science (AWIS). She also served in the 1992 Mentoring Group of the Women in Cancer Research (WICR), and she conducted the Synthetic Organic Program at the Department of Chemistry of the University of Pennsylvania. In 1994 she received the ACS's Philadelphia Organic Chemists' Club Award and Henry Hill Award.

Joullié is a fellow of the New York Academy of Sciences and has been a Fullbright Lecturer. She is also the coauthor of a number of scientific articles and books.

See also American Chemical Society (ACS); American Institute of Chemists (AIC); Association for Women in Science (AWIS); Biotechnology; Brown, Rachel Fuller; Francis P. Garvan–John M. Olin Medal; Hazen, Elizabeth Lee; Medicine/Medical Technology
References "Madeleine Joullié Wins Henry Hill Award," *Chemical and Engineering News* (5 September 1994); Shearer, Benjamin F., and Barbara S. Shearer, eds., *Notable Women in the Physical Sciences: A Biographical Dictionary* (1997); Joullié Research Group, "Madeleine M. Joullié," available at http://www.sas.upenn.edu/~carrollp/joullie.html (cited 1 March 1999); University of Pennsylvania, Department of Chemistry, "Madeleine M. Joullié," available at http://www.sas.upenn.edu/chem/faculty/joullie/joullie.html (cited 1 March 1999); Women in Cancer Research (WICR), "WICR Handbook on Mentoring," available at http://www.mrl.ucsb.edu/~bettye/wicr/1.html (cited 1 March 1999).

Joyner, Marjorie Stewart (1896–1994)

In 1928, the U.S. Patent and Trademark Office issued patent No. 1,693,515 for a permanent waving machine. The machine, an electrical device that used curling irons and clamps to add waves to women's hair, was invented by African American Marjorie Stewart Joyner. Although the machine was widely used, the profits from its development were not realized by Joyner but by the company to which she had assigned the patent rights and for which she worked—the Madame C. J. Walker Cosmetics Company.

Marjorie Stewart Joyner was born in Monterey, Virginia, in 1896. She later moved to Chicago, Illinois, where she studied cosmetology. In the 1920s, Joyner joined the Madame C. J. Walker Cosmetics Company in Chicago, where she worked as a Walker Agent—a sales representative who used company products to style the hair of customers in their homes. It was while working as an agent that Joyner developed the idea for her permanent waving machine. Although Joyner did not profit directly from the machine, she was made national supervisor of the beauty schools operated by Walker's company.

In 1945, Joyner, working with noted African American educator Mary McCleod Bethune, cofounded the United Beauty School Owners' and Teachers' Association, an organization made up of about 25 schools. These schools, which offered classes at a reasonable cost that could be paid in installments, provided numerous African Americans with an opportunity to develop skills in the cosmetics professions. Joyner also worked with Bethune to raise funds for black colleges. For her work in the cosmetics industry, the *Washington Post* dubbed Joyner the "Grande Dame of Black Beauty Culture." For her lifelong commitment to aiding African Americans, Joyner was recognized at the national convention of the National Council of Negro Women in 1989, in its "Salute to Black Women Who Make It Happen."

See also Newman, Lyda; Walker, Madame C. J.
References Macdonald, Anne L., *Feminine Ingenuity: How Women Inventors Changed America* (1992); Smith, Jessie Carney, ed., *Black Firsts: 2,000 Years of Extraordinary Achievement* (1994); Alleman, Nanette, et al., "Notable Chicago African Americans," available at http://www.chipublib.org (cited 9 June 1999).

Karle, Isabella L. (b. 1921)

This crystallographer's use of electron and X-ray diffraction techniques revolutionized the way in which the molecular structure of crystals is analyzed. Using instruments she designed and built, Karle photographed the diffracted images of crystalline structures. She then applied mathematical formulas developed by her husband, Nobel Prize–winning physical chemist Jerome Karle, to identify patterns among interatomic distances and angles. Data obtained by Isabella Karle provided a means by which the structure of crystalline molecules could be identified, replicated, and synthesized in the laboratory, previously a time-consuming and costly task.

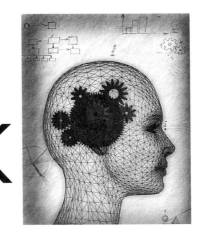

Isabella Lugoski Karle was born in Detroit, Michigan. While in high school, she chose science as her career and was awarded a scholarship to the University of Michigan, from which she received her B.S. degree in physical chemistry in 1941 and her M.S. degree, also in physical chemistry, in 1942. A fellowship from the American Association of University Women (AAUW) and a Horace H. Rackham fellowship provided the financial means Karle needed to remain at the University of Michigan, where she earned her Ph.D. in physical chemistry in 1944.

Isabella and her husband Jerome worked at the University of Chicago on the Manhattan Project (a secret government project to construct an atomic bomb) and for a short while, at the University of Michigan. However, nepotism policies at the University of Michigan prevented married couples from working together, so the Karles sought employment elsewhere. The U.S. Naval Research Laboratory in Washington, D.C., offered both Karles positions. In the Naval Research Laboratory's X-ray Diffraction Group, Isabella and Jerome Karle began their groundbreaking work on diffraction studies of crystalline structures.

Throughout her career Isabella Karle has received many honors, including the Annual Achievement Award of the Society of Women Engineers (1968), the Hildebrand Award (1970), the Garvan Medal of the American Chemical Society (1976), and the Chemical Pioneer Award of the American Institute of Chemists (1985). Karle served as president of the American Crystallographic Association in 1976 and has been a member of the National Academy of Sciences since 1978. In 1986, she received the Lifetime Achievement Award from Women in Science and Engineering; she received the Secretary of the Navy's Distinguished Achievement in Science Award the following year. In 1991 the National Institutes of Health (NIH) presented her the Paul Ehrlich Prize, and in 1992 the American Peptide Society awarded her the Vincent du Vigneaud Award. In 1993, Karle became the first woman to win the Franklin Institute's prestigious Bower Award and Prize in Science. In 1995 she was inducted into the Michigan Women's Hall of Fame. That same year, President Bill Clinton presented her the National Medal of Science.

See also American Crystallographic Association (ACA); Chemical Pioneer Award; Crystallography; Emerson, Gladys Anderson; Francis P. Garvan–John M. Olin Medal; Joullié, Madeleine M.; Manhattan Project; National Medal of Science; Nepotism Policies

References Bailey, Martha J., *American Women in Science: A Biographical Dictionary* (1994); Kass-Simon, G., and Patricia Farnes, eds., *Women of Science: Righting the Record* (1990); McMurray, Emily M., ed., *Notable Twentieth-Century Scientists,* vol. 2: (F–K) (1995); Nobel, Iris, *Contemporary Women Scientists of America* (1979); Shearer, Benjamin F., and Barbara S. Shearer, eds., *Notable Women in the Physical Sciences: A Biographical Dictionary* (1997); National Science Foundation, "Isabella Karle," available at http://www.nsf.gov/nsf/ nmos/moskarle.htm (cited 26 June 1998); Sankaran, Neeraja, "National Medal of Science Winners Contributed To Birth of Their Fields," *The*

Scientist, available at http://www.thescientist.library. upenn.edu/ yr1995/oct/heros_951030.html (cited 26 June 1998); Silverman, Edward R., "Naval Lab 'Experimentalist' Honored With Bower Award," *The Scientist,* available at http://www.thescientist.library. upenn.edu/yr1994/ jan/silverman_p4_940110.html (cited 26 June 1998).

Kaufman, Joyce Jacobson (b. 1929)

Joyce Jacobson Kaufman is most known for her applications of theoretical quantum chemistry (a branch of chemistry that focuses on the electron configuration of molecules and the energy they possess) to pharmacology. Kaufman uses her research findings to configure drugs and to predict their toxicity. She was among the first research chemists to apply the principles of quantum chemistry to large molecules, increasing our knowledge about the molecular structure of tranquilizers, narcotics, and carcinogens. Kaufman's methods also enable researchers to predict the effects of new drugs being developed for use in the treatment of mental disorders. Because of her pioneering work in applying quantum chemistry to pharmacology, many pharmaceutical laboratories now employ quantum chemists.

Joyce Jacobson was born in New York City. Following her parents' separation, she moved with her mother to Baltimore, Maryland, where she was raised. In 1937, Jacobson participated in a summer program for gifted children at Johns Hopkins University. This experience triggered her desire to pursue studies in chemistry. Twelve years later, she graduated with honors and a B.S. degree in chemistry from this same university. While working toward this degree, Jacobson met and married engineer Stanley Kaufman.

After receiving her bachelor's degree, Kaufman worked as a technical librarian at the Army Chemical Center in Baltimore. While there, she developed an indexing system for cataloging the center's technical reports. In 1950, Kaufman became a research chemist at the center. She remained in this position only two years before returning to Johns Hopkins University to study chemical physics. She received her master's degree in 1959 and her Ph.D. in 1960.

In 1960, Kaufman accepted a position at the Martin Company's Research Institute for Advanced Studies. There, while serving successively as scientist, staff scientist, and head of the quantum chemistry group, she investigated the theoretical applications of quantum mechanics to problems in chemistry. Kaufman remained at Martin until 1969, at which time she returned to Johns Hopkins University. There she served as principal research scientist in the Department of Chemistry and as associate professor in the Department of Anesthesiology and Clinical Care Medicine at the School of Medicine. Since 1970, Kaufman has served as a consultant to the National Institutes of Health (NIH).

Kaufman's work has earned her many honors and awards. In 1964, 1965, and 1966, she received the Martin Company's Gold Medal for Outstanding Scientific Accomplishments. She was elected fellow of the American Institute of Chemists in 1965 and was named fellow of the American Physics Society (APS) the next year. Kaufman received the Garvan Medal from the American Chemical Society (ACS) for her work in quantum chemistry in 1974. That same year, she was chosen outstanding chemist in the Maryland section of the ACS and presented the Maryland Chemist Award. In 1981, she was elected to the American Society for Pharmacology and Experimental Therapeutics.

See also Biomedical Engineering; Biotechnology; Computers/Computer Technology; Elion, Gertrude Belle; Francis P. Garvan–John M. Olin Medal; Medicine/Medical Technology; Pharmacology; Richardson, Jane Shelby
References Green, Jay E., ed., *McGraw-Hill Modern Scientists and Engineers* (1980); Grinstein, Louise S., Rose K. Rose, and Miriam Rafailovich, eds., *Women in Chemistry and Physics: A Biobibliographic Sourcebook* (1993); Shearer, Benjamin F., and Barbara S. Shearer, eds., *Notable Women in the Physical Sciences: A Biographical Dictionary* (1997).

Keichline, Anna W. (1890–?)

Anna Keichline was the first registered woman architect in the state of New York and is recognized for her design of homes and public buildings in several cities. She is most known for her contributions to domestic architecture and planning. Keichline received patents for several domestic appliances, including a combination sink-washboard. She also received patents for efficient kitchen designs based on the most effective use of time and movement.

Anna Keichline was born in Bellefonte, Pennsylvania. Her creative talents and penchant for detail were demonstrated at age 14, when an oak card table and walnut chest she had designed and built won first prize at a county fair. There are few accounts of Keichline's early life, but it is known that she attended Cornell University's School of Architecture. She received her architectural degree in 1911, becoming New York's first female registered architect.

Shortly after graduating, Keichline turned her talents to home efficiency. Her patented kitchen designs and arrangements of ranges, sinks, and countertops were based on cost, time, and motion economy. In addition to her creativity and inventiveness in the kitchen, Keichline also designed furniture, children's toys, and a room divider that created space for children to play. She patented a wall-mounted folding bed and a compressed-air radiator, and developed colorful, prescored, soundproof, and fireproof clay blocks for use in reinforcing walls in areas prone to flooding and tornadoes.

See also Benjamin, Miriam E.; Bethune, Louise Blanchard; Bevier, Isabel; Cochran, Josephine G.; Gabe, Frances Bateson; Gibreth, Lillian Moller; Home Economics; Lin, Maya; Stanley, Louise
References Macdonald, Anne L., *Feminine Ingenuity: How Women Inventors Changed America* (1992); Lemelson-MIT Program, "Women's History Month: Home Inventions," in Invention Dimension Inventor of the Week archives, available at http://web.mit.edu/invent/www/inventorsR-Z/whm3.html (cited 23 May 1999).

Keisler, Hedwig
See **Lamarr, Hedy**

Kempf, Martine (b. 1958)
Martine Kempf is the inventor of Katalavox. Katalavox, derived from the words *katala* (Greek, "to

understand") and *vox* (Latin, "voice"), is a control system used to operate voice-activated equipment. Kempf's Katalavox system has widespread applications. For example, it permits microsurgeons a means for making hands-free magnification adjustments. It also provides persons with disabilities the ability to operate wheelchairs and automobiles through speech.

Kempf first developed Katalavox on her Apple computer in 1981, when she was only 23. Kempf's father was the primary inspiration for her work. A victim of polio, he had designed hand controls for his car and subsequently began customizing automobiles for operation by drivers with special needs. Additional inspiration for her product were the many teenagers in Bonn, Germany, who had been left with deformities as a result of their *in utero* exposure to the drug thalidomide during their mothers' pregnancies. (Use of thalidomide was later banned throughout most of Europe and in the United States as a result of the efforts of U.S. physician Helen Brooke Taussig in the early 1960s.) Kempf first applied her Katalavox control system in a voice-activated automobile. Collaboration between Martine Kempf and Daimler-Benz led to an automobile with 50 Katalavox-controlled functions. The demonstration model was exhibited at the April 1984 industrial exposition in Tokyo, Japan.

Martine Kempf was born and raised in France. The microsurgical applications of her creation led to Kempf's receipt of the Prix Grande Siècle Laurent Perrier in 1985. Another recipient of this award was noted oceanic explorer Jacques Cousteau. The same year that she received this award, Kempf moved to the United States where she founded Kempf-Katalavox, a firm in California that refines and manufactures Katalavox-based systems. Since its development, Katalavox systems have been implemented for use by residents of more than 14 countries.

See also Blount (Griffin), Bessie J.; Computers/Computer Technology; Gilbreth, Lillian Moller; Hopper, Grace Murray; Keichline, Anna W.; Kenner, (Mary) Beatrice Davidson; Taussig, Helen Brooke
References Stanley, Autumn, *Mothers and Daughters of Invention: Notes for a Revised History of Technology* (1993); Vare, Ethlie Ann, and Greg Ptacek, *Mothers of*

Martine Kempf demonstrates her computerized voice-activated device, which has uses in both medicine and the aerospace industry. (Reuters/Corbis)

Invention: From the Bra to the Bomb, Forgotten Women and Their Unforgettable Ideas (1988); Kempf-Katalavox, "Who Is Martine Kempf?" available at http://www.katalavox.com/martine.htm (dated 6 October 1998; cited 8 August 1999).

Kendrick, Pearl Luella (1890–1980)

In 1932, bacteriologists Pearl Kendrick and Grace Eldering developed the first successful vaccine for pertussis (whooping cough). Before this vaccine was developed, pertussis infections were causing as many as 6,000 deaths each year in the United States. Most of these deaths occurred in children under age five. By 1939, the vaccine developed by Kendrick and Eldering was ready for commercial production. Its use eventually reduced the incidence of pertussis by as much as 90 percent.

Pearl Kendrick was born in Wheaton, Illinois, the daughter of a Methodist preacher who moved frequently with his family. Because of these frequent moves, Kendrick began school in Herkimer, New York, but attended many schools throughout the state before graduating from high school in Sherburne, in 1908. Kendrick then taught at rural schools (1908–1911) before enrolling at Greenville College in Illinois. She later transferred to Syracuse University, from which she received her B.S. degree in science in 1914. For the next four years, Kendrick worked as a science teacher and a high school principal. During the summers, she attended Columbia University to study bacteriology and protozoology.

Kendrick pursued employment as a bacteriologist. She accepted a job with the New York State Department of Health Laboratory in 1919. One year later, she moved to the Michigan State Department of Health Laboratories in Lansing. Kendrick worked as a microbiologist at these labs for the next six years, performing a variety of diagnostic laboratory procedures. She also assisted R. L. Kahn in the development of laboratory methods for use in the diagnosis of syphilis.

In 1926, Kendrick moved from the Lansing laboratory to the newly established state laboratories in Grand Rapids, where she served as associate director. Three years later, she took a leave of absence to pursue a doctorate at the School of Hygiene and Public Health at Johns Hopkins University. She was awarded an Sc.D. in public health in 1932, after which she returned to the Grand Rapids Branch of the Michigan State Department of Health Laboratories.

Grace Eldering joined Kendrick at the Grand Rapids facility in 1932. The women began studies of pertussis that included laboratory experiments and field tests. In a short time, they grew the organism that caused pertussis, which had been identified in 1906, in the laboratory. Only a few months later, in January 1933, they prepared a small amount of vaccine for field testing. The results of these tests were promising, and Kendrick presented a report about the vaccine to the American Public Health Association (APHA) in 1935. Additional testing in other parts of the country that took place following this meeting also showed good results and led to mass production of the vaccine by 1939. Later, diphtheria and tetanus toxoids were added to the pertussis vaccine to create a DPT vaccine. Today, all infants in the United States receive a series of DPT vaccinations.

Kendrick retired from the Michigan Department of Health in 1951. She immediately joined the faculty of the University of Michigan department of epidemiology. There she taught basic research practices. She remained at the university until her retirement in 1960.

While Kendrick was working at the Grand Rapids laboratory and the University of Michigan, she also served as a consultant to health groups from many countries, helping them develop effective pertussis vaccines. Her work with such agencies included service with Great Britain's Medical Research Council in 1949. The following year, she headed a UNICEF program of immunization in Colombia, Chile, and Brazil. She also served as a consultant to the World Health Organization (WHO) and the Pan American Health Organization until 1964. As part of this work, she participated in the WHO conference on diphtheria and pertussis vaccinations in Yugoslavia in 1952 and was involved in a pertussis vaccination project in Mexico in 1961. She also was involved with immunization programs in Russia and France.

Throughout her career, Kendrick was active in the APHA; she served as its vice president in 1946. She was a diplomate of the American Board of Microbiologists and held memberships in the Microbiology Society, the American Board of Bacteriologists, and the American Academy of Microbiologists. In 1950, Kendrick was made an honorary member of the medical staff of Blodgett Hospital in Grand Rapids. Ten years later, the Michigan legislature passed a resolution honoring Kendrick for her contributions to health in Michigan. In addition, in 1983, Kendrick was posthumously inducted into the Historical Honors Division of the Michigan Women's Hall of Fame.

See also Alexander, Hattie Elizabeth; Baker, Sara Josephine; Dick, Gladys Rowena Henry; Eldering, Grace; Elion, Gertrude Belle; Evans, Alice Catherine; Williams, Anna Wessels

References "DIED, Pearl Luella Kendrick, 90," [obituary] in "Milestones," *Time* (20 October 1980); O'Hern, Elizabeth Moot, *Profiles of Pioneer Women Scientists* (1986); Stanley, Autumn, *Mothers and Daughters of Invention: Notes for a Revised History of Technology* (1993); Greater Grand Rapids Women's History Council, "Dr. Pearl Kendrick, Dr. Grace Eldering," available at http://www2.gvsu.edu/~whc/ge.htm (cited 20 March 1999).

Kenner, (Mary) Beatrice Davidson (b. 1912)

Mary Beatrice Kenner, who generally is referred to simply as Beatrice Kenner, is recognized as the most prolific African American woman inventor. Between 1956 and 1987, Kenner applied for and received five patents for her inventions, although she claims to have actually devised as many as 152 different articles or devices. Despite her accomplishments as an inventor, Kenner never manufactured any of her inventions and thus never profited from their creation.

Mary Beatrice Davidson was born in 1912 in Charlotte, North Carolina. She considered inventing to be a family trait because her father, her grandfather, and her sister Mildred Austin Smith also had invented a variety of devices. Beatrice's father, Sydney Davidson, was by vocation a preacher; however, he also was an inventor who received patents on three inventions. One of these, a pants presser that ironed pants while they were packed away inside a piece of luggage, brought Sydney Davidson an offer of $20,000 from a company in New York in 1914. However, believing that he would make more money if he developed and sold the invention himself, Sydney Davidson turned down the offer—a decision that proved unwise, since he only made one of his pants pressers, which he sold for only $14.

Beatrice Davidson got the idea for her first invention when she was only six. The idea was for a self-oiling door hinge that would eliminate the squeaking that sometimes occurred when a door was opened or closed. Beatrice tried to construct such a hinge, but her lack of mechanical skills led her to abandon the idea. Another of her youthful ideas was an umbrella tip made from a sponge. Her thinking was that the sponge could soak up the water that ran off the umbrella after it had been closed, thus preventing puddles from gathering on the floor.

When Beatrice was 12, her family moved to Washington, D.C. While living there, Beatrice regularly visited the U.S. Patent and Trademark Office (PTO), conducting research to determine if any of her ideas had already resulted in inventions patented by others. Although some of them had, she was delighted to discover that many had not.

Beatrice received much of her education while living in Washington, D.C. She graduated from Dunbar High School in 1931. She then attended Howard University, but was forced to leave when her family could no longer afford to pay her tuition. To help support her family, Kenner took a variety of different jobs. In her spare time, she continued to think up ideas for new inventions.

During World War II, Beatrice worked for the federal government, first with the Census Bureau and later with the General Accounting Office (GAO). In 1945, she married a soldier she had met at a dance, but the marriage did not last, and the couple divorced five years later. In 1981, Beatrice married a second time. Her second husband, James "Jabbo" Kenner, also worked for the federal government.

Kenner continued to work for the federal government through the 1950s, while independently pursuing patents for her inventions. On 15 May 1956, Beatrice Kenner was issued her first patent (No. 2,745,406), for an invention she had envisioned when she was 18 years old. The patent was for a sanitary belt that was secured in place through the use of adhesive tabs. In interviews, Kenner has stated that a company was interested in marketing her invention, until they discovered it had been devised by a black woman. Undaunted by this setback, Kenner continued inventing and was issued a second patent (No. 2,881,761) on 14 April 1959, for an improvement on the sanitary napkin.

After retiring from her government job, Kenner opened a flower shop, which she ran for more than twenty years. In May 1976, she received her third patent (No. 3,957,071), for a carrier attachment for use on walkers and wheelchairs. Kenner's development of this idea resulted from her desire to help her sister Mildred, who suffered from multiple sclerosis and needed a walker to move about. Kenner's next patent (No. 4,354,643) came six years later. This patent was for a bathroom tissue holder.

In September 1987, at the age of 75, Kenner received her fifth patent (No. 4,696,068). The patent was issued for a back washer constructed of foam and terry cloth. The device was designed to be attached to a shower wall and allow bathers to wash their backs by rubbing against it. Although advancing in age, today Kenner continues to develop inventions in her spare time. Since receiving her last patent, she has developed ideas for a device for attachment to the shoulder harness of a car's seat belt that she calls the "Nickless." The device is intended to prevent the shoulder harness from scraping against the wearer's neck, a problem faced by many people of short stature, such as Kenner herself. Kenner has also developed a protective, retractable hood for use on automobile windshields, to keep snow and ice from accumulating in this area. Kenner has expressed concern over how few African Americans have become involved in the invention process, and hopes that her achievements in this area will inspire future generations.

See also Blount (Griffin), Bessie J.; Brown, Marie Van Britton; Eglin, Ellen F.; Henry, Beulah L.; Kempf, Martine; Mangin, Anna; Patent
References Hine, Darlene Clark, Elsa Barkley Brown, and Rosalyn Terborg-Penn, eds., *Black Women in America: An Historical Encyclopedia,* vol. 1: (A–L) (1993); Jeffrey, Laura, *American Inventors of the 20th Century* (1996); Stanley, Autumn, *Mothers and Daughters of Invention: Notes for a Revised History of Technology* (1993); Louisiana State University Libraries, Baton Rouge, Louisiana, "African American Women Inventors: Historical," in *The Faces of Science: African Americans in the Sciences,* available at http://www.lib.lsu.edu/lib/chem/display/women_inventors.html (cited 9 June 1999).

Kies, Mary (1742–?)

Mary Kies (nee Dixon) is recognized as the first American woman to receive a U.S. patent. The patent was issued on 5 May 1809, for Kies's invention of a process of "weaving straw with silk or thread." At the time the patent was issued, Kies was a 57-year-old resident of South Killingly, Connecticut. Little else is known about her life. However, despite the lack of information about Kies's life, it is known that her weaving process was largely used by the New England hat-making industry. Use of the method resulted, in part, from a ban on the importation of European goods that had been imposed by the federal government in response to the Napoleonic Wars in Europe. Beginning in 1821, use of Kies's weaving process declined in favor of a new method for using various grasses in the making of bonnets, which was developed by Sophia Woodhouse Welles of Wethersfield, Connecticut.

See also Goode, Sarah E.; Masters, Sybilla Righton; Metcalf, Betsey; Patent; Patent Act of 1790; Slater, Hanah Wilkinson (Mrs. Samuel); Textiles; Welles, Sophia Woodhouse
References Macdonald, Anne L., *Feminine Ingenuity: How Women Inventors Changed America* (1992); Trager, James, *The Women's Chronology* (1994); U.S. Patent and Trademark Office, *A Quest for Excellence* (1994); Vare, Ethlie Ann, and Greg Ptacek, *Mothers of Invention: From the Bra to the Bomb, Forgotten Women and Their Unforgettable Ideas* (1988); Buel, Nora, "The Long Road from Straw Hats to High Technology," *Inventors Assistance Program News* 37 (August 1994), available at http://iridium.nttc.edu/assist/inventions/invart/meetneed.html (cited 15 January 1999).

King, Helen (1869–1955)

Biologist Helen King is most noted for her work in breeding pure strains of laboratory animals—specifically, white rats. Her research findings offered new insights regarding the inbreeding of white rats. In addition, her purebred laboratory animals became a source of pure strains and mutant forms such as those required for use in research laboratories worldwide. Although King's work did not specifically utilize available technology, the pure strains produced in her laboratory would prove essential in medical research and genetic applications, especially in the highly specialized and technological fields of genetic engineering and animal husbandry.

Helen King was born in Oswego, New York. She attended the Oswego Free Academy before entering Vassar College in Poughkeepsie, New York, from which she received an A.B. degree in 1892. Three years after graduating from Vassar, King began graduate work at Bryn Mawr College in Pennsylvania. There she majored in morphology under the supervision of noted geneticist Thomas Hunt Morgan. She minored in physiology and also studied paleontology with Florence Bascom. King was awarded a Ph.D. in 1899 and published her dissertation on the embryonic development of the common toad two years later. She remained at the college five more years to continue her research and to assist in the biology laboratory. At the same time, King taught science at Miss Florence Baldwin's School (1899–1907).

In 1906, King began working as a research fellow in zoology at the University of Pennsylvania. Two years later, she accepted a teaching position at the Wistar Institute of Anatomy and Biology, in Philadelphia. She remained at Wistar until her retirement in 1949, first advancing to assistant professor in 1913, and then to professor of embryology in 1927. She was a member of the Institute's advisory board for 24 years as well as editor of the Wistar Institute's bibliographic service for 13 years. She also was editor of the *Journal of Morphology and Physiology* from 1924 to 1927.

At Wistar, King shifted her research focus from toads to rats. She became interested in the effects of close inbreeding and began a series of experiments using albino rats. She mated two males and two females from the same litter of albino rats and continued the inbreeding, selecting only the healthiest litters, for more than 130 generations. The albino rats produced as a result of these studies became known as the King colony. These animals were widely used in research projects worldwide. King published her research findings, in which she analyzed growth, sex ratio, and other characteristics in the inbred rats. She concluded that the inbred animals compared favorably with stock albinos as far as body growth, vigor, and fertility. However, the results she obtained generated controversy in the newspapers in light of established social and religious prejudices and taboos against inbreeding. Additionally, her findings appeared to contradict the work of Darwin, who suggested that inbreeding led to degeneration of animal populations.

In addition to her studies of albino rats, King researched the effects of captivity on wild animals. Her experimental subjects were wild Norway rats that had been trapped on the streets of Philadelphia. King summarized her results, concluding that the progeny of wild rats in captivity grew faster and were ultimately larger than their wild counterparts. In addition, she demonstrated that the effects of captivity tended toward a diverse rather than a homogeneous population. She hypothesized that inbred mutations were the result of variations in germ plasm resulting from age. Many of her research findings continue to have genetic implications and have been applied to other animals, including race horses and farm animals.

In 1932, King was honored by the Association to Aid Scientific Research for Women, with the Ellen Richards Research Prize. In 1937, she served as vice president of the American Society of Zoologists. She was a fellow of the New York Academy of Sciences and held memberships in the American Association for the Advancement of Science (AAAS), the American Society of Naturalists, the American Association of Anatomists, the Society of Experimental Biology and Medicine, Phi Beta Kappa, and Sigma Xi.

See also Biotechnology; Genetic Engineering; Krim,

Mathilde Galland; Phi Beta Kappa Society; Richards, Ellen Henrietta Swallow; Stevens, Nettie Maria

References Bailey, Martha J., *American Women in Science: A Biographical Dictionary* (1994); Gillispie, Charles Coulston, ed., *Dictionary of Scientific Biographies* (1981); Ogilvie, Marilyn Bailey, *Women in Science Antiquity through the Nineteenth Century: A Biographical Dictionary with Annotated Bibliography* (1986); Shearer, Benjamin F., and Barbara S. Shearer, eds., *Notable Women in the Life Sciences: A Biographical Dictionary* (1996).

Knight, Margaret E. (1838–1914)

Margaret Knight was a prolific inventor of the late nineteenth and early twentieth centuries. She received at least 22 patents in her name or with co-patentees; however, she may have developed more than 87 inventions, some of which were never patented. The first invention, for which she never received a patent, was a safety device for use in the textile industry. The idea was conceived when Knight was only 12 years old. Knight's most notable invention was the mechanism that made possible the mass manufacture of square-bottomed paper bags.

Margaret (Mattie) Knight was born in York, Maine, but grew up in Manchester, New Hampshire. She received little formal education but was intrigued by tools and mechanical objects at an early age. Her mechanical inclination was demonstrated when at age 12, Knight observed an accident involving a machine at the cotton mill at which her brothers worked. A machine spindle broke free, injuring a worker. This incident led to Knight's development of a safety mechanism that stopped the machine if a thread broke, preventing the ejection of the spindle.

Unlike most inventions by other women inventors of her time, most of Knight's were related to machinery rather than domestic appliances. Her first patented invention, the mechanism that made possible the square-bottomed paper bag, was developed while Knight worked at a plant that produced paper bags. Although someone contested her patent on the machine, Knight was eventually awarded the patent for its creation in 1870. The invention was used worldwide and deemed of enough importance that in 1871

Knight was decorated by Queen Victoria of England. Knight refined and updated the design of the machine over the years, and a variation of it is still used today in paper-bag manufacture.

Knight also invented and patented several domestic devices. These included a dress and skirt shield (1883), a reel for a spinning or sewing machine (1884), and a spit (1885). Around 1890, Knight's inventions again involved machines. Between 1890 and 1894, she obtained patents for sole-cutting machines used in shoemaking. In 1894, she obtained patents for a window frame and sash and a numbering machine.

During the last phase of her inventive career, Knight once again focused on machinery, developing engines and related parts. Between 1902 and 1915, she received several patents for inventions on rotary engines and motors (one was awarded after her death). Knight sold rights to some of these inventions to the Knight-Davidson Motor Company of New York. Throughout her inventing career, Knight sold many of her inventions to the companies that employed her. As a result, she never truly profited from her inventions. At the time of her death, her estate was valued at only $275.

See also Blanchard, Helen Augusta; Domestic Appliances; Henry, Beulah L.; Invention/Inventors; Patent; Safety Engineering; Textiles

References James, Edward T., Janet Wilson James, and Paul S. Boyers, eds., *Notable American Women, 1607–1950: A Biographical Dictionary,* vol. 2: (G–O) (1971); Ogilvie, Marilyn Bailey, *Women in Science Antiquity through the Nineteenth Century: A Biographical Dictionary with Annotated Bibliography* (1986); Stanley, Autumn, *Mothers and Daughters of Invention: Notes for a Revised History of Technology* (1993); Vare, Ethlie Ann, and Greg Ptacek, *Mothers of Invention: From the Bra to the Bomb, Forgotten Women and Their Unforgettable Ideas* (1988); Lemelson-MIT Program, "Prolific Female Inventors of the Industrial Era," in Invention Dimension's Inventor of the Week archives, available at http://web.mit.edu/invent/www/inventorsR-Z/whm2.html (cited 14 December 1997).

Koshland, Marian Elliot (b. 1921)

Although her educational background was in bacteriology and immunology, Marian Koshland's contributions to technology evolved from her research for the U.S. military, in connection with the development of the atomic bomb. The United States became involved in World War II immediately following the bombing of Pearl Harbor in 1941. At this time, Marian Koshland was completing the requirements for a bachelor's degree at Vassar College in Poughkeepsie, New York. By the time Koshland received her M.S. degree from the University of Chicago in 1943, the United States had already been involved in the war for more than a year, and the University of Chicago was already actively involved in war research. Koshland was asked to participate in this research through work at the Office of Scientific Research and Development (OSRD), which was located at the university. She simultaneously contributed to research being done by the Commission on Air Borne Diseases at the University of Colorado. From 1945 to 1946, Koshland served as a junior chemist on the atomic bomb project at the Manhattan District in Tennessee (now the Oak Ridge National Laboratory), where studies in uranium separation and enrichment were being conducted.

At the conclusion of World War II, Koshland returned to her doctoral studies. She received a doctorate in bacteriology in 1949 from the University of Chicago. From 1953 to 1965, she worked as an associate bacteriologist at the Brookhaven National Laboratory (a nuclear research facility), located on Long Island, New York. She then accepted a teaching position at the University of California at Berkeley, where she advanced in rank to become department chair in 1983.

See also Anderson, Elda Emma; Bartlett, Helen Blair; Fink, Kathryn (Kay) Ferguson; Foster, Margaret; Goeppert-Mayer, Maria; Libby, Leona W.; Manhattan Project; Office of Scientific Research and Development (OSRD); Quimby, Edith Hinkley; Way, Katharine; Wu, Chien-Shiung

References Bailey, Martha J., *American Women in Science: A Biographical Dictionary* (1994); Jaques Cattell Press, ed., *American Men and Women of Science,* 12th ed. (1972); Torpie, Stephen L., et al., eds., *American Men and Women of Science,* 18th ed. (1992–1993) (1992).

Krim, Mathilde Galland (b. 1926)

Mathilde Galland Krim has made several significant contributions to genetics. In the early 1950s, she became the first person to observe the DNA structure of chromosomes. In 1953, she helped develop a method of determining the gender of an unborn child by examining the amniotic fluid—the watery liquid that surrounds a developing fetus. Krim used this same procedure, called amniocentesis, to identify potential genetic abnormalities in fetuses.

Mathilde Galland was born in Como, Italy, to a Swiss father and an Austrian mother. At an early age, she spoke Italian, German, and French. Later, she learned Hebrew and English. Her family moved to Geneva, Switzerland, when she was eight years old. In 1945, Galland enrolled as one of two female students in the basic science department of the University of Geneva. From there, she received her B.S. degree in genetics in 1948 and a Ph.D. in biology in 1953. It was while doing her graduate work that Galland, using an electron microscope, observed the DNA structure of chromosomes.

The same year she received her Ph.D., Galland married David Danon, a Jewish medical student from Bulgaria. She then converted to Judaism and moved with her husband to Israel. In Israel, Mathilde Danon worked as a junior scientist at the Weizman Institute of Science in Rehovot. While there, she helped develop the technique for analyzing amniotic fluid. Today, doctors worldwide use genetic information contained in this fluid to determine the gender of the fetus and to find evidence of hereditary diseases or disorders such as Tay-Sacs disease or Down's syndrome.

In 1956, the Danons divorced. In 1958, Mathilde married American movie executive Arthur B. Krim and moved to New York City, where she accepted a position as research associate in virology at Cornell Medical College. Three years later Mathilde Krim transferred to the Sloan-Kettering Institute of Cancer Research. In 1970, she was asked to prepare a report on the history of cancer. The report influenced the passage of the National Cancer Act of 1971. In 1975, Krim helped establish the Interferon Evaluation Program at Sloan-Kettering, which she headed

Academy of Sciences (NAS) in 1988. More recently, Krim was honored with the Scientific Freedom and Responsibility Award of the American Association for the Advancement of Science (AAAS) in 1994.

> **See also** Biotechnology; Genetic Engineering; Joullié, Madeleine M.; Medicine/Medical Technology; Stevens, Nettie Maria
> **References** Harris, Laurie, *Biography Today*, vol. 1 of 3, *Scientists and Inventors Series, Profiles of People of Interest to Young Readers* (1996); Moritz, Charles, ed., *Current Biography Yearbook, 1987* (1987); Hadassah, "Medical Research: Mathilde Krim, Ph.D.," available at http://www.hadassah.org/85th_pages/w_o_d.htm (cited December 1998); "Krim, Mathilde," in BIOGRAPHY Online Database, available at http://search.biography.com/print_record.pl?id=16678 (cited December 1998).

Geneticist Mathilde Krim conducted groundbreaking work that led to development of the test known as amniocentesis. (Mitchell Gerber/Corbis)

from 1981 to 1985. At this time, she and several colleagues had discovered that interferon was an effective treatment for one kind of leukemia. In 1985, Krim secured funding, with a grant of $5 million from the National Institutes of Health (NIH), for construction of a molecular-virology laboratory at St. Luke's-Roosevelt Hospital Center in New York City. She remains associated with St. Luke's Hospital.

In addition to her groundbreaking work in genetics, Krim has been in the forefront of AIDS research and was instrumental in raising funds for that cause. For her many achievements in science, she has been the recipient of many awards. Among them are the Spirit of Achievement Award from Albert Einstein College of Medicine (1972), the Human Rights Achievement Award of the American Association of Physicians (1987), and the Charles A. Dana Award for Pioneering Achievements in Health issued by the National

Kurtzig, Sandra L. Brody (b. 1946/1947?)

Founding one of the fastest-growing publicly held companies in the United States may have been the last thing on Sandra Brody Kurtzig's mind in 1972 when she was looking for a way to supplement her family income while raising her two sons. However, Kurtzig did just that and in the process succeeded in a traditionally male-dominated arena—the development of computer software. Her contributions in this area have led some to describe her as one of the "heroes of Silicon Valley."

Sandra Brody was born in Chicago in 1947 and moved with her family to California when she was 11. Throughout her childhood, Brody was exposed to an entrepreneurial mind-set at home. Dinner conversations between her parents often revolved around the ups and downs of her father's residential real estate development company.

In her college years, Brody focused on areas less frequently entered by women than by men. After high school graduation, she attended the University of California at Los Angeles (UCLA), where she majored in chemistry and mathematics. A strong achiever, she completed her degree program in only three years, receiving a B.S. in both chemistry and mathematics in 1968. Brody then attended graduate school at Stanford University, where she earned a master of science degree in aerospace engineering, also in 1968.

After earning her M.S. degree, Brody worked for several years, first for the TRW Company as a math analyst, and later for General Electric (GE) Corporation as a marketing representative, selling software. During this period of her life, she also married Arie Kurtzig.

In 1972, at the age of 25, Sandra Kurtzig was a stay-at-home mother with two young sons. Looking for a part-time job that would permit her to remain at home with her children, she took her $2,000 severance pay from her earlier position at General Electric and began a home-based computer software business. She named it ASK Computer Systems, a name developed from the first initials in the names Arie and Sandra Kurtzig. In the company's first few years, Sandra Kurtzig developed several unique software packages that were adopted for use by publishing, manufacturing, and sales organizations to monitor inventory and employee information. Software she developed also was used to distribute corporate data to the appropriate departments within a company. Initially, Kurtzig was providing and developing software mostly for small companies. However, she later obtained projects that involved work with the Hewlett-Packard and Boeing corporations. By 1983, ASK Computer Systems employed 200 people and was generating $22 million per year in sales.

Kurtzig decided to step down from her position as chief executive officer and president of ASK in 1985. She groomed a successor from within the company to replace her as CEO, but remained chair of the company's board of directors. Over the next few years, Kurtzig traveled and spent time with her boys. She joined the morning television program *Good Morning America* as a commentator covering women in business, gave lectures at Stanford University, and wrote the book *CEO: Building a $400 Million Company from the Ground Up*, which was published in 1991. However, while Kurtzig was enjoying her time off, it became apparent that her successor and her company were in trouble.

Kurtzig returned to ASK Computer Systems,

resuming her positions as president and CEO. In addition, she instituted changes in the company's product line. The company began to develop portable software applications that could operate on multiple computer platforms and began to adapt software for market niches in new areas, such as the automotive industry. Kurtzig also increased the company's research budget from 20 percent to 50 percent of sales. In time, the sales figures increased to $100 million annually. With the company again doing well, in 1993, Kurtzig retired a second time.

Never one to rest, in May 1996, Kurtzig joined forces with her son Andy to found E-Benefits, a provider of insurance and human resource solutions for small businesses. Since small companies typically spend double the amount that large corporations spend on human resource costs, the purpose of E-Benefits is to provide automated human resource functions that small companies could afford to maintain.

See also Computers/Computer Technology; Estrin, Thelma; Goldstine, Adele Katz; Hoover, Erna Schneider; Hopper, Grace Murray; Kempf, Martine

References Hanauer, Mark, "Technology: A Friendly Frontier for Female Pioneers," *Fortune*, vol. 109 (25 June 1985); Rudolph, Barbara, "Why Can't a Woman Manage More Like . . . A Woman?" *Time* (Fall 1990); Schumacher, Mary Louise, "Sandra Kurtzig, Multiple Success: Establishing Company and Raising Two Sons," *San Jose Mercury News* (1999); Stanley, Autumn, *Mothers and Daughters of Invention: Notes for a Revised History of Technology* (1993).

Kwolek, Stephanie Louise (b. 1923)

Chemist Stephanie Kwolek discovered the technology that led to the development of Kevlar®, a high-strength, high-stiffness fiber five times stronger than an equal mass of steel and resistant to rust, corrosion, fire, and stress. First used in the cords in steel-belted tires, Kevlar® now is used in spacecraft, underwater cables, safety helmets, skis, and brake linings. The material is also used to make bullet-resistant vests worn by military and law-enforcement personnel worldwide.

Stephanie Kwolek was born in New Kensington, Pennsylvania. She showed an interest in the natural sciences at an early age—an interest that

Textile chemist Stephanie Kwolek is best known for her development of Kevlar®. (Courtesy of Dupont)

continued through her school years and led her to enroll at the Carnegie Institute of Technology in Pittsburgh (now Carnegie-Mellon University) in 1942. Kwolek graduated with a B.S. in chemistry in 1946 and began working at E. I. Du Pont de Nemours and Company, in Buffalo, New York. Four years later she moved to the Textile Fibers Pioneering Research Laboratory at DuPont's Experimental Station in Wilmington, Delaware, where she researched and developed synthetic fibers.

Kwolek worked with low-temperature polymers (long-chained molecules) that when dissolved could be drawn into thin fibers. One group of polymers on which she worked produced strong fibers, but the fibers decomposed when subjected to high temperatures. In 1965, Kwolek discovered the liquid crystalline polymer solution that could be made into the fiber that would come to be known as Kevlar®. She received a patent for this unique fiber in 1971.

Stephanie Kwolek retired in 1986, but she continues to serve as a consultant to both the Dupont Company and the National Research Council of the National Academy of Sciences (NAS). During her 40-year career, Kwolek received a total of 17 patents. She also received numerous honors and awards, including the Delaware Section Publication Award from the American Chemical Society (ACS) (1959), an honorary D.Sc. from Worcester Polytechnic Institute (1981), and the Carnegie-Mellon University Alumni Association Merit Award (1983).

Although Kwolek was involved in the development of many materials, most of the awards bestowed upon her resulted from the development of Kevlar®. Among the more significant of these are the Howard N. Potts Medal for liquid crystalline solutions of polymers and resulting fibers, from the Franklin Institute of Philadelphia (1976); the Materials Achievement Citation for Kevlar®, from the American Society of Metals (1978); the American Institute of Chemists' (AIC) Chemical Pioneer Award; and the Creative Invention Award in 1980, from the American Chemical Society (ACS). In 1992, Kwolek was inducted into the Engineering and Science Hall of Fame in Dayton, Ohio. The next year, she was honored with the National Salute to Corporate Inventors, by the National Inventors' Hall of Fame. In 1995, Kwolek received the American Innovator Award from the U.S. Patent and Trademark Office and became the fourth woman to be inducted into the National Inventors' Hall of Fame. Her most notable honor is the National Medal of Technology, which was presented to her by President Bill Clinton in 1996.

See also Lemelson-MIT Program; Materials Engineering; National Inventors' Hall of Fame; National Medal of Technology; Patent; Textiles

References Altman, Linda Jacobs, *Women Inventors: American Profiles* (1997); Torpie, Stephen L., et al., eds., *American Men and Women of Science,* 18th ed. (1992–1993) (1992); Vare, Ethlie Ann, and Greg Ptacek, *Women Inventors and Their Discoveries* (1993); Lemelson-MIT Program, "Stephanie Louise Kwolek (1923–)," in Invention Dimension, Inventor of the Week archives, available at http://web.mit.edu/invent/www/inventorsI-Q/kwolek.html (cited 14 December 1997); "National Medal of Technology: Stephanie Kwolek," in Dupont Science and Technology, available at http://www.dupont.com/corp/science/kwolek.html (cited 5 December 1998); "Stephanie Kwolek," in WITI Hall of Fame, available at http://www.witi.org/center/witimuseum/halloffame/previousinducte/1996/skwolek.shtml (cited 10 December 1997).

Lamarr, Hedy (1914–2000)

Actress Hedy Lamarr is most noted for her beauty and her success in films during the 1940s. Few people know about her coinvention of a revolutionary wireless antijamming device for use in radio-controlled torpedoes during World War II. This invention affects communications technology even today.

Hedy Lamarr was born Hedwig Maria Eva Kiesler, in Vienna, Austria. In 1933, she married Fritz Mandl, a powerful munitions manufacturer. During the early years of World War II, it was rumored that Mandl was a Nazi sympathizer who was selling war materiel to Germany. He also was investigating weapon control systems—specifically, wireless devices such as radio signals—for use in guiding torpedoes and other explosive devices. Mandl, always furtive, distrustful, and seeking to impress his clients, kept his wife Hedwig at his side, even during highly technical business meetings. It was during these meetings that Hedwig gradually came to understand the underlying technology used in wireless guidance systems.

In 1938, Austria fell to Germany. Hedwig fled from her husband and made her way to England. There she met MGM executive Louis B. Mayer and came to the United States as Hedy Lamarr. After arriving in Hollywood, Lamarr met musician George Anthiel. Anthiel was experimenting with mechanical music, such as that used in player pianos. In addition, Anthiel, who had been driven from Nazi Germany during the early 1930s, was committed to helping the war effort.

Inspired by the slotted paper rolls used to produce music in the player piano and by the effects of synchronization, Lamarr and Anthiel combined their creative talents to develop what became known as the Secret Communication System. They were awarded a patent for the system in 1942. A main feature of the device was "frequency hopping," the jumping of a radio signal from one frequency to another at rapid intervals. This feature prevented detection, jamming, or deciphering of the signal without a synchronized receiver.

Although the device developed by Lamarr and Anthiel was never used in guiding torpedoes, applications of the same technology today allow

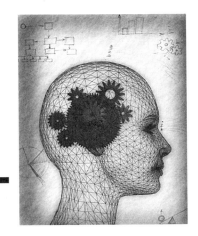

Actress Hedy Lamarr coinvented an antijamming device for use aboard naval vessels. (Corbis/ Bettmann-UPI)

multiple users to share radio frequencies at the same time without interfering with each other. This technology, known as spread-spectrum, provides a means of high-speed wireless access to the Internet and is used in satellite communications. In recognition of their achievement in advancing wireless communications, Lamarr and Anthiel received the Electronic Frontier Foundation (EFF) Pioneer Award in 1997.

See also Bradberry, Henrietta M.; Computers/
Computer Technology; Ordnance
References "Film Beauty Hedy Lamarr Dead at Age
86," [obituary] *Delaware County Daily Times* (20 January 2000); Macdonald, Anne L., *Feminine Ingenuity:
How Women Inventors Changed America* (1992);
"Screen Star Hedy Lamarr Dead at 86: Legendary
Beauty Seen in Many Motion Pictures," *Long Island
Newsday* (20 January 2000); Stanley, Autumn, *Mothers
and Daughters of Invention: Notes for a Revised History
of Technology* (1993); Couey, Anna, "The Birth of Spread
Spectrum: How 'the Bad Boy of Music' and 'the Most
Beautiful Girl in the World' Catalyzed a Wireless
Revolution—in 1941," online article appearing in
MicroTimes, available at http://www.microtimes.com/
166/coverstory166.html (cited 5 May 1999).

Lamme, Bertha (1869–1954)

The details of Bertha Lamme's engineering career are not well documented. However, it is known that she applied mathematics to the design of motors and generators, preparing the way for today's computer-aided design. It is also known that Lamme was part of the team that developed the turbogenerator and power system at Niagara Falls.

Bertha Lamme was born in a rural community near Springfield, Ohio. In 1893, she graduated from Ohio State University (OSU) with a degree in mechanical engineering and a specialty in electricity. She became the first woman at OSU and only the second woman in the United States to graduate with an engineering degree. Following graduation, Lamme was hired by the Westinghouse Company in Pittsburgh, Pennsylvania. For 12 years, she was a member of a design team that included her brother Benjamin G. Lamme and her future husband, Russell Feicht. Bertha Lamme's job was to oversee the mathematics program for the engineering department. In this role, she contributed to the designs of some of the company's early generators and motors. She also played a role in the development of many inventions for which the Westinghouse Electric and Manufacturing Company was issued patents.

One year after Lamme joined the engineering group, her brother designed a commercial induction motor and a rotary converter. Later, Feicht

designed a three-phase, 80-horsepower AC motor for a boat-pulling machine used on the Miami Canal. A few years later, he also designed the world's largest induction motor. This device powered the water cascade at the World's Fair in St. Louis in 1904. The next year, Bertha Lamme resigned her position with Westinghouse to become a wife and mother. Her only daughter, Florence, who became a physicist, was born in 1910.

Although her exact contributions as an engineer are unclear, Bertha Lamme received several honors. Ohio State University named a laboratory for both Benjamin and Bertha Lamme. In 1973, the Society of Women Engineers (SWE) honored Lamme by creating the annual Westinghouse Bertha Lamme Scholarship to help attract young women to engineering.

See also Clarke, Edith; Electrical and Electronics
Engineering; Knight, Margaret E.; Mechanical
Engineering
References Kass-Simon, G., and Patricia Farnes,
eds., *Women of Science: Righting the Record* (1990);
Stanley, Autumn, *Mothers and Daughters of Invention:
Notes for a Revised History of Technology* (1993);
LeBold, William K., and Dona J. LeBold, "Women
Engineers: A Historic Perspective," available at http://
www.asee.org/pubs/html/women_engineers.htm (cited
27 June 1998); San Jose State University, "Bertha
Lamme," available at http://www.sjsu.edu/depts/
Museum/lam.html (cited 27 June 1998); Society of
Women Engineers, "SWE Scholarship Program: The
Westinghouse Bertha Lamme Scholarships," available at
http://www.eas.asu.edu/-wise/money.html (cited 27
June 1998).

Lemelson-MIT Program

The Lemelson-MIT Program was established in 1994 by inventor Jerome Lemelson (1923–1997) and his wife, Dorothy, at the Massachusetts Institute of Technology (MIT). The program's missions are to raise awareness of the importance of science and technology to America's economic growth and to motivate new generations to become scientists and inventors. Toward these ends, it provides honor and recognition, cash awards, and educational information about American inventors and technical achievers.

The program at MIT is one of several in the United States funded by the Lemelson Foundation, a private philanthropy established by Lemelson and his family in 1993 and maintained by the reinvestment of earnings from Lemelson's worldwide licensing agreements on the more than 500 patents he was awarded during his 40-year career.

The Lemelson-MIT Program offers awards in four areas. The most well known is the Lemelson-MIT Prize, which each year awards one-half million dollars to one person, in recognition of a single invention or innovation. The Lemelson-MIT Prize is the single largest award of its kind in the world. A second award, the Lemelson-MIT Lifetime Achievement Award, also has been granted annually since 1994. Winners are selected from among the fields of medicine and health care, computing, technology, environmental science, engineering, and industrial and consumer product development.

In its first five years, the Lifetime Achievement Award has twice been given to women. Nobel Prize–winning research chemist Gertrude Belle Elion (1918–1999) was recognized with the Lemelson-MIT Lifetime Achievement Award in 1997, for lifelong endeavors in the development of drugs that are now used to treat leukemia, herpes, and immune disorders. In 1999, the award honoree was retired DuPont chemist Stephanie Kwolek, who received the award for her work in the polymer sciences, which led to the development of such fibers as Kevlar®, Lycra®, Spandex®, and Nomex®.

The Lemelson-MIT Program also promotes the inventive spirit in America's youth through its Student Prize and Invention Apprenticeship. The Student Prize is a $30,000 cash award given to an MIT senior who shows promise as an inventor. The Lemelson-MIT Invention Apprenticeship was instituted in 1998 to recognize an American high school student who shows promise as an inventor. The recipient receives an opportunity to participate in a summer mentoring partnership, where he or she does projects in science or engineering entrepreneurship. Its first winner was Krysta Morlan, who developed the "Cast Cooler," a forced-air device that helps alleviate the irritation and discomfort associated with plaster casts

by carrying soothing cool air to the skin beneath the cast, through a piece of tubing.

In addition to recognizing inventors with awards, the Lemelson-MIT Program maintains an archive of information on inventors and their inventions. The archive, which profiles the achievements of women and men, is accessible via computer through the Lemelson Foundation's Invention Dimension® Web site. The profiles are updated weekly, after a new individual has been selected as Inventor of the Week.

See also Brown, Rachel Fuller; Elion, Gertrude Belle; Gabe, Frances Bateson; Grandin, Temple; Hazen, Elizabeth Lee; Kwolek, Stephanie Louise; Low, Jeanie S.; National Inventors' Hall of Fame; National Medal of Technology; Nobel Prize; Walton, Mary
References Lemelson-MIT Program, http://web.mit.edu/invent/www/ProgInfo.html (cited 20 July 1999); Lemelson-MIT Program, "Winner's Circle," in Invention Dimension, available at http://web.mit.edu/invent/www/Winners.html (cited 20 July 1999).

Leonard, Helen Louise
See **Russell, Lillian**

Levi-Montalcini, Rita (b. 1909)

Rita Levi-Montalcini is recognized for her groundbreaking contributions in neuroembryology, a highly specialized branch of science that deals with the early growth and development of nerve cells. Through laboratory investigations involving cancerous tumors in mice, she hypothesized that nerve cell growth is triggered by the presence of a substance associated with the tumor. Further experiments using chick embryo extract convinced her of the presence of the nerve-stimulating substance, which she called nerve growth factor (NGF). For her discovery, Levi-Montalcini shared the Nobel Prize for physiology/medicine with biochemist Stanley Cohen, her research partner. Levi-Montalcini became only the fourth woman awarded the Nobel Prize in this area.

Rita Levi was born into a secular Jewish family in Turin, an industrial city in northern Italy, and received a public education. Soon after graduating from high school, Levi learned that her former governess had fallen ill with cancer. Helpless and stunned by this news, Levi set her mind to becoming a doctor. She studied Latin, Greek, mathematics, philosophy, and history. She passed the qualifying exams for entrance into the University of Turin Medical School in 1930; received her M.D. degree in 1936; and four years later, received an additional degree for specialization in neurology and psychiatry.

While training in her specialty, Rita Levi studied at the University of Turin Clinic of Neurology and Psychiatry, under noted histologist and embryologist Giuseppe Levi. While working as Giuseppe Levi's assistant, Rita learned new and dramatic staining techniques, in which silver salts were used to produce clarity and detail in the organelles of stained chick nerve cells. Giuseppe became Rita's friend and mentor and stimulated her interest in neuroembryology—the area to which she devoted her life's work. During this early period of her professional career, Rita Levi added her mother's maiden name, Montalcini, to her own surname.

In 1936, Italy's Fascist government began a campaign of persecution against Jews as a sympathetic gesture to the Nazi cause. Two years later, Fascist government decrees mandated that Jews could not attend a university, hold a university position, or practice medicine. It was during this time that Rita Levi-Montalcini was working as an assistant to Giuseppe Levi. Barred from continuing her work at the university, Levi-Montalcini left Italy for Brussels, Belgium, in 1939. There she briefly continued her research at the Neurologic Institute of Brussels. However, when the Germans invaded Belgium later that year, Levi-Montalcini once again returned to Italy.

Unable to practice medicine, Levi-Montalcini set up a laboratory in her bedroom, where she secretly conducted her research for the next three years. Using a homemade incubator, crude but effective laboratory instruments that she fashioned from sewing needles and watchmakers' tools, and her microscope, Levi-Montalcini applied her new staining techniques in studying the growth, development, and differentiation of chick embryo nerve cells—specifically, motor neurons (nerve cells that cause muscles to contract and limbs to move). Based on her observations, Levi-Montalcini hypothesized that as an embryonic limb (arm or leg) develops, motor nerves begin to grow inside the limb. However, if the developing limb is removed in an embryo, the motor nerves that have begun to grow inside the limb will die. This concept established nerve cell death as a part of normal nerve development. It also suggested that the nerve's growth was being triggered and controlled by some unknown substance produced within the limb (a substance she would later identify and name nerve growth factor, or NGF). Unable to publish her research findings in Italian journals, Levi-Montalcini submitted her writings to the science journals of other countries. Her data were published in Swiss and Belgium journals and read as far away as the United States.

When the Allied forces liberated Italy in 1944, Levi-Montalcini provided field medical services for the U.S. Army in an Italian refugee camp. She continued this work until mid-1945, when she returned to the University of Turin to continue her research. Around this same time, Levi-Montalcini's published research findings on nerve growth and development came to the attention of Viktor Hamburger, a neurobiologist at Washington University in St. Louis, Missouri. Hamburger had been investigating nerve cell growth and had conducted experiments similar to those done by Levi-Montalcini. He was intrigued by her research, noting that her conclusions differed from his own. Hamburger believed that nerve cells did not begin to grow into a limb that had been removed. Hamburger invited Levi-Montalcini to the United States to discuss her findings and to work with him in researching nerve cell growth. Levi-Montalcini accepted the invitation and traveled to the United States, where she accepted a position as a research associate at Washington University in 1947. She remained associated with the university for the next 30 years, becoming a full professor in 1958.

In 1952, Levi-Montalcini traveled to Rio de Janeiro to study tissue culture techniques. Using these new methods, she combined mouse tumor tissue with embryonic chick nerve cells. The rapid growth of new nerve tissue convinced her of the presence of a nerve stimulating substance. These studies provided clear evidence that cancerous tumors in mice carried a substance that promoted or triggered nerve growth. She named this substance nerve growth factor (NGF). In 1953, Levi-Montalcini, now an associate professor, was collaborating with biochemist Stanley Cohen at Washington University. Their research indicated that NGF was a protein and was present not only in mouse tumors but also in even greater amounts in snake venom and in the salivary glands of adult male mice.

Cohen was successful in purifying NGF and determining its chemical structure. He also produced NGF antibodies (substances that inhibited the action of NGF). Cohen then discovered another substance that, like NGF, stimulated the growth of skin cells and cells in the cornea of the eye. He called this substance epidermal growth factor (EGF).

In the early 1960s, Levi-Montalcini established a research laboratory at the Higher Institute of Health, in Rome, which worked in collaboration with Washington University to research nerve growth factors. In 1969, Levi-Montalcini established the Laboratory of Cell Biology of the Italian National Research Council in Rome. She remained associated with the laboratory until her official retirement in 1979, after which she continued her research on NGF independently.

The discovery of NGF has significantly affected science and medicine. In 1986, Levi-Montalcini discovered that NGF affects nerve cells in the brain, spinal cord, and other nerve bundles. Such findings provide powerful insights into the potential uses of NGF in the study of degenerative nerve disorders such as Alzheimer's and Parkinson's disease. NGF and EGF also might prove effective in burn therapy and in the detection and treatment of human cancers.

In recognition of her accomplishments in neuroembryology, Levi-Montalcini was a corecipient of the Nobel Prize in physiology/medicine in 1986. She shared the award with biochemist Stanley Cohen, with whom she collaborated. In addition, Levi-Montalcini has received numerous other awards and honors. In 1968, she was elected to the National Academy of Sciences (NAS). In 1974, she received the William Thompson Wakeman Award of the National Paraplegic Foundation. She received the Lewis S. Rosenstiel Award for Distinguished Work in Basic Medical Research in 1982. The following year she was awarded the Louisa Gross Horwitz Prize of Columbia University. In 1986, the same year she was awarded the Nobel Prize, Levi-Montalcini received the Albert Lasker Basic Medical Research Award. The next year, she was presented the National Medal of Science, the nation's highest scientific award, in a ceremony in the White House Rose Garden.

In addition to her awards, Levi-Montalcini has received honorary doctorates from the University of Uppsala, the Weizmann Institute of Science, St. Mary College, and the Washington University School of Medicine. She is a member of the American Association for the Advancement of Science (AAAS); the American Academy of Arts and Sciences; the Belgian Royal Academy of Medicine; the National Academy of Sciences of Italy; the European Academy of Sciences, Arts, and Letters; and the Academy of Arts and Sciences of Florence. Levi-Montalcini also was the first and only woman member of the Pontifical Academy of Sciences in Rome.

See also Cori, Gerty Theresa Radnitz; Elion, Gertrude Belle; Goeppert-Mayer, Maria; Medicine/Medical Technology; National Academy of Sciences (NAS); National Medal of Science; Nobel Prize; Yalow, Rosalyn Sussman

References Bailey, Martha J., *American Women in Science: A Biographical Dictionary* (1994); McGrayne, Sharon B., *Nobel Prize Women in Science* (1993); Moritz, Charles, ed., *Current Biography Yearbook, 1989* (1989); Parry, Melanie, ed., *Larouse Dictionary of Women* (1996); Wasson, Tyler, ed., *Nobel Prize Winners: An H.W. Wilson Biographical Dictionary* (1987); Yount, Lisa, *Twentieth-Century Women Scientists* (1996).

Libby, Leona W. (1919–1986)

Leona Woods Libby was an expert and authority in the field of molecular spectroscopy. She gained renown for her pioneering contributions in the area of nuclear fission—specifically, in the development of the neutron detection technology that was required in order to monitor the fission chain reactions crucial to the success of the Manhattan Project (a top-secret U.S. government initiative aimed at developing the world's first atomic bomb). Libby also was noted for her analysis of isotopes (the various forms of an element, which differ in the number of neutrons in their nuclei) contained in tree samples as a means of determining the characteristics of ancient climates.

Leona Woods was born in LaGrange, Illinois, a small suburb of Chicago, and received her early education there. After completing high school, Woods enrolled at the University of Chicago. She received a B.S. degree in chemistry from this school in 1938 and went on to graduate studies. It was while working toward her graduate degree that Woods was inspired to focus on diatomic molecular spectroscopy (spectroscopy of molecules composed of two atoms of the same element). Inspiration came first from Nobel laureate James Franck, who had come to the university to introduce the new field of quantum chemistry, and later through Robert Mulliken (who would later receive a Nobel prize). Woods received her Ph.D. in chemistry in 1943.

While Woods was working toward her doctorate, the University of Chicago became one of several sites at which the highly secret research on the development of the atomic bomb was being conducted. The research at Chicago took place under the direction of Nobel physicist Enrico Fermi. The research facility established at the university was named the Chicago Metallurgical Laboratory—an innocuous wording, selected to deflect attention from the actual research being conducted there on the development of the first nuclear fission reactor. Woods, who was still a graduate student, was invited by Fermi to join the research team. It was during this time that she garnered considerable knowledge in the area of nuclear physics.

Woods married fellow researcher and physicist John Marshall, Jr. in 1943. It was during this time that the research team was involved in the development of the boron trifluoride neutron detector, an instrument that is essentially a highly sophisticated counter for use in monitoring fission chain reactions. The following year, Leona W. Marshall gave birth to a son. The family moved that year to Hanford, Washington, where both Marshalls continued their research—this time focusing on plutonium production reactors at the Hanford Engineer Works. This facility was another of the many facilities established under the umbrella of the Manhattan Project.

At the conclusion of World War II, Leona W. Marshall was awarded a fellowship at the University of Chicago's Institute for Nuclear Studies, directed by Fermi. Marshall and her family returned to Chicago. There she continued her work in nuclear physics, eventually broadening her scope of interest to include fundamental particle physics, a field of study then in its infancy and one in which Marshall was considered a pioneer. Over time, Marshall advanced in position at the university, becoming a research associate (1947) and then an assistant professor in the year of Fermi's death (1954).

After Fermi died, Leona Marshall left Chicago to accept a fellowship at Princeton University's Institute of Advanced Studies. This move was to become one of many, as she would later accept academic positions as a scientist, a professor, and a consultant at the Brookhaven National Laboratory (1958–1960) in New York, New York University (1960–1963), and the University of Colorado at Boulder (1963–1966), respectively. She later served as a consultant at the Los Alamos Scientific Laboratory in New Mexico.

In 1966, Leona Woods Marshall and John Marshall divorced. That same year, Leona married Nobel Prize–winning chemist Willard Libby (Libby had been awarded the Nobel Prize in chemistry in 1960, for his work on radiocarbon dating). In 1970, Leona Woods Libby became a visiting professor of engineering at the University of California at Los Angeles. There she developed an intense interest in ancient climates, work in which her husband was involved. She developed a research program and conducted studies in

Architect Maya Lin displays her model of the Vietnam Veterans Memorial. (Corbis-Bettmann/UPI)

which she analyzed the isotopes present in tree samples. This work eventually led to the publication of many professional papers and two books on this subject, *Carbon Dioxide and Climate* (1980) and *Past Climates: Tree Thermometers, Commodities, and People* (1983).

Leona Libby died in 1986. At the time of her death, she held the position of adjunct professor of environmental science and engineering at the Los Angeles campus of the University of California. She also was working as a consultant at the Los Alamos Scientific Laboratory. In recognition of her work, she was elected a fellow of the Royal Geographical Society (RGS) and the American Physical Society (APS).

See also Anderson, Elda Emma; Gardner, Julia Anna; Goeppert-Mayer, Maria; Manhattan Project; Nuclear Physics; Ordnance; Quimby, Edith Hinkley; Spectroscopy
References Bailey, Martha J., *American Women in Science: A Biographical Dictionary* (1994); "Dr. Leona Libby, 67; Worked on Atomic Bomb" [obituary], *New York Times* (12 November 1996); Grinstein, Louise S., Rose K. Rose, and Miriam H. Rafailovich, eds., *Women in Chemistry and Physics: A Biobibliographic Sourcebook* (1993); Rossiter, Margaret W., *Women Scientists in America: Before Affirmative Action, 1940–1972* (1995); Shearer, Benjamin F., and Barbara S. Shearer, eds., *Notable Women in the Physical Sciences: A Biographical Dictionary* (1997); Torpie, Stephen L., et al., eds., *American Men and Women of Science,* 18th ed. (1992–1993) (1992).

Lin, Maya (b. 1959)

Maya Lin is a nationally recognized architect whose creative works combine the principles of geometry, art, materials science, and mechanics. She is best known for her simple yet dramatic design of the once controversial Vietnam Veterans Memorial in Washington, D.C. Dedicated in 1982, the memorial contains the names of nearly 60,000 people who were killed or listed as missing in action during the Vietnam War.

Maya Lin was born in Athens, Ohio. Her parents had settled there after fleeing Shanghai, China, just before the Communist Revolution of 1949. Lin attended Athens High School, where she excelled in mathematics and took college-level courses. While taking a course in which she studied existentialism, Lin developed a curiosity about death.

Lin graduated from high school as covaledictorian in 1977 and entered Yale University that same year. While at Yale, she often visited a nearby cemetery to observe how the living remembered the dead through memorials, statues, and headstone epitaphs. During her junior year, while studying abroad, she visited many cemeteries in Denmark, France, and England. These visits would have a significant influence on her future architectural creations.

Lin returned to Yale for her senior year in 1980. During this year, she took an architecture course in which she studied memorials and monuments for the dead. She also entered a contest being held to develop a memorial to veterans of the Vietnam War. Hers was the winning design.

Maya Lin earned her master's degree in architecture in 1986 from Yale University. The following year, she received an honorary doctorate in fine arts from Yale. In 1988, she received the Presidential Design Award for her work on the Vietnam Veterans Memorial. The same year, she was asked to design a memorial honoring those who died in the struggle for civil rights. Inspired by the words of Martin Luther King, Jr., Lin used black granite and running water for the Civil Rights Memorial, which was dedicated in Montgomery, Alabama, in 1989. Lin's most recent architectural design, The Women's Table, honors the tradition of coeducation at Yale. The Table records the number of women who attended Yale between 1701 and 1991.

See also Architecture; Barney, Nora Stanton Blatch; Bethune, Louise Blanchard; Gabe, Frances Bateson; Irwin, Harriet; Loftness, Vivian; Morgan, Julia
References Coleman, J., "First She Looks Inward," *Time,* vol. 34, no. 19 (6 November 1989); Graham, Judith, ed., *Current Biography Yearbook, 1993* (1993); Mooney, Louise, ed., *Newsmakers* (1990); Lemelson-MIT Program, "Inventor of the Week," in Invention Dimension Inventor of the Week Archives, available at http://web.mit.edu/invent/www/inventorsIQ/mayalin.html (cited 4 August 1998).

Loftness, Vivian (n.d.)

Vivian Loftness is an architect who has combined the technical elements of the fine arts with the concepts and principles of mathematics, science, and engineering. In her architectural designs, Loftness attempts to create structures that are more than just aesthetically pleasing. She also takes into account how the materials selected for a structure are best suited to the environmental and climatic factors of the region in which the structure is built and how such materials might improve the utility of the structure. For example, she has used computer simulations to determine how climate might impact building design and then has used these data to apply principles of energy conservation, solar heating, and natural ventilation in her design.

Vivian Loftness began her studies in architecture at the Massachusetts Institute of Technology (MIT) at the close of the 1960s. She completed the traditional six-year program, which culminates in both a bachelor's and a master's degree, in only five years. Thus, she was awarded her B.S. in architecture in 1974 and her M.Arch. in 1975. While working toward these degrees, Loftness also took courses outside her major at both MIT and Harvard in such diverse areas as chemistry, materials science, and environmental engineering. Her belief was that the knowledge she obtained in these courses would someday serve a purpose in her work as an architect.

After receiving her architectural degrees, Loftness accepted a position with the American Institute of Architects Research Corporation. While working with this group, she did contract work for several government agencies. Her research centered on studies that tied climatic factors and energy conservation to structural and architectural design. In addition, Loftness later held a position with a New York engineering firm that specialized in designing energy-efficient systems for commercial buildings. Her primary role at this company was to help ensure effective communication between architectural and engineering personnel in order to successfully incorporate the concepts and concerns of each group in the eventual structure.

In the early 1980s, Loftness completed various projects, among them one in which she was asked to design energy-conserving homes for use by low-income people living in Greece. Her designs for these homes made use of passive solar energy concepts to provide adequate heat during cold periods as well as to ensure good ventilation and cooling during warmer periods. The next year, Loftness accepted a contract with the World Meteorological Organization in Geneva, Switzerland, to conduct a study on how architecture is affected by global climates.

After completing her work for the World Meteorological Organization, Loftness accepted a position at Carnegie-Mellon University in Pittsburgh, Pennsylvania. At about this same time, she and her husband, Volker Hartkopf, who also is an architect, were asked to do a job for the Canadian government. The project for which they were hired involved investigating why commercial structures built to be energy efficient only a decade earlier were not performing as designed. While conducting this investigation, Loftness and Hartkopf developed an assessment concept that they called the "Total Building Performance Initiative"—a concept that involves determining how the needs of the people who will use a structure can best be met, while taking into account factors such as conservation, the environment, and building design. Loftness has since returned to Carnegie-Mellon, where as a professor and department head she incorporates ideas from the Total Building Performance Initiative in her instruction.

See also American Institute of Architects (AIA); Architecture; Barney, Nora Stanton Blatch; Bethune, Louise Blanchard; Gabe, Frances Bateson; Hayden, Sophia Gregoria; Keichline, Anna W.; Lin, Maya; Materials Engineering; Solar Technologies; Telkes, Maria

References Ambrose, Susan A., et al., *Journeys of Women in Science and Engineering: No Universal Constants* (1997); Carnegie-Mellon University, "CMU Architectural Profile," available at http://arc.arc.cmu.edu/profile/loft (cited 16 July 1999).

Logan, Myra Adele (1908–1977)

In keeping with a family tradition of health-care careers, Myra Adele Logan chose a career in medicine. Among her contributions to this field was the use of a larger and slower-than-conventional X-ray tube to detect the dense breast tissue that indicates the presence of tumors. X-rays are produced in an X-ray tube when electrons (subatomic particles) accelerated by an electric field strike a copper plate and are converted into electromagnetic radiation (X-rays). The rate at which the X-rays are generated is relative to the velocity of the electrons striking the copper plate. Differences in velocities affect how the X-rays are able to move through tissues of different densities. This technological breakthrough provided a means of detecting breast cancer that could not be observed through physical examination or traditional X ray. It became the basis for the present technology of mammography.

Myra Logan was born in Tuskegee, Alabama. She attended a laboratory elementary school affiliated with the Tuskegee Institute. After graduating from Tuskegee High School with top honors in 1923, she enrolled at Atlanta University, in Atlanta, Georgia, from which she graduated in 1927 as valedictorian. Logan then attended Columbia University in New York City, from which she received a master's degree in psychology.

After receiving her M.S. degree, Logan joined the staff of a YWCA in Connecticut. She remained there until 1929, when she was awarded the Walter Gray Crump $10,000 four-year scholarship for African American women, enabling her to attend New York Medical College. Logan received her M.D. degree in 1933 and served her internship, residency, and most of her professional career at Harlem Hospital in New York City.

Under the supervision of Louis T. Wright, Logan worked as a surgeon and a researcher. In 1943, she became the first woman to perform open heart surgery—a surgery that had been previously performed only nine times. About ten years later, Logan began focusing her attention on breast cancer. She was most interested in developing a means of detecting breast tumors that could not be located through physical examination or existing X-ray procedures. This research led to a modification in X-ray tubes used for breast X rays.

In 1951, Logan was elected a fellow of the American College of Surgeons. She was the first African American woman to join this prestigious organization. Logan was also active in several organizations, including the New York State Committee on Discrimination, the National Association for the Advancement of Colored People (NAACP), and Planned Parenthood. After her retirement in 1970, she also served as a member of the Physical Disabilities Program of the New York State Workmen's Compensation Board.

See also Medicine/Medical Technology
References Bernstein, Leonard, Alan Winkler, and Linda Zierdt-Warshaw, *African and African American Women of Science* (1998); "Dr. Myra Adele Logan, 68; Physician in Harlem" [obituary], *New York Times* (15 January 1977); Haber, Louis, *Women Pioneers of Science* (1979); Hine, Darlene Clark, Elsa Barkley Brown, and Rosalyn Terborg-Penn, eds., *Black Women in America: An Historical Encyclopedia,* vol. 1: (A–L) (1993); McMurray, Emily M., ed., *Notable Twentieth-Century Scientists,* vol. 3: (L–R) (1995).

Low, Jeanie S. (n.d.)

With an invention to her credit before she completed kindergarten, Jeanie S. Low is certainly among America's youngest inventors. Low's inventive spirit was awakened by a contest held at her school in Houston, Texas. Impatient with the plastic step-stool she was using at home to reach the bathroom sink, Low decided to create an attractive, built-in fixture that would fit at the base of the bathroom vanity as her entry for the contest. Her invention, which was called the "Kiddie Stool," won the five-year-old first place in her school contest; two years later, it won top prize at Houston's first annual Invention Fair. With two first-place awards for her invention, Low, with the help of an attorney, applied for a patent for her creation in 1990. She was issued U.S. Patent No. 5,094,515, for a "folding step for cabinet doors," two years later, on 10 March 1992.

Now a young adult, Jeanie Low has not stopped inventing. Among other ideas, she has developed a bathtub alarm that sounds when the tub is about to overflow or when a small child is in danger of drowning. Two other inventions of Low's are a doormat with automatic

brushes and an easy-grip doorknob for people with arthritis.

See also Blount (Griffin), Bessie J.; Galloway, Betty; Kenner, (Mary) Beatrice Davidson; Knight, Margaret E.
References Lemelson-MIT Program, "Jeanie Low: The Kiddie Stool," in Invention Dimension, Inventor of the Week Archives, available at http://web.mit.edu/invent/www/inventorsI-Q/low.html (cited 19 July 1999); U.S. Patent and Trademark Office, Full Text and Image Database—Number Search, available through the U.S. Patent and Trademark Office Depository, at http://www.uspto.gov/go/ptdl (cited 19 July 1999).

Lucid, Shannon Wells (b. 1943)

Shannon Lucid is probably best known as the American astronaut who has logged the greatest number of hours in space. Although Lucid has five space flights to her credit, most of these hours were accumulated during a single, 188-day stay aboard the Russian space station *Mir,* from 22 March 1996 to 26 September 1996. Her number of hours in space is in itself a significant accomplishment, but Lucid also has made several contributions to technology as a participant in the NASA space program, in the deployment of satellites and of the *Galileo* spacecraft and in numerous scientific experiments conducted in space.

Shannon Wells was born in Shanghai, China, where her parents were serving as missionaries, in 1943. Wells spent much of her early childhood with her parents in a Japanese internment camp during the Japanese occupation of China. Following their release from this camp, the family returned to the United States and settled in Oklahoma. There Wells attended public schools, graduating from Bethany High School in 1960.

After high school, Wells attended the University of Oklahoma, where she majored in chemistry. She obtained her B.S. degree in 1963. She then accepted a position at the university as a teaching assistant, which she held for one year. Over the next four years, Wells worked as a laboratory technician at the Oklahoma Medical Research Foundation (1964–1966) and later, as a chemist at Kerr-McGee in Oklahoma City (1966–1968).

In 1968, Shannon Wells married Michael F. Lucid. The following year, she became a graduate assistant at the University of Oklahoma. She re-

Astronaut Shannon W. Lucid has clocked more flying time than any other American astronaut. (UPI/Corbis-Bettmann)

mained at the university until 1973, during which time she earned both her M.S. and Ph.D. degrees in biochemistry. In the same year that she received her doctoral degree, Lucid also applied to the space program. Four years passed before she was selected for admission into this program, during which time she worked as a research assistant for the Oklahoma Medical Research Foundation, in Oklahoma City, Oklahoma.

Lucid began her astronaut training in 1978 as one of the first six American women selected for participation in the space program. She completed her training in August 1979, at which time she was qualified as a mission specialist. Lucid spent the next six years learning the various technical skills she would be called upon to use during future space flights.

Since then, Lucid has gone into space five times. Aboard her first three flights, she served as a mission specialist. The first of these flights was a seven-day mission aboard *Discovery* (Space Transportation System, or STS-51G), in June

1985. The responsibilities of the crew during this mission included the deployment of four satellites, one of which was later retrieved using the shuttle's Remote Manipulator System (RMS), or robotic arm.

Lucid's next space flight took place aboard the *Atlantis* (STS-34), from 18 October to 23 October 1989. The major event of this flight was the deployment of the *Galileo* spacecraft—a vehicle programmed to explore the planet Jupiter. The crew also mapped the distribution of ozone in the atmosphere using a device called the Shuttle Solar Backscatter Ultraviolet Instrument and conducted a variety of other experiments. Lucid's third space flight was a nine-day mission aboard the *Atlantis* (STS-43) in 1991. During this flight, the crew conducted numerous experiments and launched a Tracking and Data Relay Satellite.

On 18 October 1993, Lucid traveled into space a fourth time, aboard *Columbia* (STS-58). During this fourteen-day mission, the crew carried out numerous physiological experiments with laboratory animals and crew members. Tests related to engineering also were conducted. In March 1996, Lucid made what became her most significant flight into space. The *Atlantis* (STS-76) carried Lucid into space to rendezvous with the Russian space station *Mir,* where she was to spend the next four months carrying out experiments as a member of the Russian-American team. As a result of mechanical problems with the shuttle that was supposed to retrieve her and due to severe weather conditions on Earth, Lucid's stay in space was increased by seven weeks. Despite these problems, Lucid was eventually retrieved on 26 September 1996 by the shuttle *Atlantis* (STS-79).

Lucid's historic 1996 adventure renewed interest in America's space program. It also propelled Lucid into the limelight. In recognition of this and other achievements, Lucid was awarded a Space Medal of Honor by President Clinton in December 1996, becoming the first woman to receive this medal. She also was presented with the Order of Friendship Medal—the highest award that can be bestowed on a non-Russian—by Russian President Boris Yeltsin. In 1998, Lucid was inducted into the National Women's Hall of Fame in Seneca Falls, New York.

See also Jemison, Mae; National Aeronautics and Space Administration (NASA); National Women's Hall of Fame; Ochoa, Ellen; Resnik, Judith A.; Ride, Sally Kirsten; Space Exploration

References National Aeronautics and Space Administration, *Astronaut Fact Book* (1992); Pollock, Sean R., ed., *Newsmakers97* (1997); Read, Phyllis, and Bernard L. Witlieb, *The Book of Women's Firsts* (1992); National Aeronautics and Space Administration, "Biographical Data: Shannon W. Lucid," available at http://www.jsc.nasa.gov/Bios/htmlbios/lucid.html (cited 24 July 1999).

Macdonald, Anne L. (n.d.)

Author, former teacher, and former head of the history department at the National Cathedral School in Washington, D.C., Anne L. Macdonald felt great empathy for the women subjects of her 1992 book, *Feminine Ingenuity: How Women Inventors Changed America.* Macdonald, a resident of Bethesda, Maryland, also was an inventor who had tackled the patent process and eventually emerged with a patent and a product that she has successfully marketed through her mail-order business.

Macdonald invented a device that helps people who knit avoid tangling yarn when they are doing projects that require them to work with multiple skeins of yarn. She initially used a patent attorney to file her patent applications, but the applications were twice rejected. After dismissing the attorney, she did further research on her own and personally made a third presentation detailing the merits of her creation to the patent examiners. Feeling confident about their positive response to her presentation, Macdonald hired another attorney to restate her claims and in 1985 received U.S. Patent No. 4,548,055 for her invention, "a method of hand-knitting a patterned fabric."

In addition to her work as an inventor, Macdonald has contributed to the history of American women inventors through the publication of her book, *Feminine Ingenuity.* Macdonald is the author also of the book *No Idle Hands: The Social History of American Knitting.*

> **See also** Kies, Mary; Masters, Sybilla Righton; Metcalf, Betsey; Textiles; Welles, Sophia Woodhouse
> **References** Macdonald, Anne L., *Feminine Ingenuity: How Women Inventors Changed America* (1992); U.S. Patent and Trademark Office, Full Text and Image Database—Number Search, available through the U.S. Patent and Trademark Office Depository, at http://www.uspto.gov/go/ptdl (cited 19 July 1999).

Mack, Pauline Beery (1891–1974)

Pauline Mack was a pioneer and leader in nutrition and health sciences. She studied the chemistry of foods, textiles, and detergents and the chemistry and physics of household equipment

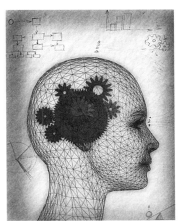

and materials. Among her most significant work was her use of X rays as a means of measuring calcium retention and bone density in higher forms of animals. For this work, Mack was awarded the Garvan Medal of the American Chemical Society (ACS) in 1950.

Pauline Beery Mack was born in Norborne, Missouri. She entered Missouri State University with an interest in opera and Latin. However, she later majored in chemistry, choosing minors in physiology and mathematics. In 1913, Mack received an A.B. degree with honors in chemistry and mathematics; she also was inducted into Phi Beta Kappa. After graduating, Mack returned to her high school, where she worked as an administrator and as a science teacher for six years. At the same time, she attended Columbia University during the summers.

Mack received her M.A. from Columbia in 1919. She then accepted a position at Pennsylvania State College, teaching freshman chemistry to home economics and liberal arts students. To promote science among her students, Mack began publishing the weekly magazine *Chemistry Leaflet* in 1927. She remained editor of the magazine for seventeen years and watched it evolve into the official publication of the ACS under the title *Chemistry.*

While teaching at Pennsylvania State College, Mack continued her graduate studies at that school. She was awarded a Ph.D. in biological

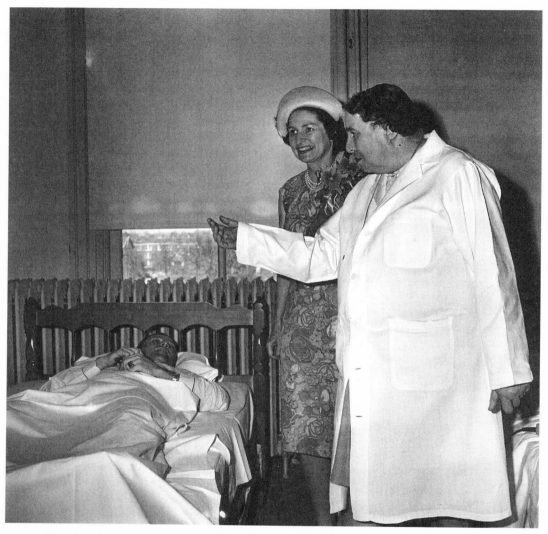

Pauline Beery Mack (right) conducted experiments at NASA to determine the effects of space travel on bone density. (Bettmann/Corbis)

chemistry in 1932. Three years later, Mack began to study human nutrition. Her primary goal was to determine whether differences existed in the diet and nutritional habits of families with different economic backgrounds. Her work attracted the attention of the Pennsylvania Department of Health and led to a state initiative called the Pennsylvania Mass Studies in Human Nutrition. In 1940, the Ellen H. Richards Institute was established as a department of the college, to continue the studies begun by Mack. Mack became the institute's first director, serving from 1935 to 1952. During this time, Mack developed the technique of using X rays to measure the mineral content of bones— research that earned her the Garvan Medal.

In 1962, Mack served as dean and director of the Research Institute of the College of Household Arts and Sciences at Texas Women's University in Denton, Texas. There she conducted studies on bone density and demonstrated that bone density decreases as a result of calcium loss. Mack's research was of interest to the National Aeronautics and Space Administration (NASA) because astronauts tend to lose bone calcium during space flights. Studies of this phenomenon have been conducted by NASA as recently as the 1992 shuttle flight, in which Mae Jemison took part, and the 1999 shuttle mission, in which former U.S. Senator and NASA astronaut John Glenn participated.

In addition to her 1950 Garvan Medal, Mack was awarded the Distinguished Daughters of Pennsylvania Medal in 1949. In 1952, she received honorary doctorates of science from Moravian College for Women, in Bethlehem, Pennsylvania, and from Western College for Women, in Oxford, Ohio. In 1970, Mack became the first woman to receive the Astronaut's Silver Snoopy Award from NASA, for her work on bone density studies in the *Gemini* and *Apollo* programs.

Mack was a fellow of the American Public Health Association (APHA), the American Institute of Chemists (AIC), the Society for Research in Child Development, and the American Association for the Advancement of Science (AAAS). She was a member of the American Association of University Professors and the Texas Academy of Science and served as national president of the Iota Sigma Pi sorority from 1945 to 1948.

See also Francis P. Garvan–John M. Olin Medal; Home Economics; Jemison, Mae; Medicine/Medical Technology; National Aeronautics and Space Administration (NASA); Phi Beta Kappa Society; Richards, Ellen Henrietta Swallow; Stanley, Louise; Textiles

References Debus, Allen G., ed., *World Who's Who in Science* (1968); Grinstein, Louise S., Rose K. Rose, and Miriam H. Rafailovich, eds., *Women in Chemistry and Physics: A Biobibliographic Sourcebook* (1993); Roscher, Nina Matheny, "Women Chemists," *ChemTech* (December 1976); Rothe, Anna, ed., *Current Biography, 1950* (1951); Shearer, Benjamin F., and Barbara S. Shearer, eds., *Notable Women in the Physical Sciences: A Biographical Dictionary* (1997); Vercellotti, Sharon V., ed., *ISP News* (the national newsletter of Iota Sigma Pi) (1986).

Macy-Hoobler, Icie Gertrude (1892–1984)

Icie Macy-Hoobler is noted for her pioneering research in the field of physiological chemistry, a branch of chemistry that studies the interrelationships of nutrition, diet, metabolism, growth, and development. She specialized in the nutritional requirements of women and children, contributing a great deal to our present understanding of malnutrition and its effects on mothers-to-be and their developing fetuses.

Icie Macy was born in a farming community in Daviess County, Missouri. She completed her first five years of public education in a one-room schoolhouse, then attended a girls' boarding school. Although inspired by one of her science teachers, Macy succumbed to her father's wishes and studied music. She attended Central College for Women and received a B.A. degree and a teaching certificate in music in 1914. Macy then entered Randolph-Macon Women's College. There her interest in science was rekindled, and she studied chemistry. One year later, she transferred to the University of Chicago, from which she received a B.S. degree in chemistry in 1916.

Following graduation from the University of Chicago, Macy accepted a position as a teaching assistant in freshman chemistry at the University of Colorado at Boulder in 1917. The next year, she taught physiological chemistry at the university's medical school while working toward her master's degree. Macy received her M.A. degree from the University of Colorado in 1918. She then left Colorado to pursue studies in physiological chemistry at Yale University.

World War I was already under way when Macy began her studies at Yale. The war effort placed demands on food crops, and wheat shortages resulted in a reduction in the amount of wheat flour available. For this reason, cottonseed and products derived from the seed were being substituted for wheat. Concern surfaced when it was determined that animals that had been fed cottonseed became ill. Macy was assigned a project to investigate the toxicity and nutritional value of cottonseed. She determined that the agent responsible for the illnesses in the animals that had eaten cottonseed was a poison present in the seeds. Upon completion of her research, in 1920, Macy received her Ph.D. in physiological chemistry, becoming the fourth woman to receive a doctorate in this field from Yale University.

After completing her studies at Yale, Macy accepted a position as a biochemist at the West Pennsylvania Hospital in Pittsburgh. She was the first woman to hold such a position at the hospital. In addition to her laboratory work, she taught hematology and urinalysis to hospital interns. It was also during this time that she began research on the calcium and magnesium content in human fetuses. These studies prompted her to analyze and compare the composition of the blood of mothers and their newborn infants.

In 1921, Macy accepted an invitation from biochemist and nutritionist Agnes F. Morgan to teach food chemistry in the Department of Household Science at the University of California at Berkeley. Two years later, she became the director of the Nutrition Research Laboratory of the Merrill-Palmer School for Motherhood and Child Development, in Detroit. In 1932, Macy gave up her job at the Merrill-Palmer School to become director of the Research Laboratory of the Children's Fund of Michigan, located at Detroit's Children's Hospital. She remained in this position until her retirement in 1954. During this 22-year period, Macy performed much of her research on long-term nutritional effects in large populations of children. She also studied the metabolism of women during their reproductive cycles, the composition of human milk, and infant growth and development. Macy's nutritional research studies of human milk resulted in the establishment of national standards for vitamin D and B supplements in cow's milk. The addition of vitamin D in milk eventually led to a decline in the disease rickets. Macy's research on vitamin C helped establish minimum daily requirements of this vitamin for infants and young children.

While working at Children's Hospital, Macy met B. Raymond Hoobler, a professor of pediatrics at Wayne State University and director of Detroit's Children's Hospital. They married in 1938. Under Macy-Hoobler's directorship, the laboratory published 265 papers. Macy-Hoobler also authored several books dealing with maternal nutrition, child health, and diet. The best known of these was *Hidden Hunger*, published in 1945.

For her work in nutrition, Macy-Hoobler received many honors. In 1938, she was presented the Norlin Achievement Award of the University of Colorado. One year later, she received the Borden Award from the American Home Economics Association (AHEA). For her work in food chemistry and her research on the composition of mother's milk, Macy was granted an honorary doctorate from Wayne State University in 1945 and the Garvan Medal of the American Chemical Society (ACS) one year later. The American Institute of Nutrition granted her its Osborn and Mendel Medal in 1952 and the Modern Medicine Award in 1954. In 1972, she accepted the Distinguished Service Award of the Michigan Public Health Association.

Macy-Hoobler held membership in many professional societies. In 1932, she became a fellow of the America Association for the Advancement of Science (AAAS). She also was a member of the American Chemical Society (ACS) and the American Institute of Chemists (AIC). In 1944, she served as president of the American Institute of Nutrition (AIN). She was elected a fellow of AIN in 1960. Macy-Hoobler also held memberships in Phi Beta Kappa, Sigma Xi, and Iota Sigma Pi.

See also American Society for Nutritional Sciences (ASNS); Bevier, Isabel; Emerson, Gladys Anderson; Francis P. Garvan–John M. Olin Medal; Mack, Pauline Beery; Morgan, Agnes Fay
References Bailey, Martha J., *American Women in Science: A Biographical Dictionary* (1994); Debus, Allen G., ed., *World Who's Who in Science* (1968); Grinstein, Louise S., Rose K. Rose, and Miriam H. Rafailovich, eds., *Women in Chemistry and Physics: A Biobibliographic Sourcebook* (1993); "Icie Macy Hoobler" [obituary], *Chemical and Engineering News* 62: 7 (February 1984); Williams, Harold H., "Icie Gertrude Macy Hoobler (1892–1984): A Biographical Sketch," *Journal of Nutrition* 114 (1984).

Mangin, Anna (n.d.)

Woodside, New York, native Anna M. Mangin was issued U.S. Patent No. 470,005 on 1 March 1892. Mangin received the patent for her design of an improved pastry fork. Although the development of such an implement may not seem to be of great practical importance, it does establish Mangin as

one of only five African American women to be issued a patent in the whole of the nineteenth century, and thus makes her worthy of mention. The
other women with whom Mangin shares this distinction include Sara E. Goode (inventor of a folding cabinet bed), Miriam E. Benjamin (inventor of
a gong and signal chair), Sarah Boone (inventor of
an improved ironing board), and Lyda Newman
(inventor of a hair brush with a detachable unit
permitting easy cleaning).

See also Benjamin, Miriam E.; Boone, Sarah;
Domestic Appliances; Goode, Sara E.; Kenner, (Mary)
Beatrice Davidson; Newman, Lyda
References Hine, Darlene Clark, Elsa Barkley
Brown, and Rosalyn Terborg-Penn, eds., *Black Women
in America: An Historical Encyclopedia,* vol. 1: (A–L)
(1993); Stanley, Autumn, *Mothers and Daughters of
Invention: Notes for a Revised History of Technology*
(1993); Louisiana State University Libraries, Baton
Rouge, Louisiana, "African American Women Inventors:
Historical," in *The Faces of Science: African Americans
in the Sciences,* available at http://www.lib.lsu.edu/
lib/chem/disply/women_inventors.html (cited 9 June
1999).

Manhattan Project

Established by the U.S. Army Corps of Engineers
in the summer of 1942 under the code name
Manhattan Engineer District, the Manhattan
Project was America's most secret and costly military effort: to research, construct, and deliver the
first atomic bomb. In 1939, Albert Einstein sent a
letter to President Franklin D. Roosevelt advising
him that fission of uranium could be used to produce an atomic bomb and that Nazi Germany
might seek to develop such a bomb. This letter
served as the catalyst for authorization to research and build the atomic bomb. The project to
develop the device was turned over to the U.S.
Army and placed under the command of Major
Leslie R. Groves.

The Manhattan Project was a monumental scientific, technological, and industrial undertaking
that cost more than $2 billion. Nearly 45,000 civil-
ian and military personnel were carefully
screened and recruited for the project, including
some of the world's most brilliant scientists. Ironically, many of the scientists who fled the Nazis
and came to the United States during the early
1930s became involved in the development of the
bomb. Highly secret industrial complexes and scientific research facilities were established at more
than 36 sites throughout the United States and
Canada. In addition, physics and chemistry research facilities were expanded and redesigned at
several major universities, including the University of Chicago, which housed the Argonne National Laboratory. This laboratory, headed by Enrico Fermi, was where the first nuclear pile was
constructed and where the first controlled nuclear
chain reaction was observed and analyzed. Diffu-
sion experiments conducted at Columbia University in New York City under Harold Urey were
aimed at identifying a means of enriching uranium and separating U-235 from U-238. Similar
experiments occurred at the newly constructed
uranium enrichment and separation plant at Oak
Ridge, Tennessee. Plutonium production was carried out at the Hanford Engineering Works in
Hanford, Washington. Among the many research
physicists working at that facility were Leona W.
Libby and her husband, John Marshall, Jr. Among
Libby's many contributions at this facility was the
development of a sophisticated device (the boron
trifluoride neutron detector) used in monitoring
fission chain reactions.

The requirements of the Manhattan Project
placed a great strain on industrial, scientific, and
natural resources and created an immediate and
urgent need for physicists, chemists, and engineers. It also provided numerous opportunities
for women in the sciences to join in the war effort. Lise Meitner, the Austrian physicist whose
pioneering work in uranium fission paved the
way for nuclear weapons research, was asked to
participate in the project to develop the atomic
bomb but refused, hoping the development of the
device would prove impossible.

Noted nuclear physicists Maria Goeppert-
Mayer and Chien-Shiung Wu worked with Urey
at Columbia on uranium isotope separation.
Goeppert-Mayer then worked at the Los Alamos
site. Wu, however, was called to the Argonne National Laboratory at the University of Chicago to
assist Enrico Fermi in solving a problem that was

critical to the success of the fission process. Both Wu and Goeppert-Mayer went on to have significant careers in nuclear physics after the conclusion of their service to the Manhattan Project. Wu confirmed research that led to a Nobel Prize being awarded to Princeton physicists Chen Ning Yang and Tsung-Dao Lee in 1956; Goeppert-Mayer's study of stable isotopes earned her the Nobel Prize in Physics in 1963.

J. Robert Oppenheimer, the noted American physicist, directed the design and construction of the bomb at the Los Alamos, New Mexico, site. The experimental detonation of the device, code-named Trinity, took place at a remote desert site near Alamogordo, New Mexico, on 16 July 1945. Among the many scientists witnessing this event was Elda Emma Anderson, who had performed critical research in neutron scattering and nuclear reactor design, two vital factors in the development of the atomic bomb. Anderson later became a leader in the field of health physics, an area that focused on protecting people and the environment from the hazards associated with radiation.

The successful detonation of the atomic bomb in the desert marked the conclusion of the Manhattan Project. In August of that year, atomic bombs were dropped on the Japanese cities of Hiroshima and Nagasaki, leading to the unconditional surrender of Japan and an end to World War II.

See also Anderson, Elda Emma; Argonne National Laboratory; Bartlett, Helen Blair; Fink, Kathryn (Kay) Ferguson; Goeppert-Mayer, Maria; Koshland, Marian Elliot; Libby, Leona W.; Nobel Prize; Nuclear Physics; Office of Scientific Research and Development (OSRD); Ordnance; Quimby, Edith Hinkley; Way, Katharine; Wu, Chien-Shiung
References Abbott, David, ed., *The Biographical Dictionary of Scientists: Physicists* (1984); Groueff, Stephane, *The Manhattan Project: The Untold Story of the Making of the Bomb* (1967); McNeil, Ian, ed., *An Encyclopedia of the History of Technology* (1996); Rhodes, Richard, *The Making of the Atomic Bomb* (1986); Rossiter, Margaret W., *Women Scientists in America: Before Affirmative Action 1940–1972* (1995).

Manning, Ann Harned (ca. 1790–1870s)

Noted inventor Cyrus McCormick received the first of several patents for what came to be known as the McCormick reaper (a harvesting machine used to cut and collect grain) in 1834. In his patent application, McCormick cited an earlier machine known as the Manning Mower as a device that influenced his design. The Manning Mower was invented around 1817 or 1818; however, a patent for this machine was not issued to William Manning of Plainfield, New Jersey, until May 1831. Some records from the era suggest that the true inventor of the Manning Mower was not William Manning at all, but rather his wife, Ann Harned Manning. Ann Manning also is believed by many to have been the inventor of a second machine, called a clover cleaner, for which her husband William obtained a patent on 24 November 1830.

See also Agriculture; Greene, Catherine Littlefield
References Abbot, Charles Greeley, *Great Inventions* (1932); Andrews, Edmund L., "An Exhibit of Inventions by Women," in Patents, *New York Times* (20 January 1990); Mozans, H. J., *Woman in Science* (1976); Stanley, Autumn, *Mothers and Daughters of Invention: Notes for a Revised History of Technology* (1993).

Maria Goeppert-Mayer Award
See **Goeppert-Mayer, Maria**

Martinez, Lissa Ann (b. 1954)

Lissa Martinez is an ocean engineer who specializes in pollution prevention. In her work, Martinez has used her technical experience and expertise to inspect the equipment and devices on ships and other oceangoing vessels to ensure that such equipment performs properly and complies with federal pollution regulations. In addition, Martinez also has worked in the shipbuilding industry.

Lissa Martinez obtained her undergraduate degree in ocean engineering from the Massachusetts Institute of Technology (MIT) in 1976. In the year she received her degree, only 5 of the 132 degrees conferred nationally in ocean engineering were issued to women—about 3.7 percent. After receiving her B.S. degree, Martinez was unable to find a job in her field, so she accepted a position with the Maritime Administration, a shipbuilding agency within the federal government. Martinez remained in this position for two years before returning to MIT, with government funding, to pursue a master's degree in technology and public policy, with a major in ocean engineering. As part of her funding arrangement, Martinez was required to serve an additional three years of government service after completing her studies.

Lissa Martinez began working for the U.S. Coast Guard after receiving her master's degree. It was while working for the U.S. Coast Guard that Martinez became responsible for inspecting safety and pollution equipment on oceangoing vessels, to make sure they were in good operating order and in compliance with U.S. pollution laws. In 1984, she left this position to accept a fellowship with the National Academy of Engineering. When her term as NAE fellow ended, Martinez launched her own consulting firm. Among other clients, she currently advises the U.S. Coast Guard and the U.S. Environmental Protection Agency (EPA) about ways in which ocean pollution (oil, garbage, and sewage) can be prevented.

Lissa Martinez is an active member of the Society of Hispanic Professional Engineers (SHPE). Through this organization, she works to improve awareness of the work done by engineers. She also speaks to groups of young people, encouraging them to pursue careers in science and technology. As part of this commitment, she and her husband, Brian Hughes, who is also an engineer, have created a scholarship fund at MIT to provide grants to students in the engineering program.

See also Earle, Sylvia; Environmental Engineering; Silbergeld, Ellen Kovner; Walton, Mary
References Bernstein, Leonard, Alan Winkler, and Linda Zierdt-Warshaw, *Latino Women of Science* (1998); Dates, Karen E., "Professional Profile: Coast Guard Ocean Engineer Lisa [sic] Martinez," *Hispanic Engineer* (Fall 1987); Telgen, Diane, and Jim Kamp, eds., *Notable Hispanic American Women* (1993); U.S. Department of Education, Office of Educational Research and Improvement, National Center for Education Statistics, *Chartbook of Degrees Conferred, 1969–70 to 1993–94* (December 1997).

Masters, Sybilla Righton (?–1720)

Sybilla Righton Masters, of Burlington Township, New Jersey, is often credited as being the first woman inventor in the United States; however, the patent for her first invention, a device used to clean and cure Indian corn, was actually issued to her husband, Thomas Masters, in London, England, in 1715. Because eighteenth-century records were poorly maintained and incomplete, the birthdate and -place of Sybilla Righton are unknown, and little is known about her early life. We do know, however, that during the mid-1690s, Sybilla married Thomas Masters, a wealthy merchant and politician, and settled in Philadelphia. There Thomas Masters held several political offices, including judge, alderman, mayor, and councilman. Sybilla remained at home, tending to the family, while also tinkering with things mechanical.

During the early 1700s, there was no patent office in Colonial America. Thus, in 1712, the Masterses traveled to London to secure a patent for two of Sybilla's inventions. As was the practice under English common law, the patent was issued in Thomas's name, since women were not permitted to own property. British Patent No. 401 was granted to Thomas Masters for "the sole use and benefit of 'a new invention found out by Sybilla, his wife, for cleaning and curing the Indian Corn growing in the several colonies in America.'"

In 1716, British Patent No. 403 was issued to Thomas Masters for a device, also invented by Sybilla, used for staining and working palmetto leaves for adorning bonnets and hats. Soon after the patent was issued, Sybilla opened a millinery shop in London, where she produced and sold bonnets, hats, baskets, and woven plant matting for chairs and other furniture. However, several months after opening the shop, Sybilla closed the business so that she and Thomas could return to America. Upon their return, Thomas Masters petitioned the provincial council to have Sybilla's patents issued in Pennsylvania. In 1717, the petition was granted and the patents were recorded and published. Sybilla Masters died in 1720.

See also Kies, Mary; Metcalf, Betsey; Patent; Patent Act of 1790; Patent and Trademark Office, U.S. (PTO); Welles, Sophia Woodhouse

References Bernstein, Leonard, Alan Winkler, and Linda Zierdt-Warshaw, *Multicultural Women of Science* (1996); Read, Phyllis J., and Bernard L. Witlieb, *The Book of Women's Firsts* (1992); Stanley, Autumn, *Mothers and Daughters of Invention: Notes for a Revised History of Technology* (1993); "New Jersey Women's History, Period I: 1600–1775," available at http://scc01.rutgers.edu/njwomenshistory/1600–1775period.htm (cited 1 March 1999).

Materials Engineering

Materials engineering has only recently emerged as a discipline distinct from other branches of engineering. The primary concerns of individuals working in this area are to research, create, or modify substances for a specific use, and to develop the technology required to produce new materials. The growth of diverse technologies—for example, those of telecommunications, computers, and space and undersea probes—has resulted in an increasing demand for the development of new materials having very specific properties of strength, mass, electrical conductivity, stability (especially under extreme temperatures), and aesthetics.

Until recently, the responsibility for identifying substances suited to a particular use fell to engineers working within their own specific disciplines, or possibly to chemists or physicists. However, the increasing demand for materials with new and unusual properties led to the emergence of materials engineering as a separate branch of engineering, albeit one closely intertwined with the others. The first significant numbers of materials engineers began to emerge in the early 1970s. For example, according to the U.S. Department of Education, only 76 baccalaureate degrees were issued in materials engineering between 1970 and 1971. Of these degrees, only three were conferred upon women, a number representing 0.39 percent. For the same period, 124 master's degrees also were issued, six (0.48 percent) of which went to women; and 78 Ph.D.s were issued, only one (0.012 percent) of which was obtained by a woman. By the mid-1990s, the field of materials engineering had grown significantly, and the number of women obtaining degrees in this field increased commensurately. For example, by the academic year 1994–1995, 501 baccalaureate degrees in materials engineering were issued, 130 (25.9 percent) of which went to women. During the same period, women earned 23.3 percent (118 out of 506) of the master's degrees, and 17.6 percent (64 out of 363) of the Ph.D.s issued in this area.

Many women have made contributions to the science of materials engineering, even before it was recognized as a separate field of study. For example, in the mid-1800s, artist Harriet Hosmer introduced a new material called faux marble for use in creating statues. Similar products continue to be developed and used today in walls, flooring, and countertops. An architect by training, Louise Blanchard Bethune was one of the first people to make use of a combination of steel and poured concrete in the foundations of buildings. Today, this combination of materials is commonly used in the construction of buildings, bridges, and retaining walls. Chemist Katherine Burr Blodgett applied her knowledge of materials to the development and application of nonreflective glass. Similarly, much of the work done by physical chemist Joan Berkowitz involved researching the use of alloys of molybdenum, tungsten, and zirconium for use in rockets and space vehicles. Patricia Eng specializes in materials suitable for use in radiation shielding. Solid state physicist Mildred Dresselhaus devoted much of her career to the study of the electronic properties of semiconductors. All of this work today would be considered materials engineering.

See also Benerito, Ruth Rogan; Berkowitz, Joan; Blodgett, Katherine Burr; Dresselhaus, Mildred S.; Eng, Patricia L.; Fitzroy, Nancy D.; Flanigen, Edith M.; Hosmer, Harriet; Kwolek, Stephanie Louise; Metals and Metallurgy; Textiles

References Barnes-Svarney, Patricia, ed., *The New York Public Library Science Desk Reference* (1995); U.S. Department of Education, Office of Educational Research and Improvement, National Center for Education Statistics, *Chartbook of Degrees Conferred, 1969–70 to 1993–94* (1997).

Mathematical Association of America (MAA)

The Mathematical Association of America (MAA) was founded in 1915. Today it is the largest professional mathematics society in the world, with a membership of about 30,000 research mathematicians, college and university teachers and administrators, high school teachers, graduate and undergraduate students, and government and corporate workers.

The MAA's main objective is to promote interest in mathematics among Americans, especially high school and college students. The organization also seeks to stimulate effective teaching, learning, and assessment in the mathematical sciences; to foster scholarship among mathematicians; to enhance general interest in the field; and to influence public policy by advocating the importance of the mathematical sciences. The MAA's goals are carried out through publications and meetings. The organization provides models for collegiate curricula, guidance to teachers and institutions, and standards for collegiate programs in the mathematical sciences.

Several women have received special recognition from or have held key positions in the MAA. Among them are Mina Rees, who was honored with the association's first Award for Distinguished Service to Mathematics, in 1962. Dorothy Lewis Bernstein became the first woman to serve as president of the MAA, in 1979. The following year, Gloria Gilmer became the first African American woman to serve on the MAA board of governors. Following Gilmer's term of service in this role (1980–1982), the board adopted a policy of appointing a governor-at-large for minorities.

See also American Mathematical Society (AMS); Bernstein, Dorothy Lewis; Mathematics

References Hine, Darlene Clark, Elsa Barkley Brown, and Rosalyn Terborg-Penn, eds., *Black Women in America: An Historical Encyclopedia,* vol. 1: (A–L) (1993); Maurer, Christine, and Tara E. Sheets, eds., *Encyclopedia of Associations: An Associations Unlimited Reference,* 33rd ed., vol. 1, parts 1–3 (1998); Young, Margaret Labash, ed., *Scientific and Technical Organizations and Agencies Directory,* 1st ed. vol. 1 (1985); "Biographies of Women Mathematicians: Dorothy Lewis Bernstein," available at http://www.agnesscott.edu/lriddle/women/bern.htm (cited 14 March 1999);

Mathematical Association of America, "Mission and Goals," available at http://www.maa.org/aboutmaa/mission.html (cited 14 March 1999).

Mathematics

Mathematics is the branch of science that is primarily concerned with the relationships among numbers, quantities, and shapes. This area of science, which has been in existence for more than 5,000 years, often is divided into several major branches: arithmetic, geometry, algebra, and pure mathematics. Arithmetic is the branch of mathematics that focuses on numbers and calculating (addition, subtraction, multiplication, and division). The area of mathematics that focuses on shapes (lines, angles, and figures) is geometry. Algebra is the branch of mathematics that makes use of mathematical shorthand, or symbols, to represent unknown quantities, while pure mathematics is concerned with whole numbers and how they behave. The concerns of mathematics impact virtually every other area of science and technology. For example, practitioners of architecture, all areas of engineering, physics, computer science, the exploration of space, and medicine, all draw on some aspects of mathematics in their work.

Applied mathematics is one of the few scientific fields into which women have been readily welcomed since antiquity. Women who obtained work in this area were generally offered positions as *computers,* a term used to describe women whose primary job responsibilities involved making mathematical computations. Such was the case with the six women who were hired to help program the ENIAC, the first computer produced in the United States. These women included Frances Bilas Spence, Marlyn Wiscoff Meltzer, Elizabeth Jennings, Elizabeth Snyder Holberton, Kathleen McNulty, and Ruth Lichterman Teitelbaum. All six of these women had their formal training in mathematics.

During the late 1930s, American mathematician Dorothy Lewis Bernstein became an early supporter of the inclusion of applied mathematics in the college mathematics curriculum. Following the success of ENIAC, more computers were built. Each successive computer seemed to have the potential to do even more tasks than its predecessors, making these machines increasingly more useful. Having seen the potential of these machines, Bernstein became a proponent of the implementation of computer science courses in college mathematics curricula. She later was instrumental in having computers and computer programming courses incorporated into many high-school mathematics programs.

Isabella Karle spent much of her time in the 1940s using mathematical formulas developed by her husband, Jerome Karle, to identify the crystalline structure of molecules. Once identified, the molecular structure could be replicated and molecules synthesized in the laboratory. The techniques developed by Karle revolutionized how crystalline structures of molecules were analyzed and eliminated previous procedures that were time-consuming and costly.

In 1942, Mary G. Ross began applying her mathematical skills to the area of ballistics, the study of the movement of objects such as cannon shells, rockets, or missiles as they are projected through air or space. Ross's job involved the development of defense systems for the U.S. military. She was again called upon to use these skills by the National Aeronautics and Space Administration (NASA) in the 1960s, when she was asked to assist in the development of the *Agena* rocket that was used in the *Apollo* space program.

As a junior mathematician at the National Laboratory, Margaret K. Butler was involved in making computations that pertained to the design of a prototype nuclear reactor for use aboard the *Nautilus* submarine (America's first nuclear submarine) in 1948. During the early 1950s, Evelyn Boyd Granville used her skills in applied mathematics to solve problems associated with the detonating devices on missiles. She also was responsible for the development of computer programs that were used during the *Mercury* and *Apollo* space programs. More recently, mathematician Christine M. Darden has made use of her mathematical abilities in the development of computer simulations that are used to improve

the designs of supersonic airplanes to lessen the effects of the large sonic booms produced by such aircraft. Darden has been conducting such work since the early 1980s.

In 1983 Katherine Coleman Goble Johnson made use of her mathematical calculations to supply space mission astronauts with navigational procedures. Mathematician Annie Easley also has contributed her talents to NASA. Her major work was in the area of energy conversions. In this role, she made calculations of the potential life span of batteries used for energy storage. She also developed and implemented computer code for use in calculating the amount of energy resulting from wind and solar energy projects being carried out by NASA.

The number of women who have contributed their mathematical skills to the advancement of technology is quite large. Since 20 percent of the undergraduate degrees conferred in mathematics are currently being issued to women and new technologies are being developed more rapidly than ever before, it is likely that the contributions of women in these areas also will increase.

See also Aeronautical and Aerospace Engineering; American Mathematical Society (AMS); Architecture; Bernstein, Dorothy Lewis; Butler, Margaret K.; Computers/Computer Technology; Darden, Christine M.; Granville, Evelyn Boyd; Johnson, Katherine Coleman Goble; Karle, Isabella L.; Mathematical Association of America (MAA); Ross, Mary G.

References Grinstein, Louise, and Paul J. Campbell, eds., *Women of Mathematics: A Biobibliographic Sourcebook* (1987); Henrion, Claudia, *Women in Mathematics* (1997); Kass-Simon, G., and Patricia Farnes, eds., *Women of Science: Righting the Record* (1990); Kenschaft, Patricia C., "Black Women in Mathematics in the United States," *American Mathematical Monthly* 88:10 (October 1981); Stanley, Autumn, *Mothers and Daughters of Invention: Notes for a Revised History of Technology* (1993).

Mather, Sarah (n.d.)

Few women have been involved with the development of instruments and other technological devices for use in ocean environments. However, a telescope designed for use in underwater environments, developed by Sarah Mather in the 1840s, has been used with success in such diverse areas as defense, shipping, and ocean exploration. Mather's invention was deemed of enough significance to be included in an 1870 publication of Matilda Gage titled *Woman as Inventor*. In this work, Gage praised Mather for her creative genius and compared the importance of her underwater telescope to that of the telescope used for viewing the heavens.

In 1845, Massachusetts native Sarah Mather was issued U.S. Patent No. 3,995, for her invention of a submarine lamp and telescope—essentially, a tube with a lamp attached at one end. Mather was one of about 30 women who had been issued a federal patent by 1845; less than 1 percent of the total number of patentees at that time were women. Mather's underwater telescope was intended to provide a means for examining a ship's outer surface for defects (such as cracks) while the vessel was in the water, thus eliminating the need for the costly and time-consuming process of dry-docking. In addition, the telescope could search the ocean floor for underwater objects, such as sunken vessels or rocks, that might impair navigation. Mather later modified and improved upon the design of her original telescope. Following the outbreak of the Civil War, the improved device was widely used by the Union Navy, which fitted its submarines with the telescope and lamp, to gather intelligence information about Confederate vessels. Other military applications of Mather's invention included its use in searching for lost or errant torpedoes and in identifying the location of potential navigation hazards.

See also Astronomy; Coston, Martha J.; Earle, Sylvia; Martinez, Lissa Ann; Ordnance

References Macdonald, Anne L., *Feminine Ingenuity: How Women Inventors Changed America* (1992); Stanley, Autumn, *Mothers and Daughters of Invention: Notes for a Revised History of Technology* (1993).

Maury, Antonia (1866–1952)

An expert in stellar spectroscopy, Antonia Maury developed a method of classifying stars based on their spectra (arrays of colors or lines produced when starlight passes through a spectroscope) and on the width and sharpness of their spectral lines. Maury's system of classification is considered one of the fundamental steps that led to the establishment of theoretical astrophysics. Ejnar Hertzsprung adopted Maury's system and used it as the basis for the Hertzsprung-Russell diagram. This diagram shows the relationship between the luminosities (brightnesses) and surface temperatures of stars—data that are significant to the study of modern astrophysics. In addition, Maury was one of the first astronomers to discover and investigate double (binary) star systems.

Antonia Maury was born into a family of prominent scientists in Cold Springs, New York. In 1840, her maternal grandfather, physician John William Draper, produced the first photographic image of the moon in daguerreotype (a photograph produced on a silver plate or a silver-covered copper plate). In 1843, Draper produced the first photograph of the sun's spectrum. Maury's uncle Henry Draper, also a physician, photographed the first stellar spectrum in 1872. Her father's cousin Matthew F. Maury was an oceanographer. Her younger sister, Carlotta Joaquina Maury, would become a distinguished paleontologist (a scientist who studies fossils).

Maury was educated at home by her father, Mytton Maury, who was a minister, an amateur naturalist, and the editor of a geographical magazine. Antonia excelled in her studies and was familiar with the classics at an early age. Later she attended Vassar College, in Poughkeepsie, New York, where she studied under noted astronomer Maria Mitchell. She obtained her B.A with honors in astronomy, physics, and philosophy in 1887.

One year after graduation, Maury obtained a position at the Henry Draper Memorial section in the Harvard College Observatory, where she worked as an assistant to Edward C. Pickering. (The Henry Draper Memorial was established with funding from the Draper family, in honor of Maury's uncle, Henry Draper.) Maury's tasks at the observatory included assisting Pickering in identifying binary stars (pairs of stars that revolve around one another) and classifying northern stars according to their spectra.

Spectra of individual stars may be obtained as starlight passes through a glass prism that is located in front of the objective lens of a telescope.

Each star produces a band of color that is broken by vertical lines, or bands, which are related to the chemical composition of that star. Maury quickly mastered the technique of spectral analysis. She also discovered that the thicknesses and resolution (clarity) of the spectral lines could be useful in stellar classification. Furthermore, Maury's classification system yielded more comprehensive data than systems used by other observatory workers; however, her system also required her to take more time on her work than Pickering believed necessary. Constant differences in opinion between Maury and Pickering about the time-consuming nature of her work resulted in Maury's leaving the observatory in 1896.

After leaving the Harvard Observatory, Maury worked for about twenty years as a teacher and lecturer at several colleges. She periodically returned to the observatory to continue working on her system of stellar classification and published her findings in 1897, in the *Annals of the Harvard College Observatory*. Following Pickering's retirement, in 1918, Maury returned to the Harvard Observatory as a research associate and continued her studies of binary stars. Maury remained at the observatory until 1935, at which time she retired. She then accepted a position as curator of the Draper Park Observatory and Museum, which is located in Hastings-on-Hudson, New York. She remained in this job for three years before leaving to pursue her interests in ornithology (the study of birds) and conservation. Among her activities in this latter area was her advocacy for preservation of the California redwoods.

Maury was a member of several professional organizations, including the American Astronomical Society, the Royal Astronomical Society, and the National Audubon Society. In 1943, she was awarded the Annie J. Cannon Prize of the American Astronomical Society, for her significant contributions to astronomy and astrophysics. Antonia Maury died on 8 January 1952 in Dobbs Ferry, New York.

See also Astronomy; Burbidge, (Eleanor) Margaret Peachey; Rubin, Vera Cooper; Sitterly, Charlotte Moore; Spectroscopy; Whiting, Sarah Frances
References Bernstein, Leonard, Alan Winkler, and

Linda Zierdt-Warshaw, *Latino Women of Science* (1998); Kass-Simon, G., and Patricia Farnes, eds., *Women of Science: Righting the Record* (1990); "Miss Antonia Maury" [obituary], *New York Times* (10 January 1952); Ogilvie, Marilyn Bailey, *Women in Science Antiquity through the Nineteenth Century: A Biographical Dictionary with Annotated Bibliography* (1986); Sicherman, Barbara, and Carol Hurd Green, eds., *Notable American Women: The Modern Period* (1980).

Mayer, Maria Goeppert
See **Goeppert-Mayer, Maria**

McCardell, Claire (1905–1958)
Claire McCardell was born in Frederick, Maryland, in 1905. After completing high school, she began studies at Hood College, which was located in her hometown. She later transferred and completed her education at the New York School of Fine and Applied Arts (subsequently renamed the Parsons School of Design).

McCardell became a fashion designer and developed a stretch leotard as well as several other articles of ready-to-wear clothing. Her first big success came in 1938, with the design of the tent dress. This became one of the first popular creations developed by an American designer. In addition, the low cost of denim prompted McCardell to use this fabric in the creation of her "Popover" house dress. This item became popular because it was sturdy, inexpensive, and easy to launder. In recognition of her achievements as a clothing designer, McCardell was featured on the cover of *Time* magazine in 1955.

See also Butterick, Ellen; Crosby, Caresse; Demorest, Ellen Curtis; Rosenthal, Ida Cohen
References "The American Look," *Time* (2 May 1955); Merrill, J. F., "Designing Woman," *Scholastic* (16 February 1955); Vare, Ethlie Ann, and Greg Ptacek, *Mothers of Invention: From the Bra to the Bomb, Forgotten Women and Their Unforgettable Ideas* (1988).

Mechanical Engineering
Mechanical engineering is concerned with the planning, designing, and testing of power tools, engines, machines, and other mechanical equip-

ment. Mechanical engineering requires a thorough knowledge of mathematics, materials, and the physical sciences and the ability to apply this knowledge in developing economical and feasible solutions to engineering problems.

Mechanical engineers work in almost all industries, making mechanical engineering the broadest engineering discipline. Mechanical engineers are involved in almost every phase of product development, from machine and tool design to construction, installation, testing, and training. One of the first women to receive a degree in mechanical engineering was Bertha Lamme. She later helped develop the Niagara Falls power system. Another woman who made early contributions to mechanical engineering was Kate Gleason, who in 1914 became the first woman awarded membership into the American Society of Mechanical Engineers (ASME). Although not trained as mechanical engineers, Lillian Moller Gilbreth and Donna Shirley have since been recognized by ASME in this field. In 1966, Lillian Gilbreth became the first woman to receive the Hoover Medal from ASME. Thirty-two years later, Donna Shirley of the Jet Propulsion Laboratory (JPL) was issued ASME's Holley Medal.

Examples of machines developed by mechanical engineers include those that produce power from gasoline, steam, coal, nuclear fuels, and other energy sources. These machines include the internal combustion engine, rocket and jet engines, and steam and gas turbines. Mechanical engineers also develop and build machines that use power. Such machines include aircraft, boats, automobiles, refrigerators, heaters, air conditioners, and industrial equipment. Many mechanical engineers today try to create designs that will result in more energy-efficient and cost-effective machines, including motor vehicles. Robots and computers are often used in the testing, production, and maintenance of these machines.

See also American Society of Mechanical Engineers (ASME); Gleason, Kate; Lamme, Bertha; Society of Women Engineers (SWE)

References Barnes-Svarney, Patricia, ed., *The New York Public Library Science Desk Reference* (1995); Franck, Irene M., and David M. Brownstone, *Women's World: A Timeline of Women in History* (1995); U.S.

Department of Labor, Bureau of Statistics, *Occupational Outlook Handbook, 1994–1995,* Bulletin 2450 (1994).

Medicine/Medical Technology

Medicine—the science and art of healing—has been practiced since earliest recorded times. In its infancy, medicine was based more on trial and error than on sound knowledge of how the body functioned. This approach frequently led to treatments that were either ineffective or that caused more harm to the body than the original illness.

However, through gradual advances in knowledge of anatomy, physiology, chemistry, physics, and technology, the practice of medicine has emerged as a true science, comprising many highly specialized branches. Many advances in medical technology have been made by women working in these specialized areas.

Pediatrics. Pediatrics is the branch of medicine that specializes in maintaining the health of and treating illnesses in children. Among the many women who have contributed to technological advances in this field are Sara Josephine Baker, Virginia Apgar, and Helen Brooke Taussig, all of whom were physicians. Baker is most well known for her involvement around 1900 in tracking the source of a typhoid epidemic to a food service worker who came to be known as "Typhoid Mary." However, this was not Baker's only contribution to medicine. Baker was responsible also for the development of a disposable eyedropper for use with newborns. The dropper provided a clean and disposable mechanism through which sterile silver nitrate solution (then used to prevent congenital blindness) could be administered into the eyes of newborns just after birth. This device helped decrease the incidence of infection in infants' eyes caused by the reuse of droppers. Baker also designed safer clothing for infants, which was deemed of enough importance that the patterns for the clothing were distributed by one major insurance company to its policyholders.

In the 1940s, pediatrician Helen Brooke Taussig developed a surgical procedure for use on infants suffering from a condition known as "blue baby syndrome." Having observed a number of children suffering from this condition, which caused the skin to acquire a bluish tinge, Taussig determined that the underlying problem was a heart defect that resulted in an inadequate supply of blood (and oxygen) throughout the body. After drawing this conclusion, Taussig consulted and worked with a cardiac surgeon to develop a surgical bypass procedure that could be performed on the hearts of children afflicted with the condition. Since its development, the procedure has been successfully performed numerous times, saving the lives of countless children.

Virginia Apgar was an anesthesiologist who worked primarily with women giving birth. After observing numerous infants immediately following their birth, Apgar devised a scoring system that could provide a quick indication of the overall health of a newborn. The system, known as the Apgar Score, has become a standard diagnostic tool used with newborns throughout the world since its introduction in 1952.

Ophthalmology. The medical specialty involved with diagnosing and treating eye problems is known as ophthalmology. Among the women who have made significant technological advances in this area are Gertrude Rand and Patricia Bath. Gertrude Rand is an ophthalmology researcher and a specialist in optics. While working with her husband, she developed a device called the Ferrand-Rand perimeter, which can be used to observe the physical structure and function of the retina of the eye. (The retina is a structure at the back of the eye on which the image an individual perceives is formed. Abnormalities in the shape or function of this structure affect sight.) In addition to her development of this device, Rand conducted extensive studies at Johns Hopkins University on lighting systems. Her findings in this area led to illumination systems that produce less glare, which are used today in many office buildings and other public facilities.

Patricia Bath is an ophthalmologist and a surgeon. In the early 1990s, she developed an improved laser system for use in the removal of cataracts. Her Laser Cataract Surgery Device combines a laser-powered probe, irrigator, and

aspirator to vaporize the cataract and then wash away and remove the debris resulting from this vaporization. Bath has received patents for her device in the United States, Canada, and several European countries.

Neurology. The medical specialty that focuses on the diagnosis and treatment of problems with the brain and nervous system is called neurology. Among the many women who have made contributions in this highly specialized field are Thelma Estrin, Rita Levi-Montalcini, Joanna Fowler, and Candace Pert. Thelma Estrin is an electronics engineer who has devoted her career to developing diagnostic tools that use computers to study the brain. These tools, which measure the electrical activity in the brain, have been used by neurologists and brain surgeons to map regions of the brain according to their function. Such maps, in turn, can be used to pinpoint a part of the brain that is not functioning as it should due to injury or disease.

Rita Levi-Montalcini was awarded a shared Nobel Prize in physiology/medicine with biochemist Stanley Cohen in 1986 for groundbreaking work that led to the identification of nerve growth factor (NGF). This substance has been identified as the chemical responsible for the development of nerves and nerve tissue in developing embryos and infants. Unlike most other tissues of the body, damaged nerve tissue does not generally regenerate itself throughout an individual's life. However, the findings of Levi-Montalcini and Cohen may eventually enable doctors to stimulate new nerve growth in adults whose nervous systems have been damaged by injury or disease.

Working independently, both Joanna Fowler and Candace Pert have conducted research that has led to a better understanding of the biochemical processes associated with drug addiction, cancer, and other diseases. Both women made use of a technological process called radioimmunoassay (developed by Nobel Prize–winning scientist Rosalyn Yalow) to trace the movement of radioactive molecules through the brain and other parts of the body. Work done by Fowler has been used by doctors worldwide to study neurological and psychiatric diseases; Fowler also has obtained eight patents on the radiolabeling procedures she has developed. Work done by Candace Pert helped other scientists identify endorphins, chemicals produced naturally by the body to regulate sensations such as pain and pleasure. Identification of these substances, in turn, is being used by doctors to help treat certain forms of drug addiction.

Oncology. The medical specialty that is concerned with the diagnosis and treatment of cancers is called oncology. Throughout the twentieth century, the number of individuals working to find better ways of diagnosing, treating, or curing some forms of cancer has grown substantially. Among the many women who have made significant contributions in this area are Edith Quimby, Myra Adele Logan, Charlotte Friend, and Catherine Fenselau.

At the time that Edith Quimby was beginning her career (around 1919), physicians were just beginning to use X rays, radium, and radioactive isotopes in the detection and treatment of cancers. Because such treatments were just beginning, very little was known about what dosage of radiation could safely be administered to the body, producing the desired effects without also causing harm to other healthy tissues. Quimby focused her work on this issue and, after conducting numerous studies, established standards for radiation dosages. Myra Adele Logan, in her work with cancer, discovered a new way of locating tumors in the breast that could not be discovered by physical examination in 1953. She used a larger and slower-than-conventional X-ray tube to identify the dense breast tissue that could serve as an indicator that a tumor was present. Her apparatus and procedure were precursors to those used in modern-day mammography.

In 1957, Charlotte Friend became the first person to develop a vaccine that prevented mice from acquiring a form of leukemia induced by a virus. Fifteen years later, she uncovered a way to make a mouse cell showing signs of leukemia behave more like a normal cell. Although her work did not conclusively prove that viruses cause cancer in humans, it did open new avenues for research. In the early 1970s, Catherine Fenselau used mass

spectrometry (a procedure of separating mixtures of molecules or atoms into their component parts) to identify and analyze certain anticancer drugs. She also investigated how these drugs reacted within the body, a study that provided insight into why some patients develop a resistance to drugs being used to treat their cancer.

Bacteriology and Virology. Many diseases are caused by bacteria or viruses. Bacteriology is the scientific study of bacteria; virology is the study of viruses. Many women have focused their careers on the study of bacteria and viruses. Often such study is conducted to find out what diseases such agents may cause. Other times, these agents are studied to find a means of preventing them from causing disease or to find an effective means for treating a disease they do cause. Among the many women who have devoted much of their careers to studying these disease-causing agents are Cornelia Downs and Rita Colwell.

Cornelia Downs developed a quick and inexpensive method of identifying viruses and bacteria. In 1959, she perfected an antibody staining technique that pathologists throughout the world began to utilize as a diagnostic tool for distinguishing among sickness-producing organisms. When she became the first person to recognize that the infectious human viral disease known as tularemia (rabbit fever) was transmitted from animals to humans, she simultaneously provided insights into how other diseases, such as rickettsia and Rocky Mountain spotted fever, might be transmitted from animal to human hosts.

Rita Colwell developed a way to use computers in identifying bacteria. In 1966, she also conducted research that uncovered the fact that the bacteria that cause cholera are present inside zooplankton—microscopic, animal-like organisms present in estuaries. Estuaries are regions of brackish water formed where fresh water running off the land meets salt water from oceans. Building on this finding, Colwell further demonstrated that filtering water in which zooplankton live through several layers of cloth was an effective way to remove these microorganisms from the water and thus render the water safe for drinking. These findings have proved useful in developing nations, where people must often rely on untreated, natural sources of water, such as ponds, for their drinking water supply.

During the mid-1950s, Rachel Fuller Brown and Elizabeth Lee Hazen identified and isolated an antibiotic from soil bacteria. This antibiotic, called nystatin, became the first effective treatment for fungal infections of the skin, digestive system, and female reproductive system. It also was used to treat trees infected with Dutch elm disease and to eliminate mold growth in livestock feed and on artwork in museums. Later, these women developed two additional antibiotics—phalamycin and capacidin.

Gertrude Belle Elion shared a Nobel Prize in physiology/medicine in 1988 with her colleague George Hitchings and with Sir James W. Black of England. All three scientists were recognized for their lifelong contributions to the development of life-saving drugs, a technological field known as pharmacology. In the early 1950s, Elion discovered a drug that proved effective in treating some forms of leukemia. Although the drug was not 100 percent effective, it did offer the possibility of a cure for this disease when it was used in combination with radiation and other drugs.

Elion's major contribution in the field of pharmacology did not rest solely in the new drugs she created, but in the methods she used to develop these drugs. When she began her work in this field, the discovery of most new drugs resulted from a trial-and-error approach; if one drug was unsuccessful at treating a particular problem, another was tried in its place, until a desired result was observed. Elion's method studied the chemistry and metabolic processes of infected cells. She then applied her knowledge of chemistry to develop compounds that would interfere with the diseased cell's metabolic processes without affecting the surrounding healthy cells. As a result of her work, Elion developed drugs for which she received more than 40 patents. These drugs proved effective in the treatment of such diseases as chicken pox, shingles, herpes infections, leukemia, malaria, and gout. In addition, the methods she developed for producing new drugs have been adopted for use by many other scientists, including those now working to find effective treatments or cures for such devastating diseases as cancer and AIDS.

Diagnostic Procedures. The proper treatment of illnesses often cannot occur until a physician is able to identify the underlying cause of the ailment. Although some diseases and disorders are fairly easy to identify from their symptoms, others are more difficult. Many women have developed technologies that are now used to diagnose disease. Among them are Gladys Rowena Henry Dick, Florence Seibert, Helen Free, and Rosalyn Yalow.

Gladys Dick, together with her husband, developed a skin test that could be used to detect how susceptible an individual was to scarlet fever. This test has come to be called the Dick test. In 1923, the Dicks isolated the toxin produced by the hemolytic streptococci bacteria that cause scarlet fever. They then used this toxin to develop a vaccine that prevented people from developing the disease as well as an antitoxin that was used to treat those who had become infected with the illness.

Tuberculosis, TB, and consumption are all names for the same highly contagious disease. The disease is caused by tubercle bacilli (rod-shaped bacteria). Before the mid-twentieth century, TB was a leading cause of death in many parts of the world. However, the disease has become less problematic through a diagnostic test that was developed by Florence Seibert in the 1940s. Like the Dick test, Seibert's test is a skin test that can identify a person who has been infected by the bacteria that cause TB. The test is commonly called a tine test, and its use has resulted in a much lower incidence of TB.

Helen Free did not work on any specific diseases; however, she did develop several laboratory techniques that made testing for a variety of diseases easier, safer, more efficient, and less costly. Free formulated more reliable chemical reagents for use in the laboratory and improved on existing laboratory procedures. The reagents she created and the procedures she developed are standard now in urinalysis, blood chemistry, histology (tissue study), and cytology (cell study), in laboratories around the world.

In 1977, Rosalyn Sussman Yalow received a Nobel Prize in physiology/medicine for a diagnostic technique called radioimmunoassay (RIA). RIA uses radioisotopes (radioactive elements) to trace and measure small amounts of substances throughout the body. For example, radioactive iodine is used in diagnosing problems of the thyroid that may be treated with medication or surgery. RIA has been used to investigate the metabolic pathways of insulin in the body, as a means of learning more about diabetes. RIA also can be used to detect nutrients, hormones, enzymes, drugs, and viruses in the body or in body fluids. Before blood is used for transfusion, for example, RIA is used to screen it for contaminants. In addition, RIA is used in the detection and treatment of leukemia, peptic ulcers, neurotransmitter imbalances, and dwarfism.

Medical Tools and Instruments. Many tools and devices have been developed to aid in the detection and treatment of various medical problems. As in other aspects of medicine, here, too, women have made substantial contributions. Lisa M. Vallino and Betty M. Rozier, Alice Bryant, and Mary Thompson are only a few of the women who have developed tools and instruments having medical uses.

Lisa M. Vallino and Betty M. Rozier are a daughter and mother who worked together to design and market a device that prevents intravenous (IV) needles and catheters from being dislodged from the patient. Vallino knew from her firsthand experience as a nurse that this was a common problem. Keeping IV needles in place helps ensure that patients receive the necessary fluids, nutrients, and medications. It also increases the safety of health-care providers by preventing their repeated exposure to pathogens carried in body fluids; and it saves the health-care facility money.

Alice G. Bryant was an ear, nose, and throat (ENT) specialist who began practicing medicine in the late 1800s. She also is responsible for the invention of several instruments used by otolaryngologists. Otolaryngology is the medical specialty that deals with problems affecting the ear, nose, and throat. A tonsil tenaculum and

nasal polypus hook developed by Bryant aided her in the surgical removal of tonsils and of nasal polyps, respectively. These instruments have become standard equipment for ENT surgeons. Bryant also invented a special kind of tongue depressor called a tonsil separator; a tonsil cannula (inserted tube); and a bone-gripping forceps. In addition, she invented an electrical foot-switch that permitted her to control much of the diagnostic and therapeutic equipment she used in her office, while keeping her hands free.

Mary H. Thompson became one of the best abdominal and pelvic surgeons in the United States in the late 1800s. During the 1870s, she developed a surgical needle for use in abdominal surgery. This needle has proven so effective that it is still in use by surgeons working in many hospitals today.

Many other women have made significant technological contributions to the practice of medicine. Such contributions have emerged from virtually all areas of science and all medical specialties. Since the number of women entering scientific and medical fields in all areas has steadily increased in the past quarter century, it is likely that women's contributions to the technologies of medicine also will continue to increase.

See also Apgar, Virginia; Baker, Sara Josephine; Bath, Patricia; Biotechnology; Blount (Griffin), Bessie J.; Brown, Rachel Fuller; Bryant, Alice G.; Colwell, Rita Rossi; Dick, Gladys Rowena Henry; Downs, Cornelia Mitchell; Elion, Gertrude Belle; Estrin, Thelma; Fenselau, Catherine Clarke; Fowler, Joanna S.; Free, Helen Murray; Friend, Charlotte; Genetic Engineering; Hazen, Elizabeth Lee; Kempf, Martine; Kenner, (Mary) Beatrice Davidson; Levi-Montalcini, Rita; Logan, Myra Adele; Pert, Candace Bebe; Pharmacology; Quimby, Edith Hinkley; Radioimmunoassay; Rand, (Marie) Gertrude; Seibert, Florence Barbara; Taussig, Helen Brooke; Thompson, Mary H.; Vallino, Lisa M., and Rozier, Betty M.; Yalow, Rosalyn Sussman
References Altman, Linda Jacobs, *Women Inventors* (1997); Shearer, Benjamin F., and Barbara S. Shearer, eds., *Notable Women in the Life Sciences: A Biographical Dictionary* (1996); Sicherman, Barbara, and Carol Hurd Green, eds., *Notable American Women: The Modern Period* (1980); Stanley, Autumn, *Mothers and Daughters of Invention: Notes for a Revised History of Technology* (1993); Vare, Ethlie Ann, and Greg Ptacek, *Mothers of Invention: From the Bra to the Bomb, Forgotten Women and Their Unforgettable Ideas* (1988).

Metals and Metallurgy

Metals are naturally occurring elements that have several distinguishing characteristics. For example, metals readily reflect light; thus, they appear shiny. All metals, with the exception of mercury (a liquid), are solids at room temperature. Metals also are good conductors of heat and electricity; are malleable (capable of being hammered into various shapes); and are ductile (capable of being drawn out into wires).

Most metals are found in Earth's crust, its outermost rocky layer. Few exist in a pure metallic state. Most metals exist as compounds; that is, they occur in combination with other elements, as hard or rocky deposits called ores. Metallurgy is the branch of chemistry that studies metals and their uses and the means by which metals may be separated or extracted from their ores.

The labor involved in the mining and refining of metals has over the centuries traditionally been provided by men. There are, however, several American women who have made contributions to technology in this area. Among the most notable is Carrie Jane Everson of Colorado. In the mid-1880s, Everson obtained a patent for a physical process designed to separate gold and silver from a mixture of sediments. Everson's process involved placing the sediments into an oil-acid mixture that was then vibrated to thoroughly mix the ingredients. In this process, the nonmetallic components of the sediments adhered to the oil and floated to the surface, while the heavier metal (gold or silver) settled to the bottom. At the time Everson developed her process, male miners found their traditional methods of obtaining metal satisfactory and thus felt no need to adopt a process developed by a woman. However, around the turn of the twentieth century, when many metals became less accessible than before, some miners began exploring the use of the method developed by Everson. By the time this process was finally adopted for common use, Everson's patent had expired; thus, she never profited from its use.

At about the same time that Everson was developing her oil flotation process for separating metals from sediments, Julia Hall and her brother Charles were developing a process that used electricity to obtain aluminum from its ore. The Halls were working in a laboratory they built in their home in Ohio. Although Julia was not immediately given adequate recognition for her role in the development of this process, over time, her contributions became better known. Her efforts also were instrumental in introducing aluminum to the marketplace and in the founding of the Pittsburgh Reduction Company (which later became known as the Aluminum Company of America, or simply Alcoa).

Most of the work done by women in the area of metallurgy took place in the laboratory and has involved finding new uses for existing metals or developing new alloys. Alloys are metallic substances produced when two elemental metals are combined. The properties of alloys generally differ slightly from the properties of the component metals from which they are formed.

Many women have studied the physical and chemical properties of metals in an attempt to determine how these metals might best be used. Among the earliest was Charlotte R. Manning, who received two patents for processes involving the covering of metals with other substances as a means of decreasing corrosion. The first of these patents was issued in 1903 for electroplating, a process in which an electric current is used to cover, or plate, one metal with another metal. Manning's second patent, which was issued in 1907, involved the "enameling of metal hollowware," the coating of metal containers such as cooking pots and the insides of certain appliances with an enamel covering.

Laurence Delisle Pellier, a research metallurgist working in Connecticut used electron microscopy to study the structure and properties of metals. In addition, she also sought ways to use alloys of titanium and stainless steel in chemical plants and the making of surgical instruments. By the early 1960s, Pellier had received a patent for gold plating surgical needles. A contemporary of Pellier was Joan D. Berkowitz, a physical chemist who focused her research on high-temperature oxidation of transition metals and their alloys. Her research led to the use of alloys of tungsten, zirconium, and molybdenum in rockets and space vehicles.

Industrial research chemist Mary Lowe Good applied her knowledge of metallurgy to the development of coatings that are used to prevent barnacles (sea animals) from attaching to the hulls of ships, an occurrence that increases the drag on the ship as it moves through the water. Similarly, Doris Kuhlmann-Wilsdorf also has applied her knowledge of metallurgy to the sea. While working for the U.S. Navy, she designed metal brushes for use in electrical motors. The brushes are designed to generate electrical current as they rub against contacts. The development of motors using this technology may permit the Navy to replace their heavy, diesel-powered engines with lighter, electrical motors.

Another area of interest to women metallurgists is the effect of temperature on metals. Two women working in this area are Julia Weertman and Mary Johnson. Weertman's research focuses on how very high temperatures affect the structure of metals at the atomic level. Changes in the atomic structure of metals can affect such properties as tensile strength and brittleness. Johnson's studies of metals involve how their properties change both at very high temperatures and at very low temperatures. Specifically, her findings are being applied to spacecraft—in particular, to metal parts in these vehicles that might malfunction at extreme temperatures.

Traditionally, studies of the properties of metals have been conducted by people working in the fields of chemistry and physics. More recently, such studies have become a concern of individuals working in materials science and materials engineering. As technology continues to result in the development of new products, research in this area will undoubtedly continue to increase in importance.

See also Berkowitz, Joan; Everson, Carrie Jane; Good, Mary Lowe; Hall, Julia Brainerd; Materials Engineering; Weertman, Julia
References Bailey, Martha J., *American Women in Science, 1950 to the Present: A Biographical Dictionary* (1998); Kass-Simon, G., and Patricia Farnes, eds., *Women of Science: Righting the Record* (1990); Macdonald, Anne L., *Feminine Ingenuity: How Women Inventors Changed America* (1992); Stanley, Autumn, *Mothers and Daughter of Invention: Notes for a Revised History of Technology* (1993).

Metcalf, Betsey (1786–1867)

Several people from New England have received patents for processes used in making straw hats and bonnets. However, much evidence suggests that Betsey Metcalf (sometimes spelled Betsy Metcalf) started the New England straw-weaving industry. At age 12, Metcalf discovered how to weave a bonnet from seven strands of straw. This was not a new invention but a recreation of a weave she had observed on an imported bonnet displayed in a store window. With help from an aunt, Metcalf also learned to bleach the straw by placing it in air-tight barrels suspended over hot coals sprinkled with sulfur. Metcalf was advised to patent her process, but refused because she did not want the notoriety. More than ten years later, in 1809, Mary Kies became the first American woman awarded a patent for a straw-weaving process—a process based on Metcalf's discovery.

Metcalf, who lived in Providence, Rhode Island, taught women in surrounding communities how to make her braids and bonnets. These women taught others, and eventually an industry evolved. After Metcalf married Obed Baker, the couple moved to West Dedham, Massachusetts (also known as Westwood).

See also Kies, Mary; Masters, Sybilla Righton; Welles, Sophia Woodhouse
References Buel, Nora, "The Long Road from Straw Hats to High Technology," *Inventors Assistance Program News* 37 (August 1994) (also available at http://iridium.nttc.edu/assist/inventions/invart/meetneed.html [cited 17 December 1998]); Macdonald, Anne L., *Feminine Ingenuity: How Women Inventors Changed America* (1992); Stanley, Autumn, *Mothers and Daughters of Invention: Notes for a Revised History of Technology* (1993); Gilbreath, Christine A., "Maid in America: Women in the Straw Hat Industry," in American Museum of Straw Arts, available at http://www.2xtreme.net/christyg/Maid_in_America.html (cited 18 December 1998).

Miller, Elizabeth Smith (1822–1911)

Elizabeth Miller was the inventor of the enormously popular fashion garment of the mid-1800s that came to be known as bloomers. Miller, a homemaker from New York City, designed the garment, which consisted of Turkish pantaloons worn under a loosely belted skirt that fell to just below the knees, to provide her with a pragmatic outfit for use while gardening. Miller, who was a cousin of noted women's rights activist Elizabeth Cady Stanton, wore her outfit while visiting Stanton in Seneca Falls, New York, during the first women's rights convention in 1848. The outfit was immediately admired by feminist writer Amelia Jenks Bloomer, who not only began wearing the garment but also praised its comfort in her writings for the magazine *Lily.* As a result of these writings and Amelia Bloomer's frequent wearing of the garment in public, Miller's design came to be called bloomers.

See also Converse, Susan Taylor; Strickland, Sarah; Women's Rights
References Kane, Joseph Nathan, Steven Anzovin, and Janet Podell, *Famous First Facts,* 5th ed. (1997); Read, Phyllis J., and Bernard L. Witlieb, *The Book of Women's Firsts* (1992).

Missiles
See **Ordnance**

Moore, Ann (b. 1940)

Ann Moore, a pediatric nurse, and her husband, Mike, joined the Peace Corps in the early 1960s, with the intention of improving the quality of life for the people living in a developing nation. Their experiences in Togo, West Africa, inspired Ann to develop an infant carrier that made life easier for herself. In time, this product also proved helpful to many other young mothers throughout the world.

In Togo, Moore observed the special bond between mother and infant that she attributed to the custom of transporting babies in cloth back-carriers. American thinking at the time postulated that such constant closeness between mother and infant would "spoil" a child. However, Moore's observations of Togo women and their infants convinced her otherwise.

A few months after she returned to the United States, Moore gave birth to a daughter. Eager to foster the same closeness with her child that she had observed in Togo, she fashioned a carrier that became the basis for a product that would evolve into the "Snugli." Ann's carrier saw a lot of use as she and the baby traveled around the country, accompanying her husband to his various job sites. As the family traveled from place to place, Moore and her daughter inadvertently became a walking advertisement for the carrier. They were frequently stopped by women who admired the creation, who inquired about how to obtain a similar carrier for themselves. Moore gradually accumulated orders for her creation and began to realize a capital gain from its sale.

Ann Moore began working with her mother, Lucy Aukerman, a woman with 30 years of sewing experience, to produce the carriers for others. In time, Ann's mother improved on the original design to make the carrier more secure. In a one-night sewing spree, Aukerman created a carrier consisting of two pouches—one nested inside the other—with zippers on each pouch. She then added straps to the double-pouched carrier, which crisscrossed the wearer's shoulders. Aukerman also added a waistband that secured the pack to the wearer's waist. This improved design was nearly perfect. Over the next few years, minor modifications and improvements were made to the carrier to provide the wearer increased comfort.

As the number of requests for Moore's carrier increased, she and her mother decided to apply for a patent. The patent for the "Snugli" was issued in 1969. In the patent application, the pair described their creation as a "pouch-like infant carrier that is comfortable to wear, safe, versatile, inexpensive, easy to use, sanitary, washable, rugged, trouble-free and decorative." When a writer mentioned the "Snugli" in the *Whole Earth Catalog,* sales dramatically increased. Orders rose from 15 to 25 to almost 300 per month. This led Moore and Aukerman to incorporate in 1972.

Ann's husband, Mike Moore, served as president of the company, and Ann became director of consumer relations. At this point, Aukerman assigned her patent rights to her daughter. To make the Snugli more affordable, the company began producing a less expensive model at a factory in Lakewood, Colorado. In 1980, they added a diaper bag with a side-mounted changing pad that would lie flat when unsnapped.

Most mainstream buyers did not take the Snugli seriously. However, after *Consumer Reports* assigned the Snugli its highest rating for soft carriers for babies six months or younger, sales grew rapidly. By 1982, sales had reached $4 million; in 1984, they were up to $6 million. In 1985, the family sold the rights to manufacture the Snugli to Gerico, a Huffy Company.

After selling her rights to the Snugli, Moore invented yet another carrier product. This product, called Airlift, was a padded, portable, and adjustable carrier in which an oxygen cylinder could be easily transported. Because it is worn on the body, the carrier allows a greater range of movement to people, such as those with emphysema, who require oxygen to assist them in breathing. The Airlift is styled for use either as a shoulder carrier or as a carrier that can be attached to the back of a wheelchair or a walker.

See also Domestic Appliances; Donovan, Marion; Kenner, (Mary) Beatrice Davidson; Proudfoot, Andrea H.

References Stanley, Autumn, *Mothers and Daughters of Invention: Notes for a Revised History of Technology* (1993); Vare, Ethlie Ann, and Greg Ptacek, *Mothers of Invention: From the Bra to the Bomb, Forgotten Women and Their Unforgettable Ideas* (1988).

Morgan, Agnes Fay (1884–1968)

Agnes Fay Morgan (born Jane Agnes Fay) was one of the founders of nutritional science. In 1915, she became the first person to introduce a course in scientific nutrition at a university. The course later developed into a program of animal and human nutrition and food technology. In her work, Morgan analyzed nutrients in foods, the influence of food processing on proteins and vitamins, and how vitamin deficiencies affected the body. She also patented a process of dehydrating a liver pudding called scrapple.

Morgan was born in Peoria, Illinois, where she attended Peoria High School. She later enrolled at Vassar College, in Poughkeepsie, New York, but soon transferred to the University of Chicago. There Morgan majored in chemistry, receiving her B.S. degree in 1904 and her M.S. degree in 1905. In 1914, she received a Ph.D. in organic chemistry from the same university. She began working as an assistant professor in the division of nutrition at the University of California at Berkeley and, in time, became a full professor. She established a graduate program in nutritional science at Berkeley and a food science program at the college's Davis campus. She also worked as a biochemist in the Agricultural Experiment Station.

Morgan researched nutrition and food chemistry throughout her career. Much of this research centered around developing standards for human nutrition. She specifically studied the effects of sulfur dioxide (a preservative) on vitamin C. She studied the roles of vitamin D and calcium on the parathyroid gland to determine their effects on bone growth. Morgan also studied phosphorus metabolism and discovered that pantothenic acid (a B vitamin) was needed for proper adrenal function and to maintain proper pigmentation of the hair and skin. In 1949, she was awarded the Garvan Medal by the American Chemical Society for this work. Five years later, she also received the Borden Award from the American Institute of Nutrition.

Other honors presented to Agnes Fay Morgan include the naming of the home economics building at the Davis campus of the University of California as the Agnes Fay Morgan Hall. In addition, a research award was named for her at the 1969 convention of the Iota Sigma Pi Society. The professional organizations in which Morgan was active included the American Chemical Society (ACS), the American Association for the Advancement of Science (AAAS), the American Institute of Nutrition (AIN), and the Society of Biological Chemists.

See also American Society for Nutritional Sciences (ASNS); Emerson, Gladys Anderson; Farmer, Fannie

Merritt; Francis P. Garvan–John M. Olin Medal; Home Economics; Richards, Ellen Henrietta Swallow
References Bailey, Martha J., *American Women in Science: A Biographical Dictionary* (1994); Kass-Simon, G., and Patricia Farnes, eds., *Women of Science: Righting the Record* (1990); Shearer, Benjamin F., and Barbara S. Shearer, eds., *Notable Women in the Physical Sciences: A Biographical Dictionary* (1997); Sicherman, Barbara, and Carol Hurd Green, eds., *Notable American Women: The Modern Period* (1980); Crystal, David, ed., "Morgan, Agnes Fay," in *The Cambridge Biographical Encyclopedia,* available at http://www.biography.com/find/bioengine.cgi?cmd=1&rec=12073 (cited 30 June 1998).

Morgan, Julia (1872–1957)

Julia Morgan is recognized for her outstanding achievements in American architecture during the first half of the twentieth century. She contributed to the design or construction of more than 800 structures in California, Utah (Salt Lake City), Illinois, and Hawaii. Her unique style, originality, and influence were both a source of pride and an inspiration to women entering the field of architecture.

Julia Morgan was born in San Francisco and raised in Oakland, California. After graduating from Oakland High School, Morgan attended the University of California at Berkeley to study architecture; she was the first female student in the College of Engineering. She graduated from UC–Berkeley in 1894. Two years later, she traveled to France, hoping to attend the Ecole des Beaux-Arts, in Paris. After several attempts to pass the school's entrance exam, she was admitted into the architectural school in 1898—the first woman to be admitted into the architectural section. In 1902, Morgan became the school's first woman graduate.

Morgan returned to California, where she became the first woman in California to receive an architect's license. For the next several years, she worked on the design of two buildings, including a Greek theater on the University of California (Berkeley) campus. She also was commissioned to design several structures for Phoebe Apperson Hearst, mother of publisher and movie magnate William Randolph Hearst. Additional architectural commissions included the redesign and construction of the Fairmont Hotel, which had been destroyed in the California earthquake and fires in 1906. The hotel, considered a landmark, helped establish Morgan's reputation as an architect. Morgan also designed the bell tower, library, and several other buildings for Mills College and Berkeley's St. John's Presbyterian Church, also a landmark. Morgan's work is recognizable by its Spanish Revival motifs, a popular architectural style of the time.

As Morgan's reputation developed, so did demand for her work, which was admired by women's groups and organizations, which took pride in her success. After Morgan was commissioned to design YWCA residence halls in several California cities, she hired and trained several women architects and drafters to assist her in this work.

At the conclusion of World War I, Morgan was once again commissioned by the Hearst family. Beginning in 1919, and for the next 20 years, Morgan undertook a series of assignments, beginning with the design of a castle (La Cuesta Encantada), guest houses, and a wildlife preserve on the Hearst estates in San Simeon, California, and in Mexico. The Hearsts also hired Morgan to design newspaper plants in several California cities, including Los Angeles and San Francisco. During the late 1920s and early 1930s, the Hearsts experienced financial setbacks resulting from the Great Depression. Work on their estates slowed, allowing Morgan to take on other projects. She collaborated on designs for the new campus planned for Principia College at Elsah, Illinois. She also traveled to Salt Lake City and Hawaii, where she continued designing residence halls for the YMCAs.

World War II resulted in severe shortages of labor and materials. As a result, many new construction projects were suspended. These events led to a slowing in Morgan's workload that continued until her retirement in 1946.

See also Architecture; Barney, Nora Stanton Blatch; Bethune, Louise Blanchard; Cambra, Jessie G.; Hayden, Sophia Gregoria; Keichline, Anna W.; Lin, Maya; Loftness, Vivian
References Cullen-DuPont, Kathryn, *The Encyclopedia of Women's History in America* (1998);

Heinemann, Susan, *Timelines of American Women's History* (1996); Parry, Melanie, ed., *Larousse Dictionary of Women* (1996); Sicherman, Barbara, and Carol Hurd Green, eds., *Notable American Women: The Modern Period* (1980).

Morrill Act of 1862

The Morrill Act (or Land-Grant Act) of 1862 allotted 30,000 acres of public land to each state for each senator or representative it had in Congress. Under the terms of the grant, the land was to be sold and its proceeds used to establish and maintain colleges for agriculture and the mechanical arts (manufacturing).

The Morrill Act was named for Vermont congressman Justin Smith Morrill, who introduced the first bill establishing land-grant colleges in 1857. The bill was signed into law by President Abraham Lincoln in 1862. Similar land-grant legislation that supported and extended the original bill was framed in 1868 and 1890. The latter bill provided a monetary grant of $25,000 to all land-grant colleges.

The Morrill Act had a profound impact on the training of scientists, agricultural engineers, and home economists in American colleges and universities. It also created educational opportunities for women. The initial bill and supporting legislation provided the means by which new colleges were constructed and established facilities were expanded. The University of California, the University of Illinois, and Cornell University are examples of land-grant colleges.

See also Agriculture; Home Economics
References Macdonald, Anne L., *Feminine Ingenuity: How Women Inventors Changed America* (1992); Weatherford, Doris, *American Women's History: An A to Z of People, Organizations, Issues, and Events* (1994); Zophy, Angela Howard, ed., *Handbook of American Women's History* (1990).

Mount Holyoke College

Founded by Mary Lyon in 1837 as the Mount Holyoke Female Seminary, Mount Holyoke College of South Hadley, Massachusetts, first opened its doors to 80 young women "who wanted an education more sound in content and serious in purpose than was being offered" by other female seminaries of that time. The college is an original member of the Seven Sister Colleges and boasts many graduates who have made significant contributions to science and technology. Among its most noteworthy alumni and faculty are chemist Emma Perry Carr, zoologist Cornelia Maria Clapp, chemist Dorothy Hahn, naturalist Lydia White Shattuck, and zoologist Ann Haven Morgan.

With more than 25,000 women graduates, Mount Holyoke College boasts a long tradition of academic excellence in the education of women. In fact, Mount Holyoke is the oldest continuing institution for women in the United States. The college, which is accredited by the New England Association of Schools and Colleges, is an independent liberal arts college that offers both undergraduate and graduate degrees. It shares educational resources with neighboring Amherst, Hampshire, and Smith Colleges and with the University of Massachusetts.

See also Carr, Emma Perry; Hahn, Dorothy Anna; Seven College Conference; Sherrill, Mary Lura
References Bailey, Martha J., *American Women in Science: A Biographical Dictionary* (1994); Mount Holyoke College, *Bulletin and Course Catalogue (1997–1998),* available at http://www.mtholyoke.edu (cited 23 April 1998).

Muller, Gertrude (1887–1954)

Child safety was uppermost in importance to Gertrude Muller when she began inventing child care products. With her sister, Muller designed a collapsible toilet seat for children that fit onto a standard one. She later designed children's steps, a car seat that permitted children a safe view through the window, and a pediatric urine specimen collector.

Gertrude Muller was born in Leo, Indiana, in 1887. Her father died when she was six, necessitating the relocation of the Muller family to Fort Wayne, where Gertrude attended public school. After high school, Muller attended the International Business College in Fort Wayne to train as a secretary. She spent her free time reading about health, nutrition, and human development.

From 1904 to 1910, Muller worked as a

stenographer for the General Electric Company. She then worked at the Van Arnam Manufacturing Company, a manufacturer of toilet seats, where she was assistant to the president and later an assistant manager. While Muller was with this company, she and her sister designed a children's toilet seat. The seats were soon being manufactured by Van Arnam and sold through plumbers, who were the primary buyers of the company's products.

Muller formed her own company, the Juvenile Wood Products Company, in 1924. The company manufactured products for children, which were sold through baby shops and department stores. Its first product was Muller's toilet seat, which was now called the "toidy seat." As the company grew, Muller introduced new products. These included "toidy two-steps" to help toddlers reach sinks; "the comfy-safe auto seat"; and a folding booster seat, and other items. Muller also wrote pamphlets to accompany her products. One of them, "Training the Baby," which was first printed in 1930, underwent twenty-six printings and was widely distributed to parents by pediatricians and used in home economics classes.

Muller believed products for children should be safe. To accomplish this, she had auto crash tests conducted to improve the safety of her car seat. In recognition of her commitment to safety, she was selected by the National Safety Council as one of the first three women members admitted to its National Veterans of Safety. In 1954, she was an invited guest at President Eisenhower's White House Conference on Highway Safety.

Muller was a member of the Business and Professional Women's Club and the American Home Economics Association. In 1944, her company was renamed the Toidy Company. She served as its president and provided jobs to many members of her family until her death in 1954 from cancer of the spine.

See also Baker, Sara Josephine; Donovan, Marion; Home Economics; Low, Jeanie S.; Medicine/Medical Technology; Safety Engineering; Vallino, Lisa M., and Rozier, Betty M.
References "Head of Child-Aids Firm, Ill 6 Months, Dies" [obituary], *Fort Wayne Journal Gazette* (1 November 1954); Logan, Vivian Crates, "Fort Wayne Women At Work," *Fort Wayne News-Sentinel* (3 May 1940); Mort, Cynda, "Career Built on Child Safety," *Fort Wayne News-Sentinel* (20 March 1976); Sicherman, Barbara, and Carol Hurd Green, eds., *Notable American Women: The Modern Period* (1980); Stanley, Autumn, *Mothers and Daughters of Invention: Notes for a Revised History of Technology* (1993).

National Academy of Engineering (NAE)

The National Academy of Engineering (NAE) was established under a charter of the National Academy of Sciences (NAS) in 1964 to serve as a parallel organization to the NAS with the responsibility of advising the federal government on matters of technology. The membership of the academy comprises primarily engineers working in the United States. In addition to its advisory responsibilities, the NAE also encourages research and education in engineering and recognizes achievements of engineers. To meet this last goal, the academy created the Draper Prize in 1988. Considered the engineering equivalent to the Nobel Prize, the Draper Prize carries a monetary award of $375,000.

Admittance into the National Academy of Engineering is determined by election and is regarded as one of the highest honors that can be bestowed upon an engineer. Individuals are elected for admission in recognition of their contributions to the knowledge and science of engineering and technology. Some women who have received this honor include Grace Murray Hopper, Betsy Ancker-Johnson, Mildred Dresselhaus, Jean Sammet, Ruth M. Davis, and Nancy D. Fitzroy.

> **See also** Ancker-Johnson, Betsy; Dresselhaus, Mildred S.; Edwards, Helen Thom; Fitzroy, Nancy D.; Hicks, Beatrice Alice; Hopper, Grace Murray; National Academy of Sciences (NAS); Widnall, Sheila
> **References** Kass-Simon, G., and Patricia Farnes, eds., *Women of Science: Righting the Record* (1990); Leitch, Alexander, *A Princeton Companion* (1978); Olsen, Kirstin, *Chronology of Women's History* (1994); "Beyond the Blueprint, Directions for Research on Head Start's Families: About Participating Organizations," available at http://ericps.ed.uiuc.edu (cited 5 May 1999).

National Academy of Sciences (NAS)

Incorporated on 3 March 1863 by an act of the U.S. Congress, the National Academy of Sciences (NAS) is a private, nonprofit society that was established for the purpose of advising the U.S. government on scientific and technological mat-

ters. Among the fifty founders of the NAS was Frederick Barnard—the advocate of higher education for women and president of Columbia College (1864–1889) for whom Barnard College was named.

Admittance into the NAS is considered one of the highest honors that can be bestowed upon a scientist. It occurs through election, based on an individual's contributions to knowledge of science and technology. In 1925, anatomist Florence Rena Sabin became the first woman admitted to the NAS. Other prominent women scientists who have been accorded this honor are psychologist Margaret Washburn (1931), geneticist Barbara McClintock (1944), biochemist Gerty Cori (1948), physicists Maria Goeppert-Mayer and Chien-Shiung Wu (1956), neurobiologist Rita Levi-Montalcini (1968), chemist Mildred Cohn (1971), pediatric cardiologist Helen Brooke Taussig (1973), physicist Rosalyn Yalow (1975), oncologist Charlotte Friend (1976), astronomer Margaret Burbidge and chemist Isabella Karle (1979), biologist Lynn Margulis and biochemist Joan A. Steitz (1983), geneticist Liane B. Russell (1986), engineer Esther Conwell and chemist Gertrude Belle Elion (1990), biochemist Jane Richardson (1991), geophysicist Susan Solomon (1992), and molecular biologist Elizabeth Blackburn (1993).

Since its inception, some responsibilities of the NAS have been designated to other councils and organizations that have been established under NAS charters. The first such organization was the National Research Council, created in 1916. This organization is charged with coordinating the scientific activities of scientists in industry, government, and universities. In 1964, the National Academy of Engineering was established as a parallel organization to the NAS. Its members include engineers who have made important contributions to their fields, who advise the federal government on matters of technology. In addition, the Institute of Medicine was established in 1970 to advise the government on matters dealing with public health.

> **See also** Blackburn, Elizabeth Helen; Burbidge, (Eleanor) Margaret Peachey; Conwell, Esther Marly; Cori, Gerty Theresa Radnitz; Elion, Gertrude Belle; Friend, Charlotte; Goeppert-Mayer, Maria; Karle, Isabella L.; Levi-Montalcini, Rita; National Academy of Engineering (NAE); Richardson, Jane Shelby; Taussig, Helen Brooke; Wu, Chien-Shiung; Yalow, Rosalyn Sussman
> **References** Leitch, Alexander, *A Princeton Companion* (1978); Olsen, Kirstin, *Chronology of Women's History* (1994); "Beyond the Blueprint, Directions for Research on Head Start's Families: About Participating Organizations," available at http://ericps.ed.uiuc.edu (cited 4 April 1999).

National Aeronautics and Space Administration (NASA)

The National Aeronautics and Space Administration (NASA) is an independent, quasi government agency with the mission of initiating, promoting, and coordinating a space program focused on research, exploration, and technological development. NASA was established by the U.S. Congress in 1958—in part as a response to the former USSR's launching of its first space satellite (*Sputnik*) in 1957—through the National Aeronautics and Space Act.

Although a formal space agency was not created until 1958, NASA actually had its beginnings in the National Advisory Committee for Aeronautics (NACA), founded in 1915. This was a time of great social and cultural change in the United States, coupled with advances in technology, especially in automobile manufacture and other machine-based industries. The formation of NACA stemmed from growing concern that the

U.S. aviation program was not on a par with comparable European aviation initiatives. These concerns were heightened by the threat of war.

The Langley Memorial Aeronautical Laboratory (now the Langley Research Center) of Virginia, which opened in 1917, was the first NACA research installation. The Ames Aeronautical Laboratory (now the Ames Research Center) was opened in California in 1941. The next year, the Aircraft Engine Research Laboratory (now the Lewis Research Center) opened in Ohio. Since then, additional research facilities have been established, including the Goddard Space Flight Center (Maryland), the Lyndon B. Johnson Space Center (Texas), and the John F. Kennedy Space Center (Florida)—a major launching site for spacecraft. The Jet Propulsion Laboratory, or JPL (in California), and the George C. Marshall Space Flight Center (in Alabama), formerly under the Department of Defense (DoD), were transferred to NASA in 1960.

NASA headquarters are located in Washington, D.C., and it is here that the overall planning and development of various elements of the space program take place. The particular activities of NASA installations are managed by four Strategic Enterprises, each of which administers a specific portion of the agency's efforts. The NASA Enterprises are the Office of Aero-Space Technology, the Office of Earth Science, the Human Exploration and Development of Space Enterprise (HEDS), and the Office of Space Science.

The Office of Aero-Space Technology is responsible for the research, development, transfer, application, and commercialization of technologies necessary for meaningful and successful space exploration. Its efforts focus on aircraft, space and launch vehicles, nuclear and other propulsion systems, electronics, and biotechnology. The Office of Earth Science (formerly the Mission to Planet Earth Enterprise) uses space as an orbital platform to gather data about Earth's environment that may not be gathered by any other means. Included in this are data dealing with ozone depletion and climate change. The Exploration and Development of Space Enterprise seeks to broaden the space frontier and to expand the human experience of outer space. The mission of the Office of Space Science is the scientific exploration of space and the solar system, which includes the discovery of planets among other star systems, the search for life beyond Earth, and the charting of the evolution of the universe.

Since its beginnings, women have played significant roles in the space program. Until recently, this work occurred behind the scenes, with women being prohibited from participating in space flights. Despite this limitation, the work of women in such areas as mathematics, engineering, biology, physics, chemistry, astronomy, meteorology, and geology has contributed much to the success of the space program. For example, Joan Berkowitz conducted research that led to the use of alloys of molybdenum, tungsten, and zirconium in rockets and space vehicles. Aerospace engineer Yvonne Brill developed rocket propulsion systems in the 1970s that are still used today. Astronomer Margaret Burbidge helped develop a spectrograph that was launched with the Hubble Space Telescope. Mathematicians Evelyn Granville and Katherine Coleman Johnson calculated orbital trajectories for the *Apollo* spacecraft, and aerospace engineer Barbara Crawford Johnson helped develop the backup guidance system used during the reentry of these vehicles. Engineer Beatrice Hicks developed an environmental sensor that was used in the Saturn V rockets that powered the *Apollo* spacecraft. Caroline Herzenberg used spectroscopy to analyze the composition of lunar samples obtained during the flight of *Apollo 11*. Pauline Beery Mack used her expertise in nutrition to develop methods for measuring calcium loss that were used by NASA.

In 1959, NASA began selecting *astronauts,* a new word derived from two Greek words, meaning "sailor among the stars." Seven test pilots were selected in the first astronaut group. Included in this group was Alan B. Shepard, Jr., who would become the first American astronaut. Additional astronaut groups were formed in 1962, 1963, 1965, 1966, and 1969. Until 1969, all NASA pilots and scientist astronauts were men. Even though Russia had sent the first woman into space in 1963 (cosmonaut Valentina Tereshkova, aboard *Vostok 6*), NASA continued its policy of selecting only men to participate in space flights well into the 1970s.

In 1978, NASA changed its policies regarding women on space flights. In that year, it named 20 mission specialists and 15 pilots for its space shuttle program. Six of the 35 participants were women, all of whom were selected to serve as mission specialists. These women were Sally K. Ride, Judith A. Resnik, Anna Fisher, Margaret Seddon, Shannon Lucid, and Kathryn D. Sullivan.

As mission specialists, these women were responsible for deploying and recovering satellites, deploying the Hubble Space Telescope, and conducting scientific and medical experiments. *Challenger* astronaut and physicist Sally K. Ride was the first American woman to go into space, in June 1983; she also was the youngest American to orbit Earth. Prior to this flight, Ride and Judith Resnik worked together on the design and development of the Remote Manipulator System (RMS), a robotic arm for use aboard spacecraft.

Electrical engineer Judith Resnik became the second American woman to go into space, aboard the first flight of *Discovery* in 1984. Resnik was scheduled for a second space flight, aboard the *Challenger* in 1986; however, the flight was never realized because the shuttle exploded seconds after taking off, killing all crew members aboard.

Physician Anna Fisher served as mission specialist aboard the orbiter *Discovery* in 1984. During this voyage, she participated in the deployment of two telecommunications satellites and in the first space salvage mission in history, in which two communications satellites were successfully retrieved.

Margaret Seddon, a physician and the first woman to achieve the rank of astronaut, served as mission specialist and payload commander aboard flights of *Discovery* (1985) and *Columbia* (1991, 1993).

Astronaut Shannon Lucid also journeyed into space in 1985. Lucid has since been a crew member aboard *Atlantis* (1989 and 1991), and *Columbia* (1993) shuttle missions, and made history in 1996, as the astronaut who had spent the longest period of time in space. This accomplishment took place during a six-month period in space (22 March through 26 September) aboard the Russian space station *Mir.* In recognition of her achievement, Lucid was awarded the Congressional Space Medal of Honor by President Bill Clinton, becoming the first woman to receive this prestigious award. In addition, she was awarded the Order of Friendship Medal by Russian President Boris Yeltsin. This is the highest award that can be presented to a noncitizen of Russia.

In 1984, geologist Kathryn D. Sullivan became the first woman to walk in space, as a member of the extravehicular activity (EVA) team on the *Challenger,* demonstrating in-flight satellite refueling. She also was a crew member aboard the shuttle *Discovery* when it deployed the Hubble Space Telescope in 1990.

Since NASA's selection of the first six women astronauts in 1978, the agency has continued to select women for participation in the astronaut program, where they have trained as mission specialists, payload commanders, and pilots. To date, more than 25 women have undergone astronaut training, of whom at least 15 have participated in space missions. Included among these women are Mae Carol Jemison, who in 1992 became the first African American woman to go into space; Ellen Ochoa, who became the first Latino woman to go into space in 1993; and Eileen Collins, who in 1995 became the first woman to pilot the space shuttle during a mission to rendezvous with the *Mir* space station. In addition, numerous other women continue to contribute their talents to NASA through their work at the agency's Strategic Enterprises and various field installations.

See also Aeronautical and Aerospace Engineering; Astronomy; Berkowitz, Joan; Brill, Yvonne Claeys; Burbidge, (Eleanor) Margaret Peachey; Darden, Christine M.; Fitzroy, Nancy D.; Flügge-Lotz, Irmgard; Gardner, Julia Anna; Granville, Evelyn Boyd; Herzenberg, Caroline Littlejohn; Hicks, Beatrice Alice; Jemison, Mae; Jet Propulsion Laboratory (JPL); Johnson, Barbara Crawford; Johnson, Katherine Coleman Goble; Lucid, Shannon Wells; Mack, Pauline Beery; Ochoa, Ellen; Resnik, Judith A.; Ride, Sally Kirsten; Ross, Mary G.; Simpson, Joanne; Sitterly, Charlotte Moore; Space Exploration; Widnall, Sheila; Wu, Ying-Chu (Lin) Susan

References Anderson, Frank W., Jr., *Orders of Magnitude: A History of NACA and NASA, 1915–1976* (1976); Felder, Deborah G., *A Century of Women: The Most Influential Events in 20th Century Women's History* (1999); Franck, Irene M., and David M. Brownstone, *Women's World: A Timeline of Women in History* (1995); National Aeronautics and Space Administration, *Astronaut Fact Book* (1992); National Aeronautics and Space Administration, History Office, at http://www.hq.nasa.gov/office/pao/History/history.html (cited 29 May 1999).

National Engineers Week

National Engineers Week is a one-week period set aside annually to promote awareness of the work of engineers and the engineering profession. Established in 1951 by the National Society of Professional Engineers, the event occurs during the week of President George Washington's birthday (February 22), in recognition of his work as a land surveyor and military engineer and his role in helping to establish the nation's first engineering school at West Point. Each year, a different professional engineering society and corporation cosponsor National Engineers Week events, including classroom visitations by practicing engineers, junior- and senior-high school design competitions, and community exhibits.

Several engineering societies, including the Society of Hispanic Professional Engineers (SHPE), use this week to help promote participation by individuals who are members of underrepresented groups, including women and Latinos, in engineering fields. In addition, the week is recognized by the U.S. Congress through statements made by its members and in an annual message presented by the president of the United States.

See also Society of Hispanic Professional Engineers (SHPE); Society of Women Engineers (SWE)
References National Engineers Week, available at http://www.eweek.org (cited 15 March 1999).

National Institute of Standards and Technology (NIST)

The National Institute of Standards and Technology (NIST) is a nonregulatory agency of the U.S. Commerce Department's Technology Administration. NIST oversees a number of interrelated initiatives with the collective mission of advancing measurement science and developing techniques and standards to support industry, commerce, scientific institutions, and all branches of government. In addition, NIST assists U.S. industries (in particular, metallurgy, transportation, communications, and power) by developing programs designed to speed the commercialization of new and emerging technologies and to enhance international competitiveness.

In addition to maintaining standard systems of measurement (time, length, and mass), NIST communicates with its counterpart organizations worldwide to promote and support technological advances. NIST also performs research and provides technical services in the fields of computer science, technology, electronics, materials science, and building and fire safety.

NIST originally was established as the Office of Weights and Measures (a branch of the Treasury Department) by the U.S. Congress in 1824. At that time, agency responsibilities were to establish uniform weights and measures for use by U.S. customs houses and state and foreign governments. In 1901, the agency's name was changed to the National Bureau of Standards (NBS). Three years later, the NBS was made part of the Department of Commerce. It became the primary government agency for research in chemistry, physics, engineering, and metallurgy. In 1945, Charlotte Moore Sitterly, an astrophysicist specializing in spectral analysis of celestial bodies, joined the NBS in the spectroscopy section of its atomic physics division. In 1988, the agency's name once again was changed, this time to the National Institute of Standards and Technology (NIST), which remains its name today.

See also Computers/Computer Technology; Granville, Evelyn Boyd; Materials Engineering; Metals and Metallurgy; Safety Engineering; Sitterly, Charlotte Moore
References Considine, Douglas M., ed., *Van Nostrand's Scientific Encyclopedia*, 8th ed., vol. 2: (J–Z) (1990); Levy, Richard C., *Inventing and Patenting Sourcebook* (1990); National Institute of Standards and Technology, "NIST and You," http://www.nist.gov/public_affairs/history.htm (cited 12 May 1999); National Institute of Standards and Technology, "NIST's Fast

Facts," http:// www.nist.gov/public_affairs/fact sheet/fast facts2.htm (cited 12 May 1999).

National Inventors' Hall of Fame

The National Inventors' Hall of Fame is a nonprofit organization that honors U.S. inventors. It was established in 1973 by several patent attorneys and representatives of the U.S. Patent and Trademark Office who by honoring past inventors, hoped to encourage the development of future inventions. The Hall of Fame promotes creativity through various programs, traveling exhibits, and video presentations.

Nominations for inclusion in the Hall of Fame are accepted from various sources through the submission of a nomination form. Once received, the form is reviewed by a selection committee comprising representatives from technical and scientific organizations in the United States. Committee members then vote on the nominee by considering whether the nominee has received a U.S. patent, how the invention contributes to the welfare of the nation, and the invention's success in promoting progress in the sciences and useful arts.

Inductees are honored at a ceremony held in Akron, Ohio. In addition, an annual recognition ceremony is held on National Inventors' Day at the U.S. Patent and Trademark Office in Arlington, Virginia. Until 1995, National Inventors' Hall of Fame inductees received recognition only through exhibits displayed at the U.S. Patent and Trademark Office. However, through private funding, the organization has established a permanent residence known as Inventure Place, in Akron, Ohio.

In 1991, Nobel Prize–winning scientist Gertrude Belle Elion became the first woman inducted into the National Inventors' Hall of Fame, for her development of the leukemia-fighting drug, 1-Amino–6-Mercaptopurine. Three years later, Elizabeth Lee Hazen and Rachel Fuller Brown were inducted for their coinvention of nystatin (the world's first successful antifungal medication) and a means of producing it. The next year, chemist Stephanie Louise Kwolek became an inductee, largely for her development of Kevlar®, a fiber that is used in the manufacture of bullet-resistant vests worn by military and law enforcement officials. The first woman to serve as president of the National Inventors' Hall of Fame was Mary Ann Tucker, who served a term from 1997–1998.

See also Brown, Rachel Fuller; Elion, Gertrude Belle; Hazen, Elizabeth Lee; Kwolek, Stephanie Louise; Patent; Patent and Trademark Office, U.S. (PTO)
References Macdonald, Anne L., *Feminine Ingenuity: How Women Inventors Changed America* (1992); Read, Phyllis J., and Bernard L. Witlieb, *The Book of Women's Firsts* (1992); National Inventors' Hall of Fame, available at http://www.invent.org (cited 6 January 1998).

National Medal of Science

The National Medal of Science recognizes individuals for their outstanding contributions to knowledge in the physical, biological, mathematical, engineering, behavioral, or social sciences. Recipients of the award, which is presented annually, are determined from recommendations made by nationally represented scientific and engineering organizations and the National Academy of Sciences (NAS) to the President's Committee on the National Medal of Science.

The National Medal of Science was established by the U.S. Congress in 1959 as a presidential award. The first award was presented in 1962. As of 1997, more than 350 of America's leading scientists and engineers have been recognized for their contributions to science and engineering as well as the potential effects on advancing scientific thought. Just over 20 of these recipients were women, four of whom are also Nobel Prize recipients.

The first National Medal of Science presented to a woman was received by geneticist Barbara McClintock (also a Nobel Prize recipient) in 1970 for her work on "jumping genes." Other women who have received this prestigious award include Chien-Shiung Wu (1975), Rita Levi-Montalcini (1987), Rosalyn S. Yalow (1988), and Gertrude B. Elion (1991). Wu received the award for her contributions to elementary particle physics (she established nonconservation of parity in beta par-

ticle decay and conservation of vector current in beta particle decay). Levi-Montalcini received her award for her discoveries and research of nerve growth factors (NGFs). Rosalyn S. Yalow received the National Medal of Science for radioimmunoassay (RIA), a system whereby substances in the body may be radioactively tagged and traced. Elion was granted her award in recognition of her contributions in chemotherapy, which advanced the treatment of gout, leukemia, and cancer, and in the use of immunosuppressants during transplant surgeries.

See also Burbidge, (Eleanor) Margaret Peachey; Dresselhaus, Mildred S.; Elion, Gertrude Belle; Karle, Isabella L.; Levi-Montalcini, Rita; National Medal of Technology; Nobel Prize; Patrick, Ruth; Rubin, Vera Cooper; Wu, Chien-Shiung; Yalow, Rosalyn Sussman
References Siegman, Gita, ed., *Awards, Honors, and Prizes,* vol. 1: *United States and Canada,* 10th ed. (1992); National Science Foundation, "National Medal of Science Recipients, 1997–1962," available at http://www.fastlane.nsf.gov/a7/A7Winners.htm (cited 15 May 1998); National Science and Technology Medals Foundation, "About the Medals," available at http://www.asee.org/nstmf/medals.html (cited 15 May 1998).

National Medal of Technology

The National Medal of Technology is the highest honor that can be bestowed on an American innovator. The award, which is presented annually by the president of the United States, is granted to an individual, team, or company in recognition of their development of technological innovations that significantly improve products, services, or processes. To be considered for the award, individuals and team members must be U.S. citizens. Similarly, a company that receives the award is required to have more than 50 percent of its shares or assets held by U.S. citizens.

The National Medal of Technology was created in 1980 when Congress passed the Stevenson-Wydler Technology Act. The first awards were granted in 1985 and recognized the accomplishments of 15 individuals, teams, and corporations. Women who have been honored by the National Medal of Technology include Helen Edwards (1989), Grace Murray Hopper (1991), and Stephanie L. Kwolek (1994).

Edwards received the award as one of four members of the Fermi National Accelerator Laboratory team who designed, constructed, and initially operated the TEVATRON particle accelerator, a device that has been instrumental in exploring the properties of matter and in the design of a newer accelerator called the Superconducting Super Collider.

Retired naval officer Grace Murray Hopper received her National Medal of Technology jointly with the Digital Equipment Corporation, for her pioneering achievements in the computer industry—specifically, in the development of computer languages.

Like Hopper, Stephanie Kwolek was retired at the time her award was granted. Her award was presented for her discovery and application of crystal processing to the development of new fibers that have been used internationally to create products that save lives and benefit humankind.

See also Edwards, Helen Thom; Hopper, Grace Murray; Kwolek, Stephanie Louise; National Medal of Science
References National Science and Technology Medals Foundation, "About the Medals," available at http://www.asee.org/nstmf/medals.html (cited 11 May 1998); National Science and Technology Medals Foundation, "Medal 1: The National Medal of Technology," available at http://www.ta.doc.gov/medal/ (cited 11 May 1998); National Science and Technology Medals Foundation, "The National Medal of Technology: 1985–1997 Recipients," available at http://www.ta.doc.gov/medal/Recipients.htm (cited 11 May 1998).

National Science Foundation (NSF)

Created by the National Science Foundation Act of 1950, the National Science Foundation (NSF) is an independent agency within the executive branch of the U.S. government, established to support research and education in science and engineering in the United States. The agency accomplishes its goals through monetary awards, including fellowships, grants, and contracts that fund research and graduate study in mathematics; physical, biological, computer, and social sciences; and engineering.

The NSF also encourages the exchange of scientific research and information and supports the development and use of computers and other scientific methods and technologies. It administers U.S. research activities in the Arctic and Antarctic and supports and coordinates research centers and facilities throughout the United States, including the National Center for Atmospheric Research (Colorado), the National Optical Astronomy Observatory (Arizona), and the National Astronomy and Ionosphere Center (Arecibo, Puerto Rico).

See also National Academy of Engineering (NAE); National Academy of Sciences (NAS)
References Maurer, Christine, and Tara E. Sheets, eds., *Encyclopedia of Associations: An Associations Unlimited Reference*, 33rd ed. (1998), vol. 1, parts 1–3; Office of the Federal Register, National Archives and Records Administration, *The United States Government Manual 1997/98* (1997).

National Women's Hall of Fame

The National Women's Hall of Fame is a nonprofit organization that highlights the contributions of women in America, past and present, to the nation's well-being. The organization was established to educate the public about the important roles women have played throughout American history as well as to pay tribute to particular women whose contributions in the arts, athletics, business, education, government, the humanities, philanthropy, and science have enhanced the general quality of life.

The National Women's Hall of Fame was founded in 1969 in Seneca Falls, New York—the site of the first women's rights convention, in 1848. The Hall of Fame houses a research library, exhibits, and a learning center that contains historical memorabilia, including artifacts, photographs, and audiovisual materials. The Hall of Fame also creates traveling exhibits for use by organizations throughout the United States.

The first induction ceremony of the National Women's Hall of Fame was held in 1973, when 25 women were selected for inclusion. Present members recognized for their contributions to the sciences and technology include Nobel Prize–winning pharmacologist Gertrude B. Elion; former U.S. Surgeon General Antonia Novello; physicians Elizabeth Blackwell, Alice Hamilton, Florence

Sabin, and Helen Brooke Taussig; anthropologist Margaret Mead; and environmentalist Rachel Carson. A list of additional inductees in the fields of science and technology appears in Table A.2 in the Appendix.

References Cullen-DuPont, Kathryn, *The Encyclopedia of Women's History in America* (1998); Tinling, Marion, *Women Remembered* (1986); Zophy, Angela Howard, ed., *Handbook of American Women's History* (1990); National Women's Hall of Fame, "Our History," available at http://www.greatwoman.org/history.htm (cited 14 December 1998); National Women's Hall of Fame, "The Women of the Hall," available at http://greatwomen.org/grtwmn.htm (cited 7 January 1998).

National Women's History Month

In 1987, both houses of the U.S. Congress approved the National Women's History Month Resolution, establishing the month of March as National Women's History Month, a period set aside for recognizing the achievements of American women in the humanities, the sciences, medicine, and technology. Since the passage of this resolution, schools, workplaces, and communities throughout the country have made special efforts during this month to increase public awareness of women's achievements, through sponsorship of a variety of activities and programs.

The celebration and designation of National Women's History Month grew out of two earlier events—the establishment of March 8 as International Women's Day and the expansion of this celebration to a week-long period known as Women's History Week. The first International Women's Day was celebrated in Denmark, Austria, Switzerland, and Germany in 1911, to commemorate a labor rally held in New York City on 8 March 1857 by seamstresses who were demanding better working conditions.

In 1978, the Education Task Force of the Sonoma County (California) Commission on the Status of Women initiated a Women's History Week Celebration for their school district, to address concerns about the lack of instruction on women's history in the local curriculum. Soon other school districts throughout the country began establishing their own guidelines for increasing instruction about women's history. By 1981, interest in the local programs begun by Sonoma County was so great that the U.S. Congress adopted a resolution declaring one week in the month of March as National Women's History Week.

Celebration of National Women's History Week in the schools was seen as one vehicle by which gender equity might be reached in the classroom. This, combined with the increased availability of curriculum materials related to women's history, led the National Women's History Project (NWHP) to petition Congress to expand the week-long celebration to a month-long celebration. With the passage of the 1987 resolution, National Women's History Month became an annual event.

See also National Engineers Week; Women's Rights
References Felder, Deborah G., *A Century of Women: The Most Influential Events in 20th Century Women's History* (1999); National Women's History Project, "A Look at Women's History Month," available at http://www. nwhp.org (cited 11 April 1999).

Nepotism Policies

Nepotism is the practice of hiring or assigning business or political positions to members of one's family. The term *nepotism* derives from a Latin word meaning "nephew." To avoid conflicts of interest and ensure that only the most qualified individuals are hired and that they perform the obligations of their position objectively, many government agencies, corporations, colleges, and universities throughout the United States have at one time or another instituted policies prohibiting the simultaneous employment of related individuals. Institutions having such policies would not hire members of the same family (whether immediate or extended). More recently, however, many institutions have revised their policies to restrict the employment of related individuals only when one of the employees involved is in a position to make decisions that affect the other. Such decisions may include matters of retention, transfer, promotion, salary, and supervision.

Although nepotism policies were not explicitly directed against women, social values often led to a male relative's being given priority in employment over a woman, regardless of the qualifications of the individuals. In many instances, if a man and woman working for the same company married, the woman was dismissed from the company. In other cases, women were permitted to remain with a company but were asked to do their jobs without salary or recognition. Examples of such cases are provided by two women Nobel laureates: Gerty Cori and Maria Goeppert-Mayer. Both women had difficulty gaining positions and recognition as a result of the nepotism policies that were in place at the universities for which their husbands worked.

See also Affirmative Action; Cori, Gerty Theresa Radnitz; Goeppert-Mayer, Maria; Lamme, Bertha; Women's Rights
References Rossiter, Margaret W., *Women Scientists in America: Before Affirmative Action, 1940–1972* (1995); Duke University, "Employment of Relatives (Nepotism)," in *Personnel Policy Manual,* available at http://www.hr.duke.edu/policy/ppm/a–15.htm (cited 12 May 1998); University of Rochester, "Conflicting Employment Relationships (Nepotism)," in *Personnel Policies and Procedures,* available at http://www.rochester.edu/Admin/HR/policies/1215.HTM (cited 12 May 1998).

Newman, Lyda (n.d.)

Little is known about the life of Lyda Newman. However, this New York City resident is known to have received the last of only four patents issued to African American women during the nineteenth century. Newman was granted U.S. Patent No. 625,446 on 15 November 1898, for a hairbrush with a detachable bristle unit that permitted easy cleaning. This hairbrush is believed to have been the first with synthetic bristles.

See also Goode, Sarah E.; Joyner, Marjorie Stewart; Patent; Walker, Madame C. J.
References Hine, Darlene Clark, Elsa Barkley Brown, and Rosalyn Terborg-Penn, eds., *Black Women in America: An Historical Encyclopedia,* vol. 1: (A–L) (1993); Stanley, Autumn, *Mothers and Daughters of Invention: Notes for a Revised History of Technology* (1993); Lemelson-MIT Program, "African American Inventors of the Early 20th Century," available at http://web.mit.edu/invent/www/inventorsA-H/AAweek3.html

(cited 4 April 1998); Louisiana State University Libraries, Baton Rouge, "African American Women Inventors: Historical," *The Faces of Science: African Americans in the Sciences,* available at http://www.lib.lsu.edu/lib/chem/display/women_inventors.html (cited 9 November 1997).

Nobel, Alfred
See **Nobel Prize**

Nobel Prize

These international awards are granted annually to recognize individuals of outstanding achievement in the fields of chemistry, physics, physiology or medicine, literature, and the promotion of world peace. A sixth Nobel Prize in the area of economics was created in 1968, through an endowment of the national bank of Sweden, with the first award in this area being granted in 1969. The first Nobel Prizes were presented in 1901 by the king of Sweden.

Nobel Prizes are granted by the Nobel Foundation as designated in the will of Alfred Bernhard Nobel (1833–1896), a Swedish chemist and philanthropist who invented dynamite and blasting gelatin. Because of these inventions Nobel was sometimes referred to as the "Merchant of Death." In an attempt to improve his image, Nobel changed his will so that the interest on his $9 million estate would be distributed annually to those who improved the human condition in specific branches of science. Nobel Prizes dealing with technology are granted in the areas of physics, chemistry, and physiology or medicine. Per Nobel's will, prizes in physics and chemistry are awarded by the Royal Swedish Academy of Sciences; and those in physiology or medicine are awarded by the Karolinska Institute in Stockholm.

The Nobel Prizes, which are considered the highest honors that can be bestowed upon individuals, consist of a monetary award, a diploma, and a gold medal. To date, ten women have been awarded Nobel Prizes for their work in science and technology. Descriptions of these women and their achievements appear in Table A.3 in the Appendix.

See also Cori, Gerty Theresa Radnitz; Elion, Gertrude Belle; Goeppert-Mayer, Maria; Levi-Montalcini, Rita; Yalow, Rosalyn Sussman

References Famighetti, Robert, et al., eds., *World Almanac and Book of Facts, 1994* (1994); Heinemann, Susan, *Timelines of American Women's History* (1996); Olsen, Kirstin, *Chronology of Women's History* (1994); Simmons, John, *The Scientific 100: A Ranking of the Most Influential Scientists, Past and Present* (1996); Stuart, Sandra Lee, ed., *Who Won What When* (1980).

Nuclear Physics

Nuclear physics is the study of the subatomic particles that make up the nucleus of an atom and of the activities or interactions among these particles. This branch of science had its beginnings in 1911, when Nobel Prize–winning chemist Ernest Rutherford proposed the existence of the atomic nucleus. Since this discovery, numerous other scientists and engineers have devoted their careers to the study of atomic nuclei.

The atomic nuclei of all elements except hydrogen are composed of two types of subatomic particles—protons and neutrons (the hydrogen nucleus is made up of a single proton). Protons are subatomic particles having a positive charge; the number of protons in an atom determine that atom's atomic number. Neutrons have no electrical charge and thus are neutral; the number of neutrons in the nucleus of an atom, combined with the number of protons in the same atomic nucleus, determine that atom's mass.

Within the nucleus of an atom, there are binding forces that hold the particles of that nucleus in close proximity to one another. Because protons all carry a positive electrical charge, the protons within an atom have a natural tendency to repel one another (electrical charges that are the same repel each other). However, the binding forces within a nucleus are greater than those forces that would tend to push the protons apart. This concept is most apparent in atoms with lesser atomic numbers (those having relatively few protons). However, in individual atoms having large nuclei, the binding forces are weaker due to the greater distances between protons, and these atoms have a greater natural tendency to be unstable, or radioactive. Radioactivity is the spontaneous break-down of the nucleus of an atom, which results in the emission of alpha particles (helium nuclei), beta particles (electrons), or gamma radiation (electromagnetic shortwaves).

Marie Curie, working in France, was the first woman to extensively study radiation and to identify radioactive elements. In fact, she is credited with coining the term *radioactivity*. She, her husband, Pierre, and Henri Becquerel shared the 1903 Nobel Prize in physics for their research into radioactivity. In 1911, Marie Curie was again awarded a Nobel Prize, this time in chemistry, for her discovery of the element radium. (Curie remains the only scientist to have won Nobel Prizes in two different areas.)

In 1917, Lise Meitner and Otto Hahn in Berlin were seeking to identify radioactive elements other than uranium that were present in pitchblende. In this search, the pair identified the element that came to be called protactinium. Seven years later, Irène Joliot-Curie (Marie and Pierre's daughter) shared a Nobel Prize in physics with her husband, Frederic Joliot, for their work in the creation of artificial radiation. In the years following these events, many other scientists discovered additional radioactive elements, or synthesized them in the laboratory.

Meitner made a second major contribution to the area of nuclear physics in 1939 when she introduced the term *fission* to describe the process by which the nucleus of an atom could be caused to break apart when bombarded by a neutron. The process had been demonstrated to be feasible less than one year earlier by Otto Hahn and Fritz Strassman, who were working in Germany. In the fission process, which Meitner and Otto Frisch described in 1939, the splitting of the nucleus results in new elements and free neutrons, and releases a tremendous amount of energy.

Within a few years of Meitner's description of nuclear fission, scientists in the United States began working to use the energy released during the fission reaction to develop an atomic weapon. This secret initiative came to be known as the Manhattan Project. Research leading to the development of an atomic bomb was conducted at a variety of sites located throughout the United States and Canada.

Although most of the work at these sites was performed under the supervision of male scientists, a great number of women (physicists, chemists, and engineers) were called upon to participate in the project in a variety of roles. Among the most well known were Maria Goeppert-Mayer, Chien-Shiung Wu, Edith Hinkley Quimby, Elda Emma Anderson, Leona Woods Libby, and Isabella Karle. Collectively, these women's contributions were of monumental importance in the successful development of the weapon that eventually brought an end to World War II. Many other, lesser-known scientists, including Margaret Foster, Katharine Way, Kathryn Fink, Marian Elliot Koshland, Helen Blair Bartlett, and Rose Mooney Slater, also played a significant role in the research involved with the Manhattan Project.

After the bombs resulting from the Manhattan Project were detonated in Japan, concern rapidly grew about the potential hazards of such weaponry. Following her work on the Manhattan Project, Elda Emma Anderson pioneered a new area of science called health physics—an area of study dedicated to protecting people and the environment from the harmful effects of radiation. Kathryn Fink also directed much of her post–Manhattan Project work toward these goals. More recently, engineer Patricia Eng, working with the U.S. Nuclear Regulatory Commission (NRC), has developed effective radiation shielding for spent nuclear fuels (radioactive substances such as uranium) awaiting disposal. Unlike the women associated with the Manhattan Project, Eng is most concerned about the radiation hazards presented by spent fuel from nuclear power plants.

Nuclear power plants are facilities that utilize nuclear fuels to generate electricity. Among the women who have been involved in the development or operation of nuclear power plants are physicists Ada I. Pressman and Shirley Ann Jackson. In the late 1960s, Ada Pressman helped develop controls and sensors for use in nuclear power plants. In 1995, physicist Shirley Ann Jackson was appointed to chair the NRC. Her responsibilities included the regulation and evaluation of all nuclear power plants in the United States to ensure their compliance with NRC safety guidelines. Unlike her predecessors, when Jackson discovered that plants were not in compliance, she had them closed down. Eng, too, played a role in evaluating compliance with NRC guidelines. However, unlike Jackson, Eng was involved in direct inspection of nuclear facilities.

Many women have contributed to the theory of quantum physics. Among the two most significant are Chien-Shiung Wu and Maria Goeppert-Mayer. In 1957, Chien-Shiung Wu succeeded in demonstrating that the principle of conservation of parity did not apply to all matter. In this work, Wu showed that subatomic particles given off by a decaying atomic nucleus are not all emitted in the same direction, as had been previously thought. Later that year, the scientists upon whose work she had built were awarded a Nobel Prize for the hypothesis that Wu confirmed through her work. Goeppert-Mayer's major accomplishment in this area came in the early 1960s when she developed her spin orbit theory. The theory held that particles in the nucleus, like those outside the nucleus (electrons), were arranged in a predictable pattern. For this work she was awarded the Nobel Prize in physics in 1963. In addition, Goeppert-Mayer was able to apply her research to explain why some isotopes (atoms of the same element that have different numbers of neutrons) are more likely to be radioactive than others.

Many astrophysicists today are building upon the work of early nuclear physicists to determine the structure and composition of stars and galaxies. They are using this work also to develop an understanding of how the universe evolved.

See also Anderson, Elda Emma; Astronomy; Bartlett, Helen Blair; Eng, Patricia L.; Fink, Kathryn (Kay) Ferguson; Foster, Margaret; Goeppert-Mayer, Maria; Jackson, Shirley Ann; Karle, Isabella L.; Koshland, Marian Elliot; Libby, Leona W.; Manhattan Project; Ordnance; Pressman, Ada I.; Quimby, Edith Hinkley; Spaeth, Mary; Way, Katharine; Wu, Chien-Shiung
References Benson, Harris, *University Physics* (1991); Bernstein, Leonard, Alan Winkler, and Linda Zierdt-Warshaw, *Multicultural Women of Science* (1996); Rossiter, Margaret W., *Women Scientists in America: Before Affirmative Action, 1940–1972* (1995); Vare, Ethlie Ann, and Greg Ptacek, *Mothers of Invention: From the Bra to the Bomb, Forgotten Women and Their Unforgettable Ideas* (1988).

Ochoa, Ellen (b. 1958)

Ellen Ochoa is a physicist, an electrical engineer, and an inventor who holds three patents related to optical systems and processes. In addition, Ellen Ochoa will forever be known as America's first Hispanic female astronaut—an achievement recognized when she completed her astronaut training in July 1991. Two years later, Ochoa became the first Hispanic American female astronaut to go into space during a nine-day mission aboard the shuttle *Discovery*. She has since made two additional space flights, in 1994 and in 1999.

Ellen Ochoa was born in Los Angeles, California, in 1958. While she was in junior high school, Ochoa's parents divorced, and Ellen moved with her mother, Roseanne Ochoa, to La Mesa, a small town in southern California. There Ellen continued her secondary school education and graduated from Grossmont High School as class valedictorian in 1975. Following high school, Ochoa attended San Diego State University. She earned a B.S. degree in physics and graduated at the top of her class in 1980.

After receiving her B.S. degree, Ochoa pursued graduate studies in electrical engineering at Stanford University. While there, she was granted two fellowships: the Stanford engineering fellowship (1980–1981) and an IBM predoctoral fellowship (1982–1984). She received her M.S. degree in 1981 and a Ph.D. in 1985, both in electrical engineering. In her research for her doctoral dissertation, Ochoa developed an optical system in which she used photorefractive (light-scattering) crystals to filter images. Several years later, she was issued a patent for this system.

Immediately after obtaining her Ph.D., Ochoa joined the Imaging Technology Branch at Sandia National Laboratories in Livermore, California, as a research engineer. There Ochoa's research focused on various uses for optical processing systems—mechanisms that use optical devices to gather and analyze information. This work led to Ochoa being listed as the coinventor on three optics-related patents: one for an optical inspection system, one for an optical object-recognition method, and one for a method used to remove noise (distortions) and provide increased resolu-

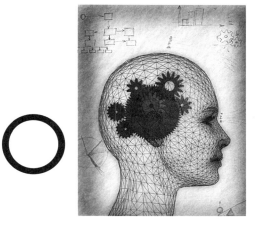

tion in images. Previously, noise reduction and resolution enhancement could be accomplished only through computer alteration of images.

Ochoa applied for admission to NASA's astronaut training program in 1985, just after receiving her Ph.D. In 1987, she was selected (as one of the top 100 finalists) to join the program. The next year, she became a researcher in the Intelligent Systems Technology Branch at NASA's Ames Research Center, at Moffett Field Naval Air Station, in Mountain View, California. At Ames, Ochoa's first job was to manage a research group working on optical systems for use in space automation. Within six months, she was promoted to the position of chief of the Intelligent Systems Technology Branch. In this role, she directed a team of researchers who were developing high-performance computational systems for use in space missions.

Ochoa began her astronaut training in January 1990, at the Johnson Space Center in Houston, Texas. She completed this training and became an astronaut in July 1991. In April 1993, Ochoa took part in her first space mission, serving as a mission specialist (an astronaut trained in spacecraft operations) aboard the *Discovery*. During the nine-day mission, the primary role of the crew was to study how solar activity affects Earth's climate and environment. To obtain the data, Ochoa had to use the shuttle's Remote Manipulator System (RMS), a robotic arm, to deploy

Ellen Ochoa was the first Hispanic woman astronaut in the United States. (Associated Press/AP)

and later recapture the *Spartan* satellite. The satellite was launched to obtain photographs and other important information about the sun's corona (the outermost layer of the sun).

In November 1994, Ochoa made a second space flight, during which she served as payload commander aboard the space shuttle *Endeavor.* The payload commander is a specialist trained in the performance of scientific research. Here, as aboard her earlier *Discovery* mission, Ochoa again used the RMS to capture the *CRISTA-SPAS* atmospheric research satellite at the end of its eight-day data-gathering mission.

Among NASA's most recent space projects are its involvement in the construction of the International Space Station, a cooperative enterprise involving the space agencies of several nations, including the United States, Canada, and Russia. In May 1999, Ochoa once again traveled into space to participate in the second space mission dealing with this ambitious project. Among the seven-member *Discovery* crew involved with this mission were three women: American astronauts

Ellen Ochoa and Tammy Jernigan and Canadian astronaut Julie Payette. The major objectives of this mission included linkup with the part of the station that had been constructed and the transfer of equipment and supplies from the shuttle to the station (including two cranes that would be used to assemble components of the station).

In recognition of her achievements as an engineer and an astronaut, Ellen Ochoa has received many awards. She was the recipient of the Hispanic Engineer National Achievement Award for the Most Promising Engineer in Government in 1989. The following year she received the Pride Award from the National Hispanic Quincentennial Commission. In 1993, she was named Houston YWCA Outstanding Woman in Science and Technology and was awarded the Congressional Hispanic Caucus Medallion of Excellence. She received the Women in Science & Engineering (WISE) Engineering Achievement Award in 1994. In addition, Ochoa has been honored by NASA with three Space Flight Medals (1993, 1994, 1999), an Outstanding Leadership Medal (1995), and NASA's Exceptional Service Medal (1997).

See also Askins, Barbara; Dunbar, Bonnie J.; Jemison, Mae; Lucid, Shannon Wells; Resnik, Judith A.; Ride, Sally Kirsten; Space Exploration

References Kanellos, Nicolás, ed., *The Hispanic American Almanac,* 2nd ed. (1966); Telgen, Diane, and Jim Kamp, *Notable Hispanic American Women* (1993); Unterberger, Amy, ed., *Who's Who Among Hispanic Americans, 1991–1992* (1994); National Aeronautics and Space Administration, "Astronaut Bio: Ellen Ochoa" (dated January 1996), available at http://www.jsc. nasa.gov/Bios/htmlbios/ochoa/html (cited 15 June 1999); National Aeronautics and Space Administration, "Preflight Interview—Ellen Ochoa," available at http:// spaceflight.nasa.gà6/crew/intochoa.html (cited 15 June 1999).

Office of Scientific Research and Development (OSRD)

In 1939, prior to U.S. involvement in World War II, events were unfolding in the United States and in Europe that would have political, social, and military consequences for many years to come. In that year, noted Nobel Prize–winning physicist (1921) Albert Einstein sent a letter to President

Franklin Delano Roosevelt, informing him that German scientists were already conducting research for the purpose of developing an explosive nuclear device (one year earlier, German physicists Otto Hahn and Fritz Strassmann had successfully demonstrated nuclear fission, a significant step toward and precursor to developing such a device). Given the early German conquests in Europe and the threat of continued Nazi aggression, Roosevelt created an Advisory Committee on Uranium and gave it a mandate to determine whether an explosive atomic device could be built. After being informed in 1941 that the development of such a device was possible, Roosevelt and members of the United States Congress created the Office of Scientific Research and Development (OSRD) and charged it with the responsibility of developing the world's first atomic bomb. Vannevar Bush, an electrical engineer and dean of the engineering school at the Massachusetts Institute of Technology (MIT), was named director of the agency.

Bush soon created the Manhattan Engineer District (later renamed the Manhattan Project), naming U.S. General Leslie R. Groves as its director. Noted physicist J. Robert Oppenheimer was placed in charge of all research that would be conducted toward the development of the bomb. Almost immediately, industrial facilities and research centers were created in Oak Ridge, Tennessee; Hanford, Washington; Los Alamos, New Mexico; and at the University of Chicago, Columbia University in New York City, and the University of California at Berkeley.

The Manhattan Project was one of the costliest and most ambitious defense research initiatives ever conducted in the United States. The project required the expertise of physicists, chemists, geologists, biologists, engineers, and scientists in numerous other specialties and disciplines. With an almost limitless budget, and given that many men had been called into military service, the project offered women an opportunity to obtain employment in factories and in the research centers and laboratories associated with the development of each component of the bomb. The project also opened doors to new

fields of research, including nuclear medicine and peace-time applications of nuclear power.

Among the most noted women scientists who participated in the Manhattan Project were Chien-Shiung Wu, Maria Goeppert-Mayer, Leona Woods Libby, Elda Emma Anderson, Edith Hinkley Quimby, and Isabella Karle. Lesser known but no less important were the contributions of Margaret Foster, Katharine Way, Kathryn Fink, Marian Koshland, Helen Blair Bartlett, and Rose Mooney Slater.

Wu, best known for her work on parity in nuclear beta decay, brought to the project expertise in radiation detection and an understanding of events that occur during a chain reaction. Her combined knowledge in these areas was instrumental in solving a problem that dealt with an interruption in the rate of reaction in an atomic pile. Goeppert-Mayer, now known for her research in spin-orbit coupling and nuclear shell structure (for which she shared a Nobel Prize in physics in 1963), conducted research on uranium isotope separation by means of photochemical actions. Foster, a geochemist, also conducted research on radioactive isotope separation—specifically, the separation of thorium from uranium. Koshland conducted similar research on uranium separation and enrichment at the Oak Ridge facility. Anderson contributed her expertise in spectroscopy, neutron scattering, and nuclear reactor design. After completing her work on the Manhattan Project, Anderson became involved in the field of health physics—an area that studies ways in which people and the environment may be protected from the harmful effects of radiation. Quimby and Fink also have contributed much to present-day understandings of the biological effects of radiation. Libby worked at the University of Chicago, where she was involved in the development of nuclear fission reactors. Libby also developed a sophisticated neutron detector designed to monitor fission chain reactions.

After fulfilling their wartime commitments to OSRD, many of the women scientists returned to their former careers as researchers or university teachers. Many continued to work in the area of nuclear physics, applying their knowledge in this area to medicine, electrical power generating facilities, and regulation of the use of nuclear materials.

See also Anderson, Elda Emma; Bartlett, Helen Blair; Fink, Kathryn (Kay) Ferguson; Foster, Margaret; Goeppert-Mayer, Maria; Karle, Isabella L.; Koshland, Marian Elliot; Libby, Leona W.; Manhattan Project; Ordnance; Quimby, Edith Hinkley; Way, Katharine; Wu, Chien-Shiung

References Ambrose, Stephen E., *New History of World War II* (1997); Groueff, Stephane, *The Manhattan Project: The Untold Story of the Making of the Atomic Bomb* (1967); Rhodes, Richard, *The Making of the Atomic Bomb* (1986).

Ordnance

Ordnance refers to military supplies and equipment, including weapons, ammunition, propellants (explosives that are used to propel rockets, missiles, and other projectiles), and pyrotechnic substances (explosives that are used to create visual signals or illuminate an area of specific interest). Until recently, American women were barred from participating in combat; however, women's involvement with the development of ordnance dates back more than a century.

One of the earliest contributions to the field of pyrotechnics was made by Martha J. Coston. Coston developed Pyrotechnic Night Signals—maritime flares—for which she received a patent in 1871. These pyrotechnic devices were particularly useful during the Civil War and on the seas and battlefields during World War I and World War II.

In 1899, M. J. Alsbau of New York made a modification to a torpedo that had previously been created by T. W. Just of England. Alsbau's modification included the addition of a "false head" to the torpedo. This head separated from the main body of the torpedo after launch in such a way as to strike the target at which it was aimed at a location above the surface of the water. Simultaneously, the main body of the torpedo struck the same target below the waterline, as in the original design. In honor of Alsbau's contribution, the weapon was renamed the Just-Alsbau torpedo.

Hertha Ayrton made several contributions that benefited the military during World War I.

The first of these involved the development of electric searchlights that she made with her husband. Her second, more notable contribution was known as the Ayrton antigas fan. This device was used by soldiers in the trenches to redirect potentially toxic gases launched by enemy forces.

Several women made significant contributions to the war effort during World War II. Most noted among these are film actress Hedy Lamarr, Henrietta Bradberry, Lillian Greneker, and Mary Babnick Brown. Lamarr developed a wireless antijamming device designed for use with radio-controlled torpedoes. Although Lamarr's device was never actually used by the Navy, the technology has been adopted for use in modern satellite communications, including Internet applications. African American inventor Henrietta Bradberry developed what was termed a "torpedo discharge means": a device that used compressed air to discharge a torpedo from an undersea vessel. Like Lamarr's, Bradberry's invention, which is similar to the currently used pneumatic system, was never adopted by the military.

In peacetime, Lillian Greneker designed mannequins for use in the theater. Oddly, her experience with papier-mâché enabled her to assist the military in solving a key problem in the production of vulcanized rubber fuel tanks for use aboard submarines and fighter aircraft. Mary Babnick Brown had the dubious distinction of donating a strand of her hair for use in the development of the crosshairs (the sighting component) of the top-secret Norden bombsight, a precision bombing instrument.

World War II saw the design and development of missiles and rocket systems never before used in wartime. Again, women were at the forefront in the development and testing of many of these new weapon systems. In 1948, Margaret K. Butler, a senior computer scientist at the Argonne National Laboratory, worked on the design of the nuclear reactor for the *Nautilus* submarine. During the 1950s, Mary G. Ross, a mathematician, applied her genius in ballistics and orbital mechanics to evaluating the performance of ballistic and defense missile systems. She also researched the effects of ocean wave movements on submarine missile launches. Elise F. Harmon developed brushes for use in aircraft generators, and printed circuitry for use in missiles. During this same period, Evelyn Boyd Granville developed computer programs that were used to analyze rocket trajectories. She also applied mathematical solutions to missile fuse problems.

A few years after World War II, physicist Marguerite M. Rogers worked within several different offices of the U.S. Navy, applying her physics expertise to the design and development of weapons systems. Through this work, which continued until 1980, Rogers became an authority on aerial rocketry and air support weapons systems. For her work with the Navy, Rogers was presented a Distinguished Civilian Service Award from the Secretary of Defense in 1981.

Further developments in missiles and lasers continued to be made during the 1960s and 1970s. Barbara Crawford Johnson, an aerospace engineer, developed guidance systems for use in military aircraft. She also played a major role in the development of an air-to-ground missile used aboard the B-52 bomber. Research physicist Mary Spaeth developed a tunable dye laser, a device capable of changing the frequency of the light being emitted. Spaeth also developed a damage-resistant, resonant reflector for use in range finders. Range finding devices increase accuracy in the delivery of certain types of ordnance and are currently mounted on tanks and missile-carrying aircraft.

In addition to the women involved in the de-sign, development, and testing of conventional weapons and weapons systems, a small but significant number of women participated in the Manhattan Project, the secret government program designed to produce the world's first atomic bomb. The Manhattan Project research was occurring at the same time as World War II and resulted in the production of the bomb that brought about an end to this war. Among the many women involved in this project were Maria Goeppert-Mayer, Chien-Shiung Wu, Elda Emma Anderson, Helen Blair Bartlett, Kathryn Ferguson Fink, Margaret Foster, Marian Elliot Koshland, Leona Woods Libby, Katharine Way, and Rose Mooney Slater.

See also Anderson, Elda Emma; Bartlett, Helen Blair; Bradberry, Henrietta M.; Butler, Margaret K.; Coston, Martha J.; Fink, Kathryn (Kay) Ferguson; Foster, Margaret; Goeppert-Mayer, Maria; Granville, Evelyn Boyd; Greneker, Lillian; Harmon, Elise F.; Hopper, Grace Murray; Johnson, Barbara Crawford; Koshland, Marian Elliot; Lamarr, Hedy; Libby, Leona W.; Manhattan Project; Mather, Sarah; Office of Scientific Research and Development (OSRD); Quimby, Edith Hinkley; Rogers, Marguerite M.; Ross, Mary G.; Spaeth, Mary; Way, Katharine, Wu, Chien-Shiung

References Ambrose, Stephen E., *New History of World War II* (1997); Salerno, Heather, "Mothers of Invention: Though Unsung and Ignored, Women Have Pushed Technology's Frontiers," *Washington Post* (12 March 1997); Sluby, Patricia Carter, "Black Women and Inventions," *Sage: A Scholarly Journal on Black Women*, vol. 6, no. 2 (Fall 1989); Tsipis, Kosta, *Arsenal: Understanding Weapons in the Nuclear Age* (1983); "Woman Perfects Torpedo: Dr. M. J. Alsbau Masters the Principle of Steering It," *New York Times* (17 December 1899).

Parker, Ivy (1907–1985)

In 1966, chemist and research engineer Ivy Parker gained the title of "first lady of petroleum" for her contributions to the development of pipeline technology in the petroleum industry. Parker was a specialist in the causes and prevention of pipeline corrosion. She also developed an electrolytic titration method for assessing the amount of chloride in crude oil. This was important to pipeline corrosion technology, since chlorides affect the refining process of crude oil and facilitate pipeline corrosion.

Ivy Parker was born near Tucumcari, New Mexico. After graduating from high school, she attended West Texas State College in Canyon, Texas, receiving her bachelor's degree in chemistry in 1928. She was granted a master's degree by the University of Texas (UT) in 1931 and four years later became the first woman awarded a Ph.D. in chemistry from that school.

Parker began her career working as a chemist at a refinery in Deer Park, Texas. It was while at Deer Park that Parker developed her electrolytic titration methods. During the 1940s, Parker worked as a corrosion engineer for the Plantation Pipe Line Company in Atlanta, Georgia. In 1944, she became the first editor of *Corrosion,* the journal of the National Association of Corrosion Engineers (NACE). In 1962, *Corrosion* changed from a quarterly to a monthly publication. At the same time, NACE began a second publication, *Materials Protection.* Parker accepted a position as editor of *Materials Protection,* remaining in that role until 1968.

Parker's work as editor, researcher, and contributing writer to *Corrosion* and *Materials Protection* was instrumental in the development and promotion of NACE's publications. In 1969, NACE awarded Parker a certificate of appreciation and created the Ivy Parker Award, a Southeast Region Award that was established and presented to Parker for her outstanding contributions to the organization. In 1973 and 1974, respectively, she received the Citation of Recognition for Outstanding Contributions to NACE and the R. A. Brannon Award, also for outstanding contributions to the advancement of NACE.

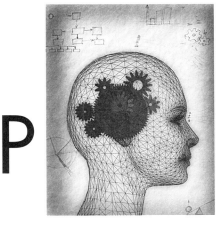

In addition to her affiliation with NACE, Parker chaired the Society of Women Engineers (SWE) Board of Trustees for 16 years. She was elected a fellow of the organization in 1982. She also held memberships in the American Chemical Society (ACS), the American Institute of Chemists (AIC), the American Association for the Advancement of Science (AAAS), the Electrochemical Society, Sigma Xi, Iota Sigma Pi, and the Georgia Academy of Sciences.

See also Chemical Engineering; Everson, Carrie Jane; Flanigen, Edith M.; Gardner, Julia Anna; Good, Mary Lowe; Petroleum Engineering; Society of Women Engineers (SWE)

References "Ivy M. Parker to Receive Brannon Award," *Materials Protection and Performance* (December 1973); "Ivy Parker—First Lady of Corrosion" [editorial], *Corrosion,* vol. 41, no. 11 (November 1985); Kass-Simon, G., and Patricia Farnes, eds., *Women of Science: Righting the Record* (1990).

Patent

A patent is a document or grant issued by the government that provides an inventor or discoverer the right to exclude others from producing, selling, or using the invention in the United States for a stipulated period of time. The history of the U.S. patent dates back to the Constitutional Convention of 1787. Under Article 1, Section 8 of the Constitution, Congress was empowered "to promote the progress of . . . the useful arts." The first patent law, signed by President George Washington, was the Patent Act of 1790. The first U.S. patent was issued the same year to Samuel Hopkins for his soap-making formula. In 1809, Mary Kies became the first woman to receive a U.S. patent, for inventing a method of weaving straw with silk or thread.

Patents are granted for inventions or discoveries that are new or original, useful, and have not been patented or described in any printed or published works in the United States or any foreign country. Upon meeting these requirements, an applicant must file an application, pay an application fee, and provide documentation describing the invention for the patent being sought. The patent applicant must also take an oath stating that the invention is original. Experts in science and technology are employed by the U.S. Patent and Trademark Office to study and review all applications. They research previously filed patents and related technical documents to determine whether the invention meets the criteria of "new, useful, and not previously patented or described."

There are three kinds of patents: utility patents, plant patents, and design patents. A utility patent is issued for a new process, machine, or composition of matter, such as the invention or discovery of a synthetic or composite material. A plant patent is issued for new or distinct varieties of plants, such as those cultivated for their unique flowers or fruit. Plant patents may also be issued for laboratory-produced organisms, such as bacteria, or for transgenic, or genetically engineered, fruits and vegetables. A design patent is granted for a new or original design for an article of manufacture.

The term of a patent defines the period of time during which the inventor has a legal monopoly on the invention. The term for utility and plant patents is 20 years from the date of issue. Design patents have a term of 14 years. During the patent term, the patentee has the right to sue anyone (excluding the federal government) who uses the invention without permission—a practice known as infringement. The federal government may produce or use any patented invention without the consent of the inventor; however, it

must compensate the inventor in such instances. The patentee may also sue for damages to reclaim money made through the improper use or sale of his or her invention. When a patent term expires, the invention becomes public property and the invention may be used, reproduced, or sold by anyone, with no legal restrictions.

Among the many patent markings, one of the most familiar is "patent pending." This marking indicates that a patent has been applied for but not yet granted. The "patent pending" mark has no legal bearing. However, many inventors use this mark to discourage others from using, producing, or selling their inventions.

See also Biotechnology; Genetic Engineering; Invention/Inventors; Kies, Mary; Masters, Sybilla Righton; Patent Act of 1790; Patent and Trademark Office, U.S. (PTO)
References Dumouchel, J. Robert, *Government Assistance Almanac, 1993–94,* 7th ed. (1993); Office of the Federal Register, National Archives and Records Administration, *The United States Government Manual, 1997/98* (1997); U.S. Patent and Trademark Office, *A Quest for Excellence* (1994).

Patent Act of 1790

The American patent system originated on 10 April 1790, when President George Washington signed the nation's first patent law. The law was inspired by the English Statute of Monopolies of 1624, which granted an inventor safeguards for 21 years. During the Constitutional Convention of 1787, it was recognized and agreed that the ingenuity and creativity of the people must be protected. Article 1, Section 8 of the United States Constitution provided Congress with the power "to promote the progress of science and useful arts by securing for limited times to authors and inventors the exclusive right to their respective writings and discoveries." Unlike the British system, which granted patents to court favorites or to those who could afford to purchase one, U.S. patent law provided patent rights to every American citizen.

Under the Patent Act of 1790, President Washington created a patent commission to review and issue patents. The commission was made up of the secretary of state, the secretary of war, and the attorney general. Today, the issuance of patents is the responsibility of the U.S. Patent and Trademark Office (PTO), an agency within the Department of Commerce. The first U.S. patent was granted to Samuel Hopkins, for his soap formula, on 31 July 1790. The first patent issued to a woman came in 1809, when Mary Kies was awarded a patent for a process of weaving straw with silk or thread.

See also Invention/Inventors; Kies, Mary; Patent; Patent and Trademark Office, U.S. (PTO)
References Cardwell, Donald, *The Norton History of Technology* (1995); Macdonald, Anne L., *Feminine Ingenuity: How Women Inventors Changed America* (1992); U.S. Patent and Trademark Office, *A Quest for Excellence* (1994); National Patent Association, "A Brief History of the U.S. Patent," available at http://www.nationalpatent.com.history.html (cited 11 March 1998).

Patent and Trademark Office, U.S. (PTO)

Founded in 1870, the U.S. Patent and Trademark Office (PTO), a federal agency, was originally established as the Patent Office, a subdivision of the Department of State, in 1802. At that time, the Patent Office had numerous responsibilities, including handling copyrights, collecting and disseminating agricultural information, and collecting weather data. Over time, as new patent legislation was passed, many of these responsibilities were transferred to other government agencies. It was not until the passage of revised patent laws in 1836, and again in 1870, that the primary responsibility of the Patent and Trademark Office became what it is today: the registration and issuance of patents and trademarks.

In 1925, the responsibilities and functions of the Patent and Trademark Office were transferred from the Department of State to the Department of Commerce. Today, the function of the PTO is to accept and evaluate applications for patents and trademarks. After specific legal requirements are met, the PTO grants patents and approves and registers trademarks. The PTO also provides public search centers for researching applications and maintains scientific libraries and files that contain more than 30 million documents for searches of U.S. and foreign patents and trademarks.

See also Invention/Inventors; Patent; Patent Act of 1790
References Dumouchel, J. Robert, *Government Assistance Almanac, 1993–94,* 7th ed. (1993); Office of the Federal Register, National Archives and Records Administration, *The United States Government Manual 1997/98* (1997); U.S. Patent and Trademark Office, *A Quest for Excellence* (1994).

Patent Medicine
See **Pinkham, Lydia Estes**

Patrick, Ruth (b. 1907)

Ruth Patrick is a world renowned expert and authority in the field of limnology, the branch of science that studies freshwater ecosystems—specifically, lakes and rivers. Patrick has studied freshwater ecosystems throughout the United States, Mexico, Brazil, and Peru for more than a half century. Her research focus has been a particular species of microscopic, single-celled algae known as diatoms. These aquatic organisms inhabit both fresh- and salt water. Through her research, Patrick demonstrated that diatoms living in freshwater ecosystems may be used to determine the presence of pollutants in these ecosystems. Using a device she invented, called a diatometer, Patrick developed a method of using diatoms to monitor water pollution.

Ruth Patrick was born in Topeka, Kansas, in 1907. Her father, Frank Patrick, was an attorney who possessed more than a casual interest in the natural sciences. It was his latter interest that influenced Ruth, who often accompanied her father on nature excursions. Ruth Patrick attended Coker College in South Carolina. She graduated with a B.S. degree in 1929. She then enrolled at the University of Virginia at Charlottesville, where she received both her master's degree (1931) and her doctorate (1934) in botany. The topic of her doctoral dissertation was the relationship between diatoms and water pollution. While pursuing her graduate degrees, Patrick participated in summer programs at several notable research facilities, including those at Woods Hole (Massachusetts), Cold Spring Harbor (New York), and the University of Virginia laboratory at Mountain Lake. It was while working at the Cold Spring Biological Laboratory that Ruth Patrick met Charles Hodge IV, whom she married in 1931. Following the marriage, Ruth elected to retain her maiden name.

Patrick worked as a research assistant at Temple University in Philadelphia, Pennsylvania, after receiving her Ph.D. In 1939, she accepted a position as an assistant curator in the microscopy department of the Academy of Natural Sciences in Philadelphia. At the Academy of Natural Sciences, Patrick also created the department of limnology. She became chair and curator of the department in 1947. While serving in these positions, Patrick also taught botany at the University of Pennsylvania, where she became a full professor in 1970. She remained affiliated with both of these institutions until the mid-1970s, at which time she was appointed to the Francis Boyer Research Chair (1973), and later, to chair the board of directors of the Academy of Natural Sciences (1976) Patrick was the first woman to hold the latter position.

Patrick's interest in diatoms predates her doctoral studies; and after she received her Ph.D., her continued interest and research on these unique organisms led her to uncover their importance as a means of recognizing the nature of pollution in freshwater ecosystems. While studying the ecology of freshwater ecosystems, Patrick discovered that the population size of diatoms at a given site as well as the size of individual organisms was directly related to the presence and extent of pollution. This discovery led her to develop the diatometer.

Patrick has conducted research on the health of freshwater ecosystems throughout the United States. She also has participated in research expeditions in Mexico, Brazil, and Peru. Her unique means of detecting and studying freshwater ecosystems have been used by limnologists and environmental researchers worldwide. In addition, her research and numerous publications, including her book *Groundwater Contamination in*

the United States (1983), have prompted scientists to consider the diversity of organisms in an environment a determinant of the health of that environment. Her expertise was called upon when she was invited to participate in framing the federal Clean Water Act (CWA), which was enacted by the U.S. Congress in 1963. The CWA, amended several times since then, is still the key piece of water pollution legislation in the United States.

Ruth Patrick has received many awards in recognition of her pioneering work in freshwater ecology and environmental conservation. In 1969, she received the Gimbel Philadelphia Award. The following year she was a recipient of the Pennsylvania Award for Excellence in Science and Technology. In 1972, the Ecological Society of America presented her its Eminent Ecologist Award. She received the highly prized John and Alice Tyler Ecology Award in 1975 and the Governor's Medal for Excellence in Science and Technology in 1988. In 1996, Patrick was awarded the National Medal of Science by President Bill Clinton. This is the highest award the U.S. government can bestow upon an American scientist. In addition, Patrick has been awarded honorary degrees by a number of prestigious institutions, including Princeton University, Swarthmore College, and the University of Massachusetts.

Patrick has served as an environmental adviser to several U.S. presidents. She also has been active in a number of professional organizations. In 1970, she was elected to membership in the National Academy of Sciences (NAS) and also became the first woman named to chair the board of the Academy of Natural Sciences. She has served as president of the Phycological Society of America (1954–1957) and of the American Society of Naturalists (1975–1977). Patrick also holds memberships in the Botanical Society of America, the American Society of Plant Taxonomists, the American Society of Limnology and Oceanography, and the American Institute of Biological Sciences.

See also Earle, Sylvia; Environmental Engineering; Martinez, Lissa Ann; National Academy of Sciences (NAS); National Medal of Science; Richards, Ellen Henrietta Swallow

References Olsen, Kirstin, *Chronology of Women's History* (1994); O'Neill, Lois Decker, ed., *The Women's Book of Records and Achievements* (1979); Saari, Peggy, and Stephen Allison, eds., *Scientists: The Lives and Works of 150 Scientists* (1966); Watkins, T. H., et al., "One Hundred Champions of Conservation." *Audubon* 100:66 (November–December 1998).

Payne-Gaposchkin, Cecelia (1900–1979)

Cecelia Payne-Gaposchkin, one of the outstanding astronomers of the twentieth century, is noted for her extensive studies of variable stars (a binary system, the brightness of which appears periodically to change according to the positions of the stars within the system) and of the composition and structure of galaxies. Payne-Gaposchkin used the information contained on photographic plates to determine the magnitudes and distances of stars. She then used these data in combination with information about star color to establish a standard scale for magnitude. Payne-Gaposchkin also discovered a method of accurately correlating the color of a star to its temperature. In addition, her doctoral dissertation incorporated studies of stellar atmospheres, which led her to conclude that stars are composed mostly of the elements hydrogen and helium—an idea that was contrary to the popular beliefs of that time.

Cecelia Payne was born in Wendover, England, in 1900. By the time she was 12, she was fluent in several languages and had already developed an interest in science and mathematics. In 1919, Payne entered the Newnham College of Cambridge University on a scholarship. There she studied biology, chemistry, and physics and received her A.B. in 1923. She also was awarded a National Research Scholarship, which permitted her to pursue graduate studies in astronomy at Radcliffe College in Cambridge, Massachusetts. While engaged in these studies, she also worked as a technical assistant at the Harvard Observatory (also located in Cambridge).

Payne was awarded a Ph.D. in astronomy from Radcliffe College in 1925, becoming the first person to be awarded such a degree by this school.

By this time, she also had published several research papers. Her dissertation, *Stellar Atmospheres,* indicated that variations in the absorption lines of star spectra resulted from differing atmospheric temperatures rather than from variations in the composition of the stars. She also suggested that the atmospheres of stars were composed primarily of the elements hydrogen and helium. Payne's findings were not immediately accepted; however, within a short time, they began to gain support from the astronomy community.

Payne became a permanent member of the staff of the Harvard Observatory in 1927. In 1931, she became an American citizen, and three years later, she married Russian astronomer Sergei Gaposchkin. Payne and her husband together conducted extensive studies of variable stars. They reported about how these stars change in brightness, color, and size. They also suggested how and why the atmospheres of such stars change over time. Cecelia Payne-Gaposchkin also made studies of novae and supernovae (explosions marking the births and deaths of stars, respectively).

In 1938, Payne-Gaposchkin was promoted to astronomer and lecturer at the Harvard Observatory. Eighteen years later, she became the first woman to be appointed a full professor of astronomy at Harvard. At the same time, she was named chair of the Department of Astronomy, becoming the first woman to hold this prestigious post. She remained in this position for ten years before retiring in 1966, at which time she was named professor emerita.

For her work in astronomy, Payne-Gaposchkin was presented many honors. While a student at Newnham College, she was elected to membership in the Royal Astronomical Society of England. In 1924, she became a member of the American Astronomical Society; ten years later this society chose her as the recipient of its Annie J. Cannon Prize for significant contributions to astronomy. Radcliffe College presented her its Award of Merit for outstanding scientific achievements in 1952. Nine years later, she was awarded the Rittenhouse Medal of the Franklin Institute of Philadelphia, Pennsylvania. Payne-Gaposchkin was again honored by the American Astronomical Society in 1976, when she was awarded its Henry Norris Russell Prize (she was the first woman to receive this honor). The following year, an asteroid (a minor planet formerly called 1974 CA) was renamed Payne-Gaposchkin in her honor.

Payne-Gaposchkin was presented honorary degrees from Wilson College (1942), Smith College (1943), Western College (1951), Cambridge University (1952), Colby College (1958), and the Women's Medical College of Philadelphia (1961). In 1957, the American Association of University Women (AAUW) honored Payne-Gaposchkin with a $2,500 award for her use in future research projects. Payne-Gaposchkin authored several books, including *Variable Stars* (1938), *Stars in the Making* (1952), *Variable Stars and Galactic Structure* (1954), *Introduction to Astronomy* (1954), and *Galactic Novae* (1957).

See also Astronomy; Burbidge, (Eleanor) Margaret Peachey; Maury, Antonia; Rubin, Vera Cooper; Sitterly, Charlotte Moore; Spectroscopy; Whiting, Sarah Frances
References Debus, A. G., ed., *Current Biography, 1957* (1957); Kass-Simon, G., and Patricia Farnes, eds., *Women of Science: Righting the Record* (1990); Kidwell, Peggy A., "Cecilia Payne-Gaposchkin: The Making of an Astrophysicist," in *Making Contributions: An Historical Overview of Women's Role in Physics* (1984); Lankford, John, and Rickey L. Slavings, "Gender and Science: Women in American Astronomy, 1859–1940," *Physics Today* (March 1990); Rossiter, Margaret W., *Women Scientists in America: Before Affirmative Action, 1940–1972* (1995).

Pearce, Louise (1885–1959)

African sleeping sickness is a tropical disease caused by a parasitic protozoan that infects humans and other mammals. This protozoan often resides in the body of an insect called the tsetse fly and enters the body of a mammalian host as a result of the insect's bite. Once in the body, the protozoan produces toxins that destroy red blood cells. The destruction of the red blood cells results in fever, fatigue, anemia, and a feeling of general weakness. If left untreated, African sleeping sickness can result in death. There is no known cure for this disease; however, it has been

controlled through the use of the drug tryparsamide. Among the principal researchers and developers of this drug was pathologist and physician Louise Pearce.

Louise Pearce was born in Winchester, Pennsylvania, in 1885. When she was still very young, the Pearce family moved to California. There Pearce received her early education and attended high school at the Girls' Collegiate School in Los Angeles, from which she graduated in 1903.

Pearce remained in California for the first stage of her college education, attending Stanford University in Menlo Park (a suburb of San Francisco). She graduated from this university in 1907 with an A.B. degree in histology (the study of tissues) and physiology. Pearce then traveled to the other side of the United States to attend medical school at Boston University, where she remained for two years. She then transferred to Johns Hopkins University in Baltimore, from which she received her M.D. degree in 1912. After receiving her M.D. degree, she remained at the university to complete a one-year internship before accepting a research fellowship at the Rockefeller Institute for Medical Research (now Rockefeller University) in New York.

Pearce spent her entire career at the Rockefeller Institute (from 1913 to 1951). When she first joined this facility, she and a colleague, Wade Hampton Brown, were assigned the task of determining whether arsenic compounds (which had been shown by other researchers to be somewhat successful in treating syphilis) might be an effective treatment for African sleeping sickness. This disease was very prevalent in tropical areas at this time. Six years after beginning their research, Pearce and Brown reported in the *Journal of Experimental Medicine* in 1919 that tryparsamide, a drug they developed, had been shown to be effective in treating African sleeping sickness.

Although preliminary tests on tryparsamide had met with success in the laboratory, Pearce needed to determine its effectiveness in a human population. To conduct this research, she traveled to a region of equatorial Africa. Tests she conducted there were successful. Upon her return to the United States in 1923, Pearce received a promotion at the Rockefeller Institute to the position of associate member.

Pearce and Brown again began a collaboration on a research project—this time, focused on the causative agent of syphilis in rabbits, with the purpose of determining how the disease affected the body's major organs. Once they established how syphilis affected rabbits, they began treating the infected animals with arsenic compounds to determine the effects of these drugs on the disease. Pearce and Brown then conducted similar studies of these drugs on humans.

During the late 1920s and early 1930s, Pearce and Brown again changed their research focus. They began a study of malignant tumors (later named the Brown-Pearce carcinoma) in rabbits. In this work, Pearce and Brown intentionally transplanted tumors to a number of rabbits for the purpose of developing a population that could be studied to learn more about comparable tumors in humans. While conducting their studies on rabbit cancer, Pearce and Brown also investigated how heredity and other factors affect a rabbit's sensitivity to and response to disease. Several times, the results of the research being conducted by Pearce and Brown was threatened by an outbreak of rabbit pox in their laboratory. However, the collaborators took advantage of the outbreak to study the disease. This study led to the discovery and identification of the causative agent of rabbit pox—a virus. In spite of this success, Pearce, Brown, and their laboratory animals had to be moved to another facility (in Princeton, New Jersey) to prevent the spread of disease from their rabbits to those being used by other researchers at the institute.

Shortly after they moved their laboratory, Brown became ill and had to abandon his research. Pearce, however, continued the studies they had begun together on her own. Within five years, she had identified several hereditary and deforming diseases that occurred in rabbits. She continued her research on disease in rabbits until her retirement in 1951.

Pearce was active in many professional organizations, including the American Association of University Women (AAUW), an organization in which she served as director from 1945 through 1951. She also served with the General Advisory Council of the American Social Hygiene Association (1925–1944) and as president of the Women's Medical College of Pennsylvania (1946–1952).

For the work she did on the production of a successful drug for the treatment of African sleeping sickness, Pearce was awarded the Order of the Crown of Belgium from that country's government in 1921. She was again recognized by this country's government in 1953, with the King Leopold II Prize (a $10,000 monetary award) and the Royal Order of the Lion. Pearce also received honors for her work from several organizations in the United States. These included the Elizabeth Blackwell Award (1951) of the New York Infirmary for Women and Children. In addition, she received at least five honorary doctoral degrees and was inducted into several honor societies, including Phi Beta Kappa, Sigma Xi, Phi Beta Phi, and Alpha Omega Alpha.

See also Alexander, Hattie Elizabeth; American Association of University Women (AAUW); Baker, Sara Josephine; Brown, Rachel Fuller; Dick, Gladys Rowena Henry; Eldering, Grace; Elion, Gertrude Belle; Evans, Alice Catherine; Hazen, Elizabeth Lee; Hollinshead, Ariel; Medicine/Medical Technology; Pharmacology; Seibert, Florence Barbara; Williams, Anna Wessels
References "Dr. Louise Pearce, Physician, 74, Dies" [obituary], *New York Times* (11 August 1959); Saari, Peggy, and Stephen Allison, eds., *Scientists: The Lives and Works of 150 Scientists* (1966); Weatherford, Doris, *American Women's History: An A to Z of People, Organizations, Issues, and Events* (1994).

Peden, Irene Carswell (b. 1925)

Electrical engineer Irene Carswell Peden has made significant contributions to radio science and has emerged as an expert on radio wave transmission and antennas. Using technologies known as radio wave propagation (the transmission of energy at radio frequencies) and wave scattering (the dispersal of waves over an area), Peden investigated the characteristics of deep glacial ice in Antarctica. She also used these technologies to analyze the characteristics of the portion of the atmosphere known as the lower ionosphere over the continent of Antarctica. The information gathered from these experiments has provided scientists with a better understanding of the formation and features of glaciers near the poles. It also has helped scientists learn more about the characteristics and composition of the atmosphere over the South Pole.

Irene Carswell was born in Topeka, Kansas, in 1925. She became interested in science while she was in high school and later turned this interest into a lifelong career in engineering. After graduating from high school, Carswell began her college studies at Kansas City Junior College. She graduated with an associate's degree in science in 1944. Carswell then attended the University of Colorado in Boulder, where she studied electrical engineering. She received a bachelor of science in electrical engineering (BSEE) in 1947.

Following her graduation from the University of Colorado, Carswell worked for two years at the Delaware Power and Light Company (known today as Delmarva). She left this company in 1949 and moved to California to join the staff of the Aircraft Radio Systems Lab of the Stanford Research Institute in Menlo Park (just outside San Francisco).

In 1958, Carswell received her master's degree in electrical engineering from Stanford University. She remained at Stanford to pursue her doctoral degree, while also teaching electrical engineering and physics at the university. Carswell received her Ph.D. in 1962. With her receipt of this degree, she also received the distinction of becoming the first woman to acquire a doctorate in any field of engineering from Stanford University. The same year that she received her doctoral degree, Carswell married attorney Leo J. Peden.

Irene Peden accepted a position at the University of Washington in Seattle as an assistant professor of electrical engineering, and spent her entire professional teaching career at that institution. While there, she advanced in academic rank, becoming an associate professor in 1964 and a full professor in 1971. In addition to her teaching responsibilities, Peden worked as a researcher in the university's Electromagnets and Remote Sensing Laboratories. From 1971 to

1976, she served as associate dean of the College of Engineering. In addition, she was associate chair of the Department of Electrical Engineering from 1983 to 1985.

While teaching at the University of Washington, Peden also periodically served as a consultant to various government and professional science organizations, including the United Nations (UN), the Food and Drug Administration (FDA), the National Science Foundation (NSF), and the Department of Defense (DoD). During the late 1960s, few women became scientists and engineers. Working as a consultant to UNESCO, Peden and others conducted research to determine why this was the case. The findings were published in a UNESCO report titled "Access of Women to Technical Careers in the West Coast Region of the United States of America, 1966–1970." This report became one of the first to document and recognize the role of gender discrimination in discouraging women from pursuing technological and scientific careers or from obtaining meaningful employment in such careers.

In 1970, Peden made history by becoming the first woman engineer from the United States to live and perform fieldwork in the interior of Antarctica. Peden visited this continent from October through December to conduct studies on glacial ice. Before these studies began, Peden, who had just completed the UNESCO study that identified gender discrimination as a problem for women in the sciences, herself became the target of such discrimination. When Peden planned to begin her research, the U.S. Navy, which operated the laboratories in Antarctica, barred her from the test site because she was a woman. However, the National Science Foundation (NSF) later aided Peden in gaining access to the area so she could conduct her experiments. In these experiments, Peden used very high frequency (VHF) radio waves to locate subsurface structures in the glacial ice. She also developed the mathematical models and the technological tools needed to interpret the data collected.

During the latter part of the 1970s and the 1980s, Peden served on the boards of several government agencies in the role of consultant.

Among these posts were her service from 1978 through 1987 on the Army Science Board, where she was vice chair (1983–1985) and chair (1986–1987). During part of this same period (1983–1985), she also was a member of the National Research Council (NRC). In addition, in 1988, she was a member of the National Aeronautics and Space Administration's (NASA) Space Station Crew Selection and Advisory Panel.

Peden retired from her position as professor at the University of Washington and was named professor emerita in 1994. Since her retirement, she has remained active in many of the professional organizations of which she is a member. These organizations include the Institute of Electrical and Electronics Engineers (IEEE), the American Association for the Advancement of Science (AAAS), the American Society of Engineering Educators (ASEE), and the Society of Women Engineers (SWE). Since 1995, Peden also has served on the Army Science Board, where she advises the secretary of the Army and the chiefs of staff about research, development, and acquisitions; the Polar Research Board; and the Naval Research Advisory Committee (NRAC). In this last post, Peden advises the Navy about technical and scientific matters. She also has served as vice chair of NRAC's Information Warfare—Defense Panel.

Peden has received numerous awards both for her work in electrical engineering and for her attempts to increase women's access to engineering careers. Among these honors are the Achievement Award of the Society of Women Engineers (SWE), which she received in 1973; the U.S. Army's Outstanding Civilian Service Medal (1987); and the NSF's Engineer of the Year award (1993). She is a fellow of the IEEE and was presented its Centennial Medal in 1984 and its Harden Pratt Award in 1988. In 1993, the ASEE inducted Peden into its Hall of Fame and presented her with its Centennial Medal. The following year, she was elected a fellow of this organization and was honored with honorary doctorates from Michigan State University and Southern Methodist University.

See also Barney, Nora Stanton Blatch; Electrical and Electronics Engineering; Environmental Engineering; Institute of Electrical and Electronics Engineers

(IEEE); Lamarr, Hedy; National Science Foundation (NSF)

References Litzenberg, Kathleen, *Who's Who of American Women,* 18th ed., 1993–94 (1995); McMurray, Emily M., ed., *Notable Twentieth-Century Scientists,* vol. 3: (L–R) (1995); Torpie, Stephen L., et al., eds., *American Men and Women of Science,* 18th ed. *(1992–1993)* (1992); Winkler, Alan, e-mail correspondence with Irene Peden (9 July 1999); Naval Research Advisory Committee, "Dr. Irene Peden," available at http:// nrac.onr.navy.mil/webspace/ members/peden.html (cited 19 April 1999); Virginia Polytechnic Institute and State University, Bradley Department of Electrical and Computer Engineering, "Irene C. Peden," available at http://www.ee.vt.edu/ ~museum/women/peden/peden.html (cited 19 April 1999).

Pennington, Mary Engle (1872–1952)

Bacteriologist and chemist Mary Engle Pennington contributed greatly to the technology of refrigeration and its use in preventing food spoilage. During World War I, while working with the Perishable Products Division of the U.S. Food Administration, Pennington suggested a change in the design and construction of home and commercial refrigerators and refrigerated storage areas that improved their performance. This change greatly improved upon current technologies, helping to increase the shelf life of perishable foods by decreasing spoilage resulting from bacterial growth.

Mary Engle Pennington was born in Nashville, Tennessee, but spent most of her early life in Philadelphia, Pennsylvania. In 1890, Pennington enrolled in the Towne Scientific School of the University of Pennsylvania, where she studied chemistry and biology. After only two years, Pennington completed the course work required for a bachelor's degree, but was instead issued a Certificate of Proficiency in biology because of a school policy that prohibited the issuance of a bachelor's degree to a woman. Pennington then enrolled at the Electrochemical School of Edgar Fahs Smith (part of the University of Pennsylvania), where she majored in chemistry. She received her Ph.D. in 1895.

After receiving her Ph.D., Pennington remained at the University of Pennsylvania for one year as a fellow in chemical botany. She spent an additional year as a fellow of physiological chemistry at Yale University before returning to Philadelphia. Although opportunities for work in science were not readily available to women, Mary Pennington devised a way to practice her profession. After securing promises of business from several local physicians, she and Elizabeth Atkinson opened the Philadelphia Clinical Laboratory, where they conducted bacteriological and chemical analyses of medical specimens. The laboratory was very successful, and Pennington's work was so well respected that she was granted an appointment as a lecturer at the Women's Medical College of Pennsylvania. Around the same time, Pennington also served as a bacteriologist with the Philadelphia Bureau of Health.

While working at the Philadelphia Bureau of Health, Pennington began research into bacteriological contamination of dairy products and how current methods of preserving such products might be improved to reduce spoilage. Results of this research led her to devise new standards for milk inspection in Philadelphia as well as many other regions of the country.

Harvey W. Wiley, the chief of the Bureau of Chemistry at the U.S. Department of Agriculture (USDA), was a family friend of the Penningtons. He followed Mary Pennington's work at the Philadelphia Bureau of Health and asked for her assistance in evaluating refrigeration as a means of preserving food. In 1905, Wiley asked Pennington to take the civil service examination required by federal employees. To hide the fact that Pennington was a woman (which would likely lower her chance of employment), Wiley suggested that she take the exam using only her initials. Following his suggestion, Pennington took and passed the exam as M. E. Pennington and was appointed to a position as a bacteriological chemist with the USDA before they realized she was a woman. The next year, Wiley named her chief of the newly formed Food Research Laboratory of the Bureau of Chemistry. Under Pennington's supervision, the Food Research Laboratory focused its efforts on methods to prevent bacterial spoilage of fish, poultry, milk, and eggs. The laboratory's research

findings resulted in the development of techniques and practices that eventually became industry standards in the handling, packaging, movement, and distribution of foods.

During World War I, Pennington served as a researcher for the Perishable Products Division of the U.S. Food Administration, investigating the combined effects of humidity and freezing on food preservation. She also monitored the effectiveness of insulation and air circulation in refrigerated railroad cars in maintaining uniform temperatures designed to prevent spoilage of perishable foods. Her studies led to the development of design standards for refrigerated railroad cars that transported perishable foods nationwide. Her design for ice-cooled and motor-driven refrigerator cars remained in place until about 1950, when more effective mechanical cooling and refrigeration systems were developed.

Pennington resigned her post with the USDA in 1919 and accepted a position with a firm that manufactured insulating materials. Three years later, she started her own consulting company, which focused on matters of food handling, transportation, and storage. During this time, Pennington continued her research on food chemistry and preservation, now centering her attention on freezing as a method of retarding spoilage of perishable foods. Her continued efforts in the area of food preservation advanced the design and construction of household refrigerators and commercial food storage facilities. Her expertise also contributed to the development and processing of frozen foods.

Pennington has been recognized and honored for her many pioneering contributions in the area of refrigeration and food preservation. For her work during World War I, she was presented with the Notable Service Medal from the Hoover administration in 1919. She received the Garvan Medal from the American Chemical Society (ACS) in 1940. That same year, Pennington became the first woman elected to the American Poultry Historical Society's Hall of Fame. Later, she became the first woman member of the American Institute of Refrigeration, an organization in which she was serving as president at the time of her death in 1952. In 1947, Pennington was elected a fellow of the American Society of Refrigeration Engineers. Other organizations of which she was a member include the American Association for the Advancement of Science (AAAS), the American Chemical Society, the American Society of Biological Chemists, and the Society of American Bacteriologists.

See also American Society of Heating, Refrigerating and Air-Conditioning Engineers (ASHRAE); Baldwin, Anna; Caldwell, Mary Letitia

References Bailey, Martha J., *American Women in Science: A Biographical Dictionary* (1994); Grinstein, Louise S., Rose K. Rose, and Miriam H. Rafailovich, eds., *Women in Chemistry and Physics: A Biobibliographic Sourcebook* (1993); "Mary Pennington, Engineer, 80, Dead" [obituary], *New York Times* (28 December 1952); Read, Phyllis J., and Bernard L. Witlieb, *The Book of Women's Firsts* (1992); Sicherman, Barbara, and Carol Hurd Green, eds., *Notable American Women: The Modern Period* (1980).

Pert, Candace Bebe (b. 1946)

Candace Pert is a neurophysiologist, a scientist who studies the workings of the brain and nervous system. Through her work in this discipline, Pert has emerged as one of the leading experts on how certain chemicals affect brain function. Using the technology known as radioimmunoassay (RIA), Pert introduced radioactively labeled synthetic opiates (pain-killing drugs derived from opium) into the body and then identified sites (chemical receptors) within the brain to which these substances attached, producing an expected result. From this observation, she hypothesized that the presence of such sites in the brain suggests that the brain itself has a natural ability to produce substances having opiate-like effects. This hypothesis was later supported through the discovery of endorphins, naturally produced compounds of the brain that have been shown to induce pleasure and relieve pain. Pert also has done significant research with neurotransmitters (chemical substances that transmit nerve impulses throughout the body) and peptides.

Candace Bebe Pert graduated from Bryn Mawr College in Pennsylvania with an A.B. in 1970. She then attended Johns Hopkins University School of Medicine in Baltimore, Maryland, where she pursued a doctoral degree in pharmacology. It was while working toward this degree that Pert did the opiates research that led her to identify the presence and location of chemical receptors in the brain. For this research, Pert was awarded her Ph.D. in pharmacology in 1974.

The research that Pert did toward her doctorate laid the groundwork for the discovery of endorphins, a discovery made in 1973 by Scottish scientists Hans Kosterlitz and John Hughes. For this discovery, Kosterlitz and Hughes shared a Lasker Award in Medicine with Pert's Ph.D. professor and mentor, Solomon Snyder, in 1978. Pert's omission from this award was recognized by some members of the medical and scientific community as unjust, and it became an issue of controversy. Pert's predoctoral research also provided a basis for understanding opiate dependency (a common form of drug abuse).

After receiving her doctorate, Pert was awarded a one-year fellowship by the National Institutes of Health (NIH), which allowed her to continue doing research at Johns Hopkins. After the fellowship ended, she held several other posts within the university and advanced to the position of resident pharmacologist. In 1982, Pert accepted the position of chief of the Brain Chemical Section at the National Institutes of Mental Health (NIMH). She remained with the NIMH, where much of her work focused on neurotransmitters, until 1987. This work led to the identification and location of receptor sites for such addictive and commonly abused drugs as Valium® and PCP (angel dust).

Pert also researched immune systems and the nature of viruses, including HIV (the virus responsible for AIDS). In this research, she investigated the use of amino acid molecules (peptides) and their ability to attach to receptor cells. Continued research led her to conclude that specific peptides may have the ability to attach to and block receptor sites to which viruses such as HIV may attach. Much of the research now being conducted into AIDS and discovering a means of preventing this disease is based on similar receptor cell studies.

Pert left the NIMH in 1987 to open her own research facility, called Peptide Design, which she operated for three years. She then accepted a post as an adjunct professor in Georgetown University's Department of Physiology. In addition to teaching, Pert continues her research into AIDS.

See also Elion, Gertrude Belle; Medicine/Medical Technology; Pharmacology; Radioimmunoassay (RIA); Yalow, Rosalyn Sussman
References Bailey, Martha J., *American Women in Science, 1950 to the Present: A Biographical Dictionary* (1998); Jaques Cattell Press, ed., *American Men and Women of Science*, 16th ed. (1986); Stanley, Autumn, *Mothers and Daughters of Invention: Notes for a Revised History of Technology* (1993).

Petermann, Mary Locke (1908–1975)

Mary Petermann, a research pioneer and expert in protein chemistry, is best known for her work in protein structure, composition, and synthesis. Petermann was one of the first to isolate and determine the physical and chemical structure of mammalian ribosomes (cell organelles associated with protein synthesis). Her findings have contributed much to the current understanding of the mechanism of protein synthesis at the molecular level.

Mary Petermann was born in Laurium, Michigan. After graduating from high school in 1924, she attended a preparatory school in Massachusetts. One year later, she entered Smith College in Northampton, Massachusetts, where she obtained her B.A. degree with high honors in chemistry in 1929. She was also elected into the Phi Beta Kappa Society.

Following graduation, Petermann worked for one year at Yale University as a technician in the psychology department. She spent the next four years at the Boston Psychopathic Hospital as a researcher. In 1936, Petermann began doctoral studies in physical chemistry at the University of Wisconsin. She received her Ph.D. in physical chemistry in 1939 and worked at the University of Wisconsin as a research chemist in the physical chemistry department until 1945, becoming the first woman chemist on the staff. During this six-

year period at Wisconsin, Petermann researched the use of gelatin and pectin and developed methods for purifying human blood serum albumin (a protein) for use as a blood substitute. She also described the characteristics of diphtheria toxins and antitoxins and helped develop a method of purifying antibodies that are now used in treating mumps. In addition, her observations of the affects of certain enzymes on protein antibodies became the basis for Rodney Porter's Nobel Prize–winning work on the structure of immunoglobulins (antibodies) in 1972. Around this time, Petermann successfully isolated and characterized the ribosome. During much of her protein research, she used techniques involving high-speed centrifugation and electrophoresis (devices used to separate the components of mixtures based upon molecular properties such as size, weight, and electrical charge).

In 1945, Petermann began work as a research chemist at Memorial Hospital in New York City, studying the relationship of plasma proteins and cancer. The next year, she became a Finney-Howell Foundation Fellow at the Sloan-Kettering Institute for Cancer Research. In 1960, Petermann became an associate member of the institute and, in 1963, its first woman member. While at Sloan-Kettering, Petermann also taught biochemistry in the Sloan-Kettering Division of Cornell University's Graduate School of Medicine, becoming the first woman professor at Cornell in 1966. When she retired in 1973, she was named member emerita.

Petermann has received many honors and awards for her contributions to protein chemistry. In 1963, she received the Alfred P. Sloan Award for her work on proteins and nucleoproteins. She received the Garvan Medal from the American Chemical Society (ACS) in 1966 for her work on ribosomes. That same year, Petermann was given the Distinguished Service Award of the American Academy of Achievement and awarded an honorary D.Sc. degree by Smith College.

Petermann was a member of Sigma Xi, Sigma Delta Epsilon, the American Society of Biological Chemists, the American Association for the Advancement of Science (AAAS), the American Association for Cancer Research, the Biophysical Society, the Harvey Society, and the Enzyme Club. She was a fellow of the New York Academy of Sciences and was instrumental in organizing the Sloan-Kettering Institute chapter of the Association for Women in Science (AWIS). Petermann also helped organize the Memorial Sloan-Kettering Cancer Center Association for Professional Women (MSKCCAPW) and served as its president in 1974. In 1976, the American Women in Science Educational Foundation named a scholarship in her honor. The next year, the MSKCCAPW established a study carrel in the Lee Coombe Library in her honor.

> **See also** Association for Women in Science (AWIS); Francis P. Garvan–John M. Olin Medal; Jeanes, Allene Rosalind; Medicine/Medical Technology; Richardson, Jane Shelby
> **References** Bailey, Martha J., *American Women in Science: A Biographical Dictionary* (1994); Grinstein, Louise S., Rose K. Rose, and Miriam H. Rafailovich, eds., *Women in Chemistry and Physics: A Biobibliographic Sourcebook* (1993); McMurray, Emily M., ed., *Notable Twentieth-Century Scientists,* vol. 3: (L–R) (1995); Shearer, Benjamin F., and Barbara S. Shearer, eds., *Notable Women in the Physical Sciences: A Biographical Dictionary* (1997).

Peterson, Edith Runne (1914–1992)

Edith Peterson was a pioneer in organotypic tissue culturing, a process in which tissues removed from an organ and placed in a culture medium grow and simulate the structure and function of the organ from which they were taken. In 1948, Peterson became the first scientist to grow myelin—the insulating tissue sheath that surrounds nerve cells—in a test tube. Her work in this area has been applied to studies of muscular dystrophy, a disease resulting in the degeneration of the myelin in the brain and spinal cord.

Edith Runne was born in Brooklyn, New York, but spent some of her early years in Germany. She and her mother returned to the United States in 1926 following the sudden death of her father. Runne attended Barnard College, where she majored in zoology and graduated with a B.S. degree in 1937. Two years later she received an M.S. degree in zoology from Columbia University. In 1941, Edith Runne married Charles Peterson, a commercial artist.

During the early 1940s, Edith Peterson worked as a researcher at Columbia University's College of Physicians and Surgeons. There she developed a technique for growing nerve cells, using cultures containing chick embryos. Using organotypic tissue culture techniques, Peterson succeeded in growing nerve cells, brain cells, and myelin. In 1966, Peterson became a research associate in the department of neurology at the Albert Einstein College of Medicine of Yeshiva University in the Bronx, New York. There she focused her research efforts on muscular dystrophy, a degenerative disease of skeletal muscle. She also researched the effects of taxol, a natural substance obtained from the bark of yew trees, on nerve cells. Her studies showed that in the body taxol acts as a toxin and prevents nerve cells from reproducing. (Taxol has since been used as an experimental drug in cancer research). Peterson also did research to identify substances that would lead to the survival and recovery of damaged nerve cells.

Peterson coauthored 55 publications and 45 abstracts. In 1986, she was awarded an honorary Doctor of Humane Letters degree by Albert Einstein College of Medicine. She also was principal associate emerita in Einstein's Department of Neuroscience. She continued working at her laboratory even after her retirement in 1990.

> **See also** Levi-Montalcini, Rita; Medicine/Medical Technology
> **References** "Edith R. Peterson, 78; Studied Cell Cultures" [obituary], *New York Times* (20 August 1992); Gardner, Karen, Media Relations Manager at Albert Einstein College of Medicine, mail communication with Alan Winkler (20 March 1999); McMurray, Emily M., ed., *Notable Twentieth-Century Scientists,* vol. 3: L–R (1995).

Petroleum Engineering

Petroleum engineering applies the principles and practices of geology, chemistry, physics, and engineering to the exploration, recovery, development, and processing of oil and natural gas. Once a productive reservoir of oil or gas is located, petroleum engineers study the surrounding rock formation to determine its properties. These data are used to establish guidelines for efficient and cost-effective drilling and production procedures. Petroleum engineers are sometimes called upon to design equipment and strategies that will achieve the greatest recovery of oil or natural gas. Computer models may also be employed to simulate reservoir yield based on various recovery techniques.

Usually, only 40 to 60 percent of the oil or gas in a reservoir reaches the surface as a result of pressure exerted deep in the reservoir. Thus, petroleum engineers often use enhanced recovery techniques to maximize a reservoir's yield. These techniques include injecting water, chemicals, or steam into a reservoir to increase pressure and force oil or gas to the surface.

Once crude oil has been recovered, petroleum engineers often work with chemists and research engineers to determine the quality and purity of the product. A woman who has made significant contributions in this area is chemist Edith M. Flanigen. During her career, Flanigen obtained more than 100 patents for molecular sieves, crystalline compounds with molecule-sized pores that are used to separate parts of a mixture. Her most notable invention was for a crystalline compound called zeolite that is used by the petroleum industry in the refining process. Impurities in crude oil affect the refining process and may lead to pipeline corrosion. Research engineer Ivy Parker pioneered technology to assess the causes of pipeline corrosion and means of preventing it.

See also Computers/Computer Technology; Environmental Engineering; Flanigen, Edith M.; Gardner, Julia Anna; Parker, Ivy

References Barnes-Svarney, Patricia, ed., *The New York Public Library Science Desk Reference* (1995); Cosgrove, Holli R., ed., *Encyclopedia of Careers and Vocational Guidance,* 10th ed., vol. 4 (1996); U.S. Department of Labor, Bureau of Labor Statistics, *Occupational Outlook Handbook,* Bulletin 2500 (1998–1999).

Pharmacology

In its strictest sense, pharmacology is the study of the effects that chemicals have on living things, particularly as such substances relate to the prevention, treatment, or cure of illness or disease. However, this definition of pharmacology does not take into account the mostly accidental discoveries by the earliest peoples that certain plant and animal products or minerals relieved symptoms of pain and illness. Over time, such discoveries emerged into a primitive practice of medicine by people often called healers, who made use of specific mixtures of herbs and other ingredients, which they prepared for use in the treatment of specific illnesses. Later, the making of such preparations became the work of apothecaries, the predecessors of today's pharmacists. As these individuals, as well as doctors and others, gained a greater understanding of chemistry, physiology, and medicine, the science of pharmacology, as it is known today, emerged.

Early in American history the treatment of illness generally relied on home remedies composed largely from herbs, roots, animal parts, and other materials that were mixed together according to a "formula" passed down from generation to generation. Later, such remedies were replaced by what came to be called patent medicines. Such medicines were prepared, packaged, and sold to the public with promises of cures for a variety of ailments. Among the most notable of these was Lydia E. Pinkham's Vegetable Compound, which was first introduced around 1875. This compound was marketed as a cure for "female complaints," and by 1881, Pinkham was selling $250,000 worth of this product annually.

Patent medicines and other similar concoctions continued to gain in sales and popularity until the passage of the Pure Food and Drug Act of 1906. Following this act, the government became more involved in making sure that products lived up to their advertised claims. As a result, many patent medicines ceased production, allowing for increased sales of pharmaceutical products sold by recognized pharmaceutical companies. Women played an important role in the production and development of many such pharmaceutical products.

In the 1930s, physician Hattie Alexander developed a serum in rabbits that was used to treat people infected with influenzal meningitis, a bacterial disease that affects the nervous system. Alexander demonstrated that this serum, when used in conjunction with antibiotics, could result in as much as a 90 percent reduction in the fatality rate associated with this disease. At the same time that Alexander was working on treatment for influenzal meningitis, Pearl Kendrick and Grace Eldering were working together to develop a vaccine for pertussis (whooping cough). They were successful in producing such a vaccine in 1939, the same year that Alexander's vaccine became available. The pertussis vaccine was later combined by Kendrick and Eldering with a vaccine for tetanus (lockjaw).

In 1949, Margaret Pittman standardized the diphtheria–pertussis–tetanus vaccine, commonly known as DPT. In this process, she worked with the pertussis-tetanus vaccine developed by Kendrick and Eldering ten years earlier as well as the diphtheria vaccine developed by Anna Wessels Williams in the 1890s. Pittman also standardized the vaccine for cholera about the same time.

The first antibiotic, penicillin, was discovered in 1928 but was not made available for use until 1941. Around this time, Gladys Hobby was working as a microbiologist with the Pfizer Corporation, where she helped develop the antibiotics streptomycin and viomycin. She also codiscovered the antibiotic Terramycin® in 1950. These antibiotics, including penicillin, proved very effective in treating a variety of bacterial infections in humans. However, it was not until the mid-1950s, that the first successful antibiotic for the treatment of fungal infections was developed. This development resulted from the combined efforts of Rachel Fuller Brown and Elizabeth Lee Hazen, who were working for the New York State Department of Health. The drug they developed, called nystatin, was used to treat fungal infections of the digestive system, skin, and female reproductive system. Several years later, Brown and Hazen developed two other antibiotics: capacidin and phalamycin.

Among the best-known women working in the field of pharmacology is Gertrude Belle Elion, who in 1988 was recognized for her lifelong contributions in this area with a Nobel Prize in medicine/physiology. Elion shared the prize with her mentor and colleague George Hitchings and with British scientist Sir James W. Black. During her more than thirty-year career, Elion developed a number of drugs that proved successful in the treatment of gout, leukemia, herpes, shingles, and other viral infections. In addition, her work resulted in drugs that reduced the incidence of tissue rejection following organ transplant surgery. The drugs resulting from Elion's work earned her nearly fifty patents.

Not all of the work in pharmacology deals with the development of new drugs. Many people working in this area have devoted at least part of their careers to removing potentially harmful drugs from the marketplace. Such was the case with physician Helen Brooke Taussig of Maryland. During the 1960s, Taussig conducted research that showed that use of the drug thalidamide by pregnant women often resulted in serious birth defects (including malformed limbs and blindness) in their children. Based on this research Taussig launched a successful campaign to have this drug removed from the market in both the United States and Europe.

Other women have focused their attention on determining the potential side effects of drugs for the purpose of eliminating or reducing these effects. Others are seeking ways to improve the effectiveness of certain drugs by decreasing the body's resistance to these drugs. For example, Catherine Clarke Fenselau has devoted much of her career to studying anticancer drugs. Fenselau researched the interactions of these drugs with proteins in the body to learn why some people develop a resistance to some drugs and others do not.

See also Alexander, Hattie Elizabeth; Brown, Rachel Fuller; Eldering, Grace; Elion, Gertrude Belle; Fenselau, Catherine Clarke; Hazen, Elizabeth Lee; Hobby, Gladys Lounsbury; Kendrick, Pearl Luella; Pert, Candace Bebe; Pinkham, Lydia Estes; Pittman, Margaret; Taussig, Helen Brooke; Williams, Anna Wessels

References Bouton, Katherine, "The Nobel Pair," *New York Times Magazine* (29 January 1989); Rossiter, Margaret W., *Women Scientists in America: Before Affirmative Action, 1940–1972* (1995); Stanley, Autumn, *Mothers and Daughters of Invention: Notes for a Revised History of Technology* (1993).

Phi Beta Kappa Society

The letters *Phi, Beta,* and *Kappa* are the first initials of Greek words meaning "Philosophy is the Guide to Life." The Phi Beta Kappa Society is a national undergraduate college and university honor society for men and women. The nation's oldest and most prestigious fraternity, Phi Beta Kappa was organized in 1776 at the College of William and Mary in Virginia, as a secret society for literary and philosophical debates and exercises. Membership was based on unity and mutual appreciation. The secrecy requirement ended in 1883.

In 1988, the organization's name changed to the Phi Beta Kappa Society. The society recognizes, encourages, and supports scholastic achievement and academic excellence in the liberal arts and sciences. New members are elected from the ranks of undergraduate juniors and seniors with high academic standing by participating college faculty.

The Phi Beta Kappa Society has a membership of approximately 500,000, with active chapters in 248 colleges. The first chapter at an American women's college was founded at Vassar College in 1898. The Phi Beta Foundation sponsors several awards, including scholarships and book awards. Among its publications are *The Key Reporter* and the *American Scholar,* a quarterly journal containing essays, poetry, and reviews.

> **See also** Berkowitz, Joan; Elion, Gertrude Belle; Granville, Evelyn Boyd; Hopper, Grace Murray; Mack, Pauline Beery; Miller, Elizabeth Smith; Pool, Judith Graham; Sitterly, Charlotte Moore; Vassar College
> **References** Maurer, Christine, and Tara E. Sheets, eds., *Encyclopedia of Associations: An Associations Unlimited Reference,* 33rd ed., vol. 1, parts 1–3 (1998); Phi Beta Kappa Society, http://www.pbk.org/aboutphi.htm.

Pinckney, Eliza Lucas (1722–1793)

Eliza Lucas was born in 1722 on the island of Antigua, in the British West Indies. She is noted for her successful experimentation in growing and breeding the indigo plant during the mid-1700s. During this period, indigo was extremely important to the textile industry in England because of its use as a coloring agent for clothing. Her introduction of indigo to the South provided this region with a significant cash crop that had great economic value. As a result, indigo became one of the South's leading agricultural products, along with rice. In addition, the successful cultivation of this crop released the South from its dependence on France (from which the dye was previously imported) and Britain (to whom crops and dye products became a major export).

Eliza's father, George Lucas, was a military man. He was the lieutenant governor of Antigua, and he often treated his daughters, Eliza and Polly, much as he treated the soldiers in his command. Lucas was dogmatic in stressing that Eliza attain an education, so he sent her back to England to be educated.

Lucas moved his family to South Carolina in 1737. At the time of the move, Eliza was 15 years old. The family settled on Wappoo, one of three plantations owned by Lucas. Only two years after settling in South Carolina, Lucas was called back to Antigua for military duty. Eliza was left in charge of his plantations because she was the oldest of the children and her mother was disabled.

Although she was only 16, Eliza lived up to her father's expectations, and the plantation prospered under her supervision. She overcame the gender bias of the subordinate male plantation workers and became an assertive taskmaster much like her father. In addition to her keen management skills, her knowledge of agriculture was put to good use as the plantation produced several crops, including indigo and rice.

While Eliza was in England, she had studied botany, a subject in which she had developed an interest. Her training in these classes served her well when she made the decision to import indigo seeds from the West Indies in 1740, with hopes of growing this crop on her plantation. The indigo plant, from which a blue dye could be obtained, was in great demand in countries that manufactured clothing. Eliza experimented with growing and breeding different strains of indigo until she was able to successfully develop a strain suited to cultivation on the Wappoo plantation.

After successfully producing indigo on her

own land, Eliza shared the seeds of her crop with several neighbors. This generosity proved advantageous to plantation farmers in the young colony of South Carolina. Eliza's success with creating hybrid strains of indigo and selling the seeds had a significant economic impact on the region. Within three years, South Carolina was exporting approximately 100,000 pounds of indigo to England. By the 1760s, they were producing more than 1 million pounds of this crop each year. The South Carolina indigo boom begun by Eliza Lucas lasted until the Revolutionary War, when a trade blockade occurred between the colonies and England.

In many ways, Eliza Lucas's behavior and attitudes might have placed her in the company of feminists, had she lived in the twentieth century. She was a trailblazer also in her personal life: She chose her own husband rather than participate in an arranged marriage. In addition, as she had done on her father's plantation, she would one day run the plantation belonging to her husband.

Eliza Lucas married the widower Charles Pinckney, an attorney and active politician, in 1774. Their union yielded four children, two boys and two girls. When Charles was appointed to a political position in London, the Pinckneys moved to England, where they lived from 1753 until 1758. Although they had left the colonies as a family of six, they returned as a unit of four, having left the boys behind in England to pursue their educations.

Eliza Pinckney never allowed business to interfere with her family life. When her husband died in 1758, just two weeks after they returned to South Carolina, she continued raising her girls while also managing Charles's seven plantations. Following the eruption of the Revolutionary War, Eliza discontinued contact with her friends in England and supported her two sons, who had returned stateside to work for the colonial revolution.

In time, Eliza Pinckney's sons would become respected politicians in the Old South—one would become a signer of the Declaration of Independence. Her eldest son, Charles Cotesworth Pinckney, was a delegate to the Constitutional Convention; Thomas, the younger son, was the

governor of South Carolina by the end of the Revolutionary War. Eliza Lucas Pinckney was such an influential figure within the colonies, that at the time of her death in 1793, President George Washington requested the honor of serving as one of her pallbearers.

See also Agriculture; Fox, Sally; Genetic Engineering; Metcalf, Betsey; Welles, Sophia Woodhouse
References Barker-Benfield, G. J., and Catherine Clinton, *Portraits of American Women: From Settlement to the Civil War,* vol 1. (1991); Berkin, Carol, *First Generations: Women in Colonial America* (1996); Clarke, Joni Anderson, "Bringing the Past to Life," *Women's Review of Books,* vol. 14, no. 3 (December 1996); "Hypatia's Sisters: Biographies of Women Scientists Past and Present," Women in Science course, Women Studies Program, University of Washington (Summer 1975); "Business: Women in the Workplace," *Women's History Feature* (Spring/Summer 1996), available at http://www.thehistorynet. . . . icles/19962_text.htm (cited 13 July 1999).

Pinkham, Lydia Estes (1819–1883)

Born into a Quaker family in Lynn, Massachusetts, in 1819, Lydia Estes Pinkham became the first American woman to earn a substantial living from the development of nonprescription pharmaceutical products during the late nineteenth and early twentieth centuries. Pinkham and her family began their pharmaceutical empire with the production of Lydia E. Pinkham's Vegetable Compound—a product advertised as a cure-all for premenstrual and menstrual ailments. The formula was a success until the mid-1930s, when the medical establishment, using the power granted it under the Pure Food and Drug Act of 1906, attacked the product's claims as fraudulent. Despite this attack, Pinkham's formula is still produced and bottled today in Puerto Rico, under the auspices of a major pharmaceutical company.

Pinkham's family-run empire began when Lydia brewed an herbal tonic for herself in her kitchen. Some historians have reported that the recipe for the tonic was given to Lydia's husband, Isaac Pinkham, as payment for a debt owed by a local machinist. Lydia Pinkham brewed the herbal mixture, adding 18 percent alcohol for use

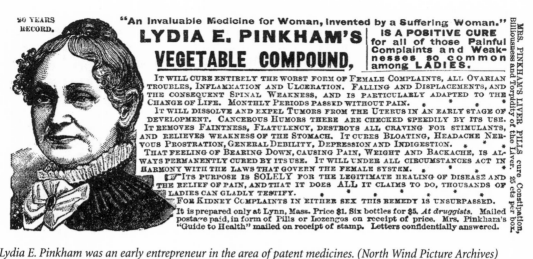

Lydia E. Pinkham was an early entrepreneur in the area of patent medicines. (North Wind Picture Archives)

as a preservative. She discovered the resulting product to be quite invigorating.

As Lydia Pinkham began sharing the tonic with friends and neighbors, word spread throughout her hometown of Lynn, Massachusetts, about the benefits the tonic provided for what were termed "women's weaknesses." As a result of these unsolicited endorsements, a business slowly began to develop. Evidence of the potential success of the product came in 1875, when women from Salem, Massachusetts, traveled to Lynn, eager to purchase Pinkham's elixir. Reports of this incident indicate that Pinkham sold the women six bottles of the elixir for $5. At the time of this transaction, Pinkham was in her mid-fifties. However, with the birth of Lydia E. Pinkham's Vegetable Compound, Pinkham, a former schoolteacher and active abolitionist, proved that it is never too late to become an entrepreneur. Within one year, Pinkham began advertising her product in area newpapers and sales began to flourish. The popularity of the product was fortuitous, since the Pinhkam family was undergoing a period of great financial hardship.

Pinkham's Compound became one of the earliest patent medicines (a medicinal product for which a U.S. letters patent was issued) in the United States. It also was the most successful such product of the late nineteenth and early twentieth centuries. Much of the product's suc-

cess derived from the groundbreaking methods used by the Pinkhams in the marketing and promotion of their product. These methods included printing Lydia Pinkham's image on the product's label (an idea suggested by Pinkham's son Dan) in 1879. Soon after this promotional tactic was essayed, business doubled. By 1881, the company's ledger books showed $250,000 in annual sales. The family immediately placed $150,000 of these earnings back into advertising by providing the major newspapers throughout the country with woodcuts of Lydia Pinkham's image. The woodcuts were to be used as a means of placing Pinkham's logo alongside her advertisements. The Pinkhams also began producing trading cards, compact sewing kits, and promotional booklets written by Pinkham herself that provided advice on health, home management, recipes, and beauty, along with testimonials of the benefits of Pinkham's product.

Many believed Pinkham's Compound was successful because it provided "respectable" ladies of the era with a means of satisfying their desire for alcohol. However, research conducted in the 1940s reported the finding of estrogen-like properties in the original formula for the compound. These data provided the therapeutic possibility that the formula actually had benefits for those suffering with "female complaints." Many modern-day herbalists defend Pinkham's original herbal mixture as an effective means for strengthening and toning the female reproductive system. The original recipe contained a combination of herbal roots and seeds in an 18-percent alcohol solution. With an alcohol content of between 13 and 20 percent, the mixture was typical of any herbal tincture. In addition, the active ingredient in Pinkham's Compound, Black Cohosh, continues to be widely used in the treatment of menstrual problems because it contains a natural form of estrogen.

Prior to her death in 1883, Lydia Pinkham became a model for both the American dream and the forthcoming feminist movement. She managed her household, established a thriving family business, and remained an outspoken advocate of women's rights and of the abolishment of slavery.

See also Pharmacology; Richards, Ellen Henrietta Swallow; Walker, Madame C. J.
References Oleson, Charles W., *Secret Nostroms and Systems of Medicine: A Book of Formulas* (1892); Stage, Sarah, *Female Complaints: Lydia Pinkham and the Business of Women's Medicine* (1979); Varro E., "The Bright Side of Black Cohosh," *Prevention* (April 1997); Cowles History Group, Inc., "TheHistoryNet: Picture of the Day, June 30," available at http://www.thehistorynet.com/picture/0630.htm (cited 19 June 1998); Floyd, Barbara, "From Quackery to Bacteriology," available at http://www.cl.utoledo.edu/quackery/quack3c.html (cited 28 June 1999).

Pittman, Margaret (1901–1995)

Vaccines are successful against diseases if they possess an effective potency and cause no serious side effects. As a member of the research staff of the Bureau of Biologics of the National Institutes of Health (NIH), which today is a division of the U.S. Food and Drug Administration (FDA), Margaret Pittman produced, tested, and standardized vaccines that were used to prevent cholera, typhoid, tetanus, and pertussis (whooping cough). In 1933, immunization with the diphtheria–pertussis–tetanus (DPT) vaccine was not available. Approximately 250,000 cases of pertussis (with more than 5,000 deaths) occurred in the United States in that year. Through the development and use of vaccines initially standardized by Margaret Pittman, by 1995 the incidence of pertussis had

been reduced to between 3,000 and 5,000 cases (with deaths resulting in only 10 to 15 cases).

Margaret Pittman was born in Prairie Grove, Arkansas, in 1901. Her mother was a relative of reaper inventor Cyrus H. McCormick, and her father was a physician. While still in their teens, both Margaret and her older sister assisted their father in the administration of anesthesia to patients for whom he was setting broken bones. This experience no doubt influenced Margaret's decision to pursue a career in medicine. After completing high school in her hometown of Prairie Grove, she attended an academy in a nearby community for an additional two years. She then enrolled at Hendrix College in Conway, Arkansas. At Hendrix, Margaret majored in biology and mathematics. She graduated *magna cum laude* with an A.B. degree in 1923.

After receiving her degree, Pittman taught at the Girls' Academy of Galloway College in Searcy, Arkansas. She became principal of the school after only one year. By the end of her second year, Pittman had saved enough money to continue her education, so she resigned her position at the academy to attend the University of Chicago. There she studied bacteriology and medical laboratory work. She received her M.S. degree in bacteriology in 1926.

Pittman remained at the University of Chicago an additional two years, during which time she worked toward her doctorate on a research fellowship from the Influenza Commission of the Metropolitan Life Insurance Company. In 1928, she interrupted her doctoral studies to accept a position as a research scientist at the hospital of the Rockefeller Institute for Medical Research in New York. While there, she studied a bacterium (*Hemophilus influenza*) that was believed to be the cause of influenza. At the same time, she investigated the bacteria-destroying activity of animal serum (the liquid part of the blood that does not contain any clotting factors). During her work, Pittman identified two strains of *H. influenza,* one of which (the capsule-enclosed strain) was determined to be the agent responsible for the disease known as meningitis. After making this positive identification, Pittman developed an antiserum for this disease—an antiserum that was later perfected by Hattie Elizabeth Alexander.

While performing her research at the Rockefeller Institute, Pittman worked to complete her doctoral dissertation during the evenings. She briefly returned to the University of Chicago, where she completed her doctoral requirements and earned her Ph.D. in bacteriology, during the summer of 1929. She then returned to the Rockefeller Institute to continue her studies on *H. influenzae* (she would eventually identify six distinct strains of this organism).

Pittman left the Rockefeller Institute and accepted a position as an assistant bacteriologist at the New York State Department of Health laboratories in 1934. Two years later, she resigned from this post to work as a bacteriologist at the National Institutes of Health (NIH) in Washington, D.C. She also applied her knowledge of statistics to the development of standards for an antimeningococcus serum—a method still used in testing biological agents.

In 1941, when the NIH moved to Bethesda, Maryland, Pittman was given her own research laboratory; seven years later, she was promoted to the position of senior bacteriologist. At this time, she resumed her research on *H. influenzae*. However, shortly after World War II began, Pittman was called upon to study blood contaminants and other factors that cause chills, fever, and other reactions that frequently accompanied serum therapy, including transfusion. Her research findings suggested that incubation temperature and the chemical composition of the culture medium used in the processing of blood plasma, serum, and albumin contributed to the chills, fever, and other, often fatal, reactions associated with transfusion therapies.

In 1944, Pittman was called upon to develop a pertussis vaccine. Working from her NIH laboratory in Bethesda, Pittman collaborated with Pearl Kendrick of the Michigan State Laboratory to develop a potency standard for the pertussis vaccine earlier developed by Kendrick and Grace Eldering. This vaccine produced a tenfold drop in mortality resulting from pertussis; however, its use often produced serious side effects, including

fever, localized swelling, seizures, and in some cases death. Pittman and Kendrick succeeded in developing the required potency standard for the pertussis vaccine in the United States in 1949. As standards improved and requirements for the production of the pertussis vaccine were upgraded during the 1950s and 1960s, the vaccine became safer, confidence in its use increased, and greater numbers of children were vaccinated.

In 1958, Pittman became the first female NIH laboratory chief when she was named chief bacteriologist of the Laboratory Bacterial Products Division of Biological Standards. In this position, she served as a consultant to the World Health Organization (WHO) as well as carrying on with her research responsibilities at the NIH laboratories. In 1959–1960, she consulted with the WHO on a cholera vaccine. During the 1960s, she worked with the WHO to develop standards for a typhoid vaccine. She again served as a consultant to the WHO in Cairo and in Madrid from 1971 to 1972.

Pittman retired from the NIH in 1971. Following her retirement, she served as a guest worker and a consultant at the Center for Biological Evaluation and Research, under the aegis of the U.S. Food and Drug Administration (FDA), until 1975. Even after her retirement, Pittman continued to serve as a consultant to health agencies in many countries seeking to develop vaccines for the prevention of such diseases as pertussis, cholera, and yellow fever. Among the countries she worked with were Switzerland, France, Brazil, Pakistan, Czechoslovakia, Canada, Iran, Scotland, and the Netherlands.

Pittman was highly revered by her contemporaries, as evidenced by her service as president for both the Washington Branch of the American Society of Microbiology (1949–1950) and the Washington Academy of Sciences (1955), as well as her inclusion on the Board of Governors of the American Academy of Microbiology (1963–1969). She also held memberships in the American Association for the Advancement of Science (AAAS), the Society for Experimental Biology and Medicine, and the International Association of Biological Standardization.

In recognition for her achievements in the

development and standardization of vaccines, Hendrix College presented Pittman the Hogan Mathematics Medal in 1922, elected her to Sigma Xi as a graduate student, and awarded her an honorary LL.D. in 1954. She received the Superior Service Award (1963) and the Distinguished Service Award (1968) from the U.S. Department of Health, Education and Welfare (HEW). In addition, the University of Chicago Alumni Association presented her its Professional Achievement Award in 1973. Pittman also is a recipient of the Federal Woman's Award of the U.S. government (1970) and the Alice Evans Award of the American Society for Microbiology (1990). In 1994, the NIH instituted a lecture series in her honor.

See also Alexander, Hattie Elizabeth; Antibiotics; Baker, Sara Josephine; Biotechnology; Brown, Rachel Fuller; Dick, Gladys Rowena Henry; Eldering, Grace; Elion, Gertrude Belle; Evans, Alice Catherine; Hazen, Elizabeth Lee; Kendrick, Pearl Luella; Medicine/Medical Technology; Pharmacology; Williams, Anna Wessels
References Bailey, Martha J., *American Women in Science: A Biographical Dictionary* (1994); O'Hern, Elizabeth Moot, *Profiles of Pioneer Women Scientists* (1986); Stanley, Autumn, *Mothers and Daughters of Invention: Notes for a Revised History of Technology* (1993); Torpie, Stephen L., et al., eds., *American Men and Women of Science*, 18th ed. (1992–1993) (1992).

Pool, Judith Graham (1919–1975)

Physiologist Judith Pool developed the technology used to isolate and prepare antihemophilic factor (AHF), a clot-forming protein missing from the blood of individuals with hemophilia. Her procedure revolutionized the treatment of bleeding associated with hemophilia and became the standard for treating hemophiliac patients. Pool also codeveloped a refined microelectrode, a device used to measure and record electrical impulses passing along muscle and nerve tissues. Her codeveloper, Ralph Gerard, was nominated for a Nobel Prize for the development of the microelectrode in the 1950s, but Pool's contribution brought her no recognition.

Judith Pool was born in Queens, New York, where she attended Jamaica High School. She attended the University of Chicago, from which she received a B.S. degree in 1939. Pool then re-

mained at the university, taking graduate courses and working as an assistant in physiology. In 1942, she accepted a position as an instructor in physics at Hobart and William Smith Colleges in Geneva, New York. However, she left this post to return to the University of Chicago, receiving her doctorate in physiology in 1946. During the early to mid-1940s, Pool performed research leading to the development of the microelectrode.

In 1950, Pool and her family moved to California, where she worked as a research associate at the Stanford Research Institute until 1953. She later became a research fellow at Stanford University School of Medicine and eventually rose through the ranks to the position of full professor. She spent the remainder of her career at Stanford. During this time Pool also carried out research on clotting factors and hemophilia and discovered the antihemophilic factor (AHF) in 1959.

For her research on hemophilia, Pool received many awards. Among them were the Murray Thelin Award of the National Hemophilia Foundation (1968), the Elizabeth Blackwell Award of Hobart and William Smith Colleges (1973), and the Professional Achievement Award of the University of Chicago (1975). In 1971, she served as copresident of the Association for Women in Science (AWIS). In addition, she was the first chairperson of the Professional Women of Stanford University Medical Center.

Pool held memberships in the American Association for the Advancement of Science (AAAS), the American Physiological Society, and the Society for Experimental Biology and Medicine. Following her death in 1975, the National Hemophilia Foundation renamed its Research Fellowships Awards the Judith Graham Pool Research Fellowships.

See also Association for Women in Science (AWIS); Blackburn, Elizabeth Helen; Hyde, Ida Henrietta
References Bailey, Martha J., *American Women in Science: A Biographical Dictionary* (1994); Kass-Simon, G., and Patricia Farnes, eds., *Women of Science: Righting the Record* (1990); Sicherman, Barbara, and Carol Hurd Green, eds., *Notable American Women: The Modern Period* (1980); Stanley, Autumn, *Mothers and Daughters of Invention: Notes for a Revised History of Technology* (1993).

Potts, Mary Florence Webber (1851–?)

Mary Florence Potts endeared herself to countless women when at the age of only 19 she patented her modifications to the flat, or "sad," clothes iron in 1870. The safety, value, and comparative ease-of-use positioned "Mrs. Potts' Cold Handle Sad Iron" at the top of a long list of competing products—a place it held until the introduction of the electric iron.

In developing her iron, Potts combined knowledge she had gleaned as the daughter of a plasterer with her firsthand experience of the annoyances of using the old-style "sad" (an archaic word meaning "heavy") iron. The original design for her iron consisted of a thick iron base attached to a thinner upper frame that was filled with plaster of Paris—a modification intended to shield the user's hand from the intense heat that frequently scorched fingers. Later modifications to the iron included the addition of a double-pointed base, which permitted the user to iron in either direction, along with a detachable wooden handle that fit the three bases included in the set.

Potts and her husband, Joseph, initially sought to market the iron on their own; however, they came close to bankruptcy in the process. The couple then moved to Joseph's hometown of Philadelphia, Pennsylvania, where they turned over sales of the iron to the American Enterprise Manufacturing Company. The company's use of advertising cards at the 1876 Centennial Exposition in Philadelphia, featuring Mrs. Potts and the iron in a variety of whimsical cartoons, made the iron popular throughout the country. Even today, collectors pursue these trading cards, as well as the irons themselves, which provide a glimpse into the history of women in America.

Following the success of her iron, Mary Potts and her husband copatented yet another invention, described as a "remedial medical appliance" that used heat in a therapeutic manner, in 1892. At the time that this second invention was patented, the couple had relocated from Philadelphia and was living in Austin, Illinois.

See also Blanchard, Helen Augusta; Blount (Griffin), Bessie J.; Centennial Exposition; Domestic Appliances;

Eglin, Ellen F.; Gilbreth, Lillian Moller; Henry, Beulah L.; Hibbard, Susan; Invention/Inventors; Jones, El Dorado; Knight, Margaret E.; Patent

References Grossman, Bob, "Mrs. Potts Advertising Trade Cards," *Iron Talk: Journal of Antique Pressing Irons,* Issue 11 (May/June 1997); Macdonald, Anne L., *Feminine Ingenuity: How Women Inventors Changed America* (1992); "Mrs. Florence Potts: The True Story," *Iron Talk: Journal of Antique Pressing Irons,* Issue 11 (May/June 1997); Stanley, Autumn, *Mothers and Daughters of Invention: Notes for a Revised History of Technology* (1993); Walker, Jimmy, editor and publisher of *Iron Talk,* e-mail correspondence with Alan Winkler (1 July 1999).

Pressman, Ada I. (b. 1927)

At a time when fewer than 1 percent of American women pursued degrees in engineering and obtained employment in their chosen area of study, Ada I. Pressman not only achieved both these goals but emerged as a leader in her profession. Although she held only a bachelor's degree throughout much of her career, Pressman helped establish systems-and-control engineering as a discrete engineering area, earning recognition as an authority in the design of power plant instrumentation and control systems. Her work eventually resulted in the use of sensor technology in the monitoring mechanisms of nuclear power plant shutdown systems. Such monitoring capabilities prevent equipment damage and radiation leakage, thus making work in such plants safer for employees, as well as decreasing the likelihood that harmful radiation will be released into the environment.

Ada Pressman was born in Sidney, Ohio, a small town in Shelby County. Pressman had intended to pursue a secretarial career after graduating from high school; however, at her father's urging, she instead attended college. In 1948, she entered Ohio State University as a mathematics major. She later changed her area of study to engineering, and earned a B.S. degree in mechanical engineering in 1950, after only two years of study.

After receiving her bachelor's degree, Pressman accepted a position as project engineer at the Bailey Meter Company in Cleveland, Ohio. While working at the Bailey Meter Company, she began developing her skills in instrumentation and control systems technology. At Bailey, her work focused primarily on the use of such systems at electricity-generating power plants and on U.S. Navy ships that used fossil fuels (coal, oil, or natural gas) as their energy source. Pressman would later apply the skills honed in this position to develop and implement similar control technologies at facilities generating electricity from nuclear fuels.

Pressman moved to Vernon, California, accepting a position as process and instrument engineer for the Bechtel Power Corporation in 1955. She remained with Bechtel, advancing through various engineering and managerial positions, for thirty-two years. In the ten-year period between 1964 and 1974, she served first as an instrument engineer and later as instrument group leader. In these roles, Pressman developed automatic controls and reliable sensors for equipment and power generating systems. In the latter position, she also directed a team in the design and construction of four nuclear power generating units. In 1968, Pressman was promoted to the position of assistant chief control system engineer, a position she held for four years.

Pressman was promoted to the position of control systems engineering group supervisor at the Rancho Seco Nuclear Power Plant in 1971. This plant was the first nuclear power facility constructed at a site that was not located near a major body of water. While working at Rancho Seco, Pressman designed a secondary cooling system for the facility. This cooling system was powered by a diesel generator that operated independently of other power sources, to ensure that the power to the system would continue to operate if the main power generators shut down. Around this same time, Pressman began a campaign to have control systems engineering classified as a discrete engineering field in the state of California. She was successful in this goal and became the first person to register as a systems engineer in that state.

In 1974, Pressman received an M.B.A. in business administration from Golden Gate University. At the same time, she became chief control system engineer in Bechtel's Los Angeles division. In this role, Pressman was responsible for the development and maintenance of control systems at more than fifteen major power projects worldwide. Pressman's next promotion came in 1979, when she was named engineering manager. She remained in this position until her retirement from the Bechtel Power Corporation in 1987.

Pressman has been a member of several professional organizations, including the American Society of Mechanical Engineers (ASME), the American Nuclear Society, the Institute for the Advancement of Engineering's College of Fellows, and the Society of Women Engineers (SWE), an organization in which she has been active since 1954. In 1979, Pressman was elected president of the SWE, serving in this role until 1980. In 1983, Pressman was elected a fellow of the SWE, an honor bestowed in recognition of her achievements in the field of engineering as well as for her efforts at helping women to become more involved in the engineering profession. Pressman also served as vice president of the Instrument Society of America from 1973 to 1978.

In recognition of "her significant contributions in the field of power control systems engineering," Pressman was awarded the Achievement Award of the SWE in 1976. Other honors bestowed on Pressman include the Distinguished Alumna Award from Ohio State University (1974), the E. G. Bailey Award from the Instrument Society of America, the Outstanding Engineer Merit Award (1975), and the Twin Award from the YWCA (1981).

See also Anderson, Elda Emma; Clarke, Edith; Eng, Patricia L.; Environmental Engineering; Lamme, Bertha; Mechanical Engineering; Safety Engineering; Society of Women Engineers (SWE)

References McMurray, Emily M., ed., *Notable Twentieth-Century Scientists,* vol. 3: (L–R) (1995); Society of Women Engineers, "Ada Irene Pressman, 1927–," available at http://www.swe.org/SWE/PastPresident/pressman.htm (cited 10 April 1999); Virginia Tech, "Ada Irene Pressman," in the Virtual Museum, available at http://www.ee.vt.edu/~museum/women/ada/Ada'spage.html (cited 10 April 1999).

Proudfoot, Andrea H. (n.d.)

In the late 1970s, Ann Moore of Colorado obtained a patent for an infant carrier she called the Snugli. The carrier provided women with a means of toting infants from one place to another in a pouch-like device that rested on the chest. After receiving one of these carriers as a gift, Andrea Proudfoot of Eugene, Oregon, made a modification to the Snugli. Her modified carrier was designed to carry the baby on the mother's back, in a manner similar to today's backpacks, instead of in front.

On the basis of this innovation, Proudfoot obtained a patent for her infant carrier. She has since begun manufacturing her creation, which is known as Andrea's Baby Pack, in moderate quantities. The development of this new carrier provides an example of how one invention may build on the idea of another.

See also Donovan, Marion; Moore, Ann; Wells, Jane
References Vare, Ethlie Ann, and Greg Ptacek, *Mothers of Invention: From the Bra to the Bomb, Forgotten Women and Their Unforgettable Ideas* (1988).

Quimby, Edith Hinkley (1891–1982)

Edith Quimby is recognized as a pioneer and expert in radiology—the science of radioactive substances and radiation (e.g., X rays, radium, and the like), particularly as it applies to medical diagnosis and treatment of illness. Quimby is recognized for three significant accomplishments in this area. The first is her use of radioactive isotopes (forms of the same element that vary in the number of neutrons in their nuclei) in the diagnosis and treatment of cancer and other diseases. Her second contribution lay in her establishment of standardization in the dosages of radiation used in the treatment of various cancers. In addition, Quimby contributed to the war effort when she was called upon during World War II to conduct research for the Manhattan Project, the U.S. program that resulted in the development of the world's first atomic bomb.

Edith Quimby was born Edith Hinkley, in Rockford, Illinois, in 1891. While she was a child, her family moved frequently; thus Quimby received her early education at schools located in several different states. Eventually, she completed her education in Boise, Idaho, where she graduated from the Boise High School with a four-year scholarship that allowed her to attend Whitman College in Walla Walla, Washington.

At Whitman, Hinkley majored in both physics and mathematics. She received her B.S. degree in 1912 and then accepted a position as a high school science teacher in Oregon. After teaching for two years, Hinkley was awarded a fellowship that permitted her to attend the University of California at Berkeley. While at UC–Berkeley, Edith Hinkley met Shirley L. Quimby, a graduate student in physics. The couple married in 1915, the year before Edith Quimby received her M.A. degree in physics.

After receiving her master's degree, Edith Quimby again returned to teaching high school science—this time at a school in Antioch, California. In 1919, the Quimbys moved to New York after Shirley Quimby accepted a position as a physics instructor at Columbia University. Edith obtained a position as a researcher at the New York City Memorial Hospital for Cancer and Allied Diseases. It was while working at Memorial Hospital that she began her studies in radiation, becoming the only woman in America to hold a research post in the area of medical physics.

When Edith accepted her post at Memorial Hospital, the use of radiation (in the form of X rays and radium) as a treatment for cancer and similar diseases was in its infancy. Because it was such a new field, most doctors making use of such treatments were unaware of the radiation dosages required for effective treatment. This issue became the driving concern behind Edith Quimby's research. Over the next twenty years she conducted numerous studies, which culminated in a recommendation of standardized dosages (in roentgens, the unit of measurement for radiation in use at the time) of radium and X rays that would effectively treat tumors with minimal negative side effects.

Quimby remained at Memorial Hospital until 1943; in her final years there, she also taught courses in radiology at the medical college of Cornell University. She then accepted a position in radiology at the College of Physicians and Surgeons at Columbia University. Quimby would spend the remainder of her professional career at this facility.

At Columbia, Quimby became a pioneer in the field now known as nuclear medicine when she cofounded the Radiological Research Laboratory. Among her major studies within this laboratory

Nuclear physicist Edith Quimby worked on the Manhattan Project and pioneered research into the development of standards for use in radiology. (Corbis-Bettmann)

During World War II, Quimby divided her time at Columbia University between medical research and research that was essential to the production of the first atomic bomb. Following the war, Quimby continued her service to the federal government by serving as a consultant to the Atomic Energy Commission (AEC)—an agency established by the government in 1946 for the purpose of regulating the production and use of atomic (nuclear) energy.

For her pioneering work in the safe use of radioactive substances, Edith Quimby became the first woman to be awarded the Janeway Medal of the American Radium Society in 1940. She later received awards from the Radiological Society of North America (1941) and the American Cancer Society (1957). In addition, Quimby was a member of many professional organizations, including the American Radium Society (of which she served as president in 1954), the American Roentgen Ray Society, and the Radiological Society of North America. She also was a fellow of the American Physical Society and the American College of Radiology.

See also Anderson, Elda Emma; Eng, Patricia L.; Goeppert-Mayer, Maria; Manhattan Project; Nuclear Physics; Ordnance; Radioimmunoassay (RIA); Yalow, Rosalyn Sussman

References Bailey, Martha J., *American Women in Science: A Biographical Dictionary* (1994); Grinstein, Louise S., Rose K. Rose, and Miriam H. Rafailovich, eds., *Women in Chemistry and Physics: A Biobibliographic Sourcebook* (1993); Rothe, Anna, ed., *Current Biography, 1949* (1949); Saari, Peggy, and Stephen Allison, eds., *Scientists: The Lives and Works of 150 Scientists*, vol. 3 (1966); Saxon, Wolfgang, "Edith Quimby Dies; Radiation Expert" [obituary], *New York Times* (13 October 1982).

were experiments involving the use of radioactive isotopes (including the newly developed synthetic radioactive sodium) in the diagnosis and treatment of disease. Among the conditions studied were thyroid disorders and brain tumors. In addition to her efforts at treating patients with radioactive substances, Quimby also was very concerned with how the handling of such substances might affect medical personnel. She spent a great deal of her time addressing this latter concern.

Radioimmunoassay (RIA)

Radioimmunoassay (RIA) involves the use of radioisotopes to quickly label, trace, and measure tiny amounts of hormones, proteins, vitamins, enzymes, viruses, drugs, and other substances in blood or other body tissues. The term *radioimmunoassay* is a compound of three words: *radio-* (relating to radiation—that is, the spontaneous release of particles or energy); *immuno-* (having to do with the body's physiological response to the presence of antigens); and *assay* (a test used to determine the quantity of a substance). A relatively new technology that was first made public in 1959, RIA is the coinvention of doctors Rosalyn Sussman Yalow and Solomon A. Berson. Yalow was awarded the Nobel Prize in physiology/medicine for her groundbreaking work with RIA in 1977. Berson did not share the prize, having died in 1972.

When foreign agents (antigens), such as bacteria, viruses, or hormones, enter the blood or the other tissues of an animal, the body's immune system responds by producing antibodies (proteins) to protect against these antigens. Antibodies destroy or deactivate antigens by binding with them at specific locations (called binding sites) along the antibody surface. The metabolic activity or pathway of an antigen can be traced by "labeling" it, that is, chemically binding it to a radioisotope. Once the molecule has been labeled in this way, its movements can readily be traced and measured. When antibodies and labeled antigens contact one another, a radioactive antigen-antibody complex is formed. If an unknown concentration of nonradioactive antigen is now introduced, both nonradioactive and radioactive forms of the antigen compete for the same binding sites on the antibody. During this time, some of the already bound antigen is displaced. Using a device called a scintillation counter, the ratio of radioactivity levels along binding sites is then determined and compared to prepared standards (known amounts of radioactive and nonradioactive antigen).

Radioimmunoassay is considered one of the most significant achievements of the twentieth century. Not limited solely to the study of antigen-antibody reactions, RIA has powerful re-

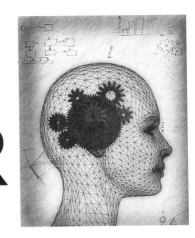

search and diagnostic applications in other areas of medicine and biochemistry. For example, RIA can be used to study binding reactions between proteins (including enzymes) and hormones. The procedure also has uses in blood screening for drugs and infectious agents. Other applications of RIA include its use in detecting infertility problems, hormone-secreting cancers, and endocrine disorders.

See also Fowler, Joanna S.; Frantz, Virginia Kneeland; Nobel Prize; Yalow, Rosalyn Sussman
References Parker, Sybil P., *McGraw-Hill Encyclopedia of Science and Technology*, 8th ed., vol. 15 (1997); Saari, Peggy, and Stephen Allison, eds., *Scientists: The Lives and Works of 150 Scientists*, vol. 3 (1996); Stanley, Autumn, *Mothers and Daughters of Invention: Notes for a Revised History of Technology* (1993).

Railroads

A railroad is a permanent system of transportation composed of cars that travel along a pair of parallel steel rails (tracks) that are held in place at a fixed distance through the use of wooden beams called ties. The rails are mounted to the ties through the use of heavy metal nails called spikes. Depending upon their location and use, the tracks upon which a train moves may be located on the ground or may be elevated above ground level by means of steel and concrete girders. Railroads typically provide transportation either for people (passenger trains) or for cargo (freight trains); however, a single train may serve both purposes.

The design and construction of railcars, tracks, and rail facilities have typically been carried out by men. However, a few women have made contributions in these areas. Among them are Jane G. Swisshelm, Mary Walton, and Mary Engle Pennington. In the 1840s, Jane G. Swisshelm of Pennsylvania observed that on dark evenings it was difficult for an individual to identify when the last car of a moving train had passed. She believed that this problem may have explained why earlier in the week a train that had stopped in the dark was struck in the rear by a second train traveling in the same direction. These thoughts prompted Swisshelm to write a local newspaper with the suggestion that the last car (or caboose) of trains be equipped with a red light, the presence of which would indicate the end of the train. Soon after her suggestion was printed in the newspaper, Swisshelm observed that trains running along the track on which the accident had previously occurred were now equipped with such lights. Within a few years, the policy of placing red lights on the rear platforms of trains had been adopted by most railroads.

In the late 1800s, Mary Walton of New York City devised a means of dampening the sound produced by elevated trains running along their metal tracks. Walton's concern in this area arose because the noise generated from the moving trains near her home was so great, it was keeping her up at night. Walton's solution to the problem was a soundproofing system consisting of tar-coated boxes filled with sand and cotton upon which the railroad tracks could be secured. This combination of materials effectively absorbed the vibrations produced by the track, thus greatly reducing the noise. For this invention, Walton was issued a patent in 1881. Her device was immediately adopted by the New York City Metropolitan Railroad. In time, it also was incorporated by other elevated railway systems throughout the country.

Mary Engle Pennington's contribution to the railroad industry stemmed from the years of research she conducted to determine the effects of temperature and humidity on perishable foods. As a result of her work in this area, Pennington helped develop standards for use in the construction of refrigerated railroad cars used to transport foods. In addition, she later assisted in the design of ice-cooled and motor-driven refrigerator cars. These designs were so effective that they remained in use for nearly thirty years before newer technologies permitted the development of more sophisticated railroad cooling and refrigeration systems.

See also Beasley, Maria E.; Pennington, Mary Engle; Walton, Mary
References Convis, Orville R., "Why Trains Have Red Taillights," *Christian Science Monitor* (4 August 1986); Sicherman, Barbara, and Carol Hurd Green, eds., *Notable American Women: The Modern Period* (1980); Stanley, Autumn, *Mothers and Daughters of Invention: Notes for a Revised History of Technology* (1993).

Rand, (Marie) Gertrude (1886–1970)

Gertrude Rand, a prominent researcher in ophthalmology and physiological optics, is best known for the codevelopment, with her husband, Clarence Ferree, of the Ferree-Rand perimeter—an optical device that detailed the structure and function of the retina. The device provided data about the retina's perceptual abilities and became an important instrument for diagnosing vision problems.

Gertrude Rand was born in Brooklyn, New York. She attended Cornell University, from which she received her B.A. degree in experimental psychology in 1908. She continued her studies in psychology at Bryn Mawr College in Pennsylvania, earning both an M.A. and a Ph.D. in 1911. Rand remained at Bryn Mawr, serving in various research and teaching positions, until 1927. While at Bryn Mawr, she married her former mentor, Clarence Ferree, and collaborated with him in research on color perception and on light sensitivity of the retina; this research led to the development of the Ferree-Rand perimeter.

In 1928, Rand and her husband moved to the Wilmer Ophthalmological Institute of the Johns Hopkins University School of Medicine. There

Gertrude taught research ophthalmology, then physiological optics, before becoming associate director of the Research Laboratory of Physiological Optics in 1936. During this period, Rand and Ferree served as consultants in lighting technology and developed instruments and lamps for use in ophthalmology and reduced-glare illumination systems for public facilities, including the Johns Hopkins University Hospital and New York's Holland Tunnel.

After her husband's death in 1943, Rand moved to New York City and became a research associate at the Knapp Foundation of the Columbia University College of Physicians and Surgeons. She remained in this position until her retirement in 1957. There Rand researched color blindness. This research led to the development of diagnostic plates that accurately measured the type and degree of color vision defects in individuals.

In recognition of her many achievements and contributions, Rand became the first woman elected a fellow of the Illuminating Engineering Society of North America (IESNA) in 1952. She was awarded the society's Gold Medal in 1963. For her outstanding research in vision, Rand became the first woman to receive the Edgar D. Tillyer Medal of the Optical Society of America in 1959. She also was a member of the American Association for the Advancement of Science (AAAS) and the American Psychological Association.

See also Bath, Patricia; Blodgett, Katherine Burr; Bryn Mawr College; Greenewalt, Mary E. H.; Illuminating Engineering Society of North America (IESNA)
References Bailey, Martha J., *American Women in Science: A Biographical Dictionary* (1994); Franck, Irene M., and David M. Brownstone, *Women's World: A Timeline of Women in History* (1995); Read, Phyllis J., and Bernard L. Witlieb, *The Book of Women's Firsts* (1992); Sicherman, Barbara, and Carol Hurd Green, eds., *Notable American Women: The Modern Period* (1980).

Ray, Dixy Lee
See **Atomic Energy Commission (AEC)**

Resnik, Judith A. (1949–1986)

Electrical engineer Judith Resnik became only the second American woman to go into space during the maiden voyage of the space shuttle *Discovery* in 1984. Two years later, Resnik was scheduled for a second space flight, aboard the *Challenger;* however, the flight was never realized and the entire crew perished when the *Challenger* exploded only seconds after liftoff from the Kennedy Space Center in Florida. Although most known for her service as an astronaut, this was not Resnik's only contribution to science and technology. She also worked with Sally Ride, the first American woman in space, to design and develop the Remote Manipulator System (RMS)—a robotic arm for use aboard shuttle missions; created software; developed procedures for deployment of a Tethered Satellite System; and worked as a biomedical engineer and staff fellow with the National Institutes of Health (NIH).

Judith Resnik was born in Cleveland, Ohio, on 5 April 1949. She grew up in Akron, where she attended public schools and also received religious instruction in Judaism. While attending Akron's Firestone High School, Resnik demonstrated outstanding abilities when she achieved perfect scores of 800 points on both the verbal and the math sections of the SAT. After graduating from high school, she attended Carnegie-Mellon University in Pennsylvania as an electrical engineering major. Resnik received her B.S. in electrical engineering in 1970. Soon after, she began work as a design engineer with the RCA Corporation.

In 1974, Resnik left RCA to work at the NIH in Bethesda, Maryland. She served as staff scientist and biomedical engineer in the neurophysiology laboratory, where she did work involving the physiology of visual systems, while also working toward her doctoral degree. She received this degree from the University of Maryland in 1977. She then accepted a position as a senior systems engineer with the Xerox Corporation in El Segunda, California.

While working at Xerox, Resnik applied to NASA for admission into its astronaut program. In 1978, she was selected as an astronaut candidate for the space shuttle program. That same year, Resnik married engineering student Michael Radak. They separated five years later.

In 1984, Resnik made her first space flight, serving as mission specialist aboard the earth orbiter *Discovery*. During the 144-hour flight, Resnik operated the robotic arm she had helped design, removing ice particles from the outer shell of the orbiter. She also carried out solar-power experiments and assisted in the deployment of three satellites. In recognition of her achievements, she was awarded the NASA Space Flight Medal that same year. Resnik, while still with the space program, also worked as a commentator for ABC television. Her job was to report on events aboard the fourth shuttle mission. Two years later, Resnik was selected to serve as one of three mission specialists on the *Challenger*. Teacher Christa McAuliffe, who was to be the first civilian in space, also was part of the seven-member crew. During this flight, Resnik's major task was to photograph Halley's Comet. However, immediately after liftoff on 28 January 1986, the *Challenger* exploded, killing all aboard.

Resnik was a member of several professional organizations, including the Society of Women Engineers (SWE) and the Institute of Electrical and Electronics Engineers (IEEE). To celebrate Resnik's accomplishments, the SWE created the Resnik *Challenger* Medal in her honor in 1986. The award is presented to an individual woman having more than ten years of exceptional engineering accomplishments who has contributed to advancements in space exploration and technology. The award was presented to engineer Yvonne C. Brill in 1993. The IEEE also has named an award in Resnik's honor. The IEEE Judith A. Resnik Award is presented annually to an individual who has made outstanding contributions to space engineering. In 1993, engineer and astronaut Bonnie J. Dunbar was presented the award for her "significant contributions to the processing and development of electronic materials in space."

See also Biotechnology; Brill, Yvonne Claeys; Dunbar, Bonnie J.; Institute of Electrical and Electronics Engineers (IEEE); Jemison, Mae; National Aeronautics and Space Administration (NASA); Ochoa, Ellen; Ride, Sally Kirsten; Society of Women Engineers (SWE); Space Exploration

References "Judith A. Resnik" [obituary], *New York Times Biographical Service* (1986); Levitan, Tina, *First Facts in American Jewish History: From 1492 to the Present* (1996); Slater, Elinor, and Robert Slater, *Great Jewish Women* (1998); Institute of Electrical and Electronics Engineers, "IEEE Judith A. Resnik Award," available at http://www.ieee.org/about/awards (cited 7 May 1999); Society of Women Engineers, "Resnik Challenger Medal," available at http://www.swe.org/SWE/Awards/resnik.htm (cited 7 May 1999).

Richards, Ellen Henrietta Swallow (1842–1911)

Ellen Swallow Richards is recognized as one of the founders of home economics because of her work in promoting healthful living and safe environments. When Richards began her work, home economics was called domestic science and incorporated issues that today are part of ecology, such as air and water quality, as well as concerns regarding nutrition and household products. Through her work in home economics and ecology, Richards became a pioneer in many areas of science and technology. These included her establishment of the first laboratory open to women at the Massachusetts Institute of Technology (MIT) in 1876 and her role in the development of the nation's first sanitary engineering program in 1890. In addition, Richards's continued efforts at breaking down gender barriers provided women greater access to education in the sciences.

Ellen Swallow was born in Dunstable, Massachusetts. Her parents, who were teachers, farmers, and merchants, educated their daughter at home. When Ellen was seventeen, her family moved to Westford, Massachusetts. Ellen enrolled at the Westford Academy, where she studied French, Latin, and mathematics. She graduated in 1863 and worked for the next five years to raise tuition money to attend Vassar College.

Swallow received her B.A. from Vassar in 1870. She then attended MIT as a special student, where she studied chemistry. Her admission as a special student arose from the school's policy of denying women entry; however, the "special student" admission did establish her as the first woman to attend a scientific school in the United

Ellen Swallow Richards was a pioneer in water analyses as they related to water purification. (Sophia Smith Collection, Smith College)

States. Three years later, Swallow became the first woman to receive a B.S. degree from MIT. At the same time, Vassar awarded Swallow a master's degree in chemistry based upon a thesis she had submitted earlier.

After graduating from MIT, Swallow remained at the school for two years to pursue postgraduate studies, but she was never awarded a doctoral degree, ostensibly because MIT did not wish its first D.S. in chemistry to be granted to a woman. However, this same school did grant Swallow a position as its first woman chemistry teacher in 1873. She remained in this position, albeit without pay, until 1878.

In 1876, Swallow helped establish a Women's Laboratory at MIT using money obtained from the Boston Women's Education Association. The laboratory provided women an opportunity to participate in scientific studies. It also provided Swallow with more secure employment when

MIT hired her in 1878 to serve as an instructor of chemistry and mineralogy at the laboratory. Recognizing the achievements of women in the sciences, the Women's Laboratory of MIT was shut down in 1883 when the school changed its policies and began admitting women using the same standards as it applied to men.

Swallow married Robert H. Richards, chair of the Mining and Engineering Department at MIT, in 1875. While assisting her husband in his research, she became an expert in mineral analysis. Her work was recognized by the American Institute of Mining and Metallurgical Engineers when they elected Richards as their first woman member in 1879. A few years later, Richards's interests turned toward sanitation. She helped develop a chemical laboratory for the study of sanitation at MIT in 1884. Six years later, MIT became the first university in the United States to offer a complete program in sanitary engineering. Until her death in 1911, Richards worked as an instructor of the sanitary chemistry laboratory and also taught courses in mineralogy at MIT. The year before her death, she received an honorary doctoral degree in chemistry from Smith College.

While a student at MIT, Richards had assisted her professors in analyses of inland water supplies. While teaching in the sanitation engineering program, she returned to this work, analyzing 40,000 water samples for the Massachusetts State Board of Health between 1887 and 1889. Richards extended her sphere of influence when she served as a nutrition expert for the U.S. Department of Agriculture (USDA). She also became involved in combustion experiments with fuel oils, which led to the design of the Aladdin oven. In addition, Richards invented an artificial gastric juice composed of pepsin and hydrochloric acid that facilitated laboratory studies of the digestive process. She is also credited with revolutionizing the dry cleaning industry by discovering a process of using naphtha to clean wool. Richards helped establish the Seaside Laboratory in Massachusetts (now known as Wood's Hole).

Richards wrote more than 30 books, pamphlets, and articles about proper food preparation and cooking techniques. She also helped establish school lunch programs and demonstrated sanitary methods for preparing low-cost nutritional meals. In 1885, Richards published *Food Materials and Their Adulterations*. This publication influenced the passage of the first Pure Food and Drug Act in the state of Massachusetts. In 1899, Richards helped organize a school of housekeeping. This school later evolved into the department of home economics at Simmons College. She also was instrumental in creating a nutrition department at the University of Chicago.

In addition to academics, Richards was active in many professional organizations and helped found two of them—the Association of Collegiate Alumnae (now the American Association of University Women) in 1882, and the American Home Economics Association in 1908. She served as the first president of the latter organization, remaining in the position for two years. Richards also was appointed to the National Education Association's (NEA) Council to supervise home economics teaching in schools throughout the nation in 1910.

See also Affirmative Action; American Association of University Women (AAUW); American Society for Nutritional Sciences (ASNS); Baker, Sara Josephine; Bevier, Isabel; Cochran, Josephine G.; Columbian Exposition; Donovan, Marion; Emerson, Gladys Anderson; Evans, Alice Catherine; Farmer, Fannie Merritt; Fieser, Mary Peters; Home Economics; Jones, Amanda Theodosia; Metals and Metallurgy
References Bailey, Martha J., *American Women in Science: A Biographical Dictionary* (1994); Breton, Mary Joy, *Women Pioneers for the Environment* (1998); Ogilvie, Marilyn, *Women in Science Antiquity through the Nineteenth Century: A Biographical Dictionary with Annotated Bibliography* (1986); Shearer, Benjamin F. and Barbara S. Shearer, eds., *Notable Women in the Physical Sciences: A Biographical Dictionary* (1997); Stanley, Autumn, *Mothers and Daughters of Invention* (1993).

Richardson, Jane Shelby (b. 1941)

Molecular biologists Jane Shelby Richardson and her husband, David Richardson, are recognized for their application of X-ray crystallography (a tool that uses X-ray diffraction to reveal the three-dimensional structure of molecules) to protein molecules. Jane Richardson also is noted for her application of computer technology to help illustrate the process of protein folding, a mechanism whereby long chains of amino acids bend, fold, and coil to produce a protein with a specific shape and structure. The new tools developed by Richardson provide the biotechnology necessary for mass-producing proteins such as human insulin as well as for designing new protein molecules not presently found in nature.

Jane Shelby was born in Teaneck, New Jersey. In 1958, her science talents became evident when she won third place in the national Westinghouse Science Talent Search (a science competition for high-school students) for the project "Calculating the Orbit of *Sputnik* from Naked-Eye Observations." After graduating from high school, Shelby attended Swarthmore College in Pennsylvania. She graduated *cum laude,* with a B.A. degree in philosophy and minors in math and physics, in 1962. That same year, she married chemist David C. Richardson.

After graduating from Swarthmore, Jane Richardson attended Harvard University in Massachusetts, where she continued her studies in philosophy. She left Harvard after one year and briefly pursued a teaching career. In 1964, she joined the department of chemistry at Massachusetts Institute of Technology as a technician. It was during this time that the Richardsons began applying X-ray crystallography to the study of the molecular structure of proteins. While working at MIT, Jane also resumed her studies at Harvard University. She received an M.A. in philosophy of science and an M.A.T. in natural sciences in 1966.

Jane Richardson left MIT in 1969, to work in the Laboratory of Molecular Biology at the National Institutes of Health (NIH) in Bethesda, Maryland. Within the year, she moved to Durham, North Carolina, where she accepted a position as associate professor in the department of anatomy at Duke University. Fourteen years later, in 1984, Richardson became medical research associate professor in the department of biochemistry at Duke University. She was named James B. Duke Professor of Biochemistry in 1991.

During her tenure at Duke, Richardson continued her studies of protein structure. She also developed computer programs that displayed three-dimensional models of protein chains and demonstrated the folding mechanism that takes place as amino acids join together to form proteins. In addition to her ongoing research, Richardson also teaches both graduate and undergraduate biochemistry and serves as codirector of the Comprehensive Cancer Center at Duke University Medical Center.

Jane Richardson has been recognized for her achievements and pioneering research in the field of X-ray crystallography, applying technology to unraveling the code contained within the sequencing of folds in protein molecules. She was named a MacArthur Fellow and received the MacArthur "Genius" Award in 1985. That same year, she, her husband, David, and Bruce Erikson were jointly recognized in *Science Digest,* in the article "The Year's Top 100 Innovations." Swarthmore College awarded her an honorary doctorate of science the following year. In 1990, Richardson

received an honorary doctorate from Duke University. She was elected into both the National Academy of Sciences (NAS) and the American Academy of Arts and Sciences (AAAS) in 1991. In addition, the University of North Carolina at Chapel Hill presented her with an honorary doctorate in 1994.

> **See also** Biotechnology; Computers/Computer Technology; Crystallography; Genetic Engineering; National Academy of Sciences (NAS)
> **References** "Secret of Proteins Is Hidden in Their Folded Shapes," *New York Times* (14 June 1988); Shearer, Benjamin F., and Barbara S. Shearer, eds., *Notable Women in the Physical Sciences: A Biographical Dictionary* (1997); "Biochemical Michelangelos— SCULPTing large molecules with computers," available at http://www.sdsc.edu/MetaScience/Articles/sculpt.html (cited 23 February 1999); "Jane Shelby Richardson: James B. Duke Professor of Biochemistry," available at http://marini.biochem.duke.edu/Faculty/Richardson.html (cited 20 February 1999).

Ride, Sally Kirsten (b. 1951)

Sally Kirsten Ride will forever be known as the first American woman to go into space; however, her most significant contributions lie not in her space flights but in her role in developing new technology that continues to figure importantly in the space program. Specifically, Ride is the coinventor (with Judith A. Resnik) of the Remote Manipulator System (RMS)—a robotic arm for use in deploying or capturing satellites or other objects in space. Ride also played a key role in helping to investigate the cause of the explosion of the space shuttle *Challenger* in 1986, which resulted in the deaths of all seven of its crew members.

Sally Kirsten Ride was born in Los Angeles, California, on 26 May 1951. She is the daughter of Dale Ride, a political science professor at Santa Monica Community College, and Joyce Ride, a counselor at a women's correctional institution. Ride attended the Westlake School for Girls of that city, from which she graduated in 1968. She distinguished herself as a superior student and athlete during her teen years; she was ranked eighteenth on the national junior tennis circuit.

After graduating from high school, Ride began undergraduate studies in physics at

Swarthmore College in Pennsylvania. After her freshman year, she left Swarthmore to pursue a career in tennis; however, she soon decided to continue her education, and in 1970, enrolled at Stanford University. Ride graduated from Stanford in 1973, with bachelor's degrees both in physics and in English literature. A consummate scholar, Ride remained at Stanford after receiving her bachelor's degree and completed the requirements for an M.S. in physics in 1975 and a Ph.D. in astrophysics in 1978.

In 1977, while Ride was completing her Ph.D., she decided to respond to a classified ad placed by the National Aeronautics and Space Administration (NASA), which was seeking individuals to work as mission specialists. Ride had always wanted to go into space, so she applied for admission to NASA. Out of the more than 8,000 applicants, Ride was selected as one of only thirty-five to enter the astronaut training program in 1978. Six of these thirty-five individuals were women—the first ever to be selected for astronaut training by NASA.

Ride trained as an astronaut for two years. She was educated about computer systems, the launching of spacecraft, and flight maneuvering. During this training period, Ride and Resnik also developed the 50-foot robotic arm (the RMS) that would later become an essential part of NASA's shuttle program. The RMS provides a means of launching and retrieving satellites carried into space aboard the shuttle. Ride would have an opportunity to operate this robotic arm during her first flight into space, aboard the *Challenger* (mission STS-7), in 1983. Prior to this space flight, Ride had served as an on-orbit capsule communicator for the STS-2 and STS-3 missions, which also involved the *Challenger*.

Ride's historic six-day mission into space began on 18 June 1983. On that mission, she was responsible for monitoring various science experiments and operating the RMS. Ride made a second journey into space (aboard shuttle mission 41-G) from 5 to 13 October 1984. During this eight-day flight, Ride served as a mission specialist and assisted other crew members in the deployment of the Earth Radiation Budget Satellite.

Like her first flight, Ride's second flight into space also was historic because it marked the first space walk by a woman—crew member Kathryn D. Sullivan. Sullivan and crew member David C. Leestma carried out a space walk, known as an EVA (extravehicular activity), to demonstrate the capability of in-flight satellite refueling.

Ride was scheduled for a third trip into space in summer 1986, aboard shuttle mission 61-M. However, following the explosion of the *Challenger* on 28 January 1986, all subsequent shuttle launches were canceled until a cause for the disaster could be ascertained. It was also during this disaster that Ride lost her astronaut training classmate and RMS collaborator, Resnik. A commission was established following this incident to investigate the cause of the *Challenger* explosion. Ride was appointed to the commission, which was known as the Presidential Commission on the Space Shuttle Challenger Accident. She later went to work at NASA headquarters in Washington, D.C., where she served as special assistant to James Fletcher, the administrator for long-range and strategic planning. While working for Fletcher, Ride wrote a report, now known as the "Ride Report," in which she suggested changes in NASA's space exploration program.

Ride retired from NASA in fall 1987 to accept a fellowship in International Security and Arms Control at her alma mater, Stanford University. Two years later, she left Stanford to accept her current position as the director of the California Space Institute at the University of California at San Diego. For her work in the space program and as a role model for young American women, Sally Ride has received several awards and honors. Among them are two NASA Space Flight Medals (1983, 1984). In 1988, she also was inducted into the National Women's Hall of Fame.

See also Dunbar, Bonnie J.; Jemison, Mae; Lucid, Shannon Wells; National Aeronautics and Space Administration (NASA); National Women's Hall of Fame; Resnik, Judith A.; Space Exploration
References Chaikin, Andrew, "Sally Ride, 1983: The First American Woman in Space," *Working Woman* (November/December 1996); Felder, Deborah G., *A Century of Women: The Most Influential Events in 20th Century Women's History* (1999); National Aeronautics

and Aerospace Administration, *Astronaut Fact Book* (1992); Read, Phyllis J., and Bernard L. Witlieb, *The Book of Women's Firsts* (1992); "Sally Kirsten Ride: Pioneer in Space," in WIC Biography, available at http://www.wic.org/bio/sride.htm (cited 13 July 1999).

Rigas, Harriet B. (1934–1989)

Electrical engineer Harriet Rigas was known for her work in computer technology and computer engineering education. She created the technology that makes it feasible to update computer operating systems (analog and digital) through the use of automatic patches, such as that available today in software referred to as "upgrades." Such software eliminates the need to reinstall entire programs, saving both time and money. Rigas also improved methods used to create the codes used by computers to store and manipulate data.

Harriet Rigas was born in the Canadian city of Winnipeg, Manitoba. She attended Queens University in Ontario, and received a B.Sc. degree in 1956. For the next year, she worked as an engineer at the Mayo Clinic. She then began graduate studies at the University of Kansas in Lawrence, from which she received an M.S. degree in 1959 and a Ph.D. in electrical engineering in 1963. From 1963 to 1965, Rigas worked as an engineer at the Lockheed Missile and Space Company in Sunnyvale, California, and as an assistant professor at San Jose College.

Rigas joined the faculty of Washington State University (WSU) in 1965 and remained there until 1980, becoming manager of the school's Hybrid Facility in 1968 and professor of electrical engineering in 1976. At WSU, Rigas also created the university's computer engineering program, developed its curriculum, and raised funds to support the program.

While working at WSU, Rigas served also as a professor at the Naval Postgraduate School in Monterey, California. In 1980, she was named chair of the electrical engineering department at that school. In 1987, Rigas joined the faculty of Michigan State University, where she served as professor and chair of the electrical engineering department until her death in 1989.

Rigas participated on many panels and advisory committees. In the 1970s, she chaired the Commission on the Status of Women and served as president of the Association for Faculty Women. In 1975–1976, Rigas was a program director for the National Science Foundation (NSF); she later became a member of its Electrical, Computer, and Systems Engineering Advisory Committee. She also was a member of the Navy Research Advisory Committee and the National Academy of Sciences Advisory Committee.

In 1980, Rigas received the Engineer of the Year Award from the Spokane Section of the Institute of Electrical and Electronics Engineers (IEEE); she received IEEE's national Engineer of the Year Award in 1983. In 1982, she received the Achievement Award of the Society of Women Engineers (SWE) in recognition of her "significant contributions in electrical engineering and computer technology." The following year, the University of Kansas presented her with its Distinguished Engineering Service Award. Rigas was named a fellow of the IEEE in 1984. She also served on its board of directors and was an IEEE representative to the Accreditation Board for Engineering and Technology. She received that organization's Meritorious Award in 1988. Following her death in 1989, the IEEE posthumously bestowed on her its Rare Fellow Award; it also established the Harriet B. Rigas Award, to be presented annually to a woman who is an outstanding engineering educator. The Association for Faculty Women also instituted a Harriet B. Rigas Award, which recognizes a student for outstanding work in a doctoral program.

See also Butler, Margaret K.; Computers/Computer Technology; Conway, Lynn Ann; Electrical and Electronics Engineering; Granville, Evelyn Boyd; Hopper, Grace Murray; Institute of Electrical and Electronics Engineers (IEEE)

References McMurray, Emily M., ed., *Notable Twentieth-Century Scientists*, vol. 3: (L–R) (1995); Stanley, Autumn, *Mothers and Daughters of Invention: Notes for a Revised History of Technology* (1993); Hewlett Packard, "Harriett B. Rigas," available at http://www.hpl.hp.com/univafrs/awards/hrigas.htm (cited 13 March 1999).

Rockwell, Mabel MacFerran (1902–1979)

Formally trained as an electrical engineer, Mabel MacFerran Rockwell is credited with several innovations that have had an impact on a variety of engineering fields. One of her more noted accomplishments was her development of a method for locating transmission breakdowns in complex electrical systems (systems composed of many circuits). Rockwell also took part in the design and construction of the Colorado River Aqueduct power system and the installation of the electrical components at the Boulder Dam. In addition, she developed a method of streamlining aircraft production and lowering costs; helped design underwater propulsion and navigation systems; and participated in the design of the *Polaris* and *Atlas* missile launch control systems.

Mabel MacFerran was born to Edgar O. and Mabel Alexander MacFerran in Philadelphia, Pennsylvania, in 1902. She received her education at the Friends' School in the Germantown section of that city and later enrolled at nearby Bryn Mawr College. MacFerran was at Bryn Mawr only a short time before transferring to the Massachusetts Institute of Technology (MIT), where she was awarded a bachelor's degree in science in 1925. She graduated first in her class. The following year, she traveled to the opposite coast of the United States to pursue a master's degree at Stanford University in Menlo Park, California. She received a master's degree in electrical engineering in 1926, again graduating at the top of her class. In addition, MacFerran was elected a member of Sigma Xi.

After receiving her master's degree, MacFerran worked as a technical assistant for the Southern California Edison Company. There she developed a method of locating multiple electrical transmission failures transpiring concurrently at different locations within the system. This work permitted the company to increase the system's reliability. MacFerran's next position was with the Metropolitan Water District (MWD) of Southern California. At the MWD she was involved in the design of the power system that was used in the Colorado River Project. This system involved the construction of a vast hydroelectric power plant and of Hoover Dam (now Boulder Dam). MacFerran was the only woman actively involved with electrical installations at this dam. Shortly after this project's completion, MacFerran worked briefly for the U.S. Bureau of Reclamation, where her responsibilities included designing systems to carry and distribute water from the Central Valley Project dams to irrigation districts in Southern California.

Mabel MacFerran married electrical engineer Edward W. Rockwell in 1935. (The couple divorced in 1962.) One year after their marriage, they had their only child, a daughter named Margaret. Two years later, Mabel Rockwell returned to work, accepting a position as a plant electrical engineer with the Lockheed Aircraft Corporation in Burbank, California. When Rockwell started at Lockheed, she was involved with production research. Within two years, she was promoted to the position of production research engineer, where she was responsible for supervising more than twenty technicians who were working to develop methods that would speed the production of aircraft for use by the military. While working on this problem, Rockwell demonstrated that spot welding was far superior to riveting in aircraft assembly because it resulted in stronger bonds, accelerated production rates, and lowered production costs. She also developed techniques that provided the cleaner surfaces that were essential to strong welds as metals were fused. In addition, Rockwell studied ways to provide the large amounts of electrical power needed to obtain the high temperatures used in the welding process.

During and shortly after World War II (from 1941 to 1948), Rockwell worked for the U.S. Navy and the U.S. Air Force. Her responsibilities with the Navy included developing instrumentation for underwater propulsion systems and submarine guidance. She later served as an engineer at both the Naval Installation at Mare Island and the Naval Ordnance Test Station at Pasadena, in California. When she concluded her responsibilities with the Navy, Rockwell worked as an engineer at the McClellan Air Force Base in California, where she designed electric substations.

Following the war, Rockwell worked briefly for the Westinghouse Corporation. It was while working at Westinghouse that she was asked to design the electric control system for the *Polaris* missile launcher. Rockwell later did similar work at Convair, where she helped develop the launching and ground controls for the *Atlas* guided missile system.

In 1948, Rockwell returned to Stanford University to work as a consulting technical editor for the electrical engineering department. In this position, she edited the dissertations submitted by doctoral candidates as well as articles written by her colleagues. She remained in this position through much of the 1970s. During the 1960s and 1970s, Rockwell also served as a consulting technical writer for several companies located in the San Francisco Bay area of California.

Rockwell was well recognized for her many contributions to engineering. In 1958, President Dwight D. Eisenhower named her Woman Engineer of the Year. That same year, the Society of Women Engineers (SWE) presented her its Achievement Award in recognition for her contributions to the development of electrical control systems. Several papers Rockwell wrote, detailing the benefits of spot welding to the aircraft industry, also brought her awards.

See also Clarke, Edith; Electrical and Electronics Engineering; Fitzroy, Nancy D.; Granville, Evelyn Boyd; Johnson, Barbara Crawford; Ordnance; Rogers, Marguerite M.; Strong, Harriet R.
References Goff, Alice C., *Women Can Be Engineers* (1946); McMurray, Emily M., ed., *Notable Twentieth-Century Scientists*, vol. 3: (L–R) (1995); Stanley, Autumn, *Mothers and Daughters of Invention: Notes for a Revised History of Technology* (1993); Virginia Polytechnic Institute and State University, Bradley Department of Electrical Engineering, "Mabel MacFerran Rockwell," available at http://www.ee.vt.edu/~museum/women/rock/rock.html (cited 30 April 1999).

Rodgers, Dorothy (1909–1992)

Dorothy Rodgers developed a variety of inventions, for which she was awarded at least seven patents. Her earliest creation was a personal cooling device that she designed in the 1930s: a wristband that held a refrigerant near the wearer's wrist veins, cooling the body. Rodgers planned to exhibit this device at the scheduled 1939 New York World's Fair but was unable to do so due to World War II.

Rodgers's most notable invention was a sanitary cleaning device for toilets, which came to be called the "jonny mop." She sold her rights to the jonny mop to a manufacturing company for $10,000 plus royalties. However, she was forced into litigation when the company declined to pay the royalties due her for the invention. The manufacturer claimed it had changed the design of the mop, thus nullifying its royalty obligations to Rodgers. The courts, however, disagreed with this assertion, and Rodgers was awarded due compensation.

Another invention for which Rodgers obtained a patent was a device that allowed children to escape a refrigerator if they became trapped inside. This device was never put to use because refrigerator manufacturers claimed it would be too costly to install, even though the estimated cost of doing so was only about $1 per machine.

Rodgers later patented a reusable pattern that she sold to McCall's. The "try-on" patterns were made of fabric, allowing them to be washed, ironed, altered, and reused. The patterns were primarily used by dressmakers and schools offering dressmaking classes. Rodgers also developed an educational toy: a book that aided children who were learning to read, do arithmetic, or learn a foreign language. This idea was purchased by the Ideal Toy Company.

Although Rodgers's inventions brought her a measure of financial success, she referred to herself as a "substandard inventor"—perhaps unfavorably comparing her achievements to those of her famous husband, composer Richard Rodgers, whose credits included the Broadway hits "The King and I," "Carousel," and "The Sound of Music."

See also Butterick, Ellen; Demorest, Ellen Curtis; Domestic Appliances; Safety Engineering
References Grimes, William, "Dorothy Rodgers is Dead at 83; Writer, Inventor, and Decorator," *New York Times* (18 August 1992); Showell, Ellen H., and Fred M. B. Amram, *From Indian Corn to Outer Space: Women Invent in America* (1995); Vare, Ethlie Ann, and Greg Ptacek, *Mothers of Invention: From the Bra to the Bomb, Forgotten Women and Their Unforgettable Ideas* (1988).

Roebling, Emily Warren (1843–1903)

The dedication plaque on the Brooklyn Bridge lists Emily Warren Roebling, her husband, Washington Roebling, and her father-in-law, John Roebling, as builders of the bridge. Despite this fact, Emily Roebling rarely receives recognition for her contributions to the building of this famous structure. Shortly after construction began, John Roebling died from injuries suffered in an accident on the bridge. His son Washington also became a bridge casualty when he was paralyzed, lost his hearing and speech, and was partially blinded from caisson disease (the bends) in 1872. Washington developed the disease while working on the bridge's foundation. Following these problems with her family members, Emily Roebling took over the job of construction engineer on the project. As the only person able to communicate with her husband, she carried instructions and progress reports between him and bridge workers. Using her husband as a resource, Emily Roebling quickly learned about materials strengths, bridge specifications, and the higher mathematics needed to calculate the curves formed by free-hanging cables. She also learned the intricacies of cable construction. For 11 years, Roebling supervised the daily construction of the bridge. She was, in fact, the nation's first woman field engineer.

Emily was born in Cold Springs, New York. She traveled extensively with her husband, learning much about bridge construction and engineering. In 1882, she gave a speech before the American Society of Civil Engineers (ASCE) in which she pleaded that her husband be permitted to finish his work on the Brooklyn Bridge. This occasion marked the first time a woman addressed the ASCE. The speech proved effective, as the Roeblings were permitted to complete the construction they had begun. The bridge was completed the next year.

In addition to her contributions to the Brooklyn Bridge construction, Emily Roebling raised a son, John Roebling II. This remarkable woman proved that no task was too great a challenge, when at the age of 55 she earned a law degree from New York University.

See also American Society of Civil Engineers (ASCE); Bridges; Cambra, Jessie G.; Civil Engineering
References Kass-Simon, G., and Patricia Farnes, eds., *Women of Science: Righting the Record* (1990); Mann, Elizabeth, *The Brooklyn Bridge* (1996); Petroski, Henry, *Engineers of Dreams: Great Bridge Builders and the Spanning of America* (1995); ASEE, "Earliest Pioneers: Emily Warren Roebling," available at http://www.asee.org/pubs3/html/women_engineers.htm (cited 7 June 1998); Purdue University, Department of Engineering, "Emily Warren Roebling," in the Engineering-Specific Career Advisory Problem-Solving Environment, available at http://www.ecn.purdue.edu/ESCAPE/special/women/Histore/wiehistm.html (cited 7 June 1998).

Rogers, Marguerite M. (1916–1989)

Physicist Marguerite Rogers contributed to the design and development of weapon systems for the U.S. Navy, particularly those intended to be launched at ground targets by aircraft. Through this work, Rogers became an authority on the use of gunfire on military targets; aerial rocketry; and the effectiveness of air support weapons. She also developed the technology that makes possible the use of computerized electronic devices related to weaponry in aircraft.

Records documenting Rogers's early life are scarce. It is known that she attended Rice University, from which she received her bachelor's, master's, and doctoral degrees, all in physics. In 1940, she became an assistant professor at the University of Houston. She joined the Naval Avionics Facility in Indianapolis three years later. Here she managed the facility's Optics Section and Research Department.

From 1946 to 1948, Rogers worked as a research associate at the University of North Carolina. She then served as a senior physicist at the Oak Ridge National Laboratory for one year before joining the staff of the Naval Ordnance Test Station (NOTS), in China Lake, California. In 1953, Rogers left NOTS to join the faculty of Columbia College in South Carolina as a professor of physics and as chairperson of the science division.

In 1957, Rogers returned to NOTS, which was later renamed the Naval Air Warfare Center Weapons Division (NWC), as an electronics scientist. The following year, she became head of the

Heavy Attack Systems Analysis Branch. This position made her the first woman department head at the NWC.

In 1962, Rogers led the Air-to-Surface Weapons Division at the NWC. Four years later, she headed the Weapons Systems Analysis Division. In this position, Rogers became part of a team that was working to change the Navy's emphasis on use of nuclear weaponry to more conventional, but improved ordnance devices. During this time, she also aided in the development of a weapon series (known as the "eye") that proved effective during the Vietnam War. Rogers retired from the NWC in 1980.

In 1966, the NWC presented Rogers its highest honor—the L. T. E. Thompson Award—for her work in Naval weapons development. The same year she also received the Naval Air Systems Command Superior Civilian Service Award. She was presented both the Harvey C. Knowles Award of the American Ordnance Association and the Achievement Award of the Society of Women Engineers (SWE) in 1967. Nine years later, she was awarded the Federal Woman's Award. Rogers was presented the Department of Defense (DoD) Distinguished Civilian Service Award by the Secretary of Defense in 1981, becoming only the seventh woman to receive this honor. The award is the highest honor a civilian employee can be granted by the DoD.

See also Aeronautical and Aerospace Engineering; Computers/Computer Technology; Flügge-Lotz, Irmgard; Hopper, Grace Murray; Ordnance
References McMurray, Emily M., ed., *Notable Twentieth-Century Scientists,* vol. 3: (L–R) (1995); "Rogers Led the Way for Women—Devoted Her Life to Science" [obituary], *China Lake Rocketeer* (17 March 1989); Vare, Ethlie Ann, and Greg Ptacek, *Mothers of Invention: From the Bra to the Bomb, Forgotten Women and Their Unforgettable Ideas* (1988).

Rose, Mary Davies Swartz (1874–1941)

Educator Mary Rose helped establish nutrition as a scientific discipline. She is most known for her writings about nutrition and for organizing a nutrition department at Teachers College of Columbia University in New York; the department became a training center for teachers of nutrition. Rose also developed nutrition education programs for public schools.

Rose was born Mary Swartz in Newark, Ohio; she was raised in Wooster. After graduating from Wooster High School, she enrolled at Shepardson College (later part of Denison University) in 1894. Rose interrupted her studies in 1897 to teach at her alma mater; she then returned to Shepardson where she received a bachelor of letters degree in 1901. The following year, Swartz studied home economics at Mechanics Institute in Rochester, New York. After graduating there, she spent three years teaching home economics to high school students.

In 1905, Swartz entered Teachers College of Columbia University to study household arts. She received a B.S. degree the following year. Swartz then enrolled at Yale University, where she majored in physiological chemistry. She received a Ph.D. in 1909 and returned to Teachers College as its first full-time instructor of nutrition and dietetics.

Swartz married biochemist Anton R. Rose (a fellow graduate student at Yale) in 1910. The same year, she became an assistant professor of nutrition in the newly established department of nutrition at Teachers College's new School of Household Arts. Mary Rose later was promoted to associate professor (1918) and full professor (1921). At Teachers College, Rose developed instructional methods to help students acquire sound foundations in the scientific aspects of nutrition. She focused on energy metabolism and the nutritive values of vitamins and proteins in the body. Rose also published many books about the importance of nutrients in the body. Two of these, *A Laboratory Handbook for Dietetics* (1912) and *The Foundation of Nutrition* (1927), became important texts in the area. Other books by Rose include *Feeding the Family* (1916), *Everyday Foods in War Time* (1918), and *Teaching Nutrition to Boys and Girls* (1932).

Rose became a leading nutritional expert in the United States. During World War I, she was deputy director for New York City at the Bureau of Conservation of the Federal Food Administration. In 1935, she was appointed by the Health Committee of the League of Nations to study the physiological basis of nutrition. Five years later, the same year she retired from Teachers College, Rose became an advisor on nutrition to the Council of National Defense.

Rose was a member of the American Association for the Advancement of Science (AAAS), the American Society of Biological Chemists, the Society of Experimental Biology and Medicine, the American Home Economics Association, and the American Public Health Association. In 1919, she was elected an honorary member of the American Dietetic Association. She also was a charter member of the American Institute of Nutrition (now the American Society for Nutritional Sciences [ASNS]. Rose was associate editor of ASNS's *Journal of Nutrition* from 1928 to 1936 and served as its president from 1937 to 1938. To honor Rose's work, Teachers College created a scholarship in her name. In 1948, the Nutrition Foundation, Inc., established the Mary Swartz Rose Fellowship. The fellowship is presented by the American Dietetic Association to a graduate student working toward a Ph.D. in dietetics.

See also American Society for Nutritional Sciences (ASNS); Bevier, Isabel; Emerson, Gladys Anderson; Farmer, Fannie Merritt; Home Economics; Morgan, Agnes Fay; Richards, Ellen Henrietta Swallow
References Bailey, Martha J., *American Women in Science: A Biographical Dictionary* (1994); James, Edward T., Janet Wilson James, and Paul S. Boyers, *Notable American Women, 1607–1950: A Biographical Dictionary*, vol. 3: (P–Z) (1971); "Mary S. Rose Dead; Nutrition Expert," [Obituary], *New York Times* (2 February 1941); Merriam-Webster Inc., *Webster's Dictionary of American Women* (1996).

Rosenthal, Ida Cohen (1886–1973)

Ida Kaganovich was born in Minsk, Russia, in 1886. When she was in her late teens, she and her family emigrated because of the political unrest in their country. They came to the United States and eventually settled in Hoboken, New Jersey. There they adopted the name Cohen as the family surname. Shortly after arriving in Hoboken, Ida Cohen opened a small dressmaking shop.

Some time later, she married William Rosenthal, who assisted her in the shop.

Business flourished and the Rosenthals moved to larger quarters, on Manhattan's upper East Side. Around this time, Ida designed a bra that greatly improved upon the bra design of Caresse Crosby. Rosenthal's innovative creation consisted of cups intended to support the breasts and was offered in several sizes—a new feature. In addition, Rosenthal's garment was designed so that clothing worn over it draped naturally.

Rosenthal's bra was at first given away at no cost with each dress a woman purchased. However, women increasingly entered the shop, seeking to purchase only the bra. In response to the overwhelming demand for her product, Ida and her husband obtained the funds necessary to begin their own bra-making company, which they called the Maiden Form Brassiere Company, in 1923. By the late 1930s, the company was bringing in more than $4 million annually; 20 years later, the figure had reached a staggering $40 million. At the same time, facilities for production of the Maiden Form Bra were being established in Canada, England, and Puerto Rico.

William Rosenthal died in 1958, and Ida became president of the company, which was now called Maidenform, Inc. In 1973, when she contracted pneumonia and died, Maidenform, Inc. was taken over by Beatrice Coleman, her daughter.

See also Butterick, Ellen; Converse, Susan Taylor; Crosby, Caresse; Demorest, Ellen Curtis; Rodgers, Dorothy; Strickland, Sarah
References Felder, Deborah G., *A Century of Women: The Most Influential Events in 20th Century Women's History* (1999); Vare, Ethlie Ann, and Greg Ptacek, *Mothers of Invention: From the Bra to The Bomb, Forgotten Women and Their Unforgettable Ideas* (1988).

"Rosie the Riveter"

When the United States entered World War II in 1941, many of the nation's men left their jobs in industry to join the armed forces. Their departure resulted in a shortage of skilled workers. This shortage was most problematic in the factories and industries that made materials and products needed by the military to support the war effort. To address this workforce shortage, the federal government initiated a campaign designed to attract American women into the skilled labor force. In time, "Rosie the Riveter" emerged as the symbol of this campaign and the women who worked in the nation's factories.

Most married women did not work outside the home prior to World War II. Twenty-six states actually had laws prohibiting married women from working outside the home, while nepotism policies instituted by the federal government and many private industries also forbade the employment of women if their husbands also were employed by that facility. When the United States became involved in World War II, the need for skilled laborers forced the government and industry to drastically change these policies. In his Columbus Day speech of 1942, President Franklin Delano Roosevelt urged the industrial community to abandon their former prejudices and policies against women in the workplace as a means of filling the available jobs in America's defense-related industries.

More than 15 percent of married women joined the workforce to take war-related jobs between 1942 and 1944. Most of these women had no previous training or experience with technology or machinery. However, campaigns to entice women into technical fields played not only on their patriotism but on the idea that women who could operate such homemaking devices as a sewing machine or clothes wringer could learn to operate machinery such as a riveter or a drill press.

The release of the song "Rosie the Riveter," written by Redd Evans and John Jacob Loeb, in 1943, acknowledged the work being done by American women. Further acknowledgment came in a 29 May 1943 *Saturday Evening Post* cover featuring "Rosie the Riveter," a creation by noted American artist Norman Rockwell. Rockwell's depiction virtually institutionalized the character Rosie the Riveter as a representative of America's working women. Soon thereafter, in an attempt to bring even more women into the factories that were part of the war effort, the U.S. government began using Rockwell's creation to signify that defense-related jobs were "women's work."

See also Lamarr, Hedy; Manhattan Project; Ordnance
References Felder, Deborah, *A Century of Women: The Most Influential Events in 20th Century Women's History* (1999); Gluck, Sherna Berger, *Rosie the Riveter Revisited: Women, the War, and Social Change* (1987); Tobias, Sheila, and Lisa Anderson, "What Ever Happened to Rosie the Riveter?" *Ms.* (June, 1973).

Ross, Mary G. (b. 1908)

Mary Ross was an early leader in the research, development, and application of technology to ballistics, orbital mechanics, and astrophysics. Ross applied her mathematical skills to the area of ballistics when she was a member of an engineering team that developed defense systems for use by the U.S. military. Her skills in orbital mechanics and astrophysics were called into use again, when she was involved in developing the Agena rockets used in the *Apollo* space program as well as the *Polaris* reentry vehicle used during NASA's manned space flights. Prior to her retirement, Ross also conducted research that was essential to the development of the space probes that were sent to explore the planets Venus and Mars. Along with these professional contributions, Ross has devoted much time to encouraging young people to pursue careers in technology.

Mary Ross was born into a Cherokee family in Oklahoma in 1908. She is a descendant of John Ross, who served as the principal chief of the Cherokee Nation from 1828 to 1866. Throughout her life, Ross has maintained pride in her Cherokee heritage and has been recognized as a scholar of Cherokee culture and history. At a very early age, she developed interests in math and physics. She did well in her studies and graduated from high school at the age of 16.

Following high school, Ross entered Northeastern State Teachers' College in Tahlequah, Oklahoma, where she majored in mathematics. She graduated with a B.A. degree in 1928. For the next eight or nine years, Ross worked in public schools as a teacher of mathematics and science. During this same period, she also served as a girls' adviser at a coeducational school for students of Pueblo and Navajo heritage. Desiring to continue her own education, Ross returned to college, attending Colorado State Teachers' College (now the University of Northern Colorado at Greeley). There she obtained a master's degree in mathematics in 1938.

In 1942, Ross went to Burbank, California, to work as an assistant mathematician with Lockheed Aircraft Corporation. At the time, the country was embroiled in World War II, and Lockheed was one of the many companies working on projects that supported the war effort. Ross's responsibilities in this area involved formulating the calculations needed by the engineers who were working on problems related to the development of fighter and transport aircraft.

While she was working at Lockheed, Ross's supervisors recommended that she consider becoming an engineer. To achieve this, Ross continued her education, taking courses in aeronautical and mechanical engineering at the University of California, Los Angeles (UCLA). She graduated with a degree in mechanical engineering and in 1949 was registered as a professional engineer. After she had received this degree, Ross's work at Lockheed turned to engineering problems involving payloads and stress analysis. She also worked on problems related to supersonic aircraft—those able to break the sound barrier.

In 1954, Lockheed formed its Missiles Systems Division. Ross was the only female engineer selected to join the group. For the next five years, much of her work involved evaluating the performance of defense and ballistic missile systems. She also studied the effects of ocean wave velocities on ships and how water and pressure affected missiles launched from submarines.

In 1958, Lockheed became involved in new projects, and Mary Ross's career shifted from defense systems to space exploration. This change was largely due to the launch of the *Sputnik* satellite by the USSR in 1957—an event that initiated a space race between the United States and Russia. Ross was promoted to the position of research specialist. In this role, she studied satellite orbits and made the orbital calculations used by the Agena rockets that powered the *Apollo* space vehicles.

Ross received yet another promotion, this time to the position of advanced systems engineer. In this position, she worked on the *Polaris* reentry vehicle as well as engineering systems for use in manned space flights. Prior to her retirement in 1973, Ross also was involved in the design of the space probes being sent to Mars and Venus, which were to gather data as they flew past the planets.

Since her retirement, Ross has spent much of her time working with mentoring and career guidance programs. Through this work, she hopes to encourage more young girls and Native Americans to consider careers in technology, science, and mathematics. In recognition of this work, the Santa Clara Valley Section of the Society of Women Engineers (SWE) has established a scholarship in Ross's name. She also was honored with the Woman of Achievement Award from the California State Federation of Business and Professional Women's Clubs (1961); the Woman of Distinction Award from the *San Francisco Examiner* (1961); and the Contributions to Engineering and Community Award from Region VII of the Society of Manufacturing Engineers (1985). In 1990, she was honored with the Jessie Bernard Wise Women Award from the Center for Women Policy Studies. In recognition of her professional achievements, Ross has been presented with Achievement Awards from both the Council of Energy Resource Tribes and the American Indian Science and Engineering Society, both in 1985. In 1992, she was inducted into the Silicon Valley Engineering Hall of Fame.

Ross also holds memberships and is active in several professional organizations. Among them are the American Indian Science and Engineering Society and the Society of Women Engineers (SWE), in which she holds lifetime memberships. With the SWE, she has served as national treasurer (1969–1971) and national audit committee chairman (1977–1978) and on the Fellowship Selection Committee (1983–1984).

See also Aeronautical and Aerospace Engineering; Brill, Yvonne Claeys; Computers/Computer Technology; Granville, Evelyn Boyd; Hicks, Beatrice Alice; Johnson, Barbara Crawford; Johnson, Katherine Coleman Goble; Ordnance; Space Exploration

References Champagne, Duane, ed., *The Native North American Almanac: A Reference Work on North*

American Indians in the United States and Canada (1993); McMurray, Emily M., ed., *Notable Twentieth-Century Scientists*, vol. 3: (L–R) (1995); "Mary G. Ross," in Silicon Valley Engineering Hall of Fame, available at http://www.svec.org/hof/1992.html#ross (cited 7 May 1999).

Rozier, Betty
See **Vallino, Lisa M. and Rozier, Betty M.**

Rubin, Vera Cooper (b. 1928)

Astronomer Vera Cooper Rubin is an authority on the structure and rotation of galaxies and the movements of stars within them. She also is an expert in cosmology, the branch of astronomy that examines the structure and origin of the universe. Rubin was a pioneer in developing the technology that is now used to track and photograph astral spectra (an array of colors resulting when starlight passes through a prism). By examining these spectra, Rubin was able to determine the velocity and direction of movement of the stars comprising a galaxy. The results of this research led her to conclude that much of the universe is made up of matter that is "dark," or invisible to the unaided eye. Other astronomers have since corroborated her hypothesis.

Vera Cooper was born in Philadelphia, Pennsylvania, in 1928. By the age of 12, she had already decided that she would one day become an astronomer. Vera's father, Philip Cooper, an electrical engineer, was a significant figure in his daughter's early life. He helped her build her first telescope when she was only 14. He also accompanied her when she attended local amateur astronomy meetings. Vera attended Coolidge High School in Washington, D.C., and graduated in 1945. That same year she was offered a scholarship to attend Vassar College in Poughkeepsie, New York. At that time, Vassar, an all-female college, was among a small number of colleges that offered a program in astronomy to women. Cooper was the only astronomy major in the school.

In 1947, Cooper met Robert Rubin, a graduate student in physical chemistry at Cornell University in Ithaca, New York. The following year they married, and Vera Rubin also graduated with a B.A. degree in astronomy from Vassar College. She had hoped to pursue graduate studies in astrophysics at Princeton University; but after she learned that Princeton did not accept women into its graduate astrophysics program, she decided to attend Cornell University.

Vera enrolled at Cornell as a graduate student in astronomy. She received her M.A. from that school in 1951. While pursuing her graduate degree, she studied the motions of galaxies—a subject that would become the focus of her master's thesis and of her life's work. Prior to receiving her master's degree in 1950, Rubin delivered a presentation at a conference of the American Astronomical Society. Her presentation introduced her belief that galaxies might be rotating around some yet-to-be-defined center, while moving outward at the same time, in accordance with the theory of the expanding universe. At the time, her work was viewed with much skepticism, partly because there was no other proof to support such findings, and partly because Rubin was a 22-year-old female graduate student.

In 1951, Rubin received her master's degree and her husband received his Ph.D. The Rubins then moved to Washington, D.C., where Robert had been offered a position at the National Bureau of Standards (now the National Institute of Standards and Technology). Vera enrolled at Georgetown University, where she began her doctoral studies. She received her Ph.D. in astronomy in 1954. While conducting her doctoral research, Rubin showed that galaxies were not randomly dispersed, as scientists previously thought, but that they were in fact grouped closely together.

After receiving her Ph.D., Rubin accepted a position teaching mathematics and physics at Montgomery County Junior College. The following year, she accepted a position as a research associate at Georgetown University. In 1963, Rubin took a one-year leave to conduct research at the University of California at San Diego. There she shared her theories and collaborated with noted astrophysicist Margaret Burbidge and her husband, who were conducting research on quasars (quasi-stellar radio sources). The Burbidges were noted for their pioneering research on the fusion theory they developed to explain the presence of heavier elements in stars in the early 1950s.

Rubin left Georgetown University in 1965 and accepted a position as an observational astronomer with the Department of Terrestrial Magnetism at the Carnegie Institution in Washington, D.C.; she remains in this position today. During the 1970s, Rubin's research emphasis shifted back to the work she had done while preparing her master's thesis—the motions of galaxies. Rubin, in collaboration with core-searcher and physicist W. Kent Ford, conducted spectroscopic studies of galaxies. Her research findings strongly suggested that stars orbiting the galaxy at its outer edge traveled as fast as those closer to the center of the galaxy. This finding clearly contradicted an earlier supposition—namely, that stars orbiting at the outer edge of a galaxy traveled more slowly that those closer to the center, much like the motion of planets orbiting the sun. Rubin suggests that some enormous, yet-to-be explained, invisible mass is exerting a gravitational force strong enough to keep the stars in their orbits. She refers to this invisible, ill-defined mass as "dark matter." After conducting additional research, Rubin and Ford theorized that a large number of galaxies are moving rapidly with respect to the rest of the universe. This theory, known as the "Rubin-Ford effect," suggests that matter is not evenly distributed throughout the universe but exists in clumps. Furthermore, these clumps exert enormous gravitational forces that have an accelerating effect on the movements of galaxies.

Rubin has authored many articles published in journals such as the *Astrophysical Journal,* the *Astronomical Journal,* and the *Bulletin of the American Astronomical Society.* She has served as an associate editor for the *Astronomical Journal* and the *Astrophysical Journal* Letters, and as a member of the editorial board of *Science* magazine. In 1981, she was elected a member of the National Academy of Sciences (NAS). She holds honorary D.Sc. degrees from Harvard, Yale, and Creighton Universities. Rubin was awarded the National Medal of Science by President Bill Clinton in 1993.

See also Astronomy; Burbidge, (Eleanor) Margaret Peachey; Maury, Antonia; Payne-Gaposchkin, Cecelia; Sitterly, Charlotte Moore; Spectroscopy; Whiting, Sarah Frances

References Ambrose, Susan A., et al., *Journeys of Women in Science and Engineering: No Universal Constants* (1997); Bailey, Martha J., *American Women in Science, 1950 to the Present: A Biographical Dictionary* (1998); Fins, Alice, *Women in Science* (1979); McMurray, Emily M., ed., *Notable Twentieth-Century Scientists,* vol. 3: (L–R) (1995); Yount, Lisa, *Contemporary Women Scientists* (1994); San Jose State University, "Vera Cooper Rubin," in Virtual Museum, available at http://www.sjsu.edu/depts/Museum/rubinv.html (cited 24 July 1999); "Vera Rubin to Speak on 'What Hubble Didn't Know about Galaxies,'" available at http://myhouse.com/NCA/Vera_Talk_intro.htm (cited 24 July 1999).

Russell, Lillian (1861–1922)

It is not known who coined the phrase "Necessity is the mother of invention"; however, this phrase certainly applied to Lillian Russell's invention of a dresser-trunk. When Russell designed her invention, her career as a stage singer and actress required frequent travel. She wished to make her life easier by having a dressing trunk, complete with drawers, mirrors, and lighting fixtures, that kept her clothing and makeup organized during performances yet folded to a smaller size for shipping. The trunk for which Russell received U.S. Patent No. 1,014,353 on 16 January 1912 met her needs. Unfortunately, it did not catch on with the traveling public as she had hoped.

Lillian Russell was born Helen Louise Leonard in Clinton, Iowa, in 1861. After studying acting in Chicago, she obtained her first professional job in a New York City production of Gilbert and Sullivan's *H.M.S. Pinafore* (1879) as a chorus member. For the next 20 years, Russell sang in various opera companies in England and the United States. She later joined the Weber and Fields burlesque company of New York, for whom she worked until 1904. With this company, Russell became the highest paid actress of her day, earning as much as $1,200 per week.

In 1904, voice problems forced Russell to give

up her singing career. She turned her attention toward comedy until 1908, when she briefly resumed her singing career. She then worked as a columnist for the Pittsburgh *Leader,* a newspaper owned by her fourth husband, Alexander Pollock Moore. Later, she turned her talents toward raising money for the World War I war effort. She sold war bonds, raised money for the American Legion, and served as a recruiter for the U.S. Marine Corps. Russell served her country again in 1922, when President Harding asked her to tour Europe as a special investigator for immigration. Russell died that same year, shortly after completing her tour.

See also Domestic Appliances; Goode, Sarah E.; Invention/Inventors; Lamarr, Hedy

References Macdonald, Anne L., *Feminine Ingenuity: How Women Inventors Changed America* (1992); Vare, Ethlie, and Greg Ptacek, *Mothers of Invention: From the Bra to the Bomb, Forgotten Women and Their Unforgettable Ideas* (1988); University of Rochester Library, "D.18: Lillian Russell Papers, 1876–1886," available at http://rodent.lib.rochester.edu/RBK/ LRUSSELL.HTM (cited 15 March 1999).

S., Mary (ca. 1851–1880)

The existence of the inventor known only as Mary S. of St. Louis, Missouri, was revealed by Charlotte Smith, in her 1891 periodical *The Woman Inventor*. According to Smith's reports, Mary S. developed at least 53 inventions worthy of patents during her brief life, even though no patents exist in her name. This achievement makes her one of the most prolific women inventors of her time. However, like many early women inventors, Mary S. sold the rights to her inventions to male agents for a small fee, instead of applying for patents in her own name. The agents, in turn, obtained patents for the inventions in their names. The agents who bought rights to Mary S.'s inventions were able to profit greatly from her work, but Mary died in poverty at the age of 30.

See also Eglin, Ellen F.; Inventions/Inventors; Kies, Mary; Patent; Patent Act of 1790

References Stanley, Autumn, *Mothers and Daughters of Invention: Notes for a Revised History of Technology* (1993); Lemelson-MIT Program, "Prolific Female Inventors of the Industrial Era," in Invention Dimension Inventor of the Week archives, available at http://web.mit.edu/www/invent/inventorsR-Z.whm2.html (cited 17 January 1999).

Safety Engineering

Safety engineering is concerned with eliminating unsafe or hazardous practices and conditions that can result in personal injury or property damage in industrial plants, construction sites, mines, and transportation systems (rails, highways, and waterways). Safety engineers identify potential physical and environmental hazards then develop and design programs and systems to monitor, control, or eliminate these hazards. In addition, safety engineers coordinate safety and first-aid training and instruct workers and supervisory staff on how to implement safe practices and programs.

Safety engineers use many techniques to identify potentially hazardous conditions. They check and test equipment and conduct surveys. They also make recommendations on the use and type of protective clothing as well as fixtures and structures dealing with fire, chemical, and elec-

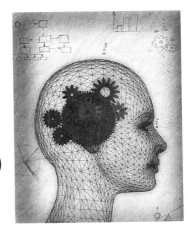

trical safety. Recently, safety engineers have played an expanded role in making home products safer. In this role, they consult with design engineers and other engineering specialists to improve the quality and design of home products, electrical appliances (including tools and power equipment), and items designed for use by children, such as toys, clothing, and furniture.

See also Anderson, Elda Emma; Baker, Sara Josephine; Hamilton, Alice; Industrial Engineering; Knight, Margaret E.

References Barnes-Svarney, Patricia, ed., *The New York Public Library Science Desk Reference* (1995); Cosgrove, Holli R., ed., *Encyclopedia of Careers and Vocational Guidance,* 10th ed., vol. 4 (1996); U.S. Department of Labor, Bureau of Labor Statistics, *Occupational Outlook Handbook,* Bulletin 2500 (1998–1999).

Scott, Charlotte Agnes
See **American Mathematical Society; Bryn Mawr College**

Seibert, Florence Barbara (1897–1991)

Tuberculosis, commonly called TB (or in earlier times, consumption), is a highly infectious respiratory disease that is caused by a rod-shaped bacterium, or bacillus. The early symptoms of this disease often are similar to those of the common cold or flu, and like these illnesses, TB can

Biochemist Florence Seibert developed a skin test for use in diagnosing tuberculosis. (Bettmann-Corbis)

rapidly spread throughout a population if not detected. When undetected and untreated, TB can be fatal. Today, TB is easily detected through the use of a diagnostic skin test called a tine test. Among the more common skin tests now used to detect TB in humans is one that was developed between the late 1930s and early 1940s by American biochemist Florence Barbara Seibert.

Florence Barbara Seibert was born in Easton, Pennsylvania, in 1897. As a child, she contracted polio (a common disease at that time), which affected her legs. Damage resulting from this childhood illness required her to walk with a cane throughout her life. It may also have been her early exposure to disease that led Seibert to pursue a career related to medicine.

After completing her high school education, Seibert enrolled at Goucher College in Baltimore, Maryland, where she studied chemistry and zoology. She earned her bachelor's degree from this school in 1918. Seibert then accepted employ-

ment as a chemist with a paper mill located in Garfield, New Jersey. She submitted her application for this position in response to a call to America's women to help fill positions in industrial and technological fields that had been vacated by men who enlisted in the military during World War I. Seibert later left this position to enroll in a graduate program at Yale University in New Haven, Connecticut.

At Yale, Seibert focused her studies on determining why people often developed fevers in response to injections of medications composed of proteins. While researching this subject, Seibert discovered that it was not the proteins that were causing the reaction but contaminants present in the distilled water with which the proteins had been mixed to provide an injection medium. To remedy this problem, Seibert developed a distillation apparatus that produced nearly sterile distilled water. This apparatus would later play a significant role in the development of safer intravenous (IV) treatments. For her work in this area, Seibert was awarded a doctorate from Yale in 1923.

Seibert was awarded a one-year fellowship to the University of Chicago upon completion of her doctoral program. After completing this fellowship, she joined the faculty of the University of Chicago, where she taught and continued her research on distilled water and fever-causing bacteria for the next nine years.

In 1932, Seibert left the University of Chicago to accept a research position at a facility within the University of Pennsylvania that was studying tuberculosis. Seibert began her research in this area by revisiting earlier research that had been carried out by noted bacteriologist Robert Koch in the 1890s. In his research, Koch had succeeded in demonstrating that if a sample of culture medium on which TB-causing bacteria had previously been grown was injected beneath the skin of an individual who was infected with TB, a distinctive reaction would result at the injection site. Koch was unable to explain why this reaction occurred. He did, however, speculate that the reaction might result from the presence of a protein in the culture medium.

Building on Koch's hypothesis, Seibert successfully identified and isolated the protein Koch had speculated about, in pure, crystalline form. She then used this protein to develop a skin test that proved successful in detecting the presence of the TB-causing bacillus in the body of a person infected with the disease. By 1941, methods for purifying the test protein were perfected and reproduced in a manner that made the test widely available. The following year, the test was standardized and approved for use throughout the world. Despite its approval, however, it would take several years before many physicians would adopt the test in their practices.

After Seibert developed the skin test—for which she is best-known—she remained at the University of Pennsylvania, where she worked as both a professor and a researcher, until her retirement in 1959. During her last years at the university, she continued her efforts to gain wider usage of the TB test she had developed earlier. The onset of World War II occurred at about the same time that Seibert's TB test was developed. This event, combined with a reluctance on the part of many members of the male-dominated medical community to make use of a test developed by a woman, prevented the test's wide acceptance and use. In 1952, Seibert appeared before the World Health Organization (WHO), where she successfully argued for acceptance and standardization of her TB test.

After retiring from the University of Pennsylvania in 1959, Seibert moved to Florida. She lived there until her death in 1991.

Seibert was well recognized for her work on developing a test for TB. Among the many awards bestowed upon her were the Trudeau Medal of the National Tuberculosis Association (1938); the Garvan Medal of the American Chemical Society (1942); the Gimbel Philadelphia Award (1945); the Distinguished Daughters of Pennsylvania Medal (1950); and the John Elliot Memorial Award (1962). Seibert was elected to the National Women's Hall of Fame in 1990.

See also Dick, Gladys Rowena Henry; Francis P. Garvan–John M. Olin Medal; Logan, Myra Adele; Medicine/Medical Technology; National Women's Hall of Fame; Pharmacology

References Block, Maxine, ed., *Current Biography, 1942* (1942); Lambert, Bruce, "Dr. Florence B. Seibert, Inventor of Standard TB Test, Dies at 93" [obituary], *New York Times* (31 August 1991); Saari, Peggy, and Stephen Allison, eds., *Scientists: The Lives and Works of 150 Scientists* (1966); Weatherford, Doris, *American Women's History: An A to Z of People, Organizations, Issues, and Events* (1994).

Seven College Conference

During the mid- to late nineteenth century, a number of small, private, liberal arts colleges, most of which were located in the northeast, opened their doors for the specific purpose of educating women. These schools offered young women coursework that was intended to provide the foundations necessary to perform long-established domestic responsibilities, which included maintaining a home and raising children.

In 1926, seven of these colleges, namely Mount Holyoke College, Vassar College, Wellesley College, Smith College, Radcliffe College, Bryn Mawr College, and Barnard College established educational and philosophical ties that led to the creation of a coalition of these schools, then known as the "Seven Sister Colleges" and today known as the Seven College Conference. M. Carey Thomas, educator, suffragist, and president of Bryn Mawr College (1894–1922), assumed a leadership role when she advocated educational change that would lead to academic and professional excellence. High tuition costs, financial support provided by the families of students in attendance at these colleges, and the generosity of alumni, ensured a quality education that often was compared to that offered in all-male Ivy League schools. This educational excellence was demonstrated in the sciences as well as in the humanities.

See also Barnard College; Bryn Mawr College; Carr, Emma Perry; Mount Holyoke College; Vassar College; Wellesley College; Whiting, Sarah Frances
References Cullen-DuPont, Kathryn, *The Encyclopedia of Women's History in America* (1998); Heinemann, Susan, *Timelines of American Women's History* (1996); Olsen, Kirstin, *Chronology of Women's History* (1994).

Seven Sister Colleges
See **Seven College Conference**

Shaw, Mary (b. 1943)

Mary Shaw is a computer science expert whose research has contributed much to the current understanding of computer software—specifically, to its development, design, and applications. Shaw has devised algorithms (mathematically precise procedures for carrying out a process) for solving complex computer problems. In addition, she has increased the speed and efficiency of computational processes by evaluating the mathematical expressions used in these processes—an area known as software architecture. Shaw also has improved programmer productivity by creating powerful computer languages and has devoted much of her time to establishing the design and development of software systems as a distinct engineering discipline.

Mary Shaw was born in Washington, D.C., in 1943. She began expressing an intense interest in mathematics, science, and electronics during her middle school years. While attending high school in Bethesda, Maryland, Shaw participated in an after-school program involving computers that was conducted by an IBM employee. It was while participating in this program that she had an opportunity to visit the IBM Space Computer Center in Washington, D.C., an event that sparked her interest in computers. During her junior and senior years and for one year after her high school graduation, Shaw also participated in a summer program involving computers for advanced students sponsored by the Operation Research Office of Johns Hopkins University in Baltimore, Maryland.

After graduating from high school, Shaw enrolled in 1961 at Rice University in Houston, Texas, where she expressed an early interest in studying mathematics. However, she changed her focus to computer programming after visiting and then participating in the Rice Computer Project, a group of faculty members and graduate students involved in the construction of a computer called the Rice I. While participating in this

project, Shaw developed a programming language and worked on routines that were used to increase the speed and efficiency of the system. She remained with the project for the duration of her undergraduate studies.

After completing her junior year at Rice University, Shaw attended a summer institute at the University of Michigan. While there, she met Alan Purlis, a professor from Carnegie Mellon University. She became very intrigued by his work. After Shaw graduated from Rice University *cum laude* with a B.A. degree in mathematics in 1965, she enrolled in the newly created Department of Computer Sciences at Carnegie Mellon University, in Pittsburgh, Pennsylvania. Alan Purlis, whom she had met during the summer while studying at the University of Michigan, became her adviser.

At Carnegie Mellon, Shaw continued her computer studies and became involved in researching compilers—programs that convert human language into a language form that can be used by computers. Shaw received her Ph.D. in computer science in 1971. She then joined the Computer Science Department at Carnegie Mellon University, becoming its first woman faculty member. For the next several years, Shaw continued her work on compilers. It was also during this time that she began doing research on algorithms and software architecture. She collaborated with Joseph Traub in developing the Shaw-Traub algorithm—a means of evaluating a mathematical expression (consisting of one or more variables) that increases the speed and efficiency of a computer.

In addition to her work on compilers and algorithms, Shaw developed an interest in finding ways to improve software design—specifically, by organizing data in computer programs. From 1974 to 1978, she developed programs called abstract-data types (ADTs). ADTs serve as tools for program development by organizing and grouping the related sets of data and operational procedures used by a computer program. The final elements of Shaw's work in simplifying complex computer programs came about with the development of Alphard, a computer language that implements ADT. She developed Alphard in collaboration with two other computer scientists, William A. Wulf and Ralph L. London. She also simplified programming abstracts so that they were more closely related to the computer language than they were to the operational limitations of the machine itself.

In 1981, Shaw formed a group consisting of college faculty members and undergraduate students at Carnegie Mellon University for the purpose of designing a curriculum that would lead to an undergraduate degree in computer science. The curriculum developed by the group was implemented by Carnegie Mellon, and later, adopted by many other universities. In addition, Shaw has worked with the Information Systems Division at IBM, where the curriculum she developed is used as an in-house training program.

Shaw was instrumental in creating the Software Engineering Institute (SEI) at Carnegie Mellon University in 1984. She served as its chief scientist until 1987. She then became involved in software architecture—a new engineering discipline that supports the design and development of software systems.

Shaw became a member of Sigma Xi in 1972. She received the Association for Computing Machinery's (ACM) Recognition of Service Award in 1985, and again in 1990. In 1990, she also was elected a fellow of the Institute of Electrical and Electronics Engineers (IEEE). Her papers on "Prospects for an Engineering Discipline of Software" and "An Introduction to the Construction and Verification of Alphard Programs" also have received recognition. In 1992, Shaw was elected a fellow of the American Association for the Advancement of Science (AAAS). The next year she was presented the Warner Prize for contributions to software engineering and systems development methods. Shaw was named to the Alan J. Purlis chair of computer science in 1995 and the next year became a fellow of ACM. Currently, Shaw holds an appointment at the Software Engineering Institute and serves as its Associate Dean for Professional Programs. For the 1997–1998 school year, Shaw received a fellowship at the Center for Innovation in Learning, at Carnegie Mellon University.

See also Bernstein, Dorothy Lewis; Butler, Margaret K.; Computers/Computer Technology; Conway, Lynn Ann; Estrin, Thelma; Granville, Evelyn Boyd; Hopper, Grace Murray; Mathematics; Rigas, Harriet B.
References Ambrose, Susan A., et al., *Journeys of Women in Science and Engineering: No Universal Constants* (1997); Bailey, Martha J., *American Women in Science, 1950 to the Present: A Biographical Dictionary* (1998); Torpie, Stephen L., et al., eds., *American Men and Women of Science,* 18th ed. (1992–1993) (1992); Ross, Leslie, "Mary Shaw, Woman in Computing," available at http://cc.kzoo.edu/~k96Ir01/maryshaw.html (cited 11 June 1999).

Sherman, Patsy O. (b. 1930)

The product that has come to be known as Scotchgard® is present in many homes throughout the world. In addition, this product is used on many materials used in home decorating, such as carpeting and upholstery, before they ever leave the factory. One might expect such a product to result from years of market research and laboratory work. However, this product actually resulted, in part, from a laboratory accident.

Patsy Sherman, the product's inventor, became a research chemist for the 3M Company in 1952. Among her first assignments with the company was a mandate to develop a rubber material that was not prone to decomposition, for use in making jet fuel hoses. While Sherman's team was working on this project, the latex emulsion they developed was accidentally spilled onto a pair of shoes. It was while trying to clean up the spilled chemical that Sherman observed it had some unusual and potentially useful properties. First, the substance resisted removal from the shoes, even when a variety of solvents had been applied to it. In addition, the product actually repelled water and other liquids. These observations led the research team to conclude that the properties of this substance might make it useful as a protective agent for fabrics. Sherman's team proposed their idea for such a product to the company and obtained permission to conduct further research to develop their idea. The product now known as Scotchgard® emerged in 1956. This product has had a great impact on the textile industry and is now used worldwide.

Sherman and her main collaborator, Sam Smith, obtained a patent for the Scotchgard® formula, and immediately assigned the patent rights to the 3M Company. Sherman and Smith also obtained patents for several other materials they developed while working for 3M. In addition to having her name appear on these patents, Sherman was recognized for her role as an inventor through her induction into the Minnesota Inventors' Hall of Fame in 1989. The following year, Patsy Sherman's invention was displayed along with those of other women inventors in a special exhibit at the U.S. Patent and Trademark Office titled "Woman's Place Is in the Patent Office." Patsy Sherman retired from the 3M Company in 1992.

See also Gabe, Frances Bateson; Greneker, Lillian; Kwolek, Stephanie Louise; Patent; Textiles
References Flanaghan, Barbara, Resource Center Coordinator, 3M Public Relations, e-mail correspondence with Alan Winkler (11 August 1999); Macdonald, Anne L., *Feminine Ingenuity: How Women Inventors Changed America* (1992); Showell, Ellen H., and Fred M. B. Amram, *From Indian Corn to Outer Space: Women Invent in America* (1995); Smithsonian Institution, "Innovative Lives," available at http://www.si.edu/lemelson/Lect11.htm (dated 5 February 1999; cited 23 July 1999).

Sherrill, Mary Lura (1888–1968)

Mary Sherrill used her skills as a chemist to synthesize and purify organic compounds for use in spectroscopic analysis. The data obtained from these purified compounds were used by Sherrill's colleague at Mount Holyoke College, Emma P. Carr, to test new theories about molecular structure. During World War I, Sherrill developed and patented several gases that caused sneezing when mixed with illuminating gas to prevent accidental asphyxiation. During World War II, she investigated the synthesis of antimalarial drugs to replace quinine, which had become unavailable. Sherrill was also responsible for obtaining the first National Research Council (NRC) instrument grant to a women's college when she received monies to purchase a vacuum spectrograph for Mount Holyoke College.

Mary Sherrill was born in Salisbury, North Carolina. She entered Randolph-Macon Women's College in Lynchburg, Virginia, in 1906 and received an A.B. in chemistry three years later. She remained at Randolph-Macon, taking graduate courses and working as a chemistry assistant. In 1911, she received an M.A. in physics and joined the Randolph-Macon staff to teach chemistry. In the summer of 1914, Sherrill entered the University of Chicago; she spent the next two summers and the entire 1916–1917 academic year working toward a Ph.D. in chemistry. She was awarded this degree in 1923.

Sherrill worked at Randolph-Macon as an adjunct professor of chemistry from 1917 to 1918, and as associate professor of chemistry at North Carolina College for Women from 1918 to 1920. During World War I, she was experimenting with gases as a research associate with the Chemical Warfare Service (CWS). In September 1921, she became assistant professor of chemistry at Mount Holyoke College, rising to associate professor in 1924, full professor in 1930, and department chair in 1946. She held this last position until her retirement in 1954.

Sherrill was awarded the Garvan Medal from the American Chemical Society (ACS) in 1947 for her outstanding work in education and with antimalarial drugs. The next year, the University of North Carolina presented her with an honorary D.Sc. degree. In 1957, she shared with Emma Carr the James Flack Norris Award of the Northeastern Section of the ACS, for outstanding teaching of chemistry.

See also Carr, Emma Perry; Elion, Gertrude Belle; Francis P. Garvan–John M. Olin Medal; Mount Holyoke College; Patent; Spectroscopy
References Grinstein, Louise S., Rose K. Rose, and Miriam H. Rafailovich, eds., *Women in Chemistry and Physics: A Biobibliographic Sourcebook* (1993); Robertson, Patrick, ed., *The Book of Firsts* (1975); Shearer, Benjamin F., and Barbara S. Shearer, eds., *Notable Women in the Physical Sciences: A Biographical Dictionary* (1997); Mount Holyoke College, Archives and Special Collections, "Chemistry Department Records, 1897– ," available at http://www.mtholyoke.edu/offices/library/arch/col/rg18ii.htm (cited 5 February 2000).

Shirley, Donna (b. 1941)

Oklahoma native Donna Shirley is the Director of the Mars Exploration Program at the Jet Propulsion Laboratory (JPL). In the late 1990s, Shirley's work in this program resulted in the exploration of Mars by a small vehicle similar in apearance to a child's remote-controlled car, called the Sojourner. The Sojourner was the first such vehicle used in the exploration of another planet.

Donna Shirley was born in Wynnewood, Oklahoma, in 1941. At the age of ten, she had already decided that she wanted someday to become an aeronautical engineer. Throughout her childhood, Shirley developed an avid interest in flying and space. To encourage this interest, her parents gave her flying lessons for her fifteenth birthday. After completing these lessons, by age 16, Shirley had earned her pilot's license; she was flying solo before she graduated from high school.

Following high school, Shirley attended the University of Oklahoma at Norman. Having been discouraged by a professor from pursuing her chosen major in aeronautical studies, Shirley changed her major to writing. She earned a bachelor's degree in this field in 1963. After obtaining her degree, Shirley accepted a position as a technical writer with McDonnell Aircraft, in St. Louis, Missouri. Knowing that she did not want to be a techical writer for the rest of her life, Shirley decided to return to college. She again attended the University of Oklahoma, from which she received a B.S. degree in aerospace engineering in 1965.

After receiving her engineering degree, Shirley again worked with McDonnell Aircraft. In 1966, she joined the staff of the Jet Propulsion Laboratory (JPL) of the National Aeronautics and Space Administration (NASA) as an aerodynamist. Shirley spent part of her first year at the JPL designing spacecraft that would someday be sent to Mars. When the funding for this project was cut, Shirley was for a brief time left without work. After completing her master's degree in aerospace engineering at the University of Southern California, she was able to obtain another position with the JPL. This project involved the development of an automated drug-identification system. However, due to the limits of available technology, research in this area was halted.

Around 1970, Shirley began work as a mission analyst for the *Mariner* Venus–Mercury expedition, which was to take place in 1973. During the development of the project, Shirley was promoted to the position of project engineer. The *Mariner 10* mission was considered a success despite numerous mechanical difficulties. Shirley was later presented a Group Achievement Award for her work on this project.

Late in 1979, Shirley began work on a vehicle that would orbit and drop probes into the atmospheres of Saturn and Titan (one of Saturn's moons). This preliminary work led to the *Cassini* mission, which was launched in 1997. Shirley joined and later headed a team studying the feasibility of creating a space station. While working on this project, Shirley developed a knowledge of robotics. For her work on the space station development, Shirley received a second NASA Group Achievement Award, in 1985.

In 1987, NASA again began investigating the possibility of sending a spacecraft to Mars. The goal of the mission would be to collect samples from Mars and then return to Earth. Shirley was asked to lead the team that was assembled to design a rover for this mission. The team designed a one-ton rover that was expected to cost approximately $10 million to construct. This high cost led to the revocation of funding for the project in 1990.

Shirley believed that a smaller, lighter, and much less expensive rover could be developed to explore Mars. Although most of her team members did not believe a small machine could be successful in this area, Shirley was given an opportunity to seek funding for her idea. She did obtain the necessary financial support, and the design of the minirover was begun. In addition to designing a smaller rover, a means needed to be developed to get the rover onto the surface of Mars. The rover was placed aboard the *Pathfinder* landing craft. Once the *Pathfinder* was on the surface of Mars, it released the Sojourner rover. The small vehicle moved about the planet at a low speed, analyzing the composition of the planet's soil and rocks. This information was then sent back to the *Pathfinder,* which radioed the data back to scientists on Earth.

The most notable problem that occurred during the mission was a temporary, unexplained loss of radio contact between the Sojourner and the *Pathfinder.* Despite this problem, the Sojourner was generally perceived as a success, and it is likely that similar technologies will be used in space exploration projects in the future. In the meantime, Shirley continues to head the JPL's Mars Exploration Program.

Shirley also participates in a number of professional organizations such as Women in Technology International (WITI), hoping to encourage other women to pursue scientific and technical careers.

See also Askins, Barabara; Jet Propulsion Laboratory (JPL); National Aeronautics and Space Administration (NASA); Resnik, Judith A.; Ride, Sally Kirsten; Space Exploration
References Corcoran, Elizabeth, "Women in Techology Compare Experiences, Challenges at Meeting," *Washington Post* (27 June 1998); Schick, Elizabeth A., ed., *Current Biography Yearbook, 1988* (1988).

Silbergeld, Ellen Kovner (b. 1945)

Ellen Silbergeld is one of this country's leading authorities on lead poisoning. While working for the Environmental Defense Fund (EDF) in the 1980s, Silbergeld's studies of lead in the environment became instrumental in leading the U.S. government to require a phasing-out of leaded gasolines for use in automobiles in favor of unleaded, or lead-free, gasolines. She also worked to have stricter regulations applied to the use of carcinogens such as dioxin, asbestos, and formaldehyde. In addition to her work as a researcher and an environmental lobbyist, Silbergeld has made several significant contributions to technology. Among these are her development of assays—tests used to identify the presence of chemicals in biological tissues or the environment—for lead and mercury. For these tests, she has been issued two patents.

Ellen Kovner was born in Washington, D.C., in 1945. Following high school, she entered Vassar College in Poughkeepsie, New York, on a full scholarship. She graduated *summa cum laude* with an A.B. degree in modern history and English in 1967. In addition, Kovner was elected to Phi Beta Kappa and received a Fulbright Fellowship, which enabled her to pursue a doctoral degree in economics at the University of London in England. However, after only one semester of study, Kovner returned home to Washington, D.C.

After returning to the United States, Kovner briefly worked as a file clerk. Then she obtained a job with the National Academy of Sciences (NAS), where she worked both as a secretary and as a program officer on various committees. While working at the NAS, she developed an interest in science, an area of study she had avoided throughout her college years. This new interest was sparked largely by concerns being raised about the effects of environmental degradation on human health. To learn more about these effects, she enrolled at the Johns Hopkins University in Baltimore, Maryland, and pursued a doctoral degree in environmental engineering.

While at Johns Hopkins, Kovner became interested in biochemical toxicology (poisons). During her second year of graduate school, she married Mark Silbergeld, a lawyer she had met in 1968. Ellen Silbergeld received her Ph.D. in environmental engineering sciences in 1972. After receiving this degree she remained at the university three additional years to conduct postdoctoral research at the School of Hygiene and Public Health. It was during this time, while working with some of the leading toxicologists in the country, that Silbergeld's interest in lead poisoning was piqued.

In 1975, Silbergeld began work as a staff fellow at the National Institutes of Health (NIH) in Bethesda, Maryland. Five years later, she became head of the newly created Neurotoxicology Section of the National Institute of Neurological and Communicative Disorders and Stroke. In this position, Silbergeld conducted research on the effects of lead compounds and certain food dyes on the central nervous system. Silbergeld left the NIH in 1982 to become senior toxicologist at the Environmental Defense Fund (EDF) in Washington, D.C. This position allowed her to make use of her scientific expertise to affect pending litigation involving hazardous chemicals and environmental issues.

While at the EDF, Silbergeld played a key role in raising public awareness about the dangers that lead poses to humans, particularly children. This awareness helped Silbergeld convince the federal government to require a phasing-out of leaded gasoline. She also helped strengthen environmental regulations regarding PCBs (polychlorinated biphenyls), substances that give off dioxin and other harmful chemicals when burned. Her role in this area involved convincing the government to demand removal of large electrical transformers that contained PCBs. Silbergeld was a member of an EDF group that persuaded the McDonald's restaurant chain to stop using polystyrene packaging in favor of paper. In addition, Silbergeld served as a consultant to the government of Bermuda regarding trash incineration.

In 1991, Silbergeld became a professor in the pathology department at the University of Maryland Medical School in Baltimore. The next year, she became a member of the department of epidemiology and preventative medicine there. At the same time, she taught classes at Johns Hopkins Medical School and served as an adjunct professor in the department of pharmacology and experimental therapeutics at the University of Maryland in Baltimore and as an affiliate professor of environmental law at the University of Maryland Law School.

It was during the 1990s that Silbergeld developed her lead assay. The test was designed to rapidly detect lead in biological tissues. This test differed from earlier assays in its ability to produce results quickly, rather than months after a sample was taken. Silbergeld submitted the specifications for her lead assay to the U.S. Patent and Trademark Office in May 1993. On 11 October 1994, she was issued Patent No. 5,354,652 for the test, the rights to which she assigned to the University of Maryland at Baltimore.

Silbergeld continues to teach at both the University of Maryland and Johns Hopkins University. Using funds from a $290,000 grant awarded

her by the John D. and Catherine T. MacArthur Foundation in 1993, she also does independent research on toxic chemicals that present an environmental hazard to humans. She used much of this money to finance studies on mercury in the Amazon River basin. In this area, mercury is commonly used to extract gold from sediment deposits. Silbergeld has invented a second assay for the detection of mercury in soil samples, for which she has been granted a patent.

Silbergeld has served as consultant to many committees and advisory boards. She is a reviewer of grants for both the National Foundation of the March of Dimes and the National Science Foundation (NSF). She also is a prolific writer and a member of the editorial board of the *American Journal of Industrial Medicine* and *Chemical and Engineering News.* When not working on research or as an instructor, Silbergeld devotes much of her time to the organization of symposiums and workshops on environmental issues as well as to workshops regarding attitudes toward women in the sciences.

See also Berkowitz, Joan; Environmental Engineering; Richards, Ellen Henrietta Swallow
References Torpie, Stephen L., et al., eds., *American Men and Women of Science,* 18th ed. (1992–1993) (1992); Shearer, Benjamin F., and Barbara S. Shearer, eds., *Notable Women in the Life Sciences: A Biographical Dictionary* (1996); "Ellen Kovner Silbergeld, Class of 1967," in the Vassar College Women in Science Hall of Fame, available at http://www.vassar.edu/SciWomen/index.html#Silbergeld/Carty (cited 23 June 1999); Environmental Defense Fund, "EDF People: Dr. Ellen K. Silbergeld," available at http://www.edf.org/pubs/EDF-Letter/1987/Oct/m_silbergeld.html (cited 23 June 1999).

Simpson, Joanne (b. 1923)

Joanne Simpson became the first woman in the world to hold a Ph.D. in meteorology, the branch of science dealing with the study of the atmosphere, particularly weather phenomena and climate. In addition, Simpson has the distinction of being the first woman to serve as chief scientist for meteorology at the Goddard Space Flight Center (GSFC) of the National Aeronautics and Space Administration (NASA), in Greenbelt, Maryland.

Through her work as a meteorologist, Simpson has become an authority on tropical cloud systems. She also is recognized for her work in helping to develop the computer simulation technology that is now used to alter the dynamics of cumulus clouds to produce rain. However, her many accomplishments and achievements in meteorology did not come easy. Throughout her career, Joanne Simpson often experienced both disappointment and discrimination.

Joanne Simpson was born in Boston, Massachusetts, in 1923. She received her entire elementary and secondary school education at private schools. At the beginning of World War II, she was attending the University of Chicago. During this time, the university was offering a government-sponsored program in meteorology encouraging college students to become instructors of meteorology for the purpose of training military personnel to identify potential weather conditions that might affect wartime maneuvers. In 1943, Simpson was issued her bachelor of science degree. She then went to New York University, where she served as an instructor of meteorology. After one year in New York, Simpson returned to the University of Chicago, where she also taught meteorology.

While teaching at the University of Chicago, Simpson also began graduate studies. She completed these studies and was awarded a master's degree in meteorology in 1945. Although Simpson wished to continue her graduate studies, the university faculty discouraged her because they believed that with the war over, women should return to the home rather than pursue academic endeavors. She was refused fellowship assistance and had great difficulty finding a faculty member who was willing to supervise her work; she did eventually get an adviser, but this came with the price of continual harassment.

While working toward her Ph.D., Simpson continued to work as an instuctor of meteorology at the school. In 1948, Joanne Simpson married a man who was an assistant professor of meteorology at the University of Chicago. The day after they married, she was discharged from her position as an instructor because of the university's nepotism policies, which held that when a couple employed in the same department at an institution married, the woman must relinquish her post in favor of her husband. To secure the financial support necessary to complete her doctorate, Simpson accepted a position as an instructor of physics and meteorology at the Illinois Institute of Technology. This position entitled her to free admission to courses at that school, so she completed most of her work there and then transferred her credits to the University of Chicago, from which she received her Ph.D. in meteorology in 1949.

Simpson continued to teach in the fall and spring at the Illinois Institute of Technology from 1949 to 1951, spending her summers working as a meteorologist at the Woods Hole Oceanographic Institution in Massachusetts. While she was pursuing her career, her marriage ended in divorce. In 1951, she accepted a full-time position as a research scientist and meteorologist at Woods Hole, where she remained for several years. There she focused on research of hurricanes and trade winds.

In 1960, Simpson accepted a position as a professor of meteorology at the University of California at Los Angeles (UCLA). She remained at UCLA until 1965. That year, she again married a fellow meteorologist, and the couple moved to Florida, where Simpson had accepted a position as director of the Experimental Meteorological Laboratory of the National Oceanic and Atmospheric Administration (NOAA) in Coral Gables. It was here that she made her first major contribution to technology, in carrying out a nine-year investigation into the process of cloud seeding (the injection of substances into clouds to induce rain). Under Simpson's direction, airplanes conducted a massive seeding operation in which pyrotechnics (fireworks) were used to release silver iodide smoke into cumulus clouds. This seeding technique caused the clouds to release their water as rain.

While working for NOAA, Simpson also served as an adjunct professor of atmospheric sciences at the University of Miami. After leaving NOAA in 1974, she was appointed professor of environmental science at the University of Virginia; two years later she was named to the William W. Corcoran Chair. While teaching at Virginia, Simpson and her husband formed a private meteorological consulting service—Simpson Weather Associates.

In 1979, Simpson was appointed to head the Severe Storms Branch of the Goddard Space Flight Center (GSFC) of the National Aeronautics and Space Administration (NASA) in Maryland. She later became chief scientist for meteorology, the first woman to hold this position. While at NASA, Simpson produced the first computer-simulated model of a cumulus cloud. She has since extended her work in this area to include the development of computer models of tropical clouds, tropical rain processes involved in the hydrologic (water) cycle, and means of measuring rainfall in tropical areas from space. In recognition of her work with NASA, the GSFC in 1997 named its fastest supercomputer in Simpson's honor; such an honor is rarely bestowed on a living individual.

In addition to having a computer named for her, Joanne Simpson has been the recipient of numerous other honors and awards throughout her career. In 1962, she received the Meisinger Award from the American Meteorological Society (twenty-one years later this organization honored her again with the Carl-Gustaf Rossby Research Medal—its highest award). She was given the Silver Medal of the Department of Commerce in 1967 and their Gold Medal in 1972. In 1975, the University of Chicago Alumni presented Simpson their Professional Achievement Award. NASA presented her its Exceptional Science Achievement Medal in 1982. Two years later, she was presented the V. J. Schaefer Award of the Weather Modification Association. Simpson also has received the Women in Science and Engineering (WISE) Lifetime Achievement Award (1990).

Simpson is a member of Phi Beta Kappa and Sigma Xi. She was elected a fellow of the American Meteorological Society in 1968 and became that organization's first woman president in 1989. In 1988, Simpson was elected into the National Academy of Engineering; in 1994, she was elected a fellow of the American Geophysical Union.

See also Computers/Computer Technology; National Academy of Engineering (NAE); National Aeronautics and Space Administration (NASA); Nepotism Policies; Phi Beta Kappa Society; Van Straten, Florence Wilhelmina; Women's Rights
References Bailey, Martha J., *American Women in Science, 1950 to the Present: A Biographical Dictionary* (1998); Bernstein, Leonard, Alan Winkler, and Linda Zierdt-Warshaw, *Multicultural Women of Science* (1996); Litzenberg, Kathleen, ed., *Who's Who of American Women,* 18th ed., 1993–1994 (1995); Williams, Jack, "NASA Chief Kept Her Head in the Clouds," *USA Today* (22 December 1998); NASA, Earth and Space Data Computing Division, "Chief Meteorologist Joanne Simpson Honored at T3E Dedication Ceremony," available at http://www.hq.nasa.gov/hpcc/reports/annrpt97/accomps/ess/WW95.html (cited 31 May 1999).

Sitterly, Charlotte Moore (1898–1990)

Charlotte Moore Sitterly was an astrophysicist and a leading authority on the composition of the sun. Her interpretations of solar spectra (a band of lines or colors produced by the absorption of radiant energy, which indicates the presence of specific elements) reflected the most comprehensive summary of atomic, spectroscopic, and solar spectrum data available and continue to be used worldwide as models for interpreting the spectra of distant celestial bodies. Sitterly's research also produced evidence that the element technetium existed in nature.

Charlotte Moore was born in Ercildoun, Pennsylvania, where she attended local public schools. After graduating from Coatesville High School in 1916, she enrolled at Swarthmore College as a mathematics major. Moore graduated Phi Beta Kappa with a B.A. in mathematics in 1920. That same year, she began her career at the Princeton University Observatory, where she made measurements and performed the mathematical calculations that were at the time considered "women's work" in astronomy. She also began conducting her own research on atomic spectra. Moore remained at the Princeton Observatory for five years. During this time, she worked with noted astronomer and Princeton professor Henry Norris Russell, whose stellar evolution theory and diagram of star classification (known as the Hertzberg-Russell diagram) have become standard points of reference for astronomers.

In 1925, Moore accepted a position at the Mt. Wilson Observatory in Pasadena, California, similar to her position at Princeton; at Mt. Wilson, she prepared solar spectra data obtained at the observatory for publication. The results of her work, which were published in a monograph in 1928, were a major astronomical reference for almost 40 years.

Moore returned to Princeton in 1928; however, she left one year later to pursue graduate work in astronomy on a Lick Fellowship at the University of California at Berkeley. She received her Ph.D. in astronomy in 1931 and then returned to Princeton as an assistant spectroscopist. Within five years, she was promoted to the position of research associate. In this role, she prepared tables of atomic spectra. This work led to the publication of *A Multiple Table of Astrophysical Interest* in 1933.

In 1937, Charlotte Moore married fellow astronomer Bancroft Walker Sitterly, whom she had met at Princeton. That same year, she was awarded the Annie J. Cannon Prize for her contributions to astronomy. Around this time, scientists working in Italy identified a substance that had been produced in a particle accelerator at Berkeley and whose existence had previously been only theoretically assumed. The substance, later named technetium, was predicted to be the "missing" element that would fill in an unexplained gap in the periodic table of elements. Sitterly detected this newly discovered element in the solar spectrum, a finding that indicated that the element existed in nature and not just in the laboratory. Technetium has since been discovered in the spectra of other distant stars.

In 1945, Charlotte Sitterly accepted a position at the National Bureau of Standards (now the National Institute of Standards and Technology). She worked in the Spectroscopy Section of the Atomic Physics Division, supervising the preparation of the energy tables that were published between 1949 and 1958 in several volumes titled *Atomic Energy Levels*. For her work on this project, Sitterly was awarded the Gold Medal of the Department of Commerce in 1960. The next year, she became one of the first six women to receive the newly created Federal Woman's Award for outstanding government service. In addition, she was presented with the Annie Jump Cannon Centennial Medal in 1963.

Sitterly authored or coauthored nearly 100 professional papers and monographs during her career. She also was an active member of several professional organizations, including the American Association for the Advancement of Science (AAAS); the American Physical Society (APS); and the American Astronomical Society, of which she served as vice president from 1958 through 1960. She became a fellow of the Optical Society of America, and in 1949 the Royal Astronomical Society of London elected her its first woman foreign associate. In addition, Sitterly was awarded honorary doctoral degrees from Swarthmore College, the University of Michigan, and the Universität zu Kiel in Germany.

See also Astronomy; Burbidge, (Eleanor) Margaret Peachey; Goeppert-Mayer, Maria; Maury, Antonia; National Institute of Standards and Technology (NIST); Spectroscopy

References "Charlotte Sitterly, 91, Physicist; Devoted Career to Sunlight Studies" [obituary], *New York Times* (8 March 1990); Moritz, Charles, ed., *Current Biography, 1962* (1962); Shearer, Benjamin F., and Barbara S. Shearer, eds., *Notable Women in the Physical Sciences: A Biographical Dictionary* (1997).

Slater, Hannah Wilkinson (Mrs. Samuel) (n.d.)

British-born textile entrepreneur Samuel Slater established what became the nation's first successful water-powered cotton mill. The success of the mill, which opened in 1790 in what is today Pawtucket, Rhode Island, is believed to be due in part to the perfection of a cotton thread by Slater's wife, Hannah Wilkinson Slater. Although much information exists about the life and achievements of Samuel Slater, very little information exists about the life of Hannah Wilkinson Slater. Records do indicate, however, that Mrs. Samuel Slater was issued a U.S. patent for a perfected cotton thread in 1793. This date should establish Mrs. Slater as the first "American" woman to receive a U.S. patent. However, the U.S. Patent and Trademark Office generally bestows this honor on Connecticut native Mary Dixon Kies. Kies received a patent in 1809 for "a method to weave straw with silk or thread." It is not known why the discrepancy over which woman was actually the first to be issued a U.S. patent exists. However, possible explanations include the fact that Kies received her patent in her own name, whereas the Slater patent was issued to "Mrs. Samuel" Slater, thus recognizing and crediting the name of Samuel Slater, a male, as was the custom. The discrepancy may also arise from the citizenship of Mrs. Samuel Slater, who like her husband, might have been foreign-born.

See also Greene, Catherine Littlefield; Kies, Mary; Masters, Sybilla Righton; Patent; Textiles; Welles, Sophia Woodhouse

References Olsen, Kirsten, *Chronology of Women's History* (1994); Stanley, Autumn, *Mothers and Daughters of Invention: Notes for a Revised History of Technology* (1993); Trager, James, *The People's Chronology* (1992); Trager, James, *The Women's Chronology* (1994); U.S. Patent and Trademark Office, *A Quest for Excellence* (1994); Prewitt, Pamela, "Women's History Month 1996: 'See History in a New Way'" (internet document from the Topical Research Program at the Defense Equal Opportunity Management Institute, July 1995), available at http://www.pafb.af.mil/DEOMI/whm96.htm (cited 23 January 2000).

Society of Hispanic Professional Engineers (SHPE)

The Society of Hispanic Professional Engineers (SHPE) is an organization composed of engineers, student engineers, and scientists whose common goal is to increase the number of Hispanic engineers by providing motivation, support, and incentives to students desiring to enter the profession. SHPE sponsors competitions, provides scholarships, and conducts educational programs to prepare students for technical careers. The organization also develops retention programs for students at the postsecondary level, organizes conferences and workshops on career enhancement, and organizes forums on technical information.

Founded in 1974, the SHPE now numbers about 6,000 members, with 6 regional groups and 33 local groups. There are also more than 200 student chapters. Among SHPE's more well-known members are civil engineer Margarita Colmenares, who founded the San Francisco chapter of SHPE in 1982 and became the national president of SHPE in 1989. Ocean engineer Lissa Martinez founded the Washington, D.C., chapter. Other noted members of SHPE include planetary geologist and Jet Propulsion Laboratory (JPL) employee Adriana Ocampo, construction engineer Hermelinda Renteria, and industrial engineer Carol Sanchez.

Awards sponsored by SHPE include the Hispanic Engineer National Achievement Award for Most Promising Engineer in Government, the Community Service Award, and the Pioneer Award. SHPE's journal *Hispanic Engineer* is published quarterly and features articles about Hispanic engineers who serve as role models for the Hispanic community.

See also Jet Propulsion Laboratory (JPL); Martinez, Lissa Ann; Society of Women Engineers (SWE)

References Chabrán, Richard, and Rafael Chabrán, eds., *The Latino Encyclopedia*, vol. 5 (1996); Maurer, Christine, and Tara E. Sheets, eds., *Encyclopedia of Associations: An Associations Unlimited Reference*, 33rd ed., vol. 1, parts 1–3 (1998); Montney, Charles B., ed., *Hispanic Americans Information Directory*, 3rd ed. (1994); Society of Professional Hispanic Engineers, available at http://www.engr.umd.edu/organizations/shpe (cited 12 December 1998).

Society of Women Engineers (SWE)

The Society of Women Engineers (SWE) is a nonprofit educational service organization composed of engineering graduates and people having equivalent engineering experience. Through its publications, meetings, and career development and guidance conferences, the SWE disseminates information about opportunities for women and achievements of women in engineering. The organization encourages young women to pursue careers in engineering and assists women engineers who have left work for extended periods of time in returning to employment.

The SWE was established when 50 women

representing independent groups of women engineers and women engineering students from various cities met at the Green Engineering Camp of the Cooper Union in New Jersey in 1950. The organization has since grown; current membership (which is not limited to U.S. citizens) is approximately 16,000, with 84 sections throughout the United States. Student sections have been chartered at nearly 300 colleges, universities, and engineering schools. Membership was opened to men in 1976.

In addition to promoting the involvement of women in engineering, the SWE sponsors several award programs. The Distinguished New Engineer (DNE) Award recognizes outstanding women engineers who have less than ten years' engineering experience. Only SWE members are eligible to receive this annual award. In 1986, the SWE created the Resnik Challenger Medal. This award honors astronaut and mission specialist Judith A. Resnik, who was killed along with other crew members aboard the *Challenger* that year. The Resnik Challenger Medal pays tribute to engineering achievements in space exploration. Recipients of this award include astronaut Bonnie J. Dunbar (1992) and aerospace engineer Yvonne C. Brill (1993).

The highest and most prestigious award given by the Society of Women Engineers is the Achievement Award. This award is presented annually to a woman, who need not be a member of the society, who has made significant, long-term contributions to engineering. A list of SWE Achievement Award winners for the years 1952–1997 appears in Table A.4 in the Appendix.

See also Aeronautical and Aerospace Engineering; Dunbar, Bonnie J.; Resnik, Judith A.; Ride, Sally Kirsten; Space Exploration
References Maurer, Christine, and Tara E. Sheets, eds., *Encyclopedia of Associations: An Associations Unlimited Reference,* 33rd ed., vol. 1, parts 1–3 (1998); Society of Women Engineers, "About the Society of Women Engineers," available at http://www.swe.org (cited 31 May 1998); Society of Women Engineers, "Achievement Award," available at http://www.swe.org/SWE/Awards/achiev.htm (cited 1 June 1998); Society of Women Engineers, "Resnik Challenger Medal," available at http://www.swe.org/SWE/Awards/resnik.htm (cited 1 June 1998); Society of

Women Engineers, "Distinguished New Engineer (DNE) Award," available at http://www.swe.org/SWE/Awards/dne.htm (cited 1 June 1998).

Solar Technologies

The sun gives off a great deal of energy in the form of light, heat, and other types of electromagnetic radiation. This energy makes life on Earth possible, maintaining global temperatures in a range that can support life and driving the process of photosynthesis—the food-making process of plants. Solar technologies are methods and devices that have been developed to harness the sun's energy for practical purposes, including the heating and cooling of buildings, the heating and distillation of water, the generation of electricity, and the cooking of food.

Maria Telkes was a pioneer in the use of solar technology for heating and cooling homes. In 1939, Telkes joined a team of researchers at the Massachusetts Institute of Technology (MIT) who were conducting research on solar energy conversions. While working at MIT, Telkes designed a solar energy system that was intended to be used as the heating system for a home during the winter months. In addition, the same system could be used to cool the home during the warmer, summer months. In 1948, the system designed by Telkes was installed in a prototype home in Dover, Massachusetts, where it worked as planned. That same year, Telkes, in collaboration with architect Eleanor Raymond, received a patent for a house that made use of such a system. Many years later, another structure that Telkes had been involved in designing was constructed on the campus of the University of Delaware. This structure, called Solar One, not only incorporated heat transfer systems but also made use of materials specifically designed to store heat for other home uses.

Telkes's work with solar technologies was not limited to home heating and cooling systems. She also developed several distillation systems that were designed to use the energy from the sun as a means of obtaining freshwater from saltwater. Among her earliest work in this area was her development of portable distillation units during World War II. The units were designed for use by military personnel on life rafts. Telkes later designed larger solar distillation units (also for obtaining freshwater from saltwater) for use by people living in the Virgin Islands.

Other solar technologies developed by Maria Telkes include her work with solar water heaters, solar food dryers, and thermoelectric generators intended for use aboard spacecraft. The importance of this last development is that it reduces the space requirements and potential weight of a spacecraft's load by eliminating the need to carry batteries and other electricity-generating devices.

Telkes was a pioneer and is well known for her work in developing solar technologies, but she is not the only woman to make contributions in this area. Another is Countess Stella Andrassy, who worked with Telkes for a time at Princeton University. Andrassy obtained at least ten patents for devices that make use of solar energy by the end of the 1970s—at least one of which she holds jointly with Telkes. Among the devices for which Andrassy was issued patents are solar water heaters, stoves, food dryers, and stills.

Yet another woman who has obtained a patent for a solar stove is Mildred L. Clevett of Englewood, Colorado. The patent for this portable and foldable stove (U.S. Patent No. 4,130,106), of which Clevett is the copatentee, was issued 19 December 1978.

See also Loftness, Vivian; Telkes, Maria
References Rothe, Anna, ed., *Current Biography, 1950* (1950); Stanley, Autumn, *Mothers and Daughters of Invention: Notes for a Revised History of Technology* (1993); U.S. Patent and Trademark Office, Full Text and Image Database—Number Search, available through the U.S. Patent and Trademark Office Depository, at http://www.uspto.gov/go/ptdl (cited 15 July 1999).

Sound
See **Acoustical Engineering**

Space Exploration
People have had visions of journeying into space to explore its vast, mysterious expanses almost since the beginning of recorded time. They dreamed of walking on the moon or of visiting the planets or the stars. The earliest studies of space began on Earth in the field of astronomy, through observations at first made with the unaided eye and later with telescopes and other types of optical devices.

The field of astronomy has advanced through the efforts of many people, and women have played an active role in this area of science for centuries. In the United States, the most significant studies carried out by women in astronomy began during the nineteenth century, with the work of Maria Mitchell, Sarah Frances Whiting, Mary Whitney, Antonia Maury, Annie Jump Cannon, and Henrietta Swan Leavitt. Work done by these women led to the discovery of many new stars and a means of classification for stars.

This work was continued and built upon in the twentieth century by other women, including Charlotte Moore Sitterly, Cecelia Payne-Gaposchkin, and Vera Rubin. Like their predecessors, these women carried out many studies on stars, using a technology known as spectroscopy. However, their work went beyond that of earlier women, as they discovered new galaxies and new types of stars and even began to provide evidence about the composition of stars. Despite these advances, virtually all of these women had to limit their exploration of space to observations that could be made from Earth using telescopes or other devices.

Before humans could journey into space, they had to develop a means of escaping Earth's gravity. This feat was accomplished during the 1940s when scientists and engineers succeeded in building and propelling rockets into space to a distance of 250 miles above Earth's surface. On 4 October 1957, Russia launched the first artificial satellite, *Sputnik 1,* which orbited Earth for 95 days at a height of approximately 550 miles. The launching of this satellite marked the beginning of the space age. At the end of its journey, *Sputnik 1* reentered Earth's atmosphere and quickly incinerated. The launch of *Sputnik 1* deepened the Cold War between the United States and Russia and goaded the United States into action toward developing space exploration vehicles that could outperform those built by the Russians. In keeping with this goal, the National Aeronautics and Space Administration (NASA) of the United States launched its first satellite, *Explorer 1*, on 31 January 1958. *Explorer 1* journeyed more than 1,500 miles above Earth's surface, surpassing the distance achieved by Russia one year earlier.

In 1959, Russia launched the first of its space probes, the *Luna 1*. A space probe is a rocket that carries sophisticated equipment that is used to make a variety of measurements that can then be relayed back to Earth via radio transmissions. *Luna 1* was sent on a flyby mission to the moon. Three months later, the United States launched its space probe, *Pioneer 4*. This probe made a journey of more than 400,000 miles in space before its radio stopped transmitting, resulting in a loss of contact between the probe and Earth.

The first human did not go into space until cosmonaut Yuri Gagarin of Russia made an orbit around Earth on 12 April 1961 aboard the *Vostok 1*. This flight was followed by a U.S. flight the next month, when Alan B. Shepard, Jr. made a 15-minute suborbital flight aboard *Freedom 7*. John Glenn became the first American astronaut to orbit Earth when in February 1962 he circled Earth three times aboard *Friendship 7*. Both of these flights, which were part of America's *Mercury* program, demonstrated that the United States had the technological capability needed to send humans into orbit around Earth.

The *Mercury* program was dominated by men, particularly those who had served as jet pilots in the military. However, in 1961, twenty-six women pilots were selected to be tested for physical and psychological capabilities of becoming astronauts. The tests were quite stringent. Thirteen of the women did as well as their male counterparts, but for some reason all of the women were dropped except for Jerrie Cobb. This veteran pilot did complete the entire program, but was never permitted to take part in a space flight. Thus, until the mid-1970s, all of America's astronauts were men.

Russia again sent a probe into space to photograph the side of the moon that cannot be observed from Earth. During the mid-1960s, U.S. *Ranger* probes were successful in sending lunar photographs back to Earth; the *Surveyor* probe later made a soft landing on the moon and gathered data that were used by scientists on Earth to analyze the lunar surface. All of the U.S. efforts in this area were in preparation for the *Apollo* mission, the goal of which was to place a human on the moon's surface—a goal reached by the United States in 1969.

Although NASA did not open its astronaut program to women until the 1970s, women did work in various capacities behind the scenes in the space program, making contributions that were crucial to its success. For example, Alice Chatham, a sculptor, was hired by NASA to design the space helmets that would be worn by the astronauts. She had previously served as an employee of the U.S. Air Force, where she was responsible for designing the helmets worn by its test pilots.

During the early 1960s, mathematician Katherine Coleman Goble Johnson was employed by NASA. Her job responsibilities included developing emergency navigational maps and charts for use by the astronauts. She also helped develop navigational procedures that could be used by NASA engineers to track spacecraft trajectories. At the same time, Barbara Johnson helped develop the Entry Monitor System (EMS)—a graphic display designed to aid astronauts in their navigation by monitoring the spacecraft's angle of reentry. Between 1965 and 1967, Catherine Fenselau helped develop methods that made use of the technologies of mass spectrometry to search for evidence of living things in the rocks that had been collected from the moon by the space probes.

The Equal Employment Act of 1972 strengthened the responsibilities of the Equal Employment Opportunity Commission (EEOC), making it more difficult for employers to discriminate against people on the basis of their gender as had NASA with regard to women astronauts. Realizing that as a part of the federal government it could no longer continue to maintain its discriminatory policies regarding women in space, NASA finally opened its astronaut program to women. In January 1978, NASA selected six women to become the first women astronauts. Among this group was Sally Ride, who in 1983 became the first American woman to travel into space, aboard the seventh flight involving a space shuttle—a reusable spacecraft developed by NASA. During their astronaut training, Ride (a physicist) and Judith Resnik (an engineer who was one of the original six women selected to participate in the astronaut program) developed the Remote Manipulator System (RMS)—a robotic arm that is used by shuttle crew members to deploy and recapture satellites. Resnik later met with tragedy when she perished along with the other crew members aboard the second scheduled flight of the shuttle *Challenger,* which exploded shortly after takeoff.

Another of the original six women astronauts was Kathryn D. Sullivan. She made history in 1984 when she became the first woman to walk in space. In 1992, Mae Carol Jemison became the first African American woman to travel into space. Jemison, a physician and an engineer by training, traveled into space aboard space shuttle flight STS-47 (*Discovery*), where she served as a mission specialist and conducted studies of motion sickness and calcium loss associated with weightlessness. In 1996, Shannon Lucid made history when she set a record for the longest consecutive period spent in space by any American astronaut—six months. Lucid spent those months working aboard the Russian space station *Mir.*

Women also continue to contribute to space exploration in other ways. In the early 1990s, noted astronomer Margaret Burbidge helped design a spectroscope that was to be launched into space along with the Hubble Space Telescope. After being placed into orbit, the Hubble Space Telescope failed to perform as planned, as a result of technical problems involving its mirrors; however, the spectroscope developed by Burbidge functioned perfectly, allowing astronomers to gather new data about distant space objects.

In 1993, astronaut Kathy Thornton went into space to repair the Hubble Space Telescope. The repairs were successful and have allowed the telescope to provide astronomers on Earth improved views of stars and other objects in space. That same year, Ellen Ochoa, an engineer who holds several patents in optical processes, became the first Hispanic American woman to travel into space. The first Asian American woman astronaut, Chiaki Makai, traveled into space aboard a shuttle the following year.

Among the more recent developments in space exploration are the use of space stations—structures placed into orbit for long periods of time that provide a short- or long-term habitat for astronauts. The first such station was the *Mir,* which was produced in Russia. Since the end of the Cold War between the United States and Russia, the two countries have worked together on many projects aboard this space station. In 1995, Bonnie J. Dunbar and Ellen Baker became the first women to dock their module with the Russian space station. Prior to becoming an astronaut, Dunbar had conducted studies on the use of ceramic tiles as a thermal protection barrier for space vehicles.

Not all of NASA's endeavors in the latter part of the 1990s involved the space shuttle. In 1997, NASA launched the *Pathfinder* spacecraft. This probe carried along with it a small remote-operated device called the Sojourner (named for African American figure Sojourner Truth) to Mars. Once on the surface of Mars, the Sojourner, which was designed under the direction of Donna Shirley of the Jet Propulsion Laboratory (JPL), transmitted photographic data of the Mars surface as well as data about its soil composition to scientists on Earth. The Sojourner did experience some minor technical problems while it journeyed along the surface of Mars; however, the project was generally considered a technological success.

More recently, the United States has begun to carry out shuttle flights that are transporting materials needed for the construction of the *International Space Station.* This station will provide astronauts a long-term habitat in space, replacing the *Mir,* which suffered from numerous mechanical and electrical problems during its last years in operation. In December 1998, Nancy J. Currie used the RMS arm to connect the U.S. *Unity* module with the Russian *Zarya* in the first stage of the new space station's construction.

In July 1999, Eileen Collins made history when she served as the first female commander of a space shuttle mission. Among this mission's major technological accomplishments was the launch of an X-ray telescope that will provide space scientists on Earth a greater range of data about stars, planets, and other objects in space. NASA has plans also to send other probes into space to obtain photographs of and data about several other planets.

See also Astronomy; Burbidge, (Eleanor) Margaret Peachey; Dunbar, Bonnie J.; Fenselau, Catherine Clarke; Jemison, Mae; Johnson, Barbara Crawford; Johnson, Katherine Coleman Goble; Lucid, Shannon Wells; Maury, Antonia; Ochoa, Ellen; Payne-Gaposchkin, Cecelia; Resnik, Judith A.; Ride, Sally Kirsten; Rubin, Vera Cooper; Sitterly, Charlotte Moore; Spectroscopy; Whiting, Sarah Frances

References Ambrose, Susan A., et al., *Journeys of Women in Science and Engineering: No Universal Constants* (1997); Bernstein, Leonard, Alan Winkler, and Linda Zierdt-Warshaw, *Multicultural Women of Science* (1996); Graham, Judith, ed., *Current Biography Yearbook, 1993* (1993); National Aeronautics and Space Administration, *Astronaut Fact Book* (1992); Schick, Elizabeth A., ed., *Current Biography Yearbook, 1998* (1998); Sherr, Lynn, "Remembering Judy: The Five Women Who Trained with Judy Resnik Remember Her . . . and That Day," *Ms. Magazine* (June 1986); Vare, Ethlie Ann, and Greg Ptacek, *Mothers of Invention: From the Bra to the Bomb, Forgotten Women and Their Unforgettable Ideas* (1988); National Aeronautics and Space Administration, "NASA-Women Astronauts Timeline," available at http://www.nasa.gov/women/index.htm (cited 5 August 1999).

Spaeth, Mary (b. 1938)

The laser (an acronym for *l*ight *a*mplification by *s*timulated *e*mission of *r*adiation) is a device that produces a beam of high-intensity, monochromatic (single frequency or wavelength), coherent light. Six years after the introduction of the first working laser, physicist Mary Spaeth invented what came to be called the tunable dye laser. This device made it possible to change the frequency of the light emitted by a laser while it is in use. As fre-

quency changes, so does the light's color. With this improvement, the laser became a more versatile tool for use in biology, chemistry, physics, medicine, and other areas. Spaeth also was involved in the development of a damage-resistant resonant reflector that is used by the military in the ruby range finder—an optical device used to determine distances—and in high-peak power lasers.

Mary Spaeth was born in Houston, Texas, in 1938. As a child, she loved to build things. Her parents encouraged this interest, providing their daughter with her own set of carpentry tools when she was very young. By the time Mary was 8, she had used her creative talents and abilities to devise the method that is today used to reseal cardboard cereal boxes.

After high school, Mary Spaeth entered Valparaiso University in Indiana. There she performed optical research and studies on saturable (soluble) dyes. She received a B.S. degree in 1960, with a dual major in physics and mathematics. It was in this same year that Theodore Maiman created the first working laser. This laser could produce light in various colors; however, once the laser was in use, the color selected could not be changed. At the time that Maiman's device was unveiled, Spaeth was at Wayne State University near Detroit, Michigan, working toward her master's degree in nuclear physics. She was awarded this degree in 1962. She then joined the technical staff at Hughes Aircraft Company.

In 1966, scientists Peter Sorokin and J. R. Lankard demonstrated that certain dyes could be used to change the color of the light produced by a laser. Using data from their research and data from her own experiments involving a variety of dyes, Spaeth successfully produced a tunable dye laser. The ability of a tunable dye laser to change the frequency of light made it a useful tool for identifying and then separating isotopes (forms of an element having different numbers of neutrons in their nuclei) for study. Because the chemical structure of each isotope of an element differs slightly, each isotope absorbs a specific wavelength of light differently. As this occurs, each isotope also gives off a different amount of energy. This energy changes the size, shape, and electrical charge of the isotope, making it easier to separate it from its sister isotopes. Prior to the development of the tunable laser, the identification and separation of isotopes proved to be expensive and tedious.

The tunable dye laser was first used to separate isotopes of uranium and plutonium for use in the production of nuclear weapons. It was later used to obtain isotopes of these same elements for use as fuels in nuclear reactors. More recently, the tunable dye laser also has been applied to astronomical studies. In this area, it is used to improve the resolution of the telescopes used at observatories; it may improve this resolution to the point where it equals that of telescopes, such as the Hubble Space Telescope, that are in orbit.

In 1974, Spaeth left Hughes Aircraft Company to work as a physicist at the Lawrence Livermore National Laboratory in California, where she used the principles on which the tunable dye laser was based to help identify fuels for use in nuclear power plants. Shortly thereafter, she became a member of the Atomic Vapor Laser Isotope Separation (AVLIS) Project at Lawrence Livermore. She remained with this group for about fifteen years, attaining the title of deputy associate director. In 1990, Spaeth retired and began a career as a graphic artist. She continued working as a graphic artist for about ten years, before returning as a consultant to the laboratory where she had last worked.

See also Astronomy; Burbidge, (Eleanor) Margaret Peachey; Nuclear Physics; Spectroscopy
References Bailey, Martha J., *American Women in Science, 1950 to the Present: A Biographical Dictionary* (1998); Brown, Kenneth A., *Inventors at Work: Interviews with 16 Notable American Inventors* (1988); Salerno, Heather, "Mothers of Invention: Though Unsung and Ignored, Women Have Pushed Technology's Frontiers," *Washington Post* (12 March 1997); Spaeth, Mary, e-mail communication with Alan Winkler (17 June 1999); Strong, C. L., "Tunable Dye Laser," *Scientific American* (February 1970); Travers, Bridget, ed., *World of Scientific Discovery* (1994).

Spectroscopy

Spectroscopy is a field of study that investigates the manner in which both visible and invisible light (electromagnetic radiation) interact with matter. Visible light (also referred to as the visible spectrum) includes all the light observed when a beam of white light passes through a prism and separates into its constituent or component colors, in an array commonly called a spectrum. The visible spectrum makes up an extremely small part of the entire band of electromagnetic radiation, which also includes radio waves, microwaves, infrared, the visible spectrum, ultraviolet (UV) radiation, X rays, and gamma rays.

When electromagnetic radiation strikes an object, it can be reflected (bounced off the object), transmitted (passed through the object), absorbed (taken in by the object), or cause the object itself to emit light (fluoresce). Electromagnetic radiation that is absorbed by an object interacts with that object; it is this electromagnetic radiation that is the subject of analysis and interpretation in spectroscopy.

The spectroscope, a device used to produce and observe spectra for observation and study, is the primary instrument of spectroscopy. One of the earliest and simplest devices used to separate white light into its component colors was the triangular glass prism used by Sir Isaac Newton in 1666. Newton observed that as sunlight passed through the prism, it was dispersed, forming a continuous spectrum. The spectrum consisted of an array of colors ranging from red through violet, with no interruption or gap in the sequence. Newton's observation of the scattering of sunlight into its component colors was a precursor to modern spectroscopy.

Nearly 150 years after Newton reported his observations of light passing through a prism, German physicist, astronomer, and lensmaker Joseph von Fraunhofer developed the prism spectrometer. This device consisted of a collimator (a device that produces parallel rays of light), a prism (used to bend the light rays), and a telescope (used to view the resulting color components of the spectrum produced). Using this improved spectroscope, Fraunhofer in 1814 advanced Newton's findings, observing that thin, dark lines (today called Fraunhofer lines) interrupted the sun's otherwise apparently continuous spectrum.

In 1848, French physicist Jean Bernard Foucault noted that placing sodium into a flame caused the flame to burn with a characteristic yellow color. It was later observed that other elements placed into flames also resulted in a flame of a particular color. Additional advances in spectroscopy resulted from improved spectroscope designs and innovations provided by Robert Bunsen and Gustav Kirchhoff in 1859. Using the burner that now bears his name, Bunsen and Kirchhoff superheated the various elements known at that time. Building upon the observations of Foucault, they observed and classified each element according to its unique spectra. They also discovered the elements cesium and rubidium. In addition, Kirchhoff successfully explained the presence of the Fraunhofer lines as characteristics of sunlight that result from interactions between the elements in the sun's cooler atmosphere and those in the sun's hotter interior. Kirchhoff's explanation paved the way for identifying the elements in the sun, and it continues to be applied in determining the chemical composition of stars.

The earliest principles and practices of spectroscopy dealt with visible light and applications of simple spectroscopes that made use of a glass prism to separate white light into its spectrum. However, since the early twentieth century, spectroscopy has been expanded beyond the study of the visible spectrum. In 1912, physicists Sir William Henry Bragg and (his son) Sir William Lawrence Bragg used a spectroscope to study the spectral patterns of X rays. This was accomplished by replacing the glass prism with a diffraction grating—a lens, mirror, or crystal that contained many closely patterned, parallel grooves, each of which assisted in the dispersal of light. The device the Braggs developed resulted in one of the earliest X-ray spectroscopes; it also provided the foundation for X-ray crystallography. Since this development, spectroscopes designed to study other specific regions of the electromagnetic spectrum have been developed. For example, today's technology allows scientists to make use of spectroscopes that help them analyze ultraviolet radiation, microwaves, mass, electrons, and infrared radiation.

Although the earliest studies in spectroscopy and the development of most spectroscopes and spectrometers resulted from the work of men, many significant applications of this technology have resulted from the work of women. For example, in the early 1900s, chemist Emma Perry Carr became a pioneer in the use of ultraviolet spectroscopy—the use of ultraviolet (UV) radiation to analyze the composition of substances. In her work, Carr sought to determine the relationship between the molecular structure of a compound and the ultraviolet spectra given off by that compound. Carr conducted her studies on organic compounds while working as a professor and researcher at Mount Holyoke College in Massachusetts. Later, two of her students, Dorothy Hahn and Mary Lura Sherrill, conducted similar studies at Mount Holyoke on hydrocarbons—specifically, those consisting of molecules possessing double bonds between carbon atoms.

During the 1940s, astrophysicist Charlotte Moore Sitterly used optical spectroscopy as a means of analyzing the composition of the sun and other stars. Later, while working at the National Bureau of Standards (today the National Institute of Standards and Technology), Sitterly extended her use of optical spectra to the analysis of elements. These data were used to compile tables of the atomic energy levels in different elements.

Among the most significant uses for spectroscopy are those in astronomy. In the late 1800s, Antonia Maury obtained spectra of stars by photographing starlight as it passed through a prism placed in front of a telescope. Using the data she observed from the resulting spectra, Maury improved the existing classification system for stars and also proved that the star at the center of the Big Dipper was not a single star but a binary star system. Working at the same observatory as Maury, noted astronomer Annie Jump Cannon used spectroscopy to identify and classify stars. In this work, Cannon was able to classify so many stars that she often is referred to as the "census taker of the sky."

During the 1950s, astrophysicist Margaret Burbidge used what was described as astronomical spectroscopy to research the formation of stars. Based upon her spectroscopic observations and analyses of the surface environment of stars, she correctly hypothesized that heavy elements present in stars form from lighter ones through the process of nucleosynthesis (nuclear fusion).

In the late 1960s, biochemist Catherine Fenselau used mass spectroscopy—a spectroscopic technique that deflects substances in a certain pattern according to their mass and electrical charge—to analyze the composition of rocks that had been collected from the surface of the moon. More recently, she has used this same process to help identify the composition of substances that have been shown effective in the treatment of cancer. This technology provides a means for such substances to be replicated in the laboratory.

In the late 1950s, research chemist Mary Lowe Good made use of infrared and Mössbauer spectroscopy (a technique that uses gamma ray absorption and emission to determine the chemical composition of solid substances) to develop ways of separating or synthesizing complex metals. Several years later, Caroline Littlejohn Herzenberg used this same technology to analyze the makeup of lunar samples and of rocks and minerals that are present on Earth. Jeannette Grasselli Brown was a pioneer in the use and applications of the infrared spectrometer, an instrument that can both identify and quantify the molecules present in a substance.

See also Astronomy; Burbidge, (Eleanor) Margaret Peachey; Carr, Emma Perry; Fenselau, Catherine Clarke; Good, Mary Lowe; Hahn, Dorothy Anna; Herzenberg, Caroline Littlejohn; Maury, Antonia; Sherrill, Mary Lura
References Abel, George, *Exploration of the Universe,* 2nd ed. (1969); Chaison, E., and Steve McMillan, *Astronomy Today,* 3rd ed. (1999); Grinstein, Louise S., Rose K. Rose, and Miriam H. Rafailovich, eds., *Women in Chemistry and Physics: A Biobibliographic Sourcebook* (1993); Kass-Simon, G., and Patricia Farnes, eds., *Women of Science: Righting the Record* (1990); Semat, Henry, *Fundamentals of Physics,* 3rd ed. (1958); Strong, C. L., "Ocular Spectroscope," *Scientific American* (December 1952); Strong, C. L., "Ultraviolet Spectrograph," *Scientific American* (October 1968).

Stanley, Louise (1883–1954)

Louise Stanley, a leader in the field of home economics and nutrition, holds the unique distinc-

tion of becoming the first woman to serve as a bureau chief for a department of the federal government when she was named director of the newly created U.S. Bureau of Home Economics, an agency within the U.S. Department of Agriculture (USDA), in 1923. Stanley assumed this post several years after her service as chair of the Legislative Committee of the American Home Economics Association. In her work, Stanley's professional interests were closely allied with her personal goals. She was an advocate for improving the quality of life in the home and sought to secure federal support for home economics programs.

Louise Stanley was born in Nashville, Tennessee, on 8 June 1883. When she was orphaned at the age of four, she and her younger brother went to live with an aunt who lived nearby. Stanley received her early education in Nashville, where she attended both the Peabody Demonstration School and Ward's Seminary. Stanley had an insatiable desire to learn and, because of her inheritance, the money to do so. She attended Peabody College of the University of Nashville in Tennessee, from which she earned an A.B. degree in 1903. She then enrolled at the University of Chicago, where she received a B.Ed. in 1906. The next year she attended Columbia University in New York City, where she obtained an A.M. degree. In 1911, she was awarded a Ph.D. in biochemistry from Yale University.

While Stanley was involved in her collegiate pursuits, a new field of study, called home economics, was beginning to emerge. This new discipline allied the sciences with education and provided employment opportunities for women with combined interests in these areas. Stanley was more than qualified on both counts. She fully understood the value of home economics as a tool for promoting health and wholesome family living; she also understood the importance of proper diet and the relationship of nutritious foods to good health and longevity.

In 1911, shortly after Stanley received her doctorate, Secretary of Agriculture Henry C. Wallace named her chief of the newly created Federal Board of Vocational Education. While serving in this position, she conducted research in the area of nutrition that would later become the basis for creating dietary plans for families with different economic levels. She also conducted housing surveys and prepared guidelines for consumer purchasing.

Stanley became an instructor in the department of home economics at the University of Missouri at Columbia in 1917. She remained at the university until 1923, advancing through the academic ranks to professor and then department chair. During her tenure at the University of Missouri, Stanley joined a circle of other professionals who viewed home economics as a means of improving the lives of individuals. The group also sought federal support for home economics education. Along with her colleagues, Stanley served as head of the American Home Economics Association's legislative committee. To her credit, she and her colleagues successfully lobbied for the passage of the Smith-Hughes Act in 1917. This act provided federal funding for industrial, agricultural, and home economics education in public schools.

Having distinguished herself in the field of home economics, Stanley was appointed director of the U.S. Bureau of Home Economics upon its formation within the USDA in 1923. During her tenure in this post, she encouraged research that led to the development of standardized food plans based upon nutrition and economics and the standardization of clothing sizes based upon studies of body measurements. Her food plans were adopted for use in government programs and aided consumers during the Great Depression and World War II. Under her direction, the bureau also conducted extensive home efficiency studies, designed to reduce time and extra steps in maintaining a home.

At times, Stanley's programs and policies placed her in the midst of conflicts between farmers and the Congress, such as when it was claimed that public funds were being used to discourage the consumption of sugar and wheat products, thus jeopardizing the livelihood of farmers. Never swayed from her mission to serve the consumer and provide a better quality of life for those in need, Stanley continued to promote her nutritional programs.

Stanley was supported in her efforts by several prominent women's organizations, including the Daughters of the American Revolution (DAR). However, when invited to join this group, she declined the offer because of the organization's discriminatory membership policies: The DAR refused membership to African Americans and other people of color. Such a practice was in direct opposition to Stanley's political beliefs and her overall mission of serving those in need.

During the 1940s, Stanley served as special assistant to the administrator of the Human Nutrition and Home Economics Bureau (a division of the Agricultural Research Administration), a position she held until 1950. At this time, she extended her sphere of influence when she conducted research and developed educational home economics programs in Latin American countries, including Venezuela, Brazil, and Mexico. Stanley also participated in the United Nations Conference on Food and Agriculture in 1943 and worked with the United States National Commission for UNESCO.

Following her retirement in 1950, Stanley served as a home economics consultant with the office of Foreign Agriculture Relations of the USDA until 1953. She was instrumental in institutionalizing home economics and was one of the first women to gain acceptance and influence among political leaders. In recognition of her outstanding work in developing and promoting the field of home economics, the American Home Economics Association established the Louise Stanley Latin American Scholarship in her honor in 1953. Stanley died of cancer in 1954, in Washington, D.C. The home economics building on the campus of the University of Missouri was dedicated in her name in 1961.

See also Baker, Sara Josephine; Bevier, Isabel; Gilbreth, Lillian Moller; Home Economics; Morrill Act of 1862; Pennington, Mary Engle; Richards, Ellen Henrietta Swallow

References "Louise Stanley" [obituary], *New York Times* (16 July 1954); Sicherman, Barbara, and Carol Hurd Green, eds., *Notable American Women: The Modern Period* (1980).

Stevens, Nettie Maria (1861–1912)

Biologist Nettie Stevens performed research in three major areas. Her earliest work focused on the structure and classification of ciliate protozoa. Stevens next turned her research skills to studying specialized regenerative processes in certain flatworms. However, the research for which Stevens is most noted is her study of chromosomes and their connection to heredity. In 1905, Stevens published findings that showed that the gender of offspring is determined by the chromosomes contributed by male sex cells (sperm cells). This discovery continues to have broad implications today, particularly in the field of animal husbandry. For example, animal breeders working in the dairy industry can apply Stevens's findings to breed dairy cattle with particular characteristics.

Nettie Stevens was born in Cavendish, Vermont, and was raised in Westfield, Massachusetts, where she attended public school. Stevens graduated from the Westford Academy in 1880. Between 1880 and 1896, she alternately taught school, worked as a librarian, and continued her education. She graduated from the Westfield Normal School in 1892. Four years later, at age 35, she enrolled at Stanford University as a special student; the following year, she was admitted into the freshman class. At Stanford, Stevens earned her A.B. degree (1899) and her master's degree (1900), both in physiology. She then spent a year studying in Italy and Germany. Upon returning to the United States, Stevens enrolled at Bryn Mawr College, where she was awarded a Ph.D. in 1903. The focus of her doctoral research was the structure and classification of ciliate protozoa.

After receiving her Ph.D., Stevens remained at Bryn Mawr for the remainder of her career. While there, she conducted studies on the tissue processes involved in regeneration (the ability of an organism to replace lost body parts) in hydroids and planaria, a flatworm. Stevens later changed the focus of her research to chromosomes and sex determination. In this research, she indicated the presence of an "accessory chromosome" in sperm cells. Further investigations, focused on mealworms, prompted Stevens to conclude that two kinds of sperm cells existed—one containing an X chromosome and the other, a Y chromosome. Stevens also noted that unfertilized egg cells contained two X chromosomes. Using these observations, she correctly hypothesized that an egg cell fertilized by a sperm cell containing the X chromosome would result in a female embryo, while an egg cell fertilized by a sperm cell containing the Y chromosome would result in a male embryo.

Stevens verified her research findings using mosquitos, flies, spiders, and plants. She published her initial findings in 1905, and almost 40 other articles before her death in 1912. Similar research and conclusions were simultaneously reached by Edmund B. Wilson, a biologist working independently of Stevens at another facility. Until recently, Wilson generally had been credited for the discovery. Today, Stevens is also acknowledged for her research findings. In recognition of her research on chromosomes and sex determination, she was inducted into the National Women's Hall of Fame in 1994.

See also Bryn Mawr College; Genetic Engineering; Krim, Mathilde Galland; National Women's Hall of Fame
References Bailey, Martha J., *American Women in Science: A Biographical Dictionary* (1994); Eicher, Dr. Eva M., Senior Staff Scientist, Jackson Laboratory, Bar Harbor, Maine, telephone interview with Leonard Bernstein (23 March 1999); Kass-Simon, G., and Patricia Farnes, eds., *Women of Science: Righting the Record* (1990); Parry, Melanie, ed., *Larousse Dictionary of Women* (1996); Shearer, Benjamin F., and Barbara S. Shearer, eds., *Notable Women in the Life Sciences: A Biographical Dictionary* (1996); Uglow, Jennifer S., ed., *The International Dictionary of Women's Biography* (1982).

Strickland, Sarah (1812–1872)

Little is known about the life of Massachusetts native Sarah Strickland. It is known, however, that she eventually settled in Vineland, New Jersey, where she actively participated in issues concerning women's rights. In this role, Strickland frequently spoke at public events on such matters as women's health, the vote, and taxation, as well as on the capabilities and accomplishments of women.

The latter part of the 1850s witnessed significant movement in the area of women's rights. Among the many issues of the time were those related to changes taking place in women's clothing, especially as these changes affected a woman's ability to carry out her daily responsibilities (whether on the farm or in the classroom). It may have been the fashion movement toward less restrictive clothing for women that prompted Strickland and a companion, Darwin E. Crosby, to develop plans for an improved clothing dryer for which they received a patent in 1869. The dryer was designed as a clothes frame that allowed dresses to dry without developing wrinkles. Strickland assigned her rights to the clothes dryer to Crosby shortly after the patent for the invention was issued.

See also Converse, Susan Taylor; Miller, Elizabeth Smith; Women's Rights
References Burstyn, Joan N., ed., *Past and Promise: Lives of New Jersey Women* (1990).

Strong, Harriet R. (1844–1929)

Harriet Strong is often called the "Walnut Queen," for her remarkable success in cultivating this crop in arid southern California. Strong also was recognized for developing several household inventions, including a device for opening windows and a window-sash holder. However, few people know about her development of a unique irrigation design that made use of a system of carefully placed dams to regulate water flow in a controlled, uniform manner. Strong's irrigation system proved so useful that it received an award from the federal Agricultural and Mining departments. Its design was copied and used by engineers as far away as Central America.

Born in Buffalo, New York, Harriet Russell spent her early years as a semi-invalid due to what was described as a spinal affliction. Her illness and seclusion allowed her to devote great amounts of time to studying art, music, literature, and history. At age 14, Strong attended the Young Ladies' Seminary of Mary Atkins at Benicia, California. She remained there for two years, becoming proficient in music, French, and English. In 1863, Russell met and married Charles Lyman Strong, a man almost twice her age. One year later, Charles Strong, who was prone to overwork and stress, suffered the first of several nervous breakdowns. This event forced him to resign his position and move his family to Oakland, California. Further breakdowns, combined with an unsuccessful mining venture, drove Charles to take his own life.

Left with four young daughters and huge family debts, Harriet sought and received medical treatment for her lifelong spinal problem, and was restored to good health. She then turned her attention to farming, deciding to plant walnuts, a popular crop at the time and one that grew well in the arid southern Californian climate. She also planted citrus fruit trees, pomegranates, and pampas grass (imported from Germany and used for decorative purposes).

To ensure success in bringing her products to market, Strong designed an irrigation system for her property. The system made use of a series of dams to store water and control flooding. She received patents for her dam designs in 1887 and 1894. In her system, each dam was carefully positioned so that the pressure of water stored in a lower dam would support the physical structure of the preceding dam.

It was also during this period that Strong developed her household inventions. One of these was a device that allowed her to open a window from her bed. Strong's success brought her much recognition. She was the first woman elected to the Los Angeles Chamber of Commerce. She also gained national notice when she demonstrated her patented irrigation and water storage system at the World's Columbian Exposition (Chicago World's Fair) in 1893.

Strong became a leading proponent of flood control and water supply. In 1918, she made a presentation before a congressional committee advocating the use of dams in the Grand Canyon to develop the Colorado River. She stressed that the project was needed to prevent flooding and to provide adequate electricity and water for the rapidly growing communities of southern California. Elements of her proposals were incorpo-

H. W. R. STRONG.

METHOD OF AND MEANS FOR IMPOUNDING DEBRIS AND STORING WATER.

No. 528,823. Patented Nov. 6, 1894.

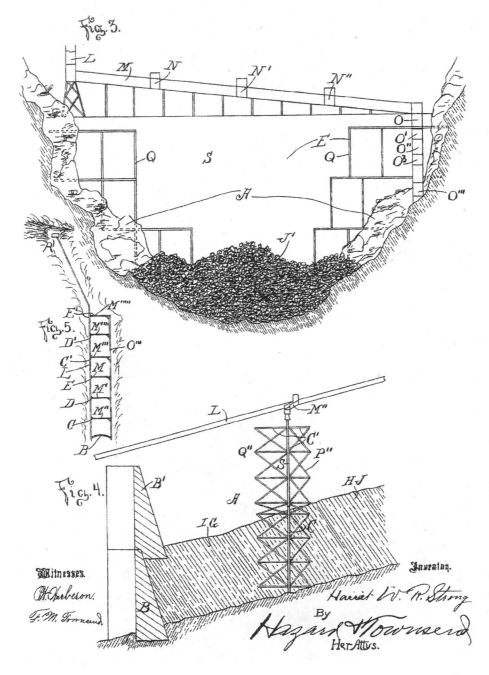

This illustration is the patent drawing for the irrigation system developed by Harriet Strong. (USPTO)

rated into the eventual development of the Colorado River.

See also Agricultural Engineering; Civil Engineering; Columbian Exposition; Environmental Engineering; Greene, Catherine Littlefield; Invention/Inventors; Patent; Pinckney, Eliza Lucas; Rockwell, Mabel MacFerran

References James, Edward T., Janet Wilson James, and Paul S. Boyers, eds., *Notable American Women: A Biographical Dictionary* (1607–1950), vol. 3: (P–Z) (1971); Stanley, Autumn, *Mothers and Daughters of Invention: Notes for a Revised History of Technology* (1993); Vare, Ethlie Ann, and Greg Ptacek, *Mothers of Invention: From the Bra to the Bomb, Forgotten Women and Their Unforgettable Ideas* (1988).

Taussig, Helen Brooke (1898–1986)

Physician Helen Brooke Taussig recognized that the "blue baby syndrome" (cyanosis) resulted from a congenital heart condition that deprived infants of oxygenated blood, causing them to appear blue. Between 1941 and 1944, Taussig and cardiac surgeon Alfred Blalock developed a surgical procedure to correct the heart defect that resulted in cyanosis. This procedure has saved the lives of thousands of babies. Years later, Taussig successfully lobbied for a ban on the sale of the drug thalidomide (a tranquilizer used by pregnant women to prevent nausea) in the United States and also helped eliminate use of this drug in Europe.

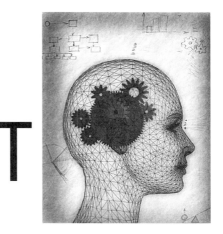

Helen Taussig was born in Cambridge, Massachusetts, in 1898. Her father was a Harvard professor, and her mother, a Radcliffe graduate. When Helen was 11, her mother died from tuberculosis. Helen, too, developed a mild case of tuberculosis and also suffered from dyslexia—a condition that delayed her high school graduation by one year. During her childhood, she also suffered from whooping cough, which resulted in her partial loss of hearing.

After high school, Taussig attended Radcliffe College for two years. While there, she became a tennis champion. She later transferred to the University of California at Berkeley, where she was elected into Phi Beta Kappa and awarded a B.A in 1921. After receiving her undergraduate degree, Taussig returned to Massachusetts. She wanted to study medicine at Harvard Medical School, but at that time, women who studied at the school were not granted degrees. At Harvard, Taussig studied histology and bacteriology. She also studied anatomy at nearby Boston University. It was at Boston University that Taussig became interested in cardiology.

Taussig applied to and was admitted to the Johns Hopkins University School of Medicine. She received her M.D. in 1927. For the next year, she worked on an Archibald fellowship at Johns Hopkins and was placed in charge of the university's new cardiac clinic. Taussig performed her internship at the Cardiology Clinic of the Harriet Lane Home (the pediatrics section of Johns Hopkins University Hospital) from 1928 to 1930. The next year, she was appointed to head the cardiac clinic, and she remained in this position until 1963.

Taussig's work at the Harriet Lane Home exposed her to many infants suffering from heart problems. Because of the hearing loss she developed as a child, Taussig could not use ordinary stethoscopes in her examinations. To overcome this limitation, she became one of the first doctors routinely to use a fluoroscope and electrocardiograph, along with physical examination, to diagnose cardiac disease. Her use of these methods led her to hypothesize that the "blue baby" condition resulted from a hole in the heart's septum (the muscular wall that separates the left and right ventricles) or from a blockage in the blood vessels that carry blood between the heart and lungs.

In 1941, Taussig contacted cardiac surgeon Alfred Blalock to discuss her ideas. The two immediately began working to find a way to allow blood flow between the heart and lungs in children who had blocked arteries. In 1944, Blalock performed surgery using a shunt (by-pass) to reroute an artery that normally went to an arm, to the lungs, where it could pick up needed oxygen. The operation was a success, and it opened the way for other types of heart surgery.

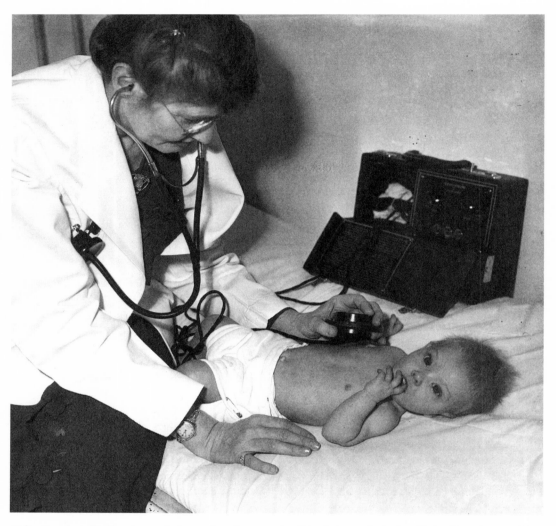

Helen Taussig codeveloped a surgical procedure for correcting "blue baby syndrome" and helped ban the use of thalidomide by pregnant women. (Corbis/Bettmann-UPI)

In 1947, Taussig published the book *Congenital Malformations of the Heart* to inform doctors worldwide about the use of fluoroscopes and electrocardiographs as methods for identifying congenital heart defects.

While working at the Harriet Lane Home, Taussig also taught at Johns Hopkins University School of Medicine. From 1930 to 1946, she was an instructor in pediatrics. In 1946, she became an associate professor of pediatrics. Finally, in 1959, Taussig became the first woman ever to be appointed a full professor at the university.

In the early 1960s, one of Taussig's former students alerted her to an outbreak of deformities that were occurring in newborns in Germany. Taussig traveled to Germany to interview the mothers of the stricken newborns, and she quickly identified the drug thalidomide as the probable cause of the defects. After returning to the United States, Taussig recommended to the U.S. Food and Drug Administration (FDA) that sale of this drug be banned in the United States. The United States did ban the drug, and many European countries followed suit. Taussig later provided testimony before a Senate committee that resulted in the development of stricter laws involving the testing and sale of drugs.

Helen Taussig received worldwide recognition for her contributions to cardiology and was granted 20 honorary degrees and more than 30 international awards. In 1947, she was presented the French Chevalier Legion d'Honneur and the Women's National Press Club Award. She was awarded the American College of Chest Physicians Medal of Honor in 1953 and the Albert Lasker Award one year later. In 1957, Taussig was the recipient of both the Eleanor Roosevelt Achievement Award and the American Heart Association's Award of Merit. During the year of her retirement, Taussig received the Achievement Award of the American Association of University Women (AAUW) and the American Heart Association's Gold Heart Award. The following year, President Lyndon B. Johnson presented Taussig the Medal of Freedom, the highest honor that can be bestowed upon a civilian. In Germany, the University of Göttingen dedicated the Helen B. Taussig Cardiac Clinic. In 1966, the American College of Physicians bestowed its John Phillips Memorial Award on Taussig for her contributions to internal medicine. The Johns Hopkins Pediatric Cardiac Clinic was renamed for Taussig in 1970, and in 1976 it presented her with the Milton S. Eisenhower Gold Medal. In 1973, Taussig was inducted into the National Women's Hall of Fame.

Helen Taussig was active in many professional organizations and held positions of leadership in several. In 1964, she became the first woman president of the American Heart Association and in 1972, the first woman master in the American College of Physicians. She was elected to membership in the National Academy of Sciences (NAS) in 1973, 28 years after Alfred Blalock received that honor. Taussig also founded the Heart Association of Maryland and served as its president from 1952 to 1953.

See also Apgar, Virginia; Baker, Sara Josephine; Kempf, Martine; Medicine/Medical Technology; National Women's Hall of Fame; Pharmacology; Phi Beta Kappa Society

References Altman, Lawrence K., "Dr. Helen Taussig, 87, Dies; Led in Blue Baby Operation" [obituary], *New York Times* (23 May 1986); Bailey, Martha J., *American Women in Science: A Biographical Dictionary* (1994); Moritz, Charles, ed., *Current Biography, 1966* (1966); Potter, Robert, "Saving Our Doomed 'Blue Babies,'" *American Weekly* (17 February 1947); Shearer, Benjamin F., and Barbara S. Shearer, eds., *Notable Women in the Life Sciences: A Biographical Dictionary* (1996); Stanley, Autumn, *Mothers and Daughters of Invention: Notes for a Revised History of Technology* (1993); National Women's Hall of Fame, "Helen Brooke Taussig, 1898–1986," available at http://www. greatwomen.org (cited 1 April 1999).

Telecommunications

Telecommunications is the term used to describe technologies that make use of optical or electrical signals to transmit information (data) by means of fibers, wires, or through the air. Telephones, computer modems, radios, televisions, communication satellites, and all other devices that make use of combinations of such machines are examples of telecommunication technologies. Use of such technologies advanced greatly throughout the twentieth century in conjunction with advances in the space program as well as computers and computer technologies.

Several women have devoted a part of their lives to developing telecommunication technologies. Among them are Hedy Lamarr, Erna Schneider Hoover, Beatrice Hicks, Clara Brinkerhoff, and Alva Matthews. Hedy Lamarr is best known for her acting career in the early part of the twentieth century. However, during World War II, Lamarr collaborated with musical composer George Anthiel to develop a device, for use with radio-controlled torpedoes, that would prevent the radio signals that controlled torpedoes from being jammed by enemy forces. This device, known simply as a Secret Communications System, earned Lamarr and Anthiel a patent in 1942. Although this particular device was not adopted by the U.S. Navy at the time, systems they later adopted did make use of the same frequency-hopping technology as that used by Lamarr and Anthiel in their antijamming device.

Beatrice Hicks is most known for her work in chemical engineering and for her work as a designer of environmental sensors used in spacecraft and other enclosed spaces. She also is known for being a founding member of the Society of Women Engineers (SWE). During part of her career, she was employed by the Western Electric Company. While working for this company, she invented several new pieces of telephone equipment. For her work in this area, Hicks received many awards from her employer.

Erna Schneider Hoover's contribution to telecommunications came about while she was employed by the telephone company. While working for Bell Laboratories in New Jersey in the 1970s, Hoover and a colleague developed computer software that was designed to prevent overloading within the telephone system. Such overloading occurred when numerous people were trying to make calls at the same time. The software developed by Hoover and Eckhart provided a means of regulating and rerouting calls so as to permit the greatest number of calls to be completed at the same time. A patent was issued for this software in 1971.

Before telephones were invented, telegraphs were a major means of long-distance communication. In 1882, a New York City music teacher named Clara M. Brinkerhoff coinvented a key for a telegraph machine with George Cumming. Their key was an improvement on older keys in that the contact points were placed around the edges of the key. After obtaining patents on this new key in the United States and England, Cumming and Brinkerhoff opened a company to sell their invention.

After the U.S. space program devised a way to place a spacecraft in orbit around the Earth, they applied this technology to placing satellites into orbit. Among the early satellites sent into orbit was one known as *Telstar*. This satellite, which was placed into orbit in 1962, made live simultaneous television broadcasts throughout the world possible. Among the major developers of the *Telstar* satellite was engineer Alva Matthews. Since the launch of *Telstar*, many other satellites having uses in television and radio broadcasting, cellular telephone transmissions, and weather broadcasting have been placed in orbit. Many of these were carried into space aboard the NASA

space shuttles and placed into orbit using the robotic arm that was designed by former astronauts Sally Kirsten Ride and Judith A. Resnik.

Telecommunications is one of the fastest-growing industries in the world. As computer technologies continue to become more complex and powerful, and as humans find more ways to make use of the rapid data transmissions made possible by telecommunications, it is likely that this industry will continue to grow and that the number of women participating in developing new technologies in this field also will increase.

See also Computers/Computer Technology; Hicks, Beatrice Alice; Hoover, Erna Schneider; Lamarr, Hedy; Resnik, Judith A.; Ride, Sally Kirsten; Space Exploration
References Showell, Ellen H., and Fred M. B. Amram, *From Indian Corn to Outer Space: Women Invent in America* (1995); Stanley, Autumn, *Mothers and Daughters of Invention: Notes for a Revised History of Technology* (1993).

Telkes, Maria (1900–1995)

Maria Telkes was among the first people to investigate practical applications of solar energy—the energy of the sun. Working with architect Eleanor Raymond, Maria Telkes designed the first solar heated house (for which she received a patent) in 1948. During the 1950s, Telkes expanded her applications of solar technology to develop a solar oven (for which she also received a patent) and solar cookers that remain the basis for modern designs. In addition, she created thermoelectric devices (apparatus that convert heat energy into electricity), solar electric generators, and solar stills used for desalination (the removal of salt from ocean water to make the water suitable for drinking).

Maria Telkes was born, raised, and educated in Budapest, Hungary. She attended Budapest University, where she studied physical chemistry, and received her B.A. degree in 1920. Four years later, she obtained her Ph.D. in the same area. After teaching physics in a Budapest school for one year, Telkes left Hungary for the United States. The purpose of the trip was to visit an uncle who was the Hungarian consul in Cleveland, Ohio. Shortly after her arrival, Telkes was asked to join the research faculty of the Cleveland Clinic Foundation as a biophysicist. She accepted the offer and remained in the United States.

At the Cleveland Clinic Foundation, Telkes's interest in energy associated with living things prompted her to conduct studies on energy sources and the changes in energy that occur when healthy cells develop into cancerous cells. She also studied the human brain and the emission of electrical energy associated with its normal functions. These studies led to the development of a photoelectric device that was capable of recording the electrical energy transmitted by the brain. Telkes reported her findings in the book *Phenomena of Life,* on which she collaborated with George Crile.

In 1937, Telkes became an American citizen. That same year, she was hired as a research engineer in the research division of the Westinghouse Electrical and Manufacturing Company in East Pittsburgh, Pennsylvania. She remained at Westinghouse for two years. During this time, Telkes focused her research on energy conversions and designed a number of devices that converted heat energy into electricity. She later received patents for these devices.

Telkes left Westinghouse and joined the Massachusetts Institute of Technology (MIT) Solar Energy Conversion Project as a research associate in 1939. At MIT, she began the work for which she is most well known—finding practical applications for solar energy. Telkes's early work at MIT involved investigating the use of solar energy in devices that could change heat energy into electricity. She also developed a new solar heating system for use in homes. This solar heating system was not the first such system developed; however, it differed from earlier solar heating systems in that a chemical (sodium sulfate decahydrate), rather than circulating water or crushed rock, was used to collect and store heat absorbed from sunlight. In Telkes's solar heating system, sunlight passing through a large glass window heats air that is trapped in a space behind the glass. The air then transfers its heat through a metal sheet and into a second air space. From this air space, circulating fans move the warmed air

into chemical-filled storage compartments located in the walls between rooms, making the walls the actual heating elements of the house.

While Telkes was at MIT, the United States entered into World War II. Telkes, who was noted for her energy research, was asked to serve as a civilian adviser to the Office of Scientific Research and Development (OSRD). While working with the OSRD, she designed a portable distillation system that used solar energy to produce drinking water from sea water. The system was designed for installation on life rafts used by military personnel. For this invention, Telkes was awarded an OSRD Certificate of Merit in 1945.

In 1948, Telkes again was asked to contribute her talents to a federal research program that was seeking a way to remedy a drinking water shortage in the Virgin Islands. Telkes applied the same distillation principles she had used in the portable distillation systems for the life rafts.

That same year, a prototype of Telkes's solar heating system was installed in an experimental house built on the estate of sculptor Amelia Peabody, in Dover, Massachusetts. The solar heating system proved highly efficient and cost-effective in heating the home during the winter months. In addition, during the hottest summer months, the chemical contained in the wall storage compartments drew heat out of the rooms of the house. The circulating system thus was reversed, and the heat was removed.

Telkes began working at the College of Engineering of New York University (NYU) in 1953. There she organized a solar energy laboratory. In 1958, she left NYU to serve as the research director of solar engineering at the Princeton Division of Curtis-Wright Corporation. At Curtis-Wright, Telkes pioneered new ways to make use of solar energy, developing solar dryers, solar water heaters, and solar thermoelectric generators for use aboard spacecraft.

Telkes again changed jobs in 1961, accepting a position at Cryo-Therm. In her two years with this company, she focused her attention on developing insulating materials to protect temperature-sensitive instruments such as those used aboard spacecraft. These materials were later used in transporting receptacles aboard the *Apollo* and *Polaris* spacecraft.

In 1963, Telkes became the leader of the solar energy application laboratories at MELPAR Company, where she again turned her attention toward experiments that used solar energy to produce freshwater. Six years later, she moved to what would be her last professional position, at the University of Delaware's Institute of Energy Conservation. At this facility, Telkes conducted research on the design of efficient heat transfer systems and developed materials that could be used to store solar energy. The construction of a solar heated building at the University of Delaware, known as "Solar One," resulted from this research. Maria Telkes retired from the University of Delaware in 1978. Upon her retirement, the university named her professor emerita.

Telkes was a member of several professional organizations, including the American Chemical Society (ACS), the Electrochemistry Society, and Sigma Xi. In 1952, she became the first recipient of the Society of Women Engineers (SWE) Achievement Award, in recognition for her work in developing means of using solar energy. Twenty-five years later, Telkes was presented the Charles Greeley Abbot Award from the American Solar Energy Society. That same year, the National Academy of Sciences (NAS) Building Research Advisory Board honored her for advancing the technology of solar heated buildings.

See also American Institute of Architects (AIA); American Society of Heating, Refrigerating and Air-Conditioning Engineers (ASHRAE); Architecture; Barney, Nora Stanton Blatch; Bethune, Louise Blanchard; Keichline, Anna W.; Morgan, Julia; Patent; Solar Technologies

References Graham, Judith, ed., *Current Biography 1996* (1996); Rothe, Anna, ed., *Current Biography Yearbook, 1950* (1950); Vare, Ethlie Ann, and Greg Ptacek, *Mothers of Invention: Notes for a Revised History of Technology* (1988); Arizona State University, College of Architecture and Environmental Design, "Telkes, Maria, 1900–1995," available at http://www.asu.edu/caed/AEDlibrary/libarchives/solar/telkes.html (cited 27 May 1999).

Tesoro, Giuliana Cavaglieri (b. 1921)

Giuliana Cavaglieri Tesoro gained prominence in the field of polymer chemistry for her development of chemicals, specifically flame retardant polymers (compounds consisting of many molecules) used in the manufacture of textiles. Tesoro has received 110 patents for textile polymers. Included among these are patents for the development of antistatic chemicals used in the production of synthetic fibers and fiber binding polymers. Tesoro also pioneered research to improve the permanent press properties of fabrics.

Giuliana Cavaglieri was born into a Jewish family in Venice, Italy. She was raised and educated in that country. However, because Italy's racial laws enacted in 1938 prevented Jews from attending universities, Giuliana went to Geneva, Switzerland, to begin her college studies and earned a diploma there as an X-ray technician. During the early 1940s, her family moved to the United States. Here, Giuliana attended Yale University, receiving her Ph.D. in organic chemistry in 1943. While at Yale, she met and married classmate Victor Tesoro.

After receiving her doctorate, Tesoro accepted a position as research chemist first with the Calco Chemical Company (1943–1944) and later, with the Onyx Oil and Chemical Company (1944). At Onyx, Tesoro became associate director of research in 1957. She held other research positions at J. P. Stevens & Company and the Princeton University Textile Research Institute and served as senior chemist at Burlington Industries. In 1971, Tesoro became research professor at Polytechnic Institute of New York. She then served as a visiting professor at the Massachusetts Institute of Technology (MIT) and as a member of the editorial board of the *Textile Research Journal,* a monthly publication of the Textile Research Institute.

In addition to her work in industry and academia, Tesoro has enjoyed membership in many professional organizations, including the New York Academy of Sciences (NYAS), the Society of Women Engineers (SWE), the American Association of Textile Chemists and Colorists (AATCC), the American Association for the Advancement of Science (AAAS), and the American Chemical Society (ACS). She also was a member of the Fiber Society and served as that organization's president in 1974. Tesoro has received many awards recognizing her achievements in polymer and textile technology. Among them are the American Dyestuff Reporter Award (1959), the Olney Medal of the American Association of Textile Chemists and Colorists (1963), and the Achievement Award of the Society of Women Engineers (1978).

See also Benerito, Ruth Rogan; Fox, Sally; Kwolek, Stephanie Louise; Textiles

References Bailey, Martha J., *American Women in Science: A Biographical Dictionary* (1994); Grinstein, Louise S., Rose K. Rose, and Miriam H. Rafailovich, eds., *Women in Chemistry and Physics: A Biobibliographic Sourcebook* (1993); Rossiter, Margaret W., *Women Scientists in America: Before Affirmative Action, 1940–1972* (1995); Stanley, Autumn, *Mothers and Daughters of Invention: Notes for a Revised History of Technology* (1993).

Textiles

Any woven product is considered a textile. The word *textile* also is used collectively to refer to all natural or synthetic fibers, threads, and yarns that have the capability of being woven. Examples of fibers used in the production of textiles include those derived from plants and animals as well as those made synthetically in the laboratory. Common plant fibers include cotton, linen, flax, and hemp. Fibers derived from animals include wool, silk, felt, and some types of fur. Synthetic, or human-made, fibers include nylon, rayon, polyester, and spandex. Products resulting from textile manufacturing include clothing, upholstery, carpeting, and a variety of other products used in homes, automobiles, offices, and industry.

In the United States, the textile industry dates back to colonial America. Among the earliest women to make a significant contribution in this area was Sybilla Masters. In 1716, Sybilla's husband, Thomas, obtained a patent in England for a process developed by his wife. The patent was issued for a means of working and staining straw for use in the making of hats and bonnets. Sybilla's process also encompassed a means of working the

leaves of the palmetto (a shrub) to create matting for use in chairs and other pieces of furniture. In his application for the patent on this invention, Thomas Masters readily admitted that the processes had been developed by his wife Sybilla. However, custom at the time prevented women from owning property, so a patent had to be obtained by Thomas rather than Sybilla Masters.

In the mid-1700s, Eliza Lucas Pinckney was living on and operating a plantation in the Carolina colonies. While trying to devise ways to make her plantation profitable, she found a way to successfully cultivate indigo and developed a means of obtaining the blue dye for which this plant is most known. The dye resulting from this process was then sold to textile mills both in the colonies and abroad for use in coloring fabrics.

Pawtuckett, Rhode Island, resident Hannah Wilkinson Slater developed an improved cotton thread for use in sewing in the late 1700s. She obtained a patent for this invention in 1793 (in the name of Mrs. Samuel Slater). The thread became widely used in the textile mills operated by Hannah's husband, Samuel Slater.

Many of the major textile mills of early America were located in the North; however, many of the plants grown for use in the production of textiles emerged from the South. Much of the success of the textile industry in America was dependent upon developments in the growing and harvesting of crops such as cotton, linen, flax, and hemp. The cotton gin played a major role in the harvesting and processing of cotton near the end of the eighteenth century. In addition, the cotton gin also made use of a combing device that permitted the fibers in the cotton boll to be easily separated from the seeds. Although the patent for the cotton gin was issued to Eli Whitney in 1794, many people believe that the true genius behind the development of this machine may have been Catherine Littlefield Greene of Georgia. It is known that Greene provided Whitney the funding and space needed to develop his machine. In addition, some evidence suggests that the idea for this development originated with Greene and that she played an instrumental role in a design change that made the machine workable.

Although cotton was a major plant used by the textile industry, by this time in history, straw also was of great importance. This was particularly evident in the New England states. Rhode Island native Betsey Metcalf became well known for a straw-weaving process she developed in 1799. This method was widely used throughout New England, but Metcalf never profited from its use because she elected not to apply for a patent. Ten years after Metcalf developed her weaving process, Mary Kies of South Killington, Connecticut, devised a means of incorporating silk or thread into the straw-weaving process. In 1809, Kies became the first American woman to be issued a patent in her own name. Her process was widely used until it was improved upon by another developed and patented by Sophia Woodhouse Welles in 1821.

The hatmakers of New England did most of their weaving by hand. However, much of the textile work being done in the United States resulted from large-scale weaving and sewing mills. In the 1860s, twelve-year-old Margaret Knight developed a safety device for use in such mills after observing an accident that occurred when a machine shuttle broke free, striking and injuring the machine's operator. Knight's device prevented similar accidents from occurring by causing the machine to stop if a thread broke, thus preventing the shuttle from being ejected by the machine. In 1894, Knight developed yet another invention for use by the textile industry—a reel for use in spinning or sewing machines. At the same time that Knight was making her contributions to the textile industry, Helen Augusta Blanchard also was making significant contributions through her development of devices related to sewing. Blanchard received 28 patents in her lifetime. All but two of these were related to sewing, with the most significant including sewing machine needles, a spool case, and a sewing machine capable of zig-zag stitching.

Throughout the early part of the twentieth century, many of the developments occurring within the textile industry were related to improvements in machinery used to make products from natural fibers. Near the middle of this century, the development of synthetic materials such as nylon, rayon, spandex, and dacron also began to greatly influence the textile industry. One woman who has made significant accomplishments in the development of new synthetic fibers is polymer chemist Stephanie Kwolek. Kwolek's major achievement in this area occurred while she was employed by the DuPont Company in Wilmington, Delaware. In 1965, she developed an unusual fiber called Kevlar. The fiber is known for its incredible strength and its resistance to corrosion and damage from fire. In 1971, Kwolek obtained a patent for this fiber (which was assigned to the DuPont Company), which has since been used in the manufacture of tires, automobile brakes, and bullet-proof vests worn by law enforcement and military personnel.

Other major accomplishments in textiles that have involved synthetic substances have resulted from the work of Giuliana Tesoro, Ruth Benerito, and Patsy Sherman. Giuliana Tesoro's major contributions in this area lie in her development of flame-retardant polymers, antistatic polymers, and polymers that resist wrinkling. Her work in this area has resulted in at least 110 patents. Ruth Benerito also has been awarded numerous patents (more than 50) for her work in the textile industry. Her major contributions in this area rest in her development of processes used to treat fabrics to make them resistant to wrinkling and to staining caused by water, dust, and oil. Patsy Sherman also developed a product intended to protect fabrics from staining. This product, which Sherman developed in 1956 while working for the 3M Company, came to be known as Scotchgard®. Since its development, Scotchgard® has been widely used at textile plants that produce carpeting, upholstery fabrics, and wall coverings. In addition, the product is available for purchase for use by individuals desiring to protect the various fabrics used in their homes and automobiles from damage by stains.

Although much of the work done in the textile industry in the past 50 years has involved the use of synthetic materials, some inventors, such as Sally Fox, concentrated on developing improvements in natural fibers. Using her knowledge of genetics and selective breeding, Fox developed a means for growing cotton that resulted in diverse naturally colored fibers she called FoxFibre®. Fox later expanded her endeavors by developing her own company, Natural Cotton Colours, Inc., which supplies the cotton from her plants to textile mills in the United States and Japan for use in making products such as clothing and towels.

See also Agriculture; Benerito, Ruth Rogan; Blanchard, Helen Augusta; Fox, Sally; Greene, Catherine Littlefield; Kies, Mary; Knight, Margaret E.; Kwolek, Stephanie Louise; Masters, Sybilla Righton; Metcalf, Betsey; Pinckney, Eliza Lucas; Sherman, Patsy O.; Slater, Hannah Wilkinson (Mrs. Samuel); Tesoro, Giuliana Cavaglieri; Welles, Sophia Woodhouse
References Bernstein, Leonard, Alan Winkler, and Linda Zierdt-Warshaw, *Multicultural Women of Science* (1996); Heinemann, Susan, *Timelines of American Women's History* (1996); Scott, Brian, "Stopping Bullets," in "Working Knowledge," *Scientific American* (March 1997); Vare, Ethlie Ann, and Greg Ptacek, *Mothers of Invention: From the Bra to the Bomb, Forgotten Women and Their Unforgettable Ideas* (1988); Smithsonian Institution, Lemelson Center, "Innovative Lives," available at http://www.si.edu/lemelson/Lect12.htm (cited 3 August 1999).

Thompson, Mary H. (1829–1895)

Mary H. Thompson was a pioneer in many areas within the medical profession. After receiving her medical degree from the New England Female Medical College in Boston, Massachusetts, in 1863, Thompson traveled to Chicago, where she founded the Chicago Hospital for Women and Children (later renamed the Mary H. Thompson Hospital) in 1865. Thompson also helped establish the Women's Medical College of Chicago.

During her career as a physician, Thompson became known as one of the most highly rated abdominal and pelvic surgeons in the United States. She also was the only woman surgeon in the Chicago area. It was through her role as a surgeon that Mary Thompson's contribution to technology emerged. In the 1870s, she developed an abdominal needle for use during surgery. This needle quickly gained in popularity and was not only adopted for use by many surgeons of the time but also continues to be used today in abdominal surgery in major hospitals throughout the country.

See also Blount (Griffin), Bessie J.; Bryant, Alice G.; Medicine/Medical Technology; Vallino, Lisa M., and Rozier, Betty M.
References Debus, Allen G. ed., *World Who's Who in Science*, 1st ed. (1968); Kane, Joseph Nathan, Steven Anzovin, and Janet Podell, *Famous First Facts*, 5th ed. (1997); Stanley, Autumn, *Mothers and Daughters of Invention: Notes for a Revised History of Technology* (1993).

Todd, E. L. (n.d.)

E. L. Todd is believed to be the first woman to invent an airplane. When she developed her invention, in 1908, Todd was an employee of the U.S. Patent and Trademark Office (PTO) in Washington, D.C. Todd demonstrated the plane she developed at an air show held in Brooklyn, New York. This plane, unlike others of the day, featured a collapsible design that allowed it to be reduced in size for easy transport. Very little else is known about this early inventor in aeronautics.

See also Jones, El Dorado
References Read, Phyllis J., and Bernard L. Witlieb, *The Book of Women's Firsts* (1992); "Woman Has New Aeroplane: Miss Todd Hopes to Exhibit the Model at Brighton Beach," *New York Times* (31 July 1908); Zilberg, Caroline, ed., *Women's Firsts* (1997).

Vallino, Lisa M. (b. 1961) and Rozier, Betty M. (b. 1939)

Perseverance, tenacity, and a vision born of necessity gave Missouri natives Lisa Vallino, R.N., B.S.N., and Betty Rozier the impetus to pursue their quest to patent, produce, and market a medical device designed to prevent intravenous needles and catheters from being accidentally dislodged from their insertion sites. At the time the idea for this invention was developed, Vallino was working as a pediatric nurse at Cardinal Glennon Children's Hospital in St. Louis, Missouri. In her work, Vallino was confronted daily with situations involving the dislodging of intravenous (IV) needles or catheters from patients. The danger of such occurrences was readily apparent: The IVs carried fluids, nutrients, and various medicines to patients in need of them. When IVs or catheters became dislodged, Vallino and her colleagues generally resorted to fashioning plastic urine cups into devices that could cover and guard the insertion areas.

However, Vallino believed that the time involved in cutting the cup and taping the rigid plastic to the patient's skin was time that skilled nurses could put to better use. To address this problem, she set out to develop and manufacture her own device. She enlisted the aid of her mother, Betty Rozier, to deal with the legal, trademark, and patent issues involved in developing such a device. She also asked Rozier to research how the manufacturing and marketing of the protector might be accomplished. Rozier, who had experience running her own firm and working with machinery, seemed a logical choice to deal with the business end of the process.

Vallino's goal was to fabricate a cover that protected both peripheral and central infusion sites from accidental bumps or the accidental or deliberate removal of the needle or the fluid supply line attached to the needle, sparing the patient needless pain. She also expected the device to improve safety for health-care workers by reducing their chances of exposure to pathogens carried in body fluids as they tried to reconnect an IV or catheter to a patient. In addition, she be-

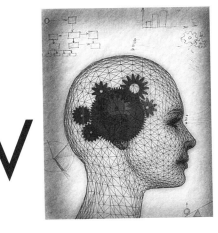

lieved that use of the device would save time and money because nursing time would not be wasted in fashioning makeshift protectors and reinserting IVs.

Vallino and Rozier had a vacuum-molded, or thermoformed, prototype of the unit developed. They then showed the device to potential buyers as a means of obtaining feedback from nurses about potential design flaws or omissions. Based on this input, the pair changed the initial design to make use of a softer plastic. They also added ventilation holes and made the device transparent, so nurses could easily observe the injection site.

Vallino and Rozier next met with a patent attorney. At the initial meeting with this attorney, they were told that their idea was too simple to qualify for a patent. In response to this information, Rozier undertook the required patent research herself and discovered that although many people had applied for similar patents, their devices were too complex or too costly to succeed. It appeared that the simplicity of Vallino's design was its strength.

Believing in their product, Vallino and Rozier founded their company, Progressive IVs, in early 1991. In January, they applied for a design patent under the name I.V. House® to protect the product's appearance from being copied and to give them the limited protection offered by a patent-pending designation. This allowed them to sell the product while they waited for the official patent to be granted. In May of the same year, they also sent an application to the U.S. Patent and Trademark Office to register the name of the device and to obtain trademark registration.

During the first production run for the I.V. House®, Vallino and Rozier had problems with the materials used. They rejected the order, found a new manufacturer, added a recessed tape guide, and changed to an injection-molding process that used latex-free polyethylene—a substance that had already obtained FDA approval for medical uses—to produce a precisely formed unit that could be packaged without additional labor. The change of materials and the added design feature of a tape guide made the device "sophisticated" enough to warrant a utility patent, for which they applied in July 1991. This patent would protect Vallino and Rozier from others who might attempt to copy the device.

After the I.V. House® was twice rejected for a utility patent, the patent attorney working with Vallino and Rozier persuaded the patent reviewer to consider the humanitarian aspects of the protector. This consideration apparently worked, and Vallino and Rozier were issued Utility Patent No. 5,167,240 on 1 December 1992. The design patent (No. D335,926) was granted on 25 May of the following year.

In 1994, Vallino and Rozier's company, Progressive IVs®, introduced an infant-sized version of its infusion site guard. Its first use was on Vallino's young son, who had contracted pneumonia. At present, the product is in use by more than 100 hospitals in the Midwest, for children and the elderly. That same year, the device was shown at the National Investors' Expo in Washington, D.C. (an event cosponsored by the U.S. Patent Office and the Intellectual Property Owners' Association), where it received an award for excellence.

Since developing their product, both Vallino and Rozier have been honored with awards from technology and entrepreneurial groups. In 1994, Rozier was granted the Advocate of the Year Award from the U.S. Small Business Administration's Missouri Women in Business. In 1997, both women were selected as Invention Ambassadors for the Lemelson-MIT Prize Fund. In addition, Vallino was presented the 1998 Woman of Distinction award during the Sigma Sigma Sigma Centennial.

See also Baker, Sara Josephine; Blount (Griffin), Bessie J.; Bryant, Alice G.; Medicine/Medical Technology; Patent

References Showell, Ellen H., and Fred M. B. Amram, *From Indian Corn to Outer Space: Women Invent in America* (1995); Vallino, Lisa, RN, BSN, "I.V. House: Pediatric Nurses Contribute to Refinement of IV Protector," *Journal of Pediatric Nursing*, vol. 13, no. 3 (June 1998); Lemelson-MIT Program, "Betty M. Rozier & Lisa M. Vallino: Intravenous Catheter Shield," in Invention Dimension, Inventor of the Week, available at http://web.mit.edu/invent/www/inventorsR-Z (cited 9 July 1999); U.S. Patent and Trademark Office, Full Text and Image Database—Number Search, available through the U.S. Patent and Trademark Office Depository, at http://www.uspto.gov/go/ptdl (cited 9 July 1999).

Van Deman, Esther (1862–1937)

Esther B. Van Deman was an acknowledged expert in archaeology, the branch of science that studies the remains of past human cultures. Her area of specialization focused on ancient Roman building construction—a subject she studied while living in Rome for more than thirty years.

Van Deman entered the University of Michigan at Ann Arbor in 1887. She received her A.B. degree in 1891 and remained at the University of Michigan to pursue her graduate studies. She received her A.M. degree the following year. After receiving her master's degree, Van Deman spent the next five years alternately teaching Latin at Wellesley College and the Bryn Mawr School in Baltimore, and taking postgraduate courses at Bryn Mawr College. In 1896, Van Deman enrolled in the University of Chicago, where she began her doctoral studies. She studied the classics and Roman archaeology, receiving her Ph.D. in 1898.

After obtaining her doctorate, Van Deman returned to the classroom, this time at Mount Holyoke College in South Hadley, Massachusetts. There she taught Latin for three years. In 1901, Van Deman accepted a fellowship offered her by the American School of Classical Studies in

Rome; she remained there until 1903, at which time she returned to the United States and became an associate professor of Latin and archaeology at Goucher College in Towson, Maryland.

In 1906, Van Deman returned to Rome as a fellow of the Carnegie Institution of Washington, D.C. Her return to Rome marked the beginning of what would become a thirty-year project. During her three decades in Rome, Van Deman studied ancient Roman buildings, centering her research on the materials used in their construction as well as on the way in which the building was constructed. As a result of her investigations and her research of available literature, Van Deman proposed that the composition of ancient brick, mortar, and other building materials as well as the architectural patterns that emerged over time provided information that could be used to date these structures.

Van Deman published her work and applied her research methods to other buildings and structures. The methods she developed for dating have become standard among archaeologists. Van Deman died in Rome at the age of 74. Until the time of her death, she was still involved in researching and perfecting standards for dating structures.

See also Architecture
References "Esther B. Van Deman, U.S. Archaeologist: Authority on the Ruins of Rome Was Carnegie Institution Associate—Dies at 74" [obituary], *New York Times* (5 May 1937); James, Edward T., Janet Wilson James, and Paul S. Boyers, eds., *Notable American Women, 1607–1950: A Biographical Dictionary*, vol. 3: (P–Z) (1971); Read, Phyllis J., and Bernard L. Witlieb, *The Book of Women's Firsts* (1992).

Van Straten, Florence Wilhelmina (1913–1992)

During World War II, the success of many military engagements, especially naval and air campaigns, was largely dependent upon the ability of meteorologists to provide accurate weather forecasts. Forecasting requires an understanding of atmospheric physics and the physical factors that combine to produce the weather. Expertise in each of these areas was provided by physical

chemist and meteorologist Florence W. van Straten, who served as a specialist in aerological engineering (meteorology) with the Naval Weather Service during World War II. Through her expertise in chemistry and meteorology, van Straten also contributed to the development of a technology known as cloud seeding, which has shown promise in allowing scientists to actually modify weather by changing the characteristics of clouds.

Florence van Straten was born in Darien, Connecticut, in 1913. She received most of her elementary and secondary school education in the New York City public schools. However, her father's position as a business executive with Metro-Goldwyn-Mayer (MGM) Pictures required the family to travel frequently. This travel provided Florence van Straten an opportunity to spend one of her secondary school years living and studying in Nice, France. She returned to the United States in 1929 and graduated later that year from the Girls' High School in Brooklyn, New York, at the age of 16.

Throughout her high school years, van Straten's desire was to attend college as an English major, to prepare for a career as a writer. However, Florence's father convinced her that it might be prudent for her also to pursue studies in another area (since many writers are not able to support themselves from their work), to provide an alternative means of income, if necessary. After some discussion with Florence van Straten's high school principal, it was decided that Florence would study chemistry at college, in addition to English.

Florence van Straten attended New York University (NYU), where she majored in both chemistry and English. During the fall semester of her senior year at NYU, van Straten was asked to teach a freshman chemistry class for a professor who had become ill. The professor did not recover from his illness, and van Straten taught the course for the remainder of the semester. When the spring semester of her senior year arrived, van Straten, who had enough credits to obtain her bachelor's degree in either English or chemistry, was offered a teaching fellowship for the following school year—on the condition that she receive her bachelor's degree in chemistry, rather than in English, and that she pursue graduate studies in chemistry. Van Straten accepted the offer, graduating *cum laude* with a B.S. degree in chemistry in 1933 and an election into Phi Beta Kappa.

After receiving her bachelor's degree, van Straten remained at NYU as both an instructor and a graduate student. She earned an M.S. degree in chemistry in 1937, and a Ph.D. in physical chemistry in 1939.

Van Straten joined the U.S. Navy's Women Accepted for Voluntary Emergency Service (WAVES) at the start of World War II, serving as a specialist in meteorology. With the WAVES, van Straten, who held the rank of ensign, was selected to attend the Massachusetts Institute of Technology (MIT) as part of her training in aerological engineering. Within only nine months, she had earned a diploma as a certified meteorologist and was immediately assigned the responsibility of providing weather data to Pacific Fleet commanders, for use in planning military strategies. It was during this time that van Straten began researching the physical factors that produced weather, as a means of improving weather forecasting—an interest that dominated the rest of her professional career.

After the war, van Straten, who now held the rank of lieutenant commander, decided to return to civilian life. However, she continued working with the Navy as the civilian technical adviser and director of the Technical Requirements Branch of the U.S. Naval Weather Service in the Office of Chief of Naval Operations. In this role, van Straten suggested changes in the design of weather balloons. Unlike earlier weather balloons, the redesigned balloons were capable of traveling lower in the atmosphere, where they could escape damage from strong winds present at higher altitudes. The balloons, which had cellophane-thin shells, also were capable of carrying heavy radio equipment that was used to transmit data back to Earth. Van Straten also theorized a procedure for cloud seeding that could create or dissipate clouds—a theory that was tested and that proved to have merit in 1958.

Van Straten continued to work as a civilian for the Naval Weather Service until her retirement in 1962. There her work and research focused on a variety of weather-related issues. One result of this work was a patented sonic device for use in preventing the formation of ice on the wings of airplanes. Another of her technical achievements involved the development of a system that automatically and simultaneously plotted radar scope data at a number of radar monitoring stations. Van Straten also provided then-classified data on weather conditions relating to missile launches and investigated the pattern of radioactive fallout in the event of a nuclear attack on the United States.

In recognition of her civilian service to the Naval Weather Service, van Straten was presented the Meritorious Service Award of the U.S. Department of the Navy in 1956. Three years later, she was presented the Woman of the Year Award by the Women's Wing of the Aerospace Medical Association. Van Straten held memberships in several professional organizations, including the American Association for the Advancement of Science (AAAS), the American Meteorological Society, and the American Geophysical Union.

Following her retirement, van Straten made her home in Green Acres, Maryland, a suburb of Washington, D.C. She continued to serve as a consultant to the U.S. Navy during her retirement. Until her death in 1992, van Straten also devoted much of her time to the writing that she had believed would be her career.

See also Anderson, Elda Emma; Patent; Simpson, Joanne; Whiting, Sarah F.

References Baker, Russell, "Navy's Tests Create and Dissolve Clouds," *New York Times* (24 September 1958); "Does Something about It: Florence Wilhelmina van Straten," *New York Times* (24 September 1958); "Florence W. van Straten Dies, Navy Atmospheric Physicist" [obituary], *Washington Post* (31 March 1992); McMurray, Emily M., ed., *Notable Twentieth-Century Scientists*, vol. 4: (S–Z) (1965); Yost, Edna, *Women of Modern Science* (1959).

Vassar College

Vassar College is a private liberal arts college located in Poughkeepsie, New York. The college was endowed and founded in 1861 by Matthew Vassar under the name Vassar Female College. Vassar was the first American college to provide young women with an education equal in quality to that offered by the finest men's colleges. Since its beginnings, Vassar has insisted upon high academic standards and emphasized a quality curriculum that included math and science. This approach to women's education soon gained popularity and became a model for several other women-only colleges that later came to be known collectively as the Seven Sisters.

On 26 September 1865, Vassar Female College admitted its first class of 353 young women. The faculty numbered 30, 22 of whom were women. The most distinguished faculty member was astronomer Maria Mitchell, for whom a chair in astronomy was created. In 1867, the word "female" was removed from the college name; however, more than 100 years passed before Vassar became coeducational and admitted its first male student.

Today, Vassar continues its rich tradition in the liberal arts; it also offers specialty and advanced courses in math and science. In addition, special programs are available in the environmental sciences, microscopy, spectroscopy, and geology. Among the notable women who received undergraduate degrees from Vassar College are electrical engineer Edith Clarke and mathematician and computer scientist Grace Murray Hopper.

See also Clarke, Edith; Hopper, Grace Murray; Seven College Conference; Spectroscopy

References Franck, Irene M., and David M. Brownstone, *Women's World: A Timeline of Women in History* (1995); Macdonald, Anne L., *Feminine Ingenuity: How Women Inventors Changed America* (1992); Weatherford, Doris, *American Women's History: An A to Z of People, Organizations, Issues, and Events* (1994); Vassar College, available at http://www.vassar.edu (cited 19 May 1998).

Walker, Madame C. J. (1867–1919)

Sarah Breedlove was born on 23 December 1867 to Owen and Minerva Breedlove, in Delta, Louisiana. At the time of Sarah's birth, her parents were slaves on a cotton plantation owned by Robert W. Burney. Despite these humble beginnings, Sarah Breedlove would later use her wit and tenacity to improve her lot in life and become the first African American millionaire.

After Sarah Breedlove reinvented herself as Madame C. J. Walker in 1906, she eventually achieved financial success and independence through the development of a line of hair-care products for African American women. These products were marketed by the Madame C. J. Walker Cosmetic Company. Walker often is credited as the inventor of the hot comb; however, that instrument, which was developed to press and style the hair of African Americans, was actually devised by Marjorie Joyner in 1928. At the time of its development, the hot comb was known as a "permanent wave machine." When she developed the "permanent wave machine," Joyner was an employee of the Madame C. J. Walker Cosmetic Company, and she immediately assigned the rights to the invention to that company.

As a child, Sarah Breedlove was orphaned when both of her parents succumbed to a yellow fever epidemic. In 1878, work became scarce in her hometown of Delta, so Sarah and her older sister Louvenia moved to Vicksburg, Tennessee, where they obtained jobs as domestics. At the age of 14, Sarah married Moses McWilliams; four years later, in 1885, Sarah McWilliams gave birth to her only child, a daughter she named Lelia.

Only two years after the birth of her daughter, Sarah McWilliams became a widow when her husband was lynched by a mob. Because of her gender and race, McWilliams had few options available to her to provide support for herself and her daughter. Determined to make her own way, Sarah McWilliams moved with her daughter to St. Louis, Missouri, where she obtained work washing clothes. She remained in this job for the next seventeen years, during which time she was able to save enough money

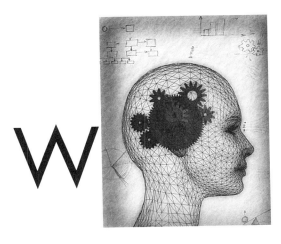

to send her daughter to Knoxville College, a private college for African Americans located in Knoxville, Tennessee.

Through much of her life, McWilliams suffered with a condition known as alopecia—a condition resulting in periodic balding—that was common among African Americans. The causes of this common ailment are numerous, and include stress, poor diet, scalp diseases, and the often harsh procedures African American women undergo to straighten their hair. To help her condition, McWilliams used a variety of hair and scalp remedies that were then available, including a product known as Malone's Wonderful Hair Grower. At one point, McWilliams actually supplemented her income by selling the product for Annie Malone, who would later become one of McWilliams's major competitors.

McWilliams moved to Denver in 1905 at age 37. At this time she had meager savings of about $1.50. It was while living in Denver that McWilliams began to experiment with different hair and scalp formulas; however, she put her faith and her funds in a formula that she claimed came to her in a dream. During this time, she briefly worked as a cook for a pharmacist named E. L. Scholtz. McWilliams tested her formula on herself, on friends, and on family; it is possible that she also consulted with her employer, Scholtz, in order to perfect her formula.

Madame C. J. Walker invented many hair care products for African American women, and she was a consummate businesswoman. (Schomberg Center)

By 1906, two significant events occurred in McWilliams's life: she married newspaper sales agent Charles Joseph Walker (C. J. Walker), and she began selling her hair-care products door-to-door. Walker's husband, C. J., became her business partner. In keeping with traditions of the time, Sarah adopted his name and began marketing her products under the name Madame C. J. Walker. The Walkers traveled throughout Denver selling the "Walker System" of hair-care products; and in time, Walker expanded her company to include a mail-order operation—a venture that was placed under the direction of her daughter. Business thrived, and Walker once again expanded her company by training sales agents and opening a beauty parlor.

In 1908, Madame C. J. Walker and her daughter, Lelia, moved to Pittsburgh, where they opened the Lelia College for Walker Hair Culturists. There hundreds of African American women were trained in the use of the Walker System. Many of these women later became Walker Agents, traveling salespeople who demonstrated the use of Walker's products in the homes of potential clients. In 1910, the headquarters for the Madame C. J. Walker Company were moved to Indianapolis, to take advantage of the city's access to numerous rail facilities.

In 1912, Lelia Walker changed her name to A'Lelia Walker and adopted a thirteen-year-old girl named Mae Bryant. Mae began working with her mother and in a short time became a model for the Walker products. Mae was well suited to the task, as she was blessed with long, thick hair. The following year, A'Lelia and Mae moved to New York and opened another Lelia College.

Around this same time, Madame Walker proved herself to be a business genius. She began to target a larger audience, making presentations throughout the United States and the Caribbean at conventions held by African American religious, civic, and fraternal organizations. Beauty parlors that made use of the Walker System opened up throughout these areas, and Walker's sales force grew. Yet while Walker's professional life was prospering, her personal life was suffering. As a result of differences regarding both personal and business ideas, Madame C. J. Walker and her husband, Charles, parted ways.

Madame Walker has become a role model for many young people. In addition to overcoming adversity to become one of America's most successful entrepreneurs, she made improving the lives of others a part of her company's mission. During the last years of her life, she became an advocate for the education of black women and supported this endeavor through generous philanthropic donations to a variety of schools and individuals. Walker also used her influence to get antilynching legislation passed. She died of complications from hypertension on 25 May 1919, at the age of 51.

Madame Walker's business gave African American women of all backgrounds the opportunity to lift themselves out of poverty as she herself had done. In addition, it provided this means without asking women to compromise their dignity. At the time of her death, Walker was living in her dream house, Villa Lewaro, in Orangeburg, New York, where she had resided for only one year. Villa Lewaro was intended to be an inspiration to all

African Americans, and it was a meeting place for black intellectuals of the time. The structure was designed by the black architect Vertner Woodson. The year Walker died, the C. J. Walker Manufacturing Company earned $500,000.

Although she has been dead more than 80 years, the legacy and inspiration provided by the life of Madam C. J. Walker live on. In 1999, she was voted one of the 100 Most Fascinating Women of the Twentieth Century by *Ebony* magazine.

> **See also** Joyner, Marjorie Stewart; Newman, Lyda
> **References** Bundles, A'Lelia P., "Madame C. J. Walker: Cosmetics Tycoon," *Ms.* (July 1983); Nulty, Peter, "The National Business Hall of Fame," *Fortune* 12:6 (23 March 1992); "The 100 Most Fascinating Women of the Twentieth Century," *Ebony* LIV:5 (March 1999); Sluby, Patricia Carter, "Black Women and Inventions," *Sage: A Scholarly Journal on Black Women,* vol. 6, no. 2 (Fall 1989); Smith, Jessie Carney, and Nikki Giovanni, *Black Heroes of the 20th Century* (1998); Steck, Robert, "The Beauty Part," *D&B Reports,* 42:2 (March/April 1993).

Walton, Mary (n.d.)

Sheer desperation probably drove Mary Walton to develop her most notable creation, a sound-dampener for elevated train tracks. While living in an apartment in Manhattan that was situated next to the elevated railroad, Walton became acutely aware of the need to quiet the annoying and seemingly constant clanking and rattling that accompanied the passing trains. Determined to solve the problem, she retreated to her basement, where she began erecting a mock-up of a section of elevated railroad track, which she balanced between two barrels. Walton framed the rails with wooden boxes she built and then coated the insides of this framing with tar. Once the tar was in place, she lined the insides of the boxes with a thin layer of cotton and packed the remaining space in the boxes with sand. She then applied a coating of tar over the sand-filled boxes to help keep the sand in place. Once her construction was complete, she tested her design by having someone strike the metal rails with a heavy hammer as she listened from a nearby room. To her delight, she found that the combination of sand, cotton, and tar absorbed the vibrations that produced the noisy clanking sound, effectively dampening the noise.

Once she was convinced that her system had merit, Walton approached a manager at the New York City Metropolitan Railroad and persuaded him to allow her to test her apparatus on an actual length of elevated track. He agreed to the test with the proviso that if it proved successful, she would acquire a patent on the noise-reduction system and sell the rights to the New York City Metropolitan Railroad. Walton agreed to the terms, successfully ran her test, and received U.S. Patent No. 327,422 on 8 February 1881. For the rights to her invention, the New York City Metropolitan Railroad paid Walton the sum of $10,000 plus an additional royalty on the invention for the remainder of her life. Walton's solution to the noisy elevated train problem won her a great deal of acclaim—especially from the nation's feminists, who delighted in the fact that a woman had been successful in solving a problem that many of the great men of the day, including Thomas Edison, had been unable to solve.

Although Walton's noise pollution device may have garnered her more attention, an earlier invention that tackled air pollution was equally impressive. In 1879, Walton was issued the first of two patents—Patent No. 221,880—for a device eliminating the release of harmful smokestack emissions into the air. This device, which could be used on smokestacks anywhere, from factories to locomotives, used pipes to direct smokestack emissions into large tanks filled with water. After a certain period of time, the tank's contents (the water and the pollutants it contained) were emptied into the local sewage system.

> **See also** Environmental Engineering; Martinez, Lissa Ann; Railroads; Safety Engineering; Silbergeld, Ellen Kovner
> **References** Macdonald, Anne L., *Feminine Ingenuity: How Women Inventors Changed America* (1992); Salerno, Heather, "Mothers of Invention: Though Unsung and Ignored, Women Have Pushed Technology's Frontiers," *Washington Post* (12 March 1997); Stanley, Autumn, *Mothers and Daughters of Invention: Notes for a Revised History of Technology* (1993); Lemelson-MIT Program, "Mary Walton: Anti-Pollution Devices," in Invention Dimension, Inventor of the Week archives, available at http://web.mit.edu/invent/www/inventorsR-Z/walton.html (cited 6 July 1999).

Waltz, Hazel Hook (n.d.)

The bobby pin, a device used to hold the hair in place, is purported to have been invented by Hazel Hook Waltz in 1916. Despite the popularity of this simple implement, Hook reportedly made no money from her creation. Instead, the substantial money made from the bobby pin was realized by a large manufacturing company that began marketing this accessory after obtaining a patent on a bobby pin with a slightly different design from that created by Waltz.

See also Greene, Catherine Littlefield; Invention/Inventors; Newman, Lyda; Walker, Madame C. J.
References Olsen, Kirstin, *Chronology of Women's History* (1994); Vare, Ethlie Ann, and Greg Ptacek, *Mothers of Invention: From the Bra to the Bomb, Forgotten Women and Their Unforgettable Ideas* (1988).

Way, Katharine (1903–1995)

Nuclear theorist Katharine Way is best known for the systems she devised to organize, evaluate, and classify the nuclear data that accumulated in the forty years following the discovery of nuclear energy. She also is recognized for her original research and publication (1954) on beta decay rates of fission products. In 1966, Way published a research paper dealing with nuclear spin parity assignments. Beta decay and nuclear spin theory (parity) are the subjects with which nuclear physicist Chien-Shiung Wu also is most closely associated.

Katharine Way was born in Sewickley, a suburb of Pittsburgh, Pennsylvania, in 1903. Beginning at age 12, Way spent two years at a boarding school in Plainfield, New Jersey. She then transferred to a school for intellectual achievers in Greenwich, Connecticut. Way enrolled at Vassar College in the late 1920s; however, she was forced to leave Vassar when it was believed that she had contracted tuberculosis. Way convalesced for two years, and upon recovering from her illness, returned to her undergraduate academic pursuits, electing to attend Columbia University in New York City. She received a B.S. degree in 1932. Way then entered the University of North Carolina at Chapel Hill, where she majored in physics; she re-

ceived a Ph.D. in that field in 1938. While preparing for her doctoral degree, Way also coauthored three papers in the field of nuclear physics.

After receiving her Ph.D., Way accepted a research fellowship at Bryn Mawr College in Bryn Mawr, Pennsylvania. The following year, she accepted a teaching position at the University of Tennessee, where she remained until 1942. While at the University of Tennessee, Way became involved in a project to produce an isotope of neptunium. This project was halted when she was called upon to join a research team at the U.S. Naval Ordnance Laboratory. There she worked on underwater mines (explosive devices) and mine sweepers (mechanical devices designed to detect and detonate mines).

Way was invited to work on the Manhattan Project, a government program created by the Office of Scientific Research and Development (OSRD), at the University of Chicago, to build the first atomic bomb. At Chicago, Way worked on reactor design, conducted experiments dealing with a self-sustaining chain reaction, and organized data on radioactive fission products. It was the latter work that led to Way's research on beta decay and to the development of the system for organizing nuclear data for which she would later became known.

Way joined the research team at the Oak Ridge National Laboratory (another Manhattan Project site) in 1945. There she continued her fission research and continued work on her classification of nuclear data. During this period, Way postulated the existence of shells within the nucleus: Maria Goeppert-Mayer later received a Nobel Prize in 1963 for her discoveries in this area.

Way accepted a position with the National Bureau of Standards (now the National Institute of Standards and Technology) in Washington, D.C., in 1947. It was here that she dedicated herself full-time to the organization and classification of nuclear data. Way recruited other physicists to assist her in this endeavor. Way institutionalized the classification process in 1953 when she formed the Nuclear Data Project (NDP), a program in which nuclear data were collected and organized into a discrete collection that came to be known as the Nuclear Data Sheets. Way remained with this project until her retirement in 1968.

Following her retirement, Way was able to concentrate more effort on a number of other personal interests: the concerns of minorities who are physically challenged, professional women, and health problems related to aging. During the early 1960s, she supported the American civil rights movement, participating in a number of public marches and demonstrations. Way also served as president of the Durham Chapter of the American Association of University Women (AAUW) in 1972–1973. The following year, she was named North Carolina Distinguished Alumnus.

See also Goeppert-Mayer, Maria; Libby, Leona W.; Manhattan Project; National Institute of Standards and Technology (NIST); Nuclear Physics; Office of Scientific Research and Development (OSRD); Ordnance; Quimby, Edith Hinkley; Wu, Chien-Shiung

References Grinstein, Louise S., Rose K. Rose, and Miriam H. Rafailovich, eds., *Women in Chemistry and Physics: A Biobibliographic Sourcebook* (1993); Torpie, Stephen L., et al., eds., *American Men and Women of Science*, 18th ed. (1992–1993) (1992); University of California at Los Angeles, Contributions of 20th Century Women to Physics, "Way, Katharine," available at http://www.physics.ucla.edu/~cwp (cited 14 August 1999).

Weaponry
See **Ordnance**

Weeks, Dorothy (1893–1990)

In 1917, Dorothy Weeks held a position with the U.S. Patent and Trademark Office (PTO) in Washington, D.C. At the same time, she worked at the National Bureau of Standards (now the National Institute of Standards and Technology). Several years later, Weeks embarked on what would become a varied career in industry and academia. In 1924, she received a master's degree in physics at the Massachusetts Institute of Technology (MIT). Soon thereafter, she studied at the Prince School of Business at Simmons College, where she obtained a second master's degree, in business. With this degree in hand, Weeks obtained a

position as a supervisor with a Boston department store. She remained in this position until 1928, at which time she began teaching physics at Wellesley College, while working toward her Ph.D. at MIT.

After becoming the first woman to receive her doctoral degree in mathematics from MIT in 1930, Weeks obtained a position as a professor and head of the physics department at Wilson College in Chambersburg, Pennsylvania, where she remained until 1956. During the two-year period between 1943 and 1945 (when the United States was involved in World War II), Weeks took a leave from her position at Wilson to work for the federal government in the Office of Scientific Research and Development (OSRD). The OSRD was using the latest science and technology to support the war effort. After the war, Weeks returned to her teaching post, where she remained until her retirement.

From 1958 until 1964, Weeks was employed at the U.S. Army arsenal in Watertown, Massachusetts. While working at this site, Weeks developed materials for use in protective shielding against nuclear radiation. Weeks next turned her efforts to astronomy. In pursuit of this interest, she accepted a post as a spectroscopist at the Harvard Observatory in Cambridge, Massachusetts. Until her retirement in 1976, Weeks also conducted studies on solar satellites. She remained in Massachusetts until her death of a stroke in 1990, at the age of 97.

See also Astronomy; Eng, Patricia L.; Quimby, Edith Hinkley; National Institute of Standards and Technology (NIST); Office of Scientific Research and Development (OSRD); Spectroscopy

References "Dorothy Weeks, 97, A Physicist Who Led in Variety of Careers" [obituary], *New York Times* (8 June 1990); Read, Phyllis J., and Bernard L. Witlieb, *The Book of Women's Firsts* (1992); Rossiter, Margaret W., *Women Scientists in America: Before Affirmative Action, 1940–1972* (1995).

Weertman, Julia (b. 1926)

Julia Weertman is a solid state physicist and metallurgist who specializes in studying the characteristics of metals. She has conducted a wide range of experiments to determine the effects that very high temperatures have on metals and their alloys, specifically with regard to how such temperatures relate to failure and fatigue. She also has been involved in the study of crystals consisting of only several atoms (a field of study known as nanotechnology), an area of work that has brought her several patents.

Julia Weertman (nee Randall) was born in Muskegon, Michigan, in 1926. At the age of 17, in 1943, she became the first woman to be admitted into the College of Engineering and Science of the Carnegie Institute of Technology (today Carnegie Mellon University) in Pittsburgh, Pennsylvania. There Randall planned to study aeronautical engineering; however, she changed her major to physics during her junior year and was awarded a B.S. degree in this area one year later. After receiving her bachelor's degree, Randall remained at Carnegie Mellon to pursue a master's degree while working as a teaching assistant. She received this degree in 1947. While working toward this degree, Randall met Johannes Weertman, a returning G.I., who also was a student. Randall and Weertman married in 1950.

After marrying, Julia Weertman continued her studies at the Carnegie Institute of Technology. She received her D.Sc. in physics in 1951. That same year, she also was awarded a Rotary International Fellowship, which permitted her to spend one year at the École Normale Supérieure in Paris, France, doing postdoctoral research.

She returned to the United States in 1952 and was named to a post as a physicist with the U.S. Naval Research Laboratory (NRL) in Washington, D.C. There she conducted studies on magnetism. She then took a brief leave to accompany her husband, who also was employed by the NRL, to London. After she and her husband returned to the United States, Johannes accepted a job in the newly formed materials science and engineering department at Northwestern University in Evanston, Illinois. Julia resigned her position at the NRL to join her husband in Illinois, but decided to remain at home with her children rather than seek employment.

After several years at home, Julia returned to

the workforce in 1972 as a visiting assistant professor of materials science and engineering at Northwestern University. The following year, she was given a permanent position at the university; she ultimately advanced through the academic ranks to chair the department of materials science in 1987. She was the first woman department chair in the engineering school. The next year, she was named Walter P. Murphy Professor of Materials Science and Engineering.

Throughout her career at Northwestern, Julia Weertman has balanced her teaching and administrative work with her ongoing research into the effects of very high temperatures on the structure of nanocrystalline materials and on the tensile strength of metals and alloys. Because of their unusually small size, nanocrystalline materials permit the detection of microstructural changes in their lattice. Weertman's research in this area has led to a better understanding of the properties of metals and other substances.

During the 1990s, this research led to developments that resulted in three patents. The first of these (No. 5,320,800) was issued to Weertman and several coworkers on 14 June 1994, for a "nanocrystalline ceramic material." A second patent (No. 4,472,749) was issued to Weertman and several colleagues in 1995, for "graphite encapsulated nanophase particles produced by a tungsten arc method." In March 1998, Weertman became the copatentee on yet another patent (No. 5,728,195), for a "method for producing nanocrystalline multicomponent and multiphase materials."

Weertman has more than 135 technical publications to her credit and has coauthored six books. In addition to her research and academic duties, she has served on numerous advisory committees, including the National Research Council (NRC), the Oak Ridge National Laboratory (ORNL), the U.S. Department of Energy (DOE), the National Bureau of Standards (now the National Institute of Standards and Technology), the Argonne National Laboratory (ANL), and the National Science Foundation (NSF). Weertman maintains memberships in Sigma Xi, the American Physical Society (APS), the American Institute of Physics, the American Society for

Metals, and the American Crystallographic Association (ACA).

For her pioneering work in materials science and engineering, Weertman has received numerous awards. These include the Creativity Award of the NSF, which she was granted in 1981 and again in 1986. In 1988, she joined the National Academy of Engineering. The next year, she received the Distinguished Engineering Educator Award of the Society of Women Engineers (SWE). She received the SWE's Achievement Award, in recognition of her pioneering work on materials failures occurring at high temperatures, in 1991. Weertman was named a fellow of the Mineral, Metals, and Materials Society in 1993.

See also Berkowitz, Joan; Materials Engineering; Metals and Metallurgy; Patent

References Bailey, Martha J., *American Women in Science, 1950 to the Present: A Biographical Dictionary* (1998); Torpie, Stephen L., et al., eds., *American Men and Women of Science,* 18th ed. (1992–1993) (1992); Weertman, Julia, e-mail correspondence with Alan Winkler (15 July 1999); Society of Women Engineers, "Julia Weertman," available at http://www.swe.org/SWE/Awards/achieve3.htm (cited 22 June 1999); U.S. Patent and Trademark Office, Full Text and Image Database—Number Search, available through the U.S. Patent and Trademark Office Depository Library, at http://www.uspto.gov/go/ptdl (cited 15 July 1999).

Welles, Sophia Woodhouse (n.d.)

The first American woman to be issued a patent was Mary Kies of Connecticut. In 1809, Kies obtained a patent for a new method of weaving straw. Kies's method, which made use of silk or thread in the weaving process, was widely adopted and drove much of the New England hat-making industry for the next 11 years. The process was then largely replaced by a new weaving method developed by Sophia Woodhouse Welles, also of Connecticut.

Welles's weaving process differed from the one used by Kies in that it made use of native grasses from the region in place of straw. For her weaving method, Welles was issued a patent in 1821. The process gained in notoriety when Welles received an award from the Hartford County Society for Promoting Agriculture and Domestic Manufac-

tures, for a hat she called the Wethersfield bonnet. Welles named the bonnet for the Connecticut town in which she lived. Welles also received praise from England when she was granted both a silver medal and a monetary award for her hat from the British Society of Arts. The money sent by the organization was meant as payment for a published description of Welles's process as well as some seeds of the plants from which the hat had been woven. However, once Welles notified the group that she had already obtained a patent for the process, they abandoned their interest in the hat.

The hat made by Welles was soon copied by many businesspeople throughout New England. In one case, a copy of Welles's bonnet, made by a man from New York who had discovered her process, was sent to Secretary of State John Quincy Adams as a gift for his wife, Louisa. Adams was so impressed with the hat that he actually praised its quality in an entry in his journal.

See also Kies, Mary; Metcalf, Betsey; Textiles

References Hong, Karen E., "Early Women Inventors," *Cobblestone: The History Magazine for Young People,* vol. 15 (1994); Macdonald, Anne L., *Feminine Ingenuity: How Women Inventors Changed America* (1992); Stanley, Autumn, *Mothers and Daughters of Invention: Notes for a Revised History of Technology* (1993).

Wellesley College

One of the Seven Sisters (now the Seven College Conference)—a group of seven women's colleges in the northeastern United States—Wellesley College was founded in 1870 as a private women's liberal arts school, in Wellesley, Massachusetts. Since then it has been an academic leader in all areas of the liberal arts and has been particularly strong in mathematics and the sciences.

The entrance requirements for admission into Wellesley have always been among the most demanding in the nation. In its first few years of operation, Wellesley applicants were required to pass a rigorous entrance examination, and a preparatory course was offered for this purpose. This course was later dropped, but the academic requirements for admission into Wellesley remain among the highest in the nation.

The mathematics program at Wellesley has long been considered among the strongest in the United States. The emphasis on mathematics emerged during the tenure of two of the school's first six presidents, both of whom were promoted to that administrative post from the mathematics faculty: Helen A. Shafer and Ellen Fitz Pendleton. In addition, until 1940, more graduates of Wellesley continued their studies in mathematics and obtained doctorates in this field than graduates from any other U.S. college.

In the sciences, two areas in which Wellesley has consistently excelled are physics and astronomy. Programs in both fields were established by noted educator Sarah F. Whiting, who in 1878 developed one of the first physics teaching laboratories for undergraduate students in the United States. Whiting later established a meteorology program at the school, complete with weather data-gathering apparatus. Data gathered by the school's program were used by the U.S. Weather Service. In addition, Whiting obtained the funding necessary to have an observatory constructed at Wellesley, an event that resulted in Wellesley's becoming a leader in astronomy. Among the school's most notable graduates in this area were Annie Jump Cannon and Caroline Furness.

Wellesley remained strictly a women's college until the 1970s. It continues its rich academic tradition today.

See also Astronomy; Barnard College; Seven College Conference; Vassar College; Whiting, Sarah Frances
References Cullen-DuPont, Kathryn, *The Encyclopedia of Women's History in America* (1998); Kass-Simon, G., and Patricia Farnes, eds., *Women of Science: Righting the Record* (1990); Lankford, John, and Rickey L. Slavings, "Gender and Science: Women in American Astronomy, 1859–1940," *Physics Today* (March 1990); Weatherford, Doris, *American Women's History: An A to Z of People, Organizations, Issues, and Events* (1994).

Wells, Jane (n.d.)

In 1872, Jane Wells of Chicago, Illinois, patented a child-care item that continues to be found in many homes throughout the world. This item, the baby-holder jumper, was designed to provide a child old enough to sit upright without assistance a means of bouncing up and down on its feet and swinging, while securely confined. The device also is designed to occupy the child's attention, freeing parents or caretakers to carry out other tasks.

Wells's husband worked as a plant manager at the nearby Occidental Manufacturing Company. After obtaining her patent on the jumper, Wells permitted this company to develop and sell the product. Enclosed in the product's package was information identifying it as the creation of a "Chicago mother" and as having been constructed almost entirely by women.

See also Donovan, Marion; Knight, Margaret E.; Moore Ann; Proudfoot, Andrea H.
References Macdonald, Anne L., *Feminine Ingenuity: How Women Inventors Changed America* (1992); Vare, Ethlie Ann, and Greg Ptacek, *Mothers of Invention: From the Bra to the Bomb, Forgotten Women and Their Unforgettable Ideas* (1988).

Whiting, Sarah Frances (1847–1927)

Sarah Whiting's most significant technological achievement was her production of the first X-ray photograph in the United States, in the early 1900s. Yet despite the significance of this achievement, Whiting is much better known for her pioneering work in using technology to educate women in the sciences. At Wellesley College, Whiting established what was only the second undergraduate physics laboratory in the United States. Like the college's founder, she believed that laboratory work was an essential part of science education for women. Whiting designed the laboratory and purchased and installed the equipment needed for its operation. Years later, Whiting also established a meteorology program that made use of the technical instruments available at the time as well as an observatory for the study of astronomy.

Sarah Whiting was born in Wyoming, New York, in 1847. Her father, Joel Whiting, was a teacher of Latin, Greek, mathematics, and physics. Sarah's interest in science emerged at an early age as she assisted her father in his preparation of physics demonstrations for his classes. By the time Sarah Whiting began her college education at Ingham University in LeRoy, New York, she already was well advanced in Latin, Greek, and mathematics, as a result of the tutoring she had received from her father. After receiving a bachelor's degree in 1865, Whiting taught briefly at Ingham. She later accepted a position as a teacher of mathematics and the classics at the Brooklyn Heights Seminary for girls, a position she held until 1876.

While teaching in Brooklyn, Whiting often visited Manhattan to attend scientific lectures given by prominent scientists. She also visited various laboratories to learn about and observe the use of the latest scientific equipment. Whiting then used this information in her teaching at the Brooklyn Heights Seminary. Whiting's reputation as a fine teacher and an innovator in the use of laboratory equipment for instructional purposes attracted the attention of Wellesley College founder Henry F. Durant. In 1875, Durant offered Whiting a position as the teacher of physics at Wellesley, an institution of higher learning for women that featured an all-female faculty. To prepare Whiting for this position—a field in which she had not formally studied—Durant made arrangements for her to audit the physics classes of Professor Edward C. Pickering at the Massachusetts Institute of Technology (MIT). In addition, Whiting also traveled to other area colleges, examining their physics programs. As a result of her observations, she was able in 1878 to establish an instructional physics laboratory at Wellesley equipped with apparatus she had developed herself or purchased from places as far away as Europe.

Whiting also was the first woman member of the New England Meteorological Society. With a newfound interest in this science, she established a course in meteorology at Wellesley. To teach the course, Whiting set up a weather station equipped with a variety of data-gathering weather apparatus. The weather station soon became the primary source of weather information in the region, and regularly reported its findings to the U.S. Weather Bureau.

The teaching methods and demonstrations Whiting used in her work were influenced by many acclaimed scientists, including Alexander Graham Bell and Thomas Edison, both of whom Whiting met during demonstrations of their inventions involving light and sound. In 1879, Whiting was invited by Edward Pickering, who was then the director of the Harvard Observatory, to examine equipment in use there. Whiting became fascinated by the spectroscopic studies of stars conducted at Harvard and introduced a course in astronomy at Wellesley the following year. Noted U.S. astronomer Annie Jump Cannon was a student in Whiting's astronomy class.

From 1888 to 1889, Whiting took a sabbatical to study at the University of Berlin and to visit laboratories in Germany and England. While in England, she attended lectures at the British Association and met Lord Kelvin, a scientist known for his work in thermodynamics and magnetism.

Whiting took a second sabbatical between 1896 and 1897 to study at Edinburgh University in Scotland. While here, she developed a close friendship with Lady Huggins, the wife of and primary assistant to astrophysicist Sir William Huggins. In recognition of this friendship, Lady Huggins donated many of Sir William's astronomical instruments to Wellesley College after her husband's death.

In 1901, German physicist Wilhelm Conrad Roentgen was awarded the first Nobel Prize in physics, for his discovery of X rays (a discovery made in 1895). Using data contained in reports of Roentgen's findings, Whiting immediately built the equipment needed to produce the first X-ray photographs in the United States. In the year prior to her production of the X-ray photograph, construction of the Whitin Observatory at Wellesley was completed. The observatory was designed according to plans developed by Whiting and was equipped with a 12-inch refracting telescope, a spectroscope, a photometer, and other equipment needed to carry out serious astronomical studies. Sarah Whiting became the observatory's director.

Whiting was a member of the American Astronomical Society and the American Physical Society (APS). In 1883, she was elected a fellow of the American Association for the Advancement

Aeronautical engineer Sheila Widnall became the first woman to serve as Secretary of the U.S. Air Force in 1993. (Agence France Presse/Corbis-Bettman)

of Science (AAAS). In 1905, she was awarded an honorary degree from Tufts College in recognition for her activities in education. She retired from Wellesley's physics department in 1912, but remained as director of the Whitin Observatory until 1916. Following her retirement, Whiting moved to Wilbraham, Massachusetts, where she lived with her sister. She died 11 years later, at the age of 80.

> **See also** Astronomy; Maury, Antonia; Simpson, Joanne; Sitterly, Charlotte Moore; Spectroscopy; Van Straten, Florence Wilhelmina; Wellesley College
> **References** Guernsey, Janet B., "The Lady Wanted to Purchase a Wheatstone Bridge: Sarah Frances Whiting and Her Successor," in *Making Contributions: An Historical Overview of Women's Role in Physics* (1984); Lankford, John, and Rickey L. Slavings, "Gender and Science: Women in American Astronomy, 1859–1940," *Physics Today*, vol. 43., no. 3 (March 1990); Ogilvie, Marilyn, *Women in Science Antiquity through the Nineteenth Century: A Biographical Dictionary with Annotated Bibliography* (1986).

Widnall, Sheila (b. 1938)

In 1993, aeronautical engineer Sheila Widnall made history when President Bill Clinton appointed her to serve as secretary of the Air Force. With this appointment, Widnall—an expert on fluid mechanics as it relates to aircraft—became the first woman ever to head a branch of the U.S. military. She served in this post until November 1997 and then returned to her academic responsibilities with the Massachusetts Institute of Technology (MIT).

Sheila Widnall was born in Tacoma, Washington, in 1938. She received her entire primary and secondary education at Catholic girls' schools, before enrolling as an engineering student at MIT in 1956. Widnall majored in aeronautics, and received her S.B. degree in aeronautics and astronautics in 1960; she was one of only ten women in a graduating class of 900. She remained at MIT for an additional four years to pursue graduate studies, receiving her S.M. (1961) and her Sc.D. (1964) both in aeronautics and in astronautics.

While working toward her advanced degrees, Widnall focused her studies on fluid dynamics—specifically, on how air flowing around wings, rudders, and propellers relates to turbulence, noise (acoustics), and aircraft stability. Today she has an international reputation as an expert on wake turbulence and on the spiraling vortices created by the movement of helicopter blades.

After receiving her Sc.D., Widnall joined the MIT engineering faculty as its first woman member. In 1979, she became the first woman at MIT to serve as a faculty chair. Prior to her nomination as secretary of the Air Force, Widnall was appointed associate provost of the university (1992–1993).

As secretary of the Air Force (1993–1997), Widnall's responsibilities included setting policies affecting the recruiting, equipping, and training of active duty personnel in the Air Force, Air National Guard, and Air Reserve. She also was responsible for equipment maintenance, research and development, and issues related to the welfare of personnel. Widnall focused much attention on quality of life issues that she believed were important to military women, such as improved housing, child care facilities, and revisions in pay and medical benefits.

After retiring from her position as secretary of the Air Force and returning to MIT in 1997, Widnall devoted much of her time and energy to encouraging more women and minorities to pursue careers in science and technology. In addition, she is well recognized for her service to a variety of professional groups, including the American Association for the Advancement of Science (AAAS), where she became the fifth woman to serve as president. In 1993, she also served as vice president of the National Academy of Engineering. Honors and awards bestowed on Sheila Widnall include the 1986 Abby Rockefeller Mauze Professor of Aeronautics and Astronautics Award from MIT and a 1998 Living Legacy Award issued by the Women's International Center (WIC).

See also Aeronautical and Aerospace Engineering; American Association for the Advancement of Science (AAAS); Darden, Christine M.; Flügge-Lotz, Irmgard; National Academy of Engineering (NAE)

References Ambrose, Susan A., et al., *Journeys of Women in Science and Engineering: No Universal Constants* (1997); Brown, Mike, "Secretary of Air Force Dr. Sheila Widnall Flies JPATS Trainer," press release of Raytheon Aircraft (23 May 1996); Carlin, Peter Ames, and Linda Kramer, "Air Force One: Secretary Sheila Widnall Navigates Stormy Skies," *People* 48:14 (6 October 1997): 143–144; Sherrow, Victoria, *Women in the Military: An Encyclopedia* (1996); Wright, Sarah H., "Widnall Fêted by Fellow Women Faculty," *MIT Tech Talk* (4 November 1998), available at http://web.mit.edu/newsof . . . 8/nov04/widnall.html (cited 14 March 1999).

Williams, Anna Wessels (1863–1954)

Bacteriologist Anna Williams helped develop methods for treating the infectious diseases diphtheria and rabies. In 1894, she isolated the *Corynebacterium diphtheriae* bacillus, a strain of diphtheria bacteria that was used to produce the antitoxin that proved successful in almost eliminating this childhood disease. Four years later, Williams's work led to the mass production of a vaccine to combat rabies. Several years later, she also developed a quick method for diagnosing this disease. Her technique provided accurate diagnosis of rabies in minutes rather than days.

Anna Wessels Williams was born in Hackensack, New Jersey, in 1863. Until the age of 12, she was educated at home. She then attended the State Street Public School, where her interest in science was piqued when she was permitted to look through a microscope belonging to a teacher. Williams continued her education, graduating from the New Jersey Normal School in Trenton in 1883. She then worked as a teacher for two years.

Williams decided to pursue a career in medicine after witnessing her sister's near death following the birth of a stillborn child. She entered the Women's Medical College of the New York Infirmary in 1887; four years later, she received her M.D. degree. Williams remained at the infirmary an additional year, working as an instructor of pathology and hygiene. From 1891 to 1895, she also served as an assistant to the department chair at the New York Infirmary, except for the one-year period between 1892 and 1893, when she studied abroad at the universities of Vienna, Heidelberg, Leipzig, and the Royal Fräuen Klinik of Leopold in Dresden.

In 1894, Williams began assisting in the bacteriology laboratory of the New York City Department of Health—the first municipal diagnostic laboratory in the nation—as a volunteer. It was during this time that she isolated the strain of diphtheria bacillus that led to the development of an antitoxin for diphtheria. Williams published two papers detailing this discovery and its results; however, the culture was initially named the Park strain, after the laboratory director William H. Park, who actually was on vacation at the time of the discovery. Later, the culture came to be known as Park-Williams #8, indicating at least a partial recognition of Williams's contribution. The antitoxin produced from Williams's culture was quickly made available to physicians and showed immediate results in lowering cases of diphtheria. In time, the antitoxin was combined with the vaccine for pertussis developed by Pearl Kendrick and Grace Eldering, and with the vaccine for tetanus. This combined vaccine, known as DPT, continues to be used today and has almost eradicated diphtheria worldwide.

In 1895, Williams accepted a full-time position as an assistant bacteriologist with the New York City Department of Health. While in this job, she conducted numerous investigations on streptococcal and pneumococcal infections (the causes of strep throat and pneumonia, respectively) and on trachoma and other eye infections. The following year, Williams traveled to the Pasteur Institute in France to obtain a toxin for possible use in producing a scarlet fever antitoxin. Although she was unsuccessful at producing a scarlet fever antitoxin, she was successful at developing a culture for the rabies virus, using samples she obtained in France. This achievement led to the development of a rabies vaccine in 1898.

Williams observed distinctive cell structures in the brain tissue of the rabid animals she studied during her research on rabies. These same structures were observed simultaneously by Italian physician Adelchi Negri. Because Negri published his findings before Williams, the structures were named "Negri bodies." Despite this disappointment, Williams continued her work with rabies and in 1905 published a description of a staining method she had devised that reduced the time needed to diagnose the disease from ten days to less than 30 minutes. In recognition of this important discovery, Williams advanced in position to assistant director of the laboratory. Two years later, the American Public Health Association appointed her chair of its Committee on the Standard Methods for Diagnosis of Rabies.

Other public health problems studied by Williams included influenza, venereal diseases (sexually transmitted diseases), meningitis, poliomyelitis, and smallpox. Her research on these diseases led to her being asked to train American and European military medical workers in identifying carriers of meningitis during World War I. In addition, the importance of Williams's work was recognized by her peers, as evidenced by her election as president of the Women's Medical Association in 1915 and her service as vice chairperson of the laboratory section of the American Public Health Association in 1931.

Williams published many articles in New York City Department of Health bulletins and publications. Books she authored and coauthored with Park became widely used by persons interested in infectious disease. Although she had an extraordinarily fruitful career, Williams was forced to retire from the New York City Department of Health in 1934 because of a new policy instituted by mayor Fiorella LaGuardia requiring city employees over age 70 to retire. In 1936, the New York Women's Medical Society honored Williams with a testimonial dinner for her service to the city of New York and her work in advancing the cause of women doctors.

See also Alexander, Hattie Elizabeth; Antibiotics; Baker, Sara Josephine; Brown, Rachel Fuller; Dick, Gladys Rowena Henry; Downs, Cornelia Mitchell; Eldering, Grace; Evans, Alice Catherine; Free, Helen Murray; Hazen, Elizabeth Lee; Kendrick, Pearl Luella; Pittman, Margaret
References "Anna W. Williams, Scientist, Is Dead" [obituary], *New York Times* (21 November 1954): 86;

Bailey, Martha J., *American Women in Science: A Biographical Dictionary* (1994); O'Hern, Elizabeth Moot, *Profiles of Pioneer Women Scientists* (1986); Shearer, Benjamin F., and Barbara S. Shearer, eds., *Notable Women in the Life Sciences: A Biographical Dictionary* (1996); Sicherman, Barbara, and Carol Hurd Green, eds., *Notable American Women: The Modern Period* (1980).

Women's Hall of Fame
See **National Women's Hall of Fame**

Women's Rights

The event that initiated the women's rights movement in the United States was a convention held in Seneca Falls, New York, on 19 and 20 July 1848. Women attending the convention were educators, suffragists, and women's rights advocates. The organizers of the event included Elizabeth Cady Stanton, Lucretia Mott, Jane Hunt, Mary Ann McClintock, and Martha Coffin Wright. It was at this event that Stanton and others presented the Declaration of Rights and Sentiments. This document, which was signed by the convention attendees, became the founding document of the American women's movement.

The Declaration of Rights and Sentiments was modeled after the Declaration of Independence. Its language was intended to emphasize the need for women to have equal rights with men in such areas as education, career opportunities, property rights, and the vote.

In 1854, Stanton addressed the New York state legislature, urging lawmakers to expand the married women's property act that it had passed in 1848. Unfortunately, her speech did not have the desired result. The 1848 act had provided married women with some property rights. At the time of its passage, it was the only act in the United States that gave married women any property rights. The practical significance of the act for technological advances lay in the fact that it permitted women who had developed an invention to profit from their work. Prior to the passage of this act, any invention made by a married woman would have become the property of her husband.

The Civil War (1861–1865) was a period of turmoil that divided the country philosophically, socially, and culturally. The dominant issue of the war dealt with slavery, a socioeconomic institution supported in the South and opposed in the North. Cady Stanton joined forces with Susan B. Anthony, a suffragist she had met years earlier, speaking out publicly against slavery. Stanton and Anthony saw the ownership of slaves as similar to the dominance of women by men.

Stanton and Anthony joined forces again in 1869 to found the National Woman Suffrage Association, an organization devoted to getting women the right to vote. In 1890, this organization would merge with the American Woman Suffrage Association. Although both women died in the first decade of the twentieth century, other suffragists continued their work until women got the vote with the passage of the Nineteenth Amendment to the U.S. Constitution, in 1920.

At the same time as Stanton and the other suffragists fought to get the vote, they also continued their earlier quest to obtain equal rights for women in all areas. In 1876, during the Centennial Exposition in Philadelphia, Stanton and others successfully lobbied for a special exhibition building to commemorate women's achievements. This building, known as the Women's Pavilion, showcased the artistic and technological achievements of many American women. Inside were irons developed by Mary Florence Potts, a washing machine developed by Margaret Plunkett Colvin, and maritime signal flares developed by Martha Coston. In addition to showcasing women's achievements, Stanton and her followers held numerous conferences during the exposition at which they tried to rally support for their cause. Among their followers were Matilda Joslyn Gage, Susan B. Anthony, Sara Andrews Spencer, Lillie Devereaux, and Phoebe Couzins.

At one point during the exposition, Stanton and Gage read a document they had prepared, which they called the Declaration of the Rights of Women. This document emphasized that women had been denied equal status with men for the first 100 years of American history, and it was time for a change, for equal rights under the law.

After women won the vote in 1920, the momentum of the women's movement slowed for a period. It did not become active again until around the time of the civil rights movement. The major goal of this latter movement was to gain equal rights for African Americans with regard to education, voting, and other essential life activities. Women began to recognize the similarities between their rights and those afforded African Americans. These battles for group rights continued throughout the 1950s and early 1960s. In 1964, Congress passed the Civil Rights Act, which provided African American and other minority men the same rights as white men in housing, education, and employment but did not guarantee these rights to women. The act also established an Equal Employment Opportunity Commission (EEOC). The job of the EEOC was to investigate reported violations of the Civil Rights Act (which did not take effect until 1965).

Many women were stunned and appalled that the Civil Rights Act failed to address their concerns. They joined forces again to obtain redress from Congress in the form of an amendment to the act. The National Organization for Women (NOW) formed in 1966 largely to address these concerns. Through the efforts of the participants, Congress in 1972 was moved to amend the Civil Rights Act to forbid discrimination on the basis of gender and to increase the enforcement powers of the EEOC. As a result of these changes, women gained access to educational and employment opportunities that previously had eluded them. This was particularly evident from the influx of women into technological areas once solely occupied by men.

Despite these gains, progress has been slow in achieving public recognition of women's achievements. To help remedy this situation, the month of March was designated National Women's History Month in 1987. Since then, popular awareness of the struggles and triumphs of women has increased through educational programs and media attention.

See also Centennial Exposition; Columbian Exposition; Morrill Act of 1862; National Women's Hall of Fame; National Women's History Month; Seven College Conference

References Ashby, Ruth, and Deborah Gore Ohrn, eds., *Herstory: Women Who Changed the World* (1995); Felder, Deborah G., *A Century of Women: The Most Influential Events in 20th Century Women's History* (1999); Olsen, Kirstin, *Chronology of Women's History* (1994).

Women's World Fair
See **Columbian Exposition**

Wood, Elizabeth Armstrong (b. 1912)

Elizabeth Armstrong Wood has spent most of her professional career studying crystals. She is an authority on the use of X-ray diffraction techniques for determining and better understanding the structure and physical properties of crystals. She also was among the pioneer researchers at Bell Laboratories who investigated new methods of producing synthetic (laboratory-grown) crystals. Wood did this work when crystal technology and its applications to electronic and electrical devices were in their infancy. Such work allowed for the development of products that make use of solid state components as well as lasers. In addition, Wood has been involved in studying the geology and petrology of igneous and metamorphic rocks.

Elizabeth Wood (nee Armstrong) was born and raised in New York City. From kindergarten through the twelfth grade, she attended the Horace Mann School (a private school affiliated with Columbia University). She then enrolled at Barnard College, the sister school to Columbia University, where she majored in geology. Armstrong received her B.A. degree in 1933. After receiving this degree she attended graduate school at Bryn Mawr College in Pennsylvania. She was awarded an M.A. in 1934 and then remained at Bryn Mawr an additional year to work as an instructor of geology. Armstrong then accepted a position as an instructor of geology and mineralogy at Barnard College, but returned to Bryn Mawr again one year later to teach geology. In

1938, Armstrong returned to Barnard both to work as a lecturer and to pursue a doctoral degree. She was awarded a Ph.D. in geology from Barnard in 1939 and remained at the school as a lecturer. In 1941, she was promoted to the position of research assistant.

Between 1942 and 1943, Armstrong served as a National Research Council (NRC) Fellow at Columbia University. She then joined the Physical Research Department at Bell Telephone Laboratories, where she worked as a research physicist and crystallographer. About the time that Armstrong began working at Bell Laboratories, interest was being generated in the production and use of synthetic (laboratory-made) crystals. Synthetic crystals were being explored for their potential uses in radios, watches, and directional instruments, such as compasses, and for use in jewelry as semiprecious stones. Such crystals later became instrumental in the development of semiconductors, superconductors, and lasers. Soon after Armstrong joined the Bell Laboratories research team, she met Ira Eaten Wood, who also was involved in finding ways to grow crystals for use with electrical and electronic devices. Armstrong and Wood married in 1947.

Elizabeth Armstrong Wood remained a member of the research staff at Bell Laboratories until 1967, at which time she retired. From 1963 to 1965 she also served as an adjunct professor of physics at Fairleigh Dickinson University (FDU) in New Jersey. While she was working at both Bell Laboratories and FDU, she authored or coauthored two books for publication. The first of these, *Crystal Orientation Manual,* was published in 1963. *Crystals and Light: An Introduction to Optical Crystallography* was published the following year. Both are still recommended reading for those entering the field of optical crystallography.

From 1965 to 1971, Wood was involved in creating a physical science program for nonscience students, on behalf of the National Science Foundation (NSF). She authored yet another book, *Science for the Airplane Passenger,* which was published in 1969. During the course of her career, she also contributed more than 40 articles to technical journals.

Elizabeth Wood is a member of the American Crystallographic Association (ACA) and was elected its president in 1957. She also is a member of the American Association of Physics Teachers and the American Association for the Advancement of Science (AAAS). In addition, Wood was elected to Phi Beta Kappa and Sigma Xi and is a fellow of both the American Physical Society (APS) and the Mineralogical Society of America. She has been awarded honorary D.Sc. degrees by Wheaton College, in Norton, Massachusetts (1963); Western College, in Oxford, Ohio (1965); and Worcester Polytechnic Institute, in Worcester, Massachusetts (1970). In 1977, the ACA created the Elizabeth A. Wood Science Writing Award for those who have written books or articles that bring science to the attention of a wide audience of nonscientists.

See also American Crystallographic Association (ACA); Crystallography; Emerson, Gladys Anderson; Karle, Isabella L.; Richardson, Jane Shelby
References "Elizabeth Armstrong Wood," biography mailed to Alan Winkler from the Hauptman-Woodward Medical Research Institute, Inc. (representative of the American Crystallographic Association); Kass-Simon, G., and Patricia Farnes, eds., *Women of Science: Righting the Record* (1990).

Woodhouse, Sophia
See **Welles, Sophia Woodhouse**

Wu, Chien-Shiung (1912–1997)
Nuclear physicist Chien-Shiung Wu is best known for experiments she conducted regarding beta decay, which led to her confirmation that a principle in physics known as the conservation of parity did not hold true for all matter. According to this principle, when the nucleus of a radioactive element breaks down, it emits particles consistent with the direction in which the nucleus is spinning. This principle had been assumed by physicists to be true for more than 30 years. However, when Wu tested this hypothesis using radioactive cobalt, she determined that subatomic particles emitted from the nucleus were actually given off in two directions—one consistent with

Chien-Shiung Wu, a nuclear physicist, served on the Manhattan Project to develop the atomic bomb. (Corbis)

the direction of the spin of the nucleus, and the other, opposite this direction. This discovery is considered a major achievement in the field of nuclear physics, but it was not Wu's only contribution to science and technology. Approximately 15 years before Wu made this discovery, she was asked to serve as a member of the team of scientists working on the Manhattan Project at Columbia University in New York. The Manhattan Project was the secret military initiative to develop the world's first atomic bomb.

Chien-Shiung Wu was born in Liu Ho, a village located outside the city of Shanghai, China, in 1912. Wu received her early education as well as her undergraduate education in China. She attended that country's National Central University of Nanking, from which she received a bachelor of science degree in physics in 1934. Two years later, Wu traveled to the United States to pursue graduate studies in physics. These studies took place under the direction of Ernest Lawrence (inventor of the cyclotron) at the University of California at Berkeley. Her graduate research focused on two separate scientific areas. One area dealt with how the electromagnetic properties of charged particles changed as their velocities decreased (as when passing through matter). Her other area of research focused on the types of matter that are emitted as a uranium nucleus undergoes fission (i.e., as it is split). For this work, Wu was awarded her doctoral degree in physics in 1940.

After receiving her Ph.D., Wu spent the next four years teaching and lecturing at various colleges and universities, including Berkeley, Smith, and Princeton. At Princeton, Wu's responsibilities included teaching physics to officers of the U.S. Navy. During this period, Wu also married fellow physicist Chai Liu (Luke) Yuan.

In 1944, Wu was invited by the Division of War Research at Columbia University in New York to participate in the Manhattan Project. Her chief responsibilities included developing a means for obtaining uranium–235 (the proposed fuel for the atomic bomb) and developing radiation detectors necessary for determining the amount of radiation to which workers might be exposed. In addition, Wu assisted in solving a critical problem involving the chain reactions being produced at another site participating in the Manhattan Project. Enrico Fermi believed that the fission chain reactions elemental to the success of the bombs were being disrupted by a substance given off during the fission process. Unable to determine the cause of this interference, he called on Wu for assistance. Drawing on data she had obtained while carrying out her doctoral research, Wu was able to identify and help solve the problem.

Following her service to the Manhattan Project, Wu remained at Columbia University, where she conducted research and taught until her retirement in 1981. In 1956, two physicists from Princeton—Chen Ning Yang and Tsung-Dao Lee—questioned the validity of the long-held physics principle called conservation of parity because they had observed that some recently discovered subatomic particles (K-mesons) did not seem to behave according to this principle. After consulting with Wu about their hypothesis, they asked her to carry out experiments to determine whether her observations supported theirs. Wu carried out these experiments using the laboratories at the National Bureau of Standards (now the National Institute for Standards and Technology). It was through these experiments that Wu confirmed Yang and Lee's hypothesis. That same year, Yang and Lee were awarded the Nobel Prize in physics for their findings. Wu did not share in the award.

After completing her groundbreaking work related to the principle of parity, Wu returned to her teaching and research at Columbia University. In addition, she coauthored a book, *Beta Decay,* which was published in 1965. From 1975 until 1982, Wu served as a member of the Advisory Committee to the Director of the National Institutes of Health (NIH) in Bethesda, Maryland. In 1997, she died of a stroke at a hospital in New York City.

In addition to her teaching and research, Wu was active in several professional organizations. These include the National Academy of Sciences (to which she was elected in 1958); the American Physical Society (of which she served as president in 1975); the American Academy of Arts and

Sciences; the Royal Society of Edinburgh; the Chinese Academy of Sciences; and the American Association for the Advancement of Science (an organization of which she was a fellow). In addition to these memberships, Wu was presented honorary doctor of science degrees by Smith and Goucher Colleges and by Princeton, Rutgers, and Yale Universities, among others.

In recognition of her outstanding contributions to the field of nuclear physics, Wu received numerous awards and honors. Among the more significant of these were the 1962 Woman of the Year Award from the American Association of University Women (AAUW), the 1964 Cyrus B. Comstock Prize of the National Academy of Sciences, a 1975 National Medal of Science, and the 1978 Wolf Prize in Physics. Wu is the only woman who has been issued both the Comstock and the Wolf Prizes. In 1990, an asteroid was named after Wu, making her the first living scientist to be so honored. In addition, Wu was inducted into the Women in Technology International (WITI) Hall of Fame in 1996 and the National Women's Hall of Fame in 1998.

> **See also** Argonne National Laboratory; Bartlett, Helen Blair; Comstock Prize; Eng, Patricia L.; Fink, Kathryn (Kay) Ferguson; Foster, Margaret; Goeppert-Mayer, Maria; Koshland, Marian Elliot; Libby, Leona W.; Manhattan Project; Ordnance; Quimby, Edith Hinkley; Way, Katharine
>
> **References** Dicke, William, "Chien-Shiung Wu, 84, Dies; Top Experimental Physicist" [obituary] *New York Times* (18 February 1997); Rossiter, Margaret W., *Women Scientists in America: Before Affirmative Action, 1940–1972* (1995); Schick, Elizabeth A., ed., *Current Biography Yearbook, 1997* (1997); Torpie, Stephen L., et al., eds., *American Men and Women of Science,* 18th ed. (1992–1993) (1992); University of Washington, Women Studies Program, Women in Science course, *Hypatia's Sisters: Biographies of Women Scientists Past and Present* (1975).

Wu, Ying-Chu (Lin) Susan (b. 1932)

Aerospace engineer Susan Wu is a leading authority on the development of an energy technology known as magnetohydrodynamics, or MHD. In MHD, a high-temperature fluid called plasma is used in place of the coil of wires typically found in a generator used to produce electricity. The

MHD process has been shown to be more efficient in its production of electricity than are traditional methods. Because it is more efficient, it also tends to be less polluting to the air than other coal-burning power generation processes.

Susan Wu, whose given name is Ying-Chu Lin, was born, raised, and educated in Beijing, China. Although women in her country were traditionally discouraged from seeking higher education, Lin, with encouragement from her mother, decided to enroll in an engineering program at the National Taiwan University. She completed the program and graduated with a bachelor of science degree in mechanical engineering from this university in 1955. After graduating, Lin accepted a position as an engineer with the Taiwan Highway Bureau, but remained with them for only one year. She soon discovered that other employment opportunities in her field were virtually nonexistent because most Chinese companies did not employ women, believing that they would not remain with the company once they married and had children. To improve her opportunities for employment in her field, Lin left China in 1957 and traveled to the United States, where she has remained.

Soon after coming to the United States, Lin enrolled at Ohio State University to pursue her graduate studies. She received a master's degree in aeronautical engineering in 1959. That same year, she also married Jain-Ming (James) Wu. The Wus then moved to California, where Susan Wu began studies for a doctoral degree at the California Institute of Technology in Pasadena. She was awarded this degree in aeronautical engineering in 1963.

After receiving her doctorate, Susan Wu obtained a position as a senior engineer at Electro-Optical Systems Incorporated in Pasadena. She remained with the optics engineering company until 1965, when she accepted a position as an assistant professor of aeronautical engineering at the University of Tennessee Space Institute (UTSI) at Tullahoma. It was at UTSI that Wu began her work in magnetohydrodynamics (MHD).

In MHD, chemicals in the form of plasma (a phase of matter existing only at very high temperatures) are used in place of the heavy wire coils that make up the armature of an electric generator. The plasma substances are better conductors of electricity than are the metals used in the wire coil, and therefore they generate electricity more efficiently. In a power plant that makes use of MHD technology, the burning of coal is still required to provide the energy needed to operate the generators. However, the efficiency gained through the use of the plasma decreases the amount of coal that must be burned to drive the process. The reduction of coal, in turn, results in less pollution being released from the facility and also helps to conserve coal resources for the future.

During her tenure at UTSI, Wu was awarded several promotions. She became an associate professor (1967), a full professor (1972), and administrator of UTSI's Energy Conversion Research and Development Programs (1981). She held this last position for seven years before resigning to open her own engineering and consulting firm, ERC, Inc.

Wu currently serves as president of ERC, Inc., a rapidly growing company with offices in several U.S. cities. Among the company's clients are several government agencies, including the National Aeronautics and Space Administration (NASA), the Department of Energy (DOE), and the Argonne National Laboratory, as well as several private corporations. Under Wu's direction, the company has become well known for its engineering work and also has been recognized for its role in providing employment opportunities to women and minorities. In 1993 and 1994, ERC received Minority Contractor of the Year awards from NASA's Marshall Space Flight Centers.

In addition to awards received by her company, Wu herself has been the recipient of many awards and honors. While working toward her graduate degrees, she was granted the Amelia Earhart Fellowship in 1958, 1959, and in 1962.

She is the first person to receive this fellowship award three times. Wu was presented the Institute of Aerospace Science's Best Scholastic Award at Cal Tech in 1962. In 1973 and again in 1975 she received the Outstanding Educators of America Award. Three years later, she was presented the University of Tennessee Chancellor's Research Scholar Award.

Wu became the first minority woman to receive the Achievement Award of the Society of Women Engineers (SWE) in 1985, in recognition of her research and work with MHD and for her work as an educator and administrator. The Achievement Award is the highest honor presented by the SWE, and Wu's receipt of the award was deemed to be of enough importance to be read into the *Congressional Record* of the United States Senate on 15 July 1985. In 1994, Wu was awarded the American Institute of Aeronautics and Astronautics Plasmadynamics and Laser Award.

In addition to her work in education and at ERC, Wu has testified before Congress as an expert on issues dealing with energy and engineering. She also is a U.S. presidential appointee to the advisory board of the Smithsonian Air and Space Museum. In addition, Wu holds memberships in several professional organizations, including the American Society of Mechanical Engineers (ASME), the SWE, and the American Institute of Aeronautics and Astronautics, an organization in which she is an associate fellow.

See also Aeronautical and Aerospace Engineering; Argonne National Laboratory; Clarke, Edith; Environmental Engineering; Lamme, Bertha; National Aeronautics and Space Administration (NASA)

References Bailey, Martha J., *American Women in Science, 1950 to the Present: A Biographical Dictionary* (1998); McMurray, Emily M., ed., *Notable Twentieth-Century Scientists,* vol. 4: (S–Z) (1995); "Society of Women Engineers Achievement Award to Dr. Susan Wu," *Congressional Record—Senate* (15 July 1985); Torpie, Stephen L., et al., eds., *American Men and Women of Science,* 18th ed. (1992–1993) (1992).

Yalow, Rosalyn Sussman (b. 1921)

In 1977, medical physicist Rosalyn Sussman Yalow became only the second woman to win the Nobel Prize in physiology/medicine, for her development of the technology known as radioimmunoassay (RIA). RIA combines immunology, chemistry, mathematics, and nuclear physics in using radioisotopes to trace the production, pathways, and metabolism of chemical substances in the body. Yalow's interest in nuclear physics was spurred by her reading of the biography of Marie Curie, the first woman to be awarded a Nobel Prize, and the only scientist ever to receive two Nobel Prizes. Yalow was further inspired after attending a conference in 1939 presented by Nobel laureate Enrico Fermi at Columbia University.

Rosalyn Sussman was born in the Bronx, New York. She attended neighborhood public schools and then Walton High School, where she developed a strong interest in mathematics and chemistry. After graduating from high school at age 15, Sussman entered Hunter College. She was elected to the Phi Beta Kappa honor society. In 1941, she graduated *magna cum laude* with a B.A. degree in physics and chemistry.

After receiving her B.A., Sussman accepted a graduate teaching fellowship in physics at the University of Illinois, in Urbana. She received an M.S. degree in physics in 1942. The following year, she met and married physics classmate A. Aaron Yalow. The Yalows continued their education, with Rosalyn receiving a Ph.D. in nuclear physics in 1945. Part of her doctoral research required her to design, construct, and use a device for measuring radioactivity—expertise she would later put to good use.

After receiving their degrees, the Yalows returned to New York City. Unable to obtain a position in nuclear physics, Rosalyn worked as an electrical engineer at the Federal Telecommunications Laboratory of International Telephone and Telegraph (ITT). She left this job one year later to accept a position teaching physics at Hunter College, where she remained until 1950.

During the mid-1940s, the Bronx Veterans Administration (VA) Hospital began a research pro-

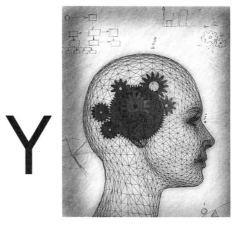

gram in which radioisotopes were used as an alternative to the more traditional and costly radium therapy, to diagnose and treat cancers. Yalow was hired as a consultant to the program in 1947. Using her background in nuclear physics, she designed the needed equipment and established a research facility to carry out her research. In 1950, she was named physicist and assistant chief of the radioisotope unit. That same year, she met Solomon A. Berson, a medical internist who had just completed his residency at the VA hospital, with whom she began a collaboration that would last 22 years.

Yalow and Berson began using radioactive iodine as a means of diagnosing and treating thyroid disorders. This research led to the use of radioisotopes to label and trace hormones and proteins in the body. Later, the duo focused on diabetes and the rate at which insulin metabolism occurred after it entered the bloodstream. Yalow and Berson were able to trace the metabolic pathway of insulin using a radioisotope of iodine. The methods they successfully employed and perfected provided a gateway to the development of radioimmunoassay (RIA), first announced in 1959.

Yalow and Berson remained a research team until his death in 1972. In 1973, following a series of departmental promotions, Yalow was named director of the newly created Solomon A. Berson Research Laboratory of the VA Medical Center—

Rosalyn Yalow was the recipient of the 1977 Nobel Prize in physiology/medicine for her role in the development of radioimmunoassay (RIA). (Corbis/Bettmann-UPI)

a facility she requested be named to honor Berson. From 1968 to 1979, she also served as a research and distinguished service professor in the department of medicine at the Mount Sinai School of Medicine. In 1980, Yalow was appointed departmental chair at New York's Montefiore Hospital. At the same time, she served as distinguished professor at Albert Einstein College of Medicine. She held both positions until 1985 and retired from the VA hospital in 1991.

Since its discovery and use with hormones and proteins, RIA has been applied to the study and detection of vitamins, enzymes, drugs, and viruses and other infectious agents. RIA is also used to screen blood for contaminants prior to transfusion. Many physicians and research scientists consider RIA one of the most significant medical breakthroughs in the diagnosis and treatment of leukemia, peptic ulcers, neurotransmitter imbalances, and hormonal disorders such as diabetes, dwarfism, and hypothyroidism.

In recognition of her distinguished career and outstanding accomplishments in medical physics, Yalow was a corecipient of the Nobel Prize in physiology/medicine in 1977. The Nobel Prize is the highest and most prestigious award that can be presented to an individual. Yalow shared the prize with the neuroscientists who applied RIA to the discovery of neurotransmitters in the brain. In addition to the Nobel Prize, Yalow has received numerous other awards. In 1975, she received the A. Cressy Morrison Award in Natural Sciences of the New York Academy of Sciences and the Scientific Achievement Award of the American Medical Association (AMA). The following year, she became the first woman to receive the Albert Lasker Prize for Basic Medical Research and Modern Medicine's Distinguished Achievement Award. Yalow was enshrined by the Engineering and Science Hall of Fame in Dayton, Ohio, in 1987. In 1993, she was inducted into the National Women's Hall of Fame in Seneca Falls, New York. Yalow has also been awarded at least 47 honorary doctorate degrees from U.S. institutions such as Columbia University, Princeton University, New York Medical College, and Johns Hopkins University, as well as from the University Claude Bernard at Lyon, France and the University of Ghent, in Belgium.

Yalow has contributed nearly 300 articles to professional journals and has served on the editorial board of Mt. Sinai's *Journal of Medicine, Diabetes, and Endocrinology* (1976–1979). She was a member of the Editorial Advisory Board for *Encyclopaedia Universalis* (1978). Yalow's professional memberships include the Radiation Research Society, the American College of Radiology, and the American Diabetes Association. In addition, she was elected to the National Academy of Sciences in 1975, served as president of the Endocrine Society from 1978 to 1979, and was elected a fellow of the New York Academy of Sciences.

See also Cori, Gerty Theresa Radnitz; Elion, Gertrude Belle; Fowler, Joanna S.; Frantz, Virginia Kneeland; Goeppert-Mayer, Maria; Levi-Montalcini, Rita; Medicine/Medical Technology; Nobel Prize; Radioimmunoassay (RIA)

References Ambrose, Susan A., et al., *Journeys of Women in Science and Engineering: No Universal Constants* (1997); Bailey, Martha J., *American Women in Science: A Biographical Dictionary* (1994); Grinstein, Louise S., Rose K. Rose, and Miriam H. Rafailovich, eds., *Women in Chemistry and Physics: A Biobibliographic Sourcebook* (1993); Kotulak, Ronald, "Dr. Yalow Talks about Her Work," *Boston Globe* (5 January 1981); Moritz, Charles, ed., *Current Biography Yearbook, 1978,* (1978); O'Neill, Lois Decker, *The Women's Book of World Records and Achievements* (1979); Rossiter, Margaret W., *Women Scientists in America: Before Affirmative Action, 1940–1972* (1995); Stanley, Autumn, *Mothers and Daughters of Invention: Notes for a Revised History of Technology* (1993); Uglow, Jennifer S., ed., *The International Dictionary of Women's Biography* (1982).

Appendix: Award Winners

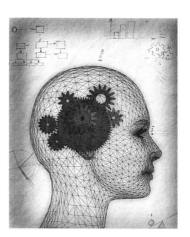

Table A.1 Garvan Medal Winners

1937 Emma P. Carr*	1958 Arda A. Green*	1979 Jenny P. Glusker
1938 No award presented	1959 Dorothy V. Nightingale	1980 Helen M. Free*
1939 No award presented	1960 Mary L. Caldwell*	1981 Elizabeth K. Wiesburger
1940 Mary E. Pennington*	1961 Sarah Ratner	1982 Sara Jane Rhoads
1941 No award presented	1962 Helen M. Dyer	1983 Ines Mandl
1942 Florence B. Seibert*	1963 Mildred Cohn	1984 Martha L. Ludwig
1943 No award presented	1964 Birgit Vennesland	1985 Catherine C. Fenselau*
1944 No award presented	1965 Gertrude E. Perlmann	1986 Jeanette G. Graselli
1945 No award presented	1966 Mary L. Petermann*	1987 Janet G. Osteryoung
1946 Icie G. Macy-Hoobler*	1967 Marjorie J. Vold	1988 Marye Anne Fox
1947 Mary Lura Sherrill*	1968 Gertrude B. Elion*	1989 Kathleen C. Taylor
1948 Gerty T. Cori*	1969 Sofia Simmonds	1990 Darleane C. Hoffman
1949 Agnes Fay Morgan*	1970 Ruth R. Benerito*	1991 Cynthia M. Friend
1950 Pauline Beery Mack*	1971 Mary Fieser*	1992 Jacqueline K. Barton
1951 Katherine B. Blodgett*	1972 Jean'ne M. Shreeve	1993 Edith M. Flanigen*
1952 Gladys A. Emerson*	1973 Mary L. Good*	1994 Barbara J. Garrison
1953 Leonora N. Bilger	1974 Joyce J. Kaufman*	1995 Angelica M. Stacy
1954 Betty Sullivan	1975 Marjorie C. Caserio	1996 Geraldine L. Richmond
1955 Grace Medes	1976 Isabella L. Karle*	1997 Karen W. Morse
1956 Allene R. Jeanes*	1977 Marjorie G. Horning	1998 Joanna S. Fowler*
1957 Lucy W. Pickett	1978 Madeleine M. Joullié*	1999 Cynthia A. Maryanoff

*Indicates women for whom entries appear in this encyclopedia.

Table A.2 Women's Hall of Fame Inductees Who Work in Science/Technology

Year	Inductee	Year	Inductee
1973	Barton, Clara	1994	Hopper, Grace Murray*
1973	Earhart, Amelia	1994	McManus, Louise
1973	Taussig, Helen Brooke*	1994	Mitchell, Maria
1981	Sanger, Margaret	1994	Richards, Linda
1986	McClintock, Barbara	1994	Stevens, Nettie*
1988	Ride, Sally*	1995	Apgar, Virginia*
1990	Seibert, Florence*	1995	Breckinridge, Mary
1993	Blackwell, Emily	1995	Collins, Eileen
1993	Cochran, Jacqueline	1995	Gilbreth, Lillian Moller*
1993	Evans, Alice*	1996	Goeppert-Mayer, Maria*
1993	Jacobi, Mary	1998	Calderone, Mary Steichen
1993	Jemison, Mae*	1998	Jackson, Shirley Ann*
1993	Mahoney, Mary	1998	Cori, Gerty Theresa Radnitz*
1993	Richards, Ellen Swallow*	1998	Lucid, Shannon W.*
1993	Wald, Lillian	1998	Wald, Florence Schorske
1993	Yalow, Rosalyn*	1998	Wu, Chien-Shiung*
1994	Cannon, Annie Jump		

*Indicates women for whom entries appear in this encyclopedia.

Table A.3 Women Nobel Prize Laureates in Science and Technology

Year	Award Area	Recipient(s) (nationality)	Reason for Award
1903	Physics	Marie Curie (France) and Pierre Curie (France); Henri Becquerel (France)	Research on radiation; discovery of spontaneous radioactivity
1911	Chemistry	Marie Curie	Discovery of radium and polonium and the isolation of radium
1935	Chemistry	Irène Joliot-Curie (France) and Frédéric Joliot (France)	Discovery of new artificially produced radioactive element
1947	Physiology or medicine	*Gerty Cori (United States) and Carl Cori (United States)	Production and breakdown of glycogen (an animal starch)
1963	Physics	*Maria Goeppert-Mayer (United States) and Hans Jensen (Germany); Eugene Wigner (United States)	Discovery of the shell-like structure of atomic nuclei; discovery and application of symmetry principles in nuclear physics
1964	Chemistry	Dorothy Crowfoot Hodgkin (United States)	Crystallographic determination of the structures of biochemical compounds, specifically penicillin and vitamin B_{12}
1977	Physiology or medicine	*Rosalyn Yalow (United States); Roger Guillemin (United States) and Andrew Schally (United States)	Development of radioimmunoassay techniques used to detect minute amounts of hormones in the body; discovery of hormones produced by the hypothalamus of the brain
1983	Physiology or medicine	Barbara McClintock (United States)	Discovery of ability of genes to move ("jumping genes")
1986	Physiology or medicine	*Rita Levi-Montalcini (United States) and Stanley Cohen (United States)	Discovery of nerve growth factors
1988	Physiology or medicine	*Gertrude Belle Elion (United States) and George Hitchings (United States); James Black (United Kingdom)	Developing principles that guide the design of new pharmaceutical therapies
1995	Physiology or medicine	Christiane Nüsslein-Volhard (Germany), Edward Lewis (United States), and Eric Wieschaus (United States)	Discovery of genes that control early stages of development in the body

*Indicates women for whom entries appear in this encyclopedia.

Table A.4 Society of Women Engineers Annual Awards

1952	Maria Telkes*	1976	Ada I. Pressman*
1953	Elsie MacGill	1977	Mildred S. Dresselhaus*
1954	Edith Clarke*	1978	Giuliana Cavaglieri Tesoro*
1956	Elise F. Harmon*	1979	Jessie G. Cambra*
1957	Rebecca H. Sparling	1980	Carolyn M. Preece
1958	Mabel M. Rockwell*	1981	Thelma Estrin*
1959	Desirée le Beau	1982	Harriet B. Rigas*
1960	Esther M. Conwell*	1983	Joan Berkowitz*
1961	Laurel van der Wal	1984	Geraldine V. Cox
1962	Laurence Delisle Pellier	1985	Y. C. L. Susan Wu*
1963	Beatrice Hicks*	1986	Yvonne C. Brill*
1964	Grace Murray Hopper*	1987	Nance K. Dicciani
1965	Martha J. B. Thomas	1988	Roberta Nichols
1966	Dorothy Martin Simon	1989	Doris Kuhlmann-Wilsdorf
1967	Marguerite M. Rogers*	1990	Lynn Ann Conway*
1968	Isabella L. Karle*	1991	Julia Weertman*
1969	Alice Stoll	1992	Evangelia Micheli-Tzanakou
1970	Irmgard Flügge-Lotz*	1993	Elsa Reichmanis
1971	Alva T. Matthews	1994	Elsa Garmire
1972	Nancy D. Fitzroy*	1995	Manijeh Razeghi
1973	Irene Carswell Peden*	1996	Barbara Liskov
1974	Barbara Crawford Johnson*	1997	Ilene J. Busch-Vishniac
1975	Sheila Widnall*		

*Indicates women for whom entries appear in this encyclopedia.

Abbot, Charles Greeley. *Great Inventions.* New York: Smithsonian Institution, 1932.

Abbott, David, ed. *The Biographical Dictionary of Scientists: Physicists.* New York: Peter Bedrick Books, 1984.

Abell, George. *Exploration of the Universe,* 2nd ed. New York: Holt, Rinehart and Winston, 1969.

"ACS Award—Garvan Medal: Arda A. Green." *Chemical and Engineering News* (28 April 1958): 123.

Adams, Samuel Hopkins. "The Great American Fraud." *Collier's* (7 October 1905).

Alic, Margaret. *Hypatia's Heritage: A History of Women in Science from Antiquity to the Late Nineteenth Century.* London: Women's Press, 1986.

"Allene R. Jeanes." *Chemical and Engineering News* (23 April 1956): 1984.

Altman, Lawrence K. "Dr. Helen Taussig, 87, Dies; Led in Blue Baby Operation." [Obituary.] *New York Times* (23 May 1986).

———. "Gertrude Elion, Drug Developer, Dies at 81," [obituary] *New York Times* (23 February 1999): A21.

Altman, Linda Jacobs. *Women Inventors: American Profiles.* New York: Facts on File, 1997.

Altman, Susan. *The Encyclopedia of African American Heritage.* New York: Facts on File, 1997.

Ambrose, Stephen E. *New History of World War II.* New York: Viking, 1997.

Ambrose, Susan A., Kirstin L. Dunkle, Barbara B. Lazarus, Indira Nair, and Deborah A. Harkus. *Journeys of Women in Science and Engineering: No Universal Constants.* Philadelphia: Temple University Press, 1997.

American Chemical Society. *American Chemical Society Awards 1998 Edition.* Washington, D.C.: American Chemical Society, 1998.

———. "1985 Garvan Medal." [Pamphlet prepared for presentation ceremony of Garvan Medal to Catherine Fenselau.] American Chemical Society, 1985.

"The American Look." *Time* 65:16 (2 May 1955): cover, 85–86.

American Men and Women of Science, 12th ed. Jaques Cattell Press, ed. New York: R. R. Bowker, 1990.

American Men and Women of Science, 16th ed. Jaques Cattell Press, ed. New York: R. R. Bowker, 1990.

American Men and Women of Science, 17th ed. Jaques Cattell Press, ed. New York: R.R. Bowker, 1990.

American Men and Women of Science, 18th ed (1992–1993), Stephen L. Torpie, Judy Redel, Richard D. Lanam, Tanya Hurst, Karen Hallard, and Beth Tanis, eds. New York: R.R. Bowker, 1992.

"America's Top 100 Young Scientists." *Science Digest* 92:12 (December 1984): 40–73.

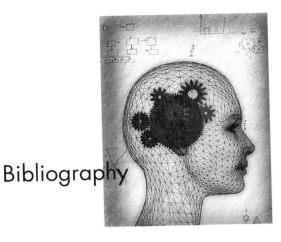

Bibliography

Anderson, Frank Walter., Jr. *Orders of Magnitude: A History of NACA and NASA, 1915–1976.* Washington, D.C.: Scientific and Technical Information Office, 1976.

Andrews, Edmund L. "An Exhibit of Inventions By Women." In Patents, *New York Times* (20 January 1990).

"Anna W. Williams, Scientist, Is Dead." [Obituary.] *New York Times* (21 November 1954): 86.

"Anthrax and Old Lace." *University of Kansas Alumni Magazine* 58:8 (May 1960).

"Arda A. Green." [Obituary.] *Chemical and Engineering News* (17 February 1958): 121.

Arenson, Karen W. "Rensselaer Polytechnic Picks New President." *New York Times* (12 December 1998): B6.

Ashby, Ruth, and Deborah Gore Ohrn, eds. *Herstory: Women Who Changed the World.* New York: Viking, 1995.

Asimov, Isaac. *Asimov's Biographical Encyclopedia of Science and Technology.* Garden City, NJ: Doubleday & Co., 1972.

———. *Asimov's Biographical Encyclopedia of Science and Technology,* 2nd ed. Garden City, NJ: Doubleday & Co., 1982.

Badger, Reid. *The Great American Fair.* Chicago: N. Hall, 1979.

Bailey, Martha J. *American Women in Science, 1950 to the Present: A Biographical Dictionary.* Santa Barbara: ABC-CLIO, 1998.

———. *American Women in Science: A Biographical Dictionary.* Santa Barbara: ABC-CLIO, 1994.

Bains, William. *Biotechnology from A to Z.* New York: Oxford, 1998.

Baker, Russell. "Navy's Tests Create and Dissolve Clouds." *New York Times* (24 September 1958): 1.

Baldwin, Sara Mullin, and Robert Morton Baldwin, eds. "Cornelia Mitchell Downs." *Illustriana Kansas* (1933).

Bamberger, Werner. "Dr. Virginia Apgar Dies at 65; Devised Health Test for Infants," [obituary]. *The New York Times Biographical Edition.* (8 August 1974): 1074.

Barker-Benfield, G. J., and Catherine Clinton. *Portraits of American Women: From Settlement to Civil War,* vol. 1 of 2. New York: St. Martin's Press, 1991.

Barnard College. *1997–1999 Catalogue,* 1997–1998 edition.

Barnes-Svarney, Patricia, ed., *The New York Public Library Science Desk Reference.* New York: Stonesong Press, 1995.

Bartels, Nancy, "The First Lady of Gearing." *Gear Technology* (September/October 1997).

Bear, Beverly, and Neil Walker. *Almanac of Famous People.* Detroit: Gale Research, 1994.

Benson, Harris. *University Physics.* New York: John Wiley & Sons, 1991.

Berkin, Carol., ed. *First Generations: Women in Colonial America.* New York: Hill and Wang, 1996.

"Berkowitz, Joan B." Biography received from Arthur D. Little, Inc (8 February 1984).

Bernikow, Louise. *The American Women's Almanac.* New York: Berkeley Books, 1997.

Bernstein, Leonard, Alan Winkler, and Linda Zierdt-Warshaw. *African and African American Women of Science.* Maywood, NJ: Peoples Publishing Group, 1998.

———. *Latino Women of Science.* Maywood, NJ: Peoples Publishing Group, 1998.

———. *Multicultural Women of Science.* Maywood, NJ: Peoples Publishing Group, 1996.

Bonta, Marcia Myers. *American Women Afield.* College Station: Texas A&M University Press, 1995.

———. *Women in the Field.* College Station: Texas A&M University Press, 1991.

Boorse, Henry, Lloyd Mofs, and Jefferson H. Weaver. *The Atomic Scientists: A Biographical History.* New York: John Wiley & Sons, 1989.

Bothamley, Jennifer. *Dictionary of Theories.* Detroit: Visible Ink, 1993.

Bouton, Katherine. "The Nobel Pair." *New York Times Magazine* (29 January 1989): 28, 60, 82, 86–88.

Bowman, J. S., ed. *The Cambridge Dictionary of American Biography.* Cambridge: Cambridge University Press, 1995.

Breton, Mary Joy. *Women Pioneers for the Environment.* Boston: Northeastern University Press, 1998.

Brittain, James E. "From Computer to Electrical Engineer: The Remarkable Career of Edith Clarke." *IEEE Transactions on Education* E28:4 (November 1985): 184–189.

Brown, Kenneth A., ed. *Inventors at Work: Interviews with 16 Notable American Inventors.* Washington, DC: Tempus Books, 1988.

Brown, Mike. "Secretary of Air Force Dr. Sheila Widnall Flies JPATS Trainer." Press release of Raytheon Aircraft (23 May 1996).

Buderi, Robert. "The Case of the Catalytic Chemist." *Business Week* (18 January 1993): 80.

Buel, Nora. "The Long Road from Straw Hats to High Technology." *Inventors Assistance Program News* 37 (August 1994).

Bundles, A'Lelia P. "Madame C. J. Walker: Cosmetics Tycoon." *Ms.* 12 (July 1983): 91–94.

Burstyn, Joan N., ed. *Past and Promise: Lives of New Jersey Women.* Metuchen, NJ: Scarecrow Press, 1990.

Butler, Margaret K. Resume sent to Alan Winkler by Margaret Butler (September 1998).

Cardwell, Donald. *The Norton History of Technology.* New York: Norton, 1995.

"Caresse Crosby, Publisher, Dies: Former Editor of Black Sun Press in Paris Was 78" [obituary], *New York Times* (25 January 1970): 7.

Carlin, Peter Ames, and Linda Kramer. "Air Force One: Secretary Sheila Widnall Navigates Stormy Skies." *People* 48:14 (6 October 1997): 143–144.

Casey, Susan. *Women Invent! Two Centuries of Discoveries that Have Shaped Our World.* Chicago: IPG, 1997.

"The Centennial." *New York Times* (10 March 1876): 1.

Chabrán, Richard, and Rafael Chabrán, eds. *The Latino Encyclopedia.* 6 vols. New York: Marshall Cavendesh, 1996.

Chaikin, Andrew. "Sally Ride, 1983: The First American Woman in Space." *Working Woman* (November/-December 1996): 43–46.

Chaison, E., and Steve McMillan, *Astronomy Today,* 3rd ed. New York: Prentice Hall, 1999.

Champagne, Duane, ed. *The Native North American Almanac: A Reference Work on North American Indians in the United States and Canada.* Detroit, MI: Gale Research, 1993.

Chandler, Lynn. "Supercomputer Named for Pioneer Researcher at Goddard." Press release of Goddard Space Flight Center (13 May 1997).

"Charlotte Sitterly, 91, Physicist; Devoted Career to Sunlight Studies." [Obituary.] *New York Times* (8 March 1990): D25.

Claire, Walter. *The Book of Winners.* New York: Harvest/HBJ Edition, 1979.

Clark, Alfred E. "Dr. Katherine Burr Blodgett, 81, Developer of Nonreflecting Glass." [Obituary.] *New York Times* (13 October 1979).

Clark, Judith Freeman. *Almanac of American Women in the 20th Century.* New York: Prentice Hall Press, 1987.

Clarke, Joni Anderson. "Bringing the Past to Life." *Women's Review of Books* 14:3 (December 1996).

Coleman, J. "First She Looks Inward." *Time* 34:19 (6 November 1989): 90.

Collins, Louise Mooney, and Geri T. Sprace, eds. *Newsmakers95.* Detroit: Gale Research, 1995.

Colowick, Sidney P. "Arda Alden Green." *Science* 128 (5 September 1958): 519–521.

Colwell, Rita. E-mail correspondence with Alan Winkler (28 February 1998).

Considine, Douglas M., ed. *Van Nostrand's Scientific Encyclopedia,* 5th ed. New York: Van Nostrand Reinhold, 1976.

———. *Van Nostrand's Scientific Encyclopedia,* 8th ed. 2 vols. New York: Van Nostrands Reinhold, 1990.

Convis, Orville R. "Why Trains Have Red Taillights." *Christian Science Monitor (*4 August 1986): 30.

Cook, Joan, "L. L. Greneker, 95: Made Mannequins with Movable Parts." [Obituary.] *New York Times (*6 February 1990): D25.

"Cora Downs." [Obituary.] *Topeka Capital-Journal (*28 January 1987).

Corcoran, Elizabeth. "Women in Technology Compare Experiences, Challenges at Meeting." *Washington Post (*27 June 1998): E1, E3.

Cosgrove, Holli R., ed. *Encyclopedia of Careers and Vocational Guidance.* Chicago, IL: J. G. Ferguson, 1997.

Cowan, Tom, and Jack Maguire. *Timelines of African American History: 500 Years of Black Achievement.* New York: Perigee, 1994.

Cullen-DuPont, Kathryn. *The Encyclopedia of Women's History in America.* New York: Da Capo Press, 1998.

Current Biography (Current Biography Yearbook, 1986–). Various editors. New York: H.W. Wilson Company, 1940–.

Daley, Marie M. "Mary Letitia Caldwell." In *American Chemists and Chemical Engineers.* Washington, DC: American Chemical Society, 1976.

Dash, Joan. *Triumph of Discovery: Women Scientists Who Won the Nobel Prize.* Morristown, NJ: Silver Burdett Press, 1990.

Dates, Karen E. "Professional Profile: Coast Guard Ocean Engineer Lisa [sic] Martinez." *Hispanic Engineer (*Fall 1987): 30–34.

Debus, Allen G., ed. *World Who's Who in Science,* 1st ed. Chicago: A. N. Marquis Co., 1968.

Derry, T. K., and Trevor I. Williams. *A Short History of Technology: From the Earliest Times to A.D. 1900.* New York: Dover Publications, 1960.

Dicke, William. "Chien-Shiung Wu, 84, Dies; Top Experimental Physicist." [Obituary.] *New York Times (*18 February 1997): B7.

Dickson, Paul. *Timelines.* Reading, MA: Addison-Wesley, 1991.

"DIED, Pearl Luella Kendrick, 90." [Obituary.] in "Milestones," *Time* 116:16 (20 October 1980): 105.

Dietz, Jean Pinanski. "The Medievalist Who Helps Make Telephones Work." *Wellesley (*Spring 1990): 7, 34.

"Does Something about It: Florence Wilhelmina van Straten." *New York Times (*24 September 1958): 52.

Donovan, Christine. "Rash Idea: Marion Donovan Helped Put Cloth Diapers Behind Us." *People Weekly (*7 December 1998): 152.

"Dorothy Weeks, 97, A Physicist Who Led in Variety of Careers." [Obituary.] *New York Times (*8 June 1990): D16.

"Dr. Alice G. Bryant, A Boston Physician: Ear, Nose and Throat Specialist Invented Surgery Instruments." [Obituary.] *New York Times (*27 July 1942): 15.

"Dr. Baker Is Dead; Health Expert, 71: Noted Woman Physician Saved Many Infant Lives as Head of Child Hygiene Bureau." [Obituary.] *New York Times (*23 February 1945): 17.

"Dr. Emma P. Carr, 91, Chemist at Holyoke." [Obituary.] *New York Times (*8 January 1972): 32.

"Dr. Esther M. Conwell Named 1960 SWE Award Winner." *SWE Newsletter (*1960): 5.

"Dr. Gilbreth, Engineer, Mother of Dozen." [Obituary.] *The New York Times Biographical Edition* (1972): 82–83.

"Dr. Leona Libby, 67; Worked on Atomic Bomb." [Obituary.] *New York Times (*12 November 1996.)

"Dr. Louise Pearce, Physician, 74, Dies." [Obituary.] *New York Times (*11 August 1959): 27.

"Dr. Myra Adele Logan, 68; Physician in Harlem." [Obituary.] *New York Times (*15 January 1977): 24.

"Dr. Rachel F. Brown, 81, Chemist." [Obituary.] *New York Times (*16 January 1980): D19.

"Dr. Temple Grandin Visits Department." *Animal Sciences.* Newsletter of the Department of Animal Sciences, University of Arkansas (Spring 1998): 1.

Dreifus, Claudia. "A Conversation with Rita Colwell: 'Always, Always, Going against the Norm.'" *New York Times Biographical Services (*February 1999): 306–307.

Dumouchel, J. Robert. *Government Assistance Almanac, 1999–2000: The Guide to Federal Domestic, Financial, and Other Programs.* Detroit, MI: Omnigraphics, Inc., 1999.

"Edith R. Peterson, 78: Studied Cell Cultures." [Obituary.] *New York Times (*20 August 1992): 19.

Edmonson, Catherine M. *365 Women Who Made a Difference.* Holbrook, MA: Adams Media, 1996.

Eicher, Eva M., Senior Staff Scientist, Jackson Laboratory, Bar Harbor, Maine. Telephone interview with Leonard Bernstein (23 March 1999).

Eisenhart, Margaret A., and Elizabeth Finkel. *Women's Science: Learning and Succeeding from the Margins.* Chicago: University of Chicago Press, 1998.

"Elda Anderson, Pioneer of Health Physics in the Atomic Energy Program, Dies at 61." [Obituary.] *Health Physics* (1961).

"Elda E. Anderson." [Obituary.] *Physics Today (*July 1961).

"The Electronic 3R's: Teaching on Home Computers (The Learning Company)." *Fortune* 107 (24 January 1983): 8.

"Elizabeth Armstrong Wood." Biography mailed to Alan Winkler by the Hauptman-Woodward Medical

Bibliography

Research Institute, Inc (representative of the American Crystallographic Association) on 1 July 1998.

"Emerson Scholarships Announced for '87." *ISP News,* National Newsletter of Iota Sigma Pi (1986): 1.

Eng, Patricia. Biographical data sent to Alan Winkler (1 July 1999).

Engelbert, Phillis, ed. *Science Fact Finder,* vol. 1: *The Natural World.* Detroit, MI: UXL, 1998.

"Esther B. Van Deman, U.S. Archaeologist: Authority on the Ruins of Rome Was Carnegie Institution Associate—Dies at 74." [Obituary.] *New York Times (*5 May 1937).

Famighetti, Robert, William A. McGeveran, Jr., Matthew Friedlander, Mark S. O'Malley, Lori P. Wiesenfeld., eds. *World Almanac and Book of Facts, 1994.* Mahwah, NJ: World Almanac Books, 1994.

Faragher, John Mack, ed. *The Encyclopedia of Colonial and Revolutionary America.* New York: Facts on File, 1990.

Felder, Deborah G. *A Century of Women: The Most Influential Events in 20th Century Women's History.* Secaucus, NJ: Birch Lane Press, 1999.

———. *The 100 Most Influential Women of All Time: A Ranking Past and Present.* New York: Citadel Press, 1996.

Fenselau, Catherine. Biographical information sent to Alan Winkler (31 March 1999).

"Film Beauty Hedy Lamarr Dead at Age 86." [Obituary.] *Delaware County Daily Times* (20 January 2000): 30.

Fins, Alice. *Women in Science.* Skokie, IL: VGM Career Horizons, 1979.

Fitzroy-Deloye, Nancy. "It's Time to Recognize the Contributions of Women Inventors." *USA Today Magazine (*1 January 1999): 66.

"Five Scientists Receive Lawrence Awards." *Physics Today (*October 1986): 137.

Flanaghan, Barbara, Resource Center Coordinator, 3M Public Relations. E-mail correspondence with Alan Winkler (11 August 1999).

"Florence W. van Straten Dies, Navy Atmospheric Physicist." [Obituary.] *Washington Post (*31 March 1992).

Fowler, Elizabeth M. "Beulah Louise Henry Has Been Called 'Lady Edison.'" *New York Times* (27 January 1962).

Fowler, Joanna S. E-mail correspondence with Alan Winkler (24 November 1998).

Francis, Raymond L. *The Illustrated Almanac of Science, Technology, and Invention.* New York: Plenum Trade, 1997.

Franck, Irene M., and David M. Brownstone. *Women's World: A Timeline of Women in History.* New York: Harper Perennial, 1995.

Franklin and Marshall, prepared in cooperation with the Higher Education Data Sharing Consortium. *Baccalaureate Origins of Doctoral Recipients: A Ranking by Discipline of 4-Year Private Institutions for the Period 1920–1995,* 8th ed. Lancaster, PA: Franklin and Marshall University, 1998.

Fuller, Edmund. *Tinkers and Genius: The Story of the Yankee Inventors.* Toronto: S. J. Reginald Saunders, 1955.

Gardner, Karen, Media Relations manager at Albert Einstein College of Medicine, mail communication with Alan Winkler (20 March 1999).

Gareffe, Peter M., ed. *Newsmakers 1989.* Detroit: Gale Research, 1989.

Garrison, Ervan. *A History of Engineering and Technology: Artful Methods.* 2nd ed. New York: CRC Press, 1999.

"Garvan Medal: Dr. Mary L. Caldwell." *Chemical and Engineering News* (18 April 1960): 86.

Geniesse, Jane F. "Dr. Ellen K. Silbergeld." *EDF People* XVIII:4 (October 1987).

Gillispie, Charles Coulston, ed. *Dictionary of Scientific Biographies.* New York: Scribner's Reference, 1981.

Giovanni, Nikki. "Shooting for the Moon." *Essence* 23:12 (April 1993): 58–60.

"Gladys A. Emerson: Tenth National Honorary Member, Elected in 1966." *ISP News,* the National Newsletter of Iota Sigma Pi (1986): 32.

Gleasner, Diana C. *Breakthrough Women in Science.* New York: Walker and Co., 1983.

Gleick, James. "Secret of Proteins Is Hidden in Their Folded Shapes." *New York Times (*14 June 1988): C1.

Gluck, Sherna Berger. *Rosie the Riveter Revisited.* New York: Penguin Books, 1987.

"The Great Exhibition, Machinery Hall." *New York Times (*17 June 1876): 3.

Goff, Alice C. *Women Can Be Engineers.* Ann Arbor, MI: Edwards Brothers, 1946.

Goggins, Tim, of the American Mathematical Society. Telephone interview with Leonard Bernstein (27 May 1998).

Goldblum, Janice, of the Archives of the National Academy of Sciences. Telephone interview with Leonard Bernstein (20 May 1998).

Granville, Evelyn Boyd. "My Life as a Mathematician." *Sage, A Scholarly Journal on Black Women* 6:2 (Fall 1989).

Green, Jay E., ed. *McGraw-Hill Modern Scientists and Engineers.* New York: McGraw-Hill, 1980.

Green, Timothy. "A Great Woman Astronomer Leaves England—Again." *Smithsonian (*January 1974).

Greenberg, Diane. "Joanna Fowler Wins DOE's Lawrence Award." *Brookhaven Bulletin* 52:42 (30 October 1998): 1–2.

Grimes, William. "Dorothy Rodgers is Dead at 83; Writer, Inventor, and Decorator," [Obituary.] *New York Times* (18 August 1992): 19.

Grinstein, Louise, and Paul J. Campbell, eds. *Women of Mathematics.* Westport, CT: Greenwood Press, 1987.

Grinstein, Louise S., Rose K. Rose, and Miriam H. Rafailovich, eds. *Women in Chemistry and Physics: A Biobibliographic Sourcebook.* Westport, CT: Greenwood Press, 1993.

Grossman, Bob. "Mrs. Potts Advertising Trade Cards." *Iron Talk* 11 (May/June 1997): 5–11.

Groueff, Stephane. *The Manhattan Project: The Untold Story of the Making of the Bomb.* Boston: Little Brown and Company, 1967.

Guernsey, Janet B. "The Lady Wanted to Purchase a Wheatstone Bridge: Sarah Frances Whiting and Her Successor." In *Making Contributions: An Historical Overview of Women's Role in Physics.* College Park, MD: American Association of Physics Teachers, 1984.

Haber, Louis. *Women Pioneers of Science.* New York: Harcourt Brace & Co., 1979.

Hanauer, Mark. "Technology: A Friendly Frontier for Female Pioneers." *Fortune* 109 (25 June 1985): 78–85.

Harris, Benson. *University Physics.* New York: John Wiley and Sons, 1991.

Harris, Ian. "JPL: Open Day 1998," *Spaceflight* 40:10 (1998): 390.

Harris, Laurie., ed. *Biography Today, Scientists and Inventors Series: Profiles of People of Interest to Young Readers,* 3 vols. Detroit, MI: Omnigraphics, 1996.

"Head of Child-Aids Firm, Ill 6 Months, Dies." [Obituary.] *Fort Wayne Journal Gazette* (1 November 1954).

Heinemann, Susan. *The New York Public Library Amazing Women in American History: A Book of Answers for Kids.* New York: John Wiley & Sons, 1998.

———. *Timelines of American Women's History.* New York: Perigee, 1996.

Hellemans, Alexander, and Bryan Bunch. *The Timetables of Science.* New York: Simon and Schuster, 1988.

Henrion, Claudia. *Women in Mathematics: The Addition of Difference.* Bloomington: Indiana University Press, 1997.

Herzenberg, Caroline. *Women Scientists from Antiquity to Present.* West Cornwall, CT: Locust Press, 1986.

Hine, Darlene Clark, Elsa Barkley Brown, and Rosalyn Terborg-Penn, eds. *Black Women in America: An Historical Encyclopedia,* 2 vols. Bloomington: Indiana University Press, 1993.

Hobby, Gladys L. *Penicillin: Meeting the Challenge.* New Haven, CT: Yale University Press, 1985.

Hogan, Kevin. "I Think, Therefore Icon." *Forbes* (13 September 1993): 70.

Hollinshead, Ariel C. Resume and e-mail correspondence with Alan Winkler (21 March 1999).

Holloway, Marguerite. "Profile: Sylvia A. Earle—Fire in Water." *Scientific American* 266:4 (April 1992): 37–38.

Hong, Karen E. "Early Women Inventors." *Cobblestone: The History Magazine for Young People* 15 (June 1, 1994): 6.

"Honoring Drug Discoverers." [Editorial.] *Boston Globe* (18 October 1988): 14.

Howard, H. "The Year's Top 100 Innovations and the Men and Women Behind Them." *Science Digest* 93:12 (December 1985): 27–63.

"I Think Icon, I Know Icon." *Working Woman* (November/December 1996): 49.

"Icie Macy Hoobler." [Obituary.] *Chemical and Engineering News* 62:7 (February 1984): 31.

"Important Women Overlooked in History Books, Says UD History Professor." *University of Dayton News* (1 July 1998).

"Inventors' Museum Moving." *New York Times* (7 September 1987): 7.

"Isabel Bevier, 82; Home Economist." [Obituary.] *New York Times* (18 March 1942).

"Ivy M. Parker to Receive Brannon Award." *Materials Protection and Performance* (Decemeber 1973): 48.

"Ivy Parker—First Lady of Corrosion." [Editorial.] *Corrosion* 41:11 (November 1985): 617.

James, Edward T., Janet Wilson James, and Paul S. Boyer, eds. *Notable American Women, 1607–1950: A Biographical Dictionary,* 3 vols. Cambridge, MA: Belknap Press, 1971.

Jeffrey, Laura. *American Inventors of the 20th Century.* Springfield, NJ: Enslow, 1996.

Jenkins-Jones, Sara, ed. *Random House Webster's Dictionary of Scientists.* New York: Random House, 1997.

Johnson, Allen, and Dumas Malone, eds. *Dictionary of American Biographies.* New York: Scribner and Son's Reference, 1977.

Jones, Edwin R., and Richard L. Childers. *Contemporary College Physics,* 2nd ed. Reading, MA: Addison-Wesley, 1993.

Jones, Stacy V. "Chemist Is Inventor of the Year." *New York Times* (27 January 1979): 30.

———. "Inventive Woman Patents 2-Way Envelope: A Single Unit Serves for Mailing and Also Returning." *New York Times* (27 January 1962): 27, 29.

"Judith A. Resnik." [Obituary.] *New York Times Biographical Service* 1986: 146.

Kane, Joseph Nathan, Steven Anzovin, and Janet Podell. *Famous First Facts,* 5th ed. New York: H. W. Wilson Company, 1997.

Kanellos, Nicolás, ed. *The Hispanic Almanac: From Columbus to Corporate America.* Detroit, MI: Visible Ink Press, 1994.

———. *The Hispanic American Almanac,* 2nd ed. Detroit, MI: Gale Research, 1966.

———. *Hispanic Firsts: 500 Years of Extraordinary Achievement.* Detroit, MI: Visible Ink Press, 1997.

Kass-Simon, G., and Patricia Farnes, eds. *Women of Science: Righting the Record.* Bloomington: Indiana University Press, 1990.

Kelly, Anne. "Breaking Barriers." *Cobblestone* 15 (1 June 1994): 2.

Keenan, Sheila. *Scholastic Encyclopedia of Women in the United States.* New York: Scholastic Reference, 1996.

Kenschaft, Patricia C., "Black Women in Mathematics in the

Bibliography

United States." *American Mathematical Monthly* 88:10 (October 1981): 592–604.

Kessler, James H., J. S. Kidd, Reneé A. Kidd, and Katherine A. Morin. *Distinguished African American Scientists of the 20th Century.* Phoenix: Oryx Press, 1996.

Kidwell, Peggy A. "Cecilia Payne-Gaposchkin: The Making of an Astrophysicist." In *Making Contributions: An Historical Overview of Women's Role in Physics.* College Park, MD: American Association of Physics Teachers, 1984.

Kittredge, Mary. *The Encyclopedia of Health: Organ Transplants.* New York: Chelsea House Publishers, 1988.

Koch, Wendy. "Mother of Invention Slowly Builds Her Base." Gannett News Service (19 November 1994).

Koppes, Clayton R. *JPL and the American Space Program: A History of the Jet Propulsion Laboratory 1936–1976.* New Haven, CT: Yale University Press, 1982.

Kotulak, Ronald. "Dr. Yalow Talks about Her Work." *Boston Globe* (5 January 1981).

Ladies' Home Journal Books. *Ladies' Home Journal 100 Most Important Women of the 20th Century.* Des Moines, IA: Meredith Books, 1998.

Lake, Mike. "A Passion to Invent Leads to Five Patents." *Virginia Gazette* (21 October 1987).

Lambert, Bruce. "Dr. Florence B. Seibert, Inventor of Standard TB Test, Dies at 93." [Obituary.] *New York Times* (31 August 1991): 12.

Lankford, John, and Rickey L. Slavings. "Gender and Science: Women in American Astronomy, 1859–1940." *Physics Today* 43:3 (March 1990): 56–65.

Leavitt, Judith Walzer. *Typhoid Mary: Captive to the Public's Health.* Boston: Beacon Press, 1996.

Leitch, Alexander. *A Princeton Companion.* Princeton, NJ: Princeton University Press, 1978.

Levin, Beatrice. *Women and Medicine: Pioneers Meeting the Challenge.* Lincoln, NE: Media Publishing, 1989.

Levitan, Tina. *First Facts in American Jewish History: From 1492 to the Present.* North Vale, NJ: Jason Aronson, 1996.

Levy, Richard C. *Inventing and Patenting Sourcebook: How to Sell and Protect Your Ideas.* Detroit, MI: Gale Research, 1990.

Litoff, Judy Barrett, and Judith McDonnell. *European Immigrant Women in the United States: A Biographical Dictionary.* New York: Garland Reference Library of Social Science, 1994.

Litzenberg, Kathleen, ed. *Who's Who of American Women.* 18th ed (1993–1994). New Providence, NJ: Reed Reference Publishing, 1995.

Logan, Rayford W., and Michael R. Winston, eds. *Dictionary of American Negro Biography.* New York: W. W. Norton & Co., 1983.

Logan, Vivian Crates. "Fort Wayne Women at Work." *Fort Wayne News-Sentinel* (3 May 1940).

Low, August, and Virgil A. Clift. *Encyclopedia of Black America.* New York: Da Capo Press, 1981.

Macdonald, Anne L. *Feminine Ingenuity: How Women Inventors Changed America.* New York: Ballantine Books, 1992.

"Machinery Hall." *New York Times* (5 June 1876): 2.

Macksey, Joan, and Kenneth Macksey. *The Book of Women's Achievements.* New York: Stein and Day, 1976.

"Madeleine Joullié Wins Henry Hill Award." *Chemical and Engineering News* (5 September 1994): 45.

Mann, Elizabeth. *The Brooklyn Bridge.* New York: Mikaya Press, 1996.

"Maria Goeppart-Mayer." [Obituary.] *New York Times* (22 February 1972).

"Marion Donovan, 81, Solver of the Damp-Diaper Problem. [Obituary.] *New York Times* (18 November 1998): B15.

Martin, Murray. "Katharine Way." *Physics Today* (December 1996): 75.

"Mary L. Caldwell of Columbia Dies: Enzyme Expert, 81, Taught Chemistry 41 Years." [Obituary.] *New York Times* (3 July 1972).

"Mary Fieser, Researcher, Writer in Organic Chemistry, Dies at Age 87." [Obituary.] *Harvard Gazette* (27 March 1997).

"Mary Pennington, Engineer, 80, Dead." [Obituary.] *New York Times* (28 December 1952): 48.

"Mary S. Rose Dead; Nutrition Expert." [Obituary.] *New York Times* (2 February 1941): 46.

Massaquois, Hans J. "Blacks in Science and Technology." *Ebony* (February 1997): 175–179.

Maulsby, Richard, and Lisa-Joy Zgorski. "Nobel Laureates to Receive Ronald H. Brown American Innovator Awards." Press release, U.S. Patent and Trademark Office (9 October 1996).

Maurer, Christine, and Tara E. Sheets, eds. *Encyclopedia of Associations: An Associations Unlimited Reference,* 33rd ed., 2 vols. Detroit, MI: Gale Research, 1998.

McCartney, Scott. *ENIAC: The Triumphs and Tragedies of the World's First Computer.* New York: Walker and Company, 1999.

McClellan, Doug. "Ellen Ochoa: Reaching for the Stars." *Los Angeles Times,* Ventura County Edition (27 May 1993): Metro, 1.

McGrayne, Sharon B. *Nobel Prize Women in Science.* New York: Carol Publishing Company, 1992.

McHenry, Robert. *Famous American Women: A Biographical Dictionary from Colonial Times to the Present.* New York: Dover, 1983.

McIntyre, Edison. "Gertrude Elion." *Cobblestone* 15 (1 June 1994): 32.

McKinney, R. E. "Sister Presidents." *Ebony* 43:4 (February 1988): 82, 84–.

McMurran, Kristan, "Frances Gabe's Self-Cleaning House

Could Mean New Rights of Spring for Housewives." *People Weekly (*29 March 1982): 38, 41.

McMurray, Emily M., ed. *Notable Twentieth-Century Scientists.* 4 vols. Detroit, MI: Gale Research, 1995.

McNeil, Ian, ed. *An Encyclopedia of the History of Technology.* London: Routledge, 1996.

McQueen, Camille Peplowski, and Margaret Cavanaugh. "Fenselau Addresses Women Chemists." *Women Chemists Newletter (*July 1985): 1.

Meeks, Fleming. "I Guess They Just Take and Forget about a Person." *Forbes (*14 May 1990).

Merrill, J. F. "Designing Woman." *Scholastic* 66 (16 February 1955): 5.

Merrill, S. "Women in Engineering." *Cosmopolitan (*April 1976): 162, 164– .

Miles, Wyndham D., ed., *American Chemists and Chemical Engineers.* Washington, DC: American Chemical Society, 1976.

Millar, David, et al. *The Cambridge Dictionary of Scientists.* Cambridge: Cambridge University Press, 1996.

Mills, Kay. "Who Is Alice Hamilton?" [Editorial.] *Roanoke Times (*11 November 1993): A15.

"Miss Antonia Maury." [Obituary.] *New York Times (*10 January 1952): 29.

"Miss Harriet Hosmer Dead: Sculptress Modeled a Notable 'Puck' of Which 30 Copies Were Made." [Obituary.] *New York Times (*22 February 1908): 7.

Montney, Charles B., ed. *Hispanic Americans Information Directory.* 3rd ed. Detroit, MI: Gale Research, 1994.

Mooney, Louise, ed. *Newsmakers90.* Detroit, MI: Gale Research, 1990.

Moore, Christopher W. [Administrative Associate, Transcript Services, UT—Austin Registrar's Office]. E-mail correspondence with Alan Winkler (5 May 1998).

Morris, Bernadine. "Three Who Directed Fashion." *New York Times (*24 February 1987): 28.

Mort, Cynda. "Career Built on Child Safety." *Fort Wayn News-Sentinel (*20 March 1976).

Mount Holyoke College. *Bulletin and Course Catalog, 1997–1998.* Mount Holyoke, MA: Mount Holyoke College, 1997.

Mozans, H. J. *Woman in Science, With an Introductory Chapter on Women's Long Struggle for Things of the Mind.* Notre Dame, IN: University of Notre Dame Press, 1991.

"Mrs. Averell, 87, Led Doll Concern: Founder of Company Here Dies on West Coast." [Obituary.] *New York Times (*28 August 1963): 33.

"Mrs. Florence Potts: The True Story," *Iron Talk* 11 (May/June 1997): 1, 3–4.

Muir, Hazel, ed. *Larousse Dictionary of Scientists.* Edinburgh, UK: Larousse, 1994.

National Academy of Sciences. *A History of the First Half-Century of the National Academy of Sciences: 1863–1913.* Washington, DC: National Academy of Sciences, 1913.

National Aeronautics and Space Administration. *Astronaut Fact Book.* PMS-011C. February 1992.

"National Presidents of Iota Sigma Pi." *ISP News,* the National Newsletter of Iota Sigma Pi (1986): 4.

Nazel, Joe. "Cataract Surgery Inventor to Be Fêted: She Returns Sight to Blind with New Laser Surgery Tools." *Wave Community Newspapers (*14 February 1996): A–B.

"No More Makeshift Site Protectors." *Nursing97 (*November 1997): 61.

Nobel, Iris. *Contemporary Women Scientists of America.* New York: Julian Messner, 1979.

Nulty, Peter. "The National Business Hall of Fame." *Fortune* 12:6 (23 March 1992): 112–118.

"Oceanographer Sylvia Earle Among 23 Individuals and Organizations to Receive UN Environment Award at World Environment Day Celebrations in Moscow." United Nations press release. UNEP/28 (26 May 1988).

Ochoa, George, and Melinda Corey. *The Timeline Book of Science.* New York: Ballantine Books, 1995.

Ochoa, Severo, and H. M. Kalckar. "Gerty T. Cori, Biochemist." *Science* 128 (1958):16–17.

Office of the Federal Register. National Archives and Records Administration. *The United States Government Manual, 1997/98.* Washington, DC, 1997.

Ogilvie, Marilyn. *Women in Science Antiquity through the Nineteenth Century: A Biographical Dictionary with Annotated Bibliography.* Cambridge, MA: MIT Press, 1986.

O'Hern, Elizabeth Moot. *Profiles of Pioneer Women Scientists.* Washington, DC: Acropolis Books, 1986.

Oleson, Charles W., *Secret Nostroms and Systems of Medicine: A Book of Formulas.* Chicago: Oleson & Company, 1892.

Oliver, Myrna. "Gertrude Elion: Nobel-Winning Scientist." [Obituary.] *Los Angeles Times (*23 February 1999): A20.

Olsen, Kirstin. *Chronology of Women's History.* Westport, CT: Greenwood Press, 1994.

"The 100 Most Fascinating Women of the Twentieth Century." *Ebony* LIV:5 (March 1999): 53, 74.

O'Neill, Lois Decker. *The Women's Book of Records and Achievements.* New York: Anchor Press/Doubleday, 1979.

Opfell, Olga S. *The Lady Laureates: Women Who Have Won the Nobel Prize.* Metuchen, NJ: Scarecrow Press, 1978.

Orenstein, Peggy, in association with the American Association of University Women. *School Girls: Young Women, Self-Esteem, and the Confidence Gap.* New York: Anchor/Doubleday, 1994.

Osen, Lynn. *Women in Mathematics.* Cambridge, MA: MIT Press, 1974.

Pabst, Georgia. "Women Are Often Mothers of Inventions." *Milwaukee Journal Sentinel* (6 April 1997).

Pankove, J. I., ed. *Electroluminescence.* New York: Springer-Verlag, 1977.

Parker, Sybil P. *McGraw-Hill Encyclopedia of Science and Technology,* 8th ed. 20 vols. New York: McGraw-Hill, 1997.

Parry, Melanie, ed. *Larousse Dictionary of Women.* New York: Anchor Press/Doubleday, 1996.

Parsons, Susan V. "1993 Resnik Challenger Medal Recipient: Yvonne C. Brill." *SWE* (September/October 1993): 18–20.

Peden, Irene Carswell. Faculty Biographical Supplement, University of Washington; and e-mail correspondence with Alan Winkler (8 July 1999; 10 July 1999).

Pelletier, Paul A., ed. *Prominent Scientists: An Index to Collective Biographies.* New York: Neal-Schuman Publishing, 1994.

Perl, Teri. *Women and Numbers: Lives of Women Mathematicians.* San Carlos, CA: Wide World Publishing/Tetra, 1993.

Petroski, Henry. *Engineers of Dreams: Great Bridge Builders and the Spanning of America.* New York: Vintage Books, 1995.

"Physicist Esther Conwell Illuminates the Behavior of Electrons in Solids." Press release of the American Physical Society, the American Institute of Physics, and Xerox Corporation (16 April 1991).

Pinkham, Lydia E. *Lydia E. Pinkham's Private Text-Book: Upon Ailments Peculiar to Women.* Lynn, MA: Lydia E. Pinkham Medicine Co (n.d.).

Plaski, Harry A., and James Williams, eds. *The Negro Almanac: A Reference Work on the Afro-American.* New York: John Wiley and Sons, 1983.

———. *The Negro Almanac: A Reference Work on the Afro-American,* 5th ed. Detroit, MI: Gale Research, 1998.

Pollock, Sean R., ed., *Newmakers97.* Detroit, MI: Gale Research, 1997.

Port, Otis. "A Plea for the Solo Inventor." *Business Week* (18 January 1993): 82.

Porter, Ray, ed. *The Biographical Dictionary of Science,* 2nd ed. New York: Oxford University Press, 1994.

Potter, Robert. "Saving Our Doomed 'Blue Babies.'" *American Weekly* (17 February 1947).

"The President in Chicago." *New York Times* (30 April 1893): 2.

"The President Presses the Button." *New York Times* (2 May 1893): 2.

"Prof. Irmgard Flugge-Lotz Dies; Taught Engineering at Stanford." [Obituary.] *New York Times* (23 May 1974).

"Profiles in Leadership." *Hispanic Engineer* (Fall 1989): 22–24.

Purl, M. "One Giant Step for Womankind: Equal Opportunity Gets off the Ground." *Working Woman* 5 (May 1980): 32–58.

Ralston, Harry A., and James Williams, eds. *Encyclopedia of Computer Science,* 3rd ed. New York: Van Nostrand Reinhold, 1993.

Read, Phyllis J., and Bernard L. Witlieb. *The Book of Women's Firsts.* New York: Random House, 1992.

Rhode Island Historical Society. Correspondence received from Linda Eppich, Chief Curator (29 December 1998).

Rhodes, Richard. *The Making of the Atomic Bomb.* New York: Simon and Schuster, 1986.

Richardson, Jane Shelby. E-mail correspondence with Alan Winkler (5 June and 8 June 1999).

Rinker, Harry L., ed. *Warman's Americana & Collectibles.* Radnor, PA: Wallace-Homestead, 1995.

Robertson, Patrick, ed. *The Book of Firsts.* New York: Crown Publishers, 1975.

"Rogers Led the Way for Women—Devoted Her Life to Science." [Obituary.] *China Lake Rocketeer* (17 March 1989): 3.

Roscher, Nina Matheny. "Women Chemists." *ChemTech #6* (December 1976): 738–743.

Rossiter, Margaret W. *Women Scientists in America: Before Affirmative Action, 1940–1972.* Baltimore: Johns Hopkins University Press, 1995.

———. *Women Scientists in America: Struggles and Strategies to 1940.* Baltimore: Johns Hopkins University Press, 1982.

Rudolph, Barbara, "Why Can't a Woman Manage More Like . . . A Woman?" *Time* 136:19 (Fall 1990): 53.

Ryan, Mary P. *Womanhood in America: From Colonial Times to the Present.* New York: New Viewpoints, 1975.

Saari, Peggy, ed. *Prominent Women of the 20th Century.* Detroit, MI: Gale Research, 1996.

Saari, Peggy, and Stephen Allison, eds. *Scientists: The Lives and Works of 150 Scientists.* 3 vols. Detroit, MI: UXL, 1996.

Sadker, Myra, and David Sadker. *Failing at Fairness: How Our Schools Cheat Girls.* New York: Touchstone, 1994.

Salem, Dorothy C., ed. *African American Women: A Biographical Dictionary.* New York: Garland Publishing, 1993.

Salerno, Heather. "Mothers of Invention: Though Unsung and Ignored, Women Have Pushed Technology's Frontiers." *Washington Post* (12 March 1997): H01.

Sammons, Vivian Ovelton. *Blacks in Science and Medicine.* New York: Hemisphere, 1990.

Sawrey, Barbara [Vice Chair for Education, Department of Chemistry and Biochemistry, University of California at San Diego]. E-mail correspondence with Alan Winkler (16 March 1998).

Saxon, Wolfgang. "Edith Quimby Dies; Radiation Expert." [Obituary.] *New York Times* (13 October 1982): A28.

Schanstra, C. "Women in Infosystems: Climbing the Corporate Ladder." *Infosystems* (May 1980): 72, 74–.

Scheff, Lynn, and Virginia Dunleavy. "Winners: Scientist Joanna Fowler." *Newsday* (15 November 1998).

Schefter, Jim. "Reaching for the Rings: The Biggest, Best, and Last of NASA's Superships, *Cassini* Takes Off for Saturn." *Popular Science* (October 1997): 60–65.

Schmeck, Harold M., Jr. "Charlotte Friend Dies at 65; Researched Cancer Viruses." [Obituary.] *New York Times* (16 January 1987): D18.

Schmittroth, Linda, Mary Reilly McCall, and Bridget Travers, eds. *Eureka!* New York: UXL, 1995.

Schumacher, Sandy [Fellow Program Coordinator, Awards/Fellow Activities, IEEE]. E-mail correspondence with Alan Winkler (16 October 1998).

"Scientist Downs Leaves Legacy of Half a Century." *Kansas Alumni Magazine* 85:5 (March 1987).

"Scientists Call for 'National Commitment' at Senate Hearings." *Science* 216 (7 May 1982): 611–612.

Scott, Brian. "Stopping Bullets." In "Working Knowledge." *Scientific American* 276:3 (March 1997): 132.

"Screen Star Hedy Lamarr Dead at 86: Legendary Beauty Seen in Many Motion Pictures." *Long Island Newsday* (20 January 2000): A6, A38.

"Secret of Proteins Is Hidden in Their Folded Shapes." *New York Times* (14 June 1988): C1, C10.

Semat, Henry. *Fundamentals of Physics*, 3rd ed. New York: Holt, Rhinehart, and Winston, 1957.

Shaw, Donna. "On the Trail of Tainted Blood: Hemophiliacs Say U.S. Could Have Prevented the Spread of AIDS." In "Reviews and Opinions." *Philadelphia Inquirer* (16 April 1995): E1–E3.

Shearer, Benjamin F., and Barbara S. Shearer, eds. *Notable Women in the Life Sciences: A Biographical Dictionary.* Westport, CT: Greenwood Press, 1996.

———. *Notable Women in the Physical Sciences: A Biographical Dictionary.* Westport, CT: Greenwood Press, 1997.

Shepard, Nona [Executive Secretary, Enrico Fermi Awards]. "The Enrico Fermi Award's 42-Year History Honors the Nuclear Age." *International Congress of Distinguished Awards* 3:1 (Spring/Summer 1998).

Sherr, Lynn. "Remembering Judy: The Five Women Astronauts Who Trained with Judy Resnik Remember Her and that Day...." *Ms.* 14:12 (June 1986): 56–58.

Sherrow, Victoria. *Women in the Military: An Encyclopedia.* Santa Barbara: ABC-CLIO, 1996.

Shiels, Barbara. *Women and the Nobel Prize.* Minneapolis: Dillon Press, 1985.

Showell, Ellen H., and Fred M. B. Amram. *From Indian Corn to Outer Space: Women Invent in America.* Peterborough, NH: Cobblestone, 1995.

Sicherman, Barbara, and Carol Hurd Green, eds. *Notable American Women: The Modern Period.* Cambridge, MA: Belknap Harvard, 1980.

Siegman, Gita, ed. *Awards, Honors and Prizes,* vol. 1: *United States and Canada.* 10th ed. Detroit, MI: Gale Research, 1992.

Simmons, John. *The Scientific 100: A Ranking of the Most Influential Scientists, Past and Present.* Secaucus, NJ: Citadel Press, 1996.

Sirica, Coimbra. "Mildred S. Dresselhaus, 1997 AAAS President." *AAAS News & Notes* (29 November 1996).

Slater, Elinor, and Robert Slater. *Great Jewish Women.* New York: Jonathan David Publishers, 1998.

Sluby, Patricia Carter. "Black Women and Inventions." *Sage: A Scholarly Journal on Black Women* VI:2 (Fall 1989): 33–35, 54.

———. "Black Women & Inventions." *Women's History Network News* (January 1993): 5.

Smith, Darrel L., ed. *Hispanic American Information Directory, 1990–91,* 1st ed. Detroit, MI: Gale Research, 1992.

Smith, Jessie Carney, ed. *Black Firsts: 2,000 Years of Extraordinary Achievement.* Detroit, MI: Gale Research, 1994.

———. *Notable Black American Women.* Detroit, MI: Gale Research, 1992.

Smith, Jessie Carney, and Nikki Giovanni, eds. *Black Heroes of the 20th Century.* Detroit, MI: Visible Ink Press, 1998.

"Society of Women Engineers Achievement Award to Dr. Susan Wu." *Congressional Record—Senate* (15 July 1985).

Spaeth, Mary. E-mail correspondence with Alan Winkler (17 June 1999).

Stage, Sarah, *Female Complaints: Lydia Pinkham and the Business of Women's Medicine.* New York: Norton, 1979.

Stanley, Autumn. *Mothers and Daughters of Invention: Notes for a Revised History of Technology.* Metuchen, NJ: Scarecrow Press, 1993.

Steck, Robert. "The Beauty Part." *D&B Reports* 42:2 (Mar/Apr 1993): 52.

Stewart, Jeffrey C. *1001 Things Everyone Should Know about African American History.* New York: Main Street Books/Doubleday, 1996.

Stille, Darlene R. *Extraordinary Women of Medicine.* New York: Children's Press, 1997.

Stinson, Stephen. "Edith M. Flanigen Wins Perkin Medal." *Chemical and Engineering News* (9 March 1992): 25.

———. "Kwolek Wins Lifetime Achievement Award." *Chemical and Engineering News* (3 May 1999): 11.

"Strategies for Change: Don't Just Say 'Do This.'" *Working Woman* (July 1990): 54.

Strong, C. L. "Ocular Spectroscope." *Scientific American* (December 1952).

———. "Tunable Dye Laser." *Scientific American* (February 1970).

———. "Ultraviolet Spectrograph." *Scientific American* (October 1968).

Stuart, Sandra Lee, ed. *Who Won What When: The Record Book of Winners.* Secaucus, NJ: Lyle Stuart, 1980.

Sullivan, Otha Richard, ed. *Black Stars: African American Inventors.* New York: John Wiley & Sons, 1998.

Sullivan, Walter. "Charlotte Sitterly, 91, Physicist; Devoted Career to Sunlight Studies." [Obituary.] *New York Times* (8 March 1990).

"SWE Personality Profile: Y. C. L. Susan Wu, 1985 Achievement Award Winner." *U.S. Woman Engineer* (March–April 1990): 31–32.

Telgen, Diane, and Jim Kamp, eds. *Notable Hispanic American Women.* Detroit, MI: Gale Research, 1993.

Thomas, Robert McG., Jr. "Marion Donovan, 81, Solver of the Damp-Diaper Problem." [Obituary.] *New York Times* (18 November 1998): B15.

Thornton, P. R. *The Physics of Electroluminescent Devices.* London: Spon, 1967.

"350 Women Who Changed the World, 1976– 1996." *Working Woman* 21:11 (November– December 1996): 32–50.

Tinling, Marion. *Women Remembered.* Westport, CT: Greenwood Press, 1986.

Tobias, Sheila, and Lisa Anderson. "What Ever Happened to Rosie the Riveter?" *Ms* (June 1973).

"Tomorrow's Achiever." In *Black Achievers in Science.* Chicago: Museum of Science and Industry, 1988.

Townsel, L. J. "Husbands of Powerful Women." *Ebony* 51:9 (July 1996): 115–118.

Trager, James. *The People's Chronology.* New York: Henry Holt, 1992.

———. *The Women's Chronology.* New York: Henry Holt, 1994.

Travers, Bridget, ed. *World of Science Discovery.* Detroit, MI: Gale Research, 1982.

———. *World of Scientific Discovery.* Detroit, MI: Gale Research, 1994.

Trescott, Martha Moore, ed. *Dynamos and Virgins Revisited: Women and Technological Change in History.* Metuchen, NJ: Scarecrow Press, 1979.

Tsipis, Kosta. *Arsenal: Understanding Weapons in the Nuclear Age.* New York: Simon & Schuster, 1983.

Tuttle, Elizabeth E. "Historic Treasure of the Week." *Vigo County Historical Society* (28 October 1984).

Uglow, Jennifer S., ed. *The International Dictionary of Women's Biography.* New York: Continuum Publishing, 1982.

U.S. Department of Education. Office of Educational Research and Improvement. National Center for Education Statistics. *Chartbook of Degrees Conferred, 1969–70 to 1993–94.* NCES 98–071. Thomas D. Snyder, Project Officer. Washington, DC: GPO, 1997.

———. *Degrees and Other Awards Conferred by Degree-Granting Institutions 1995–96.* NCES 98–256. Frank B. Morgan, Project Officer. Washington, DC: GPO, 1998.

U.S. Department of Energy. *Black Contributors to Science and Technology.* DOE/OPA-0035. Washington, DC: Office of Public Affairs, 1979.

U.S. Department of Labor, Bureau of Labor Statistics. *Occupational Outlook Handbook,* Bulletin 2500 *(1998–1999).* Washington, DC: Government Printing Office, 1999.

———. *Occupational Outlook Handbook, 1994–1995.* Bulletin 2450. Washington, DC: Government Printing Office, 1994.

U.S. Patent and Trademark Office. *A Quest for Excellence.* Washington, DC: Government Printing Office, 1994.

University of Washington, Women Studies Program, Women in Science course. *Hypatia's Sisters: Biographies of Women Scientists Past and Present.* Seattle: University of Washington, 1975.

Unterberger, Amy, ed. *Who's Who among Asian Americans, 1994–1995.* Detroit, MI: Gale Research, 1994.

———. *Who's Who among Hispanic Americans, 1991–1992.* Detroit, MI: Gale Research, 1994.

Vallino, Lisa. "I.V. House: Pediatric Nurses Contribute to Refinement of IV Protector." *Journal of Pediatric Nursing* 13:3 (June 1998):196–198.

Van Sertima, Ivan. *Blacks in Science, Ancient and Modern.* New Brunswick, NJ: Transaction Publishers, 1995.

Van Vleck, Richard. "Early Cow Milking Machines." *Scientific Medical & Mechanical Antiques* 20 (1996).

Vare, Ethlie Ann, and Greg Ptacek. *Mothers of Invention: From the Bra to the Bomb, Forgotten Women and Their Unforgettable Ideas.* New York: William Morrow and Company, 1988.

———. *Women Inventors and Their Discoveries.* Foreword by Ruth Handler. Minneapolis: Oliver Press, 1993.

Varro, E. "The Bright Side of Black Cohosh." *Prevention* 49:4 (April 1997): 76–80.

Veglahn, Nancy. *Women Scientists.* New York: Facts on File, 1992.

Vercellotti, Sharon V., ed. *ISP News* (the national newsletter of Iota Sigma Pi), 1986.

Verheyden-Hillard, Mary Ellen. *An American Women in Science Biography.* Bethesda, MD: Equity Institute, 1985.

"Virginia Frantz, Teacher, Is Dead." [Obituary.] *New York Times* (24 August 1967).

Walker, Jimmy [editor and publisher of *Iron Talk*]. E-mail correspondence with Alan Winkler (1 July 1999).

Wallis, C. Rime. "Baby Fae Stuns the World." *Time* 124 (November 1984): 70–72, 88–89.

Warren, Rebecca Lowe, and Mary H. Thompson. *The Scientist within You.* 2 vols. Eugene, OR: ACI Publishing, 1994/1995.

Wasson, Tyler, ed. *Nobel Prize Winners: An H. W. Wilson Biographical Dictionary.* New York: H. W. Wilson, 1987.

Watkins, T. H., Todd Wilkinson, Frank Graham, Jr., Ted

Levin, Kenn Kaufman, David Seideman, Jon R. Luomo, Chris Chang, Yi Shun Lai, Gretel Schueller, and Carolyn Shea. "One Hundred Champions of Conservation." *Audubon* 100:66 (November–December 1998): 120, 130.

Weatherford, Doris. *American Women's History: An A to Z of People, Organizations, Issues, and Events.* New York: Prentice Hall Reference, 1994.

Weertman, Julia. E-mail correspondence with Alan Winkler (15 July 1999).

"What the Women Have Done." *New York Times* (30 April 1893): 19.

"Where Are They Now?" *Ebony* (February 1997): 170J.

Wiemann, Jeanne Madeline. *The Fair Women: The Story of the Woman's Building, World's Columbian Exposition, 1893.* Chicago: Academy Chicago Publications, 1981.

Wilkes, Joseph A., ed. *Encyclopedia of Architecture, Design, Engineering & Construction.* 4 vols. New York: John Wiley & Sons, 1988.

Williams, Harold H. "Icie Gertrude Macy Hoobler (1892–1984): A Biographical Sketch." *Journal of Nutrition* 114 (1984).

Williams, Jack. "NASA Chief Kept Her Head in the Clouds." *USA Today* (22 December 1998).

Williams, Trevor. *Biographical Dictionary of Scientists.* Glasgow, UK: HarperCollins, 1994.

"Woman Has New Aeroplane: Miss Todd Hopes to Exhibit the Model at Brighton Beach." *New York Times* (31 July 1908): 12.

"Woman Inventor Dies in Poverty: El Dorado Jones Spent Recent Years Seeking Backing for Airplane Muffler." [Obituary.] *New York Times* (27 November 1932).

"Woman Perfects Torpedo: Dr. M. J. Alsbau Masters the Principle of Steering It." *New York Times* (17 December 1899): 8.

"Women and the Centennial." *New York Times* (10 March 1876): 8.

"Women Who Are Inventors." *New York Times* (19 October 1913): 11.

Wood, Elizabeth Armstrong. Curriculum vitae received from the Hauptman-Woodward Medical Research Institute (1 July 1999).

Wright, Sarah H. "Widnall Fêted by Fellow Women Faculty." *MIT TechTalk* (4 November 1998).

Yost, Edna. *American Women in Science.* Philadelphia: Lippincott, 1943.

———. *Women of Modern Science.* New York: Dodd Mead and Co., 1959.

Young, Margaret Labash, ed. *Scientific and Technical Organizations and Agencies Directory,* 1st ed. Detroit, MI: Gale Research, 1985.

Yount, Lisa. *Black Scientists.* New York: Facts on File, 1991.

———. *Contemporary Women Scientists.* New York: Facts on File, 1994.

———. *Twentieth-Century Women Scientists.* New York: Facts on File, 1996.

"Yvonne C. Brill, 1986 Achievement Award Winner." *U.S. Woman Engineer* (September/October 1986): 20–21.

Zia, Helen, and Susan B. Gall, eds. *Notable Asian Americans.* Detroit, MI: Gale Research, 1994.

Zilberg, Caroline, ed. *Women's Firsts.* Detroit, MI: Gale Research, 1997.

Zophy, Angela Howard, ed. *Handbook of American Women's History.* New York: Garland, 1990.

Selected Web Sites

The main web site of each organization is listed here. Additional information about these organizations and their programs may be obtained through use of the hypertext links provided at these sites.

American Association for the Advancement of Science
    http://www.aaas.org
American Association of University Women
    http://www.aauw.org
American Chemical Society
    http://www.acs.org
American Institute of Chemical Engineers
    http://www.aiche.org
American Mathematical Society   http://www.ams.edu
American Physical Society   http://www.aps.org
American Society for Electrical Engineering
    http://www.asee.org
American Society of Civil Engineers, California State Council   http://www.asce-ca.org
American Society of Heating, Refrigerating and Air-Conditioning Engineers   http://www.ashrae.org
American Society of Mechanical Engineers
    http://www.asme.org
Association for Women in Science   http://www.awis.org
Discovery Channel Online   http://www.discovery.com
Institute of Electrical and Electronics Engineers
    http://www.ieee.org
Lemelson Center of the Smithsonian Institution
    http://www.si.edu/lemelson
Lemelson-MIT Program, Invention Dimension
    http://web.mit.edu
Louisiana State University Libraries, Baton Rouge
    http://www.lib.lsu.edu
National Academy of Engineering   http://www.nae.edu
National Aeronautics and Space Administration
    http://www.nasa.gov
National Institute of Standards and Technology
    http://www.nist.gov
National Inventors' Hall of Fame   http://www.invent.org
National Science Foundation   http://www.nsf.gov
National Women's Hall of Fame   http://www.great-women.org

Bibliography

National Women's History Project   http://www.nwhp.org
Nuclear Regulatory Commission   http://www.nrc.gov
Smithsonian Institution
   http://www.si.edu
Society of Women Engineers   http://www.swe.org
U.S. Patent and Trademark Office   http://www.uspto.gov
Vassar College, Women in Science Hall of Fame

   http://www.vassar.edu
Virtual Museum of Virginia Tech
   http://www.ee.vt.edu/museum
Women in Technology International   http://www.witi.org
Wood's Hole Marine Biological Laboratory
   http://www.mbl.edu

Index

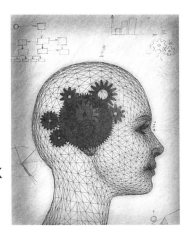

Index

Baldwin, Anna, 3, 5–6, 27
Ball, Sarah E., 5
Barbie®, 130–131
Bardeen, John, 60
Barnard College, xiii, 20, 27, 334–335
Barnard, Frederick A. P., 27, 215
Barnett Company, 127
Barney, Morgan, 28
Barney, Nora Stanton Blatch, 17, 27–28
Bartlett, Helen Blair, 18, 28–29, 225, 229, 231
Bascom, Florence, xiii, 20, 44, 108, 172
Bath, Patricia, 29, 30, 204
Baylor University Medical Center, 139
Beasley, Maria E. (nee Kenny), 29, 31, 72
Bechtel Power Corporation, 255
Becquerel, Henri, 224
Becquerel, Jean A. E. M., 50
Beecher, Catherine, 140–141
Bell, Alexander Graham, 328
Bell Telephone Laboratories, 63, 68, 142, 155, 157, 308, 334, 335
Bellevue Hospital, 15
Benerito, Ruth Rogan, 31, 96, 312
Benjamin, Miriam E., 31, 195
Bennet, William Blackstone, 133
Berkowitz, Joan, 31–32, 198, 208–209, 217
Bernstein, Dorothy Lewis, 32–33, 199–200
Berson, Solomon A., 259, 341
Beta Decay (Wu), 337
Bethune, Louise Blanchard, 17, 33, 198
Bethune, Mary McCleod, 164
Bethune, Robert Armore, 17, 33
Bevier, Isabel, 33–34
Biomedical engineering, 34, 76, 77, 91–92, 166
  dextran, 156–157
  mass spectrometry, 96–97
Biomedical Engineering Society, 92
Biotechnology, 35, 65, 91–92, 96, 98, 163–164. *See also* Genetic engineering; Medicine/medical technology
  DNA research, 7, 109–110, 35, 68
  hemoglobin research, 121–122
  laboratory animals, 172
  marine biotechnology, 58, 146–147
  nutritional research, 192–193
  serotonin research, 121–122
Black, James W., 82, 83, 247
Blackburn, Elizabeth Helen, 35, 215
Blackwell, Elizabeth, 221
Blake, Lillie Devereaux, xii
Blalock, Alfred, 305, 307
Blanchard, Helen Augusta, 36, 312
Blanchard Overseaming Company, 36
Blatch, Nora Stanton. *See* Barney, Nora Stanton Blatch
Blodgett, Katherine Burr, 8, 9, 36–38, 198

Bloomer, Amelia Jenkins, 210
Blount (Griffin), Bessie J., 38
Boeing Corporation, 76–77, 176
Boeing Science Research Labs, 13
Boone, Sarah, 38–39
Born, Max, 114
Bosch Arma Corporation, 132
Boston Cooking School, 95
Boston Cooking School Cook Book (Farmer), 95
Boston Women's Education Association, 263
Boulder Dam, 268
Bradberry, Henrietta M., 39, 230
Bradford, Governor, 66
Bragg, Elizabeth, 11, 39
Bragg, William Henry, 298
Bragg, William Lawrence, 298
Brahe, Tycho, 21
Bramley, Jenny Rosenthal, 39–40, 150
Brant, Mae, 322
Brattain, Walter H., 60
Breedlove, Sarah. *See* Walker, Madame C. J.
Bridges, 40–41, 269
Brill, Yvonne Claeys, 41–42, 150, 217, 262, 292
Brinkerhoff, Clara, 307, 308
Bronx Veterans Administration (VA) Hospital, 341–343
Brookhaven National Laboratories, 101, 174, 184
Brooklyn Bridge, 40, 53, 270
Brooks, Caroline, 52
Brown, Jeannette Grasselli, 299
Brown, Mari Van Britton, 42
Brown, Marjorie Lee, 120
Brown, Mary Babnick, 230. *See also* Ordnance
Brown, Rachel Fuller, 10, 15, 42, 53, 133–134, 206, 219, 247
Brown, Wade Hampton, 238, 239
Brown-Hazen Fund, 43, 134
Bryant, Alice G., 43–44, 207
Bryn Mawr College, xiii, 10, 20, 27, 36, 44, 96, 97, 103, 108, 127, 172, 243, 260, 268, 281, 301, 316, 324, 334
Bunsen, Robert, 298
Burbidge, Geoffrey, 44
Burbidge, (Eleanor) Margaret Peachey, 8, 23, 44–45, 215, 217, 275–276, 295, 298–299
Bureau of Animal Industry, 93
Bureau of Home Nutrition and Home Economics, 7
Bureau of Labor Statistics, 45
Bureau of Public Roads, 81
Burlington Industries, 310
Burroughs-Wellcome, 85–86
Bush, George, 75, 86
Butler, Margaret K., 45–46, 150, 230
Butterick, Ebenezer, 46
Butterick, Ellen, 46
Butterworth, Mary Peck, 47
Byron, Ada, 59

Index

Index

Index

Linda Zierdt-Warshaw is a freelance editor and a writer specializing in scientific and educational materials. **Alan Winkler** has worked several years in science education, most recently as a science resource specialist, and is the author of numerous science education texts. **Leonard Bernstein** is a noted author of science textbooks and other instructional materials and is also a science curriculum specialist. He has taught secondary school science and has founded a middle school with a focus on science and technology.